TRANSPARENCY OF STOCK CORPORATIONS IN EUROPE

This edited collection explores transparency as a key regulatory strategy in European business law. It examines the rationales, limitations and further perspectives on transparency that have emerged in various areas of European law including corporate law, capital markets law and accounting law, as well as other areas of law relevant for European (listed) stock corporations.

This book presents a clear and accurate picture of the recent reforms in the European transparency regime. In doing so it endorses a multi-dimensional notion of transparency, highlighting the need for careful consideration and contextualisation of the transparency phenomenon. In addition, the book considers relevant enforcement mechanisms and discusses the implications of disparate enforcement concepts in European law from both the private and public law perspectives.

Written by a team of distinguished contributors, the collection offers a comprehensive analysis of the European transparency regime by discussing the fundamentals of transparency, the role of disclosure in European business law, and related enforcement questions.

Transparency of Stock Corporations in Europe

Rationales, Limitations and Perspectives

Edited by
Vassilios Tountopoulos
and
Rüdiger Veil

• HART •
OXFORD • LONDON • NEW YORK • NEW DELHI • SYDNEY

HART PUBLISHING

Bloomsbury Publishing Plc

Kemp House, Chawley Park, Cumnor Hill, Oxford, OX2 9PH, UK

HART PUBLISHING, the Hart/Stag logo, BLOOMSBURY and the Diana logo are trademarks of Bloomsbury Publishing Plc

First published in Great Britain 2019

A catalogue record for this book is available from the British Library.

Library of Congress Cataloging-in-Publication data

Names: Tountopoulos, Vassilios, 1974- editor. | Veil, Rüdiger, 1966- editor.

Title: Transparency of stock corporations in Europe : rationales, limitations and perspectives / edited by Vassilios Tountopoulos and Rüdiger Veil.

Description: Oxford ; New York : Hart, 2019. | "The authors of this book presented drafts of their chapters at a conference on Chios Island on 11 and 12 May 2018 under the auspices of the University of the Aegean, the Union of Greek Commercialists and the University of Munich."—ECIP preface. | Includes bibliographical references and index.

Identifiers: LCCN 2019034175 (print) | LCCN 2019034176 (ebook) | ISBN 9781509925520 (hardback) | ISBN 9781509925544 (Epub)

Subjects: LCSH: Corporate governance—Law and legislation—European Union countries.—Congresses. | Disclosure of information—Law and legislation—European Union countries.—Congresses.

Classification: LCC KJE2460 .T73 2019 (print) | LCC KJE2460 (ebook) | DDC 346.24/066—dc23

LC record available at https://lccn.loc.gov/2019034175

LC ebook record available at https://lccn.loc.gov/2019034176

ISBN: HB: 978-1-50992-552-0
ePDF: 978-1-50992-553-7
ePub: 978-1-50992-554-4

Typeset by Compuscript Ltd, Shannon

To find out more about our authors and books visit www.hartpublishing.co.uk. Here you will find extracts, author information, details of forthcoming events and the option to sign up for our newsletters.

PREFACE

Disclosure of stock corporations has been a fundamental regulatory strategy for several decades. Nonetheless, the recent financial crisis, WikiLeaks, Panama Papers, the fight against tax evasion and terrorism as well as the frenetic pace of innovation spearheaded by crypto-technologies have revealed new aspects of the transparency phenomenon. This resulted in the adoption of new legislation on the European level enhancing disclosure obligations and fostering transparency of stock corporations across the EU.

Based on a multidimensional approach of transparency, the book presents a clear and accurate picture of the recent reforms in European law. The chapters discuss transparency in corporate law, capital markets law, business and commercial law. In addition, the book deals with enforcement mechanisms from the perspective of both private and public law. Reference to national case law is made where necessary in order to highlight the different national approaches.

This book is valuable for a wide audience. It aims to contribute to the academic discussion, but also offers practitioners and students the possibility to explore the transparency phenomenon from a dogmatic and interdisciplinary point of view.

The authors of this book presented drafts of their chapters at a conference on Chios Island on 11 and 12 May 2018 under the auspices of the University of the Aegean, the Union of Greek Commercialists and the University of Munich. We are grateful to our colleagues for their excellent contributions to this book and their dedication to the project. Moreover, we are grateful to Christopher Fischer, Nadja Weber and Eva Litina for their great support as well as to the editorial team at Hart.

The book is based on European legislation as of February 2019.

Vassilios Tountopoulos
Rüdiger Veil
Athens/Munich, June 2019

CONTENTS

PART III
DEVELOPMENTS IN BUSINESS LAW

PART IV
THE LIMITS OF TRANSPARENCY

PART V
ENFORCEMENT

PART VI
CONCLUSION

LIST OF CONTRIBUTORS

Victoria Athanassopoulou was born in Athens. She obtained her Law Degree at the Faculty of Law of the National and Kapodistrian University of Athens and her PhD at the University of Hamburg. She is Assistant Professor at the University of the Aegean, Department of Trade, Shipping and Transport and she teaches Maritime Law, Chartering, Marine Insurance and Sea Labor Law at an undergraduate as well as at a postgraduate level.

Gregor Bachmann is a full Professor of Law at Humboldt-Universität, Berlin, where he holds the chair for Civil Law and Corporate Law. His research focuses on matters of corporate governance. Prof. Bachmann was a visiting professor at the Center for Transnational Legal Studies (CTLS) in London (2016), a research fellow with King's College London 2015/2016 and Grotius Research Fellow at the University of Michigan Law School (2018).

Nicholas L Georgakopoulos is the H.R. Woodard Professor of Law in the McKinney School of Law of Indiana University. He has written several books including the *Logic of Securities Law* (Cambridge University Press, 2017; with a foreword by Richard A Posner) and *Illustrating Finance Policy with Mathematica* (Palgrave/Springer 2018) and many articles, which are broadly cited, including by the United States Supreme Court and the Securities and Exchange Commission. He specialises in the intersection of law, finance, and uncertainty.

Paolo Giudici is Professor of Business Law at the School of Economics and Management of the University of Bozen-Bolzano. He is an ECGI Research Associate and professorial fellow at Tilburg University. His research started with antitrust, moving to capital markets law and company law, with a key interest in civil liability and private enforcement. Before starting his academic career, he was a practising business lawyer for fifteen years. In the continental European tradition, he continues to serve as legal counsel and advocate in matters concerning his areas of academic expertise.

Brenda Hannigan is a Professor of Corporate Law at the University of Southampton, UK. Her interests lie particularly in corporate governance, especially corporate purpose, directors' duties, shareholder remedies and corporate reporting. She is the author of *Company Law*, 5th edition (Oxford University Press), the General Editor of Butterworths Corporate Law Service and a guest member of the Company Law Committee of the Law Society of England and Wales.

Jörn Axel Kämmerer is Professor of Public Law, Public International Law and EU Law at Bucerius Law School and was a Visiting Professor at Université Paris I (Panthéon-Sorbonne) and Seoul National University. A Director of the Institute on Company and Capital Markets Law (ICCML/IUKR) at Bucerius, he joined an advisory committee to the German Ministry of Finance on financial markets regulation in 2011. He is the author of a textbook, and co-editor of a commentary on Constitutional Law and in 2016 he was elected Secretary-General of the Societas Iuris Publici Europaei (SIPE).

Theodor Katsas is Assistant Professor of Commercial Law at the Law Faculty of Demokrition University at Thrace, Greece. He received his PhD and LLM at the Humboldt University of Belin, Germany. He is Managing Partner of the Law Firm, Marinos Katsas Liaskos & Associates and has specialised, lectured and published extensively in the areas of Business, Commercial and Company Law. He is member of numerous legislative committees.

Corrado Malberti is Associate Professor of Commercial Law at University of Trento. From 2010 to 2015 he was Associate Professor of Commercial Law at the University of Luxembourg, where he was also Director of the Master 1 in European Law. He graduated from the University of Milan. He completed an LLM at University of Chicago and a PhD in Commercial Law at Bocconi University. He has published widely in the fields of company law and financial market regulation in English, Italian and French.

Michail-Theodoros Marinos is Full professor in Law School at Demokritos University. He is a graduate of Athens Law School and holds a PhD from Hamburg in unfair competition law. His main fields of research are intellectual property, company and competition law. He is an active lawyer and has been member of various legislative committees including Partnership Law, Copyright and Trademark Law, Law implementing the Antitrust-Enforcement Directive.

Alexandra Mikroulea is Professor in Industrial Property Law, Competition Law, Banking Law and Capital Market Law at the University of Athens. She holds a JD from the University of Athens and a PhD in European Competition Law from the University of Munich. She was scientific fellow at the Max Planck Institute on Innovation and Competition in Munich, and has held research residencies in Mainz, Bonn, Hamburg, Munich, London, New York. She was a Visiting Scholar at UPenn (2010) and Visiting Professor at UCL (London, 2018). She was a member of the Hellenic Competition Committee. She has participated as organiser and speaker in numerous conferences and events, and has published several articles and books in her area of practice. She is a founding partner at Mikroulea/Staikouras Law Firm in Athens.

Jennifer Payne is Linklaters Professor of Corporate Finance Law at the University of Oxford. Her publications include *Corporate Finance Law: Principles and Policy* (Hart Publishing, with Louise Gullifer, 3rd edition 2020); *Principles of Financial Regulation* (Oxford University Press, 2016) (with John Armour et al); and *The Oxford Handbook of Financial Regulation* (Oxford University Press, 2015, with Niamh Moloney and Eilis Ferran). She is a founder editor of the *Journal of Corporate Law Studies* and of the Oxford Business Law Blog. She has been a Visiting Professor at a number of leading institutions internationally, and she was a member of ESMA's Securities and Markets Stakeholders Group 2016–18.

Evangehlos Perakis is Professor Emeritus of the University of Athens and a Member of the Athens Bar. He holds positions on the Legal Council of the Bank of Greece, Association of Greek Commercialists (Chairman), Association of Banking and Financial Law (Vice-chairman), Commission of Competition (former deputy Chairman), and is Chairman of ad-hoc Committees for the amendment of company law. He is a Member of the European Model Company Act (EMCA) Group. He has written extensively in corporate and insolvency law.

Alain Pietrancosta is Professor of Law and director of the Masters in Financial Law programme at the Sorbonne Law School (University of Paris). He is a member of the following: the Legal High Advisory Committee for Financial Markets of Paris; the Issuers Committee of the AMF; the executive committee of the LabEx Financial Regulation; the ParisEuroplace legal committee; the European Company Law Experts Group (ECLE). He is also founder of the *Corporate Finance and Capital Markets Law Review* (Thomson-Reuters). He has practised as a law consultant for the last 15 years.

Konstantinos Sergakis is Professor of Capital Markets Law and Corporate Governance and Director of the LLM in Corporate and Financial Law at the University of Glasgow. He is the author of *The Law of Capital Markets in the EU* (Palgrave Macmillan). He sits on the editorial board of the journals *Corporate Ownership and Control* and *Corporate Governance and Sustainability Review*. He also serves as a member of the Executive Board of the International Association of Economic Law.

Karsten Engsig Sørensen is a professor of law working at the Department of Law, Aarhus University. His main field of research is EU law and company law. Much of his research has focused on the internal market and in particular different aspects of the harmonisation of company law. He is one of the editors of the SSRN series *Nordic & European Company Law* and has published extensively in international law journals.

Giovanni Strampelli is Professor of Business Law at Bocconi University, Milan. He teaches and writes in the areas of corporate law, accounting law, bankruptcy law and securities regulation. His scholarship has been published in US, European and Italian leading business law journals (eg, the *Journal of Corporation Law*, *Virginia Law & Business Review*). He also author of two books. He has been a visiting scholar in many research institutes and universities.

Ulrich Torggler is a full professor at the University of Vienna School of Law, Department of Commercial and Business Law. His research and teaching focus on commercial, corporate and capital markets law as well as the law of obligations. He also co-hosts law conferences on an annual basis, namely the Vienna Commercial Law Day and the Annual Conference of the Austrian Corporate Law Society.

Vassilios Tountopoulos is a graduate of the University of Athens School of Law. He pursued further studies in Göttingen, Germany, where he obtained a PhD in company law. He is a full professor at the University of the Aegean and a member of the scientific committee of various legal journals. He is an active lawyer at the Greek Supreme Court. He has previously served as a general legal counsel at the Hellenic Post and as member of various expert groups. He has also served as non-executive Member of the BoD of various companies.

Rüdiger Veil is a Professor for Corporate Law and Capital Markets Law at Ludwig Maximilians-University, Munich/Germany. He has published numerous books, inter alia on European capital markets law, and articles in top-ranked journals, working particularly from a comparative perspective. Since 2014, he has been a member of the ESMA Securities and Markets Stakeholder Group. In 2016 he was elected as Chair of the Group. Rüdiger Veil also advises the German Federal Ministry of Finance with special focus regarding the EU financial markets law. He has acted as an expert for the German, Chinese and Russian parliaments.

Introduction

RÜDIGER VEIL

I. Introduction

This book explores transparency as a key regulatory strategy in European business law. Traditionally, disclosure obligations are designed to overcome information asymmetries and combat conflicts of interest. Yet, increasingly, behavioural finance and empirical studies have revealed weaknesses in this regulatory strategy and have criticised transparency on conceptual and other grounds. It is therefore worth examining the rationales, limitations and further perspectives on transparency that have emerged in various areas of European law, including corporate, financial markets, accounting and business law, as well as other areas of law relevant for European (listed) stock corporations.

The European disclosure regimes have grown exponentially in recent years. The European legislature has undertaken far-reaching reforms by enacting a number of directives and regulations that focus on transparency as a key regulatory tool. These reforms – which, amongst others, include the Shareholder Rights Directive (SRD), the Market Abuse Regulation (MAR), the Transparency Directive (TD), the Directive on Disclosure of Non-Financial Information and Diversity Information (SR), the Anti-Money Laundering Directive (AML) – have been of particular importance to European listed stock corporations which are expected to comply with a progressively more expansive and detailed set of transparency requirements.

This book analyses these reforms and aims to present a clear and accurate picture of the recent initiatives. In doing so, it endorses a multidimensional notion of transparency, highlighting the need for careful consideration and contextualisation of the transparency phenomenon.

II. Company Law

Company law is dealt with at the beginning. The European Union (EU) has adopted numerous directives on listed companies in order to coordinate the national safeguards required in the interests of shareholders and third parties. These are minimum harmonisation measures. Member States have a wide margin of discretion in implementing European law into their national laws. This can already be seen impressively in the example of access to information in company registers. The public can obtain information on the fundamental aspects of a listed company from the company register. This access to information is harmonised throughout Europe. Nevertheless, there are many differences in access to information because they are national registers still subject to national law.

The situation is similar with regard to shareholder and minority rights in a listed company. The EU has not yet harmonised these rights under corporate law. This makes it all the more important for shareholders to be able to inform themselves about what rights exist and how the rights can be exercised. This is of particular importance in view of the increasing internationalisation of the shareholder structure of listed companies.

Company law aims to protect shareholders and creditors. There are a number of potential conflicts of interests resulting from principal–agent relations. Disclosure is a proven strategy to prevent the risk of opportunistic access to corporate assets by the board of directors and the major shareholder. It is not possible to cover this for all relevant scenarios in this book; this would mean entering into capital raising and maintenance, conversion measures etc. Instead, the example of related party transactions is used to illustrate the effects disclosure obligations can have in order to prevent tunnelling.

Disclosure obligations are traditionally statutory obligations. However, in the EU, there are also numerous transparency rules that can be attributed to soft law. The corporate governance codes, which are now available in all Member States following the British model, are of particular practical relevance and theoretically attractive. It is characteristic that, under the comply-or-explain mechanism, the board of directors must declare whether or not it follows the recommendations of the Code. It is a powerful mechanism based on the disciplining power of transparency on capital markets and is therefore also dealt with in this book.

III. Capital Markets Law

Disclosure obligations are a central regulatory instrument in capital markets law. The numerous duties cannot be dealt with exhaustively in this book. Instead, certain disclosure obligations that are of central importance for investors' investment decisions are analysed by way of example. At the beginning, there is the obligation of an issuer to disclose inside information without delay. This obligation has now been harmonised throughout Europe. This is not without its problems because listed companies in Europe have different governance structures. In addition, the European legislature provides a principles-based disclosure obligation. It is difficult for issuers to assess when they have to make public inside information to the capital markets.

Disclosure of major shareholdings, on the other hand, remains the subject of a directive which gives Member States a wider range of scope for implementation. This can be explained by the different company laws of the Member States. Some Member States have even introduced stricter rules than European law. It is of particular interest for what reasons they provide for additional disclosure obligations.

The disclosure obligations in capital markets law are based on the efficient capital market hypothesis and aim to counter information asymmetries between investors and issuers. The European legislature wants to protect investors' confidence in the functioning of capital markets. However, investors are usually not in a position to analyse the information and draw conclusions as to whether to invest or not. There are therefore numerous information intermediaries who evaluate information. The problem is that such intermediaries can have serious conflicts of interest. These conflicts of interest can be countered by prohibitions, such as prohibiting an intermediary from publishing information about a market participant (financial analysis, rating etc) and advising this market participant at the same time. A less restrictive regulatory instrument is transparency. The example of proxy advisor shows how effective the regulatory strategy of transparency is in European law.

Finally, it will be discussed that the European legislature now also pursues environmental protection goals in capital markets law and provides for transparency obligations for this purpose. This is doubtful, as capital markets regulation traditionally aims to strengthen investor confidence in the functioning of markets and to ensure the stability of the financial system. It is not the task of capital markets law to promote the flow of funds into certain (sustainable) economic activities. Nevertheless, under certain conditions, transparency obligations are compatible with the traditional objectives of capital markets law.

IV. Business Law

Financial reporting is an essential part of business law in Europe. The EU harmonised the Member States' accounting laws at an early stage through directives. In addition, the EU has created its own accounting regime, the International Accounting Standards/International Financial Reporting Standards (IAS/IFRS). Recently, however, it has become apparent that the informative value of balance sheets can be improved.

Another remarkable development is that corporations are now obliged to inform the public about corporate governance aspects and corporate social responsibility in their annual financial statements and management reports. This narrative reporting is becoming increasingly important. It should therefore be considered whether disclosure obligations are likely to influence boardroom behaviour to reflect environmental, social and governance (ESG) risks.

Disclosure obligations are also provided for in order to protect certain public interests. A prominent example is the recently reformed rules on money laundering. However, it is doubtful whether the legislative objectives will be achieved with extended transparency obligations. One reason might be that European law does not provide for an effective system of sanctions for breaches of transparency obligations.

V. Limits of Transparency

The disclosure obligations in corporate law, capital markets law and business law do not exist without restrictions. Listed companies may have legitimate secrecy interests. It should also be borne in mind that European law attaches particular importance to the protection of personal data.

The limitations could be shown in detail for each disclosure obligation. This book takes a different path and presents a cross-sectional view of the central theme of the limits of transparency. Personal data protection and trade secrets are approached in separate chapters. It should also be shown that competition law can result in a variety of restrictions on transparency rules. The exchange of information between market participants may be prohibited for overriding reasons. The aim is to show how difficult it is to identify such restrictions correctly on a case-by-case basis.

VI. Enforcement

Finally, the book considers relevant enforcement mechanisms and discusses the implications of disparate enforcement concepts in European law. It therefore deals with enforcement questions from the perspective of both private and public law.

Private enforcement is essentially still a matter for the Member States. European law largely refrains from harmonising claims under private law to enforce disclosure obligations. For this reason, the functions that a private liability can have should be compared with US capital markets law. In the more recent academic debate in Europe, the preventive effects of private liability are playing an increasingly important role.

The principle of 'piercing the corporate veil' is also not Europeanised. It can have very different purposes, especially when creditors' interests are violated. However, it is of interest that the principle of 'piercing the corporate veil' may apply if there is a lack of transparency concerning the identity or the integrity of the corporation.

After all, public enforcement should not be missing from this book. In particular, disclosure obligations under capital markets law are traditionally enforced in Europe by means of public enforcement instruments. For a long time, European law has only laid down a few rules on public law sanctions. This has changed fundamentally since the financial market crisis. The sanctioning regimes are now detailed in European law and aim at harmonising the national laws to a great extent. Special emphasis will be placed on the new sanctions provided for in European law, the way in which they interrelate to one another as well as the remaining procedural autonomy of the national legislature.

VII. Conclusion

The book sees itself as an academic work that reviews recent reforms, analyses the disclosure philosophy from different angles, and presents perspectives for further legal developments. Therefore, it should be considered in conclusion what consequences the further digitalisation of companies, business processes and procedures can have. The question must also be raised as to what remains in the end: will we experience the end of anonymity in the *sociétés anonymes*?

PART I

Transparency and Corporate Law

1

Access to Information in Company Registers

KARSTEN ENGSIG SØRENSEN

I. Introduction

Historically, the right to set up a company was granted either by the national parliament or the Crown. When the need arose to make the formation of companies easier, most countries allowed companies to be formed if they complied with the predefined conditions dictated by the national law and register. Today, incorporation by registration is the most common form of incorporation.[1] As part of this process, the register will naturally receive some information, and some of this information may be made available to the public.

Since the adoption of the First Company Law Directive 50 years ago,[2] the EU has had rules regulating the registration of companies and the disclosure of certain information and documents. The topic was so important that it was among the first topics to be harmonised in the EU.[3] Even though the directive dealt with other topics, it was nevertheless the issue of access to corporate information that gave the directive its popular name: the Disclosure Directive. Later, this disclosure regime has been developed even further, in particular by harmonising the rules governing the framing and auditing of

[1] Some countries still allow companies to be formed by an act of parliament or royal charter; see, for instance, on UK law, PL Davies and S Worthington, *Gower's Principle of Modern Company Law*, 10th edn (London, Sweet & Maxwell, 2016) 76. In many countries, companies without limited liability may be formed without registration.

[2] See Council Directive 68/151/EEC of 9 March 1968 on co-ordination of safeguards which, for the protection of the interests of members and others, are required by Member States of companies within the meaning of the second paragraph of Article 58 of the Treaty, with a view to making such safeguards equivalent throughout the Community [1968] OJ L65/8 (hereinafter 'First Company Law Directive'). The directive has been amended several times since then, and nowadays the rules on disclosure are found in ch III, s 1 of the Codified Company Law Directive: Council Directive 2017/1132 Directive (EU) 2017/1132 of the European Parliament and of the Council of 14 June 2017 relating to certain aspects of company law [2017] OJ L169/46 (hereinafter CCLD).

[3] There are, however, historical indications that the reason for including this topic in the First Company Law Directive was not that it was the most important topic, but maybe that it was the most politically opportune topic to start with. See E Stein, *Harmonization of European Company Laws* (New York, Bobbs-Merrill Company, 1971) 199–202.

company accounts, the rules governing branches and by updating the system to the modern possibilities of electronic databases and the interconnection of these. As a result, disclosure has become a central part of EU company law.[4]

Not all countries provide for such a generous access to information.[5] Even in developed countries, the information given is often more limited. In this light, the solution found in the EU is in no way self-evident. In fact, before the harmonisation took place in 1968, the level of access to information in the Member States at that time was quite diverse and it was no easy feat to agree on the directive.[6]

In the following, the main feature of the solution found in the EU is analysed and contextualised. The purpose is to understand the aims that underlie the access to information in company registers in the EU and to see whether the adopted solutions reflect these aims. It is not possible to make a detailed comparative analysis, but it will be illustrated how the EU solution differs from those found in many other jurisdictions and it will also be shown that there are still substantial differences of how the EU Member States have allowed access to corporate information.

The focus of this chapter is on access to information about private and public limited company in the company registers.[7] As for listed companies, there is often access to more information, often in a different register.[8] It will not be possible to cover the information available to listed companies despite these registers, but a few references will be made to compare how the two systems have evolved.

The structure of the chapter is the following: first, it will be discussed how the company registers are organised (section II), then which information they will register and disclose and then who this disclosure should benefit (sections III–IV). The information is only valuable if it is correct, and therefore it will be examined how the information is proceeded in the registers and how Member States should allow for the enforcement of duty to disclose corporate information (sections V–VI). Finally, the key question of how the information may be accessed is analysed, followed by a brief discussion of the effect that disclosure has on the position of third parties (sections VII–VIII). The last section concludes.

II. Company Registers

Company registers are differently organised in different states.[9] In some states, companies need to register in business registers that aim to compile information on

[4] See also S Grundmann, *EU Company Law*, 2nd edn (Cambridge, Intersentia, 2012) 167; U Grohmann, *Das Informationsmodell im Europäischen Gesellschaftsrecht* (Berlin, De Gruyter, 2006).

[5] See section III.

[6] See the account in Stein (n 3) 203–35.

[7] The focus is on the types of companies covered by the First Company Law Directive, now listed in Annex II of the CCLD (n 2).

[8] In the EU, the duty of the Member States is to ensure at least one officially appointed mechanism for the central storage of regulated information. See the Transparency Directive: Council Directive 2004/109 of the European Parliament and of the Council of 15 December 2004 on the harmonisation of transparency requirements in relation to information about issuers whose securities are admitted to trading on a regulated market and amending Directive 2001/34/EC, art 21(2).

[9] See CM Schmitthoff in C Cheng (ed), *Clive M Schmitthoff's Select Essays on International Trade Law* (Dordrecht, Martinus Nijhoff Publishers, 1988) 77–78. For an overview of the different ways in which

both companies and enterprises conducted by physical persons. In other states, there is a special register which is dedicated to the registration of companies, such as the Companies House in the UK. The way in which these registers are organised often differs. In Germany, the business register, Handelsregister, is organised with the courts, which in this capacity perform a non-judicial function.[10] In other countries, the register is organised as part of a ministry or another public body, for instance, a chamber of commerce. In the following, the term 'company register' will be used to cover these different forms of registers. In addition, there may be private registers that function on a commercial basis.[11]

Not only are the company registers organised in different ways, but their location can also be either centralised or local. For instance, the registers in Germany are decentralised, and in the US, each individual state organises its own company register. From a historical point of view, decentralised registers made sense as most businesses were local. However, nowadays many companies conduct business nationwide and some even internationally. In this situation, decentralised registers may not be optimal as it will often not be obvious – especially not to a foreigner – where to look for the information.

When the EU embarked on a harmonisation process involving company registers, it would have been natural to consider whether the company registers could be organised differently. It seems that they did, in fact, consider creating a central EU register, but this idea was rejected.[12] Instead, the EU legislator chose to build up the harmonisation around the existing registers in the Member States. Thus, the Member States were required to open a file for each company in 'a central register, commercial register or company register',[13] thereby accepting that each Member State could organise its registers as it saw fit. Not only were the Member States free to decide who should run the register, they were also free to decide whether it should be one central register or several decentralised registers. To help those dealing with the company to find their way to the right register, companies should specify in their 'letters and order forms' the registers where the file on the company is kept and the number of the company in that register.[14]

This model – relying on national registers – was also used later when harmonising the rules on branches of companies.[15] Here EU legislators used the solution that

registers are organised in the EU nowadays, see Annex 2 of the Impact Assessment prepared by the Commission when proposing the directive on interconnecting registers, later Directive 2012/30/EU [2012] OJ L315/74, 54. This working document is available at: https://eur-lex.europa.eu/legal-content/EN/TXT/?uri=CELEX:52011SC0222.

[10] Consequently, the courts may not refer a preliminary ruling to the European Court of Justice when they act in the capacity of a registry; see Case 86/00 *HSB-Wohnbau GmbH*, EU:C:2001:394; Case C-182/00 *Lutz GmbH*, EU:C:2002:19, para 14.

[11] Public registers will normally not work on a commercial basis, and the activity of gathering information and allowing access to these will consequently not constitute an economic activity. Therefore, these registers will normally not be subject to competition law; see also regarding EU competition law Case C-138/11 *Compass-Datenbank GmbH*, EU:C:2012:449.

[12] See V Edwards, *EC Company Law* (Oxford, Clarendon Press, 1999) 19.

[13] See First Company Law Directive, art 3(1) and now CCLD (n 2) art 16(1).

[14] See First Company Law Directive, art 4 and now CCLD (n 2) art 26(1)(a).

[15] See Eleventh Council Directive 89/666/EEC of 21 December 1989 concerning disclosure requirements in respect of branches opened in a Member State by certain types of company governed by the law of another State [1989] OJ L395/36 and now CCLD (n 2), ch III, ss 2–3.

branches should register and make information available in the Member States in which they set up branches according to the rules in these Member States. A simpler solution would have been to require that the companies should list their branches and information on the branches in the Member States in which the company is incorporated and therefore has its file.[16] This solution may have been simpler for the companies, but may have made it more difficult for those who seek information on the branches. Even though a branch should list the register where information on the branch is available, it may be more difficult for those persons who seek information on branches to find their way around in a foreign company register. Additionally, there could be a linguistic challenge in accessing information through a foreign register. However, if access to foreign registers could be made easier and the linguistic problem could be overcome, it would simplify matters if all corporate information were made available by the national register where the company has its main file.[17]

More surprisingly, the same solution – relying on national registers – was used when the EU started introducing supranational corporate forms such as the EEIG, SE company and SCE company. Despite the fact that they are supposed to be supranational, they need to be registered in one Member State.[18] Also in other areas, the EU has relied on national registers instead of creating central registers – see, for instance, the *Officially Appointed Mechanism* (OAM) for the central storage of regulated information under the Transparency Directive[19] and the registration under the Insolvency Regulation.[20]

Relying on national registers made it easier to achieve harmonisation. Creating a central register does not only mean that there should be a central database, but would also require that the EU should create a supervisory and enforcement unit. This would have been controversial at the time when the First Company Law Directive was adopted, and probably would still be.

But even if the EU may not establish central registers in this area at present,[21] it could be avoided that the Member States register corporate information in different national registers. Thus, harmonisation does not prevent the Member States from establishing different registers for basic corporate information, insolvencies of companies,

[16] See also K Maresceau and M Tison, 'Cross-border Business in the European Union and Statutory Disclosure Requirements: Using IT as a Catalyst for Further Market Integration' (2008) 3 *Journal of International Commercial Law and Technology* 84.

[17] See also the recommendation in the *Report of the Reflection Group on the Future of EU Company Law*, 5 April 2011, 34.

[18] See Council Regulation (EEC) No 2137/85 of 25 July 1985 on the European Economic Interest Grouping (EEIG) [1985] OJ L199/1, art 6, 39; Council Regulation (EC) No 2157/2001 of 8 October 2001 on the Statute for a European company (SE) [2001] OJ L294/1, art 12. The lack of a central register cannot be explained by the fact that the state of registration determines the supplementary company law rules that govern these companies, as it would have been possible to achieve this solution by requiring these companies to stipulate in which Member State they have their registered office and where the supplementary rules therefore can be found.

[19] Directive 2004/109 (n 8) art 21(2). See also R Veil in R Veil (ed), *European Capital Markets Law*, 2nd edn (Oxford, Hart Publishing, 2017) 443.

[20] See Council Regulation (EC) No 1346/2000 of 29 May 2000 on insolvency proceedings [2000] OJ L160/1, art 22 and now Regulation (EU) 2015/848 of the European Parliament and of the Council of 20 May 2015 on insolvency proceedings [2015] OJ L141/19, art 24.

[21] It does, however, have a central register for EU trademarks and design: the European Union Intellectual Property Office.

beneficial owners and information disclosed under the Transparency Directive. As a consequence, gaining access to all corporate information may require not only the location of one register but several.[22]

In recent years, the EU has embarked on a different model to reduce the disadvantages of having national registers that third parties may find difficult to navigate. The solution has been to interconnect these registers to create a single entry point and to facilitate searches and access across the registers.[23] This is the solution used for company registers,[24] but similar projects have been set up for OAMs,[25] in the area of insolvency,[26] and for information on beneficial owners.[27] In the field of company law, it is now possible to search for EU and European Economic Area (EEA) companies through the e-justice portal,[28] which makes it possible to search for companies by name or alternatively by registration number. To facilitate the latter, all companies should now be provided with a unique identifier which ensures that it is possible to identify both the relevant register and the company within that register.[29]

The interconnecting of registers in the area of company law has not substantially changed the role of the national registers. To allow for the new platform to operate, they should enable access to the information stored,[30] but apart from this, there is no obligation for the Member States to change their internal systems of registers.[31] The solution of interconnecting the national registers is in no way equivalent to setting up a European central register. The EU only provides a platform for interconnecting

[22] Unless these registers are interconnected at a national level; see, for instance, the German Unternehmensregister (www.unternehmensregister.de). In *Report on the Digitalisation in Company Law*, March 2016, in Recommendation 4, the Informal Company Law Expert Group (ICLEG) suggested interconnecting all these registers in order to ensure easy access to all this information held in different registers. The report is available at: ec.europa.eu/info/sites/info/files/icleg-report-on-digitalisation-24-march-2016_en.pdf.

[23] This is not the first attempt made to interconnect company registers as there are several private platforms that have managed to connect some registers; see, for instance, OpenCorporates at opencorporates.com. However, globally, far from all registers are interconnected and often it may require a local presence to gather corporate information. Therefore, there are international company search agents who offer to gather corporate information. For an overview of how to search corporate information globally, see R Brett 'Searching International Company Registries Online' (2015) 15 *Legal Information Management* 172.

[24] The effort of interconnecting the registers was initiated with Directive 2012/17/EU of the European Parliament and of the Council of 13 June 2012 amending Council Directive 89/666/EEC and Directives 2005/56/EC and 2009/101/EC of the European Parliament and of the Council as regards the interconnection of central, commercial and companies registers [2012] OJ L156/1, which launches the Business Registers Interconnection System (BRIS).

[25] The so-called European Electronic Access Point (EEAP) operated by the European Securities and Markets Authority (ESMA). The system was supposed to be operating by now, but it appears that it has been delayed.

[26] The interconnection project is set out in the recasted Insolvency Regulation 2015/848 (n 20). It is not expected to take place before 2019; see further P Szirányi, 'EU-Wide Interconnection of Insolvency Registers' (2015) 16 *ERA Forum* 219.

[27] See the recent amendment to the Anti-Money Laundering Directive (Directive (EU) 2018/843 of the European Parliament and of the Council of 30 May 2018 amending Directive (EU) 2015/849 on the prevention of the use of the financial system for the purposes of money laundering or terrorist financing, and amending Directives 2009/138/EC and 2013/36/EU [2018] OJ L156/43, art 30(10)).

[28] See e-justice.europa.eu/content_find_a_company-489-en.do?clang=en.

[29] See CCLD (n 2) art 16(1).

[30] For details, see Commission Implementing Regulation (EU) 2015/884 of 8 June 2015 establishing technical specifications and procedures required for the system of interconnection of registers established by Directive 2009/101/EC [2015] OJ L144/1.

[31] See recital 27 of the CCLD (n 2).

the national registers, and the EU does not store information, nor does it in any way modify the information disclosed through the platform.[32] The platform is therefore far from offering a central register that examines and validates the information stored on companies.[33]

III. What Type of Information is Disclosed?

The registers may accumulate different kinds of corporate information. Some information may be collected without being disclosed. This would include information that the authorities may need to verify that the incorporation is complying with the requirements of the Companies Acts, for instance, proof that the capital has been paid up or minutes from the constitutive general meeting. Another type of information that may not be publicly available is information on shareholders and beneficial owners. Even though information on these is gathered in a number of jurisdictions, often this information is not available to the public.[34] In a European context, the Fourth Anti-Money Laundering Directive (Directive 2015/849) requires that information on beneficial owners should be registered, but need not, at the moment, be made publicly available.[35] Even if the information is not made publicly available, the information may still have the function of helping the authorities in law enforcement, in particular anti-money laundering legislation, tax law, rules on disqualification of directors etc.[36]

[32] See also ibid, recitals 25–26. Here, it is also stressed that the platform is not a distinct entity possessing legal personality.

[33] Some members of the Reflection Group on the Future of EU Company Law foresee that in the future, the increasing cross-border activities of companies may make a European central register natural; see *Report of the Reflection Group* (n 17) 33.

[34] According to *The International Business Registers Report*, 2016, prepared by the Association of Registers of Latin America and the Caribbean (ASORLAC), the Corporate Registers Forum (CRF), the European Commerce Registers' Forum (ECRF) and the International Association of Commercial Administrators (IACA), iaca.org/wp-content/uploads/International-Business-Register-Report-2016.pdf, 121–22, as many as 47 per cent of the responding registers collected information on shareholders, but only 65 per cent of the European jurisdictions that register the information made them publicly available. For the American jurisdictions that actually register the information, 87 per cent made the information publicly available. For information on beneficial owners, 20 per cent of the responding jurisdiction collected the information. Of the limited number of jurisdictions that register the information, only a minority of them made the information publicly available (as few as 17 per cent in Europe).

[35] Some Member States have, nevertheless, made the information publicly available. In 2016, the Commission proposed to amend the directive once again to require that information on beneficial owners should be made available, but not necessarily through the companies' registers. See Proposal for a Directive of the European Parliamant and of the Council amending Directive (EU) 2015/849 on the prevention of the use of the financial system for the purposes of money laundering or terrorist financing and amending Directive 2009/101/EC COM(2016) 450. In late 2017, there was an agreement on this amendment, and it is now adopted as Directive 2018/843 (n 27).

[36] Often EU law ensures that Member States share this non-disclosed information; see, for instance, Directive 2015/849, art 30(7) on information about beneficial owners, and Directive 2011/16 on tax information. The exchange of information on disqualified directors will be made possible once Directive (EU) 2019/1151 amending the CCLD (n 2) is implemented; see Directive (EU) 2019/1151 on the use of digital tools and processes in company law [2019] OJ L186/80.

Much information is made publicly available, but worldwide it differs as to which type of information that is. The most common information disclosed is the company's name, legal address, year of incorporation, type of business register and the names of the directors. This is the very basic information needed to confirm that the company exists and where to find it. Some jurisdictions also provide additional information on the corporate structure, annual return, shareholders and beneficial ownership.[37]

Consequently, the solution adopted in the EU is rather progressive. Under EU law, not only is the basic information on name, address and names of directors made available, but also the instrument of constitution and the statute of the company (and changes in this respect), information on which persons are authorised to represent the company, the capital subscribed (where there is an authorised capital), accounting documents, the winding-up of the company, appointment of liquidators and the nullity of the company.[38] The level of minimum harmonisation is further increased by the harmonisation of the information that the statute or instrument of incorporation should state, and through the harmonisation of the accounts.[39]

It is by no means the norm that countries require that companies make their accounts available to the company registers. A survey indicates that only 52 per cent of jurisdictions worldwide require that the annual accounts should be submitted to the registers, and not even all of them make the accounts public available. In comparison, 51 per cent of the jurisdictions worldwide require companies to submit their annual returns. Even though the annual returns are not always made publicly available, it is more common to make annual returns available than it is to make annual accounts available.[40] Here, the EU Member States clearly stand out as EU law does not require that the annual returns are made publicly available.[41]

One would assume that the information that the company exists is the most important information to receive. Almost as important is the information that the company is in the process of being wound up, as this information should prompt both shareholders, creditors and other stakeholders to take steps to limit the impact of the impending event (liquidation, bankruptcy etc). In the EU, the process of stating a winding-up and the appointment of a liquidator should be registered and made publicly available,[42] but

[37] See in particular World Bank, *Starting a Business: Transparency of Information at Business Registries* (2018) 40 f (doingbusiness.org/reports/case-studies/2018/sab); and *The International Business Registers Report* (n 34) 120.

[38] See CCLD (n 2) art 14.

[39] See ibid, arts 3–4; and the Directive 2013/34/EU of the European Parliament and of the Council of 26 June 2013 on the annual financial statements, consolidated financial statements and related reports of certain types of undertakings, amending Directive 2006/43/EC of the European Parliament and of the Council and repealing Council Directives 78/660/EEC and 83/349/EEC [2013] OJ L182/19, with later amendments.

[40] See *The International Business Registers Report* (n 34) 122–23.

[41] The only European respondents that indicated they receive annual returns are Denmark, Gibraltar, Guernsey, Ireland, Isle of Man, Jersey, Luxembourg and the UK. See *The International Business Registers Report* (n 34) 83. There is no information on whether the jurisdictions made the returns publicly available. In the EU, there is a proposal that multinational enterprises should publish country-by-country information on the tax paid, which may result in more transparency on taxes; see Proposal for a Directive of the European Parliament and of the Council amending Directive 2013/34/EU as regards disclosure of income tax information by certain undertakings and branches COM (2016) 198. For financial institutions, there is already some disclosure requirements according to the Capital Requirement Directive IV (Directive 2013/36) art 89.

[42] See CCLD, art 14(h) and (j).

there is no requirement that the information that the company is under insolvency proceedings should be registered. The opening of an insolvency proceeding should be registered under the Insolvency Regulation in an insolvency register.[43] Even though the insolvency register may operate as a separate register, the plan is to interconnect these registers through the e-justice platform. By facilitating public access to this information, the EU is more advanced than most jurisdictions. In the survey, performed in 2016, for the International Business Register, more than 80 per cent of the European jurisdictions reported that they register decisions about bankruptcies. In other regions, the number was much lower, and the lowest was in the Americas, where only 31 per cent of the jurisdictions register bankruptcies.[44]

Another area where it is common to register information on companies is when a company sets up a branch in another jurisdiction.[45] In the EU, the list of information and documents to be disclosed includes information on the company that sets up the branch, including information on where this company is registered and its registration number. But the Member States also need to register certain information about the branch, such as the address and activities of the branch, permanent representatives who represent the branch, if any, accounting documents of the company and the closure of the branch.[46]

The harmonisation of information on companies and branches differs in one respect. The requirements set out in Article 14 CCLD are only minimum requirements, and Member States are therefore allowed to require more information to be published. This could be information on shareholders, beneficial owners or maybe annual returns. On the other hand, the list of information that is required to be disclosed about EU companies which set up branches in other Member States are not only minimum requirements but also maximum requirements.[47] The CJEU has confirmed that the list which is now in Article 30(1) CCLD is exhaustive, although this does not prevent Member States from imposing the obligation on branches to provide information under social or tax law, or for the purpose of statistics.[48]

IV. Why Disclose Corporate Information through Registers?

It is clear that the amount of information on companies (and their branches) made publicly available differs considerably worldwide. These differences indicate that different jurisdictions evaluate the need for disclosure of corporate information differently.

[43] See Insolvency Regulation 2015/848 (n 20) art 24.

[44] See *The International Business Registers Report* (n 34) 40.

[45] See ibid 42–43. There are also a number of jurisdictions that register branches set up by a company in their home jurisdiction. In Europe, 26 per cent of the jurisdictions participating in the survey did so.

[46] See CCLD, art 30.

[47] There is, however, a list of information in art 30(2) of the CCLD that the Member States may also require to be disclosed. In addition, for companies from third countries (eg, non-EU/EEA members), the list of information required in art 37 of the CCLD is only a minimum list.

[48] See Case C-167/01 *Inspire Art*, EU:C:2003:512, para 69.

The positive effects of disclosure depend on who may benefit from disclosure. Normally, disclosure is assumed to be beneficial to commercial transactions as it makes it easier to access (reliable) information on companies. This information may be used by different groups, such as banks, consumers, suppliers and investors contemplating to buy shares.[49] When looking at the harmonisation in the EU, it also seems that the disclosure is assumed to be mainly beneficial to third parties that deal with the company.[50] Of course, those who enter into business with the company as trade partners, customers or investors can get the information from the company. But the process of collecting information through the company may be less reliable, more complex and more time-consuming than finding the information in the register. Also, if the information has to be collected from the company, there is a risk that one will not get all the information needed. Thus, easy access to reliable information may be beneficial to business transactions.[51]

In the EU, disclosure of corporate information has played an important role in the creation of the internal market. By harmonising the information to be disclosed, and in the case of annual accounts the format to be used, it has been made easier for those who come into contact with companies from other Member States to seek information about these companies, and with the interconnecting of registers, this has been made even easier. Access to information about companies has become a cornerstone of EU company law and has even to some extent supplanted the need for substantial harmonisation.[52] It has also been used to set aside national company law rules intended to protect creditors, as these are already sufficiently protected through the easy access to information about companies from other Member States. Thus, in *Centros Ltd*, the CJEU found that those dealing with a UK company operating though a branch in Denmark would be protected, mainly because it would be easy to identify that Centros Ltd was a UK company and because it was possible to find information about the company due to the harmonisation of annual accounts and disclosure rules for branches.[53] Thus, the extensive disclosure of corporate information in the EU has also been used to suppress national rules that intend to protect creditors.

It is less obvious that the rules ensuring the disclosure of corporate information will be beneficial to shareholders. Shareholders will normally have access to information about the company through the company. However, it may be easier to access information through company registers, and therefore shareholders may also find it more convenient to use these registers as a source of information.[54] For persons who are contemplating to buy shares in the company, it may seem a more reliable alternative going through the register for corporate information than getting the information from the selling shareholder or the company.

[49] See P Holden in the *International Business Registers Report* (n 34) 4–9.

[50] According to recital 7, disclosure should protect the interests of third parties.

[51] See Holden in the *International Business Registers Report* (n 34) 4–9.

[52] See also Grundmann (n 4) 140 and 167.

[53] See Case C-212/97 *Centros Ltd*, EU:C:1999:126, para 36. A similar argument was given in *Inspire Art* (n 48) para 135.

[54] In the recently proposed directive amending the CCLD by introducing new rules on cross-border conversions, mergers and division, there is a greater reliance on disclosure through the registers, also to the benefit of shareholders; see COM(2018) 241, arts 86h, 123 and 160j.

We know that the information on companies is accessed quite often in most jurisdictions, and this indicates that there is a positive effect of disclosing corporate information (see section VII below). However, the figures do not show who seeks the information.

These positive effects of disclosure of corporate information have to be balanced against the negative effects such as the cost imposed on the companies when they are required to disclose information, and the potential intrusion into the privacy of persons and the protection of business secrets. It is hardly surprising that the balancing of these contradictory considerations has resulted in different solutions in different jurisdictions. For instance, there are very different views on whether annual accounts and annual returns should be made publicly available. In the EU, it is now accepted that annual accounts should be disclosed, but when negotiating the First Company Law Directive, this was one of the most hotly debated topics, as Germany in particular was reluctant to allow for full disclosure.[55] Even today, there is information that would be controversial to disclose in many EU Member States, such as disclosure of tax returns, beneficial owners and shareholders.

Finally, information about persons registered as directors, shareholders or beneficial owners could be considered privacy information. Even though the Court of Justice of the European Union (CJEU) in the judgment in *Salvatore Manni* did not find that there was any need to restrict access to information about those who had been directors in companies that had gone bankrupt, it seems that several European countries deny access to personal data with reference to data protection rules.[56] The need to protect business secrets may also limit access to certain information. Based on the case law so far, it seems that the information which should be disclosed according to EU law is unlikely to be deemed business secrets.[57]

V. Processing the Information

The information held in the registers is only valuable to the business community to the extent that it is reliable. This requires a regular update of information and some form of control by the register. The First Company Law Directive hardly addressed the issue of how the Member States should go about processing the information they receive; thus, it was left to the Member States to decide which person should be responsible for

[55] See Edwards (n 12) 22–23; and Stein (n 3) 242–74.

[56] See the report *'It's None of Your Business!'* published in 2016 by Access Info Europe and the Organized Crime and Corruption Reporting Project (OCCRP). The report is available at: access-info.org/wp-content/uploads/CompanyRegisters_Report_7April2016.pdf.

[57] Both the CJEU and the General Court have dismissed the claim that the duty to disclose annual accounts infringes the protection of business secrets; see Joined Cases C-435/02 and C-103/03 *Springer*, EU:C:2004:552 and Case T-47/02 *Danzer*, EU:T:2006:167. In both cases, the courts inter alia relied on the fact that there are provisions in the accounting directive that allow the companies to suppress information if disclosure thereof would be 'seriously prejudicial' to the company; see Directive 2013/34/EU (n 39) arts 17(1)(g), 18(2) and 28(3).

submitting information to the register.[58] The directives do not regulate whether Member States may charge the company a fee when it registers information.[59] Also, it was left to the Member States to decide how to make a legality check on the formation of companies, as it accepted that this could either take the form of an administrative or judicial 'preventive' control, or the intervention of a notary.[60] Not only did the directive leave it to the Member States to decide who should perform the check, but also left it to them to decide what to check and how to go about doing so.[61] Apart from requiring that a file should be opened for each company,[62] it was left to the Member States to decide how to file the information. It did, however, require the Member States to publish the information in the national gazette appointed for that purpose by the individual Member State.[63] The directive did stress that the Member States should avoid any discrepancy between the information recorded in the register and what is published in the national gazette, but it did not outline how they should go about doing so.[64]

Later, EU law was amended to address some of the issues not addressed originally. Most importantly, in 2003 the directive was amended so that Member States should allow companies to decide whether to file their compulsory documents and particulars in a paper version or electronically.[65] Furthermore, the information should be kept in electronic form, and interested parties should also be able to access the information electronically.[66] This reform paves the way for the interconnection of registers that was effected in 2017. As mentioned above in section II, this reform required Member States to allow for access to some of the information held in their registers and as a consequence dictated aspects of the technical format, but the interconnection did not fundamentally change the fact that each Member State decides how to proceed the information it receives.

The 2003 amendment also dealt with the question in which language the file information should be written. The solution was in no way revolutionary as it was accepted

[58] See art 5 of the First Company Law Directive; and art 13 of the Eleventh Company Law Directive, Directive 1989/666/EEC [1989] OJ L395/36, now found in CCLD, arts 27 and 41.

[59] Such a fee was accepted by the CJEU as long as it covers the cost of the subsequent publication of the information; see Case C-453/04, *innoventif Limited*, EU:C:2006:361.

[60] See art 10 of the First Company Law Directive, now found in art 10 of the CCLD. The provision is not easy to read, but by studying its history, it makes it easier to understand. See Stein (n 3) 303–04.

[61] If the Member States do nothing or too little, they may incur liability for damages towards a third party who has relied on the false information registered; see also Grundmann (n 4) 184. Since the harmonised rules aim to protect a third party and not the public at large, it seems likely that the first condition for awarding damages is fulfilled; see in contrast Case C-222/02, *Peter Paul*, EU:C:2004:606. However, the second and third conditions still need to be fulfilled, which may not be easy to prove.

[62] The requirement for a unique identifier for each company came later on.

[63] See art 3(3)–(4) of the First Company Law Directive, now found in art 16(4)–(5) of the CCLD. Later on, the requirement for publishing in the national gazette was relaxed as Member States may decide to replace this publication with 'equally effective means'; see now CCLD, art 16(5), second paragraph.

[64] Article 4(6) and now CCLD, art 16(7).

[65] See Directive 2003/58/EC [2003] OJ L221/13. In some Member States, this does not mean that the companies themselves can submit the information electronically, as it may require that the company's representative goes to a notary or legal profession to have the documents certified before submitting them. See the Commission's Impact Assessment SWD(2018) 141, 15.

[66] Directive 2003/58/EC does not prevent the Member States from still using old-school paper versions, and an attempt to opt for only electronic registration was unsuccessful; see COM(2008) 194.

that the documents and particulars should be registered in the language permitted in the Member State where the register is situated. Member States should, however, allow the company to disclose a translation of the documents and particulars in any official language of the EU, and should also 'facilitate access' to such translations.[67]

Finally, it is now required that the changes in documents and particulars, such as amendments of articles of associations and new appointments of directors, should normally be disclosed within 21 days of receipt of the documents.[68]

But these reforms of EU law still leave some of the most important issues relating to the processing of information to the Member States. The Member States decide who is made responsible for carrying out the disclosure formality,[69] how to perform a legality check of the documents submitted, including whether such check should be performed by the register itself, a notary or by others, and finally whether to allow for the online formation of companies. By leaving these issues to the Member States, it is hardly surprising that very different solutions have been adopted,[70] and there is a risk that the quality of the data in the registers differs.[71] In recent years, these differences have increased as some Member States have allowed online registration and others have not.[72] One of the problems that need to be addressed when online registration is allowed is how to ensure that this possibility is not abused and how to prevent corporate identity theft. Both worldwide and also within the EU, this is done very differently.[73]

The recently adopted directive amending the CCLD require Member States to allow for the online registration of companies and online filing of subsequent information on both companies and branches. This will achieve some additional harmonisation since it will ensure that all Member States allow online registration. But the directives leave many of the details to the Member States, including how to ensure a secure identification of those performing the registration[74] and how to perform the legality control.[75] Apart from allowing for online registration and online filing, the proposal

[67] See now CCLD, art 21. Regarding branches, it is also accepted that the information should be provided in the official language of the Member State in which the branch is set up, and it is even allowed to require that certain documents such as the articles of association and the accounting documents are translated; see CCLD, art 32.

[68] See ibid art 15. In comparison, the proposed directive addressing online registration requires that this could be conducted within five working days; see art 13f of the proposal, COM(2018) 239. This indicates that the 21 days granted for updates is quite generous.

[69] See CCLD, arts 27 and 41.

[70] There does not seem to be any review of how the Member States ensure that the information they have submitted to the register is correct. A survey shows that globally, different strategies are used; see the overview in *The International Business Registers Report* (n 34) 130.

[71] Respondents to a consultation preceding the directive introducing the interconnecting of registers also expressed the concern that the quality of data differs and recommended that standards should be set at a European level; see the Commission Impact Assessment (n 9) 48.

[72] In 2018, 17 out of 28 Member States allowed a procedure for fully online registration of companies; see the Commission's Impact Assessment SWD(2018) 141, 14.

[73] For an overview of the different solutions adopted worldwide, see *The International Business Registers Report* (2016) 49–50; and for some detailed studies of different EU jurisdictions, see C Teichmann, 'Die elektronische Gründung von Kapitalgesellschaften' (2018) *GmbHR* 1.

[74] See art 13b of Directive (EU) 2019/1151 (n 36).

[75] See in particular recital 15 of Directive (EU) 2019/1151 (n 36). According to recital 19, flexibility is necessary in order to respect Member States' existing traditions, including the role of notaries or lawyers in the process.

also introduces the 'once-only' principle. According to this principle, the companies should only submit the information once. Thus, if the Member States still insist on publishing information in the national gazette, it should be the register office which after receiving the information submits the information to the national gazette.[76] Also, once a company has submitted information to its main register, this register should make the information available to the register in the Member States in which the companies operate branches, thus saving the companies the trouble of making a separate recording in the register where the branch is located.[77]

Even when this reform is implemented, the processing of information will still be more or less left to the Member States. If the data in the registers vary in reliability, it may become a problem as it may affect the reliability for all registers now that they are interconnected. Therefore, consideration should be given to taking steps to ensure that the legality control is conducted in a more standardised way. As mentioned above in section II, we are still very far from having a centralised European register, but there are many other ways of achieving a more standardised form of control. Examples of how to do this may be found in the harmonisation relying on the country of origin principle. To ensure that the country of origin conducts an adequate level of control, harmonisation may dictate how this control should be conducted, for instance, by stressing the duty to conduct a continuous check that the conditions for exercising the activity are still fulfilled,[78] and even specifying how often these checks must be conducted.[79] An alternative to set such standard through harmonisation is to ensure an increased coordination of the Member States' enforcement through committees and even supranational supervisory authorities.[80]

VI. Enforcement of the Duty to Provide Information

Another important aspect of ensuring reliable information is the enforcement of the duty to disclose. As explained above, it is left to the Member States to decide which persons are responsible for the registration of information.[81] The directive also lists the disclosure requirements for which the Member States, as a minimum, need to determine penalties.[82] But it is not stipulated how the Member States should ensure this

[76] See art 16(3), Directive 2019/1151 (n. 36).

[77] See art 28a–c and art 30a, Directive 2019/1151 (n. 36).

[78] See, for instance, Directive 2013/36/EU, [2013] OJ L176/338 (Credit Institutions), arts 14(3) and 18(c), and Regulation 1071/2009 [2009] OJ L300/51 (Road Haulage Transport), recital 7 and art 12(1).

[79] This is, for instance, the case in the regulation of road haulage transport, where there has been much focus on how the continuous control is conducted. According to art 12(2) of Regulation 1071/2009, [2009] OJ L300/51 (Road Haulage Transport), the home Member State must perform a check on authorised firms every five years. According to art 12(3), they must perform individual checks on request of the Commission.

[80] A committee, for instance, exists under Directive 2010/13/EU [2010] OJ L95/1 (AVMS) – see art 29 and Directive 2006/126/EC [2006] OJ L403/18 (Driving Licences), art 9. The Commission has also established a European Regulators Group for Audiovisual Media Services; see Decision COM(2014) 462 final.

[81] See CCLD, arts 27 and 41.

[82] See ibid arts 28 and 40. This must not lead one to conclude that there is no need to introduce penalties for other provisions in these directives, as there is also a general requirement for effective sanctions; see also Grundmann (n 4) 185.

enforcement, as it is only stipulated that there should be 'appropriate penalties'. The CJEU has explained that this term is to be interpreted in the light of case law requiring that penalties adopted for infringement of EU law should be non-discriminatory, effective, proportionate and dissuasive.[83]

However, this standard may not be completely clear, but fortunately, the CJEU has had a chance to interpret the standard setting out that it both indicates a minimum threshold for penalties as well as a maximum threshold.

The first case was *Daihatsu-Händler eV*, which concerned the German rules implementing the First Company Law Directive. According to the German implementation, it was only the following groups that were allowed to address a failure to disclose the balance sheet and profit and loss account of a company: members or creditors of the company, the central works council or the company's works council. However, by interpreting the First Company Law Directive, the CJEU reached the conclusion that the rules requiring the disclosure of these documents intend to protect any third party that needs to be informed of a company's accounting or financial situation.[84] Therefore, the German implementation did not comply with the requirement for appropriate penalties required by Article 6 of the original Directive. Each interested third party should be allowed to invoke the penalties for failure to disclose the information. Yet, often penalties are not 'triggered' by a complaint, but are enforced *ex officio* by the authorities. The argument can be made that it may not be sufficient to comply with the directive to impose penalties when third parties so require, but that some sort of *ex officio* enforcement is required.[85] The judgment left this issue undecided in *Daihatsu-Händler eV*, but in other cases, the CJEU has indicated that private enforcement may not be enough to constitute efficient enforcement.[86]

Twice, it has been attempted to set aside national penalties for the reason that it either infringes the principle of proportionality or infringes fundamental rights. Here the CJEU addresses the maximum threshold set by the Directive and other parts of EU law.

The CJEU did go to some lengths in trying the national penalty in *Texdata Software GmbH*. The Austrians charged a fine amounting to €700 regarding a foreign company's failure to submit its annual accounts to the registrar in Austria in a situation where it operated a branch in Austria. The CJEU noted that this amount seemed to correspond to the average amount fined by the Member States for such infringements. It accepted that it is 'necessary to weigh the severity of that penalty against the interests of commercial partners and interested persons and the financial risks to which they might be exposed if the true financial situation of a company is not disclosed'.[87] The fact

[83] Joined Cases C-387/02, C-391/02 and C-403/02 *Berlusconi and Others*, EU:C:2005:270.

[84] See Case C-97/96 *Daihatsu-Händler eV*, EU:C:1997:581, para 22. The judgment was subsequently confirmed in Case C-191/95 *Commission v Germany*, EU:C:1998:441.

[85] See Grundmann (n 4) 186.

[86] The CJEU has stressed that the fact that individuals may be able to rely on EU law by taking action on their domestic law to enforce their rights does not relieve Member States of their duty to implement penalties; see Case 72/85 *Commission v The Netherlands*, EU:C:1986:144, para 20; and Case C-132/05 *Commission v Germany*, EU:C:2008:117, para 68.

[87] Case C-418/11 *Texdata Software GmbH*, EU:C:2013:588, para 57.

that there was no way to deviate from the minimum amount of €700 was problematic, but given that it was possible for a company to give a reasoned objection and thereby start a procedure before a national court, it was possible for a company to trigger an assessment of the special circumstances in each case. Thus, it seems that the CJEU is unwilling to accept strict penalties if it is not possible to impose less strict penalties for cases that merit a less strict punishment. Additionally, the CJEU found that the fact that the companies had nine months from the date of the final balance sheet to file the accounts would be sufficient time to comply. Also, it noted that a longer deadline would jeopardise the protection of third parties, since they would not have access to the most recent information reflecting the actual situation of the company concerned.[88] Finally, the CJEU noted that the previous penalty enforced in Austria had proven not to be effective as less than half of the companies under that regime complied with their duty to disclose. In conclusion, it did not find that there were indications that the penalty was disproportionate.[89]

The issue of whether national penalties infringe fundamental rights was also addressed in *Texdata Software GmbH*. The German company argued that the fine violated the right to effective judicial protection and the principle of respect for the rights of the defence, as entrenched in Article 47 of the Charter of Fundamental Rights of the European Union and in Article 6(2) of the European Convention on Human Rights (ECHR). The CJEU dismissed this, but not before going into detail on the argument made by the company. First, the claim was made that a 14-day period for challenging the penalty for failure to disclose is incompatible with the principle of effective judicial protection. The CJEU noted that all branches had nine months from the final balance sheet date to make the disclosure, and that this deadline could be suspended in case of an unforeseen or unavoidable event. In this situation, 14 days were sufficient in practical terms to enable an effective objection to be prepared and submitted.[90] Second, the claim was made that reliance on a legal presumption of liability by which the burden of proof is placed on the company was incompatible with the principle of effective judicial protection. This was also rejected by the CJEU, given that the company concerned need only submit a reasoned objection to the penalty in order to trigger the ordinary procedure, under which the competent court is free to consider the specific circumstances of the case.[91] Third, the claim was made that the principle of effective judicial protection was not observed, as there was an absence of prior notice before the fine was imposed and therefore a lack of any opportunity for the company concerned to make its views known. The CJEU rejected the notion that this was the case as, given the nature of the infringement, it was sufficient that it was possible afterwards to object against the decision imposing the penalty which then immediately renders that decision inoperable and triggers an ordinary procedure under which there is a right to be heard.[92] It also noted

[88] ibid para 59.

[89] ibid para 61 of the judgment. The CJEU did, however, acknowledge that it was up to the Austrian court to make the final assessment of whether or not the fines were proportionate.

[90] Case C-418/11 *Texdata Software GmbH*, EU:C:2013:588, para 81.

[91] ibid para 82.

[92] ibid para 85.

that the object was to ensure a swift disclosure to serve the general interest of ensuring protection of third parties and shareholders. Also, the procedure was not disproportional in relation to the objective pursued.[93] Fourth, the CJEU rejected the idea that certain procedural elements (such as the obligation to state reasons in the document instituting proceedings, the barring of new pleas at the appeal stage and the fact that there is no guarantee that a hearing will be held) did raise doubts as to the conformity of the system of penalties at issue with the principles of effective judicial protection and respect for the rights of the defence.[94]

In *Berlusconi and Others*, the CJEU had to address a complicated issue about the retroactive application of more lenient penalties. In 2002, Italy introduced new, more lenient criminal penalties to sanction false information submitted in violation of the First, Fourth and Seventh Company Law Directives. Berlusconi and others were accused of providing false information at a time before the new penalties entered into force. The principle of the retroactive application of the more lenient penalty, which according to the CJEU is part of EU law,[95] meant that the new more lenient sanctions should be applied. However, the prosecuting authorities took the view that the new penalties adopted in 2002 did not comply with Article 6 of the First Company Law Directive, as they were not 'appropriate' (eg, they were too lax). They argued that since the new more lenient sanctions were invalid, the old stricter penalties should be applied. The CJEU took the view that the authorities could not rely on the Directive in this case, given that this would result in aggravating the criminal liability of the accused. It is against the nature of directives to have such an effect towards individuals, eg, the inability of directives to have horizontal effect.[96] Thus, the case was not so much based on the application of fundamental rights as the lack of horizontal effect of directives.[97]

These cases show that it is not without complications to introduce the appropriate penalties required by the directive. So far, it has been held that the Member States' penalties may be too lax. More recent case law shows that, in principle, the penalties may also be too strict, either being disproportional or infringing fundamental rights, although the CJEU still does not consider this to be the case.

VII. Access to Information

The benefits of making the information in the company registers publicly available will only be realised if interested parties have easy access to the information. The First Company Law Directive required that the information listed in the directive should be made public in two ways: first, the Member State must make the information available upon application;[98] and, second, it is required that the information must be published

[93] ibid para 86.
[94] ibid para 87.
[95] *Berlusconi and Others* (n 84) para 68.
[96] ibid para 74.
[97] The judgment in *Berlusconi* was confirmed in Joined Cases C-23/03, C-52/03, C-133/03, C-337/03 and C-473/03 *Mulliez and Others*, EU:C:2006:285.
[98] According to art 16(4), it should be possible to access general copies and copies certified as 'true copies'.

in the national gazette appointed for that purpose by the Member State.[99] The publication in the national gazette may have been state of the art when the First Company Law Directive was adopted, but later the requirement for publishing in the national gazette has been relaxed, as Member States may decide to replace this publication with 'equally effective means'.[100]

All interested parties have the right to ask for the information on file in the register.[101] The Member States cannot limit the access to specific groups of persons (such as shareholders or creditors), nor can they limit it to persons who have a special interest in the information.[102]

In the original version of the First Company Law Directive, access to information was granted 'by application in writing'.[103] Since it is now possible to access information electronically, such a formal procedure can be dispensed with. Now information can either be accessed online with the relevant register[104] or after the interconnection of the registers through the e-Justice portal. Whereas online access to information seems to be the norm in OECD countries, it is still often necessary in other jurisdictions to visit the register in person to obtain certain information.[105]

But even though Member States (and many others) offer online access to corporate information, there are still some obstacles. In the EU, it is not uncommon that online access is limited to persons who register and, moreover, it is often required that a person pays a fee to preregister.[106] But the main barrier to access is that many countries require a fee for giving access to information. Fees are quite common, not only in the EU, but also worldwide.[107] These fees differ considerably. In Europe, fees differ from €0.03 to access one record in the Netherlands to €12 in Latvia and even €27.42 in Gibraltar.[108]

In the EU, it was originally fully accepted that Member States charged fees for access to information. However, it was a condition that the fee did not exceed the administrative costs of granting access.[109] Later on, it was required that the Member States should make certain basic information available through the interconnection of registers without any charge. This included information on the name and legal form of the company, the registered office and place of registration, and the registration number.[110] At this

[99] See art 3(3)–(4) of the First Company Law Directive, now found in art 16(4)–(5) of the CCLD.

[100] CCLD, art 16(5), second paragraph.

[101] See recital 10 of the CCLD.

[102] See also Case C-97/96 *Daihatsu-Händler eV*, EU:C:1997:581, para 22. Whether this also means that everyone should have access to a complete copy of all data on companies registered is debatable; see M Lutter, W Beyer and J Schmidt, *Europäisches Unternehmens- und Kapitalmarktrecht*, 6th edn (Berlin, De Gruyter, 2018) 402 with further references. It seems that such bulk access to data is often not possible, even in the EU; see *'It's None of Your Business!'* (n 56). See also the landmark ruling of BGH, NJW 1989, 2818.

[103] See First Company Law Directive, art 3(3).

[104] In some jurisdictions, there may be problems with accessing online information; see *'It's None of Your Business!'* (n 56).

[105] See World Bank (n 37) 41.

[106] See *The International Business Registers Report* (n 34) 133.

[107] See ibid 132. When preregistration is required to gain online access to information, there is often a fee for registering.

[108] See *'It's None of Your Business!'* (n 56) 17.

[109] See art 16(4), third paragraph. The provision makes a distinction between documents that are just copies and those that are certified as 'true copies'.

[110] See CCLD, art 19(2).

point, it is only possible to access this information on the e-Justice portal together with other information that Member States choose to offer without a fee. It is necessary to contact the national register to get access to information that requires payment.

In the larger scheme of things, it seems disproportionate that such fees should be allowed to restrict access to information about companies registered in the EU. Since all Member States should now make information electronically available, there will not be any (substantial) extra costs related to allowing unrestricted access. However, it seems that in some Member States, these fees are an important source for financing the registers.[111] In an attempt to balance the financial interest of the registers and the general request for more information free of charge, the recently adopted directive amending the CCLD will ensure that further types of information are added to the list of free information, but has opted not to propose that all information should be free.[112]

Despite the fee charged, it seems that the information on companies is accessed quite often in most jurisdictions.[113] For instance, there are more than three billion searches on corporate information per year in the UK Companies House.[114] In other jurisdictions, the number is considerable lower. For instance, in Ireland there were just over 300,000 searches and in Italy there were just over 5.7 million searches.[115] A global survey shows that the most popular piece of information searched for is basic company data, such as information about the existence of an entity, entity identification and entity name. Search for information relating to directors and annual accounts are not as common. Searches about how to register, laws and regulations, and information about fees are surprisingly not as common as one could imagine.[116]

VIII. The Effect of Registration of Information

If disclosure of corporate information through the registers should benefit business transactions, those who seek the information should be able to rely on this information. It would seem relatively easy to give a third party the right to rely on the information in the register, but nevertheless the solution in the EU only partially achieves this. The solution adopted in the original First Company Law Directive has rightfully been called a 'curious compromise'.[117]

The main rule is that a third party may rely on the information disclosed in the register. Even if it turns out that the persons listed as authorised to represent the company

[111] According to the impact assessment SWD(2018) 141, 52. One Member State had been paid €250,000 just for giving access to information on directors.

[112] See the amended art 19 in Directive (EU) 2019/1151.

[113] Information about the number of searches are found in both *The International Business Registers Report* (n 34) 125–26, and the Impact Assessment prepared by the Commission when proposing the directive on interconnecting registers, the later Directive 2012/30/EU (n 9) 12–13.

[114] The 2017 annual report from Companies House states that the number of searches for free access information is over 2.1 billion and the number of searches for paid information is more than 1.3 billion. In the previous year, the number of searches for free information was 1.3 billion, which indicates a growing demand.

[115] See *The International Business Registers Report* (n 34) 125–26.

[116] See ibid 126.

[117] Stein (n 3) 276.

are in fact not authorised due to an irregularity in their appointment, a third party can rely on the information disclosed. However, here – as in many other situations – a reservation is made for situations where the third party had knowledge of the irregularities, as in this case, the third party cannot rely on the disclosed information.[118]

The regulation is somewhat more complicated than this. One of the reasons is that the harmonisation is based on the principle that it is the publication in the national gazette and not the fact that the information is made available in the register that is given precedence. As a consequence, if information is disclosed in the register, but not in the national gazette, the company cannot rely on the information against a third party. Again, there is a reservation if the company can prove that the third party knew of the information or document that, so far, has not been disclosed. If, on the other hand, the third party prefers to rely on the information that, so far, has not been disclosed in the national gazette, he or she may do so.[119] Even after the information has been published in the national gazette, the third party, during a 16-day period following the event, is allowed to prove that it was impossible for him or her to know of the information and, as a consequence, the company cannot rely on the information.[120]

Another scenario is that there is a discrepancy between the information disclosed in the national gazette and that disclosed in the register. If the information disclosed in the register is false but the text disclosed in the national gazette is correct, the company may not rely on the information disclosed in the gazette. In this situation, the third party is allowed to rely on the register, unless the company can prove that the third party knew that the information in the register was false.[121] If the information in the register is correct but the text published in the gazette is false, the directive is less clear on how this situation should be resolved. However, it seems likely that the similar solution should apply whereby a third party may rely on the version in the national gazette, it knows that this is false.[122] A very similar solution is made in the event that there is a discrepancy between the information registered in the official language and the alternative translation of this information which the company – voluntarily – has chosen to register as well.[123]

The navigation of this regime is made even more difficult due to the fact that there are differences in the implementation of these rules in the Member States.[124] The navigation is made somewhat easier by the fact that the Member States are obliged to make up-to-date information available explaining the national provision as to when third parties may rely on the disclosed information.[125] With the introduction

[118] See CCLD, art 8. For a discussion of what it takes to have knowledge – which is not completely clear, either in this provision or in similar provisions found elsewhere in the CCLD – see Edwards (n 12) 29.

[119] Unless publication is constitutive. The same is the case if the third party relies on information that has not been registered in the companies file. Here third parties may, nevertheless, rely on non-registered information unless registration is constitutive; see CCLD, art 16(7), third paragraph.

[120] See ibid art 16(6).

[121] See ibid art 16(7).

[122] However, the issue is debatable; see Lutter et al (n 103) 413; and L Bock, *Der Harmonisierungserfolg der Publizitätsrichtlinie* (Baden-Baden, Nomos Verlag, 2016) 115–19, both with further references.

[123] See CCLD, art 21(4).

[124] See also the Commission Impact Assessment for the introduction of an interconnecting of registers (n 9) 26.

[125] See CCLD, art 17.

of the e-Justice portal, this information should also be made available in all official languages in the EU.[126]

Even so, the regulation appears to be more complicated than it needs to be. Given that the third party is more likely to retrieve the information registered in the company registers than by reading the national gazette, it would be simpler if all legal effects were attached to the disclosure in the register. The move towards online registration implies that often the companies themselves submit the information to the file and, in this event, it should also be their responsibility if false or incomplete information is registered.[127] This seems to be the solution adopted in the recently adopted Directive (EU) 2019/1151 amending the CCLD. According to this amendment, the disclosure in the register is the only publication needed, and therefore rules on discrepancies are no longer needed. The amendment allows that the Member States may still require an additional publication in the public gazette. If the Member States choose to do so, and there is a discrepancy of what is in the register and in the national gazette, the information in the register shall prevail, see Art 16(5) in Directive (EU) 2019/1151. There is, however, still a reservation that third parties cannot rely on information they know are false.

The current regime tries to find a balance between safeguarding third parties when they are in good faith, but protecting the company against third parties who know that the information they rely on is false.[128] The simpler solution is to allow a third party to rely on the information registered, without any reservations for the third party who knows better. By 'punishing' the third party who has access to information in this way, it may give the third party an incentive not to try to gain knowledge about the company, because in the end, this may be to his or her disadvantage. Similarly, the third party who has taken the trouble to study the articles of association of a company, including the provision stating the object of a company, also runs the risk that the agreement the third party has with the company is not binding because it falls outside the object of the company.[129] It may be preferable to aim for a situation where, no matter what you will discover, it will never have a negative impact on your legal position that you took the time to seek information in the company register. In some jurisdictions, it may be difficult to accept that a third party can rely on information that he or she knows is false. Nevertheless, it must be recalled that it is either the company or the registry that is to blame for the false information. Therefore, allowing a third party to rely on the false information ensures that those responsible for providing the information bear the burden of the mistake. As a result, the companies and the registers are given an extra incentive to make sure that such mistakes are avoided, so allowing a third party to rely on false information will serve a greater good.

[126] See ibid art 17(2).

[127] An earlier attempt to abandon the publication in the national gazette and make do with publication through the registers was unsuccessful; see COM(2008) 194.

[128] In Germany, some scholars assume that a third party can only rely on the false information if the company is in some way responsible for the fact that the false information is disclosed. This very far-reaching limitation of the main rule that third parties (in good faith) should be protected is highly controversial and seems likely to be in conflict with the directive; see Bock (n 123) 123–27.

[129] See the exception allowed by art 9(1), second paragraph of the CCLD.

IX. Conclusions

Worldwide, a wide variety of corporate information is made available through the registers. However, the amount of information, how it is processed and how it is made available differ considerably. Here the EU stands out in the sense that it has made more information publicly available than most jurisdictions and has made disclosure through the register a cornerstone in the regulation of companies. However, the regulation in the EU is still based on national registers that, to a large extent, operate independently. The recent interconnection of registers has partly overcome some of the problems caused by the existence of national registers, but not all. It is still clear that Member States perform different forms of legality checks on registration and filing, and as a consequence, the reliability on information in the different registers is likely to differ. Also, the fact that many Member States still charge fees for accessing certain kinds of information may work as a barrier to access to corporate information. Thus, there is still room for making corporate information even more reliable and accessible through the company registers in the EU.

The access to corporate information should be beneficial to both the companies and third parties. However, there have been examples where easy access to information may, in fact, impair the legal position of third parties. Thus, the knowledge they gain may make it impossible to rely on deviating information published, or it may release the company from a commitment entered into by a person authorised to represent the company. Easy access to information has also had the effect that Member States may be prevented from adopting special regulatory regimes to protect third parties when engaging with companies from other Member States. It is debatable whether easy access to corporate information should have such detrimental effects.

2

Disclosure through Minority and Individual Rights in Public Limited Liability Companies

CORRADO MALBERTI

I. Introduction

European law recognises the importance of transparency in the interests of minority or individual shareholders wishing to exercise their rights. Hence, at a European level, special rules exist regarding, among other things, the facilitation of cross-border voting, the transparency of proxy advisors and the disclosure of related party transactions. Furthermore, shareholders enjoy enhanced disclosure rights when some important decisions come up for consideration. Nonetheless, European law does not systematically recognise the information rights of minority or individual shareholders. By contrast, at a national level, in the context of general meetings, information rights of minority shareholders are often considered 'basic' or 'fundamental' rights. These rights aim at protecting shareholders and holding directors accountable through transparency. This chapter examines the various tools and approaches provided for under European and national law regarding shareholder information by analysing whether shareholder rights may help improve the transparency of European companies.

This chapter is organised as follows: section II, which is divided into two subsections, uses a functional approach to investigate the transparency rights granted to minority and individual shareholders under European law. Subsection II.A examines transparency rights in European company law and, more specifically, the disclosure rights granted by the European company law directives that are now codified in Directive 2017/1132.[1] Then, subsection II.B explores the transparency rights granted to individual and minority shareholders under European financial market regulations. Special attention is given

[1] Directive (EU) 2017/1132 of the European Parliament and of the Council of 14 June 2017 relating to certain aspects of company law [2017] OJ L169/46 (Company Law Directive or Directive 2017/1132).

to the rights included in the Shareholder Rights Directive,[2] which enacted detailed regulations on the functioning of general meetings of listed companies. In truth, in light of its content, this directive may be considered halfway between a company law and a financial market regulation. Subsection II.B also examines some disclosure rights granted to shareholders under the Transparency Directive[3] and the Takeover Bids Directive.[4] Section III examines the information rights of minority and individual shareholders provided for under national law, with specific regard, inter alia, to the right of inspection and to the right to ask for a special investigation. Section IV discusses the general framework of the information rights of minority and individual shareholders, and also explores the changes to these rights in light of the debate on the evolving role of the general meeting and of the goals pursued by disclosure obligations. Section V concludes this chapter.

II. The Disclosure Rights of Minority and Individual Shareholders in European Law

A. Rights Granted under European Company Law

i. The Disclosure of Accounting Documents

One of the first disclosure rights granted under European company law is that currently mentioned in Article 14(f) of Directive 2017/1132[5] concerning the disclosure of accounting documents. This obligation goes back to the enactment of the First Company Law Directive.[6] During the preparatory works for the directive, there was considerable debate as to whether to impose such disclosure on all limited liability companies,[7] and the final adoption of this provision only became possible after it was agreed to delay its

[2] Directive 2007/36/EC of the European Parliament and of the Council of 11 July 2007 on the exercise of certain rights of shareholders in listed companies [2007] OJ L184/17, as amended (Shareholder Rights Directive or Directive 2007/36).

[3] Directive 2004/109/EC of the European Parliament and of the Council of 15 December 2004 on the harmonisation of transparency requirements in relation to information about issuers whose securities are admitted to trading on a regulated market and amending Directive 2001/34/EC [2004] OJ L390/38, as amended (Transparency Directive or Directive 2004/109/EC).

[4] Directive 2004/25/EC of the European Parliament and of the Council of 21 April 2004 on takeover bids [2004] OJ L142/12, as amended (Takeover Bids Directive or Directive 2004/25/EC).

[5] As mentioned in this provision, the disclosure of accounts is also governed by Directive 2013/34/EU of the European Parliament and of the Council of 26 June 2013 on the annual financial statements, consolidated financial statements and related reports of certain types of undertakings, amending Directive 2006/43/EC of the European Parliament and of the Council and repealing Council Directives 78/660/EEC and 83/349/EEC [2013] OJ L182/19, as amended (Directive 2013/34/EU).

[6] First Council Directive 68/151/EEC of 9 March 1968 on coordination of safeguards which, for the protection of the interests of members and others, are required by Member States of companies within the meaning of the second paragraph of Article 58 of the Treaty, with a view to making such safeguards equivalent throughout the Community [1968] OJ L65/8, subsequently amended and codified (First Company Law Directive or Directive 68/151/EEC).

[7] See V Edwards, *EC Company Law* (Oxford, Oxford University Press, 1999) 26 ff.

entry into force for private limited liability companies.[8] The issue was that of striking a balance between the need to ensure confidentiality of accounts and the need to safeguard the general disclosure of information and particulars of European limited liability companies.

Following the enactment of this directive, the debate focused more in detail on which parties should benefit from the disclosure of annual accounts and what sanctions should be levied in cases of non-disclosure.[9] The problem was examined in several decisions of the European Court of Justice, which concluded that the First Company Law Directive precludes Member States from 'failing to provide for appropriate penalties in cases where companies limited by shares fail to effect compulsory disclosure of their annual accounts as prescribed'.[10] The European Court of Justice also made clear that Member States are precluded:

> [F]rom restricting to members or creditors of a company, the central works council or the company's works council the right to apply for imposition of the penalty provided for by the law of [a] Member State in the event of failure by a company to fulfil the obligations regarding disclosure of annual accounts.[11]

Finally, the Court clarified that such disclosure should also benefit a company's competitors,[12] even though some national courts continued to wonder whether the disclosure of accounting documents could amount to a revelation of business secrets.[13]

In brief, although the disclosure of accounting documents should benefit the general public, that disclosure is also made in the interests of shareholders. This conclusion is true in particular in those Member States where the annual accounts are approved by the general meeting.[14] In fact, given that the accounts are prepared under the responsibility of the members of the administrative, management and supervisory bodies of the company (Article 33 of Directive 2013/34), when they are made available to shareholders for their approval, they provide valuable information to them.

[8] See art 2(1)(f) of Directive 68/151/EEC.

[9] Edwards (n 7) 22 ff; S Grundmann and F Glasow, *European Company Law*, 2nd edn (Cambridge, Intersentia, 2012) 185 ff; E Stein, *Harmonization of European Company Laws* (Indianapolis, Bobbs-Merrill Company, Inc, 1971) 237 ff.

[10] Judgment of 29 September 1998, *Commission v Germany*, C-191/95, EU:C:1998:441, ruling 2.

[11] Judgment of 4 December 1997, *Verband deutscher Daihatsu-Händler eV v Daihatsu Deutschland GmbH*, C-97/96, EU:C:1997:581, ruling 1.

[12] Judgment of 23 September 2004, *Axel Springer AG v Zeitungsverlag Niederrhein GmbH & Co Essen*, C-435/02, EU:C:2004:552, para 34.

[13] The reference is to Judgment of 15 January 2002, *Lutz and Others*, C-182/00, EU:C:2002:19, para 10, decided on other grounds, in which an Austrian court asked the European Court of Justice whether European company law, which allegedly requires companies 'to reveal business secrets by imposing the obligation to disclose the balance sheet and the profit and loss account for each financial year', was compatible with the general legal principle of proportionality, the fundamental right to property and the freedom to pursue an economic activity provided by European law. It should also be mentioned that art 36 of Directive 2013/34/EU currently allows the Member States to – somewhat – delay the publication of the annual financial statements of micro-undertakings, making them less readily available to the public.

[14] For more details on these countries, see Grundmann and Glasow (n 9) 273 f; A Lafarre, *The AGM in Europe: Theory and Practice of Shareholder Behaviour* (Bingley, Emerald Publishing, 2017) 82 f.

ii. Information Rights Deriving from the Second Company Law Directive

a. The Disclosure Required in Case of Contributions in Kind

Disclosure rights that benefit minority and individual shareholders are also granted under those parts of the Company Law Directive that derive from the Second Company Law Directive.[15] Although the Second Company Law Directive is mainly concerned with the rules on the formation and alteration of the legal capital, it also provides some relevant information rights to shareholders.

For example, Article 49 of Directive 2017/1132 requires the preparation of an 'expert report'[16] when a company issues shares for consideration other than cash.[17] Public limited liability companies are required to prepare this report at the moment of their creation or when they decide to increase their capital.[18] Even though this report should be understood in the general framework of the rules governing the maintenance of the legal capital, it is also important for shareholders, since it aims at preventing the overvaluation of assets contributed in kind, which could dilute the value and the voting rights of the outstanding shares.[19] When this report is prepared ahead of a capital increase, it is essential information made available to shareholders so that they can decide whether to approve or reject the proposed capital alteration.[20]

Furthermore, Article 52 of Directive 2017/1132, which is applicable in cases of a company acquiring substantial assets belonging to persons that participated in the incorporation procedure, pursues similar goals. Since a shareholder may circumvent Article 49 of the Company Law Directive by contributing cash to the company and then having the company use that cash to acquire assets from the said shareholder, Article 52 of Directive 2017/1132 requires that, in cases of acquisition of assets of substantial value from the persons who participated in the incorporation procedure,

[15] The reference is to the Second Council Directive 77/91/EEC of 13 December 1976 on coordination of safeguards which, for the protection of the interests of members and others, are required by Member States of companies within the meaning of the second paragraph of Article 58 of the Treaty, in respect of the formation of public limited liability companies and the maintenance and alteration of their capital, with a view to making such safeguards equivalent [1977] OJ L26/1, as amended and codified (Second Company Law Directive).

[16] According to art 49(2) of Directive 2017/1132, this report must contain a description of the contributed assets and must state whether the value of the assets corresponds 'at least to the number and nominal value or, where there is no nominal value, to the accountable par and, where appropriate, to the premium on the shares to be issued for them'.

[17] See Edwards (n 7) 61 ff; Grundmann and Glasow (n 9) 220 ff.

[18] See art 70(2) of Directive 2017/1132, concerning capital increases paid with contributions in kind, which makes direct reference to art 49 of Directive 2017/1132 and extends to these transactions the obligation to prepare the expert report.

[19] See Grundmann and Glasow (n 9) 222, who highlight that this report is also prepared in the interests of shareholders.

[20] Interestingly, according to art 49(4) of Directive 2017/1132, when some conditions are satisfied, the persons who take part in the incorporation of the company may decide to waive their right to this report. On this simplification, see Edwards (n 7) 62 f; Grundmann and Glasow (n 9) 223 f; T Papadopoulos and N Moloney, 'EU Company Law' in D Vaughan, A Robertson and P Eleftheriadis (eds), *Law of the European Union* (Oxford, Oxford University Press, 2012), issue 36, § 152; D van Gerven, 'Community Rules Applicable to the Incorporation and Capital of Public Limited Liability Companies' in D van Gerven (ed), *Capital Directive in Europe: The Rules on Incorporation and Capital of Limited Liability Companies* (Cambridge, Cambridge University Press, 2014) 3, 17 f.

an expert report[21] on the valuation of these assets must be prepared. Moreover, this article also requires that the transaction be approved by the general meeting.[22] Therefore, also in this case, shareholders receive information on transactions that may be prejudicial to their interests.[23]

b. Disclosure in Cases of Acquisition of Own Shares and Financial Assistance

European company law requires public limited liability companies to disclose information when they acquire or provide financial assistance for the acquisition of own shares. Article 63(2) of Directive 2017/1132 requires public limited liability companies to disclose in their annual report information regarding the acquisition, amount and disposal of such shares.[24] As indicated above discussing the publication of annual accounts, even a general disclosure of information on own shares may benefit shareholders and be considered in their interests.[25]

The rules on financial assistance provide an even clearer example of disclosure in the interest of shareholders, since Article 64(3) of Directive 2017/1132 requires that these transactions be 'submitted by the administrative or management body to the general meeting for prior approval'. Furthermore, in view of that general meeting, the administrative or management body is also required to present a report outlining the reasons and details for the transaction, highlighting, among other things, the risks that the transaction might have for the company's liquidity and solvency.[26]

c. Limitations on Pre-emption Rights

In the context of capital increases, in addition to the obligation to prepare a report on contributions in kind (Article 70 of Directive 2017/1132), the Company Law Directive requires the preparation of a report when the prospective capital alteration involves a limitation of pre-emption rights decided by the general meeting (Article 72(4) of Directive 2017/1132). Just like any other provision that grants decision-making rights to shareholders,[27] Article 68(1) of Directive 2017/1132, which gives to the general

[21] Unsurprisingly, this report is similar to that mentioned in art 49 of Directive 2017/1132, which is directly referred to in art 52(1) of Directive 2017/1132.

[22] When certain conditions are satisfied (see arts 50 and 51 of Directive 2017/1132), the reports mentioned in arts 49 and 52 of Directive 2017/1132 are not needed.

[23] For an analysis of this provision, see Edwards (n 7) 64 ff; Grundmann and Glasow (n 9) 224 f; van Gerven (n 20) 23 f.

[24] More precisely, the following information should be disclosed: (a) the reasons for the acquisitions made during the financial year; (b) the number and nominal value or, in the absence of a nominal value, the accountable par value of the shares acquired and disposed of during the financial year and the proportion of the subscribed capital which they represent; (c) in the case of acquisition or disposal for a value, the consideration for the shares; and (d) the number and nominal value or, in the absence of a nominal value, the accountable par value of all the shares acquired and held by the company and the proportion of the subscribed capital which they represent.

[25] For further details on this disclosure, see Grundmann and Glasow (n 9) 233 f.

[26] For additional information on these disclosure obligations, see Papadopoulos and Moloney (n 20) § 239 ff.

[27] For example, art 59 of Council Regulation (EC) No 2157/2001 of 8 October 2001 on the Statute for a European company (SE) [2001] OJ L294/1, as amended (Regulation 2157/2001 or SE Regulation) states that any amendment to the statutes of a *Societas Europaea* requires a decision of the general meeting. Beyond the

meeting the competence to decide on capital increases, provides information to shareholders regarding the upcoming discussions and decisions of the general meeting, allowing them to choose whether to participate in the meeting and how to vote. Yet Article 72(4) of Directive 2017/1132, in addition to requiring a decision of the general meeting on the capital alteration, also imposes on the administrative or management body of the company a duty to prepare a written report indicating the reasons for the restriction of the pre-emption right, in particular with regard to justification of the issuance price of the offered shares.[28] In this case as well, the shareholders' interests are protected by informing them of the reasons that justify a transaction that may result in the dilution of both the value and the voting rights of the outstanding shares.

d. Reduction of the Subscribed Capital

Article 73 of Directive 2017/1132 states that any reduction in the subscribed capital that is not ordered by a court is subject to a decision by the general meeting. As mentioned in the previous paragraph, the very fact that the shareholders are involved in the decision-making process implies that they must receive information from the company at least on the intention to carry out such a transaction. In discussing the information rights of shareholders, this provision is interesting because it states that the notice convening the meeting must specify at least 'the purpose of the reduction and the way in which it is to be carried out'.[29] This enhanced disclosure obligation in the notice, which is applicable to all public limited liability companies, may give the shareholders additional useful information to assess the transaction.

e. Convocation of a General Meeting in the Case of Serious Losses

A final provision deriving from the Second Company Law Directive that grants information rights to shareholders is Article 58 of Directive 2017/1132, which concerns the measures companies must take when they incur serious losses. More precisely, according to this article, in the 'case of a serious loss of the subscribed capital', of an amount set by Member States but that cannot be set above one-half of the subscribed capital, 'a general meeting of shareholders shall be called … to consider whether the company should be wound up or any other measures taken'.[30]

In this case, the Company Law Directive does not provide additional details on the information that must be made available to shareholders, giving Member States the discretion to decide which documents are to be prepared for the general meeting and

situations in which European directives and regulations require a decision of the general meeting, it should be recalled that national company law normally gives shareholders extensive decision-making powers on disparate matters, such as the modification of bylaws and the appointment of corporate bodies. In all these cases, shareholders receive information from the company on these matters in the context of the decision-making procedure (for a recent overview of the most relevant competences of the general meeting in some important EU Member States, see Lafarre (n 14) 63 ff).

[28] For further details on the nature and the goals pursued by this provision, see Grundmann and Glasow (n 9) 237 ff.

[29] On this disclosure obligation, see Papadopoulos and Moloney (n 20) § 312.

[30] See Edwards (n 7) 67 f; Grundmann and Glasow (n 9) 230, who argue that this art provides an 'information model'.

whether to impose a 'recapitalise or liquidate' rule. However, especially in the Member States that do not require recapitalisation in the case of serious losses, these meetings are held mainly for the benefit of shareholders in order to inform them of the deterioration of the company's accounts and to give them a venue to discuss and decide on possible countermeasures.

iii. Information Rights Granted to Shareholders in Mergers and Divisions

a. National Mergers

Along with those of other stakeholders, national reorganisation procedures may directly affect shareholders' positions. For this reason, the procedure for approving mergers and divisions is surrounded by specific precautions. The interests of shareholders are mainly protected in the general meetings that are normally called to approve these transactions. From the perspective of the information rights granted to minority and individual shareholders, the rules governing national mergers and divisions deserve attention since they provide clear indications on the tools provided for under European law to ensure the protection of these persons.

For national mergers, the fact that a general meeting must vote on the transaction is a form of disclosure required in the interests of shareholders.[31] However, even more interesting are the rules concerning the prior information that must be given to shareholders in the context of the merger, normally in view of the general meeting that will decide on the transaction.[32] These documents are the draft terms of the merger, the report of the administrative or management body, the expert report[33] and the accounting statement. Barring exemptions, all these documents must be made available at the company's registered office for inspection by shareholders at least one month before the date of the general meeting.[34]

[31] It should be recalled that, according to the Company Law Directive, the approval of the general meeting is not always needed in the context of national mergers. In fact, the exceptions may be found in arts 94, 111 and 113 of Directive 2017/1132. The first and the third of these provisions, whose wording is similar (although the former gives more options of implementation than the latter), may be invoked to omit the approval of the merger by the general meeting of the acquiring company, with the essential difference that while art 94 is applicable in all cases, art 113 is applicable only in cases of a merger by acquisition by a company which holds 90 per cent or more of the shares of a company being acquired. Instead, art 111 is formulated in broader terms, and it exempts from the approval of the general meetings the transactions in which there is a transfer of all assets and liabilities by one or more companies to another company which holds all their shares. In any case, these three provisions, among other requirements, state that for their application, it is necessary that one or more shareholders of the acquiring company holding a percentage of the subscribed capital (with the possibility of excluding non-voting shares), which may not be fixed at more than five per cent, are entitled to require the convocation of the general meeting of the acquiring company to resolve on the approval of the merger. In brief, even these exemptions confirm the idea that in national mergers the general meeting is held mainly in the interests of the shareholders, with the specification that, when certain conditions are met, the general meeting may be held only if a qualified minority of shareholders so requests.

[32] On these disclosure obligations, see Edwards (n 7) 107 f; Grundmann and Glasow (n 9) 683.

[33] As provided in art 96(2) of Directive 2017/1132, this report should essentially assess whether 'the share exchange ratio is fair and reasonable'.

[34] It is important to highlight that even when the approval of the general meeting may be omitted, the preparation of all or part of these documents may still be needed. In this sense, the prior information is not strictly related to the holding of the general meeting.

Originally, this disclosure was made at the company's registered office and was therefore intended solely for shareholders. However, following the amendments introduced in the Third Company Law Directive[35] by Directive 2009/109/EC,[36] companies may also comply with this obligation by making the same documents available – arguably even to the general public – on their websites.

Although the disclosure methods for the documents prior to the general meeting have partially changed and although the disclosure obligation may be fulfilled by making these documents publicly available on the company's website, there is currently little doubt that this disclosure is essentially made in the interests of shareholders. This interpretation is supported by the wording of Articles 95(3), 96(4) and 97(1) of Directive 2017/1132, which state that, with the unanimous agreement of all the shareholders and the holders of other securities conferring the right to vote of each of the companies involved in the merger, it is possible to forgo, respectively, the report of the administrative or management body, the expert report and the accounting statement. This conclusion is also confirmed by the legislative history of the provisions governing national mergers. In fact, the original Third Company Law Directive did not mention the possibility of waiving the right to the documents prepared prior to the general meeting, and left the question open to different interpretations. It was only with Directive 2007/63/EC[37] that this possibility was made clear for the expert report. Then, Directive 2009/109/EC extended this possibility to the accounting statement and the report of the administrative or management body.

Another confirmation of the fact that the documents made available at the company's registered office are disclosed in the interest of the shareholders may be found in the procedural simplifications applicable to mergers between parent companies and subsidiaries when the former hold at least 90 per cent of the shares of the latter. When a parent company holds all the shares of its subsidiary, Article 110 of Directive 2017/1132 provides that the preparation of both the report of the administrative or management body and the expert report is not required.[38] Moreover, when a parent company holds at least 90 per cent of the shares of its subsidiary and the minority shareholders of the latter are entitled to have their shares transferred to the acquiring parent – and some other conditions are met[39] – companies are not required to prepare the report

[35] Third Council Directive 78/855/EEC of 9 October 1978 based on Article 54(3)(g) of the Treaty concerning mergers of public limited liability companies [1978] OJ L295/36, subsequently amended and codified (Third Company Law Directive).

[36] Directive 2009/109/EC of the European Parliament and of the Council of 16 September 2009 amending Council Directives 77/91/EEC, 78/855/EEC and 82/891/EEC, and Directive 2005/56/EC as regards reporting and documentation requirements in the case of mergers and divisions [2009] OJ L259/14 (Directive 2009/109/EC).

[37] Directive 2007/63/EC of the European Parliament and of the Council of 13 November 2007 amending Council Directives 78/855/EEC and 82/891/EEC as regards the requirement of an independent expert's report on the occasion of merger or division of public limited liability companies [2007] OJ L300/47 (Directive 2007/63/EC).

[38] Interestingly, this provision does not mention the accounting statement, but – apparently – nothing prevents that, at least with the unanimous agreement of all the shareholders and the holders of other securities conferring the right to vote in each of the companies involved in the merger, it would also be possible to waive the right to this document.

[39] More precisely, the minority shareholders of the subsidiary, in case they decide to take advantage of this exit right, should be entitled to 'receive consideration corresponding to the value of their shares' and 'in the

of the administrative or management body, the expert report or to comply with the disclosure obligations laid out in Article 97 of the Company Law Directive (Article 114 of Directive 2017/1132). Therefore, in such cases, an accounting statement does not have to be prepared, even in the absence of specific unanimous approval of the shareholders, since the companies involved in the transaction can avoid making a disclosure, at the registered office, of the draft terms of the merger, the accounting statement and the other documents mentioned in that provision.

By making the simplifications in the merger procedure dependent on the shareholding structure of the companies involved in the transaction, and, even more importantly, by granting the shareholders the right to waive some documents, the Company Law Directive implies that the report of the administrative or management body, the expert report and, arguably, also the accounting statement are prepared in the interests of the shareholders and the holders of other securities conferring the right to vote.

Furthermore, it can also be concluded that since it is possible to forgo these documents only with their unanimous consent, this information right belongs individually to each shareholder and each holder of securities conferring the right to vote. However, in some situations, such as when the parent company holds at least 90 per cent or all the shares of the subsidiary, European company law does not recognise these individual rights.[40] Hence, it may be concluded that these information rights are individual to the extent that the companies involved in the transaction have minority shareholders (or a qualified number of minority shareholders).[41]

b. National Divisions

Considering that the rules applicable to national divisions largely follow those of national mergers, companies' procedural disclosure obligations are, unsurprisingly, largely intended for the benefit of shareholders. It is also unsurprising that many of the procedural aspects examined above closely follow those of mergers. This is the case, for example, for the need for approval of the general meeting of all the companies involved in the division and for the prior information that must be given to the participants in the general meeting. The rules regarding the right of inspection of documents at the registered office and the possibility of making these documents available on the company's website also closely follow those for national mergers. Finally, it should be mentioned that the possibility to waive the right to the expert report,[42] the report of the administrative or management body, and the accounting statement, granted to the shareholders and the holders of other securities conferring the right to vote, did not

event of disagreement regarding such consideration' to ask that the value of that consideration is 'determined by a court or by an administrative authority' (art 114 of Directive 2017/1132).

[40] Similar conclusions may be reached with regard to the exemptions from the approval of the general meetings.

[41] Interestingly, the existence of a minority shareholder, or of a qualified minority of shareholders, may affect the rules regarding the disclosure in either the company where these minorities are found or in the other companies.

[42] The content of this report is comparable to that provided for national mergers. In fact, art 142 of Directive 2017/1132, which requires the preparation of this report in divisions, makes direct reference to art 96(2) of Directive 2017/1132.

exist in the original text of the Sixth Company Law Directive[43] and was introduced only with a subsequent amendment.[44]

Examining the other simplifications provided by the Company Law Directive, the most interesting is probably the one that is applicable when, in the context of a division by formation of new companies, the shares in each of the new companies are allocated to the shareholders of the company being divided in proportion to their rights in the capital of that company (Article 156(4) of Directive 2017/1132).[45] In fact, in that case, Member States may provide that the report of the administrative or management body, the expert report and the accounting statement are not required. By making the disclosure of these documents conditional upon the respective position of the shareholders in the dividing and in the newly formed companies, the Company Law Directive further confirms that in national divisions, just as in national mergers, these documents are prepared essentially in the interests of shareholders.

c. Cross-border Mergers

Since the rules on cross-border mergers are less detailed on the procedural aspects than those on national mergers, they only provide little additional information to understand the disclosure rights granted to minority and individual shareholders. In fact, Article 121(1)(b) of Directive 2017/1132, provides that 'a company taking part in a cross-border merger shall comply with the provisions and formalities of the national law to which it is subject'; this provision could be interpreted as giving Member States extensive powers to decide how to structure these mergers. However, this impression is incorrect since Recital (56) of Directive 2017/1132 also states that each company involved in these transactions – and each third party concerned – 'remains subject to the provisions and formalities of the national law which would be applicable in the case of a national merger'. Therefore, it must be concluded that, unless otherwise indicated, the European rules applicable to national mergers apply to cross-border mergers. Furthermore, sometimes, the few procedural rules provided for cross-border mergers closely follow the solutions adopted for national mergers.[46]

[43] Sixth Council Directive 82/891/EEC of 17 December 1982 based on Article 54(3)(g) of the Treaty, concerning the division of public limited liability companies [1982] OJ L378/47, subsequently amended and codified (Sixth Company Law Directive).

[44] It was only with Directive 2007/63/EC that this possibility was made clear for the three different documents (art 144 of Directive 2017/1132).

[45] It should be mentioned that, also in the case of a division, it is possible to avoid the approval of the general meeting of one or all of the companies that take part in the transaction. More precisely, art 140 of Directive 2017/1132 allows Member States to introduce a derogation from the need of obtaining the approval by the general meeting of the recipient company. This simplification closely resembles that applicable to the general meeting of the acquiring company in mergers (art 94 of Directive 2017/1132). Instead, art 154 of Directive 2017/1132 concerns the exemption from the requirement of approval by the general meeting of the company being divided, when the recipient companies together hold all the shares and all other securities conferring the right to vote at the general meetings of the company being divided and some other conditions are satisfied. In both cases, the prior information, where applicable, is still required and, as previously seen for mergers, it is not strictly related to the holding of the general meeting.

[46] This is the case, for example, of art 126(3) of Directive 2017/1132, which states that Member States may not require an approval of the merger by the general meeting of the acquiring company if the conditions indicated in art 94 of Directive 2017/1132, concerning the same situation for national mergers, are satisfied.

With regard to the interests protected in cross-border mergers, some indications on the main differences between these transactions and national mergers may be found in the simplifications provided for the case of a merger between a parent company and a subsidiary, when the former holds all the shares and other securities conferring the right to vote in the general meetings of the latter (Article 132 of Directive 2017/1132). Contrary to the provisions for national mergers, when a wholly owned subsidiary is acquired, only the expert report[47] is not required, while the report of the administrative or management body is still needed. This different approach is justified by the fact that, according to Article 124 of Directive 2017/1132, in cross-border mergers, the report of the administrative or management body must also discuss the implications of the cross-border merger for creditors and employees, and must be made available not only to the shareholders but also to the employees. In any case, this same provision of the Company Law Directive is clear in stating that this report is 'intended for the members' without reference to other stakeholders.[48] Therefore, it can be concluded that the report of the administrative or management body is still needed in these transactions because, given that this report should also explain the implications of the cross-border merger for creditors and employees, the fact that the cross-border merger takes place between a parent and its wholly owned subsidiary is, for those purposes, irrelevant.[49] This analysis of the rules governing cross-border mergers reveals that although the report of the administrative or management body in these transactions has a broader scope than that required for national mergers, it is expressly intended in the interests of shareholders, even though it should also be made available to other stakeholders.

B. Rights Granted by European Financial Market Regulations

i. The Shareholders Rights Directive

a. Information Prior to the General Meeting

The Shareholder Rights Directive provides extensive disclosure rights in the interests of shareholders of listed companies. Amongst these, an important role is

[47] Given that art 125 of Directive 2017/1132, which governs the expert report in cross-border mergers, makes direct reference to art 96(2) of Directive 2017/1132. Also, in these transactions the content of the expert report is similar to that provided for national mergers.

[48] However, it is less clear whether, as in national mergers, with the unanimous agreement of all the shareholders and the holders of the other securities conferring the right to vote of each of the companies involved in the merger, it would be possible to forgo this report. Bech-Bruun and Lexidale, 'Study on the Application of the Cross-border Mergers Directive' (2013), publications.europa.eu/en/publication-detail/-/publication/0291c60a-df7a-11e5-8fea-01aa75ed71a1, Main Findings 64, suggest that although this possibility is not allowed, it would be desirable. Recently, the Proposal for a Directive of the European Parliament and of the Council amending Directive (EU) 2017/1132 as regards cross-border conversions, mergers and divisions [2018] COM/2018/241 final – 2018/114 (COD), proposed amending art 124 of Directive 2017/1132 to allow a waiver of this report 'where all the members of the merging companies have agreed'.

[49] In national mergers, the report of the administrative or management body should explain the draft terms of the merger and the legal and economic grounds for them, with specific attention to the share exchange ratio. For that reason, given that in a merger between a parent and its wholly owned subsidiary there is no exchange ratio, it is easy to understand why no report is needed in such cases.

played by the right to provide information prior to general meetings (Article 5 of Directive 2007/36).[50]

In the context of the general meeting, the first information that must be disclosed is the convocation, which should be published with an appropriate period of notice using means that could reasonably ensure effective dissemination of information to the public throughout the European Union (EU). However, it is also possible for Member States to allow companies to avoid this public announcement if they are 'able to identify the names and addresses of their shareholders from a current register of shareholders, provided that the company is under an obligation to send the convocation to each of its registered shareholders' (Article 5(2) of Directive 2007/36).[51]

The convocation must include detailed information regarding the time and place of the general meeting, the procedures to participate in the meeting, the right to ask questions, the right to put items on the agenda and to table draft resolutions, the procedures for voting by proxy and, where applicable, those for casting votes by correspondence or electronic means, the details on the record date, the indications on how to obtain the documents and draft resolutions to be discussed at the meeting, and, finally, also the address of the website where the information required by Article 5(4) of Directive 2007/36 may be found (Article 5(3) of Directive 2007/36).[52]

Article 5(4) of Directive 2007/36 requires companies to make certain information available to shareholders on their websites. This information should include at least the convocation, the total number of shares and voting rights at the date of the convocation, the documents to be submitted to the general meeting, the draft resolutions or, where no resolution is proposed to be adopted, a comment for each item on the proposed agenda of the general meeting, and, where applicable, the forms to be used to vote by proxy and to vote by correspondence, unless those forms are sent directly to each shareholder. Furthermore, according to this provision, draft resolutions tabled by shareholders must be added to the company's website as soon as practicable after their reception by the company.[53]

The disclosure required for listed companies prior to the general meeting is intended to provide the shareholders with the information that is needed to take pondered decisions. It should be highlighted that the addressees of this information are, in principle, the shareholders, even though a wider dissemination is also accepted. More precisely, Article 5(2) of Directive 2007/36 states that the convocation should be publicly disclosed and, when certain specific conditions are satisfied, it may be addressed solely to shareholders. Instead, with regard to the information mentioned in Article 5(4) of Directive 2007/36 and to be provided on the company's website, it should be emphasised

[50] On this provision, see M Lutter, W Bayer and J Schmidt, *Europäisches Unternehmens- und Kapitalmarktrecht Grundlagen, Stand und Entwicklung nebst Texten und Materialien*, 6th edn (Berlin, Walter de Gruyter, 2018) 1188 f; S Kalss and C Klampfl, *Europäisches Gesellschaftsrecht* (München, CH Beck – Manz, 2015) 154 f.

[51] For more details on this provision, see Lutter et al (n 50) 1190 ff. It should also be mentioned that art 3b of Directive 2007/36, which was introduced by Directive 2017/828 (Directive (EU) 2017/828 of the European Parliament and of the Council of 17 May 2017 amending Directive 2007/36/EC as regards the encouragement of long-term shareholder engagement [2017] OJ L132/1 (Directive 2017/828)), now provides a legal framework on how the communication between companies, shareholders and intermediaries should take place.

[52] See Lutter et al (n 50) 1192 f.

[53] On this provision, see ibid 1193 f.

that, even though apparently nothing prevents wider dissemination, the Shareholder Rights Directive requires companies to make that information available 'to [their] shareholders' and not to the general public.

b. The Right to Ask Questions

One of the most important information rights granted by the Shareholder Rights Directive to shareholders of listed companies is the right to ask questions to the corporate bodies.[54] Although the EU Member States traditionally recognised the right to ask companies for information even before the enactment of Directive 2007/36, the solutions adopted in the various legal systems were not uniform.[55] In some countries, this right was strictly related to the holding of the general meeting, while in others the interaction between the company and shareholders did not necessarily take place during the meeting. Another important difference among Member States lay in terms of how they struck a balance between, on the one hand, the shareholders' right to receive information and, on the other, the companies' right to preserve business secrets and to ensure the orderly running of the general meeting.[56] To address these problems, Article 9 of Directive 2007/36 was formulated to give shareholders of listed companies the right to ask questions, but also to provide Member States with several implementation options on the exercise of this right.

A first important aspect of the right to ask questions is that it must concern matters related to items on the agenda of the general meeting (Article 9(1) of Directive 2007/36). This means that there is a relationship between the right to ask questions and the holding of the general meeting, and that shareholders are not entitled to ask questions on any matter related to the affairs of the company.[57] Inevitably, this approach limits the scope of the shareholder right examined here and also gives companies the power to maintain some confidentiality on matters completely unrelated to items on the meeting agenda.

In any case, the Shareholder Rights Directive also states that an answer should be given to the submitted questions (Article 9(1) of Directive 2007/36). However, the directive does not specify how detailed this answer must be.

One relevant option granted to Member States in implementing the directive consists of determining the conditions whereby the right to ask questions must be exercised. In fact, Member States may take or allow companies to take appropriate measures 'to ensure the identification of shareholders, the good order of general meetings and their preparation and the protection of confidentiality and business interests of companies'

[54] On this right, see Lafarre (n 14) 25 f; Lutter et al (n 50) 1205 ff; Kalss and Klampfl (n 50) 158 f; M Siems et al, 'Abuse of Shareholder Rights' in M Siems and D Cabrelli (eds), *Comparative Company Law: A Case-Based Approach*, 2nd edn (Oxford, Hart Publishing, 2018) 339 ff, who, discussing a practical case, provide a comparative overview on the right to ask questions in several jurisdictions.

[55] In general, on the right of information of shareholders, see KC Pelzer, *Das Auskunftsrecht der Aktionäre in der Europäischen Union* (Köln, Heymanns, 2004); E Perakis, 'Rights of Minority Shareholders: General Report' in E Perakis (ed), *Rights of Minority Shareholders* (Bruxelles, Bruylant, 2004) 12, 67 ff.

[56] For an overview of the current legal framework on the right to ask questions in several EU Member States, see Lafarre (n 14) 43 ff. For a comparative analysis of this right, see M Siems, *Convergence in Shareholder Law* (Cambridge, Cambridge University Press, 2008) 121 ff.

[57] On the precise content of this limitation, see Lutter et al (n 50) 1206.

(Article 9(2) of Directive 2007/36).[58] Evidently, these measures may hinder the right to ask questions, for example, by limiting the time given to shareholders to exercise this right.

Member States may also enact legislation that would allow companies to provide a single overall answer to questions that have the same content (Article 9(2) of Directive 2007/36). This possibility clearly reduces the burdens placed on companies.

Furthermore, Member States may also state that the duty to answer questions is considered to be fulfilled if the relevant information is available on the website of the company in 'a question and answer format' (Article 9(2) of Directive 2007/36). This provision is important because it makes clear that although the right to ask questions concerns matters related to the items on the agenda of the general meeting, the dialogue between shareholders and companies does not necessarily have to take place during the meeting.

Given that different national perspectives exist on the right to ask questions, that the Shareholder Rights Directive is applicable only to listed companies and that Member States may take advantage of various implementation options, some divergences persist across the EU in the application of this right, in spite of its harmonisation.

c. The Right to Put Items on the Agenda and to Table Resolutions

The Shareholder Rights Directive enhanced the information rights of shareholders by giving them the right to add items to the agenda of the general meeting and to table draft resolutions (Article 6 of Directive 2007/36).[59] When introduced by Directive 2007/36, this right was not a complete innovation for European company law, since both the Statute for the *Societas Europaea* (Article 56 of the SE Regulation) and that for the *Societas Cooperativa Europaea* granted minority shareholders at least the power to add new items to the agenda (Article 57 of the SCE Regulation).[60]

The Shareholder Rights Directive states that this right may be recognised to shareholders individually or collectively. In any case, Member States may not require that more than five per cent of the share capital be needed to exercise this right.[61]

Clearly, this right is not exclusively aimed at improving the level of information available to shareholders. However, since the notice of the convocation for the meeting has informational value, it gives shareholders useful elements to decide whether to participate and how to vote at the general meeting. In this case, the information originates mainly from the shareholders that made the proposal and not directly from the company.

In any case, communication of the updated agenda among shareholders is mediated by the company, which must make it available in the same manner as the previous agenda (Article 6(4) of Directive 2007/36). Similarly, as already mentioned,

[58] See ibid 1207.

[59] On this right, see Lafarre (n 14) 25; Lutter et al (n 50) 1195 f; Kalss and Klampfl (n 50) 155.

[60] Council Regulation (EC) No 1435/2003 of 22 July 2003 on the Statute for a European Cooperative Society (SCE) [2003] OJ L207/1 (Regulation 1435/2003 or SCE Regulation).

[61] When certain conditions are met, this right may also be complemented with the right to call the general meeting (art 6(1) of Directive 2007/36).

also the communication of the draft resolutions tabled by shareholders is mediated by the company, as these draft resolutions must be published on the company's website as soon as practicable once they have been received by the company (Article 5(4)(d) of Directive 2007/36).

The right to add items to the agenda and to table resolutions may play an important role in improving the quality of the information communicated by the company to shareholders. In fact, this right may be used as a means to expose relevant matters to the attention of the general meeting and to trigger a reaction from the company, especially when the new items or the proposed new resolutions are not welcome to the corporate bodies. In fact, in reacting to the shareholders' initiatives, the company may disclose useful information and explain the reasons that led it to organise the agenda differently.

d. Disclosure of Voting Results

Another provision of the Shareholder Rights Directive that has informational value concerns the publication on the company's website of the voting results for each resolution of the general meeting. Depending on the applicable national law, such publication must be made, at the latest, within 15 days after the general meeting (Article 14 of Directive 2007/36). This disclosure, while related to decisions taken by shareholders, is addressed to the general public and not expressly to shareholders.[62]

e. Remuneration Policy and Report

The European legislature recently amended the Shareholder Rights Directive to introduce new disclosure obligations for the benefit of shareholders.[63] These innovations concern the remuneration policy and related party transactions.[64]

Starting with the disclosure obligations concerning the remuneration policy, Directive 2017/828 gives shareholders the right to approve or reject the remuneration policy of directors, and requires companies to prepare a remuneration report, which is also subject to shareholders' approval. The rules on the approval of the remuneration policy are somewhat intricate, since the directive says that shareholders have the right to vote on that policy and that vote is binding (Article 9a(2) of Directive 2007/36). However, Member States may also decide to give this vote simple advisory status. In that case, companies are allowed to pay remuneration 'to their directors only in accordance with a remuneration policy that has been submitted to such a vote at the general meeting' (Article 9a(3) of Directive 2007/36). Moreover, if 'the general meeting rejects the proposed remuneration policy, the company shall submit a revised policy to a vote at the following general meeting' (Article 9a(3) of Directive 2007/36).[65]

[62] On this disclosure obligation, see Kalss and Klampfl (n 50) 161 f; Lutter et al (n 50) 1248 ff, who argue that the disclosure of the voting results gives shareholders the possibility to verify that their votes have been correctly taken into account by the company.

[63] These amendments were introduced by Directive 2017/828.

[64] See Lutter et al (n 50) 1209 ff.

[65] Details on what information on the remuneration policy should be provided are indicated in art 9a(6) of Directive 2007/36.

Any material change to the remuneration policy must be submitted to a vote of the general meeting and – in any case – a vote of the general meeting on the policy is required at least every four years (Article 9a(5) of Directive 2007/36). Furthermore, after the vote, both the policy and the results of such a vote must be published on the company's website and remain publicly available for the period of application of the policy (Article 9a(7) of Directive 2007/36).

The remuneration report provides a comprehensive overview of the remuneration awarded or due to directors during the most recent financial year.[66] The purpose of collecting and processing these data is that of 'increasing corporate transparency as regards directors' remuneration with the view to enhancing directors' accountability and shareholder oversight over directors' remuneration' (Article 9b(3) of Directive 2007/36). As mentioned above, the general meeting has the right to approve or reject this report, yet this vote is simply advisory in nature. In any case, the company must explain in the following remuneration report 'how the vote by the general meeting has been taken into account' (Article 9b(4) of Directive 2007/36).[67] Finally, companies must make the remuneration report available on their website for a period of 10 years (Article 9b(5) of Directive 2007/36).

The rules of the Shareholder Rights Directive on remuneration give shareholders important information and decision-making rights. The fact that the general meeting should discuss and vote on both the policy and the remuneration report proves that shareholders are the first addressees of this information. However, also in this case, the publication of these documents is not made in their exclusive interest, but also in the interests of the general public.

f. Related Party Transactions

Although the rules on related party transactions should arguably also protect the interests of minority shareholders in situations tainted by a potential conflict of interest, European law does not grant any specific information right to such shareholders. It is true that companies must announce material transactions with related parties and that this announcement should provide the necessary information to assess whether 'the transaction is fair and reasonable from the perspective of the company and of the shareholders who are not a related party, including minority shareholders' (Article 9c(2) of Directive 2007/36).[68] It is also true that Member States may provide that this announcement be 'accompanied by a report assessing whether or not the transaction is fair and reasonable from the perspective of the company and of the shareholders who are not a related party, including minority shareholders' (Article 9c(3) of Directive 2007/36). However, this information is made publicly available and is not specifically addressed to shareholders.

[66] The content of this report is indicated in art 9b(1) of Directive 2007/36.

[67] According to this provision, the companies that fall within the definition of a small or medium-sized company, as provided by Directive 2013/34/EU, may be exempted by the Member States from the obligation to submit the remuneration report to a vote, at least as long as this report is discussed as a separate item in the annual general meeting.

[68] In general, on the European rules applicable to related party transactions, see Lutter et al (n 50) 1222 ff.

Shareholders enjoy enhanced information rights only in cases of so-called 'material transactions' with related parties[69] and only if a Member State provides that these transactions must be approved by the general meeting.[70] In this case, the information given to shareholders follows the rules and procedures normally provided for general meetings with two additional particularities. First, the information disclosed to shareholders may be accompanied by a report on the fairness and reasonableness of the transaction. Second, since in the context of the approval of these transactions the voting rights of the related parties are somewhat restricted,[71] those of other shareholders may become more relevant for the approval of the resolution. Therefore, in this context, a non-related shareholder's request to receive more information is likely to be examined with greater attention by the company.

ii. The Takeover Bids Directive

a. The Opinion of the Board on the Bid

In the context of takeover law, the opinion on the offer prepared by the target company's board (Article 9(5) of Directive 2004/25/EC) is another interesting example of disclosure imposed on companies in the interests of shareholders.[72] This opinion should discuss the effects of the offer on all the interests of the company and on the strategic plans of the offeror for the company 'and their likely repercussions on employment and the locations of the company's places of business'. Given that, according to Article 9(5) of Directive 2004/25/EC, the board's opinion should be made public and also communicated to the employee representatives or, where there are no such representatives, to the employees themselves, this document is not exclusively – or expressly – addressed to the shareholders.

In any case, the board's opinion is valuable information for the shareholders to decide whether to tender their shares to the offeror. Moreover, the opinion should also be understood in the broader framework of the non-frustration rule (Article 9 of Directive 2004/25/EC). When this rule is applicable, although the board is not allowed to take actions without the prior approval of the general meeting, it is at least required to deliver an opinion on the offer. Therefore, in this case, the opinion may also become an important document for shareholders when they are called on to decide on defensive measures.

b. Shareholding Structure and Defensive Measures

The Takeover Bids Directive requires listed companies to disclose relevant information regarding their shareholding structure and the adoption of defensive measures

[69] The exact definition of these transactions is left up to the Member States within the general framework provided in art 9c(1) of Directive 2007/36.

[70] In fact, Member States may provide that the approval is given 'by the general meeting or by the administrative or supervisory body' (art 9c(4) of Directive 2007/36).

[71] For details on these limitations, see art 9c(4) of Directive 2007/36.

[72] See, for example, Grundmann and Glasow (n 9) 743 f.

(Article 10(1) of Directive 2004/25/EC).[73] This information is made available not only to shareholders but also, more generally, to the public. However, since this information must be published in the annual report of the company (Article 10(2) of Directive 2004/25/EC) and since the board is required to present the annual general meeting with an explanatory report on these matters (Article 10(3) of Directive 2004/25/EC), the shareholders' position on this information is not merely that of any potential investor, given that they enjoy enhanced information and – eventually – also some decision-making rights on it.

iii. The Transparency Directive

The Transparency Directive harmonises the transparency requirements for information of issuers of listed securities. The transparency obligations mandated by this directive are mainly provided in the interests of the general public and not specifically for those of shareholders. However, at least one provision of this directive (Article 17 of Directive 2004/109/EC) makes reference to some disclosure obligations that are directed expressly to shareholders. In fact, the directive states that issuers must ensure that 'all the facilities and information necessary to enable holders of shares to exercise their rights are available' (Article 17(2) of Directive 2004/109/EC). More precisely, inter alia, companies must: (a) 'provide information on the place, time and agenda of meetings, the total number of shares and voting rights and the rights of holders to participate in meetings'; (b) 'make available a proxy form … to each person entitled to vote at a shareholders' meeting'; and (c) 'publish notices or distribute circulars concerning the allocation and payment of dividends and the issue of new shares' (Article 17(2)(a), (b) and (d) of Directive 2004/109/EC). According to this directive, the communication from the company to shareholders may be carried out using electronic means if the general meeting so decides and certain other conditions are satisfied (Article 17(3) of Directive 2004/109/EC).[74]

Although not particularly detailed, the disclosure obligations in the interests of shareholders laid out in the Transparency Directive warrant attention as they were one of the earliest examples of the harmonisation of such obligations provided by European financial market regulations.[75] However, since this directive is addressed only to companies with listed securities, it has no implications for the vast majority of European public limited liability companies.

[73] On this disclosure obligation, see ibid 746 f; R Veil, 'Disclosure of Defensive Structures and Mechanisms' in R Veil (ed), *European Capital Markets Law*, 2nd edn (Oxford, Hart Publishing, 2018) 729 ff.

[74] On art 17 of Directive 2004/109/EC, see N Moloney, *EU Securities and Financial Markets Regulation*, 3rd edn (Oxford, Oxford University Press, 2014) 140; Veil (n 73) 449, 454 f.

[75] Before that directive, see the disclosure obligations that were imposed on listed companies by Point 2(b), Schedule C of the Annex of Council Directive 79/279/EEC of 5 March 1979 coordinating the conditions for the admission of securities to official stock exchange listing [1979] OJ L66/21 (Directive 79/279/EEC).

III. Disclosure Rights of Minority and Individual Shareholders under National Law

A. The Right of Inspection

National company law provides some rights that are not yet harmonised at the European level by either European company law or financial market regulations. Amongst these, it is common for Member States to grant individual or minority shareholders the right to inspect some company books or records.[76] Even today, this information right remains almost entirely governed by national law.

The right of inspection may take different forms and concern a variety of documents and records. Notably, this right can be entirely independent of the right to take part in the general meeting.[77] In certain jurisdictions, the right of inspection plays an important role, while other legal systems approach it with more caution.[78] Also in this case, as for the right to ask questions, a balance must be struck between the interests of the shareholders to receive information from the company and that of companies to maintain confidentiality and avoid shareholder misconduct. From this perspective, in order to prevent continuous and burdensome requests for documents and records from disrupting company life, the exercise of this right may be mediated by courts or other gatekeepers.[79]

As mentioned above with regard to mergers and divisions, the right of inspection may also concern the documents related to a specific general meeting. In that form, this right shares traits with the obligations imposed by European law on listed companies to disclose information prior to the general meeting, since in both cases the information right is granted in view of allowing shareholders to take more pondered decisions in that meeting.

In conclusion, the right of inspection is a powerful tool in the hands of individual and minority shareholders, but it is also a tool that can easily be abused by shareholders. As for the right to ask questions, if a jurisdiction sets certain limits, the risk of abuses will decrease, but the effectiveness of this right could also be undermined. Moreover, given the different national approaches to the right of inspection and the lack of harmonisation in this field, depending on the applicable national law, individual and minority shareholders may find themselves in quite different positions if they wish to exercise this right.

B. The Right to Ask for a Special Investigation

National company law frequently grants minority shareholders the right to ask for a special investigation of the company. The law may provide that the exercise of this

[76] For a comparative analysis of that right, see Perakis (n 55) 68 ff; Siems (n 56) 124 f; GH Roth and P Kindler, *The Spirit of Corporate Law* (München, CH Beck – Manz, 2013) 131 f.

[77] See Roth and Kindler (n 76) 131.

[78] Siems (n 56) 124; Roth and Kindler (n 76) 132.

[79] Perakis (n 55) 69 f.

right is mediated by a vote of the general meeting, an intervention by the company's supervisory body, or the involvement of courts or other authorities. The jurisdictions where this right exists differ depending on the circumstances that may justify the investigation.[80]

Notwithstanding national differences, the right to request a special investigation is deemed an effective corporate governance tool that may improve companies' transparency.[81] Moreover, this right is arguably less prone to abuses than other rights granted to minority or individual shareholders, because the inquiry procedure relies on corporate bodies or third parties that, acting as gatekeepers, may prevent possible abuses.

From the perspective of European law, the lack of harmonisation in this field is not attributable to a lack of interest in this right. In fact, at various moments, attempts have been made to introduce the right to ask for a special investigation in European company law.[82] However, these attempts were unsuccessful, despite legal scholarship highlighting the advantages of this right.[83]

Examining the disclosure rights of individual and minority shareholders, it is sufficient to highlight that the right to ask for an investigation is a powerful tool in the hands of shareholders to reveal information that a company would be unlikely to disclose. An innocent company that is worried about possible abuses of minority rights might consider this right more favourably than individual inspection rights, since, in this case, the investigation is not carried out directly by shareholders. Instead, if a company has something to hide, it may view the launch of an investigation with some fear, since the procedure is usually carried out by knowledgeable professionals who are granted strong inspection powers. For shareholders, this mediation has some benefits, but also some inconveniences, since the interests that should be pursued by those who carry out the investigation may not coincide exactly with those of the shareholders who triggered the procedure.

[80] For more comparative details on this right, see ibid 71 ff.

[81] KJ Hopt, 'Comparative Corporate Governance: The State of the Art and International Regulation' in AM Fleckner and KJ Hopt (eds), *Comparative Corporate Governance: A Functional and International Analysis* (Cambridge, Cambridge University Press, 2013) 3, 82, who argues that the special investigation 'may play an important role as a preventive measure for the protection of minorities'.

[82] More precisely, some reference to the right to ask for a special investigation may be found in the first drafts of the Statute for the *Societas Europaea* (*cf* European Commission, 'Projet d'un statut d'une société anonyme européenne par Pieter Sanders' (1966), aei.pitt.edu/39000/1/A3884.pdf, arts VI-7-1 ff; European Commission, 'Proposed Statute for the European Company' (1970), aei.pitt.edu/83204/1/BUL456-1970.8.pdf, arts 97 ff). More recently, the High Level Group of Company Law Experts, 'A Modern Regulatory Framework for Company Law in Europe' (2002), ecgi.org/publications/documents/report_en.pdf, ch III § 3.4, also recommended the introduction of special investigation rights for minority shareholders. That recommendation, however, was ultimately not accepted by the European Commission (see Hopt (n 81) 82).

[83] See, for example, Hopt (n 81) 81 f; KJ Hopt, 'Modern Company and Capital Market Problems: Improving European Corporate Governance after Enron' in J Armour and JA McCahery (eds), *After Enron: Improving Corporate Law and Modernising Securities Regulation in Europe and the US* (Oxford, Oxford University Press, 2006) 445, 465 ff; KJ Hopt, 'Rights of Minority Shareholders under German Law' in E Perakis (ed), *Rights of Minority Shareholders*, (Bruxelles, Bruylant, 2004) 389, 399 ff; Perakis (n 55) 71 ff.

C. Other Rights Granted by National Company Law

i. *The Right to Call the General Meeting*

As mentioned before, the Shareholder Rights Directive gives shareholders of listed companies the right to put items on the agenda of the general meeting. This directive also states that when this right is limited to the annual general meeting, shareholders should be given 'the right to call, or to require the company to call, a general meeting … with an agenda including at least all the items requested by those shareholders' (Article 6(1) of Directive 2007/36). With the exclusion of this case, the harmonisation directives do not require Member States to grant shareholders the right to call general meetings.[84]

Although not harmonised at the European level, national company law frequently gives shareholders the right to call the general meeting in public limited liability companies.[85] In the context of disclosure rights granted to minority shareholders, the role of this right is comparable to that of the right to put items on the agenda: it can be used by shareholders to draw other shareholders' attention to matters that are deemed relevant and to stimulate reactions from the company. Without going into detail on how the right to call the general meeting takes shape in national law, the most relevant difference with the right to put items on the agenda is that the former can be invoked by minority shareholders independently of the convocation of a general meeting, while the latter at least presupposes that the company takes the initiative of calling the meeting. From this perspective, all other things being equal, the right to call the general meeting is more favourable to shareholders than the right to add items to the agenda, since it does not require previous actions by the company.

ii. *Adjournment of the General Meeting*

A disclosure right granted to shareholders by national law in some countries is the right to request an adjournment of the general meeting.[86] This right warrants mention because it may be useful to allow shareholders to gather additional information regarding the items discussed in the meeting.[87] However, this right does not necessarily impose

[84] It should also be recalled that this right is provided by both the Statute for the *Societas Europaea* and that for the *Societas Cooperativa Europaea*. Art 55 of Regulation 2157/2001 states that one or more shareholders who hold at least 10 per cent of the subscribed capital of a *Societas Europaea* may request the company to convene a general meeting and draw up the agenda. Furthermore, the statutes of the company or national legislation may provide for a smaller percentage under the same conditions as those applicable to public limited liability companies. A similar right is granted for the *Societas Cooperativa Europaea* under art 55 of Regulation 1435/2003, with the difference that, in that case, the power is given, alternatively, to at least 5,000 members or to the members who have at least 10 per cent of the total number of votes. In addition, this provision also states, without making reference to national law, that these 'proportions may be reduced by the statutes'.

[85] Perakis (n 55) 75 f.

[86] ibid 76, who makes reference to Greek and Italian law.

[87] This rationale is expressly evoked in Italian law by art 2374 of the Civil Code, which provides that in order to ask for an adjournment of the general meeting, shareholders should state that they are not sufficiently informed on the proposals presented before the meeting.

specific disclosure obligations on companies, but simply allows shareholders to conduct personal research and to better process the available information.

iii. Representation of Minority Shareholders on Corporate Bodies

National law may give minority shareholders the right to appoint one or more members to the administrative or supervisory body of the company. This possibility, which, for example, is granted by Italian law for both the administrative and the supervisory body of listed companies, may give minority shareholders better access to company information, since the persons who are appointed may consult the documents that are made available to the members of the relevant body of the company.[88]

However, it should be made clear that the representatives of minority shareholders are subject to the same duties as other members of the corporate body to which they belong, including the duty of confidentiality. Furthermore, the individual information and inspection rights of the representatives of minorities may vary across jurisdictions. In any case, in the legal systems that grant this right to minorities, the persons appointed – eventually even minority shareholders – will enjoy stronger disclosure rights than those granted to ordinary shareholders, at least inasmuch as they will also be active in the corporate bodies to which they belong.[89]

IV. Framing the Disclosure Rights of Minority and Individual Shareholders

A. Framing the Disclosure Rights of Shareholders

i. Equal Treatment

The need to ensure equal treatment is an essential component of the disclosure obligations imposed on companies for the benefit of shareholders. Since disclosure rights are granted to individual – or to a minority of – shareholders, it should be ensured that companies provide the required information to all shareholders on equal terms.

It is remarkable that the principle of equal treatment is expressly mentioned in many directives examined in the previous pages, which make it applicable to the disclosure obligations provided therein. Starting with the Company Law Directive, Article 85 of Directive 2017/1132 states that, for the purposes of the implementation of the chapter of that directive concerning 'Capital maintenance and alteration', 'the laws of the Member States shall ensure equal treatment to all shareholders who are in the same position'. This provision originates from the Second Company Law Directive and has limited

[88] For additional details on the representation of minority shareholders on corporate bodies, see P Davies et al, 'General Report: Boards in Law and Practice: A Cross-country Analysis in Europe' in P Davies et al (eds), *Corporate Boards in Law and Practice: A Comparative Analysis in Europe* (Oxford, Oxford University Press, 2013) 3, 41 f, 99.

[89] According to Italian law, the members of the board of auditors also participate in the meetings of the board of directors (art 2405 of the Civil Code).

scope, since it is addressed only to transactions concerning the modification and the maintenance of the legal capital. This is also made clear in the Recitals of the Company Law Directive, where it is stated that it is necessary that the laws of the Member States 'relating to the increase or reduction of capital ensure that the principles of equal treatment of shareholders in the same position … are observed and harmonised' (Recital (46) of Directive 2017/1132). Therefore, in the context of this directive, the principle of equal treatment is applicable – without a doubt – to the disclosure obligations required in case of: (a) contributions in kind decided in the context of capital increases; (b) limitation of the pre-emption right; (c) acquisition of own shares and financial assistance; (d) reduction of the share capital; and (e) convocation of the general meeting in the case of serious losses.[90]

With regard to listed companies, the principle of equal treatment is mentioned in Article 17 of Directive 2004/109/EC concerning the disclosure obligations imposed on companies for the benefit of shareholders, which states that listed companies must 'ensure equal treatment for all holders of shares who are in the same position'.[91] Furthermore, the principle of equal treatment is stated in general terms by Article 4 of the Shareholder Rights Directive, which provides that listed companies must 'ensure equal treatment for all shareholders who are in the same position with regard to participation and the exercise of voting rights in the general meeting'. Interestingly, the focus of this provision is on the rights granted to shareholders in the context of the general meeting.[92]

Nevertheless, the importance of the principle of equal treatment should not be overemphasised, since the three directives mentioned above all state that only shareholders that are 'in the same position' should be treated equally.[93] This specification leaves room to make distinctions among shareholders, for example, depending on the number of shares they own.

Finally, the European Court of Justice interpreted somewhat restrictively the principle of equal treatment in company law. In the *Audiolux* decision, the court made clear that European law does not 'provide conclusive evidence of the existence of a general principle of equal treatment of minority shareholders'[94] and that therefore, when this principle is not expressly mentioned, it cannot be inferred from the other legislative acts that make reference to it.[95]

ii. The Addressees of Disclosure Obligations

The analysis of the different rights of information granted to shareholders reveals that, in many cases, although companies prepare and make available information for the benefit

[90] On the principle of equal treatment under the Second Company Law Directive, see Grundmann and Glasow (n 9) 215 f.

[91] Before that directive, the principle of equal treatment of shareholders was stated in similar terms in Point 2(a), Schedule C of the Annex of Directive 79/279/EEC.

[92] On the principle of equal treatment under the Shareholder Rights Directive, see Lutter et al (n 50) 1176 f.

[93] ibid.

[94] Judgment of 15 October 2009, *Audiolux SA ea v Groupe Bruxelles Lambert (GBL) and Others and Bertelsmann AG and Others*, C-101/08, EU:C:2009:626, para 52.

[95] See Grundmann and Glasow (n 9) 216.

of shareholders, that information is not necessarily made available only to shareholders. For example, in some cases, such as takeovers, the information prepared by companies is also made available to the representatives of the employees, while in other cases, such as the disclosure of accounting documents, the information is published for the interest of the general public.[96]

An initial distinction that should be made regarding the information rights of shareholders is that between disclosure for the benefit of shareholders alone and disclosure in the interests of other persons: in the first phase of the harmonisation of European company law, when the information was not expressly addressed only to shareholders, it was normally made available to the general public. At that time, the debate was mainly focused on the respective scopes of the information to be provided to shareholders and to the public, and on the possibility of maintaining the confidentiality of the information given to shareholders. Interestingly, in that phase, shareholders were seldom expressly allowed to waive their right to information.

In a second phase, shareholders were given broader possibilities to waive their rights to documents prepared in their interest. At that time, disclosure obligations concerning other specific interests – different from those of the general public – started emerging. More precisely, in some cases, employees became the object of disclosure obligations intended for shareholders, but which shareholders were not expressly allowed to waive. In other cases, these stakeholders became the addressees of disclosure obligations, alongside shareholders.

The emergence of the possibility for shareholders to waive their disclosure rights coincided with another interesting trend related to the development of the legal framework governing listed companies: since shareholders in these companies are essentially investors and since companies are arguably interested in attracting more investors, the information addressed to shareholders also becomes valuable for the general public of potential investors.[97] In this context, companies may favour broader dissemination of information: the possibility of making information available on the company's website is evidence of this trend, and, if the information is generally addressed to investors, nothing should prevent companies from making it available to an audience broader than that of the current shareholders.

The implications of this ongoing change in perspective are manifold. For example, this approach can hardly be reconciled with the idea that, at the same time, the information given to shareholders may be kept confidential. In addition, when information on other stakeholders is considered in that disclosure, it is normally provided from the perspective of a company that is disseminating information to current and future investors. Finally, this also means that in order to protect the interests of other stakeholders, new needs for disclosure obligations may arise and that the possibility of waiving the right to disclosed information – which is quite theoretical for listed companies – should be

[96] It should also be made clear that, at least for some of the rules of the Company Law Directive that derive from the Second, the Third, the Sixth and the Cross-border Merger Directives, the publication of documents is also relevant for the protection of creditors.

[97] For an insightful overview of the problems raised by some recent trends in the legislation and corporate governance principles applicable to the exchanges of information between companies and investors, see KJ Hopt, 'The Dialogue between the Chairman of the Board and Investors' (2017) 3 *Revue Trimestrielle de Droit Financier* 97.

reconsidered, at least to the extent that the disclosure is addressed not only to current but also to potential shareholders.

In the end, examining the changes to the rules on the information rights granted to shareholders, while a distinction was traditionally made between shareholders and the general public, the contrast is now shifting to one between investors and other stakeholders. In this framework, the dichotomy between disclosure obligations imposed in the interests of shareholders, on the one hand, and those required in the interests of the public, on the other, becomes less relevant if the public is viewed as the pool of potential investors. In this sense, since the interests of current and potential shareholders largely coincide, companies may decide to share with the latter the information disclosed to the former. Finally, in this same context, in view of protecting the interests of other stakeholders, such as employees, additional information obligations may become necessary.

iii. Minority, Individual and General Meeting Rights

Another interesting conclusion of this analysis is that the information rights granted to shareholders may take different forms from that of a report to be made available to shareholders in view of a general meeting. In fact, a distinction may be drawn between the rights granted to shareholders in the context of the general meeting and the rights that shareholders enjoy independently of the holding of a meeting.

Furthermore, although an information right is related to a general meeting, it does not necessarily mean that it should be exercised during that meeting. This mixed approach achieves different goals: first, maintaining the information rights linked to a specific general meeting allows companies to better control the exercise of those rights; and, second, allowing shareholders to be informed outside – but in the context – of the general meeting facilitates communication between companies and shareholders, without facing the risk of disrupting the meeting.

Another important difference among disclosure obligations imposed on companies is that, in some cases, the right of information is individual, while in other situations, the right can be activated only by a qualified minority of shareholders. However, even when the decisions on the matters for which some disclosure is required are taken by the general meeting following the majority principle, and although some other exceptions exist,[98] the right to receive prior information remains individual. Moreover, it is also worth noting that when the information is not exclusively addressed to shareholders, it is not possible to forgo it, even with their unanimous consent.

iv. Sanctions

This investigation also makes clear that although several harmonised rules exist on the information rights of minority shareholders, a harmonised system of sanctions is still lacking. In fact, depending on the jurisdiction involved, violations of disclosure

[98] For example, in the case of a simplified merger, when the parent company holds at least 90 per cent of the shares of the subsidiary.

obligations may result in different sanctions, ranging from the payment of damages, personal liability of the directors, and invalidation of the resolutions of the general meeting, to potentially the invalidation of contracts concluded by the company by virtue of a faulty resolution of the general meeting.

However, national laws tend to prevent disruptive consequences for third parties and to adopt different methods to uphold the effects of the decisions of the general meeting that are not in full compliance with the information rights of shareholders.[99] In any case, no harmonisation exists in the field of sanctions for violations of information rights,[100] and this could lead to different practical results for shareholders who want to protect their right to be informed, depending on the law applicable to the specific case.[101]

B. The Evolving Role of the General Meeting

The analysis of the information rights granted to minority and individual shareholders also makes clear the close connections between those rights and the potential role of shareholders and general meetings in corporate governance. In public limited liability companies, and especially listed companies, the idea that the general meeting is the place where informed shareholders debate and take decisions for the common best interest is far from the reality. General meetings are rarely the place where shareholder democracy is exercised and, in many cases, they are simply empty rituals in which decisions taken elsewhere receive their final sanction. In this context, it is unsurprising that the strategies for empowering shareholders and revitalising general meetings are an essential part of the company law and corporate governance debate.

Depending on the functions that the general meeting may play in company law, the information rights granted to shareholders may also pursue different goals: the more the general meeting becomes the place where company information is presented and discussed for the benefit of current and potential investors, the more the information disclosed should be made accessible to the public and focused on aspects that are relevant for investment decisions. As explained above, this is, in fact, a current trend in European law.

At the same time, attempts are being made to empower shareholders with new decision-making rights, like those on the remuneration policy. In this case as well, the information rights attached to these decision-making rights transcend the interests of current shareholders. Furthermore, the need to take into account the interests of other stakeholders becomes more and more relevant.

In conclusion, the future changes to the rules on disclosure of company information for the benefit of shareholders will definitely be influenced by the evolving role of the general meeting in company law and corporate governance. At present,

[99] See, for example, Siems et al (n 54) 371 ff.

[100] *cf* Lutter et al (n 50) 1207, discussing the absence of a harmonised framework on sanctions with specific regard to the right to ask questions.

[101] Siems et al (n 54) 374 f.

it seems that these changes may go towards extending the scope and the addressees of the disclosure rights to the benefit of some stakeholders, and blurring the distinction between the information provided to the market and to shareholders. In any case, the information rights of minority and individual shareholders will certainly evolve into something more elaborate than the current dialectic between, on the one hand, minority and individual shareholders and, on the other hand, majority shareholders and managers.

V. Conclusion

This chapter has examined the different information rights granted to the shareholders of public limited liability companies. The analysis addressed the disclosure obligations imposed on companies by both European and national law, highlighting that these rules are provided, in some cases, by company law and, in other cases, by financial market regulations.

This investigation was useful to provide a general framework on the disclosure rights granted to minority and individual shareholders. It examined, in particular, the principle of equal treatment, the persons entitled to receive information and the absence of a harmonised framework on sanctions. Finally, it discussed how changes to the role of the general meeting in company law could, in the future, transform the nature of the information rights granted under European law to minority and individual shareholders.

3

Disclosure of Corporate Governance by Codes

GREGOR BACHMANN*

I. Introduction

Following the British model of the UK Corporate Governance Code (formerly known as the 'Cadbury Code'), most European and many Asian countries have established so-called corporate governance codes that set up 'best practice' standards for the governance of publicly listed companies. Coupled with the principle of 'comply-or-explain', this regulatory strategy provides for the disclosure of governance structures and thus puts pressure on issuers to make their governance structures more transparent and to improve them.

This chapter analyses the regulatory instrument of corporate governance codes with regard to disclosure. It starts with a closer look at the term 'corporate governance' and how the governance structure of a company is disclosed in general. It continues by describing the legal nature and the function of codes, and how codes form a part of the overall disclosure regime. It next highlights and discusses questions and problems arising from the use of codes as a regulatory tool. It then closes with a summarising conclusion.

II. Corporate Governance and its Disclosure

A. What is Corporate Governance?

'Corporate governance' is a term widely used in today's literature on corporate organisation and corporate law.[1] However, it is not a clearly defined term, let alone a clear-cut legal notion. Codes sometimes define 'corporate governance',[2] but usually they tacitly

* I would like to thank Michael Goodyear, University of Michigan Law School, JD Candidate 2020, for his help with the editing work.

[1] For its origins, see V Magnier, *Comparative Corporate Governance* (Cheltenham, Edward Elgar, 2017) 1.

[2] See, eg, UK Code 2018, Introduction: 'The system by which companies are directed and controlled.'

assume a common understanding of what it means. Put broadly, 'corporate governance', as the term is used today,[3] depicts the structure of the board and its functioning, the rights of shareholders and the role of the general meeting, and, sometimes, the role of auditors. This understanding is also reflected in the rules and recommendations of most corporate governance codes, the bulk of which focus on the board of directors.[4]

In a more abstract way, three major features may be identified that characterise corporate governance: it is a *private* mode of governance (as opposed to public governance); it is of a *capitalist* nature (as opposed to other private modes of governance, such as cooperatives); and it largely involves all of those who, in a broader sense, exercise *control* over the company by making significant decisions.[5] For the purposes of this chapter, we will not dwell on matters of definition, but will put up with the general and simpler notion that corporate governance describes the way in which a corporation is governed by its organs and members.

Aspects that *are not* elements of corporate governance (at least not in the narrow sense used here) include factors that may be somehow relevant for the economic success of a company and its social reputation, but that do not directly relate to the functioning of the board or the role of shareholders. Thus, the *contractual* and *governmental relations* of the company, as well as matters of 'corporate social responsibility' (CSR),[6] are excluded from our analysis.

B. How is Corporate Governance Disclosed?

If one wants to learn about the governance of a certain corporation – for instance, how the board is composed and what powers it holds – several sources of information are available. Starting on the most abstract level, company law itself will provide some answers. Most company law statutes contain rules specifying, amongst other things, the number of directors, the power and duties of board members, and the competences of the shareholders' meeting. However, these rules are not always easy to find or to understand, nor do they always provide meaningful answers. Although legislative acts are published and can nowadays be easily accessed through the Internet, they are dense and written in language that non-lawyers sometimes find difficult to understand. In order to fully grasp the meaning of a statutory provision, it is also necessary to know how courts interpret it. Court rulings, although published as well, are sometimes even more cumbersome to read than legal provisions.

Moreover, statutes usually just provide a general framework, such as proscribing a minimum or maximum number of directors.[7] Therefore, instead of or in addition to

[3] For a different notion, pertaining more to the 'taming' of corporate (capitalist) power, see KJ Hopt and G Teubner (eds), *Corporate Governance and Directors' Liabilities: Legal, Economic and Sociological Analyses on Corporate Social Responsibility* (Berlin, De Gruyter, 1985).

[4] A prominent example is the UK Code of Corporate Governance.

[5] Magnier (n 1) 2.

[6] CSR has become more prominent in public and scholarly debate. For a comprehensive account, see B Spiesshofer, *Responsible Enterprise – The Emergence of a global economic order* (Munich, Beck, 2018). It is sometimes seen as part of corporate governance and even reflected in recent codes. See, eg, UK Code 2018, Principle A: 'generating value for shareholders and contributing to wider society'.

[7] eg, s 154(2) of the UK Companies Act 2006: 'A public company must have at least two directors.' German law requires only one director (see § 76(2), first sentence of the Aktiengesetz (AktG)). If the stated capital exceeds €3 million, the company is required to have at least two directors unless the articles of association

reading the general company law, the curious investor might want to read the Articles of Association of a certain company and, if available, additional organisational rules. These articles and rules are supplemented by other private statements of the company, such as financial reports, the prospectus and ongoing financial information, including inside information disclosed in accordance with Article 17 of the Market Abuse Regulation (MAR).[8] Not publicly available are shareholder agreements such as agreements on the joint exercise of voting rights.

Thus, a person willing to learn details about the governance structure of a certain company is faced with a difficult task. He or she has to read through a lot of rules and try to make sense of them. Even if this job is managed, our curious investor will not know whether there are additional mandatory or voluntary standards that the company and its board could or should follow, or whether such standards are actually met. Here, corporate governance standards and statements, as obliged or recommended by certain legislative or self-regulatory bodies, may play an important role.

III. Corporate Governance Codes

A. The Legal Nature and Functions of Codes

Codes, such as corporate governance codes, are often dubbed 'soft law', meaning they perform a function similar to that of legal norms by guiding people's behaviour, but are not enforceable by courts or state agencies. Whether they deserve to be called 'law' at all is a theoretical question that does not need to be discussed here.[9] It suffices to say that even those authors who highlight the normative nature of 'soft law' do not dispute the fact that it is, and remains, voluntary in nature. In any case, since soft law usually lacks democratic legitimation, one should be careful in using soft law standards to fill gaps in legal rules.

What seems more important than the legal nature of corporate governance codes is the regulatory function they serve. Two functions are common to all, or at least most, corporate governance codes. The first one is to *improve* corporate governance by setting up benchmarks that go beyond the minimum standards established by (mandatory) law. For example, corporate law may not require term or age limits for board members or specify the functions they serve, but some corporate governance codes do.[10] Also, many codes recommend an 'appropriate' number of independent directors, which is not required by law.

provide otherwise (§ 76(2) second sentence AktG). The German Code (Deutscher Corporate Governance Kodex, DCGK) recommends each issuer have more than one director (see DCGK 4.2.1). The draft of the revised DCGK omits this recommendation and instead presupposes that each company has more than one director. See DCGK 2019 (draft), principle 1.

[8] Regulation (EU) No 596/2014 of the European Parliament and of the Council of 16 April 2014 on market abuse (market abuse regulation) and repealing Directive 2003/6/EC of the European Parliament and of the Council and Commission Directives 2003/124/EC, 2003/125/EC and 2004/72/EC [2014] OJ L173/1.

[9] Answering this question in the affirmative, see, eg, Magnier (n 1) 94 ff.

[10] See, eg, UK Corporate Governance Code (2018), Provision 19: 'The chair should not remain in post beyond nine years'; DCGK 5.4.1(2): 'the composition of the Supervisory Board shall reflect … an age limit and

A second function of corporate governance codes is to make the governance structure of companies *more transparent*. This is achieved in a twofold way. First, the codes themselves contain transparency provisions that go beyond those of mandatory law. The UK Code, for example, expects 'a clear explanation' if a person holds the post of chairman of the board for more than nine years.[11] Second, many laws require companies to disclose to the public whether they follow a certain corporate governance code or not ('comply or explain'). The informational function of codes is described in more detail below.[12]

B. The Proliferation of Corporate Governance Codes in Europe (and Elsewhere)

The origin of modern corporate governance codes is in the UK. The former Cadbury Code of 1992 (the predecessor of the modern UK 2018 Code) is considered the 'mother' of all modern corporate governance codes.[13] Since the birth of the Cadbury Code, corporate governance codes have spread around the globe. Although not mandated by EU law, they are prevalent in Europe. Most countries have enacted a corporate governance code.[14] Germany, for example, promulgated its 'Deutscher Corporate Governance Kodex' in 2002.

Outside Europe, corporate governance codes can be found in Commonwealth countries, in Asia and in growing numbers of African and South American jurisdictions. A 'blind spot' is the US, where no single (or 'national') code exists, but where many separate organisations have set up their own standards of good corporate governance.[15] An impressive and comprehensive list of corporate governance codes can be found on the website of the European Corporate Governance Institute (ECGI).[16]

C. The Comply-or-Explain Mechanism

The role and function of modern corporate governance codes cannot be fully understood if one does not also consider the so-called 'comply-or-explain' mechanism. Also originating in the UK, this mechanism legally requires listed companies to *either* comply

a regular limit to supervisory board members' term of office'. The draft of the new DCGK also provides for an age limit (DCGK 2019 (draft), B.3) and for a term of three years (B.1).

[11] See, ibid, Provision 19 third sentence.

[12] See below, sections IV.C and V.

[13] See Magnier (n 1) 63 (mentioning some earlier but less influential codes in the US, Hong Kong and Ireland). Also published in 1992 were the 'Principles of Corporate Governance' by the American Law Institute (ALI), which, however, were not promulgated in the form of a code and were not coupled with a 'comply-or-explain' mechanism.

[14] See for the UK: UK Code of Corporate Governance (n 10); for Germany: Deutscher Corporate Governance Kodex; for Austria: Österreichischer Corporate Governance Kodex; for France: Code de gouvernement d'entreprise des sociétés cotées; for Italy: Codice di Autodisciplina; for Denmark: Anbefalinger for god Selskabsledelse; for Greece: Ελληνικός Κώδικας Εταιρικής Διακυβέρνησης.

[15] See, eg, *Business Roundtable: Principles of Corporate Governance* (Washington DC, BRT, 2016).

[16] See https://ecgi.global/content/faq/code.

with the provisions of the code *or* to publicly explain why the issuer does not comply with all or some of the provisions.

The 'comply-or-explain' approach is considered 'the trademark of corporate governance in the UK', which, in the words of the British Financial Reporting Council (FRC), 'has been widely imitated and internationally admired'.[17] Most European countries and many other jurisdictions have indeed followed the approach, though – for reasons still unknown – not in the US. At a higher level, the European Union (EU) has made use of the comply-or-explain mechanism in its accounting directive with regard not only to national corporate governance codes (see below), but more recently also with regard to voluntary CSR concepts.[18] Thus, the comply-or-explain principle today is not only a 'trademark of corporate governance in the UK', but is also considered 'a key feature of European corporate governance'.[19]

The basic idea of the comply-or-explain mechanism is as simple as it is effective. Issuers are left with a choice to comply or not to comply with certain corporate governance standards, thus keeping them within the realm of 'soft law'. Yet, as issuers are required to make any non-compliance public and to also publicly justify it, the mechanism puts some pressure on issuers. If the public or the markets (whether capital, products, human resources or otherwise) on which the company is trading expect compliance with the soft law standards, they will 'punish' the non-compliant issuer through methods such as abandoning its shares and refusing to buy its products. The company, on the other hand, is given the opportunity to explain its non-compliance and may thereby convince markets that the reason for its non-compliance is a good one.

Both the reactions by markets and the response of public opinion will send a signal to issuers as well as to the regulator or promulgating institution on whether a certain standard of soft law seems to be a desirable one. This, in turn enables, issuers, regulators and promulgators to reconsider their options by either moving to compliance (issuer) or by repealing, redesigning or reinforcing the respective standard (regulator/promulgator). All in all, the comply-or-explain mechanism gives some bite to soft law standards, while at the same time allowing for flexibility and experimentation.

With regard to standards that do not reflect undisputed or commonly held values, this flexible regulatory approach might be superior to mandatory law. It differs from dispositive law (default law) in that it does not allow for an opting-out from otherwise applicable rules, but rather requires an active opt-in decision plus an explanation if the company does not want to opt in to the standard. However, due to the justification requirement, it is disputed whether regulation by comply-or-explain is really a milder form of government action.[20]

[17] UK Corporate Governance Code 2016, 4. The new and slimmer version of the Code (2018) no longer contains this sentence.

[18] See art 19a of Directive 2013/34/EU, [2013] OJ L182/19 (as amended by Directive 2014/95/EU regarding the disclosure of non-financial and diversity information [2014] OJ L330/1).

[19] See Recital 6, Commission Recommendation 2014/208/EU of 9 April 2014 on the quality of corporate governance reporting ('comply or explain') [2014] OJ L109/43.

[20] For an account of the critical debate in Germany, see G Bachmann in T Kremer, G Bachmann, M Lutter and A von Werder, *Deutscher Corporate Governance Kodex (Commentary)*, 7th edn (Munich, CH Beck, 2018) fn 80 ff.

IV. Codes and the Disclosure of Corporate Governance

As mentioned above, an important function of corporate governance codes is to make the governance structure of companies more transparent.[21] This is done by requiring (or expecting) the company to publish certain statements or reports.

A. The Comply-or-Explain Statement

Even before the EU introduced the requirement to report on governance issues in the annual report (see section IV.B below), many Member States had a rule in place that mandated a statement declaring compliance or non-compliance with the recommendations of a national corporate governance code. A typical example is Germany, which, in 2002, inserted a new § 161 into its Stock Corporate Act (Aktiengesetz), which reads as follows:

> The management board and supervisory board of a listed company shall declare annually that the recommendations of the 'Government Commission German Corporate Governance Codex' published by the Federal Ministry of Justice and Consumer Protection in the official part of the Federal Gazette have been and will be complied with, or which recommendations have not been or will not be applied and why.

It is noteworthy that when it was first introduced in 2002, § 161 only required companies to declare *whether* the recommendations of the German Code were complied with or not. The obligation to justify non-compliance was introduced only in 2009 by adding the two words 'and why'. This was done in accordance with new EU law.[22] Other Member States had similar rules in place, though mostly not in their corporate laws, but rather in their rules on financial accounting or in the Listing Rules.

B. The 'Corporate Governance Statement'

In 2013, the EU amended its accounting rules and enacted a revised directive on the annual financial statements (Directive 2013/34/EU). Article 20 of this directive provides that listed companies (in EU nomenclature 'undertakings') shall include in their management report a 'corporate governance statement', which must contain at least two things: (1) a reference to the corporate governance code to which the undertaking is subject or which the undertaking has voluntarily decided to apply; and (2) additional information on the governance structure and practices of the company.

i. Reference to a Code

The directive does not oblige Member States to establish a national corporate governance code, nor does it require them to subdue their companies to any such code. Instead, it presupposes that in the majority of Member States, a corporate governance

[21] See above, section III.A.
[22] See below, section V.B.

code simply exists (which is indeed the case).[23] The directive also takes account of the fact that Member States' laws take different approaches with regard to their respective codes. Some make issuers 'subject' to their code, allowing for non-compliance only with regard to detailed recommendations, not for its principles.[24] Others leave issuers a free choice to comply with the code or to choose to follow an alternative – foreign or private – code.[25] In any case, issuers must indicate where the relevant texts of the codes to which they adhere are publicly available.

As mentioned above, the directive further mandates that if a company departs from a corporate governance code, an explanation as to which parts of the respective code it departs from and the reasons for doing so must be given. The same holds true where the issuer has decided not to refer to any provisions of a corporate governance code.[26] The directive does not specify how detailed the explanation needs to be, although a recent EU recommendation provides some guidance on this.[27]

ii. (Additional) Information on Corporate Governance Practices

The directive on the annual financial statements acknowledges that a Member State might not have a national corporate governance code. For such cases, the directive requires that the company provide all relevant information about its corporate governance practices 'over and above the requirements of national law', and that those details are made publicly available.[28] It is not entirely clear whether this obligation applies to issuers who are already subject to a corporate governance code or who have voluntarily declared compliance with such a code. However, the German legislature has answered this question in the affirmative by requiring every issuer to publish such a description, even if they declare full compliance with the German Code.[29]

In addition, the directive requires a description of the main features of the undertaking's internal control and risk management systems in relation to the financial reporting process, certain information on measures taken with regard to potential hostile takeover bids[30] and – unless the information is already fully provided for in national law – a description of the operation of shareholder meetings, an explanation of the authority of shareholder meetings, and a description of shareholders' rights and how they can be exercised.[31] Issuers must also describe in their corporate governance statement the composition and operation of their administrative, management and supervisory bodies, as well as their committees.[32] This obligation arises regardless of whether the issuer follows a certain code or not.

[23] See *Business Roundtable* (n 15).

[24] An example is the UK Corporate Governance Code (n 10). The new draft DCGK (2019) follows this example.

[25] An example is Germany, which allows issuers to declare full non-compliance with the recommendations of the German Corporate Governance Code.

[26] See art 20(1)(b) of Directive 2013/34/EU (n 18).

[27] See below, section V.C.

[28] *cf* art 20(1)(a)(iii) of Directive 2013/34/EU (n 18).

[29] See § 289f (2) Nr 2 of the Handelsgesetzbuch (HGB).

[30] For details, see art 10(1)(c)–(i) of the EU Takeover Directive (Directive 2004/25/EC [2004] OJ L142/12).

[31] See art 20(1)(e) of Directive 2013/34/EU (n 18).

[32] See ibid art 20(1)(f).

iii. Alternative Modes of Disclosure

All the aforementioned information is to be disclosed annually as part of the so-called management report (in German *Lagebericht*), which is a mandatory annex to the annual financial statements. However, Member States may permit issuers to set out the information in a separate report published together with the management report or as a publicly available document on the issuer's website, provided that reference is made to it in the management report. The separate report and the publicly available document may cross-refer to the management report, where the required information is made available in that management report.[33] Issuers therefore have a broad choice of how to publish their corporate governance statements, while investors should be easily able to find such information. This elastic approach is, again, due to the fact that Member States have different traditions of disclosure. It shall also provide issuers with as much flexibility as possible. What matters is not prescribing a rigid form of disclosure, but that investors and the public are able to find the relevant information.

C. Reporting Requirements Set up by the Codes

As mentioned above, many codes contain transparency provisions that go beyond those of mandatory law.[34] Sometimes these provisions only clarify or specify existing statutory disclosure requirements. The UK Code, for instance, recommends that the board describes the work of its committees[35] and makes their responsibilities publicly available,[36] thus meeting the Directive's obligation to describe in the corporate governance statement the composition and operation of the committees.[37] In other cases, corporate governance codes set up disclosure standards not already contained in statutory law. The German Code, for example, recommends that the supervisory board, in its election proposals to the general meeting, discloses the personal and business relationships of every candidate with the company, the governing bodies of the corporation, and any shareholders with a material interest in the corporation.[38]

Sometimes corporate governance codes merely recommend the disclosure of certain facts without stating when and where to make such disclosure. Issuers are then free to choose their own method of publicity. Although this is in conformity with the idea of flexibility, which underlies regulation by codes in general, it may be burdensome for investors searching for certain information. Companies are therefore well advised to present information about their corporate governance in a coherent and easily understandable manner. In order to support that goal, some codes make recommendations about the place of disclosure. The German Code, for instance, recommends disclosing the remuneration of supervisory board members in the notes

[33] *cf* ibid art 20(2).
[34] See UK Code (n 10) Provision 19.
[35] See ibid Provision 23 ('describe the work of the nomination committee'); Provision 26 ('describe the work of the audit committee'); and Provision 41 ('description of the work of the remuneration committee').
[36] See ibid Provision 14.
[37] See ibid Provision 19.
[38] See DCGK 5.4.1 (6) and DCGK 2019 (draft), B.14.

to the financial statements or the management report and classifying by remuneration components.[39]

In certain cases, corporate governance codes provide for special 'reports' to be published in addition to legally required reports. A typical example was the remuneration report as recommended by the German Code.[40] Today, European law mandates the publication of a remuneration report.[41] However, some details of how to describe the elements of remuneration are still left to the discretion of Member States or issuers. The German Code fills this gap by recommending the usage of model tables, which are provided as appendices to the Code.[42]

Moreover, the German Code recommends that the management board and the supervisory board report annually on corporate governance in a so-called 'Corporate Governance Report' to be published in connection with the corporate governance statement mandated by EU law.[43] The idea of the Corporate Governance Report is to provide issuers with a cohesive document that contains all relevant information on matters of corporate governance that is not already mandated by legal provisions. As the information given in such required reports naturally overlaps with that of the corporate governance statement, it makes sense to require its publication 'in connection' with the mandatory reports. The Corporate Governance Report also leaves room for comments to be provided on the so-called suggestions of the German Code,[44] code provisions that are not subject to the comply-or-explain principle.

V. Questions and Problems

As shown above, corporate governance codes can contribute to the improvement and transparency of corporate governance in a meaningful way, especially if coupled with the comply-or-explain mechanism. Nevertheless, there are some open questions with regard to the use of codes as a regulatory technique.

A. What Should a Code Contain?

A key feature of every code is its *recommendations*, voluntary provisions with which issuers are free to comply or not, provided that they explain their non-compliance ('comply-or-explain'). Although the terminology differs, such recommendations can be found

[39] See DCGK 5.4.6 (3); abolished in the DCGK 2019 (draft) with regard to new legal reporting requirements established in the German Stock Corporation Act.

[40] For the historical development of this recommendation, see Bachmann, in Kremer et al. (n 20) no 1052.

[41] See art 9b of Directive 2007/36/EU [2007] OJ L184/17, as amended by Directive 2017/828/EU [2017] OJ L132/1; transposed into German law by § 162 of the Stock Corporation Act.

[42] The draft of a revised DCGK (2019) abolishes those tables.

[43] *cf* DCGK 3.10. The DCGK 2019 (draft) has abolished this recommendation in favour of a comprehensive description of the company's corporate governance in the corporate governance statement. The draft now recommends that issuers report on how they apply the DCGK's principles ('apply and explain'); see DCGK 2019 (draft), A.19.

[44] See DCGK 3.10, second sentence. The DCGK 2019 (draft) has abolished this recommendation; see ibid.

in every code.[45] However, codes differ with regard to additional contents. Some codes contain general 'principles' which are not subject to the comply-or-explain mechanism but are more or less mandatory in nature. A typical example is the UK Code, which consists of 'principles' and more detailed 'provisions' (recommendations) that elaborate the principles. Whereas compliance with the provisions is voluntary (provided that non-compliance is justified), the principles have to be obeyed. Accordingly, the UK Listing Rules (LR) require a statement about 'how' the principles have been applied, but only a statement as to 'whether' the provisions have been followed.[46] Some countries follow a similar approach,[47] while others refrain from inserting mandatory norms into their codes.

An opposite question is whether codes should contain *mere suggestions* or rules that are not only voluntary in nature, but do not even require an explanation if they are ignored. The Austrian and the German Codes, for example, do contain such rules (although the terminology is different),[48] but critics deem them superfluous. They claim that mere suggestions lack 'teeth' and that they should therefore either be promoted to 'real' code provisions or abolished altogether, as they are useless for investors.[49] However, suggestions may not be completely ignored by issuers, as shareholders may use their right to ask questions at the general meeting, enshrined in the EU directive on shareholders' rights,[50] in order to learn about whether and how the company has implemented a certain suggestion.[51] In practice, inserting mere suggestions into a code often mirrors the fact that the 'best practice' quality of the standard in question is disputed. The German Code tries to make suggestions more meaningful by suggesting that the board provide comments on the suggestions made in the code.[52]

A similar dispute concerns the question whether a code should *repeat statutory law*. Some codes do so, mainly in order to inform foreign investors about the peculiarities of the respective jurisdiction. Germany's corporate law, for instance, is characterised by a dual board structure (a management board and a supervisory board), and employees have a right to be represented on the supervisory board. As these features are unknown in most other jurisdictions, the German Code describes it in simple terms. This is consistent with one of the objectives of the German Code, which is 'to make the German Corporate Governance system transparent and understandable' (Preamble). Nevertheless, as with mere suggestions, critics want to abolish all code provisions that simply repeat the law, claiming that a code is not a textbook and should be as concise as possible.[53]

[45] The term 'recommendation' is used, eg, by the German Code ('Empfehlungen'), the Danish Code and the French Code. The Austrian Code uses the term 'C-rules' for comply-or-explain rules, whereas 'R-rules' (recommendations) are mere suggestions that are not subject to the comply-or-explain principle.

[46] See UK Listing Rules 9.8.6R (5) and (6).

[47] *cf*, eg, the Dutch Code and the Italian Code (n 16). The new German Code draft also adopts this approach by introducing 'principles' and recommending that issuers 'apply and explain' them (see DCGK-draft 2019, A.19).

[48] The DCGK calls them 'suggestions', and the ÖCGK 'recommendations'.

[49] For a critical account see Werder, in Kremer et al (n 20) no 154 ff.

[50] See art 9 of Directive 2007/36/EC: 'Every shareholder shall have the right to ask questions related to items on the agenda of the general meeting. The company shall answer the questions put to it by shareholders.'

[51] See Werder in Kremer et al (n 20) no 154: 'cannot be ignored altogether … as shareholders may use their right to ask questions about how the company deals with the suggestions'.

[52] See DCGK 3.10, second sentence. The DCGK 2019 (draft) has abolished this recommendation (see n 43).

[53] See, eg, KJ Hopt, 'Der Deutsche Corporate Governance Kodex: Grundlagen und Praxisfragen' in G Krieger, M Lutter and K Schmidt (eds), *Festschrift fuer Hoffman-Becking* (Munich, CH Beck, 2013) 563, 578.

A possible compromise for the questions raised above would be to keep descriptive provisions as well as mere suggestions, but to make it easier for readers of a code to see whether a provision is a recommendation (subject to 'comply-or-explain'), a mere suggestion or a description of the law. This would be in line with EU law, which does not make any pronouncements with regard to the content of a code, but which recommends that codes should make a clear distinction between parts of the code that must be followed, parts which apply on a comply-or-explain basis, and parts which apply on a purely voluntary basis.[54]

B. The Truth of the Compliance Statement

In order to fulfil its function, the comply-or-explain model must rely on the truthfulness of the compliance statement. EU law does not prescribe any mechanism for ensuring true compliance statements, nor does it provide for sanctions if the compliance statement is wrong. What is provided for is that the auditor shall check that the corporate governance statement, including the compliance statement and explanations for any non-compliance, was made.[55] Empirical evidence as well as case law shows that some issuers have publicly declared compliance with a code, although they did not, or at least not fully, follow its recommendations.[56] This misleads investors and prevents a negative market reaction.

Since EU law leaves it up to Member States to cure this problem, there is no common European let alone global standard. While some jurisdictions simply trust issuers to be honest, or rely on the self-enforcing and self-detecting forces of the financial community and self-regulatory organisations (such as stock exchanges), others seek to employ more direct tools. One such tool may be to require auditors to not only check whether a compliance statement was made but also to see if the compliance statement is true. Although it may not be possible for auditors to detect every fault in a corporate governance statement, at least in some cases this should not be difficult. For example, it should be easy to find out if the chairman of a board holds that post for a longer period than is recommended by the code with which the company allegedly complies. The German Code already employs this strategy by recommending that the supervisory board arranges for the auditor to inform it if, during the performance of the audit, the auditor identifies any facts that indicate an inaccuracy in the declaration issued by the management board and supervisory board.[57]

German law also provides for a special sanction if a corporate governance statement is wrong. According to German corporate law, a resolution of the shareholders' meeting may be set aside upon an action brought by a shareholder if such a resolution violates statutory law.[58] The German Federal Court of Justice (Bundesgerichtshof – BGH) held that such an action may be successfully brought if the general meeting

[54] See Recommendation 2014/208/EU (n 19) Section I No 2.

[55] See Art 20(3) of Directive 2013/34/EU (n 18): 'The statutory auditor … shall check that the information referred to in points (a), (b), (e) and (f) of paragraph 1 of this Article has been provided.'

[56] See M Bianchi, A Ciavarella, V Novembre and R Signoretti, 'Comply or Explain? Investor Protection through Corporate Governance Codes' (2010) *ECGI – Finance Working Working Paper*, No 278/2010.

[57] See DCGK 7.2.3 (2) and DCGK 2019 (draft), A.22.

[58] See § 243 AktG.

resolved to formally approve the company's administration, although the board issued a false compliance statement.[59] In such a case, the BGH reasoned, the general meeting exceeds its powers if it nevertheless votes for approval. Although setting aside the approving resolution does not have substantial consequences for board members and is therefore more of symbolic importance,[60] management still fears the negative impact it has on its reputation.

C. The Quality of the Corporate Governance Statement

A third problem is the quality of the corporate governance statement. If companies simply declare their compliance with a code, it may remain unclear how exactly they implement its recommendations, especially if the code leaves some discretion up to the company. On the other hand, if issuers do not comply with certain recommendations, they may only have meagre explanations for doing so. However, since the law only requires an 'explanation', but does not specify its content, it is unclear how detailed or convincing the explanation needs to be.

Some codes recognise this problem and ask issuers for a meaningful statement. The UK Code, for example, explicitly addresses the topic in its Introduction, stating that 'it is important to report meaningfully … and to avoid boilerplate reporting'.[61] Accordingly, the UK Code asks for 'high-quality reporting' that 'helps investors with their evaluation of company practices'.[62] When applying the comply-or-explain principle, issuers should avoid a 'tick-the-box approach' and provide explanations that 'set out the background [and] provide a clear rationale for the action the company is taking'.[63] The German Code does not explicitly ask for a detailed statement but recommends that issuers publish a corporate governance report that gives room for more detailed information.[64]

The European Commission responded to the problem by passing Recommendation 2014/208/EU 'on the quality of corporate governance reporting ("comply or explain")'.[65] The purpose of the Recommendation is to provide guidance to Member States, bodies responsible for national corporate governance codes, companies and other parties in order to improve the overall quality of corporate governance statements published by companies in accordance with Article 20 of Directive 2013/34/EU and, specifically, the quality of explanations provided by companies in case of departure from the recommendations of the relevant corporate governance codes.[66] To that end,

[59] *cf* Bundesgerichtshof (Germany), BGHZ 182, 272.

[60] In theory, board members responsible for a false compliance statement may be held liable for damages, but in reality it is impossible to prove a causal nexus between the false corporate governance statement and a loss in share prices.

[61] See UK Code (n 10) Introduction, 2.

[62] ibid.

[63] ibid.

[64] See DCGK 3.10. This recommendation has been abolished in the DCGK 2019 (draft) in favour of a general 'apply and explain' approach (n 43).

[65] See Commission Recommendation 2014/208/EU (n 19) Recital 6.

[66] ibid Recital 1.

the Recommendation invites issuers to not only describe *whether* but also *how* they have applied the code.[67]

Issuers are further asked to provide clear, accurate and comprehensive information, to refer to the company's specific characteristics (such as size, company structure and ownership), and to make all relevant statements available on their website.[68] In the case of departure from a code, the Commission recommends that the issuer explains in what manner the company has departed and that it describes the reasons for the departure plus the measures taken instead (if any).[69] The Commission also expects the issuer to describe how the decision to depart was taken within the company, ie, who made the decision and in what manner.[70]

As the UK example shows, many Member States or code commissions have reacted to the Commission's Recommendation by requiring more or less detailed statements with regard to code compliance. Moreover, large investors or financial intermediaries (such as proxy advisors) are able to put pressure on issuers if they are not satisfied with the quality of comply-or-explain statements or corporate governance reports. Thus, even if the Recommendation does not apply enough pressure to influence companies to comply, the large investors and financial intermediaries might. If one studies actual corporate governance statements by European issuers, one gets the impression that the reporting quality has significantly improved. What is missing is a uniform reporting scheme, which is why non-professional investors may still face some difficulties in analysing and comparing such statements. At least the right to ask questions at the general meeting, enshrined in Article 9 of the EU Shareholder Rights Directive,[71] provides issuers with a chance to gather more information.

VI. Conclusion

Codes are a widespread and meaningful tool to enhance corporate governance. They contribute to the disclosure of corporate governance in two ways. First, through the so-called comply-or-explain mechanisms, codes inform investors and the public as to whether an issuer follows a certain governance standard or not. The comply-or-explain mechanism has become a key feature not only of British corporate governance but also of EU corporate law. It has spread to jurisdictions outside Europe as well. Second, codes themselves make governance structures more public by setting up disclosure requirements that go beyond what is mandated by statutory law.

Although the comply-or-explain mechanism is well established, it leaves certain regulatory questions unanswered. One is the question about what a code should contain, while another is how to ensure the truth of compliance statements. Whereas some

[67] See Recommendation 2014/208/EU (n 19) Section III No 4.

[68] See ibid, Section II No 5 and No 6.

[69] See ibid, Section III No 8.

[70] ibid.

[71] Directive 2007/36/EC of the European Parliament and of the Council of 11 July 2007 on the exercise of certain rights of shareholders in listed companies [2007] OJ L184/17.

jurisdictions trust that ethical standards and/or reputational and market mechanisms will guarantee truthful reporting, others employ additional legal sanctions in order to create incentives for boards to report correctly. A second issue is the quality of corporate governance statements, which have not always been satisfying in the past. The EU Recommendation on the quality of corporate governance reporting, issued in 2014, gives some guidance on how the reporting can be made more meaningful. Sporadic evidence indicates that this guidance has been heard. Whether more and stricter rules are needed remains to be seen.

4

Disclosure as a Legal Instrument against Potential Abusive Behaviour in the Case of Related Party Transactions

THEODOROS KATSAS

I. Introduction

A. Related Party Transactions as a Regulatory Issue

Related Party Transactions (RPTs) are an effective instrument to divert value from a company by those in control, ie, dominant shareholders (in the case of closely held corporations) or directors (in the case of corporations with sufficient dispersion of ownership).[1] RPTs appear as regular business transactions of the company, whose merits are defined and distributed between the parties in accordance with the viewpoint of the dominant related party (ie, the dominant shareholder or CEO of the company). They represent an effective means to expropriation (tunnelling) of corporate assets in favour of the related party, who may acquire private (pecuniary) benefits of control by entering into transactions with the company or one of its subsidiaries on unfair terms. For example, a director or a majority shareholder may use a partly owned subsidiary to acquire pecuniary benefits from his company, thereby engaging in tunnelling vis-a-vis the lending company.

The latter course of action indicates the intrinsic source of danger in the case of RPTs: they involve a conflict of interest between the company and its controllers,[2] the latter being positioned either directly on the other side of the transaction (self-dealing), or

[1] L Enriques, G Hertig and H Kanda, 'Related Party Transactions' in R Kraakman et al (eds) *The Anatomy of Corporate Law* (Oxford, Oxford University Press, 2009) 154; L Enriques, *Related Party Transactions: Policy Options and Real-World Challenges (with a Critique of the European Commission Proposal)*, Working Paper 2014 (papers.ssrn.com/abstract_id=2505188) 1 et seq.

[2] VA Atanasov, BS Black and CS Ciccotello, 'Unbundling and Measuring Tunneling' (2014) *University of Illinois Law Review* 101; MJ Barclay and CG Holderness, 'Private Benefits of Control in Public Corporations' (1989) 25 *Journal of Financial Economics* 374; AM Pacces, 'Procedural and Substantive Review of Related Party Transactions (RPTs): The Case for Non-controlling Shareholder-Dependent (NCS-Dependent) Directors' (2018) *ECGI Law Working Paper* No 399/2018; Enriques (n 1) 3 et seq.

having an affiliate company or even a relative deal with the company. Such opportunism on behalf of a controller is unavoidable whenever an agency relationship exists, as is the case between minority and controlling shareholders, or between managers and shareholders in companies with dispersed ownership. In such cases, the party with (de facto residual) rights of control over the corporate assets (ie, the agent) will tend to appropriate as much value as it can get away with. What distinguishes an RPT from outright theft is the fact that RPTs (need to) take the form of an ordinary business transaction.[3] Determining whether the merits of the transaction are in favour of the company or at least equally distributed between the parties usually requires a complex cost-benefit analysis, a task that even a court is usually ill-equipped to make.

Aside from the distributional concerns in the relationship between controllers (managers or dominant shareholders) and minority shareholders, tunnelling via RPTs has a negative effect on capital market as a whole and their efficiency: if a company is unable to signal its intention not to engage in tunnelling, it may endure losses in the relevant IPO market; and a high level of tunnelling may lead to distortions in the market for corporate control and in managerial and strategic choices within the company, as controllers may indulge in transactions and strategies allowing them to extract more value via tunnelling than maximise shareholder value for all investors.[4]

At the same time, no one denies that RPTs may create value for all the parties involved.[5] For example, a company's lab may start developing a new product, but due to financial constraints, it is not feasible for the firm to proceed further with the development of the product. In such a case, the dominant shareholder may be in the best position to acquire the project from the company and have a subsidiary wholly owned by himself develop it. Selling to a third party may be a worse alternative if the third party wishes to discount the higher perceived risk of failure. If the dominant shareholder buys the project for more than its net present value to the company, then the transaction is fair and efficient; this will often be the case in closely held companies where dealing with non-related parties incurs high transaction costs due to higher information costs on both sides. RPTs are also very common in the case of corporate groups, where RPTs in the form of intra-group transactions become formalised, routine transactions, which are inevitable to a certain extent (and therefore easy to justify).[6]

The stylised examples clarify the difficulties for the third parties, be they minority shareholders, auditors or litigators, to assess whether a RPT creates value for the company. To do so, third parties would need to assess on the one hand the value of the

[3] Enriques (n 1) 5 et seq.

[4] Z Goshen, 'The Efficiency of Controlling Corporate Self-Dealing: Theory Meets Reality' (2003) 91 *California Law Review* 425; RJ Gilson and A Schwartz, 'Constraints on Private Benefits of Control: Ex Ante Control Mechanisms versus Ex Post Transaction Review' (2013) 169 *Journal of Institutional & Theoretical Economics* 160, 162; J Dammann, 'Corporate Ostracism: Freezing out Controlling Shareholders' (2008) 33 *Journal of Corporate Law* 705; AM Pacces, *Rethinking Corporate Governance* (Abingdon, Routledge, 2012), 96, 151–52; AM Pacces, 'Controlling the Corporate Controller's Misbehaviour' (2011) 11 *Journal of Corporate Law Studies* 177, 193; Enriques (n 1) 5 et seq.

[5] Atanasov, Black and Ciccotello (n 2) 108; Enriques, Hertig and Kanda (n 1) 154; David Kershaw, *Company Law in Context*, 2nd edn (Oxford, Oxford University Press, 2012) 478.

[6] Enriques (n 1) 5 et seq.

relevant project for the company, if it was realised internally, and on the other hand to find a third party willing to offer a price higher than the one offered by the controller, not to mention the transactions costs related with the finding of a third buyer and negotiating with him. Last but not least, private benefits of control, like those acquired by virtue of RPTs, are hard to observe and verify by the minority shareholders, let alone by a third party such as a court or even an arbitrator.

It is the duty of corporate law makers to restrain controllers' opportunism by striking the right balance between the need to prevent the abusive behaviour of dominant shareholders and managers, and to preserve the advantages for the company when entering into fair and value-creating RPTs. Here the following fundamental questions arise: (a) who decides upon the best interest of the company in the case of an RPT?; (b) how is a screening between RPTs possible?; and (c) when should the screening procedure take place (before or after entering in an RPT?).

B. Legal Policies on RPTs

i. *Definition of RPT*

Since RPTs are common as a vehicle for tunnelling, numerous jurisdictions provided answers to these fundamental questions and developed rules addressing RPTs as such. Accounting standards, including US-GAAP and the International Financial Reporting Standards (IFRS) applicable throughout the EU, provide for a broad definition for RPTs According to International Accounting Standard 24: 'A related party transaction is a transfer of resources, services or obligations between a [corporation] and a related party, regardless of whether a price is charged.' The notion of a related party is, in turn, defined very analytically in the same Accounting Standard so as to include all legal entities and persons, such as directors and controlling shareholders, that may presumptively exercise significant influence over a corporation's decision on whether to enter a transaction and under what terms, together with their affiliates.

The accounting notion of RPTs does not mention the (broader) term of conflict of interest. One plausible explanation is that international policy debate on conflict of interests within the corporation is articulated in terms of RPTs, so domestic policy makers are receptive to that language. A second, more practical explanation is that RPTs are easier to define and regulate than the notion of conflict of interest in general; the question of whether in a given transaction a (material) conflict of interests exists is much more subjective and therefore uncertain than the question of whether someone is a related party. In other words, detecting an RPT is easier than deciding on a case-by-case basis whether in a given transaction a director or a dominant shareholder has a material interest. It is harder for a company to develop an effective compliance structure for conflicts of interest transactions than for RPTs.[7] Identifying interests requires the collaboration of directors and dominant shareholders; their discretion in this respect will be unavoidably wide because of the subjective nature of the call.

[7] ibid 13 et seq.

ii. Legal Instruments against Tunnelling

In any given jurisdiction, finding the right balance between preventing abusive tunnelling and preserving the advantages of fair and efficient RPTs requires considering context-specific factors and variables in order to determine the most efficient solution. The legal instruments applied in most jurisdictions include: (a) prohibition; (b) procedural safeguards; (c) external independent advice; (d) *ex post* standard-based review; and (e) disclosure.[8] The conditions for these instruments to be effective will be sketched out in general terms.

a. Prohibition

Prohibition is the most effective way to address the problem of tunnelling via RPTs, albeit not the most efficient one. The instrument of prohibition appears to be easy to apply and relatively straightforward; it raises the cost of tunnelling, thus making it less profitable.[9] However, there are two main arguments against its implementation. The first is that prohibition rules out value-creating RPTs, especially in the form of intra-group transactions.[10] In this respect, the automatism of prohibition may be self-defeating in the long term, as it prevents RPTs even when they are not only fair but also necessary (ie, in crisis situations) for the company. The second argument is a practical one: RPTs are one way of tunnelling corporate assets, among other things. Unless a prohibition of every sort of tunnelling is equally well enforced, prohibiting RPTs may not accomplish much; insiders would simply avoid RPTs as an appropriation technique and would apply functionally equivalent substitutes.[11] Therefore, in most jurisdictions, prohibitions selectively target a specific category of RPTs, ie, loans to a related party such as directors and executives.[12]

b. Procedural Safeguards

Most jurisdictions provide procedural safeguards for entering into RPTs. Such rules contain a broad set of conditions regarding the conclusion of RPTs; such conditions may differentiate between RPTs, ie, with regard to the related party (for instance, a director or a controlling shareholder) or to the materiality of the transaction, where quantitative or qualitative features are used to define the significance of the RPT.[13]

[8] For an analysis of legal instruments against tunnelling, see, inter alia, V Atanasov, BS Black and CS Ciccotello, 'Law and Tunneling' (2011) 37 *Journal of Corporate Law* 16; MJ Barclay and CG Holderness, 'Private Benefits from Control of Public Corporations' (1989) 25 *Journal of Financial Economics* 371 et seq; Gilson and Schwartz (n 4) 162.

[9] Enriques, Hertig and Kanda (n 1) 154; Pacces, 'Controlling' (n 4) 191; T Paredes, 'A Systems Approach to Corporate Governance Reform: Why Importing US Corporate Law isn't the Answer' (2003) 45 *William & Mary Law Review* 1055, 1149–1151.

[10] Enriques, Hertig and Kanda (n 1) 154.

[11] ibid; Pacces, 'Controlling' (n 4) 191; Paredes (n 9) 1149–51.

[12] Selective prohibitions are common in Europe and have gained traction in the US and China in the early 2000s. In view of the corporate scandals after WorldCom, it became obvious due to the magnitude of the phenomenon how loans could be used to circumvent executive compensation; China has since banned debt guarantees to shareholders from companies and their affiliates.

[13] For instance, in the UK, both for substantial property transactions and, other than in special circumstances, for related party transactions.

The procedural safeguards in most jurisdictions currently focus on the approval of a (material) RPT by a majority of independent shareholders or its approval by disinterested or independent directors. An approval by a majority of independent shareholders is currently popular among policy makers,[14] who deploy such a safeguard as a veto power over RPTs for a dominant shareholder, thus leading to a corporate resolution by Majority of Minority (MoM) or by a majority of shareholders other than the related party itself. An approval by majority of independent shareholders can only be effective when such (minority) shareholders have a real opportunity to cast their vote, their voting is the outcome of a well-informed decision-making process following the full disclosure of all material information about the RPT, and the voting takes place at a moment when vetoing the RPT is a viable choice for the company.[15] Such conditions may raise the transaction costs for the conclusion of an RPT; however, if such conditions are not met, a MOM requirement may lead to the opposite effect – that is, impeding the conclusion of a fair (ie, in the best interests of the company) RPT, as ill-informed shareholders cannot properly assess the value of the transaction.[16] For this reason, some jurisdictions provide for MOM approval only for RPTs of particularly high value (eg, above five per cent of the company's market capitalisation).[17]

Most jurisdictions deploy the involvement of independent or disinterested directors[18] as a procedural safeguard in the approval of RPTs.[19] Board approval has some obvious advantages over shareholder approval. Depending on the composition of the shareholder body, the board is likely to have a more expert view of where the company's interests lie when entering into transactions and, depending on the size of the shareholder body, board approval is likely to be quicker and less costly. On the other hand, depending on the board dynamics, the risk with board approval is that it disguises rather than neutralises conflicts of interest, even if 'interested' directors are excluded from voting. A dominant director does not necessarily need a vote to influence board decisions, and all directors may have an incentive not to enquire too closely into the terms of the transaction in exchange for similar treatment when they engage in self-dealing. Board approval can be, and normally is, accompanied by *ex post* disclosure to the shareholders in the company's annual statements of at least 'material' self-dealing transactions, but it may require a particularly persistent shareholder to work out whether the conflict of interest infected the terms of the contract.

The key issue in such a case is how truly disinterested or independent from dominant or controlling shareholders are directors expected to be, especially when they are

[14] A Hamdani and Y Yafeh, 'Institutional Investors as Minority Shareholders' (2013), 17 *Review of Finance* 691, 692; see also s 191 of the Companies Act 2006 and UK FCA Listing Rules 11.1.6 and 11.1.10; OECD, *Asian Roundtable on Corporate Governance: Reform Priorities in Asia – Taking Corporate Governance to a Higher Level* (Paris, OECD Publishing, 2013) 66.

[15] Enriques (n 1) 18; B Black and R Kraakman, 'A Self-Enforcing Model of Corporate Law' (1996) 109 *Harvard Law Review* 1911, 1959–60.

[16] Enriques (n 1) 18 et seq.

[17] For instance, the UK, Hong Kong and Singapore; MOM approval in France is only *ex post*, at the annual meeting, and denial of approval of a properly board-approved transaction has very little practical impact, if any.

[18] On the importance of independent directors, see, inter alia, C Hill and B McDonnell, 'Sanitizing Interested Transactions' (2011) 36 *Delaware Journal of Corporate Law* 903, 922–23.

[19] As is the case in Belgium (for intra-group transactions specifically) and Italy, or they make it strongly advisable, as under Delaware case law with regard to transactions with controlling shareholders.

nominated and elected by a controlling shareholder.[20] To this end, some jurisdiction provides for the nomination and appointment of directors by minority shareholders. However, even in such cases, the fact remains that independence is basically a state of mind and is therefore dependent on personal qualities, ie, on the individual's assertiveness and ability not to succumb to reputational and career concerns.[21] Additionally, his involvement may vary in intensity: in some jurisdictions,[22] independent directors offer non-binding advice on RPTs, while others provide for binding advice by independent directors, who have a veto power over the conclusion of an RPT.[23] Furthermore, it is important that independent directors are promptly involved in the negotiation process for the conclusion of the RPT: the later they express their views on the specific RPT, the more likely that a number of alternatives will no longer be available or viable. Last but not least, even if an independent director has the necessary personal qualities, his personal knowledge of the company's business may be inferior to that of non-independent directors.[24] For this reason, the efficiency of the power of an independent director depends on whether independent directors can have full access on the relevant information, but also whether they can be assisted by independent experts of their own choice.[25]

In view of the above, neither the role of independent shareholders nor that of independent directors ensures that tunnelling via RPTs will be prevented. Theoretically, a combination of both procedural safeguards could deploy the synergies between them: independent or disinterested shareholders would screen RPTs and ensure that their terms are in the best interests of the company, while independent shareholders have the power to reject unfair RPTs if it is too late for alternative solutions. The combination of both procedural guards may raise transaction costs, but it may also contribute to lowering the risk of rejecting value-creating RPTs, since an approval of a specific RPT by independent directors may act as a credible signal of a transaction's fairness to independent shareholders. However, so far, no main jurisdiction has addressed RPTs by combining both independent directors and shareholders (MOM approval).[26]

[20] Enriques (n 1) 20 et seq; M Gutierrez and M Sáez, 'Deconstructing Independent Directors' (2013) 13 *Journal of Corporate Law Studies* 86; Hamdani and Yafeh (n 14) 698.

[21] Enriques, Hansmann and Kraakman (n 1) 55, 64.

[22] The weakest involvement requirement for an independent director is non-binding advice on RPTs, like in Belgium and, limited to smaller transactions, in Italy. Such a requirement does not prevent the dominant shareholder, or at least non-independent directors, from being part of the internal decision-making process. On the other hand, the strongest form of involvement is finally the 'independent negotiating committee' (or 'special committee') Delaware courts have since long nudged boards into using these when a parent-subsidiary merger or an management buyout (MBO) is on the agenda. The crucial point is always whether one can expect independent directors to make decisions in the best interests of the company rather than those of the related party.

[23] Enriques (n 1) 21.

[24] ibid.

[25] ibid; see also Consob Regulation on Related Party Transactions, under arts 7–8 (for larger transactions, independent directors may hire advisors at the company's expense).

[26] The one which has come closest to it is Delaware: for end-of-game transactions such as MBOs and freeze-outs, its courts have held that combining both a special committee and MOM approval grants a company and its dominant shareholder the protection of the business judgment rule and therefore virtually insulates the transaction from judicial reviewl see R Booth, 'Majority-of-the-Minority Voting and Fairness in Freeze-out Mergers' (2014) 59 *Villanova Law Review Tolle Lege* 87, 93.

c. Independent Advice and Fairness Opinions

Third-party independent advice and fairness opinions are deployed in many jurisdictions[27] in order to ensure that independent directors and minority shareholders acquire the necessary information on RPTs. Some jurisdictions require that companies make an independent financial advisor's opinion available to the shareholders before the approval of a RPT; voluntary use of a fairness opinion by an independent third-party advisor is also common practice in several jurisdictions.

The efficiency of fairness opinions remains controversial: fairness valuations unavoidably imply a high degree of discretion,[28] so that their value ultimately relies upon the reputation of the expert that provided them. Moreover, outside experts, even when chosen by independent directors, may be less independent than they look, as they usually except to gain more from other roles than from conducting fairness opinions. In addition, as a piece of information, a fairness opinion per se is not particularly helpful for the shareholder. It is the information upon which a fairness opinion is based upon (management's estimations on present or future cash-flows, the assumptions and methods applied by the expert etc) that may be of (better) use for the shareholders. The content of the fairness opinion varies depending on the jurisdiction, Delaware being the only main jurisdiction that has developed a wide body of case law on the scope of required disclosure on fairness opinions.[29]

d. *Ex Post*, Standard-Based Review of RPTs

Ex post, standard-based reviews of RPTs take a look into the merits of RPTs in order to assess whether their terms are 'fair' to the company.[30] Different standards of review may apply to different RPTs within the same jurisdiction (ie, for intra-group transactions), especially when RPTs represent routine transactions.[31] *Ex post*, standard-based reviews of RPTs interact with procedural (*ex ante*) safeguards in many ways: first, an *ex post* review may strengthen (minority) shareholder protection, acting as an additional safeguard to the procedural safeguards.[32] Procedural safeguards may, so to speak, trump

[27] Such is, for example, the case in Belgium (see art 523, para 2 of Code des societes) and Singapore (see r 921 of the Singapore Exchange Mainboard Rules).

[28] See, inter alia, LA Bebchuk and M Kahan, 'Fairness Opinions: How Fair are They and What Can Be Done about it?' (1989) 27 *Duke Law Journal* 27; A Tarde, 'Die verschleierte Konzernrichtlinie' (2017) *Zeitschrift für Unternehmens- und Gesellschaftsrecht* 365 et seq; B Hartwin and T Wansleben, 'Umsetzung der überarbeiteten Aktionärsrichtlinie in das deutsche Recht: Say on Pay und Related Party Transactions' (2017) *Der Betrieb* 1190 et seq.

[29] B Rohrbacher and M Zeberkiewitz, 'Fair Summary: Delaware's Framework for Disclosing Fairness Opinions' (2008) 63 *Business Lawyer* 881, 891 et seq, 900–01; B Rohrbacher and M Zeberkiewitz, 'Fair Summary II: An Update on Delaware's Disclosure Regime Regarding Fairness Opinions' (2011) 66 *Business Lawyer* 943; Italy's Consob Regulation on RPTs (Annex 4) requires information about the contents of fairness opinions roughly equivalent to Delaware case law.

[30] MA Eisenberg, 'The Divergence of Standards of Conduct and Standards of Review in Corporate Law' (1993) 62 *Fordham Law Review* 437, 451–57.

[31] Enriques (n 1) 30 et seq.

[32] In France, prosecution for abuse of corporate assets (*abus de biens sociaux*) complements procedural safeguards relying on shareholder meeting ratification of RPTs, while in Italy, criminal penalties for tunnelling are only relevant, for practical purposes, in the event of bankruptcy, on a count of 'fraudulent bankruptcy'. In bankruptcy, actions to recover money for the benefit of creditors, such as the *actio pauliana*, can also be used

ex post standard-based review, ie, when compliance with *ex ante* applicable procedural safeguards immunises the transaction, in the sense that it prevents a judge from declaring the RPT as prejudicial to the company. In fact, the more rigorously procedural safeguards are applied, the less judges are inclined to rule that the terms of a specific RPT are substantially unfair.[33] Last but not least, *ex post* review of RPTs may weaken shareholder protection when a remedy for violations of *ex ante* safeguards is only available if the transaction is also judged to be unfair.[34]

e. Disclosure as a Means to Prevent Unfair RPTs

Procedural safeguards, fairness opinions and standard-based reviews of RPTs do not operate in a vacuum; even the most sophisticated standard of review is useless if conflicts of interest are concealed.[35] Therefore, a standard of review needs to be combined with mandatory disclosure and effective enforcement: mandatory disclosure is necessary for acquiring knowledge of violations and effective enforcement is necessary to prevent non-disclosure.[36]

Mandatory disclosure is a widely established mechanism deployed in many jurisdictions for the purpose of preventing unfair RPTs. The main task of mandatory disclosure is to cast light on RPTs.[37] Mandatory disclosure of RPT-related information has the merit of being the least intrusive legal tool, in the sense that it does not directly impede RPTs in advance; however, it is crucial in supporting internal decision making and the company's assessment of the fairness of the transaction.[38] Although firms must bear some cost to produce relevant information, the relevant costs are not prohibiting and they can be further reduced if mandatory disclosure is exempted for smaller transactions. Another advantage of mandatory disclosure is its ease of enforcement, as it is relatively easy to identify and sanction its absence or inadequacy.

In the case of RPTs, mandatory disclosure can take place on two different fronts: first, disclosure of information to the company's decision-making organs, ie, the board of directors or the General Assembly (internal disclosure); and, second, disclosure to (potential) investors outside the firm (external disclosure). The efficiency of mandatory disclosure relies upon the content of the information provided to the investors or the company's decision-making organs and the modalities concerning the diffusion of the RPT-related information. Financial reporting standards on RPTs require disclosure (and therefore the audit) of information with reference to RPTs. In addition to

to tackle tunnelling *ex post*. *Ex post* review is finally the technique tax laws use to deal with RPTs aimed at minimising a company's tax burden (so-called transfer pricing).

[33] Enriques (n 1) 27 et seq.

[34] ibid.

[35] Pacces, 'Controlling' (n 4) 192–201.

[36] RJ Gilson, 'Controlling Shareholders and Corporate Governance: Complicating the Comparative Taxonomy' (2006) 119 *Harvard Law Review* 1641, 1653.

[37] PG Mahoney, 'Mandatory Disclosure as a Solution to Agency Problems' (1995) 62 *University of Chicago Law Review* 1047, 1066–73.

[38] From a comparative perspective, see G Jiang, C Lee and H Yue, 'Tunneling through Intercorporate Loans: The China Experience' (2010) 98 *Journal of Financial Economics* 1 et seq; YL Cheung, Yuehua Qi, PR Rau and A Stouraitis, 'Buy High, Sell Low: How Listed Firms Price Asset Transfers in Related Party Transactions' (2009) 33 *Journal of Banking and Finance* 914.

accounting standards, jurisdictions in the US and the EU require extensive periodic information about RPTs for public companies.[39] Several major jurisdictions provide for ad hoc, immediate disclosure of larger RPTs in advance of the independent directors' or shareholders' meeting for approval.[40] Allowing independent directors and shareholders to know who is in a position to engage in RPTs with the company may help detect tunnelling. In any case, if directors are not truly independent, they may not be eager to delve into the information disclosed to them. The same applies if shareholders, and especially institutional investors, are not exercising the right pressure. In such a case, mandatory disclosure may fall short of generating the desired pressure. Moreover, an effective system of mandatory disclosure is dependent on the aggressive enforcement of disclosure obligations.

II. Mandatory Disclosure on RPTs: An EU Perspective

A. Introductory Remarks

RPTs have been the focus of corporate law reforms in numerous EU jurisdictions, often due to pressure from international organisations, ie, the Organisation for Economic Co-operation and Development (OECD) and the World Bank.[41] EU Member States are currently tasked with the implementation, by 10 June 2019, of Directive 2017/828, amending Directive 2007/36/EC as regards the encouragement of long-term shareholder engagement in public companies (hereinafter the 'Shareholder Rights Amending Directive' or SRAD), which requires Member States to put in place a set of rules addressing RPTs.[42]

This framework was the outcome of a serious retreat from the more prescriptive rules of the European Commission's initial proposals.[43] The proposal issued on April 2014 by the European Commission relied on three of the legal instruments analysed in section I.B.ii above, namely: disclosure, third-party independent (fairness) opinion and independent shareholder approval of larger transactions (MoM). The proposal defined RPTs by reference to International Accounting Standard (IAS) 24 and provided for three different regulatory regimes depending on the size of RPT. For RPTs that represent more than one per cent of their assets, companies would have an obligation to publicly announce them at the time of the conclusion of the transaction, and accompany the

[39] See International Accounting Standards Board, *International Accounting Standard No 24*. No mention of materiality is made in the International Accounting Standard 24; it is an overarching principle of the IFRS that disclosure is only to be made when it is material (see International Accounting Standard No 1, para 31: 'An entity need not provide a specific disclosure required by an IFRS if the information is not material').

[40] Enriques (n 1) 24.

[41] W Puchniak and U Varottil, 'Related Party Transactions in Commonwealth Asia: Complexity Revealed' (2018) *ECGI Law Working Paper* 404/2018, ssrn.com/abstract=3169760.

[42] Directive (EU) 2017/828 of the European Parliament and of the Council of 17 May 2017 amending Directive 2007/36/EC as regards the encouragement of long-term shareholder engagement [2017] OJ L132/1.

[43] See European Commission, Proposal for a Directive of the European Parliament and of the Council amending Directive 2007/36/EC as regards the encouragement of long-term shareholder engagement and Directive 2013/34/EU as regards certain elements of the corporate governance statement, art 9c, available at: eur-lex.europa.eu/legalcontent/EN/TXT/?uri=COM:2014:213:FIN.

announcement with a report from an independent third party assessing whether or not it is on market terms and confirming that the transaction is fair and reasonable from the perspective of the shareholders, including minority shareholders. However, Member States would be allowed to exempt from the independent third-party opinion clearly defined types of recurrent transactions with an identified related party in a period of no longer than 12 months after granting the exemption, should shareholders (excluding the relevant related party from the vote) resolve so.

According to the proposal, RPTs representing more than five per cent of their assets or which can have a significant impact on profits or turnover should be submitted for approval by the General Meeting of Shareholders. The related party should be excluded from voting (MOM approval) and the approval would have to take place before the conclusion of the RPT; conclusion under the condition of shareholder approval would also be permitted. An exemption could be obtained from shareholders other than the related party for clearly defined types of recurrent transactions with an identified related party in a period of no longer than 12 months after granting the exemption. Aggregation of transactions with the same related party in a 12-month period implies that if the five per cent threshold is crossed, any subsequent transactions with the same related party should be submitted to an approval by the General Meeting of Shareholders, as analysed above.

Last but not least, the 2014 proposal provided for a general exemption from all requirements in the case of transactions between the company and one or more members of its group, and provided that those members of the group are wholly owned by the company. In addition, a newly proposed Article 14b would generally provide that Member States lay down the rules on penalties applicable to infringements of the national provisions and shall take all measures necessary to ensure that they are implemented.

B. Overview of the Regulatory Provisions of Article 9c SRAD

The provisions of the proposal were heavily criticised[44] and although the SRAD shares the basic legal toolkit of the proposal on RPTs, Article 9c contains several adjustments with regard to its implementation. The regulatory programme of the SRAD focuses on the prevention of misappropriation of corporate assets by means of RPTs (tunnelling).[45] For this reason, Member States should ensure 'that material related party transactions are submitted to approval by the shareholders or by the administrative or supervisory body according to procedures that prevent the related party from taking advantage of its position and provide adequate protection for the interests of the company and of the shareholders who are not a related party, including minority shareholders'.[46]

[44] See, inter alia, Enriques (n 1) 30 et seq; M Lutter, 'Die geplante europäische Gesetzgebung zu "Related Party Transactions"' (2014) *Europäische Zeitschrift für Wirtschaftsrecht* 687–88; W Bayer and S Philipp, 'Related Party Transactions: Der neueste EU-Vorschlag im Kontext des deutschen Aktien und Konzernrechts' (2015) *Neue Zeitschrift für Gesellschaftsrecht* 7–14.

[45] See Recital 42 of the SRAD: 'Transactions with related parties may cause prejudice to companies and their shareholders, as they may give the related party the opportunity to appropriate value belonging to the company. Thus, adequate safeguards for the protection of companies' and shareholders' interests are of importance.'

[46] See ibid.

As far as the definition of RPTs is concerned, Article 9c, para 1 SRAD defines RPTs by virtue of *renvoi* to IAS 24. However, Member States may define 'material' transactions with related parties, which will fall within the scope of the provisions on RPTs. To this end, EU Member States shall take into account an RPT's relevance regarding the economic decisions of a company's shareholders and their risks for the company and its shareholders. Material transactions thus defined (including those between a related party and a company's subsidiary, and those with the same related party which cross the relevant quantitative thresholds once aggregated within a rolling 12-month period) need to be disclosed at the time that the RPT is entered into at the latest: according to Article 9c, para 2 SRAD, information has to be provided 'at least on the nature of the related party relationship, the name of the related party, the date and the value of the transaction and other information necessary to assess whether or not the transaction is fair and reasonable from the perspective of the company and of the shareholders who are not a related party, including minority shareholders'.

In addition, Article 9c, para 3 SRAD provides that Member States have an option to require that, alongside the announcement, a report be published that assesses 'whether or not the transaction is fair and reasonable from the perspective of the company and of the shareholders who are not a related party, including minority shareholders, and explaining the assumptions it is based upon together with the methods used'. The report may be prepared by a third party, the administrative or supervisory body of the company, the audit committee or any committee of which the majority is composed of independent directors (Article 9c, para 3 SRAD). In terms of process, material RPTs are to be approved either 'by the general meeting or by the administrative or supervisory body of the company according to procedures which prevent the related party from taking advantage of its position and provide adequate protection for the interests of the company and of the shareholders who are not a related party, including minority shareholders' and without the participation of the director or shareholder who is a related party. However, Member States may opt out of this last requirement, 'provided that national law ensures appropriate safeguards which apply before or during the voting process to protect the interests of the company and of the shareholders who are not a related party, including minority shareholders, by preventing the related party from approving the transaction despite the opposing opinion of the majority of the shareholders who are not a related party or despite the opposing opinion of the majority of the independent directors' (Article 9c, para 4 SRAD).

Unless Member States provide otherwise, the disclosure and procedural requirements 'shall not apply to transactions entered into in the ordinary course of business and concluded on normal market terms' (Article 9c, para 5 SRAD). Similarly, Member States are allowed (Article 9c, para 6 SRAD) to opt for additional exemptions, namely for:

a. 'transactions entered into between the company and its subsidiaries provided that they are wholly owned or that no other related party of the company has an interest in the subsidiary undertaking or that national law provides for adequate protection of interests of the company, of the subsidiary and of their shareholders who are not a related party, including minority shareholders in such transactions';
b. 'clearly defined types of transactions for which national law requires approval by the general meeting, provided that fair treatment of all shareholders and the interests of

the company and of the shareholders who are not a related party, including minority shareholders, are specifically addressed and adequately protected in such provisions of law;

c. 'transactions regarding remuneration of directors, or certain elements of remuneration of directors, awarded or due in accordance with Article 9a [SRAD]' (say-on-pay rules);
d. 'transactions entered into by credit institutions based on measures, aiming at safeguarding their stability, adopted by the competent authority in charge of the prudential supervision within the meaning of Union law';
e. 'transactions offered to all shareholders on the same terms where equal treatment of all shareholders and protection of the interests of the company is ensured.'

Given the open-ended character of the provisions on RPTs, EU Member States will have broad discretion in implementing the provisions of Article 9c SRAD. Jurisdictions with wide experience on the regulation of RTPs (ie, England, Italy and France) will change in practice only a few things on their existing provisions. Others, which have been traditionally reluctant to regulate RPTs, will have to deploy much stricter rules, especially with regard to the procedural safeguards on the approval of RPTs. In terms of procedural requirements, so long as the legislation of EU Member States prevents the related party from participating in the transaction's approval, nothing else is required, apart from subjecting the RPT to the approval of the Board of Directors.

In any case, the SRAD provides the legislation of EU Member States with specific guidelines on how to regulate RPTs for listed companies. The relevant provisions of the SRAD are flexible enough to enable national legislators to deploy the regulatory tools that effectively constrain the abusive behaviour of controlling shareholders or directors, (ie, by requiring an independent fairness opinion and providing for MOM approval of the RPT) without excluding the conclusion of fair RPTs. Whether the implementation of the SRAD will lead to a more efficient protection of the interests of minority shareholders or to a dilution of the already existing safeguards depends in the end on the interplay between pre-existing rules and the newly created safeguards.

C. The Provisions of Article 9c SRAD on Disclosure

i. Scope of the Provisions on Disclosure

The provisions on disclosure under Article 9c SRAD represent an important step towards a harmonised EU standard on the transparency of RPTs. Interestingly, the preamble to the SRAD refers to the public disclosure of RPTs as necessary 'in order to allow shareholders, creditors, employees and other interested parties to be informed of potential impacts that such transactions may have on the value of the company. The precise identification of the related party is necessary to better assess the risks implied by the transaction and to enable challenges to the transaction, including by means of legal action'. In other words, the Preamble to the SRAD seems to adopt a more pluralistic approach to the scope of disclosure, under which the interests of other stakeholders ('creditors, employees and other interested parties') are given equal status to those of the shareholders.[47] On the other hand, the proposals for the SRAD seemed to focus exclusively on the interests of the shareholders.[48]

It is questionable whether the wording of the Preamble in this respect should be interpreted as a paradigm shift on the scope of the directors' duties when applying the rules on RPTs.[49] In view of the fact that Article 9c, para 2 SRAD does not apply the same wording as the Preamble, a conservative approach in this matter seems more appropriate. The scope of the relevant provisions still focuses on the protection of shareholders;[50] the wording of the Preamble should be interpreted as an indication of neutrality on behalf of the EU legislator with respect to the shareholder versus stakeholder debate.[51] For this reason, the implementation of Article 9c SRAD is not expected to alter the scope of the legislation of EU Member States on the fiduciary duties of the company's directors.

ii. The Duty of Public Announcement of Material RPTs

According to Article 9c, para 2 SRAD, Member States shall ensure that listed companies shall publicly announce material transactions with related parties at the latest at the time of the conclusion of the transaction. The announcement shall contain at least information on the nature of the related party relationship, the name of the related party, the date and the value of the transaction, and other information necessary to assess whether the transaction is fair and reasonable from the perspective of the company and of the shareholders who are not a related party, including minority shareholders.

The means of public announcement are not specified in the SRAD; No 44 of the Preamble to the SRAD refers cursorily to the use of the company's website or 'other easily available means' as means of public announcement without any further clarifications.[52] Moreover, the SRAD does not specify whether the public announcement should be channelled by means of corporate or capital market law.[53] The rules of capital market law on the disclosure of information provide for more immediate and flexible diffusion of the

[47] R Veil, 'Transaktionen mit Related Parties im deutschen Aktien- und Konzernrecht – Grundsatzfragen der Umsetzung der Aktionärsrechte-Richtlinie' (2017) *Neue Zeitschrift für Gesellschaftsrecht* 522 et seq; Andeas Tarde, *Related Party Transactions – Empfehlungen zur Umsetzung der reformierten Aktionärsrichtlinie vor dem Hintergrund eines englisch-deutschen Rechtsvergleichs* (Cologne, Carl Heymanns Verlag, 2018) 196.

[48] Recital 19 of the SRAD; J Vetter, 'Regelungsbedarf für Related Party Transactions?' (2015) *Zeitschrift für das gesamte Handelsrecht und Wirtschaftsrecht* 301.

[49] See, in favour of such an interpretation, Veil (n 47) 522.

[50] Tarde (n 47) 196.

[51] ibid; see also a similar approach in W Schön, 'Der Zweck der Aktiengesellschaft – geprägt durch europäisches Gesellschaftsrecht?' (2016) *Zeitschrift für das gesamte Handelsrecht und Wirtschaftsrecht* 268, 279; contra P Hommelhoff, in B Boemke, M Lembke amd R Linck (eds), *Feschrift fuer Gerrick Frhr.v.Hoyiningen-Huene* (Munich, CH Beck, 2014) 141; P Hommelhoff, 'Aktuelle Impulse aus dem europäischen Unternehmensrecht: eine Herausforderung für Deutschland' (2015) *Neue Zeitschrift für Gesellschaftsrecht* 1330.

[52] See Recital 44 of the SRAD: 'Public disclosure of such transaction, for example on a company's website or by other easily available means, is needed in order to allow shareholders, creditors, employees and other interested parties to be informed of potential impacts that such transactions may have on the value of the company.'

[53] Veil (n 47) 526; U Kleiner and V Mayer, 'Geschäfte der Aktiengesellschaft mit nahestehenden Personen und Unternehmen – Bestandsaufnahme und anstehende Neuerungen durch die Umsetzung der EU-Aktionärsrechterichtlinie' (2018) *Neue Zeitschrift für Gesellschaftsrecht* 321.

relevant information in comparison with the respective provisions of corporate law;[54] a breach of corporate law provisions results in different legal consequences compared to a breach of capital market law.[55] The choice between capital market law and corporate law is also relevant for matters related to the administrative supervision of the relevant provisions on RPTs.[56]

The contents of disclosure for material RPTs are only cursorily sketched out: disclosure does not have to go further than 'the nature of the related party relationship, the name of the related party, the amount of the transaction and any other information necessary to assess the transaction'. The open-ended reference to 'any other information necessary' in Article 9c SRAD assigns corporate insiders with the discretionary power to provide additional information on RPTs (ie, financial data)[57] in order to substantiate the fair value of the specific transaction; it remains questionable as to whether self-regulation by corporate insiders is the appropriate means for efficient regulation. As far as the timeline of disclosure is concerned, Article 9c, para 7 SRAD provides that information on RPTs should be disclosed by the time of conclusion of the respective transaction.[58] Article 9c does not define when a transaction qualifies as concluded; this matter will be answered in accordance with the national legal provisions of the EU Member State jurisdictions.

Other jurisdictions, especially in the US, provide for the disclosure of details even before the conclusion of such transactions ('proposed transactions').[59] Since the SRAD does not provide for maximum harmonisation in this matter, EU Member State jurisdictions are entitled to extend the duty of disclosure at a time point before the conclusion of the transaction in order to improve the level of information for stakeholders. However, as information on RPTs may also qualify as insider information under Article 17(1) of Regulation (EU) No 596/2014 of the European Parliament and of the Council (Market Abuse Regulation (MAR)),[60] special attention should be given so that any potential regulatory overlapping does not create legal uncertainty.[61] In this respect, 7 Article 9c, para 7 provides that the provisions on RPTs apply without prejudice to the rules on public disclosure of inside information as referred to in Article 17 MAR. In all events, an ad hoc disclosure of insider information under the MAR, containing all relevant RPT details, should be considered to be satisfactory for the purposes of the SRAD.[62]

The SRAD makes no reference to the right of an issuer to abstain from the disclosure of the details on a specific RPT on specific grounds. However, the Preamble to the SRAD makes direct reference to this matter when it mentions that 'transparency

[54] Veil (n 47) 526.
[55] ibid.
[56] ibid.
[57] Kleiner and Mayer (n 53) 321.
[58] ibid.
[59] Veil (n 47) 526.
[60] Regulation (EU) No 596/2014 of the European Parliament and of the Council of 16 April 2014 on market abuse (market abuse regulation) and repealing Directive 2003/6/EC of the European Parliament and of the Council and Commission Directives 2003/124/EC, 2003/125/EC and 2004/72/EC [2014] OJ L173/1.
[61] Veil (n 47) 526.
[62] Kleiner and Mayer (n 53) 322; Veil (n 48) 526.

requirements are not intended to require companies, institutional investors, asset managers or proxy advisors to disclose to the public certain specific pieces of information the disclosure of which would be seriously prejudicial to their business position or, where they are not undertakings with a commercial purpose, to the interest of their members or beneficiaries'.[63] It remains to be seen how the EU Member State legislators will incorporate the abovementioned reference into their national jurisdictions.[64] In any case, the reference in the SRAD's Recitals must be taken into account when interpreting the national legislation of EU Member States.[65]

iii. Fairness Opinion

According to Article 9c, para 3 SRAD, Member States may provide for the public disclosure of details on RPTs to be accompanied by a report ('fairness opinion') assessing whether or not the relevant transaction is fair and reasonable from the perspective of the company and of the shareholders who are not a related party, including minority shareholders, and explaining the assumptions it is based upon, together with the methods used.

The necessity of fairness opinions in the case of RPTs has been criticised[66] – their information value relies on the data, methods and assumptions they are based on.[67] Repeat providers of fairness opinions may act as gatekeepers and care more about their reputation than about an individual client relationship. Although fairness opinions are widely applied in the case of mergers and acquisitions, it has been argued that such opinions are not only costly but that their application in RPTs does not necessarily improve the level of shareholders' protection;[68] most shareholders in listed companies lack the necessary level of expertise to appreciate the information included in a fairness opinion. In such cases, the informative value of the report may well tend to zero; its costs, however calculated, will be real. On the other hand, it can be argued that even if a fairness opinion is not fully understandable by the shareholders, it nevertheless enhances their overall level of information. In addition, such an opinion may create a sense of confidence to the shareholders on the benefits and the value of the specific RPT.[69]

[63] See Recital 45 of the SRAD: 'This Directive sets up transparency requirements for companies, institutional investors, asset managers and proxy advisors. Those transparency requirements are not intended to require companies, institutional investors, asset managers or proxy advisors to disclose to the public certain specific pieces of information the disclosure of which would be seriously prejudicial to their business position or, where they are not undertakings with a commercial purpose, to the interest of their members or beneficiaries. Such non-disclosure should not undermine the objectives of the disclosure requirements laid down in this Directive.'

[64] Kleiner and Mayer (n 53) 322.

[65] ibid.

[66] See, inter alia, the positions of Bebchuk and Kahan (n 28) 27 et seq; Tarde (n 28) 365 et seq; Veil (n 47) 527–28; Enriques (n 1) 31 et seq; H Bungert and T Wansleben, 'Grenzüberschreitende Verschmelzungen und Spaltungen aus Sicht des Europäischen Parlaments' (2017) 70 *Der Betrieb* 198.

[67] Enriques (n 1) 30–31.

[68] Bebchuk and Kahan (n 28) 27 et seq; Tarde (n 28) 365 et seq; Bungert and Wansleben (n 66).

[69] Veil (n 47) 527–28.

The provisions of Article 9c, para 3 SRAD assign the obligation of a fairness opinion to the discretion of the national legislator of the EU Member State. In some EU Member State jurisdictions, an obligation to accompany the disclosure with a fairness opinion applies to all RPTs of listed companies,[70] whereas in other jurisdictions, such an obligation applies for RPTs of a certain volume.[71]

III. Concluding Remarks

Disclosure plays an important role in corporate governance as a tool to address agency problems, especially in the case of RPTs; its main governance function is to permit the *ex post* enforcement of managers' fiduciary duties, but disclosure rules may also complement substantive rules of corporate law by dealing with the issue of asymmetrical information among shareholders. In this respect, disclosure is instrumental to shareholder empowerment as it increases managerial consciousness by forcing managers to inform shareholders in a timely manner of the events and circumstances surrounding a specific RPT.

The SRAD has been the product of several compromises. It provides a common legal framework on the regulation of RPTs by introducing a series of legal instruments widely applied in most EU Member State jurisdictions. It also provides national legislators with considerable discretion in relation to the implementation of such legal instruments and introduces a two-level approach, focusing on (a) listed companies and (b) material RPT transactions. The discretion that the SRAD provides for the national legislator may dilute the scope of harmonisation in these two areas; however, this is unavoidable as EU Member States follow different traditions with respect to RPTs. In this respect, the SRAD provides for alternative arrangements that could well work more effectively where the proposed rules may, for example, be unduly costly due to a specific legal system's anti-synergic features. On the other hand, it may allow Member States to experiment with more stringent rules in addition to them. Similarly, Member States that already have more stringent rules in at least some respects will be under pressure to loosen up their regime.

To conclude, the rules of the SRAD may improve on the status quo in at least some of the Member States, which are weak in terms of shareholder protection. The legislation process will reveal the level of harmonisation achieved in the area of RPT regulation. A comparative legal research on the implementation of the SRAD among EU Member State jurisdictions will prove helpful in assessing the level of harmonisation achieved among jurisdictions with different regulatory traditions in relation to the RPT. In all events, the attempt to provide for uniform rules in such a core area of corporate law as tunnelling is further evidence of how harmonisation is a double-edged sword.

[70] See, for example, Greece under art 101(1) of Law No. 4548/2018.

[71] See, for example, in Italy, the Consob Regulation on Related Party Transactions of greater importance, under Annex 3.

PART II

Evolution of Disclosure in Capital Markets Law

5

Disclosure of Inside Information

JENNIFER PAYNE

I. Introduction

The EU Market Abuse Regulation (MAR) places an obligation on issuers of financial instruments[1] to disclose inside information to the market 'as soon as possible'.[2] This must be done in a way that 'enables fast access and complete, correct and timely assessment of the information by the public'.[3] The information must be disseminated to the public simultaneously, or as nearly as possible, in all EEA Member States.[4] This obligation is one of the cornerstones of EU securities market regulation.

The EU regime, based on the notion of prompt disclosure, suggests that the information does not belong to the issuer at all, but rather that, as a general matter, it can be regarded as belonging to all investors and therefore should be shared with the investing public.[5] This approach is distinct from that of other jurisdictions, most notably the US. In particular, the EU regime adopts a concept of continuous disclosure, which is

[1] Under the Market Abuse Directive, Directive 2003/6/EC (hereinafter '2003 MAD') [2003] OJ L96/16, the obligation was placed on issuers admitted to regulated markets, but this was broadened considerably under the Market Abuse Regulation, Regulation (EU) No 596/2014 (hereinafter 'MAR'), [2014] OJ L173/1 to include not only issuers that have requested or approved the admission of their financial instruments to trading on a regulated market in a Member State, but also, in the case of financial instruments traded on a Multilateral Trading Facility (MTF) or Organised Trading Facility (OTF), issuers who have approved the MTF/OTF trading or request the admission to trading of their financial instrument on an MTF in a Member State: MAR, art 2(1). A similar disclosure obligation applies to emission allowances market participants (art 17(2)).

[2] MAR, art 17. This obligation to disclose inside information as soon as possible was introduced in 2003 (see 2003 MAD, art 6). The previous obligation, found in art 7 of Directive 89/592/EEC [1989] OJ L334/30, imposed an ongoing disclosure obligation in relation to material ad hoc disclosures, but Member States varied considerably in relation to their interpretation and implementation of this requirement.

[3] MAR, art 17(1).

[4] Directive 2004/109/EC, [2004] OJ L390/38, as amended by Directive 2013/50/EU (Transparency Directive) [2013] OJ L294/13, art 21. Information is required to be displayed on the company's website (although see art 17(9) MAR for a concession for SMEs), but in order to ensure that the information is disclosed simultaneously to all market participants, additional dissemination will be needed via some form of news service, such as, in the UK, a 'Primary Information Provider' approved by the Financial Conduct Authority which carries news about all companies in the market and so does not favour those who happen to be logged on to a company's website at the time the information is posted.

[5] This is subject to some exemptions, eg, delay, discussed below at section II.C.

much broader than the obligation to disclose inside information imposed on issuers in the US. Furthermore, the EU regime seeks to achieve two goals via the obligation to disclose inside information, namely to inform investors about the company and its business and also to reduce the opportunities for insider trading by robbing information of its inside character. There is thus a close relationship between the disclosure obligation and the prohibition on insider dealing. This approach is again distinct from that of the US. These differences will be explored in this chapter.

In section II, the breadth of the obligation to disclose information in the EU is analysed and compared to the position in the US. In section III, the relationship between this disclosure obligation and the prohibition of insider dealing is discussed, again with reference to the US position. The EU approach brings with it some major benefits, not least a potential increase in market efficiency and investor protection, but also raises difficulties and challenges that must be addressed. The breadth of the continuous disclosure obligation in the EU creates potential costs for issuers and investors. The close relationship between inside information disclosure and the prohibition on insider dealing also raises potential concerns, since these forms of regulation operate in quite different ways and yoking them together could have the effect of reducing market efficiency. To some extent, the MAR anticipates these problems and tackles them, but some concerns remain, particularly regarding the early disclosure of information. The EU continuous disclosure regime is to be welcomed, but needs to be operated with care in order to ensure that the benefits of such an approach are not accompanied by undue costs for issuers and investors.

II. The Breadth of the Obligation to Disclose Inside Information in the EU

Information disclosure is widely used as a technique to regulate the financial markets. It is a cheap regulatory tool, requiring little if any governmental expenditure, and it preserves the notion of empowered investors making their own investment decisions, avoiding the difficult issues of paternalism that sometimes creep into debates about financial product regulation.[6] The purpose of information disclosure in the capital markets is first and foremost to provide investors with protection.[7] It is well understood that securities are intangible goods which cannot be inspected in the same way as other consumer products. They are claims to the future income of companies,

[6] See O Ben-Shahar and C Schneider, 'The Failure of Mandated Disclosure' (2011) 159 *University of Pennsylvania Law Review* 647.

[7] In addition to providing protection for investors, information disclosure can be seen as providing assistance to shareholders, ie, mandatory disclosure has also been said to perform an important function regarding the governance of public companies. It is even suggested by some commentators that the governance functions of mandatory disclosure are its most important functions: RH Kraakman, 'Disclosure and Corporate Governance: An Overview Essay' in G Ferrarini et al (eds), *Reforming Company and Takeover Law in Europe* (Oxford, Oxford University Press, 2004) 96.

ie, the value of securities is largely contingent on the expected future performance of the issuing company. The return on the investment is therefore uncertain and the quality of these securities cannot be fully assessed in advance. Regulators and policy makers often focus on the need to provide investors with the information they need to make rational investment decisions and to remove asymmetries of information as between insiders and outsiders in the capital markets.

Although the rhetoric around information disclosure often concerns investor protection of this rather direct sort – ie, regulating the relationship between issuer and investor – such a discussion fits most comfortably with disclosure obligations in the primary market rather than disclosure in the secondary market, which is the focus of this chapter. In the secondary market, investors are purchasing their securities not from the issuer, but from other investors, and investor protection is provided indirectly by ensuring that markets operate as efficiently as possible. It is not that information asymmetries do not exist in the secondary market, since they clearly do; investors with more information (including those with inside knowledge of the company, engaged in insider trading) will enjoy systematically greater returns at the expense of uninformed investors in the market. However, dealing with these asymmetries, and providing investors with protection, is achieved not by regulating the relationship between seller and buyer per se, but rather by ensuring that prices reflect as closely as possible the underlying value of the assets.

The efficient capital market hypothesis posits that prices within the market at any given time 'fully reflect' the available information.[8] EU and US regulators have been strongly influenced by the idea of semi-strong form efficiency whereby all publicly available information about a security is reflected in its price. The fact that insiders trading in the company's shares are able to produce systematically higher returns undermines the strong version of the efficient capital market hypothesis. On the basis of the semi-strong form of the efficient capital market hypothesis, requiring issuers to produce information about themselves and their securities can promote informational efficiency, since that information, once publicly available, will help to move the prices of the securities to a new equilibrium which reflects that new information. On this analysis, investors do not need to actually read and digest the information in order to take advantage of the disclosure.[9] The analysis function is instead performed to a large extent by securities analysts and other market professionals, such as arbitrageurs, researchers, brokers and portfolio managers who spend their time acquiring and evaluating information regarding issuers and their securities. The trading by these professionals moves the market price and thereby allows the information to be assimilated. In an efficient market, unsophisticated investors can thus free-ride on the efforts of more sophisticated ones.

[8] EF Fama, 'Efficient Capital Markets: A Review of Theory and Empirical Work' (1970) 25 *Journal of Finance* 383. The information being 'fully reflected' in the price means that the price moves to a new equilibrium, rather than the fact that the price necessarily reflects the value of the underlying assets – ie, this is about informational efficiency rather than price accuracy.

[9] See R Gilson and RH Kraakman, 'The Mechanisms of Market Efficiency' (1984) 70 *Virginia Law Review* 549 for a detailed discussion of how information becomes 'fully reflected' in the prices of securities.

This provides investors with protection when they trade in securities, since the market price reflects all publicly available information and thus ensures that they will receive a fair price in whatever transaction they engage. Of course, this does not mean that market prices reflect the fundamental value of the assets and nor does it mean that unsophisticated investors can never 'lose' in a semi-strong form efficient market. In particular, unsophisticated investors, and indeed sophisticated investors such as securities analysts, can still lose out to insiders to the extent that those insiders have information that is not publicly available and then trade in the market while in possession of that information. For this reason, it is common for jurisdictions to put in place some form of prohibition on this behaviour, something which is discussed further in section III below.

As a consequence of this approach, the EU, in common with the US, places various disclosure obligations on issuers in the secondary market. Both the US and the EU mandate the periodic disclosure of significant financial information about the company, including their financial statements. In the EU, companies with securities traded on regulated markets are required to publish their audited financial statements annually[10] and a slightly lighter set of disclosures half-yearly.[11] In the US, companies are under an obligation to publish annually a significant amount of information about the company, including their audited financial statements, via a form 10-K.[12] In addition, there is a requirement to file a form 10-Q on a quarterly basis.

In addition, both the US and the EU require ad hoc disclosures. In the EU, this consists of a number of requirements to disclose, including the obligation to disclose the interests in securities of a company held by those discharging managerial responsibilities for those companies, and those connected with them,[13] and also the major shareholdings of a company.[14] However, at the centre of these obligations is the requirement to disclose inside information 'as soon as possible'. This obligation has been described as the 'bedrock' of the EU regime.[15] It creates a continuous disclosure obligation and by creating a very broad concept of information which must be publicly disclosed, it may be regarded as advancing the goal of price accuracy in the EU. The EU approach is often described as being about providing parity of information or equality of information to the market, and in one sense it does so, maximising the amount of information made available to the public, ensuring that information is released to the market as simultaneously as possible and reducing the opportunities for selective disclosure. All investors have the potential to receive the same information at the same time, although some investors (retail investors) rarely if ever read the disclosures. This concept of market egalitarianism is valuable therefore for the support it provides to market efficiency.

[10] Transparency Directive, art 4.

[11] ibid art 5 (the requirement for quarterly reporting was abolished by Directive 2013/50/EU).

[12] See Regulation S-X.

[13] MAR, art 19(1).

[14] Transparency Directive 2004/109/EC, as amended by Directive 2013/50/EU, art 9(1).

[15] See L Enriques and S Gilotta, 'Disclosure and Financial Market Regulation' in N Moloney, E Ferran and J Payne (eds), *The Oxford Handbook of Financial Regulation* (Oxford, Oxford University Press, 2015) 519.

This stands in contrast to the US, which, while it contains an obligation for ad hoc disclosures, does not operate a continuous disclosure regime.[16] In the US, there is an obligation to publish 'on a rapid and current basis' updates to the market concerning material changes in issuers' fortunes that occur between the required quarterly reports. The obligation to file a form 8-K, to update the market as to these material changes, is linked to a list of specified events that trigger the requirement for disclosure, such as the issuer filing for bankruptcy or receivership, a material modification of the rights of security holders, or significant acquisitions or dispositions. This contrasts with the EU approach which does not specify the events that trigger disclosure, but focuses instead on the consequences of the events on the share price. In the US, there is therefore no requirement to disclose inside information that arises between the quarterly filings and which falls outside this specific list of events. In other words, there is no general duty to disclose all material information to the market. The US regime is therefore said to be a system of periodic disclosure rather than continuous disclosure.[17]

The difference between the US and EU regimes may not be quite as stark as it first appears. Issuers can choose to disclose material information falling outside the specified categories if they wish to do so, and many issuers in the US do appear to make use of optional disclosure between form 10-Q filings. In relation to inside information, day-to-day circumstances can impose an affirmative obligation to disclose on US issuers, stemming from inquiries from the investment community for information and the issuer's motivation to keep that community apprised of current developments. Many US issuers consequently adopt an affirmative policy of disclosing material information, subject to exceptions such as the necessity of keeping information confidential or the protection of a legitimate business interest.[18] Furthermore, US stock exchanges can require listed companies to promptly disclose to the public information that is material to a reasonable investor.[19]

There are some potentially significant advantages to the EU approach. In particular, if it is correct that the markets in the EU operate in accordance with the semi-strong form of the efficient capital market hypothesis, then in theory the more information that is disclosed to the market, the better, since this will enable the price of the securities to

[16] Whether or not a US company conducts a public offering, it may, upon reaching a certain size or having a specific number of shareholders, be required to register its securities with the Securities and Exchange Commission (SEC) under s 12(b), 12(g) or 15(d) of the Securities Exchange Act (SEA), subjecting it to the same ongoing requirements as if it had made a public offering. Conducting a public offering or registering securities under the SEA triggers timely and current reporting requirements, including filing of annual, quarterly and current reports to the SEC (forms 10-K, 10-Q and 8-K, respectively). These reports mandate the disclosure of financial and non-financial information, and require that public companies report certain material information on a periodic basis. US companies registering pursuant to s 12(b) or 12(g) of the SEA are subject to other requirements, including beneficial ownership reporting, short-swing trading rules and tender offer and proxy rules, pursuant to ss 16, 13(d) and 12(e) of the SEA, respectively. Certain record-keeping requirements, internal accounting controls and prohibitions on foreign corrupt practices also apply to these issuers.

[17] See, eg, *Gallagher v Abbott Laboratories* 269 F.2d 806 (7th Cir 2001) per Judge Easterbrook.

[18] For discussion, see D Oesterle, 'The Inexorable March toward a Continuous Disclosure Requirement for Publicly Traded Corporations: Are We There Yet?' (1998) 20 *Cardozo Law Review* 135.

[19] See, eg, NYSE Company Manual, Fed Sec L Rep (CCH) 23, 121 (1977).

move closer to the underlying value of the assets, providing investors with protection when they trade in the securities at the market price. However, the use of mandatory disclosure comes with costs, both for investors, if the information produced is too voluminous to be useful or is simply of the wrong kind, and for issuers, since mandatory disclosure can impose both direct and indirect costs on them. The broad EU approach to the disclosure of inside information therefore needs to be assessed not only according to the potential benefits of the regime, but must also take account of the costs and disadvantages that it can bring.

Five potential problems with the broad EU approach to disclosure of inside information are considered here. The first two may be regarded as principally concerns for the recipients of the information, namely: (1) that the information provided may be too technical, too voluminous or otherwise less beneficial for investors than intended; and (2) that the EU approach may interfere with the incentives of sophisticated investors, particularly analysts, to gather and utilise information about an issuer. The remaining problems raise concern for issuers, namely: (3) that the requirement to disclose information as soon as possible may damage issuers' ability to conduct their business, unless they have the ability to delay disclosure in some circumstances; (4) that the cost of disclosure may cause problems for certain issuers, particularly small and medium-sized enterprises (SMEs), which may be excluded from the capital markets as a result of the cost of mandated disclosure; and (5) the mandatory disclosure of inside information may bring with it an enhanced litigation risk for issuers.

A. The Benefit of Inside Information Disclosure to Investors

One concern that is sometimes raised regarding mandatory disclosure is that it may not be as beneficial to investors as intended. This might be because the technical and/or voluminous nature of the information makes it difficult for investors to utilise or because it is simply the wrong sort of information and therefore not valuable to investors. There has been increasing recognition in recent years that simply providing investors, particularly retail investors, with all the relevant information will not necessarily enable them to make optimal investment decisions. Issues of bounded rationality and information overload, in particular, can be problematic.[20] Within the EU, regulators have responded to these concerns in the primary market by requiring that the prospectus published by the issuer at the Initial Public Offering (IPO) stage be accompanied by a summary which is short,[21] easy to read and is written in comprehensible, non-technical language.[22] Furthermore, the required content and format is intended to provide investors with the information they will find most useful. The 2017 Prospectus Regulation,

[20] See, eg, T Paredes, 'Blinded by the Light: Information Overload and its Consequences for Securities Regulation' (2003) 81 *Washington University Law Quarterly* 417.

[21] The limit is seven A4-size pages: Regulation (EU) 2017/1129, [2017] OJ L168/12, art 7(3).

[22] Regulation (EU) 2017/1129, art 7(3).

for example, limits the risk factors to only those specific to the issuer and/or the securities which are material to investors.[23]

The requirements for disclosing inside information, in common with other disclosures in the secondary market, are not subject to similar protections, but this should not be regarded as overly problematic. Inside information disclosed to the market 'as soon as possible' will still be valuable for sophisticated investors, even if it is not read and utilised directly by retail investors. As discussed, it is sophisticated investors that are the main users of information disclosures in the secondary market, turning information into market prices that operate as a protection for less sophisticated market participants. The market in the aggregate is capable of processing technical and voluminous information even if individual retail investors are not. Retail investors therefore receive indirect protection even if they do not read or understand the disclosures being produced by issuers.

Another concern about the value and utility of the information disclosures required of issuers is that it is regulators and policy makers that determine the information that needs to be disclosed. They are therefore making decisions about what investors will find valuable and there are a range of reasons why policy makers may not perform this task well, including regulatory capture, cognitive biases and the regulatory regime being a response to populism. Some disclosure rules can be questioned on this basis. For example, the obligation in EU law to disclose to the public any short position higher than 0.5 per cent of a company's shares[24] may be regarded as being motivated, as least in part, by a popular desire to constrain short sellers in the aftermath of the financial crisis. This low threshold can be regarded as operating as a potential curb on short selling and therefore as having a potentially negative effect on market efficiency.[25]

However, the requirement to disclose inside information seems to avoid the worst of these concerns, since at the core of the concept of inside information is the notion of what a reasonable investor will want to know. Inside information, as defined by the MAR, is

> Information of a precise nature, which has not been made public, relating, directly or indirectly, to one or more issuers or to one or more financial instruments,[26] and which, if it were made public, would be likely to have a significant effect on the prices of those financial instruments or on the price of related derivative financial instruments.[27]

[23] ibid art 7.

[24] Regulation (EU) No 236/2012, [2012] OJ L86/1, art 6.

[25] J Payne, 'The Regulation of Short Selling and its Reform in Europe' (2012) 13 *European Business Organization Law Review* 413.

[26] Note therefore that the information does not need to relate to particular securities or a particular issuer of securities, ie, it could be information which has an impact on the securities markets generally.

[27] MAR, art 7(1). As regards the concept of 'precise' for this purpose, art 7(2) provides that information about events or circumstances 'shall be deemed to be of a precise nature … where it is specific enough to enable a conclusion to be drawn as to the possible effect of that set of circumstances or event on the prices of the financial instruments'. An early draft of the Market Abuse Regulation (published 20 October 2011) had included an additional category of inside information relating to relevant information not generally available to the public (RINGA), on the basis that information can be abused before an issuer is under an obligation to disclose it. The inclusion of this category was controversial and RINGA does not appear in the final version of the MAR.

Indeed, Article 7(4) specifically includes the concept of the 'reasonable investor' within the test of what constitutes inside information:

> For the purposes of [Article 7(1)], information which, if it were made public, would be likely to have a significant effect on the prices of financial instruments … shall mean information a reasonable investor would be likely to use as part of the basis of his or her investment decisions.[28]

Tying the concept of inside information closely to the notion of what a reasonable investor will actually find useful and valuable avoids the difficulties inherent in policy makers and regulators attempting to determine this and specify it in advance.[29]

One difficult issue that has arisen relates to the question of when information about an ongoing or developing situation crosses the threshold to become inside information. This was discussed by the Court of Justice of the European Union (CJEU) in *Geltl v Daimler AG*,[30] in which it was held that information may cross that threshold before the final situation has emerged. The MAR codifies the approach in *Geltl*, stating that 'an intermediate step in a protracted process shall be deemed to be inside information if, by itself, it satisfies the criteria of inside information as referred to in this Article'.[31] Furthermore, inside information includes not only circumstances or events that already exist or have already occurred, but also those that 'may reasonably be expected'.[32]

There are a number of potential problems that arise from this judgment, including a concern for issuers if disclosure at too early a stage in events risks harming their legitimate interests, and a concern that this approach might harm market efficiency if early stage and potentially unreliable information is publicly disclosed. These issues are discussed below.[33] The focus here is on a potential investor protection problem. Requiring information about an evolving situation to be disclosed at too early a stage risks confusing investors, providing them with information about events that are still uncertain, still evolving and may well change. To some extent, this can be addressed by provisions allowing issuers to delay disclosure in situations where disclosure is likely to cause confusion to investors, discussed in section III below, but the emphasis in the EU regime is very much in favour of early disclosure, and the ability to delay is heavily circumscribed.

[28] The CJEU has held that this 'market impact' test can be satisfied even if the direction of the impact (up or down) cannot be predicted at the time of trading: Case C-628/13 *Lafonta v Autorité des marches financiers* [2015] Lloyd's Rep FC 113.

[29] In the US, whether inside information satisfies the test of materiality also depends on the view of a reasonable investor, specifically whether the information is substantially likely to be important to the reasonable investor in making an investment decision.

[30] Judgment of 28 June 2012, *Geltl v Daimler AG*, C-19/11, EU:C:2012:397.

[31] MAR, art 7(2).

[32] ibid. In *Geltl* (n 30), the CJEU considered the meaning of 'reasonable expectation' and held that it should be equated with a realistic prospect of occurrence rather than a high probability of the event or circumstance taking place.

[33] See section II.C and section III below.

B. The Impact of Information Disclosure on Analysts' Incentives

The emphasis on equality of information which is at the heart of the EU regime comes at a potential cost regarding the role of analysts. As discussed, analysts and other information intermediaries have an important role in ensuring that markets operate efficiently, turning information about issuers and an assessment of their performance into share prices. Analysts will, of course, read and analyse publicly disclosed information published by issuers, but will also seek other information about an issuer in order to give themselves a competitive advantage, and one source of such information is the directors and officers of an issuer.

The EU regime recognises that the use of analysts is a valuable means of ensuring that information is transmitted to the marketplace, but seeks to ensure that issuers do not disclose selectively to one or a small number of analysts in a way that could undermine the concept of equality of information. Article 17(8) MAR requires an issuer (or a person acting on behalf of an issuer) which discloses any inside information to any third party in the normal course of the exercise of an employment, profession or duty to make complete and effective public disclosure of the information, simultaneously in the case of intended disclosure and promptly in the case of unintended disclosure.[34] Interestingly, this is one area in which the US regime takes a very similar approach: Regulation FD (Fair Disclosure) requires that information provided to one investor is disclosed generally to the market at the same time.

Market egalitarianism would suggest that all investors should receive information on an equal basis, ie, the same information at the same time, and this is the driver behind the provisions regarding selective disclosure. However, these provisions may diminish the incentives of analysts to seek out such information because they can obtain no competitive advantage thereby and may also reduce an issuer's incentives to disclose to analysts. An issuer may be happy for information to be in the hands of a small number of sophisticated investors, but they may not be prepared to disclose this publicly, leading them to deny disclosure to either group. Consequently, these provisions may reduce the flow of information from issuers and may increase analysts' costs.

C. The Ability of Issuers to Delay Disclosure

One concern that arises for all issuers regarding the obligation to disclose inside information is that of timing – in particular, the question of when the duty to disclose crystallises. There is a danger that announcing matters at too early a stage may be problematic for issuers because it may damage the company's ability to conduct its

[34] Note, though, that art 17(8) is subject to a carve-out: where the person to whom the information is disclosed is bound by a duty of confidentiality (eg, lawyers, accountants), disclosure to that individual will not trigger a general duty of disclosure. This allows the issuer to selectively share information with, eg, a controlling shareholder as long as the latter keeps the information confidential. However, the shareholder must refrain from using the information to trade.

business and because it relates to issues that are still changing. For example, where the company is in negotiations to sell a major holding of the company, early disclosure may make it more difficult for the company to conclude these negotiations. As discussed above, there may be an investor protection element too as the disclosure may in fact be more misleading to investors than silence. If the company discloses negotiations at too early a stage, this may also make it difficult for investors to determine how to react – specifically, how likely it is that the negotiations will succeed. If they buy shares expecting the deal to be completed and then it is not, they may well feel misled.

The legislative provisions in the MAR provide some leeway to companies in such circumstances. The obligation on companies is to disclose 'as soon as possible', rather than 'immediately', giving them some flexibility. Moreover, the legislative provisions allow issuers to delay disclosure in some circumstances. Specifically, issuers can 'on their own responsibility' delay disclosure in order to protect their 'legitimate interests'. These provisions provide issuers with some room for manoeuvre, especially where early disclosure might be misleading to investors. Article 17(4) MAR deals with the difficulty potentially created by *Geltl* by acknowledging that in a protracted process, the issuer may delay the public disclosure of inside information. *Hannam v FCA*[35] provides a good example of such a scenario, though it was decided on the basis of the pre-MAR regime. It was suggested in that case that the issuer was within its rights to delay disclosure of inside information regarding drilling results on the basis that it was necessary to do so to protect its legitimate interests. Specifically, an expert witness asserted that such a delay was standard industry practice and therefore legitimised. While the Tribunal rejected the argument that an industry practice could justify delay, it did accept that it was reasonable for the issuer to delay the announcement of the results until it could provide information that avoided misleading the market. On the facts, although the drilling results gave considerable confidence that oil was present, they were not definitive and the issuer was permitted to delay until definitive results were available. The Tribunal assumed that the results were inside information, but stated that unless there is some exceptional event or fact that requires immediate disclosure, then a listed company can reasonably delay reporting to ensure that an announcement is not misleading when it is made or to finalise its financial results.

However, the ability to delay is subject to some important caveats. The non-disclosure must not be likely to mislead the public and the company must be able to ensure confidentiality on the part of those to whom the information will have to be disclosed.[36] In addition, an issuer which delays the disclosure of information in this way must inform the relevant national competent authority that disclosure of the information was delayed and must provide a written explanation of how the conditions set out here were met, immediately after the information is disclosed to the public.[37]

In general, in relation to the issue of timing, investors' interests appear to have more weight than issuers' concerns. This is distinct from the US approach, which is

[35] *Hannam v FCA* [2014] UKUT 233 (TCC).
[36] MAR, art 17(4).
[37] ibid.

more issuer-focused. As discussed, companies in the US can disclose inside information voluntarily between the required quarterly reports – for example, when there is good news to report – but they fall under no specific SEC obligation to disclose bad news, unless failing to do so will violate Rule 10b-5 because it would render another statement made a half-truth. Courts in the US have regarded the timing of disclosure between periodic reports as a matter for the directors' business judgement, so that disclosure may be delayed until the information is ripe, or withheld if a valid business reason exists, such as where premature disclosure would impair a contract.[38] In one scenario, however, the balance is shifted in the EU in favour of the issuer. Where the issuer is a financial institution and the disclosure of the information would threaten the financial viability of the issuer and of the financial system, disclosure can be delayed, subject to the confidentiality test, a public interest test and the consent of the national competent authority.[39] The view is taken in this situation that the costs to the financial system as a whole outweigh the costs to investors of the issuer in question.

D. The Impact of Information Disclosure on SMEs

Mandatory disclosure gives rise to significant fixed costs for issuers, which may prove prohibitive for certain issuers, particularly SMEs. This is a general concern within the EU capital market regime, and a major plank of recent reforms regarding the prospectus regime has been a focus on ensuring that SMEs are not denied access to the capital markets.[40] Similar concerns arise in relation to the market abuse regime, particularly given the extension of this regime beyond regulated markets by the MAR, which brought numerous SME issuers within the regime and thus subject to the inside information disclosure obligation that had previously been outside it. The MAR makes some concessions to SMEs to tackle this concern. Article 17(9) MAR allows inside information relating to issuers whose financial instruments are admitted to trading on an 'SME growth market' to be disclosed on the market's website, rather than on the issuer's website, in some circumstances. However, this is a minor concession.

E. Liability Risk

Mandatory disclosure can increase the risk of litigation for issuers, leading to an increase in costs for disclosing firms and a possible impact on market efficiency if it reduces firms' incentives to make voluntary disclosure of information which falls outside the

[38] For discussion, see, eg, J Cox, R Hillman and D Langevoort, *Securities Regulation: Cases and Materials*, 5th edn (New York, Aspen Publishers, 2006).

[39] MAR, art 17(5).

[40] See Communication from the Commission to the European Parliament, the Council, the European Economic and Social Committee and the Committee of the Region: Action Plan on Building a Capital Markets Union, 30 September 2015, COM(2015) 468 final.

mandatory regime or slows down the production of mandated information. If firms fear litigation, they may minimise this risk by taking a formalistic approach to the disclosures they are required to make and reducing the level of non-mandated disclosures. A prohibition on selective disclosure, such as exists in both the EU and US, can exacerbate these issues.

This depends to a large extent on the level of enforcement in a regime. Under the MAR, as under the 2003 MAD, supervision and enforcement is carried out through a network of National Competent Authorities (NCAs): each Member State must designate a single administrative competent authority for the purposes of the MAR.[41] However, it is increasingly recognised that effective regulation of the capital markets within the EU requires a focus on supervisory cooperation and convergence. The MAR makes provisions in both regards.

As regards supervisory cooperation, the MAR requires NCAs to cooperate with each other and with the European Securities and Markets Authority (ESMA) where necessary for the purposes of the Regulation, unless a relevant exception applies.[42] In particular, NCAs are to render assistance to each other and to ESMA[43] and, without undue delay, exchange information, and to cooperate in investigation, supervision and enforcement activities. An NCA is also required to inform relevant NCAs and ESMA where it is convinced that acts contrary to the MAR are being or have been carried out in the territory of another Member State, or that acts are affecting financial instruments traded on a trading venue situated in another Member State.[44] The MAR also addresses the issue of cooperation with third countries.[45]

As regards supervisory convergence, the MAR addresses this in a number of ways. First, it specifies the supervisory and enforcement powers that NCAs need to have in place in order to fulfil their duties under the MAR. These include a wide range of powers, such as the power to have access to documents and other data in any form, to require or demand information from any person, to carry out inspections or investigations at non-private premises with or without warning, and to enter private premises in order to seize documents and any other data as long as prior authorisation has been obtained from judicial authorities and reasonable suspicion exists that the documents or other data may be relevant to prove that an offence has been committed.[46] Second, the MAR seeks to reduce divergences in enforcement by addressing sanctioning powers directly. Member States are required to ensure that NCAs have the power to take appropriate administrative measures and sanctions.[47] Furthermore, the MAR specifies the particular breaches of the MAR, which, as a minimum, must be subject to administrative sanctions,[48] and also specifies the types of measure and sanction

[41] MAR, art 22.

[42] ibid art 25(1). The exceptions include where the communication might adversely affect the security of a Member State and where compliance would be likely to adversely affect the NCAs own enforcement activities: art 25(2).

[43] ibid art 24 specifically addresses the requirement for NCAs to cooperate with ESMA.

[44] ibid art 25(5).

[45] ibid art 26.

[46] ibid art 23(2).

[47] ibid art 30.

[48] ibid art 30(1).

which must be available.[49] In relation to a breach of the obligation to disclose inside information as soon as possible, the MAR specifies that for natural persons, the maximum administrative pecuniary sanction should be at least €1 million, while for legal persons it should be €2.5 million or two per cent of the total annual turnover.[50] This is not a maximum harmonisation obligation: NCAs may have other sanctioning powers and may impose higher levels of pecuniary sanction.

Third, the MAR specifies how administrative measures and sanctions are to be applied: NCAs are to take account of all relevant circumstances, including a range of factors specified in Article 31 MAR, such as the gravity and duration of the breach, the degree of responsibility of the relevant person and the financial strength of the person.[51] Fourth, there is a requirement that every decision imposing an administrative sanction be published by the NCA on its website immediately after the person sanctioned is informed and ESMA is notified.[52] Finally, NCAs are required to provide to ESMA annually aggregate information regarding all administrative measures, sanctions and fines imposed under the MAR, which must then be published by ESMA in an annual report.[53]

The level of attempted supervisory cooperation and convergence within the EU on this issue is therefore quite significant and this drive towards convergence looks set to continue. Nevertheless, this does not alter the fact that enforcement is performed at the level of the NCAs. There is evidence that suggests that the enforcement of measures within a market abuse regime can have quantifiable positive effects for markets,[54] but nothing in the MAR actively seeks to increase the level of enforcement undertaken by NCAs. Most notably, however, the focus of the EU regime is on enforcement by a regulator and not private enforcement by individuals. This stands in sharp contrast to the US regime, under which private enforcement by individuals both in relation to breaches of insider dealing and in relation to the timing of disclosures is possible. It has been suggested that one of the reasons for the more restrictive periodic (as opposed to continuous) disclosure regime in place in the US is this expansive enforcement regime.[55] In particular, if a continuous disclosure standard were adopted in the US, it could expose corporations to excessive liability for failing to make timely disclosures. Uncertainty as to when information becomes material and must be disclosed is often a challenging issue in a continuous regime and could lead to second-guessing in litigation. On this analysis, the focus of the EU regime on enforcement by regulators fits well

[49] ibid art 30(2).

[50] ibid art 30(2)(i), (j).

[51] ibid art 31(1).

[52] ibid art 34(1), which also specifies that there are some circumstances in which NCAs can delay publication, publish on an anonymous basis or not publish.

[53] ibid art 33.

[54] U Bhattacharya and H Daouk, 'The World Price of Insider Trading' (2002) 57 *Journal of Finance* 75; L Beny, 'Do Insider Trading Laws Matter? Some Preliminary Comparative Evidence' (2005) 7 *American Law & Economics Review* 144; U Bhattacharya and H Daouk, 'When No Law is Better than a Good Law' (2009) 13 *Review of Finance* 577; N Fernandes and M Ferreira, 'Insider Trading Laws and Stock Price Information' (2009) 22 *Review of Financial Studies* 1845.

[55] E Greene and O Schmid, 'Duty-Free Insider Trading?' (2013) *Columbia Business Law Review* 369.

with the continuous disclosure regime that has been put in place. Despite the significant changes introduced by the MAR regarding enforcement, it appears that liability risk for issuers is not significantly increased.

F. Summary

In summary, while the EU's approach to the disclosure of inside information brings with it potential benefits, particularly regarding market efficiency (and thus investor protection), it also raises some potentially problematic issues for both issuers and investors. The decision in *Geltl*, for example, brings potential difficulties for both issuers and investors; an over-expansive view of inside information disclosure, especially regarding the timing of that disclosure, could undermine the benefits of the EU regime by increasing costs for issuers and reducing the value of information disclosure for investors. The position of SMEs, and the effect of the costs of this regime on them, also requires attention. The MAR seeks to address these concerns to some extent, but only does so partially, and problems therefore remain.

III. The Relationship between the Disclosure of Inside Information and the Prohibition on Insider Dealing

In addition to the function of inside information disclosure discussed in section II above, which is common to all forms of issuer disclosure in the secondary capital markets (namely investor protection via the concept of market efficiency), the disclosure of inside information in the EU is also intended to fulfil a second function. Specifically, the disclosure of inside information is intended to help prevent insider trading: by ensuring that the information is known to the market generally, any temptation for corporate insiders to trade on it will be removed.[56] In the EU, there is thus a close link between disclosure and insider dealing regulation.

As discussed above, investor protection and market efficiency goals underlie the issuer disclosure regime. The same goals underpin the EU market abuse regime: investor confidence and the efficient operation of the market are stated in the recitals to the MAR as being core objectives of the regulation of market abuse.[57] The adverse impact of market manipulation on market efficiency and on market pricing is obvious: market manipulation generally involves the dissemination of misleading information about an issuer or its securities, or artificial transactions intended to convey false information regarding the supply and demand for investments. The core of market manipulation is an interference with the market's normal price-forming mechanisms and thus market manipulation undermines informational efficiency. The relationship between insider

[56] MAR Recital 49.
[57] ibid Recital 2.

trading and market efficiency requires a little more thought. After all, there are those who argue that if informational efficiency is the goal, then insider trading should be allowed to take place without regulatory interference, since it provides a good method for channelling information into the market place, including information that companies may not disclose publicly.[58] Without insider trading, so it is claimed, some of this information (ie, information that would not have been publicly disclosed) would not be factored into price, since in the semi-strong form of the efficient capital market hypothesis, only publicly available information is fully reflected in the price of securities. This claim is contentious. In particular, dealing alone is an inefficient way for information to be imparted to the marketplace, since it requires analysts and others to recognise that insiders are trading in the market[59] and then to decode the nature of the underlying information from the fact that an insider is trading in the market.

Instead, the EU approach is to prohibit insider dealing on the basis that such behaviour causes investors to lose confidence in the market, believing that the market is rigged against them. The parity of information approach requires that anyone who obtains material non-public information concerning an issuer or a security because of his professional activity, or misappropriates it, should either disclose it or abstain from trading, and those receiving such information from an insider (tippees) who are aware of the material and non-public nature of the information should also either disclose it or abstain from trading. This again requires a little thought. A significant component of this approach is market egalitarianism, ie, the notion that investors should have equal access to information in the marketplace. This idea of market egalitarianism has been influential in forming the EU regime,[60] and requires that investors should have equal access to information and should not be unfairly disadvantaged by insiders dealing in the market on the basis of non-public information.

Of course, if an insider is in the market trading at a price that he knows to be inaccurate – for example, selling shares that he knows are underpriced – that insider will make a gain and anyone selling in the market at that point will suffer a loss, but any other uninformed person who also happens to be in the market at that time will also make a windfall gain. It is also the case that noise traders who trade in the market are almost always going to be at an informational disadvantage, whether or not insiders happen to be in the market. This is because information traders (analysts and other arbitrageurs) will generally know more than the noise traders and will make their profits by trading with those who are less informed. This form of inequality is not regulated; indeed, it is the basis of the efficient capital market hypothesis. This activity is what enables information to be turned into price and removing this informational

[58] See H Manne, *Insider Trading and the Stock Market* (New York, Free Press, 1966).

[59] The obligation for insiders to notify the market about their trades is limited to a narrow category of insiders in the EU, principally directors and those connected to them (MAR, art 19), and even then the obligation to notify the market of the trades is not simultaneous with those trades, but has a significant time delay (the trade must be disclosed within three days), which significantly reduces the value of this information for analysts and others.

[60] N Moloney, *EU Securities and Financial Markets Regulation*, 3rd edn (Oxford, Oxford University Press, 2014) 702.

advantage for information traders would reduce or remove their incentives to operate in a way which produces this beneficial effect. In reality, then, it is unlikely that it is the confidence of the noise traders that is crucial here; instead, it is the confidence of the information traders that is key. If insiders are in the market and are able to trade on the basis of information which they have, but the information traders do not, then this reduces the incentives of the latter group to trade, or at least to trade without demanding some price for the additional risk that this brings. Furthermore, the presence of inside traders in the market is likely to cause systematic losses to market makers and, as a consequence, market makers will increase their bid-ask spreads in order to compensate themselves. These costs will be passed on to investors, making it more expensive for them to buy and sell securities. Both of these factors are likely to reduce the willingness of investors to participate in the market, and thus to increase issuers' cost of capital.[61]

This market-focused justification for prohibiting insider dealing is not adopted in all jurisdictions. In particular, the US adopts a relationship-based rationale for regulating insider dealing.[62] In the US, the offence of insider trading is not defined by statute; instead, it is based on judicial and administrative interpretations of the broad anti-fraud provisions set out in Rule 10b-5.[63] Its basis in an anti-fraud statute has various implications, including a focus on a breach of fiduciary duty of similar breach of trust or confidence in order to supply the necessary element of fraud.[64] This stands in contrast to the EU regime, which focuses on the information which the person trading has, not how he obtained it or whether or not that person intended to violate the law. Further, there is no requirement in the MAR to demonstrate that the conduct is deceptive or misleading, or that any breach of a fiduciary (or similar) duty is present. To emphasise this point, in the MAR it is clear that the prohibition extends to anyone 'who possesses inside information which that person knows, or ought to have known, is inside information',[65] ie, a passenger in a lift who overhears a conversation about a takeover offer and uses that information subsequently to purchase securities in the target company falls within the MAR if he is aware, or ought to have been aware, that the information being discussed is inside information. There is no requirement that those having the conversation in the lift are in breach of a fiduciary duty.

There are difficulties inherent in the US approach as regards the framing of the prohibition on insider trading. In particular, the requirements of a breach of fiduciary

[61] There is empirical literature suggesting that the enforcement of insider trading prohibitions can lead to more liquid markets and a lower cost of capital for issuers: Bhattacharya and Daouk (n 54); Beny (n 54) 144.

[62] For a discussion of these two approaches, see, eg, A Loke, 'From the Fiduciary Theory to Information Abuse: The Changing Fabric of Insider Trading Law in the UK, Australia and Singapore' (2006) 54 *American Journal of Comparative Law* 123. See also M Ventoruzzo, 'Comparing Insider Trading in the United States and the European Union: History and Recent Developments' (2014) *European Company and Financial Law Review* 554.

[63] See also s 16(b) of the Exchange Act, which targets specific transactions by three categories of insiders (directors, officers and 10 per cent shareholders) and provides opportunities to require disgorgement to the issuer of profits made buying or selling equity securities in certain circumstances.

[64] The parity of information approach has been rejected by the US courts as too broad in scope, given that the US insider trading provisions are based on an anti-fraud provision: *Chiarella v United States*, 445 US 222 (1980), 234.

[65] MAR, art 8(4).

duty and scienter, in order to establish the requirement of fraud, means that many circumstances that would fall within the concept of insider dealing in the EU fall outside it in the US. For example, in the US, if an employee in a financial printers manages to figure out the name of the target firm in a takeover as the takeover documents are being printed, despite the fact that codes are used, and uses this information to buy shares in the target before the bid was announced, obtaining a profit when the share price rises post-announcement, that individual will not be guilty of insider trading since there is no breach of fiduciary duty.[66] Furthermore, where a waitress in a restaurant overhears a CEO discussing inside information about her company and trades on the basis of that information to make a profit, there will be no liability for the waitress or the CEO, providing the CEO tipped the waitress unintentionally and expected no personal benefit in return for the disclosed information.[67] This will be the case even where the waitress knows that the CEO is an insider and that the information she overhears is inside information. These requirements make the US law on insider dealing very complex and can lead to unfortunate consequences. For instance, what if a computer hacker steals from a home computer the name and password that an employee (X) uses in connection with his employment at a company and then, using X's identity, hacks into the company's computer system, obtains earnings information about the company in advance of its release, and then trades on the basis of this information and realises a substantial profit? There is no breach of fiduciary duty here, so it appears to fall outside the ambit of insider dealing provisions. In order to deal with this kind of scenario, the US courts have had to create a new form of insider trading liability based on obtaining information by means of an 'affirmative misrepresentation', which would satisfy the element of deceit required for a section 10b liability to attach.[68] The US court explained that the outcome of a hacking case such as this depends on whether the computer system was hacked into using 'deceitful' behaviour, such as the use of a fake identity, which would lead to insider trading liability, or whether no deceit was used (so that, for example, the hacker exploited a weakness in the electronic code in order to access the information), in which case no insider liability would attach.[69] This highlights some of the difficulties with the US relationship-based approach.

The relationship-based approach also means that in the US there is no unity of purpose between the disclosure regime and the insider dealing regime, so that they are regarded as separate and distinct aspects of the regulatory model: the opportunity to think about disclosure and prohibition as part of the same package is lost. There are some benefits to treating information disclosure and insider dealing regulation as two parts of a single system of capital market regulation, focused on the goal of

[66] *Chiarella* (n 64). *cf* earlier case law which followed a 'disclose or abstain' approach similar to that adopted in the EU market abuse regime; see, eg, *In the Matter of Cady, Roberts & Co*, 40 SEC 907 (1961); *SEC v Texas Gulf Sulphur* 401 F 2d 833 (2nd Cir 1968).

[67] *Switzer v SEC* 590 F Supp 756 (WD Okla 1984). See also *United States v Newman* 773 F 3d 438 (2d Cir 2014); *Salman v United States*, 137 S Ct 420 (2016).

[68] *SEC v Dorozhko*, 574 F 3d 42 (2nd Cir 2009).

[69] ibid. The MAR deals with this type of scenario by explicitly providing for the situation in which the information is obtained by criminal means: MAR, art 8(4)(d).

market efficiency. There is a close complementarity between the two regimes which justifies the inclusion of the prohibition on insider dealing and the requirement to disclose inside information in the same EU Regulation (the MAR). In particular, as discussed, a potential cost of banning insider trading is the loss of a channel for the revelation of non-public information, as other investors 'decode' price movements triggered by insiders' trades. Mandating disclosure of material changes on an ongoing basis ensures that information is transmitted to the market in a timely manner and seeks to reduce this downside. The EU's continuous disclosure regime can therefore be seen as a clear complement to the decision to ban insider dealing in order to improve market efficiency and protect investors.

However, the EU approach of putting insider dealing prohibitions and inside information disclosure obligations into one package also creates potential difficulties.[70] While both the prohibition and the disclosure obligation seek to enhance market efficiency, they operate in different ways. Inside information disclosure seeks to ensure market efficiency via information regulation – ie, market efficiency is enhanced via optimal information disclosure – while the prohibition is a form of conduct regulation, seeking to enhance market efficiency by prohibiting certain abusive behaviour. The latter form of regulation would suggest that as broad a concept of inside information as possible should be adopted, with little or no opportunity for companies to delay disclosure, since this would maximise the amount of publicly available information and reduce the amount of inside information to the greatest extent possible, thereby minimising the abusive behaviour which undermines market efficiency. However, there can be potential damage to market efficiency where an overly wide disclosure obligation is adopted which prevents issuers being able to protect highly sensitive disclosures and where torrents of potentially unreliable disclosures may operate to feed market volatility, as discussed in section II above.

Before the introduction of the MAR, there were questions raised regarding the 2003 MAD, particularly about the inclusion of both the conduct regulation and information regulation concepts within the market abuse regime and about whether, for example, the definition of inside information should be the same for both purposes.[71] It had been hoped that the decision of the CJEU in *Geltl* might provide some much-needed clarity to this area, but it did not do so. The Court in *Geltl* did not address the dual nature of inside information within the 2003 MAD, and indeed the expansive view of inside information adopted by the CJEU in that decision (the idea that an intermediate step could constitute a set of circumstances or an event and so could be 'precise' for the purposes of the general definition of inside information)[72] potentially exacerbated the problems inherent in the dual function of inside information within the market abuse regime.

[70] See JL Hansen, 'The Hammer and the Saw: A Short Critique of the Recent Compromise Proposal for a Market Abuse Regulation' (2012), ssrn.com/abstract=2193871; JL Hansen and D Moalem, 'The MAD Disclosure Regime and the Twofold Notion of Inside Information: The Available Solution' (2009) 4 *Capital Markets Law Journal* 323.

[71] ESMA, 'The Market Abuse EU Legal Framework and its Implementation by Member States: A First Evaluation' (July 2007) 6.

[72] *Geltl* (n 30) paras 33–36.

When the MAR was negotiated, there was considerable pressure to adopt different definitions of inside information for the two different functions in order to address these concerns.[73] However, this suggestion was not successful and there is a single concept of inside information within the MAR that is relevant both to issuer disclosure and the prohibition on insider dealing. Further, because the MAR follows the ruling in *Geltl* and incorporates into the regime the idea that processes with multiple stages can generate inside information that needs to be disclosed at intermediate steps in the process,[74] the risk that issuers will be in breach of their disclosure obligations if they fail to disclose negotiations and other multiple-stage processes is intensified. This linking of inside information disclosure and the prohibition on insider trading therefore potentially exacerbates the difficulties which were discussed in sections II.B and II.D above.

IV. Conclusion

The requirement to disclose inside information to the market 'as soon as possible' is a key aspect of EU capital market regulation. This continuous disclosure obligation is broadly defined and although it is subject to some exemptions, such as the ability of issuers to delay disclosure in certain circumstances, these exemptions are narrowly drawn. The emphasis is on investor protection, which is achieved by maximising market efficiency. The goal of the disclosure obligation is twofold: to ensure, as nearly as possible, that all investors have the same information about companies and their securities, and also to rob the information of its inside character, thus reducing the opportunity for insider dealing. As explored in this chapter, the EU regime has significant benefits attached to it, in terms of market efficiency and thus investor protection, but these benefits have to be weighed against the potential costs to issuers and investors which this regime may bring. There are some potentially problematic aspects to the obligation to disclosure inside information. The issue of early disclosure is a particular concern and the potential difficulties are exacerbated by attempting to yoke together two different regimes, namely disclosure regulation and conduct regulation. These concerns need to be understood and managed to ensure that the benefits of the EU regime are not undermined.

[73] This was the approach adopted by the Commission in its 2011 proposal, for example: COM(2011) 651, art 12(3).

[74] MAR, art 7(2).

6

Disclosure of Major Holdings in Listed Companies

ALAIN PIETRANCOSTA

I. Introduction

The growing global demand for investor transparency is leading to an evolution, even a revolution, at the heart of the notion of a 'public company'. The 'société anonyme', as it is called in France, bears a name – so to speak – that is increasingly inaccurate. If a listed company traditionally distinguishes itself from a company of named 'persons', it has really become a company of 'personalities', whose importance justifies doing away with their anonymity.

This 'personalisation' mainly results from the ever-expanding requirements for investors to publicly disclose their major shareholdings or derivative equivalents, currently set forth in the European Union (EU) through the Transparency Directive (TD).[1] The evolution of this directive and of its financial determinants will be the focus of this chapter.

However, one should keep in mind that this general influx of *intuitus personae* is also fuelled by other technical instruments, such as:

- the introduction of private disclosure thresholds in issuers' bylaws (information available only to the said issuers);
- the right for listed issuers to initiate a shareholder identification process: a 'pull' system (as opposed to a push system) generalised across the EU by the 17 May 2017 European Shareholder Rights Directive (hereinafter 'SRD II'),[2] Member States only being able to limit the possibility to identify shareholders holding more than a certain percentage of shares or voting rights, which cannot exceed 0.5 per cent.

[1] See R Veil, European Capital Markets Law (Portland, Hart Publishing, 2017) § 20.

[2] Article 3a; *adde*, Commission implementing Regulation (EU) 2018/1212 of 3 September 2018 laying down minimum requirements implementing the provisions of Directive 2007/36/EC of the European Parliament and of the Council as regards shareholder identification, the transmission of information and the facilitation of the exercise of shareholders rights, [2018] OJ L223/1.

Although the SRD II does not provide for the public disclosure of the results, in 10 EU countries[3] this register of significant shareholders is generally available to the public or other shareholders;[4]

- the public disclosure of significant net short positions in shares provided for in the 2012 European short-selling regulation, when these positions represent 0.5 per cent of the issued share capital of the company concerned and each 0.1 per cent above that;[5]
- the European requirements on institutional investors' engagement set forth in the SRD II;
- the ad hoc disclosure requirement imposed by the Market Abuse Regulation on issuers listed both on regulated markets and Multilateral Trading Facilities (MTFs) regarding inside information that concerns them and their managers, as well as persons closely associated with the latter – which can potentially represent an aggregate group of people numbering in the hundreds of thousands – regarding the transactions conducted for their own account relating to the shares or debt instruments of those issuers or to derivatives or other financial instruments linked thereto, providing that they reach a minimum threshold.[6]

Some Member States have introduced complementary transparency mechanisms. In France, for instance, four of them can be mentioned: (1) the possibility for a company whose securities are listed on a regulated market to ask intermediaries registered on behalf of non-French owners to disclose the identity of those owners;[7] (2) the requirement to publicly disclose 'any agreement providing for preferential conditions for the sale or acquisition of shares admitted to trading on a regulated market and covering at least 0.5 per cent of the capital or voting rights' of the issuer, within five trading days of the signing of the agreement;[8] (3) the public disclosure, before a shareholders' annual meeting of a company whose shares are admitted to trading on a regulated European market, of holdings of more than 0.5 per cent of voting rights based on temporary sale transactions;[9] (4) the requirement for 'any person preparing on its own behalf a financial transaction likely to have a significant impact on the price of a financial instrument' to 'inform the public as soon as possible of the

[3] IE, FI, IT, MT, NO, RO, SI, SE, SK, and UK.

[4] See T2S Taskforce on Shareholder Transparency, Market Analysis of Shareholder Transparency Regimes in Europe (21 February 2011).

[5] Article 6 on 'Public disclosure of significant net short positions in shares': '1. A natural or legal person who has a net short position in relation to the issued share capital of a company that has shares admitted to trading on a trading venue shall disclose details of that position to the public, in accordance with Article 9, where the position reaches or falls below a relevant publication threshold referred to in paragraph 2 of this Article.

2. A relevant publication threshold is a percentage that equals 0.5% of the issued share capital of the company concerned and each 0.1% above that.'

[6] See M Ventoruzzo and S Mock (eds), *Market Abuse Regulation* (Oxford, Oxford University Press, 2017).

[7] Article L. 228-2 of the Commercial Code.

[8] ibid art L. 233-11, dated 1989.

[9] ibid art 225-126, introduced in 2010.

characteristics of this transaction', unless a legitimate reason exists for delaying disclosure and the confidentiality of the transaction is assured.[10]

In addition to such mandatory requirements, national law makers sometimes incentivise investors to register their shares in listed companies. In France, for instance, the benefit of double voting rights, which has become the default rule in French companies whose shares are listed on a regulated market since the Florange Act of 29 March 2014,[11] is exclusively reserved for registered shares, to the great displeasure of foreign investors.

Finally, one should also be aware that the decline of anonymity is not, paradoxically, restricted to listed companies. First, we can anticipate the use of public blockchains to register securities and primarily (maybe as a first step) unlisted securities. Such registration systems would at least open the way to a public pseudonymisation of shareholders and traceability of their transactions. In France, the Monetary and Financial Code, modified by an Ordinance of 8 December 2017, now provides, at the issuer's discretion, the possibility of registering securities that are not admitted to the operations of a central depositary through a distributed ledger technology.[12] If the chosen blockchain must, in any case, make it possible to identify the owners of the aforementioned securities, other conditions set forth in a decree of 24 December 2018 imply that public blockchains will be difficult to use.[13] More importantly, and this time imperatively, account should be taken of the impact of the Anti-Money Laundering (AML) Directives, which require the identification of the so-called 'beneficial owners' (ie, in the case of corporate entities), the natural persons who ultimately own or control an entity through direct or indirect ownership of a sufficient percentage – set at 25 per cent – of the shares or voting rights or ownership interest in that entity.[14] Unlike the fourth AML Directive, which made public access an option for Member States, the fifth AML Directive of 30 May 2018 requires public access to the register of beneficial owners by 10 January 2020.[15] While this obligation mainly applies to unlisted companies, precisely because listed companies are already subject to disclosure requirements that are supposed to ensure adequate transparency of ownership information, some countries have extended it to listed companies.[16] Even when restricted to unlisted

[10] Article 223–6 of the French Markets Authority (AMF) General Regulation.

[11] See A Pietrancosta, 'The Latest Reform of French Takeover Law: The "Florange Act" of March 29, 2014' (2014) 3 *Revue Trimestrielle de Droit Financier* 42.

[12] Article L. 211-7.

[13] Décret n° 2018-1226 of 24 December 2018, [2018] JORF n°0298.

[14] The demand for more ownership transparency is global: see, eg, Transparency International, *G20 Leaders or Laggards?* (2018), which reviews G20 promises on ending anonymous companies; A Lakhani, 'Imposing Company Ownership Transparency Requirements: Opportunities for Effective Governance of Equity Capital Markets or Constraints on Corporate Performance' (2016) 16 *Chicago-Kent Journal of International and Comparative Law* 122; M Biedermann, 'G8 Principles: Identifying the Anonymous' (2015) 11 *Brigham Young University International Law & Management Review* 72, 73–74; D Kalant, 'Who's in Charge Here?: Requiring More Transparency in Corporate America: Advancements in Beneficial Ownership for Privately Held Companies' (2009) 42 *John Marshall Law Review* 1049, 1050.

[15] Directive 2018/843 of the European Parliament and of the Council of 30 May 2018 amending Directive 2015/849 on the prevention of the use of the financial system for the purposes of money laundering or terrorist financing, and amending Directives 2009/138/EC and 2013/36/EU [2018] OJ L156/43; see art 30(5).

[16] Law Library of Congress, *Disclosure of Beneficial Ownership in Selected Countries* (Washington DC, July 2017); Organisation for Economic Co-operation and Development (OECD), *Disclosure of Beneficial Ownership and Control in Listed Companies in Asia* (2016).

companies, this new public access allows listed companies to refine their knowledge of the owners – beyond mere holders – of their shares. This public access to the registers of beneficial owners is certainly a major breakthrough and a vigorous attack on shareholder anonymity in millions of companies. It may even appear disproportionate to the objective of combating money laundering, to the point of making this provision questionable in the light of higher European and national norms protecting individuals' property rights and privacy.[17] It understandably reflects a desire to prevent certain criminal activities, a pathological component that remains a step removed from the intrinsic necessity for the good functioning of capital markets to ensure a sufficient degree of transparency in the ownership and control structure of listed companies.

II. The Various Functions of the Major Holdings' Disclosure and their Development

A securities market is no more than a meeting site, a financial dating service such as Meetic, or, more accurately, since it functions through a pecuniary auction system, a financial eBay. As a means of financial resources and claims reallocation based on prices, its efficiency is directly dependent on the available information relating to the opportunities offered by the traded securities.

Information is thus the vital energy of securities markets. Indeed, prices result from the adjustment of the supply and demand of securities. The market allows for an optimal allocation of resources only if the prices that serve as indicators for investors are reliable, and this reliability depends mainly on the information available to the interested parties on the securities admitted to trading. A close relationship has traditionally been established between the extent of information available, the rationality of investor behaviour and the optimal functioning – in other words, 'efficiency'[18] – of the market, the latter two elements being conditioned by the former. By contrast, opacity, by feeding the objective irrationality of behaviour as well as shielding dubious behaviour, sows doubt and ultimately discredits the entire market. In addition, investors in financial markets are encouraged to seek information in order to maximise their gains or minimise their losses. This logically makes financial markets information-rich environments, to the point of saturation, contrasting with the situation in money markets, where short-term and risk-free claims are exchanged, making the search for information much less necessary in normal circumstances.

[17] The Directive only allows Member States to provide for exemptions, on a case-by-case basis, in 'exceptional circumstances' where the public access of the register 'would expose the beneficial owner to disproportionate risk, risk of fraud, kidnapping, blackmail, extortion, harassment, violence or intimidation, or where the beneficial owner is a minor or otherwise legally incapable'.

[18] See J Armour, D Awrey, P Davies, L Enriques, J Gordon, C Mayer and J Payne, *Principles of Financial Regulation* (Oxford, Oxford University Press, 2016) § 5.2; L Enriques and S Gilotta 'Disclosure and Financial Market Regulation' in N Moloney, E Ferran and J Payne (eds), *The Oxford Handbook of Financial Regulation* (Oxford, Oxford University Press, 2015) ch 17.

Hence, unlike in money markets, which are regulated in a confidential and substantial manner by specialised regulators, on financial markets transparency has been – or become – the mantra of legislators and regulators. Indeed, according to the dominant theory, the market is unable to spontaneously produce this information in a sufficient or efficient manner, as market information presents the characteristics of a 'public good', in Samuelson's terms. In addition, the use of transparency has major methodological advantages for regulators: being a priori cheap, it allows regulation to be placed in a democratic perspective, transparency benefiting everyone, in law if not in fact, creating a 'level playing field' between investors – in other words, guaranteeing a minimum equality of access to relevant information.

In this market egalitarianism philosophy perspective, issuers of traded securities naturally appear as the main source of information expected from investors. The value of these securities is indeed supposed to integrate what is known about the issuers' situations and their prospects of evolution – hence the dizzying increase in disclosure requirements imposed on listed issuers in recent decades, to the point where we are now wondering about the adverse effects of this transparency for the good of the financial markets themselves.

From this point of view, the transparency of major holdings appears as an additional element in reducing information asymmetry in listed companies. To be sure, in the EU, the main legal source for this matter is the same directive imposing periodic disclosure requirements on listed issuers regarding their accounting and financial condition: the so-called TD.[19] However, unlike the latter, the disclosure requirements weigh not on the listed issuers, but this time on their major shareholders, whether actual or potential, which is logical since the issuers themselves do not necessarily possess this type of information.

This information is nonetheless of tantamount importance for investors in general and fulfils the same basic function in terms of market efficiency and corporate governance.[20] Contrary to the classical dogma that equates, a little too hastily, shareholders' anonymity with their indifference or substitutability, it is easy to understand the interest for investors, whoever they are, to know the identity of persons likely to exert a significant influence on an issuer's business, for better or for worse. We know for a fact that some well-known shareholders are more successful than others. 'As many empirical studies have demonstrated, key owners' identity matters.'[21] It matters in a dispersed beneficial ownership system dominated by institutional blockholders, like those in the US or the UK. It matters even more in the context of structural concentration of direct shareholder ownership,[22] which characterises most of Europe. In such a system,

[19] As Gilson argues, two forms of transparency are required for effective corporate governance: financial disclosure and ownership transparency. R Gilson, 'Transparency, Corporate Governance and Capital Markets', OECD/World Bank, 2000.

[20] See MC Schouten, 'The Case for Mandatory Ownership Disclosure' (2010) 15 *Stanford Journal of Law, Business & Finance* 127.

[21] L Enriques, M Gargantini and V Novembre 'Mandatory and Contract-Based Shareholding Disclosure' (2010) 15 *Uniform Law Review* 713, 720, 735.

[22] See E Vermeulen 'Beneficial Ownership and Control: A Comparative Study – Disclosure, Information and Enforcement' (2013), *OECD Corporate Governance Working Papers No 7*.

large shareholders with significant voting and cash flow rights may facilitate long-term growth and firm performance. However, there is a risk that such shareholders 'also have an incentive to divert corporate assets and exploit opportunities for personal gain'[23] (private benefits of control), at the expense of the companies and minority investors.

Information on major shareholdings thus plays a major role in detecting and understanding power and influence relationships within the issuer and facilitating the implementation of legal or extra-legal anti-conflict of interest mechanisms. It enables investors to assess the adequacy of the company's governance in dealing with these conflicts and its effectiveness in terms of reducing agency costs, particularly in terms of the independence of the management. This information on major holdings is therefore instrumental in solving the structural problems traditionally assigned to company law and corporate governance norms.[24] It is located at the intersection of corporate and financial concerns, as its role in investors' assessment of the ability to challenge the existing corporate control or management further demonstrates.

The identification of key shareholders based on a photograph taken at a given time and the description of its evolution over time as it emerges from the film made up of successive notifications helps to evaluate what is called in France the 'takeoverability' ('opéabilité') of a listed issuer or, at least, the contestability of its de facto control or direction/management, and the current or potential attempts in doing so. On the market for corporate control, such information given by significant shareholders themselves then complements the one imposed on issuers regarding takeover defences provided for by Article 10 of the European Directive on takeover bids. When one considers the level of the control premium received by target shareholders in the context of contested bids or simply the positive stock market prices reactions that can follow the announcement of share acquisitions deemed to be 'activist', it is only logical and critical for the efficiency and attractiveness of financial markets that investors, even the most ordinary ones, are offered the possibility to obtain an accurate mapping of voting or cash flow rights' holdings within listed companies.

The transparency of such holdings and the struggles for power, control and influence within large corporations simultaneously obey a desire for moralisation, with its democratic connotation, which participate in the effort to seduce investors.

For all the reasons above, one can understand why the OECD, in its famous Principles of corporate governance, considers this transparency of major holdings as a basic right of investors in listed companies.[25]

Finally, in addition to satisfying this private interest requirement, the identification of major shareholders serves ancillary functions of public interest, in the sense that it helps:

- securities regulators to fight market abuses;
- antitrust authorities to supervise the effects of common shareholdings on business strategies;

[23] OECD (n 16).

[24] See KE Sørensen, 'Shareholders' Duty to Disclose, Nordic & European Company Law' (2018) *LSN Research Paper Series* No 18-04; Schouten (n 20); MC Schouten and MM Siems, 'The Evolution of Ownership Disclosure Rules across Countries' (2010) 10 *Journal of Corporate Law Studies* 451.

[25] G20/OECD, *Principles of Corporate Governance* (September 2015) V § 3.

- and more generally, the monitoring and enforcement of legal or regulatory requirements based on control situations, whether in accounting, company, takeover, labour, banking or AML law.

It is therefore difficult to reduce this information on major shareholdings to a mere complement to the traditional information on their financial condition disclosed by issuers to their investors' benefit. Strikingly, this requirement reverses the perspective and the information flow, in that it fulfils a function of information of the issuers themselves by their own investors. It fills the information gap this time in favour of issuers, which has widened over the last decades in favour of investors. We have found ourselves in a situation where investors know more and more about issuers who know less and less about their investors, for both legal and practical reasons. These reasons stem in particular from the fragmentation of securities trading venues resulting from the European Markets in Financial Instruments Directive, which in many Member States has increased the opacity of transactions, particularly on blocks of securities, in the absence of a genuine European consolidated tape; changes in the way in which securities are held through chains of intermediaries (eg, omnibus accounts);[26] the institutionalisation and internationalisation of shareholdings, which make it difficult for listed issuers to identify ultimate owners; and, finally, the tremendous development of derivative financial products that can have the effect, or sometimes purpose, of concealing real positions of influence within listed companies.

All these reasons have fed issuers' general demands for more transparency imposed on major or professional investors. Such transparency can indeed be of great strategic use for issuers and those who control or manage them. It enables them to detect at an early stage the threatening rise of a particular investor, either seeking a control position or merely preparing for an activist campaign, and to put in place appropriate 'alarm systems',[27] ie, defence methods against this unwanted influence. More positively, a better knowledge of their shareholder base helps issuers to adapt their communication and to engage in dialogue with their main shareholders. These two attitudes meet, to the extent that the best protection against activism is undoubtedly for an issuer to maintain a constant dialogue with its large shareholders, which allows it to have a clear view of the company strategy.

III. The Corresponding Evolution of the Legal Framework Set Out in the Transparency Directive

The TD provisions have been described as the first and most important rules ensuring a transparent ownership and control structure in the EU. They are also the

[26] See Market Analysis of Shareholder Transparency Regimes in Europe, T2S Taskforce on Shareholder Transparency, 21 February 2011.

[27] K Sergakis, *The Law of Capital Markets in the EU* (London, Palgrave Macmillan, 2018) 121.

first disclosure rules for shareholders introduced in the EU.[28] Unsurprisingly, their evolution has reflected the above-mentioned demands for increasing transparency of major holdings. Far from being unique to Europe, this development is perceptible on a global scale.[29] Over the last few decades, ownership disclosure rules have become more stringent everywhere, with variations correlated to the degree of countries' economic development and the level of minority shareholders' protection.

This increased stringency characterises the history of European rules, which began in 1988, when the 'TD I' introduced ownership disclosure to European capital markets law[30] and laid down the foundations of the framework we know today:

- Article 4(1) of this Directive requires that any person who, following an acquisition or disposal of shares, crosses a 10 per cent, 20 per cent, one-third, 50 per cent and two-thirds threshold in respect of voting rights, must notify the company and at the same time the competent authority, within seven calendar days, of the proportion of its voting rights. The period of seven calendar days starts from the time when the owner of the major holding learns of the acquisition or disposal, or from the time when, in view of the circumstances, he should have learnt of it.
- Article 7 contains a list of eight cases in which notification requirements regarding the attribution of voting rights attached to third-party shares exist.
- According to Article 10, a company which has received a notification must in turn disclose it to the public in each of the Member States in which its shares are officially listed on a stock exchange as soon as possible, but no more than nine calendar days after the receipt of that declaration.
- Article 15 mandates Member States to provide for appropriate sanctions in cases of non-compliance.

However, the Member States and the national competent authorities (NCAs) are given a major role in this. In addition to the lack of precision in its provisions, the TD I offers many options to Member States: they may replace certain thresholds, provide for additional information for the issuer and for other methods of informing the public. More generally, due to the minimum harmonisation nature of the Directive, Member States may subject significant shareholders to stricter requirements (Article 3). For their part, NCAs are granted exemption powers: they may exempt professional dealers in securities from the notification requirement (Article 9) and issuers from notifying the public when such disclosure would be contrary to the public interest or seriously detrimental to the companies concerned (Article 11).

[28] See Sørensen (n 24).

[29] Schouten and Siems (n 24).

[30] See H Fleischer and KU Schmolke, 'The Reform of the Transparency Directive: Minimum or Full Harmonisation of Ownership Disclosure?' (2011) 12 *European Business Organization Law Review* 121; H Fleischer and K Deckert, 'La réforme de la directive transparence : harmonisation minimale ou pleine harmonisation des règles relatives aux déclarations de franchissement de seuils?' (2011) 1–2 *Revue Trimestrielle de Droit Financier* 40.

The 2004 'TD II', adopted under the European Financial services action plan, tightens up the disclosure rules for significant holdings,[31] with the intention of offering 'better information on major shareholders' interests'.[32] It:

- extends the scope of application to certain non-EU companies listed in the EU;
- lowers the first threshold to five per cent;
- introduces additional thresholds at 15 per cent, 25 per cent and 30 per cent;
- adds more specifications regarding the denominator for the calculation of the thresholds (with the inclusion of all the shares to which voting rights are attached even if the exercise thereof is suspended);
- extends the list of assimilation cases;
- imposes shorter time limits (no more than four trading days for the notification and three trading days for the public disclosure);
- widens the events giving rise to notifications, in particular passive crossings of thresholds;
- introduces a disclosure requirement for financial instruments that result in an entitlement to acquire existing shares;
- enriches the information to be included in the notifications;
- requires the issuers themselves to publicly disclose the crossing of five per cent or 10 per cent of their own voting rights;
- repeals the exemption from notifying the public when such disclosure would be contrary to the public interest or seriously detrimental to the companies concerned;
- requires the disclosure to the public by the issuer of the total number of voting rights and capital at the end of each calendar month during which an increase or decrease of the total number has occurred.

If the minimum harmonisation nature of the TD is maintained, progress is being made in terms of EU integration through the 'home country principle'. Only the home Member State (usually defined as the Member States where an EU issuer has its registered office or where a non-EU issuer is listed)[33] may make a shareholder subject to requirements more stringent than those laid down in the Directive. The exclusive competence of the home Member States avoids investors in the securities of issuers listed in several Member States having to manage a patchwork of different transparency requirements.

Also, following the Lamfalussy process, the European Commission has laid down, in a level 2 Directive 2007/14/EC of 8 March 2007, detailed rules for the implementation

[31] See Fleischer and Schmolke (n 30).

[32] 'Financial Services: European Parliament's Approval of Proposed Transparency Directive is Good News for Investors' (DN: IP/04/398, 30 March 2004).

[33] In France, the AMF may exempt a person holding equity interests in a company whose registered office is outside the territory of the EEA from the disclosure requirements mentioned in I of art L 233-7 and II of art L 233-8 of the Commercial Code 'if it considers equivalent the obligations to which that person is subject under the law of the third State applicable to him' (Monetary and Financial Code, art L 451-2-1).

of certain provisions of the TD. Regarding the disclosure of major holdings, these detailed rules include, in particular, a two-trading day limit for a shareholder to be deemed to have knowledge of this transaction (Article 9) and a list of financial instruments that result in an entitlement to acquire, on the holder's own initiative alone, shares to which voting rights are attached (Article 11).

Despite these worthwhile efforts, the Member States' capital markets laws on major holdings disclosure continue to show a high degree of differentiation. A survey conducted by the Commission in 2008 shows the disparate numbers of Member States having imposed requirements exceeding those set out in the directive in terms of reduced notification, publication periods or lower/additional thresholds.[34] Some of these thresholds are left to the issuers themselves, whose notifications are not made public; others are calculated in proportion to the issuers' capital or taking into account extensive definitions of concerted actions.

The 2009 TD Assessment Report by Mazars underlines that the TD provisions regarding the notification of major holdings are considered to be the most problematic according to the perceptions of stakeholders and the legal assessment of the legal operation in the Member States.[35] It points out that 'the possibility for Members States to adopt more stringent requirements has undermined the harmonisation attempt of the Directive'. Consequently, the TD resulted in a failure to alleviate the burden on international investors to notify their holdings in European listed companies and a missed opportunity to reduce compliance costs.[36] According to a poll, only 15 per cent of stakeholders believed at the time that the Directive had facilitated the cross-border declaration of thresholds.

Other grounds for dissatisfaction are voiced,[37] relating to:

- national differences for the notification of major holdings, in particular the lack of a common electronic form to notify the crossing of thresholds in the EU;
- the lack of transparency regarding the lending of voting rights;
- the non-aggregation of shareholdings on the one hand and of holdings of financial instruments giving access to existing shares on the other hand;
- the insufficiency of information provided by investors crossing certain significant holdings (such as 10 per cent, 15 per cent or 20 per cent) on the French or German models;
- the uncertainty surrounding the definition of 'acting in concert', the way in which depositary receipts and voting caps should be taken into account, the manner in which the denominator is computed or the scope of certain exemptions.

[34] Commission Staff Working Document, Report on more stringent measures concerning Directive 2004/109/EC, SEC(2008) 3033 final, 10 December 2008.

[35] Mazars, *Transparency Directive Assessment Report* (2009).

[36] See European Securities and Markets Authority (ESMA), Implementation of the Transparency Directive, 7 July 2011.

[37] See Review of the operation of Directive 2004/109/EC: emerging issues, Commission staff working document, Brussels, 27 May 2010, SEC(2009) 611.

However, one of the main demands concerns the inclusion of cash-settled equity derivatives in the calculation of thresholds. This reproach is therefore not addressed to the European legislator of 2004, but grew with the tremendous development of equity derivatives, with well-publicised cases showing that they could be used to circumvent transparency requirements.[38] In the *Continental/Schaeffler* case (2008),[39] the Bundesanstalt für Finanzdienstleistungsaufsicht (BaFin) decided that Contracts for Difference (CFDs) were not subject to any notification requirements. In France, the AMF reached the same conclusion in two major cases (*Wendel/Saint-Gobain* (2010)[40] and *LVMH/Hermès* (2013)).[41] However, it still managed to impose pecuniary sanctions (€1.5 million and €8 million, respectively) on the shareholders involved on the basis of general provisions requiring any person preparing a financial transaction likely to have a significant impact on the price of a financial instrument to inform the public as soon as possible of the characteristics of this transaction.[42] Following the 2009 UK reform, Germany, France and other Member States decided to establish notification requirements for cash-settled derivatives, only with significant differences.[43]

The 2013 Amended TD (ATD), whose provisions were to be implemented through national law by 26 November 2015, seeks to respond to some of these requests and raises the level of stringency of the European requirements by a further degree.

First, steps are taken to prevent national gold-plating. As a matter of principle, the ATD deviates from traditional minimum harmonisation (Article 3) as it now limits the home Member States' – whose definition is adjusted in order to match the one enshrined in the Prospectus Directive – competence to adopt more stringent rules than those provided for in the TD. However, important exceptions are listed in Article 3 when dealing with:

(i) setting lower or additional notification thresholds than those laid down in Article 9(1) and requiring equivalent notifications in relation to thresholds based on capital holdings;
(ii) applying more stringent requirements than those referred to in Article 12, relating to the process and timing of notifications; or
(iii) applying laws, regulations or administrative provisions adopted in relation to takeover bids, merger transactions and other transactions affecting the ownership or control of companies.

[38] See Views on the issue of transparency of holdings of cash settled derivatives, ESME, November 2009; CESR proposal to extend major shareholding notifications to instruments of similar economic effect to holding shares and entitlements to acquire shares, CESR/09-1215b, January 2010.

[39] BaFin, press release, 21 August 2008; T Baums and M Sauter, 'Anschleichen an Uebernahmeziele mit Hilfe von Aktienderivaten' (2009) 173 *Zeitschrift für das gesamte Handels- und Wirtschaftsrecht* 454, 467; M Schiessl, 'Beteiligungsaufbau mittels Cash-settled Total Return Equity Swaps – neue Modelle und Einführung von Meldepflichten' (2009) *Der Konzern* 291, 295; H Fleischer and KU Schmolke, 'Kapitalmarktrechtliche Beteiligungstransparenz nach §§ 21 ff. WpHG und "Hidden Ownership"' (2008) *Zeitschrift für Wirtschaftsrecht* 1501, 1506. For a dissenting opinion, see KM Schanz, 'Schaeffler v Continental: Umgehung von Meldepflichten bei öffentlichen Übernahmen durch Einsatz von derivativen Finanzinstrumenten' (2008) *Der Betrieb* 1899, 1903; DA Zetzsche, 'Hidden Ownership in Europe: BAFin's Decision in Schaeffler v Continental' (2009) 10 *European Business Organization Law Review* 115.

[40] Dec Comm AMF sanctions, 13 December 2010, Sté Wendel SA, J-B Lafonta and Sté Deutsche Bank Paris.

[41] Dec Comm AMF sanctions, 25 June 2010, Sté LVMH Moët Hennessy-Louis Vuitton.

[42] See A Pietrancosta, *Le Lamy Droit du Financement* (Alphen aan den Rijn, Wolters Kluwer, 2018) n° 2257.

[43] See G Ferrarini, 'Equity Derivatives and Transparency: When Should Substance Prevail?' in S Grundmann et al (eds), *Festschrift für Klaus J. Hopt zum 70. Geburtstag* (Berlin, De Gruyter, 2010) 1803–22.

The minimum harmonisation thus disappears, not in favour of full harmonisation, but of enhanced harmonisation.

Concomitantly, the content of the Directive is becoming tougher with a view to greater transparency, less national disharmony (sometimes at the cost of transparency) and better enforcement and access to information. This can be seen in particular through:

- the redefinition of the time limit for notifying issuers in order to speed up the information process;
- the disappearance of certain national options, replaced by European mandatory requirements, such as the exemption relating to investment firms and credit institutions' trading books;
- the institution of an electronic access point to regulated information, developed and operated by ESMA, scheduled for January 2018 (Article 21a);
- the tightening of administrative measures and sanctions applicable to breaches of the national provisions adopted in the transposition of the TD (Article 28); referring specifically to major holdings' disclosure, the ATD requires in particular the suspension of the exercise of voting rights attached to shares;
- or the number of instances where the TD provisions are to be specified by European Commission Regulatory Technical Standards (EC RTSs) drafted by ESMA.

On the substance, the most visible contribution of the ATD concerns the inclusion in the reporting thresholds of cash-settled equity derivatives, defined as financial instruments with similar economic effect to holding shares and entitlements to acquire shares (Article 13). The ATD specifies that the number of voting rights is calculated on a 'delta-adjusted' basis by multiplying the notional amount of underlying shares by the delta of the instrument. Following the UK model, this inclusion goes as far as to impose their aggregation with holdings of shares, as well as physically settled financial instruments, for the purpose of calculating the thresholds that trigger the notification requirement, contrary to the idea supported in some countries for a separate disclosure mechanism.[44]

This is indeed quite a groundbreaking stretch: if a non-shareholder could previously be required to notify on the grounds that a legal connection existed with listed shares, enabling him to acquire them or exercise influence over the corresponding votes,[45] a declaration is now imposed on a person who is not a shareholder, who probably never will be and whose relationship with the underlying shares is exclusively economic.

[44] For France, see A Pietrancosta, 'Transparence des positions en dérivés actions : un modèle français?' (2011) 1–2 *Revue Trimestrielle de Droit Financier* 3; *cf* DA Zetzsche, 'Against Mandatory Disclosure of Economic-Only Positions Referenced to Shares of European Issuers: Twenty Arguments against CESR Proposal' (2010) 11 *European Business Organization Law Review* 231.

[45] In France, the inclusion of purely indirect holdings was provided for by Ordinance No 2015-1576 of 3 December 2015 finalising the transposition of the European Transparency Directive, in order to break a restrictive case law of the Paris Court of Appeal ruling out the application of the obligation to declare the crossing of a threshold to a non-shareholder of the company concerned (Paris, pôle 5, ch 7, June 24, 2014, No 2014/06665, X c/ Eisenberg). The same Ordinance provided that control of a company, presuming a concerted action, may be held by a natural person.

Moreover, this economic link is not indestructible or irreplaceable, since it is only based on the hedging of the shares by financial intermediaries, which could very well take other forms in the future. 'However, to avoid any confusion as to the nature of holdings, the holder of shares and financial instruments would have to specify separately'[46] in the notification its respective holdings.

Level 2 and 3 measures have since been taken in order to ensure a higher degree of practical harmonisation:

- EC delegated Regulation 2015/761 of 17 December 2014 supplementing the TD 'with regard to certain regulatory technical standards on major holdings';
- ESMA, in addition to its Q&A on the TD, has issued an indicative list of financial instruments that may be subject to notification requirements,[47] guidelines on enforcement of financial information,[48] and standard forms for major holdings notifications[49] and for home Member State disclosure by issuers under the TD.[50]

The results of these EU legal developments should not be underestimated; they compare quite well internationally. The European system appears robust and modern compared, in particular, to the US system, which was introduced by the Williams Act of 1968 and has changed little in substantive terms over the past 50 years. In the US, a shareholder or a beneficial owner must always declare crossing the five per cent threshold, and the following one per cent, within 10 days. Such a delay now appears to belong to another financial era and offers a fantastic window of opportunity for shareholder activism, as evidenced by the development of 'wolf pack strategies'. Despite this criticism, attempts at strengthening the US system, announced by the 2010 Dodd-Frank Act,[51] have so far been unsuccessful. For example, the federal anti-activist piece of legislation named the Brokaw Act, introduced on 17 March 2016 and re-introduced in 2017, aims to decrease the section 13(d) of the Securities Exchange Act of 1934 period from 10 days to four business days, to protect businesses from hedge fund 'wolf packs' (by identifying these coordinated groups of hedge funds as a single group to require disclosure) and to require derivative disclosure.[52]

Nevertheless, the European system is not without its weaknesses. One of these is the counterpart to the tightening of investor disclosure requirements. Such requirements naturally represent a factor of cost for equity investors, as well as a factor of rigidification

[46] Revised Directive on transparency requirements for listed companies (Transparency Directive) – frequently asked questions, European Commission, MEMO/13/544, Brussels, 12 June 2013.

[47] See Indicative list of financial instruments that are subject to notification requirements according to Article 13(1b) of the revised Transparency Directive, ESMA/2015/1598 (22 October 2015).

[48] ESMA, Guidelines on enforcement of financial information, ESMA/2014/1293 (28 October 2014).

[49] Standard form for major holdings, ESMA (22 October 2015).

[50] ESMA/2015/1596 (22 October 2015).

[51] Dodd-Frank Wall Street Reform and Consumer Protection Act 929R, Pub Law 111–203, HR 4173 (111th Cong 2d sess. 2010), amending 1934 Act 13(d), 15 USCA 78n(d).

[52] Brokaw Act, s 2720, 114th Cong (2016); press release, baldwin.senate.gov/press-releases/brokaw-act. See D Borak and D Benoit, 'Democrats Take Aim at Activist Investors' *Wall Street Journal* (17 March 2016), wsj.com/articles/democrats-take-aim-at-activist-investors-1458251491; TN Mirvis, 'Proposed Revisions to 13(d) Beneficial Ownership Reporting Rules' (19 March 2016), corpgov.law.harvard.edu. For a critical view, see A Brav, JB Heaton and J Zandberg, 'Failed Anti-activist Legislation: The Curious Case of the Brokaw Act' (8 February 2018), available at: ssrn.com/abstract=2860167 or dx.doi.org/10.2139/ssrn.2860167.

of the market for corporate control. Indeed, it should be kept in mind that there are costs arising from ownership disclosure, which may have important chilling effects for equity research activity and potential bidders' incentives.[53] This inhibiting constraint on economic dynamism is further aggravated by the legal uncertainties that continue to surround the new provisions, as well as their delicate articulation with other information or abstention requirements imposed on investors. This is particularly true for the new European regulation on market abuse (MAR-MAD II), considering its uncertain combination with the major holdings disclosure rules of the TD in the context of an attack led by activist shareholders or of a pre-takeover stakebuilding, provided that we acknowledge the merits of such activities.[54] The uncertainty regarding the legal characterisation and possible use by an issuer of a private notification of a threshold crossing according to the issuer's bylaws is also problematic.

The other major criticism made of the European threshold crossing reporting system lies in its persisting fragmentation, despite harmonisation efforts. The transition to the principles of home Member State control and enhanced harmonisation, while improving the situation from a market integration viewpoint, is still far from giving total satisfaction. Forces of inertia and resistance are numerous and often inherent to the general state of European integration. Even within the family of regulated markets, where the TD provisions are confined, unlike the market abuse regulation provisions, the harmonisation achieved is only relative. First, one should keep in mind that, because of the home Member State principle, which refers to the issuers' *lex societatis*, harmonisation is not directly achieved market by market, but indirectly through national company law, at least for European Economic Area (EEA) issuers (whereas in the US, foreign private issuers are subject to section 13(d) requirements). Second, the TD continues to make room for many national deviations, which are very common, as shown below. Third, some major TD provisions lack precision, which is the case for the newly introduced sanctions that consist of suspending the voting rights of non-compliant shareholders who fail to notify their major shareholdings, whose application widely differs among Member States.[55] Finally, these disclosure requirements are necessarily destined to be interpreted, applied and enforced in national environments that vary significantly both in terms of market conditions and the underlying legal rules on goods, contracts, companies and tort, all local singularities and idiosyncrasies that intrinsically restrict the dream of true European integration. In this respect, it would be illusory to think that we can achieve a complete standardisation of information related to a non-uniform substance.

For the time being, it is therefore important to deal with these existing disparities in national economic and legal situations in the EU.

One way of doing this is to make these differences more apparent and understandable. In this sense, ESMA's efforts to highlight differences – through practical guides – should be welcomed. The following overview built from data drawn from

[53] Enriques, Gargantini and Novembre (n 21) 720, 735.

[54] See RJ Gilson and JN Gordon, 'The Agency Costs of Agency Capitalism: Activist Investors and the Revaluation of Governance Rights' (2013) *Columbia Law Working Paper No 438* 904 ff.

[55] KE Sørensen and M Neville, 'Suspension of the Exercise of Voting Rights: A Step towards Deterrent and Consistent Sanctioning of EU Transparency Requirements?' (2017) 14 *European Company Law* 150.

ESMA's last practical guide, dating from May 2018,[56] lets us review a wide variety of national situations. This disparity exists both in terms of thresholds (23 Member States using additional thresholds, with the UK and France having the most), triggering events or notification and publication periods (12 Member States having shorter time limits, with Denmark and Norway having the shortest).

Countries	Thresholds (%)	Triggering events - On-exchange transactions - Passive crossing	Intra-day netting	Notification to issuer	Publication
AT	3, 4, 5, 10, 15, 20, 25, 30, 35, 40, 45, 50, 75, 90	- Settlement date - Registration of new shares	Yes	2 trading days	Issuer 2 trading days
BE	5, 10, 15, 20, 25, 30, 35, 40, 45, 50, 55, 60, 65, 70, 75, 80, 85, 90, 95	- Trade date - Registration of new shares	Yes	6 trading days	Issuer 3 trading days
BG	5, 10, 15, 20, 25, 30, 35, 40, 45, 50, 55, 60, 65, 70, 75, 80, 85, 90, 95	- Settlement date - Registration of new shares	No	6 trading days	Issuer 3 trading days
CY	5, 10, 15, 20, 25, 30, 50, 75	- Trade date - Publication under Article 15 TD	Yes	5 trading days	Issuer Next trading day
CZ	1, 3, 5, 10, 15, 20, 25, 30, 40, 50, 75	- Settlement date - Capital decreases: registration date - Capital increases: date determined by the GM (not prior to the exercise of subscription rights and not later than on the registration date)	Yes	6 trading days	NCA 3 trading days

(continued)

[56] Practical Guide, National rules on notifications of major holdings under the Transparency Directive, ESMA31-67-535 (25 May 2018).

(Continued)

Countries	Thresholds (%)	Triggering events – On-exchange transactions – Passive crossing	Intra-day netting	Notification to issuer	Publication
DE	3, 5, 10, 15, 20, 25, 30, 50, 75	– Trade date – Registration of new shares	Yes (if no voting on the day of transaction)	4 trading days	Issuer 3 trading days
DK	5, 10, 15, 20, 25, 1/3, 50, 2/3, 90	– Trade date – Publication under Article 15 TD	No	Same trading day	Issuer Same day
EE	5, 10, 15, 20, 25, 1/3, 50, 2/3	– Trade date – Publication under Article 15 TD	No	6 trading days	Issuer 3 trading days
EL	5, 10, 15, 20, 25, 1/3, 50, 2/3, as well as any change equal to or greater than +/– 3 per cent over the 10 per cent threshold	– Trade date – Start of trading of shares	Yes	3 trading days	Issuer 2 trading days
ES	3, 5, 10, 15, 20, 25, 30, 35, 40, 45, 50, 60, 70, 75, 80, 90				
FI	5, 10, 15, 20, 25, 30, 50, 2/3, 90 (shares and voting rights)	– Trade date – Publication under Article 15 TD	Yes	3 trading days	Issuer As soon as possible
FR	5, 10, 15, 20, 25, 30, 1/3, 50, 2/3, 90, 95 (shares and voting rights)	– Trade date – Settlement date	Yes	4 trading days	NCA 3 trading days

(continued)

(Continued)

Countries	Thresholds (%)	Triggering events – On-exchange transactions – Passive crossing	Intra-day netting	Notification to issuer	Publication
HR	5, 10, 15, 20, 25, 30, 50, 75	– Trade date – Publication under Article 15 TD	No	6 trading days	Issuer 3 trading days
HU	5, 10, 15, 20, 25, 30, 35, 40, 45, 50, 75, 80, 85, 90, 91, 92, 93, 94, 95, 96, 97, 98, 99	– Trade date – Registration of new shares	Yes	2 calendar days	Issuer 2 calendar days
IE	For closed-ended collective investment schemes and non-Irish issuers: 5, 10, 15, 20, 25, 30, 50, 75 For all other issuers: 3 per cent and each 1 per cent thereafter up to 100 per cent	– Trade date – Publication under Article 15 TD	Yes	For closed-ended collective investment schemes and non-Irish issuers: 6 trading days For all other issuers: 4 trading days	Issuer For closed-ended collective investment schemes and non-Irish issuers: 3 trading days For all other issuers: next trading day
IS	5, 10, 15, 20, 25, 30, 35, 40, 50, 2/3, 90	– Trade date – Publication of the results of the share capital increase	Yes	1 trading day	12:00 on the next trading day
IT	3, 5, 10, 15, 20, 25, 30, 50, 2/3, 90	– Trade date – Publication under Article 15 TD	Yes	5 trading days	NCA 3 trading days
LT	5, 10, 15, 20, 25, 30, 50, 75, 95	– Trade date – Registration of new shares	No	6 trading days	Issuer 3 trading days

(continued)

(Continued)

Countries	Thresholds (%)	Triggering events – On-exchange transactions – Passive crossing	Intra-day netting	Notification to issuer	Publication
LU	5, 10, 15, 20, 25, 1/3, 50, 2/3	– Trade date – Publication under Article 15 TD	Yes (if no exercise of voting rights)	6 trading days	Issuer 3 trading days
LV	5, 10, 15, 20, 25, 30, 50, 75, 90, 95	– Settlement date – Registration of new shares	No	6 trading days	Issuer Next trading day
MT	5, 10, 15, 20, 25, 30, 50, 75, 90	– Settlement date – Publication of the results of the share capital increase	No	4 trading days	Issuer 3 trading days
NL	3, 5, 10, 15, 20, 25, 30, 40, 50, 60, 75, 95	– Trade date – Publication under Article 15 TD	Yes	Without delay	NCA Next trading day
NO	5, 10, 15, 20, 25, 1/3, 50, 2/3, 90	– Immediately/ trade date/ agreement date – Registration of new shares	No	Immediately	The regulated market No deadline
PL	5, 10, 15, 20, 25, 33, 1/3, 50, 75, 90	– Trade date – Registration of new shares	Yes	4 trading days	Issuer Same day
PT	2, 5, 10, 15, 20, 25, 1/3, 50, 2/3, 90	– Trade date – Registration of new shares	Yes	6 trading days	Issuer 3 trading days
RO	5, 10, 15, 20, 25, 33, 50, 75, 90	– Settlement date – Registration of new shares	Yes	3 trading days	Issuer 3 trading days
SE	5, 10, 15, 20, 25, 30, 50, 2/3, 90	– Trade date – Publication under Article 15 TD	Yes	6 trading days	NCA 3 trading days
SI	5, 10, 15, 20, 25, 1/3, 50, 75	– Trade date – Registration of new shares	Yes	4 trading days	Issuer 3 trading days

(continued)

(Continued)

Countries	Thresholds (%)	Triggering events - On-exchange transactions - Passive crossing	Intra-day netting	Notification to issuer	Publication
SK	5, 10, 15, 20, 25, 30, 50, 75	- Settlement date - Registration of new shares	No	6 trading days	Issuer 3 trading days
UK	For non-UK issuers: 5, 10, 15, 20, 25, 30, 50, 75 For UK issuers: 3, 4, 5, 6, 7, 8, 9, 10 and each 1 per cent threshold thereafter up to 100 per cent	- Trade date with (exceptions) - Publication of the results of the share capital increase	Yes	For non-UK issuers: 6 trading days For UK issuers: 4 trading days	For non-UK issuers: 3 trading days For UK issuers: next trading day

Note: AT: Austria; BE: Belgium; BG: Bulgaria; CY: Cyprus; CZ: Czech Republic; DE: Germany; DK: Denmark; EE: Estonia; EL: Greece; ES: Spain; FI: Finland; FR: France; HR: Croatia; HU: Hungary; IE: Ireland; IS: Iceland; IT: Italy; LT: Lithuania; LU: Luxembourg; LV: Latvia; MT: Malta; NL: the Netherlands; NO: Norway; PL: Poland; PT: Portugal; RO: Romania; SE: Sweden; SI: Slovenia; SK: Slovakia; UK: the UK.

Technological solutions, developed by private operators, also exist, offering professional investors the capacity to apprehend and facilitate the management of national legal singularities.

It is also important to continue to amend the legal framework where it deserves to be improved. In its recent 'Fitness Check on the EU Framework for Public Reporting by Companies', which was subject to public consultation until 21 July 2018, the European Commission usefully questions whether 'the disclosure and notification regime relating to major holdings of voting rights is coherent with other EU legislation and effective in strengthening investor protection and preventing market abuse'. In a summary report published in November 2018, the Commission underlined that whereas the vast majority of respondents agreed that the existing notification regime is 'effective in both strengthening investor protection and preventing possible market abuse situations', some criticised the lack of coherence between the different forms of legislation in Member States regarding the ongoing information on major holdings of voting rights, and made suggestions aiming to ensure 'that the EU framework is kept up to date to take into account the increased complexity of instruments that give a deferred or potential access to voting rights', 'to establish a mandatory standard form for reporting', to improve to coherence between the TD requirements and the MAR or to establish a more proportionate approach for small and medium-sized enterprises (SMEs).[57]

However, we are still in need of a clear vision of the objectives to be achieved and of the proper corresponding methodology. If the case for full harmonisation has been made in academia,[58] others have been more sceptical about the efficiency of one-size-fits-all solutions and have advocated a more balanced trade-off between standardisation and flexibility.[59] It is clear that the systemic choices to be made are largely influenced by political economy considerations.[60] We may legitimately favour the stability of issuers' stock market environment to the detriment of shareholder contestation methods that are deemed to be too disruptive. It is nonetheless important to conduct serious *ex ante* and *ex post* economic impact analyses designed to shed light on the various effects of these choices and, in any case, to adopt an optimal policy mix in terms of efficiency, since such a policy mix is inevitable as long as the underlying rules have not been fully standardised.

It is certainly tempting to anticipate that the developing decentralised securities and transaction registration technologies will soon make this disclosure of major holdings regulation obsolete. Certainly, within a public blockchain environment, the exact and entire share ownership, beyond the mere crossing of specific thresholds, becomes accessible to all at any time.[61] However, on the one hand, this implies that the application of such an open system should be extended to listed securities, which is not going to be implemented anytime soon. On the other hand, even if this extension were to be carried out, it is doubtful whether we could do without traditional major shareholdings disclosure regulation, which does not limit itself to making accessible (as a public blockchain would do) the mere knowledge of raw holding positions in a pseudonymised form and potentially scattered over several accounts, but mandates the occasional proactive publication by large investors of directly nominative and refined information, in particular through the aggregation of holdings of persons sharing common interests or through the inclusion of indirect or virtual investing/trading techniques. It is difficult to imagine, at least at present, replacing this complex regulatory disclosure regime developed over decades, which largely takes into account the intentions of the participants, with a purely rudimentary and mechanical public registering system.

[57] Summary Report of the Public Consultation on the Fitness Check on the EU framework for public reporting by companies, 21 March 2018–31 July 2018, 18 November 2018, p 11.

[58] See, eg, Fleischer and Schmolke (n 30).

[59] Enriques, Gargantini and Novembre (n 21) 720, 735; OECD, *Flexibility and Proportionality in Corporate Governance* (Paris, OECD Publishing, 2018), doi.org/10.1787/9789264307490-en.

[60] See Lakhani (n 14).

[61] See C van der Elst and A Lafarre, 'Bringing the AGM to the 21st Century: Blockchain and Smart Contracting Tech for Shareholder Involvement' (2017) *ECGI Working Paper Series in Law*, Working Paper No 358.

7

Climate-Related Financial Disclosure

RÜDIGER VEIL

I. Introduction

With the Paris Agreement,[1] all nations declared their intention to combat climate change and adapt to its effects. The long-term goal of the Agreement is to hold the increase in the global average temperature to well below 2°C above pre-industrial levels and to pursue efforts to limit the temperature increase to 1.5°C above pre-industrial levels, recognising that this would significantly reduce the risks and impacts of climate change.[2] To that end, financial flows should be made consistent with a shift to low greenhouse gas emissions and climate-resilient developments.[3]

The French legislature was first to implement this goal of the Agreement: the Energy Transition for Green Growth Act[4] set forth in August 2015 is a key initiative to consolidate the French low-carbon strategy.[5] Article 173 of this Act requires asset management companies and other institutional investors to disclose information on the manner in which they incorporate environmental, social, and governance (ESG) issues into their investment and risk management policies. In section II, this chapter will first introduce the French regime, analyse the rationales and the concept of the disclosure obligations under the French law, and discuss limitations of the concept. Subsequently, in section III, the proposal of the European Commission to establish a uniform transparency regime on climate-related issues for institutional investors throughout the European Union (EU) will be addressed. The chapter will then consider which regulatory approach is preferable.

[1] Paris Agreement under the United Nations Framework Convention on Climate Change of 12 December 2015 (hereinafter 'Paris Agreement' or 'Agreement').

[2] ibid art 2(1)a).

[3] ibid art 2(1)c).

[4] Energy Transition for Green Growth Act No 2015-992 of 17 August 2015.

[5] In 2018, the Swedish legislature also introduced disclosure obligations requiring mutual funds and alternative investment funds to provide information about which sustainability efforts they have shown.

II. French Law as a Regulatory Model for Climate Reporting Obligations

The provisions of the French Monetary and Financial Code[6] have been substantially amended by Article 173 of the Energy Transition for Green Growth Act and Decree No 2015-1850 of 29 December 2015. In particular, the French legislature considerably extended the content of the reporting obligations for institutional investors, such as asset management companies (managing Undertakings for Collective Investments in Transferable Securities (UCITS) and the Alternative Investment Fund (AIF)), investment companies, insurance undertakings etc.[7] The reform – described as a 'ground-breaking step'[8] – was inspired by the idea that the financial system should contribute to making the economy environmentally more sustainable. In particular, the French legislature aimed at improving the investment process with regard to sustainability, believing that investors were not fully aware of climate change risks. In addition, green investment opportunities should be made more transparent.

A. Content

i. Investor-Related Disclosure Obligations

The first pillar of climate-related reporting in annual reports consists of investor-related disclosure obligations. Asset management companies and other institutional investors – such as investment companies, insurance undertakings and pension schemes – have to fulfil several disclosure obligations in relation to how they take into account ESG issues. They are required to describe their basic approach to integrating ESG concerns into their investment policies and strategies (so-called climate strategy reporting). They must also inform investors about how they take ESG issues into account in their risk management systems.

Another element of investor-related reporting is the obligation of asset management companies to publish a list of managed UCITS that take ESG issues into account. The list shall indicate the percentage of the assets managed by these undertakings in the total amount of assets managed by the management company.

The French law also imposes an obligation on institutional investors to provide information on the use of or membership in labels, initiatives, charters and codes that address ESG issues. Such information may be useful for investors. It is sufficient for institutional investors to provide a summary description of the initiative or label in question.

[6] The main reporting obligations are laid down in art L 533-22-1 of the French Monetary and Financial Code. These general clauses are put into more detail in art D533-16-1.

[7] The following investors are entitled to provide only a minimum set information on a ESG issues: (i) entities belonging to a group which draws up consolidated accounts with a total balance sheet of less than €500 million; (ii) entities with a total balance sheet of less than €500 million; (iii) asset management companies for those investment funds managed with less than €500 million of assets.

[8] *cf* EY, 'How Have Investors Met Their ESG and Climate Reporting Requirements under Article 173-VI?' (December 2017) 2.

Where an institutional investor has established a risk management system, it must provide a general description of the internal process for identifying risks arising from ESG matters. The investor must also consider whether and how its business activities can be affected by these risks, which it also has to describe.

ii. Portfolio-Related Disclosure Requirements

The second pillar of the French climate reporting consists of portfolio-related disclosure obligations.[9] The information to be provided by institutional investors in their annual reports can be broken down into climate-related risk reporting and climate goal alignment reporting.

Institutional investors have to report on the general approach with regard to the integration of ESG issues in their investment policy and risk management.[10] To that end, they must describe the nature of the basic ESG criteria they have considered. They must distinguish between physical risks, defined as exposure to physical impacts directly induced by climate change (eg, wildfires, floods and storms), and transition risks, defined as the exposure to changes caused by the transition to a low-carbon economy (which depend on the speed of transition). The French law does not further specify these risk-reporting requirements. Therefore, suitable methods to determine the risks have to be developed by experts. This process has only just begun.[11] So far, there is only one 'top-down, cross-asset transition and physical risk model' in the market.[12]

Furthermore, institutional investors have to make public the general information of which issuers they have analysed with regard to ESG issues. In particular, investors must consider the nature of the data processed and the source of the data. The information may be financial data or non-financial data as well as internal or external analyses and ratings.

An essential element of the reporting regime is the obligation to be transparent about the approach or methodology used by institutional investors for their analysis.[13] This includes general information on the overall characteristics of the methodology of the analyses and an explanation of the relevance of the method and the selected perimeter. As different methodologies may lead to different definitions of portfolio decarbonisation, disclosure of the applied methods is essential.[14] Furthermore, institutional investors must disclose the results of the analysis of their portfolio. The abstract requirements for transparency regarding the methodology give investors leeway to develop suitable scenarios and proportionate processes. Scenario analysis is a

[9] The disclosure obligation is regulated in art D533-16-1 of the Monetary and Financial Code.

[10] This disclosure obligation goes back to the UN Principles for Responsible Investment (UN PRI). Investors signing the UN PRI commit to six principles, the main one being the integration of ESG issues into investment analysis and the decision-making process. As of March 2016, 141 French investors were PRI signatories. *cf* PRI, *French Energy Transition Law* (Paris, 2017) 10, https://www.unepfi.org/fileadmin/documents/PRI-FrenchEnergyTransitionLaw.pdf.

[11] For more detail on climate-related risks, see Task Force on Climate-related Financial Disclosures (TCFD), *Recommendations of the Task Force on Climate-Related Financial Disclosure: Final Report* (June 2017) 5–11.

[12] The 2° Investing Initiative, *Lighting the Way to Best Practice: Climate Reporting Award Case Studies* (2017) 17.

[13] The French Ministry of Environment has provided further guidance on these disclosure obligations. *cf* Trésor, Direction générale, *Notice explicative du décret n°2015-1850* (2016), available at: tresor.economie.gouv.fr/Ressources/File/422152.

[14] *cf* PRI (n 10) 14.

well-established method for developing a strategy that is able to take into account a range of plausible future developments.[15] There is no explicit rule in the French law that institutional investors should use a 2°C scenario as a reference for managing their portfolio. However, the Task Force on Climate-Related Financial Disclosures recommends that organisations 'use a 2°C or lower scenario in addition to two or three other scenarios most relevant to their circumstances, such as scenarios related to Nationally Determined Contributions (NDCs), physical climate-related scenarios, or other challenging scenarios'.[16] It is not necessary to go into further details here. However, an important aspect of the French reporting regime should be highlighted: the disclosure obligation of institutional investors extends to past, current and future measurements of greenhouse gas emissions that are directly or indirectly attributable to an issuer that is part of the institutional investors' (managed) assets ('carbon footprint assessment').

The reporting obligations under Article D 533-16-1 II 2° lit d) of the Monetary and Financial Code is linked to the transparency obligations regarding the analysis of the portfolio. Institutional investors have to comment on how they integrate the results of this analysis into their investment policy and strategy. They must describe the following aspects: (i) changes or adjustments to the portfolio structure; and (ii) strategy of influence over issuers. Disclosure on climate engagement activities is a key element of the French regime of climate reporting. Investors can influence strategies and decisions of the corporations in which they invest not only by exercising voting rights attached to shares, but also by establishing a regular dialogue with the issuers on ESG topics.

Finally, a key element of the French reporting regime is the disclosure of the alignment of voluntary decarbonisation targets with national and international goals. This obligation is laid down in Article D 533-16-1 III 4° of the Monetary and Financial Code. An institutional investor has to report on: (i) the way in which it verifies the compliance of its investment policy with the environmental objectives of French law; (ii) the way in which it verifies the indicative targets it has set itself (contribution of the portfolio to the reduction of greenhouse gas emissions); (iii) the measures it has taken following the analysis; and, finally, (iv) the reasons for possible deviations from the indicative targets it has set itself.

This transparency obligation aims to encourage institutional investors to align their portfolio with the objectives of French environmental law and international agreements (in particular, alignment with the 2°C target of the Paris Agreement). Thus, an institutional investor must report on the way in which it verifies the conformity of its investment policy with the above objectives and how, in view of the nature of its activities and investments, it determines and measures its contribution to the achievement of the environmental objectives. Furthermore, the institutional investor has to make public the indicative targets it has set itself to assess its contribution to achieving the national and global climate targets, depending on the nature of its activities and the nature of its

[15] TCFD (n 11) 25: 'Scenario analyses is a process for identifying and assessing the potential implications of a range of plausible future states under conditions of uncertainty.'

[16] ibid 27.

investments. As an example, one investor defined the following objectives: 'Reduce the carbon footprint of all investments by at least 25% in 2025 and at least 40% in 2040.'[17] A possible measure to achieve this objective would be, for example, to lower the carbon content of the portfolio by having only assets with low levels of carbon emission or by having a high proportion of assets that contribute to decarbonising the economy.

B. Flexibility

The French law provides for statutory reporting obligations on environmental matters. Asset management companies and other institutional investors are therefore obliged to disclose such information. However, they can refrain from reporting if they explain why they do not report ('report-or-explain'). There are several reasons for this regulatory approach.

First, it may be useful to give asset management companies and other institutional investors some freedom in reporting and to accept that they do not want to comment on certain aspects. In particular, reporting can be unreasonable for them because methods that can be used to fulfil ESG disclosure obligations have not been developed yet. Best practices do not yet exist for a large part of the portfolio information.[18] Furthermore, methodologies for assessing climate risks do not yet exist for all asset classes. There is only one science-based model in the market measuring 'climate goal-alignment' directly.[19] It is a Herculean task to develop climate performance metrics.[20] Therefore, it is conceivable that an investment or asset management company cannot provide meaningful information on a particular aspect of portfolio-related reporting. Thus, it is more appropriate that the institutional investor does not declare itself on this aspect and explains why it does not, instead of requiring the investor to provide information which does not have an informational value and may be misleading. After all, it can be costly for institutional investors to provide information on all relevant ESG issues. Thus, a report-or-explain mechanism also takes into account the principle of proportionality.

There are also legal reasons for a report-or-explain mechanism. Institutional investors are not always in a position to fully meet the detailed reporting requirements for their portfolios by providing highly meaningful information. Neither investment law nor corporate law grants institutional investors a right to demand information from the issuers whose shares are in the investors' portfolio. Data collection can be tedious. It is not certain that intermediaries, such as sustainability agencies, are always in a position to provide institutional investors with the information necessary for the reports. This is mainly because neither the intermediaries nor the investors have legally binding rights to get information on ESG aspects from issuers.

[17] *cf* 2° Investing Initiative (n 12) 11 (case study analysing a Dutch asset manager with €55.9 billion in assets under management).

[18] *cf* EY (n 8) 8: 'Investors need methodologies to assess risk exposure.'

[19] *cf* 2° Investing Initiative (n 12) 14 (the model focuses on key-climate-related sectors for listed equity and corporate bond portfolios).

[20] *cf* ibid 11 on backward-looking metrics and the question of how to develop forward-looking information.

C. Evaluation: Limitations and Problems

The key goal of the French law is to ensure that investors are able to assess the sustainability of an investment. France regards itself as a pioneer in the field of sustainability reporting and corporate social responsibility. It was the first country to introduce legal reporting requirements on sustainability aspects for institutional investors. France is proud of the international dynamics of its reforms.[21] It is also a declared goal to strengthen the role of Paris as a financial centre in the global market of 'green finance'.[22]

The success of the transparency reforms cannot be assessed conclusively yet. However, it is already possible to point out the limitations and problems of the new transparency regime. The first point concerns the scope and the level of detail of information on ESG issues. The abundance of the disclosure obligations and granularity of information are enormous. This is particularly true for information on the description of the analysis methodology, climate-related risks and the engagement policy. Institutional investors have to provide numerous technical details that are difficult to comprehend without a profound knowledge of the methodologies. This brings us to the question of who is expected to make use of the information – only analysts or also (private/other institutional) investors? A private investor is unlikely to be able to accurately assess an institutional investor's sustainability strategy and the quality of climate performance metrics.[23] The French law does not provide an answer to the fundamental question of who the 'ultimate user' of the information is.[24] A further problem is the need to standardise reporting on portfolio-related aspects. The French legislature therefore tried to develop a uniform reporting format. However, an analysis of 10 exemplarily selected reports has revealed that institutional investors do not necessarily adhere to these requirements.[25] This finding indicates that a national supervisory authority should monitor the fulfilment of reporting obligations. Additionally, enforcement should be ensured by providing sanctions. Experiences on this have yet to be gathered in France.

Another problem is the lack of access to information for institutional investors on investees' emissions.[26] An institutional investor has no entitlement to demand from the issuers in its portfolio to provide it with information on greenhouse gas emissions, nor can it require issuers to provide information on their decarbonisation strategy. Law does not provide for such claims because the French legislature does not have the legislating power to regulate such claims against foreign issuers. Of course, it cannot be ruled out that issuers may voluntarily provide information on these aspects. However, this does not mean that an institutional investor has all the information necessary to fulfil the portfolio-reporting obligations. Furthermore, one cannot expect that

[21] *cf* PRI (n 10) 13: 'The French law is speeding up the learning process for the entire financial community.'

[22] *cf* ibid 12, citing the former French President François Hollande, who set out the vision for France to become the 'nation of environmental excellence'.

[23] The 2° alignment test was developed by the Sustainable Energy Investing Metrics Project consortium. See in more detail 2° Investing Initiative (n 12) 14.

[24] *cf* ibid 5.

[25] *cf* R Veil, K Deckert, A Kämmerer and C Voigt, *Nachhaltige Kapitalanlagen durch Finanzmarktregulierung* (Dessau-Roßlau, Umweltbundesamt, 2019).

[26] A further problem is the quality of such data. *cf* EY (n 8) 12.

sustainability agencies will provide all the necessary information. This may be possible in the future but not at the moment. Against this background, it is right that the French legislature has provided for a report-or-explain mechanism. An institutional investor may therefore refrain from reporting if it does not have the necessary information, for example, on greenhouse gas emissions of the issuers in its portfolio.

Overall, the French disclosure obligation has not been a challenge for institutional investors that already have well-developed ESG practices.[27] Insurance companies and asset management companies were even willing to declare how their portfolios align with the objectives of French environmental law and international agreements. A report by EY, assessing the first year of implementation of the disclosure obligation, concluded that 52 per cent of the panel[28] performed assessments of the portfolio's alignment with a 2°C scenario.[29] Two-thirds of the 2°C alignment assessments performed by the panel relied on sectoral decarbonisation scenarios developed by the International Energy Agency, for sectors such as utilities, the automotive industry, and the oil and gas industry. However, investors chose various time horizons and asset class coverages when assessing the alignment of their portfolio with a 2°C scenario.[30] The Report therefore recommends that investors should provide clearer disclosure on the extent to which their portfolios and investments are aligned with a 2°C scenario and that they explain how this alignment can lead to better performance and risk management.[31]

III. The Commission Proposal from May 2018

On 24 May 2018, the European Commission published a legislative package as part of its initiative on sustainable development.[32] The proposal for a regulation 'on the establishment of a framework to facilitate sustainable investment' (COM(2018) 353 final) deals with the criteria to be used to assess the sustainability of economic activities (taxonomy).[33] This so-called 'taxonomy regulation' is the centrepiece

[27] *cf* PRI (n 10) 9.

[28] The study covered a panel of 23 entities subject to the ESG and climate reporting requirements under French law. It included 15 insurance groups, six asset management companies and two pension funds. *Cf* EY (n 8) 17.

[29] *cf* EY (n 8) 13.

[30] *cf* ibid.

[31] *cf* ibid 13.

[32] At the end of 2016, the Commission appointed a High-Level Expert Group on sustainable finance (HLEG). On 31 January 2018, the HLEG published its final report, offering a vision on how to build a sustainable finance strategy for the EU (*cf* EU High-Level Expert Group on Sustainable Finance, *Financing a Sustainable European Economy, Final Report*, 2018). On 8 March, the Commission came forward with an Action Plan on Financing Sustainable Growth, taking into account the HLEG's recommendations (COM(2018) 97 final). The Action Plan pursues three objectives: (i) re-orient capital flows towards sustainable investment in order to achieve sustainable and inclusive growth; (ii) manage financial risks stemming from climate change, environmental degradation and social issues; (iii) foster transparency and long-termism in financial and economic activity. The legislative package is the first part of the Commission's initiative on sustainable development laid down in the Action Plan.

[33] The draft regulation is supposed to apply to measures adopted by Member States or by the EU in respect of financial products or corporate bonds that are marketed as environmentally sustainable and financial market participants offering financial products as environmentally sustainable investments (*cf* art 1(2)).

of the reform.[34] It is accompanied by the proposal for a regulation 'on disclosure relating to sustainable investments and sustainability risks and amending Directive (EU) 2016/2341' (COM(2018) 354 final). This so-called 'transparency regulation' aims to introduce disclosure requirements for institutional investors. It will be discussed in more detail because it pursues objectives comparable to those of the French transparency law. It will be considered whether and to what extent the Commission proposal differs from the French regime.

The COM draft aims to harmonise transparency rules for financial market participants, insurance companies and investment firms. First, it provides for disclosure obligations on sustainability risks. Second, it wants to promote the transparency of financial products whose objective is a sustainable investment, including the reduction of CO_2 emissions. The Commission's draft regulation is characterised by a broad understanding of the concept of sustainable investment. These are: (i) investments in an economic activity that contributes to an environmental objective, as defined in the taxonomy regulation (COM(2018) 353 final); (ii) investments in an economic activity that contributes to a social objective; and (iii) investments in companies following good governance practices'.[35]

The draft Regulation on transparency is intended to apply to 'financial market participants'. According to Article 2(a) of the proposal for a regulation, this includes: (i) insurance undertakings, an Alternative Investment Fund Manager (AIFM), an investment firm which provides portfolio management, an Institution for Occupational Retirement Provision (IORP)[36] or a provider of a pension product; (ii) a manager of a qualifying venture capital fund; (iii) a manager of a qualifying social entrepreneurship fund; and (iv) a UCITS management company. The COM draft requires the relevant information to be published on the website of the financial market participant, in pre-contractual disclosures and in periodic reports. The information made available on the website must be updated. Pre-contractual information refers to prospectuses and basic information sheets. By regular reports, the COM draft refers to the publication of the annual accounts.

A. Content of the Draft EU Regulation on Disclosure of Sustainability (COM(2018) 354 Final)

The COM proposal essentially provides for two obligations which the financial market participant needs to disclose: first, investor-related transparency of sustainability risks;

To that end, the draft regulation also defines environmental objectives, such as: (i) climate change mitigation; (ii) climate change adaption; (iii) sustainable use and protection of water and marine resources; (iv) transition to a circular economy, waste prevention and recycling; (v) pollution prevention and control; and (vi) protection of healthy ecosystems (*cf* art 5). *cf* M Stumpp, 'Die EU-Taxonomie für nachhaltige Finanzprodukte – Eine belastbare Grundlage für Sustainable Finance in Europa?' (2019) 31(1) *Zeitschrift für Bankrecht und Bankwirtschaft* 71, 73–77.

[34] *cf* on the need to define sustainability F Möslein and KE Sørensen, 'The Commission's Action Plan for Financing Sustainable Growth and its Corporate Governance Implications' (2018) Nordic & European Company Law Working Paper No 18-17, available at: ssrn.com/abstract=3251731.

[35] *cf* art 2(o) of the draft Regulation (COM(2018) 354 final).

[36] IORP means an institution for occupational retirement provision authorised or registered in accordance with art 9 of Directive (EU) 2016/2341.

and, second, product-related transparency of sustainable investments. For the time being, it is not possible to reliably determine the content of the two sets of obligations because the COM proposal is to be supplemented by delegated acts of the Commission, the content of which is not yet apparent. The COM proposal is intended as a Level 1 legislative act, so that it only provides for the essential content of disclosure obligations. However, it is already possible at this stage to compare the COM draft with the French regulatory model.

i. Investor-Related Information (Climate-Related Risk Reporting)

First, financial market participants are obliged to publish written policies on the integration of sustainability risks in their investment decision-making processes.[37] Unlike in France, this is not specified in more detail in the draft Regulation.

Second, financial market participants have to ensure transparency on the integration of sustainability risks. They have to address three aspects in pre-contractual information,[38] namely information on: (a) the procedures and conditions applied for integrating sustainability risks in investment decisions; (b) the extent to which sustainability risks are expected to have a relevant impact on the returns of the financial products made available; and (c) how the remuneration policies of financial market participants are consistent with the integration of sustainability risks and are in line, where relevant, with the sustainable investment target of the financial product.

Both investor-related disclosure obligations shall apply when a financial market participant offers or sells financial products regardless of whether the product has a focus on sustainability or not. The COM draft does not provide for exemptions for financial market participants that do not reach or exceed certain thresholds.

ii. Information on Sustainable Financial Products

The second pillar of the Commission's draft regulation consists of disclosure obligations of sustainable investments. Where a 'financial product'[39] targets sustainable investments or investments with similar characteristics, a financial market participant has to provide further information in pre-contractual publications,[40] on the website of the financial market participant[41] and in regular reports.[42] The COM draft distinguishes between a financial product for which an index has been designated as a reference benchmark (category 1) and a financial product which targets the reduction in carbon emissions (category 2).

The information to be provided in 'pre-contractual information' mainly aims at allowing investors to better understand the sustainability of the financial product.

[37] *cf* Art 3 COM draft.
[38] *cf* ibid art 4.
[39] Financial product means a portfolio management, an AIF, an insurance-based investment product (IBIP), a pension product, a pension scheme or a UCITS (*cf* ibid art 2(i)).
[40] *cf* ibid art 5.
[41] *cf* ibid art 6.
[42] *cf* ibid art 7.

As to the financial products in category 1, a financial market participant has to provide information on how the designated index is aligned with the target and an explanation as to why the weighting and constituents of the designated index aligned with the target differ from a broad market index. The idea of this disclosure obligation is to enable investors assessing the appropriateness of the designated index. End-investors should have the necessary information on how the underlying assets of the indexes were selected and weighted, which assets were excluded and for what reason, how sustainability-related impacts of the underlying assets were measured or which data sources were used.[43] In relation to financial products in category 2, the information to be disclosed shall include the targeted low-carbon emission exposure.

Further information will be published on the website of the financial market participant, in particular a description of the sustainable investment target, information on the methodologies used to assess, measure and monitor the impact of the sustainable investments selected for the financial product, including its data sources, screening criteria for the underlying assets, and the relevant sustainability indicators used to measure the overall sustainable impact of the financial product.[44] This information has to be kept up to date.

The Commission seems to follow the idea that a financial market participant is able to fulfil its reporting obligations using the ESG information provided in the annual report or non-financial statement of the issuers in which it has invested (ie, information about the 'underlying assets'). However, the corporate social responsibility (CSR) reporting obligations that currently exist for 'large undertakings' are limited.[45] It is therefore by no means certain that a financial market participant has the necessary information to fulfil its transparency obligation.

B. Flexibility

The Commission proposes to regulate the disclosure on sustainable investments and sustainability risks by means of a regulation. The Level 1 legislative act is to be supplemented by delegated acts and technical standards. The experience with European legislation teaches us that these will probably be regulations as well. The transparency obligations would therefore be directly applicable in the Member States. Alternatively, the European legislature could amend existing EU directives for financial market participants (eg, UCITS, the Alternative Investment Fund Managers Directive (AIFMD) or Solvency II). However, the Commission has opposed this regulatory approach, as there

[43] *cf* ibid Recital 6.

[44] *cf* ibid art 6(1).

[45] Directive 2014/95/EU of 15 November 2014 [2014] OJ L330, 1 requires that large undertakings which are public-interest entities exceeding on their balance sheet dates the criterion of the average number of 500 employees during the financial year include in the management report a non-financial statement containing information relating to, as a minimum, environmental, social and employee matters, respect for human rights, anti-corruption and bribery matters. However, this disclosure is limited, as the information has to be provided 'to the extent necessary for an understanding of the undertaking's development, performance, position and impact of its activity'.

would be a risk of differing implementations in the Member States.[46] This argument is not convincing. Harmonisation can also be achieved through fully harmonising directives which would largely avoid the problem of diverging legal conditions in the EU and have the advantage of a coherent and consistent (sector-specific) reform.

This brings us to the question whether there will be room for the Member States to adopt stricter rules in the future. Does the European Commission propose a fully harmonising regime? This cannot be concluded solely from the fact that the Commission proposes to adopt regulations instead of directives. The Council and the European Parliament may also adopt minimum harmonisation regulations. The wording of the draft Regulations does not allow for conclusions on the type of harmonisation either. Article 1 of the draft Transparency Regulation stipulates that the Regulation provides for 'harmonised rules'. The wording does not make clear whether this means a minimum or a full (maximum) harmonisation. The other provisions of the Regulation deal neither explicitly nor implicitly with the degree of harmonisation.

However, the European Commission explained that divergent action by Member States could create barriers to the smooth functioning of the internal market and have adverse effects on financial market participants.[47] This indicates that the Commission is striving for a uniform legal framework and wishes to exclude the individual legislation of Member States. Finally, the Commission states in the Explanatory Memorandum that its proposal provides for 'full harmonisation', which is the best way to ensure 'maximum harmonisation'.[48] These phrases are a further indication for the interpretation that the Commission should be aiming for maximum harmonisation of transparency rules on sustainable investments and risks.

C. Evaluation: Limitations and Problems

On the one hand, the personal scope of application of the COM draft is wider than the French law on transparency for institutional investors. Financial service providers (in particular investment firms) are also covered by the draft. On the other hand, the COM draft does not include public authorities in the transparency regime. The French law goes further in this respect and requires employee pension funds to report on ESG issues.

The main difference is in the design of the transparency rules. The Commission confines itself to provide for investor-related disclosure requirements, in particular concerning sustainability policies, and product-related disclosure requirements enabling investors to assess the sustainability of the financial product. Investors should be able to make an 'effective comparison' of financial products. The information should 'contribute to a correct assessment of sustainability-enhancing investments'.[49] Therefore, the

[46] Commission, 'Impact Assessment' SWD(2018) 264 final 50 f.

[47] Commission, 'Explanatory Memorandum' COM(2018) 354 final 6; see also Recital 3 of the draft Taxonomy Regulation.

[48] Commission, Explanatory Memorandum, COM(2018) 354 final, 24 May 2018, 8; Commission Staff Working Document, Impact Assessment, SWD(2018) 264 final, 24 May 2018, 51.

[49] *cf* Recital 6 of the draft Transparency Regulation.

transparency regime of the COM intends primarily to achieve investor protection. Disclosure obligations on the sustainability of a financial product only become relevant if a financial market participant offers such products.

The French law goes further than the COM draft with regard to portfolio-related disclosure obligations. Its purpose is not only to ensure investor protection through disclosure of sustainability risks, but also to promote sustainable investments. According to the French law, institutional investors are encouraged to critically examine their investment behaviour with a view to sustainable investments and, if necessary, to redesign the portfolio. Due to disclosure obligations, institutional investors should feel compelled to determine the CO_2 balance of their portfolio, set their own targets for the reduction of greenhouse gas emissions and assess the portfolio's contribution to national and international environmental goals.

The COM draft does not pursue these goals.[50] Whilst it is positive that the COM draft wants to improve investor protection, it is not convincing that it only requires institutional investors to report on sustainable financial products. It is not clear why the Commission has not adopted the French model requiring portfolio-related disclosure. The Commission does not even seem to have considered the French law.[51]

Finally, it is unclear what impact the disclosure obligations will have on the fiduciary duties of asset managers. Following the recommendations of the High-Level Group on Sustainable Finance,[52] the Commission's Action Plan 'Financing Sustainable Growth' included the clarification of the obligations of institutional investors and asset managers as a measure to encourage both end-investors and asset managers to integrate sustainability aspects into their decision-making process.[53] Surprisingly, the Commission's proposals for a legislative package on sustainable finance published on 24 May 2018 does not provide for such provisions.[54]

Nevertheless, transparency on sustainable investments could also affect the fiduciary duties of managers of an asset management company.[55] Fiduciary duties are obligations generally arising from corporate law. A manager is obliged to act in the best interests of his company; otherwise he acts contrary to his duty and, as a result, could be obliged to pay damages to his company. The supervisory law for investment companies does not provide for such obligations. However, it is conceivable that supervisory law has an impact on the obligations under corporate law: on the one hand, supervisory law might have a material legal impact in the sense that a board member is obliged to make sustainable investments; on the other hand, supervisory law could have

[50] *cf* M Stumpp, 'Die EU-Taxonomie für nachhaltige Finanzprodukte – Eine belastbare Grundlage für Sustainable Finance in Europa?' (2019) *Zeitschrift für Bankrecht und Bankwirtschaft* 71, 78.

[51] *cf* Commission Staff Working Document, Impact Assessment, SWD(2018) 264 final, 24 May 2018, 99, discussing policy options, but not mentioning the French law.

[52] *cf* EU High-Level Expert Group on Sustainable Finance, *Financing a Sustainable European Economy, Final Report*, 2018, 40: 'Strengthen director duties related to sustainability.'

[53] *cf* Commission, Action Plan, Financing Sustainable Growth, COM(2018) 97 final, 8 March 2018, 10.

[54] The Commission only proposes that 'the "prudent person-rule" with respect to the consideration of environmental, social and governance risks is taken into account'. To that end, art 19 of Directive (EU) 2016/2341 on the activities and supervision of institutions for occupational retirement provision (IORPs) should be amended. *cf* art 10 of the draft Taxonomy Regulation.

[55] F Möslein and KE Sørensen, 'The Commission's Action Plan for Financing Sustainable Growth and its Corporate Governance Implications' (2018) 15 *European Company Law Journal* 221, 229: 'disclosure requirements … are supposedly the most widespread procedural instrument in conventional company law'.

a procedural impact in the sense that a manager is at least obliged to take sustainability aspects into account in his investment decision. The obligation of an asset management company to publish information on the consideration of sustainability aspects of its portfolio (under the French law) implies that the members of the board of directors of the asset management company must deal with the issue and take sustainable aspects into account when making investment decisions. The disclosure obligations under supervisory law can therefore have an effect on the obligation to serve in the best interests of the asset management company under corporate law. Thus, the manager would not be obliged to invest in green financial products, but would have to consider ESG criteria. It is therefore preferable to attribute a procedural effect to the impact that supervisory law has on disclosure obligations.

These effects on fiduciary obligations are greatest in the case of disclosure obligations under the French law, though it only provides a report-or-explain mechanism. Thus, an institutional investor does not necessarily have to fulfil the reporting obligations. However, it has to deal with all individual aspects of climate reporting and explain if it does not want to make any statements. The obligation to deal with sustainable aspects extends in particular to the CO_2 footprint of the portfolio and its current and future composition with regard to international climate protection goals. The proposal of the European Commission provides for less far-reaching publication obligations. If an asset management company does not wish to offer sustainable financial products, it only needs to report on sustainability risks, but not on the environmental sustainability of its portfolio and its development. The disclosure obligations of the Commission draft would therefore, in principle, not affect the fiduciary duties of a manager.

IV. Conclusion

The French reform on ESG in financial markets law has led to an intense discussion in the EU Member States and in the EU on sustainable finance. In particular, the French law on climate reporting is considered a turning point in carbon reporting. France is praised for the pioneering nature of its reform. Indeed, the purpose of disclosure of climate-related information in France is threefold: to make green investment opportunities more transparent to investors; to make climate change risks more transparent to investors; and to effect decisions of asset managers and incentivise them to take into account sustainability. France has implemented these approaches very well. Thus, the French regime may serve as a regulatory model for the EU.

The introduction of climate-related financial disclosure would mean a fundamental change of European investment law which is based on the assumption that investors are solely interested in maximising their (short-term) profits. It is nevertheless possible to introduce such obligations in European law without coming into conflict with the traditional principles of investment law. Thus, a disclosure regime should require information on both investor- and portfolio-related environmental aspects. This includes information about climate change-related risks and the alignment of voluntary decarbonisation targets with national or international environmental goals. Disclosure obligations for institutional investors on portfolio-related environmental aspects should be based on a report-or-explain mechanism.

8

Proxy Advisors and Disclosure of Conflicts of Interests

ULRICH TORGGLER

I. Introduction

Proxy advisors are intermediaries on the capital markets, usually engaged by institutional investors seeking to outsource the efforts associated with the exercise of voting rights and the responsibility therefor. In recent years, proxy advisors have been criticised from many sides based on a common assertion that price competition makes them susceptible to conflicts of interests. At first, it was feared that the proxy advisory industry favoured the management of issuers. Later, both issuers and large institutional investors started to suspect activist shareholders of having an undue influence on proxy advice. This chapter evaluates both the asserted biases and the legislative answers thereto. It concludes with a note of caution against further regulation.

II. The Demand for Proxy Advice

A. The (Broken) Promise of Institutional Investor Voice

Proxy advisors are relatively new players in capital markets and an additional species of intermediaries, selling voting recommendations to institutional investors.[1] To understand their emergence, let us go back a few steps to the Berle-Means corporation, the separation of ownership and control between dispersed shareholders and powerful management,[2] in most cases in Europe between diversified shareholders on the one

[1] The oldest provider, Institutional Shareholder Services (ISS), took up its operations as recently as 1986. For an early forecast of the role of proxy advisors in corporate governance, see JC Coffee, 'Liquidity versus Control: The Institutional Investor as Corporate Monitor' (1991) 91 *Columbia Law Review* 1277, 1354 f. While Coffee already anticipated a very influential industry (ibid 1358), a broader debate did not start until the late 2000s. For a seminal discussion, see T Belinfanti, 'The Proxy Advisory & Corporate Governance Industry: The Case for Increased Oversight and Control' (2009) 14 *Stanford Journal of Law, Business & Finance* 384.

[2] AA Berle and GC Means, *The Modern Corporation and Private Property* (Piscataway, NJ, Transaction Publishers, 1932).

hand and a controlling shareholder and the management on the other.[3] Symptoms were, inter alia, golden plating, corporate perks and diversion of corporate funds.[4]

Starting in the 1970s, this assessment became increasingly inaccurate due to the growing influence of institutional investors.[5] Clark called this the 'separation of savings and investment'.[6] Black even believed in a 'Promise of Institutional Investor Voice' to overcome the Berle/Means problem.[7] However, the (alleged) promise has been broken, the main reason being that institutional investors simply lack the interest in monitoring management and engaging in corporate governance issues. They are mainly interested in the liquidity and dispersion of their investments.[8] Also, (active) fund managers usually have strong incentives to outperform an index (and not invest in it) and to prefer 'exit' over 'voice'.[9]

In addition, since 2000, we have seen a remarkable rise of passive investment funds.[10] The gap between investments in passive and active funds has been growing since 2007, likely partly due to a loss of trust in fund managers' decisions in the wake of the financial crisis[11] and the low interest rates at the time.[12] A major selling point for passive funds is low management fees. Therefore, at least traditionally, these funds have little means to engage in corporate governance.[13] Only recently has the development culminated in the inception of the first no-fee tracker fund with the sale of voting rights to activist investors as its business model.[14]

[3] For the resulting conflicts, see L Enriques, HB Hansmann, RH Kraakman and M Pargendler, 'The Basic Governance Structure: Minority Shareholders and Non-shareholder Constituencies' in RH Kraakman et al (eds), *The Anatomy of Corporate Law*, 3rd edn (Oxford, Oxford University Press, 2017) 79.

[4] *cf* J Edgerton, 'Agency Problems in Public Firms: Evidence from Corporate Jets in Leveraged Buyouts' (2012) 67 *Journal of Finance* 2187 (showing that private equity fund-owned firms owned on average 40 per cent smaller aircraft fleets than similar public firms).

[5] On this development, see EP Davis, 'The Role of Institutional Investors in the Evolution of Financial Structure and Behaviour' in M Edey (ed), *The Future of the Financial System* (Sydney, Reserve Bank of Australia, 1996) 49.

[6] RC Clark, 'The Four Stages of Capitalism: Reflections on Investment Management Treatises' (1981) 94 *Harvard Law Review* 561, 563 f.

[7] BS Black, 'Agents Watching Agents: The Promise of Institutional Investor Voice' (1992) 39 *UCLA Law Review* 811. See also BS Black, 'Shareholder Passivity Reexamined' (1990) 89 *Michigan Law Review* 520; RJ Gilson and RH Kraakman, 'Reinventing the Outside Director: An Agenda for Institutional Investors' (1991) 43 *Stanford Law Review* 863.

[8] SCY Wong, 'Why Stewardship is Proving Elusive for Institutional Investors' (2010) *Butterworths Journal of International Banking and Financial Law* 406. For early scepticism, *cf* EB Rock, 'The Logic and (Uncertain) Significance of Institutional Shareholder Activism' (1991) 79 *Georgetown Law Journal* 445.

[9] Wong (n 8) 406 f; HS Birkmose, 'You Can Lead a Horse to Water, But Can You Make it Drink? Institutional Shareholders and Corporate Voting' (2009) *European Business Law Review* 717, 732 f. See also EB Rock, 'Institutional Investors in Corporate Governance' in JN Gordon and WG Ringe (eds), *The Oxford Handbook of Corporate Law and Governance* (Oxford, Oxford University Press, 2018) 363, 372–74.

[10] Recently 'Active Fund Managers Hold Fewer and Fewer Stocks' *The Economist* (10 March 2018). On this development, see V Sushko and G Turner, 'The Implications of Passive Investing for Securities Markets', *Bank for International Settlements Quarterly Review*, March 2018, 113.

[11] Studies show that most active funds significantly underperformed their benchmarks even in the post-2007 bear market; see I Barnes, 'Do Active Equity Managers Outperform Passive Funds in a Bear Market?' *Netwealth* (8 May 2018), www.netwealth.com/OurViews/2018/5/8/active-equity-managers-outperform-passive-funds-bear-market. This may have contributed to the decline of active funds; see CW Li, A Tiwariz and L Tong, 'Investment Decisions under Ambiguity: Evidence from Mutual Fund Investor Behavior' (2016) 63 *Management Science* 2509.

[12] A Mooney, 'Passive Funds Grow 230% to $6tn' *Financial Times* (29 May 2016).

[13] However, see below n 49, 84.

[14] 'How Low Can You Go? A Milestone is Reached with the First Zero-Cost Tracker Funds' *The Economist* (4 August 2018).

B. Investor Stewardship as the Regulatory Answer

The regulatory answer was the stewardship idea, ie, regulation to encourage institutional investors to play an active role in corporate governance.[15] Upon a closer look, there are two approaches to regulate what is now commonly referred to as 'shareholder duties',[16] the beneficiaries being either the funds' investors or the issuer and its shareholders.[17]

The first variant goes back to the 1988 'Avon-Letter' of the US Department of Labour (DoL), requiring managers of pension funds to exercise voting rights. It was based on the concern that fund managers were acting against the best interests of their investors. Accordingly, their behaviour towards issuers was measured against the funds' fiduciary responsibility for the administration of the entrusted investments.[18] The French Autorité des Marchés Financiers (AMF) initially followed this approach,[19] as well as the 2004 revision of the Organisation for Economic Co-operation and Development (OECD) Principles of Corporate Governance.[20]

However, as early as 2003, the Dutch Corporate Governance Code established a different view on the goal of intensified fund engagement, emphasising the responsibility for the issuers' sustainable growth.[21] This approach was subsequently adopted by a number of jurisdictions all over the world, the best-known example being the UK Stewardship Code of 2010.[22]

In its strictest interpretation, the stewardship idea entails a legal obligation to diligently exercise (at least some) voting rights in the long-term interests of the issuer,[23] as pension funds investing in domestic issuers are required under Swiss law.[24] A milder form, adopted by most countries, obliges institutional investors to publicly disclose a stewardship policy on a comply-or-explain basis.[25] The US Dodd-Frank Act chooses a middle position, providing for transparency on how funds cast their ballots on Say on Pay votes.[26]

[15] See D Arsalidou, 'Shareholders and Corporate Scrutiny: The Role of the UK Stewardship Code' (2012) 9 *European Company and Financial Law Review* 342; IHY Chiu, 'Learning from the UK in the Proposed Shareholders' Rights Directive 2014? European Corporate Governance Regulation from a UK Perspective' (2015) 114 *Zeitschrift für Vergleichende Rechtswissenschaft* 121.

[16] *cf* HS Birkmose, *Shareholders' Duties* (Alphen aan den Rijn, Wolters Kluwer, 2017).

[17] See AG Córcoles, 'Proxy Advisors in the Voting Process: Some Considerations for Future Regulation in Europe' (2016) 13 *European Company and Financial Law Review* 106, 115 ff (on the different approaches).

[18] 29 CFR § 2509.08-2; see C Mallin, 'Institutional Investors and Voting Practices: An International Comparison' (2002) 9 *Corporate Governance: An International Review* 118, 120.

[19] See E Dubois, 'Shareholders' General Meetings and the Role of Proxy Advisors in France and Japan' (2011) 4 *Kyushu Journal of International Legal Studies* 56, 85 f; but *cf* also below, n 71.

[20] OECD (2004) *Principles of Corporate Governance* 19, www.oecd.org/corporate/ca/corporategovernance principles/31557724.pdf.

[21] On the global reception of the UK Stewardship Code, see SCY Wong, 'Is Institutional Investor Stewardship Still Elusive?' (2015) *Butterworths Journal of International Banking and Financial Law* 508.

[22] Arsalidou (n 15) 348 ff, 353 f; *cf* IHY Chiu, 'International Shareholders as Stewards: Toward a New Conception of Corporate Governance' (2012) 6 *Brooklyn Journal of Corporate, Financial & Commercial Law* 387, 395 ff.

[23] Córcoles (n 17) 114–16; *cf* also Chiu (n 22) 404 ff.

[24] Verordnung gegen übermässige Vergütungen bei börsenkotierten Aktiengesellschaften of 20 November 2013, AS 2013, 4403; Y Hausmann and E Bechtold-Orth, 'Corporate Governance: Is Switzerland Outpacing Europe? A Comparative Legal Analysis of Current Developments' (2013) 14 *European Business Organization Law Review* 535, 546 f.

[25] For example, the UK Stewardship Code and the Italian Stewardship Code.

[26] § 951 Dodd-Frank Wall Street Reform and Consumer Protection Act, Pub L 111–203, HR 4173.

C. The Rise of Proxy Advisors

However, it has to be borne in mind that institutional investors a priori have no interest in engaging in corporate governance issues. Therefore, the stewardship regulation made them outsource their responsibilities. This phenomenon has been called the 'separation of voice from investment'.[27] And, as always, demand creates supply[28] – proxy advisors entered the scene! They are, so to speak, creatures of regulation.[29]

At first glance, this sounds like pretty good news:[30] professional voting should lead to better corporate governance – a 'promise of proxy advisor voice'! However, the market for proxy advice is characterised by substantial economies of scale and network effects.[31] Institutional investors require international coverage, not only regarding voting advice but also with respect to the actual exercise of voting rights.[32] The more investors rely on one advisor, the more diligent they seem to do so.[33]

Therefore, the market is characterised by substantial first mover advantages and – as a consequence – high entry barriers: established providers benefit from their large client base. In addition, quality of voting advice in terms of sustainable corporate governance is difficult to measure.[34] As a result, beginning in the 1980s, we witnessed a monopoly of Institutional Shareholder Services (ISS). This ended with the entry of Glass Lewis in 2003. So, today, we have an oligopolistic market and – on a global level – a duopoly.[35] Due to the entry barriers mentioned above, the situation does not seem to have changed. On the contrary, smaller market participants are taken over, as was the case with the German IVOX by Glass Lewis in 2015.[36] A similar fate is probably awaiting the UK Manifest – it is currently for sale.[37]

In any case, there is evidence that some competition is happening. However, it may not be the kind of competition we want; not qualitative competition, but rather price

[27] H Fleischer, 'Zur Rolle und Regulierung von Stimmrechtsberatern (Proxy Advisors) im deutschen und europäischen Aktien- und Kapitalmarktrecht' (2012) *Die Aktiengesellschaft* 2 (referring to the rise of proxy advisors as the 'fourth stage of capitalism').

[28] *cf* N Minow, 'Regulating Proxy Advisors is Anticompetitive, Counterproductive, and Possibly Unconstitutional' *Harvard Law School Forum on Corporate Governance and Financial Regulation* (2 March 2018) (recounting that ISS initially wanted to sell a different product, but was approached by institutional investors looking for proxy advice).

[29] *cf* M Chenoweth, 'Proxy Advisory Services: Making Glass (Lewis) Transparent – and ISS Too' *WLF Legal Pulse* (17 December 2013), wlflegalpulse.com/2013/12/17/proxy-advisory-services-time-for-transparency.

[30] *cf* Coffee (n 1) 1354 f on the potential positive effects of a proxy advisory industry.

[31] See Belinfanti (n 1) 411 ff; L Klöhn and P Schwarz, 'The Regulation of Proxy Advisors' (2013) 8 *Capital Markets Law Journal* 90; Fleischer (n 27) 11.

[32] P Rose, 'The Corporate Governance Industry' (2007) 32 *Journal of Corporation Law* 887, 919 ff; Center on Executive Compensation, *A Call for Change in the Proxy Advisory Industry Status Quo* (2011) 62 ff, online. wsj.com/public/resources/documents/ProxyAdvisoryWhitePaper02072011.pdf.

[33] P Rose, 'On the Role and Regulation of Proxy Advisors' (2010) 109 *Michigan Law Review First Impressions* 62, 64; Fleischer (n 27) 3; see also C Diamond and I Yevmenenko, 'Who is Overseeing Proxy Advisors?' (2008) 3 *Bloomberg Corporate Law Journal* 606.

[34] See below n 67; *cf* also section IV.C below.

[35] See recently 'Cracking the Proxy Racket – The SEC Withdraws Guidance that Built a Corporate-Governance Duopoly' *Wall Street Journal* (17 September 2018) (asserting a 97 per cent market share).

[36] Glass Lewis, 'Glass Lewis Acquires IVOX, Leading German Proxy Advisor' (11 June 2015), www.glasslewis.com/glass-lewis-acquires-ivox-leading-german-proxy-advisor.

[37] See A Mooney, 'Proxy Voting Agency Manifest Goes into Administration' *Financial Times* (16 March 2018).

competition, imposing additional entry barriers for potential competitors.[38] Again, remember that institutional investors do not really want to be stewards. Also, they do not really want to pay for corporate governance improvements. They simply want a cheap and quick way to fulfil their steward duties, if possible globally.[39]

This raises quality concerns. ISS has 370 analysts covering around 40,000 shareholders' meetings in 117 jurisdictions per year,[40] most of them in the proxy season. Therefore, a common complaint is that recommendations are based on stereotypes and do not take into account the individual corporation and its economic, social and legal environment.[41]

III. Conflicts of Interests

A. Issuer Bias

Furthermore, there are agency problems. In particular, ISS not only advises institutional investors on voting but also consults issuers on questions of corporate governance. This raises the fear of issuer bias.[42] However, there is evidence that the market entry of Glass Lewis at least mitigated the problem: in an in-depth study of the proxy advisory market from 2004 to 2011, Tao Li found significantly more contra-management recommendations by ISS once Glass Lewis covered a particular firm.[43] However, the effect depends not only on the complexity of the issue to be voted on, but also on the size of the concerned issuer: while the market entry of Glass Lewis does not appear to change recommendations in comparatively small corporations, it seemed to lead to a stricter approach towards managements of larger issuers by ISS.[44] A possible explanation for this is that, without competition, ISS is overly friendly to large issuers that are likely to be customers in corporate governance consultancy and/or proxy advice.

[38] See especially Belinfanti (n 1) 415 ff. *cf* also Center on Executive Compensation (n 32) 62 ff.

[39] See above, sections II.A and B.

[40] Institutional Shareholder Services, 'Best Practice Principles for Providers of Shareholder Voting Research & Analysis – ISS Compliance Statement' *Institutional Shareholder Services* (19 April 2017), www.issgovernance.com/file/duediligence/best-practices-principles-iss-compliance-statement-april-2017-update.pdf.

[41] For example, Rose (n 32) 918; P Böckli, 'Proxy Advisors: Risikolose Stimmenmacht mit Checklisten' (2015) *Schweizerische Zeitschrift für Wirtschaftsrecht* 209. See also CM Nathan and P Metha, 'The Parallel Universes of Institutional Investing and Institutional Voting' *Harvard Law School Forum on Corporate Governance and Financial Regulation* (6 April 2010), corpgov.law.harvard.edu/2010/04/06/the-parallel-universes-of-institutional-investing-and-institutional-voting: 'Voting decision makers do not and cannot utilize the tools of investment decision makers because it is simply not feasible to do so in the cost environment in which proxy advisors and internal corporate governance staffs are required to operate.'

[42] *cf* JN Gordon, '"Say on Pay": Cautionary Notes on the U.K. Experience and the Case for Shareholder Opt-in' (2009) 46 *Harvard Journal on Legislation* 323, 352 f. See also ESMA, *An Overview of the Proxy Advisory Industry. Considerations on Possible Policy Options* (Discussion Paper, ESMA/2012/212, 22 March 2012) paras 64 ff.

[43] T Li, 'Outsourcing Corporate Governance: Conflicts of Interest and Competition in the Proxy Advisory Industry' (2016) 64 *Management Science* 2951, 2961–64. See also R Aggarwal, I Erel and LT Starks, 'Influence of Public Opinion on Investor Voting and Proxy Advisors' (2014) *Fisher College of Business Working Paper* 2014-03-12, ssrn.com/abstract=2447012.

[44] Li (n 43) 2964-65.

B. Fund Bias

In addition, there is another and somewhat opposite concern about conflicts of interests.[45] Advisors in their core business depend on large investment companies such as Blackrock, Vanguard and State Street, which together share more than 70 per cent of the Exchange Traded Fund (ETF) market.[46] Also, the majority shareholder of Glass Lewis is the Ontario Teachers' Pension Plan board.[47] Both facts raise the concern of a fund bias.

C. Activist Bias

Finally, large institutional investors have recently expressed the concern that proxy advisors might be too open to activist shareholders lobbying for their proposals and therefore to short-term pressures.[48] As a result, the fund industry started to articulate its views and preferences through the newly formed Investor Stewardship Group.[49] This may be conceived as a countermeasure against the widespread allegation that proxy advisors are too fund-friendly,[50] or as a direct response to competition by active funds and to ensuing collective action problems in the passive fund industry,[51] or both.

IV. Legislative Options

A. The Case for Legislation in Europe

Arguably, a situation where every stakeholder has some concerns is a good compromise. Still, the quality problem mentioned above might make a case for legislation, as a market solution is unlikely, given the price-over-quality preference on the demand side.[52]

[45] *cf* ESMA, *Follow-up on the Development of the Best Practice Principles for Providers of Shareholder Voting Research and Analysis* (Report, ESMA/2015/1887, 18 December 2015) paras 46, 74 (classic conflicts of interests ameliorated).

[46] T Team, 'The Three Largest Players Have a 70% Market Share in $4 Trillion Global ETF Industry' *Forbes* (17 May 2017), www.forbes.com/sites/greatspeculations/2017/05/17/the-three-largest-players-have-a-70-market-share-in-4-trillion-global-etf-industry/#4479273861f6.

[47] Glass Lewis, 'Company Overview', www.glasslewis.com/company-overview.

[48] See, eg, Blackrock, '2017 BPP Consultation: Questionnaire' *Best Practice Principles Group* (15 December 2017) Q11, bppgrp.info/wp-content/uploads/2018/01/Blackrock.pdf; M Kahan and EB Rock, 'Hedge Funds in Corporate Governance and Corporate Control' (2007) 155 *University of Pennsylvania Law Review* 1021, 1043 f.

[49] See M Lipton, 'Promoting Long-Term Value Creation – The Launch of the Investor Stewardship Group (ISG) and ISG's Framework for U.S. Stewardship and Governance' *Harvard Law School Forum on Corporate Governance and Financial Regulation* (1 February 2017), corpgov.law.harvard.edu/2017/02/01/promoting-long-term-value-creation-the-launch-of-the-investor-stewardship-group-isg-and-isgs-framework-for-u-s-stewardship-and-governance.

[50] *cf* section III.A above.

[51] *cf* JE Fisch, A Hamdani and SD Solomon, 'Passive Investors' (2018) *European Corporate Governance Institute Law Working Paper* 414/2018, 19–20, ssrn.com/abstract=3192069.

[52] *cf* PH Edelman, RS Thomas and RB Thompson, 'Shareholder Voting in an Age of Intermediary Capitalism' (2014) 87 *Southern California Law Review* 1359, 1425: 'proxy advisory firms often function as independent verifiers of the truth of the hedge funds' claims and the target company management's counterclaims'.

This is even more true given the impact that proxy advice is believed to have on voting outcomes, in particular on directors' elections and Say on Pay votes.[53] Yet, the degree of influence is difficult to determine, cause and effect being uncertain. In a methodologically impressive paper, Malenko and Shen used an ISS policy on Say on Pay providing that compensation proposals were reviewed in depth only if the company belonged to the bottom half in terms of total shareholder return. This, they found, led to significantly more negative voting recommendations just below the cut-off than just above. The authors show that investors' votes followed this rather arbitrary pattern.[54]

However, the correlation between recommendations and actual voting behaviour depends, inter alia, on the transaction costs associated with decision-making and with voting itself. Iliev and Lowry have shown that mutual funds with above-median total net assets are significantly less likely to follow voting advice than their smaller counterparts. Other relevant factors include the length of holding periods and exposure of fund managers to social interaction.[55]

B. The European Securities and Markets Authority's Evaluation and the Amended Shareholders' Rights Directive of 2017

Transaction costs also serve as an explanation for an especially high degree of consistency between recommendations and voting behaviour when US funds invest abroad: a number of recent studies show that in Europe, where the Commission estimated in 2014 that approximately 44 per cent of the investments were foreign,[56] conformity of voting with recommendations is significantly higher than in the US.[57]

This could well be one of the reasons why the regulation of proxy advisors was first introduced in Europe, whereas a 2014 Securities and Exchange Commission (SEC) Staff Legal Bulletin only reduced the incentives to buy voting advice by expressing the opinion that institutional investors are under no legal obligation to exercise their voting rights.[58] The European Securities and Markets Authority (ESMA), on the other hand, started a consultation process in 2011 that led to the decision to 'actively encourage

[53] See S Choi, J Fisch and M Kahan, 'The Power of Proxy Advisors: Myth or Reality?' (2010) 59 *Emory Law Journal* 869; Y Ertimur, F Ferri and V Muslu, 'Shareholder Activism and CEO Pay' (2011) 24 *Review of Financial Studies* 535; P Iliev and M Lowry, 'Are Mutual Funds Active Voters?' (2015) 28 *Review of Financial Studies* 446.

[54] See N Malenko and Y Shen, 'The Role of Proxy Advisory Firms: Evidence from a Regression-Discontinuity Design' (2016) 29 *Review of Financial Studies* 3394, 3404–11.

[55] Iliev and Lowry (n 53) 453–56.

[56] Proposal for a Directive of the European Parliament and of the Council amending Directive 2007/36/EC as regards the encouragement of long-term shareholder engagement and Directive 2013/34/EU as regards certain elements of the corporate governance statement of 9 April 2014, COM(2014) 213 final 3.

[57] M Belcredi, S Bozzi, A Ciavarella and V Novembre, 'Institutional Investors' Activism under Concentrated Ownership and the Role of Proxy Advisors: Evidence from the Italian Say-on-Pay' (2017) 14 *Corporate Ownership & Control* 41. See also S McGinty and K Uchida, 'What Roles Proxy Advisors Play: Evidence from International Comparison' (2015), ssrn.com/abstract=2666078; JM Hitz and N Lehmann, 'Empirical Evidence on the Role of Proxy Advisors in European Capital Markets' (2017) 27 *European Accounting Review* 713.

[58] Securities and Exchange Commission, *Proxy Voting: Proxy Voting Responsibilities of Investment Advisers and Availability of Exemptions from the Proxy Rules for Proxy Advisory Firms* (Staff Legal Bulletin No 20, 30 June 2014). On the effects of the release (and its somewhat unclear general approach), see Rock (n 9) 378–81.

the industry to self-regulate'.[59] Subsequently, the leading proxy advisors published Best Practice Principles (BPPs) on a comply-or-explain basis 'to help clients and stakeholders understand the market'.[60]

Although these Principles are rather vague and do not go beyond the industry standard quo ante,[61] the EU seemed satisfied:[62] after some dilution in the legislative process, Article 3j, paragraph 1 of the amended Shareholders' Rights Directive of 2017 (SRD II) provides that proxy advisors have to comply with a code of conduct or explain otherwise.[63]

'Soft law' seems to be an appropriate means to promote transparency. However, in this case, the comply-or-explain mechanism is somehow perverted: in the corporate governance context, complying means to follow some substantive rule or principle that the code lays out.[64] The BPP, which is the only code that exists, provides little more than headlines. In particular, Principle Two regarding 'Conflicts-of-Interest Management' only provides that: 'Signatories should have and publicly disclose a conflicts-of-interest policy that details their procedures for addressing potential or actual conflicts-of-interest that may arise in connection with the provision of services.' The 'Guidance' to this Principle contains a list of issues to be addressed in the policy and 'Possible Conflicts for Consideration', including the advisor's ownership structure and consulting services provided to issuers.[65] Therefore, the Principles do not contain a substantive default rule that has to be followed unless explained otherwise, such as: 'The advisor does not provide consulting services to issuers covered.' On the contrary, according to the BPP, the signatories may: 'In addition to shareholder voting research and analysis services … also provide other services, such as vote agency and/or engagement and governance overlay services.'

The lack of substantive principles is possibly the reason why Article 3j, paragraph 2 SRD II provides that proxy advisors have to publicly disclose at least a number of facts about their services, including voting policies, methods and a 'policy regarding the prevention and management of potential conflicts of interests'. Interestingly, the list is more or less copied from the BPPs, which, as mentioned above, were and are the industry standard.

Article 3j, paragraph 2 SRD II thereby works as a minimum standard in relation to the comply-or-explain mechanism of paragraph 1. This twofold regulation makes gathering information on a particular advisor burdensome, especially since the reference to

[59] ESMA, *Feedback Statement on the Consultation Regarding the Role of the Proxy Advisory Industry* (Final Report, ESMA/2013/84, 19 February 2013) para 108.

[60] Best Practice Principles Group, *Best Practice Principles for Providers of Shareholder Voting Research & Analysis* (2014), bppgrp.info/wp-content/uploads/2014/03/BPP-ShareholderVoting-Research-2014.pdf.

[61] *cf* Klöhn and Schwarz (n 31) 90; Böckli (n 41) 221–22.

[62] See also ESMA, *Follow-up on the Development of the Best Practice Principles* (n 45) paras 116 ff.

[63] *cf* Recital 8 of Regulation 1060/2009/EC: 'Credit rating agencies should, on a voluntary basis, apply the Code of Conduct Fundamentals for credit rating agencies issued by the International Organisation of Securities Commissions (IOSCO Code).' On further parallels, see Fleischer (n 27) 7–10.

[64] See, eg, K Sergakis, 'EU Corporate Governance: A New Supervisory Mechanism for the "Comply or Explain" Principle?' (2013) 10 *European Company and Financial Law Review* 394, 408 f; P Leyens, 'Comply or Explain im Europäischen Privatrecht' (2016) *Zeitschrift für Europäisches Privatrecht* 388.

[65] Best Practice Principles Group, *Best Practice Principles for Providers of Shareholder Voting Research & Analysis* (2014) 10.

a code under paragraph 1 is basically worthless without an additional examination of the policy of its originator.[66]

On the whole, it seems that the EU did not want to be too troublesome to the industry. It is a paper tiger, even though Article 14b of the Directive obliges Member States to lay down measures and penalties that are effective, proportionate and dissuasive. In any case, Article 3j will most likely not help to solve the quality problem described, the transparency of this quality and accessibility being insufficient to make dispersed funds and investors rethink their preference for low-cost, high-performing funds over hardly measurable long-term benefit.[67]

C. A Comparative Look at the US

Remarkably, at first glance, the US seems to follow this lenient approach in its Corporate Governance Reform and Transparency Act of 2017, which is currently awaiting senate approval following the hearings which were held in the Senate Committee on Banking, Housing, and Urban Affairs in the summer of 2018.[68] The new § 15H (b) of the amended Securities Exchange Act would require public disclosure that more or less looks like a blueprint of Article 3j SRD II.

Still, there is an important difference: § 15H will require registration with the SEC. Duties of registered advisors include, inter alia, management of conflicts of interests and sufficient staff to produce recommendations that are based on accurate information. Proxy advisors will also have to report, for example, the number of recommendations issued in one year and the number of staff involved. The goal seems to be an indirect qualitative supervision by the SEC, similar to that of credit rating agencies under § 15E of the Securities Exchange Act.[69] Also, the SEC would be given the power to issue final rules on conflicts of interests and on behaviour that is deemed to be unfair. This proposal certainly does not look like a paper tiger.

What does this mean for Europe? An assessment of Article 3j SRD II is due in 2023 (Article 3k). The most obvious and perhaps the easiest strategy in political terms would probably be to copy US legislation if it has been passed by then. Its focus on quality

[66] *cf* K Sergakis, 'Deconstruction and Reconstruction of the "Comply or Explain" Principle in EU Capital Markets' (2015) 5 *Accounting, Economics and Law* 233, 252–53 (pointing to encouraged superficiality as a result of a minimally invasive comply-or-explain concept).

[67] *cf* Böckli (n 41) 214; HS Birkmose, 'European Challenges for Institutional Investor Engagement – Is Mandatory Disclosure the Way Forward' (2014) 11 *European Company and Financial Law Review* 214, 252; Rock (n 9) 33. See also JA Johnston and P Morrow, 'Towards Long-Termism in Corporate Governance: The Shareholder Rights Directive and beyond' in S Vitols (ed), *Long-Term Investment and the Sustainable Company: A Stakeholder Perspective*, vol III (Brussels, ETUI, 2015) 19, 29–31; similarly, on the UK Corporate Governance Code, see S Arcot, V Bruno and A Faure-Grimaud, 'Corporate Governance in the UK: Is the Comply or Explain Approach Working?' (2010) 30 *International Review of Law and Economics* 193, 197–99.

[68] Corporate Governance Reform and Transparency Act of 2017, 115th Cong, HR 4015. A similar but less intrusive proposal brought before the 114th Congress has not been adopted; Corporate Governance Reform and Transparency Act of 2015, 114th Cong, HR 5311.

[69] See (on the concerns about quality voiced by Congress) DA Katz and T Norwitz, 'Congress Increases Pressure on Proxy Advisory Firms' *Harvard Law School Forum on Corporate Governance and Financial Regulation* (23 May 2018); *cf* also S Seelig and P Arora, 'The Regulation of Proxy Advisors' *Harvard Law School Forum on Corporate Governance and Financial Regulation* (3 August 2018).

should be easy to sell to the public.[70] Beforehand, the EU would have to reach a consensus on the question of in whose interest proxy advisors are actually supposed to operate, namely as fiduciaries of their subscribers (which would correspond to the contractual relationship), as stewards for issuers (which would force proxy advisors to play a role that diverges from what they are paid for, but seems to be favoured by the French AMF)[71] or even to the benefit of society as a whole (whatever that precisely means).[72]

In any case, in my opinion, supervision by ESMA or Member States is not desirable. As a rule of thumb, a higher degree of regulation tends to benefit larger market participants. Therefore, it would raise entry barriers to an already oligopolistic market. Also, qualitative supervision is difficult to accomplish; in fact, it has to focus on process.[73] But what are the parameters? The US bill apparently chooses the number of employees per recommendation. This seems reasonable and resembles ESMA's mandate under Article 7 of Regulation 1060/2009/EC on credit rating agencies. However, proxy advisors do not seem to have a systemic importance similar to that of credit rating agencies. Also, governmental supervision would, if at all, appear appropriate if proxy advisors were to be measured against their effect on issuers, the financial markets or even society, which, as mentioned above, would not be in line with demand-side interests and therefore could probably prove inefficient. Moreover, it is questionable whether public authorities are in a good position to determine suitable benchmarks.[74]

This case against governmental supervision becomes even stronger if we recognise that proxy advisors are fiduciaries of their clients (and their clients alone) and therefore it is for the market for advice to determine the appropriate amount of quality and its price. Also, there is the question of regulatory reach. After all, the business is more or less about US firms advising US clients.[75]

Finally and perhaps most importantly: supervision adds legitimacy to recommendations. This 'certification effect' would probably increase convergence of voting behaviour and voting advice, adding to the 'lemming problem' it should instead solve. It could lead to a comply-or-explain situation in which following a recommendation is a safe

[70] *cf* J Copland, DF Larcker and B Tayan, 'The Big Thumb on the Scale: An Overview of the Proxy Advisory Industry' *Stanford Closer Look Series* (30 May 2018) 7 (arguing for qualitative intervention based on an assertion of market failure).

[71] See Autorité des Marchés Financiers, *Agences de conseil en vote* (Recommandation AMF no 2011–06, 18 March 2011), proposing that proxy advisors submit draft reports to issuers. On the (non-binding) approach, see Dubois (n 19) 102 ff.

[72] *cf* section II.B above.

[73] See G Balp, 'Regulating Proxy Advisors through Transparency: Pros and Cons of the EU Approach' (2017) 14 *European Company and Financial Law Review* 1; *cf* art 8 of Regulation 1060/2009/EC on credit rating agencies (mandating the use of 'rigorous, systematic, continuous' and validated rating methodologies and prescribing internal quality management).

[74] See the critique on the US bill in, eg, Minow (n 28); K Bertsch, 'The Regulation of Proxy Advisory Firms' *Harvard Law School Forum on Corporate Governance and Financial Regulation* (26 September 2016); *cf* also Seelig and Arora (n 69) on the arguments of the opposition.

[75] The latter part constitutes an important difference to the regulation of credit rating agencies under Regulation 1060/2009/EC, as amended by Regulation 462/2013/EU [2013] OJ L146/1. For ratings, the EU made use of a 'trick', expanding regulatory reach by restricting European lenders from using ratings of agencies not registered in the EU; *cf* R Veil, '§ 27 Rating Agencies' in R Veil (ed), *European Capital Markets Law*, 2nd edn (Oxford, Hart Publishing, 2017) paras 48 f. However, this approach is of limited use if most customers are themselves non-European. If EU legislation is too costly, proxy advisors could therefore choose to close their European establishments, escaping the scope of art 3j SRD II (*cf* art 3j, para 4).

harbour for fund managers, creating even more incentives to draw on proxy advisors in voting decisions. Therefore, supervision might well be a putative solution exacerbating the reasons why the market for proxy advice developed in the first place.[76] A similar concern was voiced in connection with the European Credit Rating Agency Regulation, but was set aside due to the profound systemic relevance of that industry.[77] As already mentioned, proxy advisory does not carry the same weight.

In addition, as mentioned above, there is at least some competition in the market for proxy advice and growing pressure from the client side.[78] Also, the quality problem is probably overestimated. Paul Calluzzo and Evan Dudley have shown that the recommendation-correlation of votings and the ISS coverage of an issuer overall appear to have positive effects on corporate governance.[79] Indeed, voting recommendations are far from perfect, but nevertheless they might be better than nothing. Finally, it appears that investment managers are becoming increasingly aware that proxy advice is a means of information and nothing more.[80] A growing number of fund managers rely on more than one advisor;[81] in Austria, the number of double-subscriptions tripled from 2010 to 2014.[82] Therefore, the market seems to mitigate the 'lemming problem', while the opposite might result from a possible 'certification effect' of increased supervision.[83]

V. Conclusion

To sum up, the author does not think that there is a case for a paradigm shift towards governmental supervision of proxy advisors in line with the US proposal. However, there is certainly ample room for improvement.

First, a market solution would benefit from increased accountability of proxy advisors. Even the industry and even more their clients emphasise the fiduciary duties

[76] Securities and Exchange Commission, *Proxy Voting*; *cf* also above n 33.

[77] *cf* Recital 49 of Regulation 462/2013/EU (n 75).

[78] See especially Rock (n 9) 381 ff.

[79] P Calluzzo and E Dudley, 'The Real Effects of Proxy Advisors on the Firm' (2017), ssrn.com/abstract=2619698. This is supported by other studies, at least when determined on the advisor's own standards: RM Daines, ID Gow and DF Larcker, 'Rating the Ratings: How Good are Commercial Governance Ratings?' (2010) 98 *Journal of Financial Economics* 439.

[80] Helping this development are clarifications by the SEC and stewardship codes that following a proxy advisor is not sufficient, eg, in the Staff Legal Bulletin No 20 (n 58) and via obligatory disclosure of the use of proxy advisors; *cf* Diamond and Yevmenenko (n 33) 606. However, see Malenko and Shen (n 54) 3420–22 (showing that proxy advisory influence does not vary with the information content of the respective recommendation).

[81] See SJ Choi, JE Fisch and M Kahan, 'Voting through Agents: How Mutual Funds Vote on Director Elections' (2011) *NYU Law and Economics Research Paper 11–29*, 45, ssrn.com/abstract=1912772; Dubois (n 19) 90; however, see the Investment Management Association and Pensions and Lifetime Savings Association, 'Stewardship in Practice – Asset Managers and Asset Owners' (2017) 16, www.theinvestmentassociation.org//assets//files/Stewardship_report_FINAL_1.pdf (more than half of respondents only used one proxy advisor in 2016).

[82] See M Hössl and U Torggler, 'Stimmrechtsberater, institutionelle Investoren und die Änderung der Aktionärsrechte-Richtlinie' (2016) *Der Gesellschafter – GesRZ* 185, 190.

[83] See A Eckstein, 'Great Expectations: The Peril of an Expectations Gap in Proxy Advisory Firm Regulation' (2015) 40 *Delaware Journal of Corporate Law* 77; GW Dent, 'A Defense of Proxy Advisors' (2014) *Michigan State Law Review* 1287.

advisors owe to their clients.[84] However, these duties do not seem to be enforced. Article 35a of the European Regulation on Credit Rating Agencies could serve as a model. It stipulates liability of credit rating agencies vis-a-vis issuers and investors for gross negligence. In the case of proxy advisors, the liability towards clients should be non-waivable, as funds have an incentive to buy cheaper advice on a non-reliance basis.[85]

Second, transparency could and should be improved, namely requiring *meaningful* information.[86] For example, Blackrock has recently demanded more 'meat on the bones' with regard to the disclosure by proxy advisors,[87] in particular regarding their interaction with activist investors.[88] Similarly, the Financial Reporting Council (FRC) in its revised UK Corporate Governance Code of July 2018 has made an effort to improve the comply-or-explain mechanism with respect to issuers, emphasising the importance of the ability of investors to evaluate the approach to governance:[89] 'By reporting on the application of the Principles in a manner that can be evaluated, companies should demonstrate how the governance of the company contributes to its long-term sustainable success and achieves wider objectives.'[90]

This approach could serve as an example for a revision of Article 3j SRD II – namely, the provision should ensure that a single document in connection with a code enables funds and investors to obtain information on the *content* of the substantive rules a proxy advisor follows with respect to critical issues, in particular regarding conflicts of interests (and not only on the existence of such rules). If the industry does not come up with suitable principles,[91] someone else would have to step in, eg, the Commission.

An alternative (or additional) proposal calls for an institutional monitoring mechanism with regard to public disclosure, entailing 'naming and shaming' actors that are not dedicated to the disclosure process.[92] However, the author is not sure whether disclosure monitoring would stand up to a cost-benefit analysis. Ultimately, it might raise similar concerns to a governmental supervision of proxy advisors.

[84] *cf* A Meyer, D Cassidy and R Kumar, 'The Investor Stewardship Group's Governance Principles' *Harvard Law School Forum on Corporate Governance and Financial Regulation* (11 May 2018), corpgov.law.harvard.edu/2018/05/11/the-investor-stewardship-groups-governance-principles.

[85] *cf* Balp (n 73) 32–34.

[86] *cf* SJ Choi, JE Fisch and M Kahan, 'Director Elections and the Role of Proxy Advisors' (2009) 82 *Southern California Law Review* 649, 659: 'Even with respect to practices about which the advisors provide substantial detail, there is no way to determine a specific recommendation from the general policies described'; DF Larcker, AL McCall and B Tayan, 'And Then a Miracle Happens! How Do Proxy Advisory Firms Develop Their Voting Recommendations?' *Stanford Closer Look Series* (25 February 2013) 1.

[87] Blackrock (n 48) Q35.

[88] ibid Q11, Q24.

[89] Financial Reporting Council, *The UK Corporate Governance Code* (July 2018) 2. For the underlying problems, see Chiu and Katelouzou, 'Making a Case for Regulating Institutional Shareholders; Corporate Governance Roles' (2017) *King's College London Law School Research Paper* 2017–13, 22–32, ssrn.com/abstract=2896748.

[90] Financial Reporting Council, *Consulting on a Revised UK Corporate Governance Code* (Feedback Statement, July 2018) 2. The preceding consultation also addressed the UK Stewardship Code and proxy advisors; Financial Reporting Council, *Consulting on a Revised UK Corporate Governance Code* 2, 24 ff; *cf* also Financial Reporting Council, *The UK Corporate Governance Code* 2; W Bischoff, 'Open Letter from Sir Win to Proxy Advisors' *Financial Reporting Council* (20 July 2018), frc.org.uk/getattachment/179a7bd1-9fef-4f6c-94b0-3ecb882c2d05/Open-letter-from-Sir-Win-to-proxy-advisors-about-2018-Code-July-2018.pdf.

[91] Starting with a consultation in 2017, an 'Independent Review on the operation of the Principles' is underway; an update to the Principles will address the transparency requirements under SRD II; see bppgrp.info/best-practice-principles-shareholder-voting-research-review-update.

[92] Sergakis (n 66) 272–83.

PART III

Developments in Business Law

9

Financial Reporting in European Stock Corporations

GIOVANNI STRAMPELLI

I. Introduction

Financial reporting is a core component of the transparency regime of joint stock companies in Europe. All European joint stock companies are required to prepare individual and (as far as parent companies are concerned) consolidated accounts for each financial year. While consolidated accounts serve only to provide information, individual accounts have a dual function. On the one hand, according to the legal capital system laid down by Directive 2012/30/EU (now merged into Directive 2017/1132/EU), individual annual accounts serve as a legal basis for shareholders' decisions concerning distributions of dividends, the reduction of capital to cover losses, increases in the share capital by the capitalisation of reserves, share buybacks or financial assistance transactions. On the other hand, individual annual financial statements (together with consolidated financial statements) are a further source of information for shareholders, creditors and (especially for public companies) investors, providing an insight into the company's circumstances and (within certain limits) its likely future development.

However, the importance of the information function of financial reporting largely depends on the size of the company and, particularly, on whether its shares (and bonds) are traded on financial markets. Moreover, such a different relevance of the information function also influences the accounting regime applicable to listed and non-listed companies, respectively.

Indeed, under European law, company accounts may be prepared in accordance with the national rules transposing the 2013 Accounting Directive (consolidating the repealed Fourth and Seventh Company Law Directives)[1] or the International Accounting Standards/International Financial Reporting Standards (IAS/IFRS) principles

[1] European Parliament and Council Directive 2013/34/EU of 26 June 2013 on the annual financial statements, consolidated financial statements and related reports of certain types of undertakings, amending Directive 2006/43/EC of the European Parliament and of the Council and repealing Council Directives 78/660/EEC and 83/349/EEC [2013] OJ L182/19 (2013 Accounting Directive).

adopted by the European Commission according to the procedure set forth by Article 3 of Regulation (EC) 1606/2002.[2]

As the European Commission believes that it is able to ensure a high degree of transparency and comparability for financial reporting,[3] the IAS/IFRS form the bedrock of the issuer accounting disclosure regime. Under the IAS Regulation, all European issuers admitted to trading on a regulated market must prepare their consolidated accounts in accordance with the IAS/IFRS adopted by the European Commission.[4] Moreover, Member States can permit or require issuers to also prepare individual accounts in accordance with the IAS/IFRS.[5]

In addition, according to Article 5 of the IAS Regulation, Member States also have the power to permit or require non-listed companies to prepare their consolidated and/or individual accounts in accordance with the IAS/IFRS. However, as has been noted by the Commission, the 'compulsory use of IFRS does not appear to have been widely extended to non-listed companies' (and individual financial statements of listed companies).[6]

The limited extension of the IAS/IFRS to non-listed companies and, especially, to medium, small and micro-undertakings is not at all surprising. Indeed, as far as these undertakings are concerned, the publication of the company's accounts plays a less crucial role, since (more sophisticated) third parties contracting with the company should be expected to already have the relevant information or to be able to contract for their own protection, including in relation to the necessary disclosure.[7] Therefore, according to the 'think small first' principle,[8] the 2013 Accounting Directive provides Member States with the power to exempt medium, small and micro-undertakings – as defined by reference to balance sheet total, net turnover and the average number of employees during the financial year – from certain obligations applicable to large undertakings that would impose excessive administrative burdens on them.[9]

Nevertheless, it remains questionable whether the two-pronged European accounting regime is capable of fulfilling the objective set forth by the Commission and, namely, to 'strike an appropriate balance between the interests of the addressees of financial statements and the interest of undertakings in not being unduly burdened with reporting requirements'.[10] On the one hand, while the IAS/IFRS seek to provide the addressees of financial statements with the relevant information, their application can prove to be too expensive for smaller listed companies.[11] On the other hand, simplifications provided under the 2013 Accounting Directive alleviate accounting-related costs for medium, small and, especially, micro-undertakings, but can significantly limit the relevance of the information contained in the annual accounts.

[2] European Parliament and Council Regulation (EC) No 1606/2002 of 19 July 2002 on the application of international accounting standards [2002] OJ L243/1 (IAS Regulation).

[3] ibid recital 7.

[4] ibid art 4.

[5] ibid art 5.

[6] Commission, 'Evaluation of Regulation (EC) No 1606/2002 of 19 July 2002 on the application of International Accounting Standard' COM(2015) 301 final 8.

[7] J Armour et al, *Principles of Financial Regulation* (Oxford, Oxford University Press, 2016) 167.

[8] Commission, 'Think Small First – A "Small Business Act" for Europe' COM (2008) 394 final.

[9] 2013 Accounting Directive, recital 4.

[10] ibid.

[11] R Kraakman, 'Disclosure and Corporate Governance: An Overview Essay' in G Ferrarini et al (eds), *Reforming Company and Takeover Law in Europe* (Oxford, Oxford University Press, 2004) 95, 102.

Against this background, in 2018, the European Commission launched a consultation with the aim of evaluating the fitness of the EU public reporting framework by assessing, among other things, whether the costs imposed by the EU financial reporting regime are proportionate to the benefits generated. The consultation has attracted considerable interest and stakeholders from 23 Member States and 25 third countries submitted 338 responses. Although the final results of the fitness check are not yet available, this chapter will consider whether the EU accounting regime is capable of meeting addressees' information needs without imposing an excessive cost burden on undertakings.

In order to achieve this aim, this chapter will proceed as follows. Section II will provide an overview of the parallel European accounting regime in place. Section III will consider whether the IAS/IFRS and the 2013 Accounting Directive are capable of meeting the information needs of addressees and will illustrate the potential shortcomings of the current regime. Section IV will analyse the cost burdens imposed on undertakings by the IAS/IFRS and the 2013 Accounting Directive. Given the doubts that have been cast on the suitability of the IAS/IFRS for fulfilling investors' information needs, based on the UK experience with the so-called Strategic Report, section V will contend that a clear and concise narrative report focusing on the essential aspects of the company's business, circumstances, strategies and governance may be useful in reducing the potential shortcomings of IAS/IFRS accounts. Section VI will set out concluding remarks.

II. The Twofold EU Accounting Regime

Both the 2013 Accounting Directive and the IAS/IFRS pursue the objective of providing the addressees of financial statements with the relevant information. According to Article 4(3) of the 2013 Accounting Directive: 'The annual financial statements shall give a true and fair view of the undertaking's assets, liabilities, financial position and profit or loss.' Similarly, paragraph 9 of IAS 1 states that: 'The objective of financial statements is to provide information about the financial position, financial performance and cash flows of an entity that is useful to a wide range of users in making economic decisions.' However, given their general wording, these provisions do not actually highlight the significant differences existing between the historical cost-based Accounting Directive and the more future-oriented IAS/IFRS.[12]

A. Directive 2013/34/EU

Under the 2013 Accounting Directive, companies' accounts seek to serve different objectives. As specified by recital 4 of the Directive: 'Annual financial statements … do

[12] See, eg, L Enriques et al, 'Corporate Law and Securities Markets' in R Kraakman et al (eds), *The Anatomy of Corporate Law: A Comparative and Functional Approach*, 3rd edn (Oxford, Oxford University Press, 2017) 252–53: 'Traditionally, valuation has looked either to historical cost, which captures the conservative thrust of continental accounting, or to "fair market value", which tracks the interests of equity holders.'

not merely provide information for investors in capital markets but also give an account of past transactions and enhance corporate governance.'

However, this statement does not tell the full story. Indeed, in order to actually understand the logic of the 2013 Accounting Directive, it is necessary to consider the interplay between a company's accounts and the legal capital rules that lie at the heart of the legal capital-based creditor protection system imposed on limited liability companies under Directive 2017/1132/EU. As is widely recognised, in continental Europe, the prudent determination of distributable profits (and taxable income) is the primary objective of individual financial statements.[13]

Therefore, notwithstanding the 'true and fair view' requirement laid down by Article 4 of the 2013 Accounting Directive, the capital maintenance-related objectives influence the overall accounting system designed by the Accounting Directive; consequently, the principle of prudence plays a major role.[14]

A first notable implication of this prudence-based approach are the principles of realisation and 'dissymmetry' (*Imparität Prinzip*), according to which, in the first place, only profits realised at the balance sheet date may be recognised and, second, losses must be recognised at the balance sheet date where they are likely to be incurred or where it is certain that they will be incurred, but the amount or date is uncertain. In addition, Article 6 of the Directive stipulates the historical cost as the chief basis for measurement, as it prevents the recognition of unrealised profits.[15]

Nevertheless, the 2013 Accounting Directive recognises the potential limits of historical cost accounting by stating that 'Member States should be allowed to permit or require undertakings to revalue fixed assets in order that more relevant information may be provided to the users of financial statements'.[16] First, Article 7 – although without making any explicit reference to the notion of fair value[17] – allows for the evaluation of the value of assets on the basis of measurement techniques other than historical cost, which substantially coincide with the fair value technique. Second, Article 8 sets forth a further derogation from historical cost accounting by allowing Member States to permit or require the recognition, measurement and disclosure of financial instruments in accordance with international accounting standards adopted under Regulation (EC) No 1606/2002.[18]

Therefore, where Member States provide for this alternative accounting treatment, the valuation of financial instruments can be based on fair value, which is determined by reference to the market value, as detected by prices on active markets, characterised by transactions that are easily and regularly available to operators. Where there are no active markets, it is necessary to refer to normal transactions or, potentially, to current market values for similar activities or even, alternatively, to the present value of cash flows generated by the asset being valued.

[13] See, eg, RU Fülbier et al, 'The Role and Current Status of IFRS in the Completion of National Accounting Rules – Evidence from Austria and Germany' (2017) 14 *Accounting in Europe* 13, 14.

[14] See, eg, K van Hulle, 'Prudence: A Principle or an Attitude?' (1996) 5 *European Accounting Review* 375.

[15] See, eg, K van Hulle, 'The True and Fair View Override in the European Accounting Directives' (1997) 6 *European Accounting Review* 711, 715.

[16] 2013 Accounting Directive, recital 18.

[17] ibid art 7, para 1, referring to revalued amounts whose content, limits and rules for application shall be defined at the national level.

[18] ibid art 8, para 7.

As the use of bases for measurement other than historical cost implies the recognition of unrealised profits, the 2013 Accounting Directive sets out safeguards aimed at preserving the function of financial statements as a basis for the calculation of distributable profits and, more generally, for the capital maintenance rules. According to Article 7(2), the amount of the difference between measurement on a historical cost basis and measurement on a revaluation basis shall be entered into the balance sheet in an undistributable revaluation reserve, which may be capitalised in whole or in part at any time and shall be reduced where the amounts transferred to that reserve are no longer necessary for the implementation of the revaluation basis of accounting.

The rule laid down by Article 7(2) shows that derogations from prudential historical cost accounting and the adoption of an alternative valuation basis that is (admittedly) capable of providing more relevant information are not necessarily at odds with the prudential calculation of distributable profits relevant under company law.

Nevertheless, only a few Member States allow for derogation from historical cost and the adoption of alternative bases for measurement. Hence, national rules transposing the 2013 Accounting Directive are generally based on a past-oriented accounting approach, which is primarily suitable to act as a basis for the calculation of distributable profits and for capital maintenance rules. Thus, although the 2013 Accounting Directive does not explicitly target any chief category of user,[19] its national transpositions seem in general to be aimed primarily at protecting the interests of creditors.

B. The IAS/IFRS

The IAS/IFRS assign to (consolidated and individual) annual accounts a merely informative role and do not consider them as the legal basis either for the annual determination of distributable profits or the proper functioning of capital maintenance rules. The sole purpose of financial statements prepared in accordance with the IAS/IFRS is 'to provide financial information about the reporting entity that is useful to existing and potential investors, lenders and other creditors in making decisions relating to providing resources to the entity'.[20] Moreover, the Conceptual Framework states that financial reports shall 'provide information to help existing and potential investors, lenders and other creditors to estimate the value of the reporting entity'.[21]

In order to achieve this objective, the IAS/IFRS allow or require (depending on the asset class considered) the use of fair value, which, according to the definition provided by IFRS 13, coincides with 'the price that would be received to sell an asset or paid to transfer a liability in an orderly transaction between market participants at the measurement date'.[22]

[19] Van Hulle (n 15) 715.
[20] IASB, *Conceptual Framework for Financial Reporting* (2018), para 1.2.
[21] ibid para 1.7.
[22] IFRS 13, para 9. See also H Brinckmann 'Periodic Disclosure' in R Veil (ed), *European Capital Markets Law* (Oxford, Hart Publishing, 2017) 316–17.

Irrespective of whether fair value is determined with reference to market values or is based on alternative valuation techniques,[23] the use of fair value implies the recognition of unrealised, merely estimated profits and losses, corresponding to increases and decreases in fair value. Unlike historical cost accounting, under which any revaluation compared to book value is only permitted in exceptional cases, fair value accounting requires, at the end of each financial year, a re-assessment of the company's assets in order to adjust their book value to fair value: if the latter has increased during the year, this will result in unrealised capital gains. Hence, annual accounts that comply with the IAS/IFRS (in theory) seek to approximate the current value of the overall business (and therefore of the company's shares) and the 'overall' income at the balance sheet date, also including as yet unrealised income components corresponding to variations in the assets' fair value. Consequently, the adoption of the fair value method clearly marks a departure from the realisation principle, since it permits the recognition of unrealised profits.[24]

Nevertheless, it is worth noting that, contrary to conventional wisdom, the relevance of fair value within the context of the IAS/FRS should not be overstated.[25] As recently observed by Christopher Nobes, during the last decade, the International Accounting Standards Board (IASB) has not significantly extended the extent of fair value accounting.[26] Moreover, and more importantly, the use of fair value in practice is quite limited, being substantially confined to financial instruments and investment property. Indeed, where the use of fair value is optional, undertakings usually opt for historical cost.[27] When considering the difference between the 2013 Accounting Directive and the IAS/IFRS, it must also be remembered that the recognition of unrealised profits does not relate only to IAS/IFRS since, as previously noted,[28] the 2013 Accounting Directive also allows a departure from historical cost.

Nonetheless, many other significant differences between the 2013 Accounting Directive and the IAS/IFRS persist. First of all, the principle of prudence is much less significant within the IAS/IFRS system, where the prudence-related principles of realisation and asymmetry play a marginal role. According to the IASB Conceptual Framework, '[p]rudence is the exercise of caution when making judgements under conditions of uncertainty' and '[t]he exercise of prudence means that assets and income are not overstated and liabilities and expenses are not understated'.[29] However, unlike the

[23] IFRS 13, para 72, establishing a fair value hierarchy 'that categorises into three levels the inputs to valuation techniques used to measure fair value. The fair value hierarchy gives the highest priority to quoted prices (unadjusted) in active markets for identical assets or liabilities (Level 1 inputs) and the lowest priority to unobservable inputs (Level 3 inputs)'.

[24] See, eg, A Moxter, 'Gewinnrealisierung nach den IAS/IFRS: Erosion des HGB-Realisationsprinzip' (2004) *ZvglRWiss* 279; J Baetge, 'Fair Value-Accounting versus Realisations-Imparitäts- und Vorsichtsprinzip' (2003) *Rechnungswesen* 230.

[25] See, eg, Enriques et al (n 12) 253.

[26] C Nobes, 'IFRS Ten Years on: Has the IASB Imposed Extensive Use of Fair Value? Has the EU Learnt to Love IFRS? And Does the Use of Fair Value Make IFRS Illegal in the EU?' (2015) 12 *Accounting in Europe* 153, 155–59, stating that 'most of the new standards (11 of the 15) written by the IASB contain no requirement or permission to use "the FV basis". The remaining four standards do contain the FV basis, but one of them merely clarifies that the permission to use it that already existed in old standards'.

[27] ibid 159–60. See also HB Christensen and VV Nikolaev, 'Does Fair Value Accounting for Non-financial Assets Pass the Market Test?' (2013) 18 *Review of Accounting Studies* 734, providing empirical evidence showing a very limited use of fair value accounting for non-financial assets.

[28] See above, section II.A.

[29] IASB (n 20) para 2.16.

2013 Accounting Directive, the IAS/IFRS do not recognise the principles of realisation and asymmetry principle, stating that '[t]he exercise of prudence does not imply a need for asymmetry, for example, a systematic need for more persuasive evidence to support the recognition of assets or income than the recognition of liabilities or expenses', unless asymmetric requirements are needed to select the most relevant information that faithfully represents what it purports to represent.[30]

A less prudential approach of this type influences the valuation of various assets and liabilities. For example, as far as goodwill and other intangible assets with an indefinite useful life are concerned,[31] IAS 38 states that such assets shall not be amortised and are exclusively subject to the periodical impairment test by comparing their recoverable amount with their carrying amount.[32] By contrast, the 2013 Accounting Directive does not draw any distinction between assets with indefinite useful life and assets with definite useful life, and states that all intangible assets shall be written off over the useful economic life of the intangible asset.[33] Where, in exceptional cases, the useful life of goodwill cannot be reliably estimated, goodwill is written off within a maximum period set by the Member State, which must not be shorter than five years and may not exceed 10 years.[34]

Another important difference between the IAS/IFRS and the 2013 Accounting Directive concerns the recognition of provisions for future expenses. According to paragraph 14 of IAS 37, a provision shall be recognised only when: '(a) an entity has a present obligation (legal or constructive) as a result of a past event; (b) it is probable that an outflow of resources embodying economic benefits will be required to settle the obligation; and (c) a reliable estimate can be made of the amount of the obligation'. As regards the present obligation to a third party requirement, IAS 37 states that 'a past event is deemed to give rise to a present obligation if, taking account of all available evidence, it is more likely than not that a present obligation exists at the end of the reporting period'. Therefore, under IAS 37, provisions for future expenses not associated with any obligation towards third parties are excluded from recognition, even when these are authorised by the board of directors.

Such accounting requirements not only provide further evidence of the less prudential approach characterising the IAS/IFRS, but, by establishing a closer relationship between the accounting value of assets and liabilities and the future cash flows associated with them, are also consistent with the objective of the IAS/FRS accounts to help users of financial reports in assessing the prospects of future net cash inflows to the company. In fact, according to the Conceptual Framework: 'Investors', lenders' and other creditors' expectations about returns depend on their assessment of the amount, timing and uncertainty of (the prospects for) future net cash inflows to the entity'.[35]

[30] ibid para 2.17.

[31] According to the para 88 of IAS 38: 'An intangible asset shall be regarded by the entity as having an indefinite useful life when, based on an analysis of all of the relevant factors, there is no foreseeable limit to the period over which the asset is expected to generate net cash inflows for the entity.' As clarified by para 91 of IAS 38, '[t]he term "indefinite" does not mean "infinite"'.

[32] IAS 38, paras 107–10.

[33] 2013 Accounting Directive, art 12, para 11.

[34] Fülbier et al (n 13) 25.

[35] IASB (n 20) para 1.3.

III. The Suitability of the EU Accounting Regimes for Meeting Addressees' Information Needs: The Potential Limitations of Historical Cost and Fair Value Accounting

Over time, scholars and practitioners have cast doubts on the actual capacity of the historical cost-based accounting regime designed by the Accounting Directive to provide users with the relevant information. While consistent with the principle of prudence, insofar as it prevents the recognition of unrealised profits,[36] historical cost accounting is generally unable to reflect the current fundamental value of an asset[37] and the underlying future expected cash flows. Although information about the cost of assets can be used as an input in predicting margins from the future sale of goods,[38] the assistance that can be provided by historical cost accounting in estimating cash flows, their timing and uncertainty is limited, as the recognised assets' value corresponds to the price paid for them and does not reflect evidence from the market.[39] Therefore, according to critics, historical cost 'is inherently irrelevant to any contemporary decision because [it is] out-of-date information and provide no guide to an entity's current financial position.'[40]

As mentioned above, the EU legislature recognises the potential limitations of historical cost accounting and believes that a derogation from it and the use of measurement bases that allow for the revaluation of the company's assets can provide users of financial statements with more relevant information.[41] In order to enhance the relevance of the information provided by financial statements and (as far as public companies are concerned) to ensure a high degree of transparency and comparability of financial statements and hence contribute to achieving a better functioning of the European capital market, the EU legislature introduced the IAS/IFRS, which, by allowing the use of fair value, aim to represent the value of assets in a manner that reflects current market conditions.[42]

More than a decade after the entry into force of the IAS Regulation, the European Commission has considered whether it has achieved its goals.[43] In spite of existing difficulties in measuring the impact of the introduction of the IAS/IFRS, the Commission contends that the benefits resulting from the implementation of the IAS Regulation

[36] Institute of Chartered Accountants in England and Wales (ICAEW), *Measurement in Financial Reporting* (2006) 20, noting that: 'Lenders and other creditors may consider that their interests are better protected if net assets are measured conservatively, as this reduces the extent to which the company's assets can be paid out as dividends.'

[37] C Laux and C Leuz, 'The Crisis of Fair-Value Accounting: Making Sense of the Recent Debate' (2009) 34 *Accounting, Organizations and Society* 826, 828.

[38] IASB (n 20) para 6.30. See also M Bromwich, 'A Comparison of Historical Cost and Fair Value Accounting Systems: General and Some Regulatory Concerns' in R di Pietra et al (eds) *Accounting and Regulation* (New York, Springer, 2014) 269, 282, noting that in order to perform such an assessment on the basis of historical cost-based financial statements, users should supplement accounting information with relevant economic information.

[39] Bromwich (n 38) 281.

[40] ICAEW (n 36) 20.

[41] 2013 Accounting Directive, recital 18.

[42] See above, section II.B.

[43] Commission (n 6) 3–8.

outweigh the associated costs. The IAS Regulation has increased the transparency and quality of financial statements, and has led to greater comparability of financial statements within and across industries and countries, although some differences persist. The Commission concludes that the objectives of the Regulation have, generally speaking, been met, although the application of the IAS Regulation can be improved.

These findings provide a relevant assessment of the effects of the adoption of the IAS/IFRS in the EU. However, they do not consider – although it is one fundamental question with which accounting institutions and regulators are faced[44] – whether issuers' financial reports really satisfy the information needs of the different categories of investor and potential users of periodical reports.[45]

Indeed, there are some concerns about the relevance of the IAS/IFRS for investors. First, since they are more heavily based on values resulting from subjective estimates and the use of data not available to the market, the IAS/IFRS grant directors broader discretion. Secondly, the adoption of the IAS/IFRS has rendered EU issuers' financial reports considerably longer and highly complex, thus exposing unsophisticated investors to information overload.[46] In fact, most unsophisticated users do not have sufficient financial, accounting and legal literacy to understand financial reports prepared under the IAS/IFRS regime.[47]

In addition, there are concerns as regards the relevance of IAS/IFRS financial statements from their users' standpoint, due to the trade-off between the discretion allowed by accounting rules and the relevance of a company's accounts.[48] On the one hand, since fair value accounting is based on future cash flows deriving from the assets, and therefore indicates the assets' current value, it theoretically offers more relevant information than historical cost accounting. On the other hand, fair value accounting can be less helpful for investors because it entails subjective estimates that can skew asset values.[49] No accounting system can fully predict the future circumstances of a company, given that new considerations may arise that require the re-interpretation or adaptation of existing accounting standards.[50] A certain degree of discretion is therefore inherent in any accounting system. However, due to their focus on future cash flows, higher discretion and greater uncertainty are hallmarks of IAS/IFRS as compared to historical cost accounting.[51]

It is therefore doubtful whether users are necessarily better off with the more forward-looking IAS/IFRS regime or with other accounting systems, even if the latter provide less relevant information.[52] Ball notes that future-oriented accounting values

[44] See, eg, ESMA, 'Public Statement: Improving the Quality of Disclosures in the Financial Statements' (2015/ESMA/1609) 1–4.

[45] S Cascino et al, 'Who Uses Financial Reports and for What Purpose? Evidence from Capital Providers' (2014) 11 *Accounting in Europe* 185.

[46] TMJ Möllers and E Kernchen, 'Information Overload at the Capital Market' (2010) *Europa e Diritto Privato* 1005, 1009–11.

[47] E Ferran, *Building an EU Securities Market* (Oxford, Oxford University Press, 2004) 178.

[48] IASB (n 20) paras 2.12–2.13.

[49] Bromwich (n 38) 285–88.

[50] C Leuz and PD Wysocki, 'The Economics of Disclosure and Financial Reporting Regulation: Evidence and Suggestions for Future Research' (2016) 54 *Journal of Accounting Research* 525, 583.

[51] Bromwich (n 38) 269–73.

[52] See, eg, R Ewert and A Wagenhofer, 'Why More Forward-Looking Accounting Standards Can Reduce Financial Reporting Quality' (2016) 25 *European Accounting Review* 487.

increase the volatility of the results presented in the financial statements. Consequently, while promising to make earnings more informative, the IAS/IFRS paradoxically make them more volatile and difficult to forecast.[53] As has been noted by the European Commission,[54] the introduction of volatility into issuers' reports can favour short-term behaviour by investors and hold back long-term investment. Furthermore, fair value does not seem to be fully consistent with the financial decision-making and stewardship functions of financial statements. Fair value is relevant only where the entity is willing to actually sell the asset. Therefore, fair values are deemed not to be relevant for fixed assets such as property, plant and equipment, or financial investments.[55]

Nevertheless, it is worth noting that, in spite of the above-mentioned potential limitations of the IAS/IFRS, there is empirical evidence to suggest that demand from institutional investors for equities has increased as a consequence of the adoption of the IAS/IFRS.[56] All in all, these findings seem to confirm the view that, even though the IAS/IFRS do not target any chief category of user and seek to provide the information set that will meet the needs of the maximum number of primary users, IAS/IFRS financial statements are de facto mainly intended – in spite of their potential limitations mentioned above – to meet the information needs of sophisticated investors.

IV. The Cost Burdens Imposed by Accounting Rules on European Joint Stock Companies

In order to assess whether the European accounting regime is capable of meeting the objective set forth by the Commission of striking an appropriate balance between the interests of the addressees of financial statements in receiving relevant information and the interests of undertakings in not being unduly burdened with reporting requirements, the cost burden imposed by the 2013 Accounting Directive and the IAS/FRS will be considered.

A. The Simplifications for Medium, Small and Micro-Closed Companies Provided by the 2013 Accounting Directive

In line with the 'think small first' principle promoted by the Small Business Act for Europe,[57] in 2008, the European Parliament recognised that, while accounting and auditing are key areas for reducing the administrative burden for European companies,

[53] R Ball, 'International Financial Reporting Standards (IFRS): pros and cons for investors' (2006) 36 *Accounting and Business Research* 5, 12. See also N Moloney, *EU Securities and Financial Markets Regulation*, 3rd edn (Oxford, Oxford University Press, 2014) 158.

[54] Commission 'Long-Term Financing of the European Economy' COM(2014) 168 final 14.

[55] W Ballwieser, 'The Limitations of Financial Reporting' in C Leuz et al (eds) *The Economics and Politics of Accounting: International Perspectives on Trends, Policy, and Practice* (Oxford, Oxford University Press, 2004) 67.

[56] A Florou and PF Pope, 'Mandatory IFRS Adoption and Institutional Investment Decisions' (2012) 87 *Accounting Review* 1993.

[57] See above n 8.

the fourth and seventh Accounting Directives were often found to be very burdensome for small and medium-sized companies, in particular for micro-entities, and asked the Commission to continue its efforts to review these Directives.[58] In 2009, the European Commission published a proposal for a directive amending the fourth Directive as regards micro-entities. In particular, it suggested establishing an option for Member States of removing micro-entities from the scope of the fourth Directive and exempting them from the requirement to draw up annual accounts.[59] In 2010, it promoted an impact assessment in order to analyse the costs of some possible simplifications of the accounting regime for small and medium-sized enterprises (SMEs) and micro-entities[60] (and the IFRS for SMEs).[61] The impact assessment showed that the simplifications proposed were appreciated by most of the SMEs and micro-entities included in the sample, and would have implied a significant saving of accounting costs for SMEs and micro-entities.[62]

In keeping with these findings, the 2013 Accounting Directive distinguishes between micro, small, medium and large-sized undertakings based on three quantitative parameters (balance sheet total, net turnover and the average number of employees) and lays down a simplified regime for small and medium-sized undertakings and a super-simplified regime for micro-undertakings. In particular, Article 14 allows Member States to permit small-sized undertakings to draw up abbreviated balance sheets and profit and loss accounts that do not show some of the items included in the full version of the financial statements. Moreover, Articles 16 and 17 exempt small and medium-sized companies from the requirement to disclose certain information that large undertakings have to include in the notes.

More radical simplifications are provided for micro-undertakings. According to Article 36 of the 2013 Accounting Directive, Member States may exempt micro-undertakings from the obligation: (i) to draw up notes to the financial statements; (ii) to prepare a management report; and (iii) to publish annual financial statements in accordance with Chapter 7 of the 2013 Accounting Directive, provided that the balance sheet information contained therein is duly filed, in accordance with national law. Moreover, micro-undertakings may be permitted to draw up super-simplified balance sheets and profit and loss accounts.

In 2017, following the entry into force of the 2013 Accounting Directive, the Commission commissioned a study on the accounting regime of micro-companies with limited liability. In addition, the comprehensive fitness check of the EU framework on

[58] European Parliament Resolution of 18 December 2008 on accounting requirements as regards small and medium-sized companies, particularly micro-entities [2008] OJ C45 E/58.

[59] Commission, 'Proposal for a Directive of the European Parliament and of the Council amending Council Directive 78/660/EEC on the annual accounts of certain types of companies as regards micro-entities' COM(2009) 83 final.

[60] Including, eg, simplification of the required format for the balance sheet and the profit and loss account, the relaxation of the requirement to report on deferred taxation or to set up appropriate provisions, simplification of the valuation rules and the reduction of disclosures on asset movements.

[61] Commission, 'Framework Contract for Projects Relating to Evaluation and Impact Assessment Activities of Directorate General for Internal Market and Services. 4th Company Law Directive and IFRS for SMEs. Final Report' (2010).

[62] ibid 35, showing that the cost percentage saved is 42 per cent for micro-companies, 22 per cent for small companies and 26 per cent for medium companies.

public reporting by companies, launched by the Commission in 2018 in keeping with Article 36(9) of the 2013 Accounting Directive,[63] seeks to assess, amongst other things, whether the simplifications for medium, small and micro-undertakings provided by the 2013 Accounting Directive are striking the right balance between preparers' costs and users' needs.[64]

Although the results of these studies are not yet available, it seems reasonable to argue that the simplified regime for small and medium-sized undertakings strikes an acceptable balance between preparers' costs and users' needs. Despite the reservations expressed by some users,[65] the simplified accounts regime for small and medium-sized companies does not deprive the users of essential information concerning the company's circumstances. By contrast, the impact of the super-simplified regime provided for micro-undertakings is more controversial. While the cost savings granted to preparers by this regime are undisputable, the exemption from both the obligations to draw up notes to the financial statements and to prepare a management report casts doubts on the relevance of the information provided by the super-simplified accounts of micro-undertakings. Indeed, it is essentially impossible (even for the most sophisticated users) to decrypt balance sheet and profit and loss account numbers without the explanations contained in the notes and the management report. In addition, the exemption from the requirement to publish accounts might sometimes make it more expensive for users to obtain the information needed.[66] Nevertheless, as noted above, it should be expected that more sophisticated third parties contracting with micro-undertakings will already have the relevant information or will be able to ensure contractual safeguards, including in relation the necessary disclosure.[67] Therefore, it is arguable that the super-simplified accounting regime provided for micro-undertakings should not generally harm the information needs of third parties.

B. The Cost Burden Posed on Listed SMEs by the IAS/IFRS: The Case for a Simplification of the IAS/IFRS for SMEs Listed on Multilateral Trading Facilities

In 2015, within the ambit of its evaluation of the IAS Regulation, the European Commission highlighted the difficulties associated with a cost-benefit analysis of the adoption of the IAS/IFRS since, according to the Commission, it is hard to quantify the costs arising from the adoption of the IAS/IFRS.[68] Although it concluded that, on the whole, the benefits of the IAS/IFRS outweigh their costs,[69] it recognised that

[63] Asking for a report on the situation of micro-undertakings, having regard to the number of micro-companies and the reduction of administrative burdens resulting from the simplifications introduced in 2013.

[64] Commission, 'Consultation Document: Fitness Check on the EU Framework for Public Reporting by Companies' (2018) 14–5.

[65] Commission (n 61) 9–11.

[66] ibid.

[67] See above text to n 7.

[68] Commission, 'Evaluation of Regulation (EC) N° 1606/2002 of 19 July 2002 on the application of International Accounting Standards' SWD(2015) 120 final 37.

[69] ibid 41.

'the ratio of costs to benefits depends on characteristics of a company such as its size and scale of international operations'.[70] In particular, the cost of adopting the IFRS may represent an obstacle for an initial public offering, especially for SMEs.[71]

The European Commission fully endorsed this opinion in its Green Paper 'Building a Capital Markets Union', where it concluded that the application of IAS/IFRS principles might have proved to be overly burdensome for SMEs. Thus, in order to facilitate their access to capital markets, according to the Commission, 'the development of a simplified, common, and high-quality accounting standard tailored to the companies listed on certain trading venues could be a step forward in terms of transparency and comparability, and if applied proportionally, could help those companies seeking cross-border investors to be more attractive to them'.[72]

Against this backdrop, it is worth mentioning that the listing rules of the vast majority of SME-dedicated Multilateral Trading Facilities (MTFs) already allow companies to use either the IFRS as adopted by the EU or generally accepted national accounting principles.[73] However, even though such an approach can favour cost savings, it features a significant drawback, since the use of local accounting principles limits the comparability of accounts of companies based in different Member States and, by doing so, hinders cross-border investments.[74]

In order to strike a more adequate balance between the interests of the undertakings concerned and those of investors, the adoption of the IFRS for SMEs could be considered,[75] even though the IASB has stated that the IFRS for SMEs are not intended for small publicly traded entities.[76] In line with the aim of building a European Capital Market Union and, especially, of promoting SME growth markets, based on a careful cost-benefit analysis, the Commission should consider adopting the IFRS for SMEs[77] as a common EU-level accounting standard for small and medium-sized companies listed on MTFs. Even though this approach might turn out to be slightly more expensive for undertakings than the application of local accounting rules,[78] it would lead

[70] ibid 5.

[71] ibid 6.

[72] Commission, 'Green Paper. Building a Capital Markets Union' COM(2015) 63 final 14.

[73] Commission, 'Impact Assessment Accompanying the document Proposal for a Regulation of the European Parliament and of the Council amending Regulations (EU) No 596/2014 and (EU) 2017/1129 as regards the promotion of the use of SME growth markets' SWD(2018) 243 final, 85.

[74] Commission, 'Feedback statement of the public consultation on building a proportionate regulatory environment to support SME listing' (2017) 4.

[75] The Commission, as mentioned in the Green Paper 'Building a Capital Markets Union', could develop its own set of simplified accounting standards for SMEs whose shares are listed on MTFs. However, such a solution presents two significant drawbacks: the need for the creation and functioning of a European accounting standard-setter and the fact that comparability will not be achieved at a global level, thereby potentially affecting the attractiveness of SMEs listed on MTFs in the EU in the eyes international investors. See Deloitte, 'Capital Markets Union' (2015) 25, www2.deloitte.com/content/dam/Deloitte/ie/Documents/FinancialServices/investmentmanagement/ie_2015_Linkn_Learn_CMU_Deloitte_Ireland.pdf.

[76] IFRS for SMEs, paras 1.2, 1.3.

[77] IFRS for SMEs, published in 2009, is an autonomous set of accounting principles aimed at meeting the needs of smaller companies. As the IFRS for SMEs is separate from full IFRSs, it can be adopted by any jurisdiction, regardless of whether or not it has adopted the full IFRSs. In designing IFRSs for SMEs, the IASB simplified some of the principles in full IFRSs for recognising and measuring assets, liabilities, income and expense; moreover, some of the disclosures required by full IFRSs are not required by the IFRS for SMEs.

[78] Commission (n 61) 27–31. See also Moloney (n 53) 161.

to the harmonisation of the accounting rules for small and medium-sized companies listed on MTFs at the EU level and would more adequately meet with the expectations of international investors.[79] Should the IFRS for SMEs prove to be inadequate to fulfil these goals,[80] the EU Commission should engage with the IASB in order to promote the development of a simplified set of the IFRS for small and medium-sized companies listed on MTFs.[81] In any case, in order to ensure a minimum level of consistency and comparability between the financial statements of all European listed companies, a crucial aspect appears to be that a simplified accounting regime should be based on the IFRS.

V. Reconciling European Issuers' and Investors' Interests: The Role of Narrative Reporting

As noted above, both historical cost accounting and fair value accounting feature potential limitations. Such limitations are deemed to be less relevant in medium, small and micro non-listed companies, since third parties contracting with them are, generally, able to contract for their protection and to receive the information required.[82] By contrast, as far as listed companies (and, sometimes, large non-listed companies) are concerned, investors and creditors that cannot require reporting entities to provide information directly to them, and must therefore rely on financial reports for much of the financial information they need, are considered to be the primary addresses of accounting disclosure. However, some doubts have been cast on the ability of the IAS/IFRS-based regime to strike a balance between the interests of such users and those of the preparers of financial statements. First, given the potential limitations of fair value accounting, the information relevance of the IAS/FRS is controversial. Second, due to their increased length and complexity, they are deemed to be incapable of adequately fulfilling the information needs of the investors as a whole and, in particular, of unsophisticated investors. Absent a prohibition on direct trading in secondary markets by retail investors, such investors will also be recipients of issuers' financial reports.

As IAS/IFRS financial statements are very extensive and complex, EU law makers should study solutions for rendering financial reports more readable and useful for retail investors lacking financial, accounting and legal literacy.

The need to make unsophisticated investors capable of reading key accounting information cannot be denied by emphasising that they usually do not read financial reports since they lack the requisite financial literacy. Indeed, available evidence shows that a good number of retail investors include financial statements among the relevant

[79] Deloitte (n 75) 25.

[80] Commission, 'Feedback Statement on the Green Paper "Building a Capital Markets Union"' SWD (2015) 184 final 6–7.

[81] Deloitte (n 75) 24, reporting that 'the IASB has expressed on 18 February 2015 in a "Statement in response to the EC's Green Paper on a Capital Market Union" willingness to cooperate with the Commission on its project for a Capital Markets Union'.

[82] See above text to n 7.

sources of information they use,[83] that, on average, individuals invest more in firms that make clear and concise financial disclosures, and that individuals' returns increase in line with clearer and more concise disclosures.[84]

The key to rendering the IAS/IFRS financial statements of listed companies more (retail) investor-friendly and to limiting their potential drawbacks mentioned above seems to be to present information in a different manner that caters to the needs of different investor categories. The narrative component of financial reports, which is by its nature easier to read and understand for users without accounting literacy, can play a crucial role to this end.[85]

In this area, the UK experience with narrative reporting offers the main point of reference. Section 414A of the 2006 Companies Act requires the directors of all companies other than those entitled to the small companies' exemption to prepare (in addition to the directors' report and the directors' remuneration report) a strategic report the contents of which are identified in section 414C–414CB. The strategic report includes a 'fair review of the company's business' and a 'description of the principal risks and uncertainties facing the company'. The contents of the strategic report are broader for listed companies, which are also required to include a description of the company's strategy and business model, and to provide detailed gender diversity disclosures. Furthermore, the strategic report includes information concerning environmental, social and employee matters, as well as human rights issues, where necessary for a better understanding of the company's conditions and perspectives.

Empirical evidence has shown that the introduction of the strategic report has enhanced the quality of UK issuers' financial reports. Following the strategic report's introduction, almost all FTSE 1000 companies now provide a detailed discussion of their business model and business objectives in their reporting, focusing to some extent on long-term objectives. Almost 80 per cent of these companies provide a link between their key performance indicators identified and overall strategy or specific strategic objectives.[86] Moreover, the FRC has concluded that the overall quality of corporate reporting has improved since the introduction of the strategic report, although there is still scope for further improvement.[87] According to the Financial Reporting Council (FRC), the introduction of the strategic report has prompted many companies to change the structure of their annual reports and to develop innovative ways of 'telling their story'.[88]

Thus, more effective narrative reporting may also be expected to reduce the potential impact of certain shortcomings of IAS/IFRS financial statements. A strategic report-like

[83] See, eg, B Pellens and A Schmidt, 'Verhalten und Präferenzen deutscher Aktionäre: eine Befragung von privaten und institutionellen Anlegern zum Informationsverhalten, zur Dividendenpräferenz und zur Wahrnehmung von Stimmrechten' (2014) *Studien des Deutschen Deutsches Aktieninstitut* 34–35, dai.de/en/what-we-offer/studies-and-statistics/studies.html?d=205.

[84] See A Lawrence, 'Individual Investors and Financial Disclosure' (2013) 56 *Journal of Accounting and Economics* 130.

[85] G Strampelli, 'The EU Issuers' Accounting Disclosure Regime and Investors' Information Needs: The Essential Role of Narrative Reporting' (2018) 19 *European Business Organization Law Review* 1.

[86] BlackSun plc, 'The Complete 100 – Making Connections – Analysis of the FTSE 100 2013 Corporate Reporting Trends' (2013), blacksunplc.com/corporate/research/index.jsp.

[87] FRC, 'Clear & Concise: Developments in Narrative Reporting' (2015) 7–23, frc.org.uk/getattachment/f8edd6c0-55e8-4bb9-a846-3c4f20f8c5d1/Clear-and-concise-developments-in-narrative-reporting.pdf.

[88] ibid 13.

narrative document focusing on the entity's strategies and perspectives may (at least in part) counterbalance possible shortcomings within financial statements associated with the broader discretion granted by the IAS/IFRS and the higher volatility of accounting figures associated with fair value.[89]

In addition, a more synthetic disclosure of strategic information may foster institutional investors' stewardship by putting them in a position in which they are better able to effectively monitor issuers' management. The excess of information and lack of a clear structure inhibits useful engagement between the company's management and institutional investors. Thus, by encouraging institutional investor engagement, the provision of a clear and brief description of the entity's strategy, objectives and business model may incentivise dialogue between the company's management and institutional investors (in keeping with the objectives set forth in Directive 2017/828/EU aimed at fostering long-term institutional shareholder engagement).[90]

Certainly, the introduction of a narrative reporting in the form of strategic reports entails additional costs for the companies concerned. However, as was highlighted by UK policy makers when assessing the impact of the narrative reporting reform, these costs are limited (and should mainly be associated with the initial application of the new regime), whereas the benefits are expected to outweigh them.[91] Moreover, non-listed medium, small and micro-undertakings adopting the IAS/IFRS (for which associated costs might be excessive) should be exempted from the requirement to prepare additional narrative reporting, and simplifications for medium and small listed companies could be considered.

VI. Conclusions

Since the adoption of the fourth Accounting Directive in 1978, the harmonisation of accounting rules has been the chief objective of the European Commission's accounting regulatory strategy. However, the IAS Regulation and the Accounting Directives have not led to the effective harmonisation of accounting rules in the EU, with the sole exception of the consolidated financial statements of listed companies (which must be prepared in accordance with the IAS/IFRS).[92] The numerous choices granted to Member States under the IAS/IFRS Regulation and the 2013 Accounting Directive give rise to significant differences in the criteria that must be used for preparing financial statements in the Member States. In particular, according to the IAS Regulation, Member States may permit or require the use of the IAS/FRS for individual financial statements of listed companies, and individual and consolidated accounts of other companies. In addition, options available under the 2013 Accounting Directive permit Member States to significantly diversify the accounting regime applicable, respectively, to large, medium, small and micro-entities.

[89] See above, text to n 53.

[90] Strampelli (n 85).

[91] Department for Business, Innovation & Skills, 'Reforming UK Narrative Reporting. Impact Assessment' (2012) 8–11, www.gov.uk/government/publications/reforming-uk-narrative-reporting-impact-assessment.

[92] Brinckmann (n 22) 323.

Although accounting harmonisation and the comparability of financial statements at the EU level is limited overall, the options provided under the IAS Regulation and the Accounting Directive have proved to be essential in limiting the accounting-related cost burden for smaller companies and, by providing for different accounting regimes based on the company's public accountability and size, in striking an adequate balance between undertakings' and investors' needs. Therefore, the Commission's proposal to introduce a simplified regime for small companies listed on MTFs is appropriate, even though it further limits the harmonisation of accounting rules for listed companies. Moreover, although it results in further differentiation within the EU accounting regime, listed companies and (based on a specific cost-benefit analysis) non-public large companies could be required – following the UK Strategic Report model – to prepare a clear and concise narrative report focusing on essential aspects of the company's business, circumstances, strategies and governance with the aim of enhancing the effectiveness of IAS/IFRS financial statements and of making them more suitable for meeting investors' needs.

In conclusion, in order to strike an adequate balance between preparers' costs and users' needs, it is essential to differentiate between applicable accounting regimes depending on the company's public accountability and size. Therefore, in contrast to conventional wisdom, the actual goal of European regulatory policy within the accounting area should be (and actually is) not to grant a full harmonisation of accounting rules, but (as is already recognised by the 2013 Accounting Directive) to establish 'minimum equivalent legal requirements at Union level as regards the extent of the financial information that should be made available to the public by undertakings that are in competition with one another'.[93]

[93] 2013 Accounting Directive, recital 8.

10

Non-financial Reporting

Evolving Demands for Transparent Enterprises

BRENDA HANNIGAN

I. Introduction

Disclosure has always been the regulatory mechanism of choice when it comes to regulating companies for the reasons so clearly stated in the G20/OECD Principles of Corporate Governance that they are worth stating here at the outset:[1]

> A strong disclosure regime that promotes real transparency is a pivotal feature of market-based monitoring of companies and is central to shareholders' ability to exercise their shareholder rights on an informed basis. Experience shows that disclosure can also be a powerful tool for influencing the behaviour of companies and for protecting investors. A strong disclosure regime can help to attract capital and maintain confidence in the capital markets … Shareholders and potential investors require access to regular, reliable and comparable information in sufficient detail for them to assess the stewardship of management, and make informed decisions about the valuation, ownership and voting of shares. Insufficient or unclear information may hamper the ability of the markets to function, increase the cost of capital and result in a poor allocation of resources. Disclosure also helps improve public understanding of the structure and activities of enterprises, corporate policies and performance with respect to environmental and ethical standards, and companies' relationships with the communities in which they operate.

Companies have always published some element of narrative reporting alongside their financial statements, but the past two decades have seen an explosion in non-financial reporting. In section II below, we consider these multiple overlapping requirements, both mandatory and voluntary, and the resulting lack of coherence, consistency and comparability. In section III, we examine the EU's Non-Financial Reporting Directive (NFRD) 2014/95/EU[2] and the recommendations of the Financial Stability Board's Task

[1] G20/OECD, *Principles of Corporate Governance* (2015) Part V, 37–38; see also B Hannigan, 'Corporate Purpose in the UK: From Shareholder Primacy to Enlightenment and the Good Corporate Citizen' in A Pruem (ed), *Cent Ans de Droit Luxembourgeois des Societes* (Brussels, Larcier, 2016) 58–61.

[2] Directive 2014/95/EU of the European Parliament and of the Council of 22 October 2014 amending Directive 2013/34/EU as regards disclosure of non-financial and diversity information by certain large undertakings and groups [2014] OJ L330/1.

Force on Climate-Related Financial Disclosure[3] (TCFD), which are emerging as key international frameworks. We also examine the EU's High Level Expert Group Report on Sustainable Finance[4] (HLEG), which has recommended that the EU Commission integrates the requirements of the TCFD into the NFRD, thus unifying these important developments. Finally, in section IV, we conclude by considering the likely three stages of development which will emerge as we progress towards transparent and sustainable enterprises.

While reporting on environment, social and governance (ESG) matters has been around for at least 20 years (ESG is a more recent articulation of corporate social responsibility (CSG), which has been around for much longer), climate-related financial reporting is the catalyst for the changing dynamic on this issue. As governments increasingly recognise the threat posed to their economies by climate change, the matter has become a political and financial priority, as evidenced by the 184 signatories to the 2015 Paris Climate Change Agreement (notwithstanding the controversial withdrawal of the US). The focus has turned to whether financial institutions and markets sufficiently understand the risks related to climate-related matters and their potential impact on value creation. Investors are increasingly concerned that they may be operating, in effect, on the basis of an incomplete, if not false, prospectus if there is insufficient recognition of and management of climate-related risk by investee companies.[5] Business perceptions may be changing too, with the UK Prudential Regulation Authority recently highlighting that financial institutions are making the transition from seeing climate change as a matter of corporate social responsibility to seeing it as a financial risk to their businesses which needs to be addressed through strategy, governance and risk management.[6] Once the financial institutions make climate change-related risk a priority, other sectors will have no option but to follow suit. Other significant environmental, social (inequalities, community issues) and governance (management structures, employee relations) factors also pose risks to the sustainability of individual businesses and sectors. The political risks of another financial shock to global markets are evident. The timeframe is urgent because the UN General Assembly in September 2015 adopted a 2030 Agenda for Sustainable Development that includes 17 Sustainable Development Goals (SDGs) addressing the 'most important economic, social, environmental and governance challenges of our time', which include the goals of economic growth, sustainable businesses, climate action and reducing inequalities. Developing effective disclosure frameworks is key to addressing the SDGs, since businesses first need to identify and report on ESG and climate-related financial risks to their sustainability so that governments can then determine their priorities.[7] As the European

[3] Financial Stability Board, 'Task Force on Climate-Related Financial Disclosure', Final Report (29 June 2017).

[4] EU High-Level Expert Group on Sustainable Finance, 'Financing a Sustainable European Economy', Final Report 2018 (30 January 2018) (hereinafter HLEG).

[5] For an overview of the issues facing investors, see the House of Commons Environmental Audit Committee Report, 'Greening Finance: Embedding Sustainability in Financial Decision-Making' Seventh Report of Session 2017–19 (June 2018) HC 1063.

[6] See Prudential Regulation Authority, 'Transition in Thinking: The Impact of Climate Change on the UK Banking Sector' (September 2018).

[7] For the impact of the SDGs on business, see OECD, *Development Co-operation Report 2016: The Sustainable Development Goals as Business Opportunities* (Paris, OECD Publishing, 2016).

Commission has noted, 'corporate transparency on sustainability issues is a prerequisite to enable financial market actors to assess properly the long-term value creation of companies and their management of sustainability risks'.[8] KPMG's *Survey of Corporate Responsibility Reporting 2017* found that the SDGs have resonated strongly with businesses worldwide, with 43 per cent of the 250 largest global companies making a connection between their company's corporate responsibility activities and the SDGs.[9]

The financial crisis of 2007–08 has also played a role in forcing greater disclosure as it provoked a wider public debate about corporate purpose. As the price for the corporate excesses that led to the crisis was paid by wider society through higher taxes, reduced credit, constrained public services and a decade-long period of austerity, civil society now seeks greater disclosure from companies of their business activities, recognising that they can pose significant risks to the social fabric. Information is sought for many different purposes – to manage economic risk, to identify revenue generation and tax compliance, to safeguard employee and pension rights, to protect the environment, to control corruption and to end gender discrimination. These pressures have led to additional corporate reporting requirements reflecting or addressing broader societal issues. For example, in the UK, companies have been required to report on human trafficking and modern slavery (reflecting societal disapproval),[10] on greenhouse gas emissions (concerns about climate change),[11] on late payment practices and policies (abuse of economic power by large companies)[12] and on the gender pay gap (gender inequality),[13] while enhanced energy and carbon reporting will come into effect for financial years on or after 1 April 2019.[14] Of course, reporting frameworks often ascribe lofty societal ideals to non-financial reporting. The OECD Guidelines on Multinational Enterprises, for example, have as their aim 'to promote a positive contribution by enterprises to economic, environmental and social progress worldwide'.[15] The Global Reporting Initiative, discussed below, in promoting sustainability reporting standards, describes their mission as being to empower decisions that create social, environmental and economic benefits for all.[16] The Principles for Responsible Investment (PRI; see below) aims 'to bring responsible investors together to work towards sustainable markets that contribute to a prosperous world for all'.[17] More specifically, the impact assessment of the NFRD suggests that non-financial reporting can 'enhance the trust citizens have in business

[8] See European Commission, 'Action Plan: Financing Sustainable Growth' COM(2018) 97 Final, 8 March 2018, para 1.3.

[9] KPMG, 'Survey of Corporate Responsibility Reporting 2017' (KPMG, October 2017) 39.

[10] See Modern Slavery Act 2015, s 54.

[11] See the Large and Medium-Sized Companies and Groups (Accounts and Reports) Regulations 2008/410, sch 7, pt 7.

[12] See Small Business, Enterprise and Employment Act 2015, s 3; Reporting on Payment Practices and Performance Regulations 2017, SI 2017/395.

[13] See Equality Act 2010, s 78; Equality Act 2010 (Gender Pay Gap Information) Regulations 2017, SI 2017/172.

[14] See the Companies (Directors' Report) and Limited Liability Partnerships (Energy and Carbon Report) Regulations 2018, SI 2018/1155; the provisions have been extended to apply not just to quoted companies but also to large unquoted companies. For the background, see UK Department for Business, Energy & Industrial Strategy, *Streamlined Energy & Carbon Reporting, Government Response* (July 2018).

[15] OECD, 'Guidelines for Multinational Enterprises' (2011 edn) Foreword.

[16] For the GRI Mission statement, see globalreporting.org/information/about-gri/Pages/default.aspx.

[17] See PRI, 'Blueprint for Responsible Investment' (2017), available at https://blueprint.unpri.org.

and in markets and enable a more efficient allocation of capital, as well as provide for better-informed decision making'.[18] However, as the Financial Reporting Council (the UK reporting regulator) has noted, it is clear that the increasing demands for better reporting are closely connected to 'changing stakeholder and societal expectations'.[19] Large businesses in particular need to adjust to this reality.

II. Reporting Initiatives and Frameworks: The Incoming Tide

For the EU, accounting disclosure has been a harmonised requirement since the Fourth Company Law Directive 78/660/EEC and the Seventh Company Law Directive 83/349/EEC, which mandated accounts and annual reports for companies and groups of companies, respectively, with the narrative aspect of the annual reports evolving for the largest companies from a relatively factual directors' report to a management report addressing a wide range of issues. The Directives themselves have evolved into the Accounting Directive 2013/34, as amended by the Non-Financial Reporting Directive 2014/95 (NFRD) where the European Commission was able, in drafting the NFRD, to draw upon many recent influential international initiatives in this area. In its guidelines on non-financial reporting which accompany the NFRD, the Commission identified 21 international frameworks of relevance. For example, there are the OECD Guidelines for Multinational Enterprises (the most recent version from 2011), which are a widely endorsed[20] framework for responsible business conduct in areas such as employment, human rights, environment and bribery.[21] ISO 26000 Social responsibility (released in 2010) is a highly regarded voluntary standard that offers guidance on reporting social responsibility.[22] The Global Reporting Initiative (GRI) sustainability standards are the most widely adopted sustainability reporting framework, according to the KPMG *Survey of Corporate Responsibility Reporting 2017*.[23] The GRI is an independent international organisation that has pioneered sustainability reporting since 1997. It works closely with the Organisation for Economic Co-operation and Development (OECD), but also with the UN Global Compact (UNGC). The UNGC is a policy initiative launched by the UN in 2000 for businesses to align themselves with Ten Principles in the areas of human rights, labour, environment and anti-corruption. The principles are derived from the Universal

[18] European Commission, 'Staff Working Document, Impact Assessment, accompanying the proposal for the NFRD', SWD(2013) 127 final, 16 April 2013, 23.

[19] FRC, 'Annual Review of Corporate Governance and Reporting 2017/2018' (2018) 4.

[20] A total of 36 OECD member countries and 12 non-OECD countries, including Argentina, Brazil, Colombia, Egypt, Tunisia and Ukraine, adhere to the Guidelines.

[21] Also important are the high-level UN Guiding Principles on Business and Human Rights (2011), which have as their objective 'enhancing standards and practices with regard to business and human rights … and thereby also contributing to a socially sustainable globalization'.

[22] International Organisation for Standardisation, *Standard ISO 26000* (2010). Other significant bodies would include the Climate Disclosure Standards Board (CDSB) and the Sustainability Accounting Standards Board (SASB), again independent standard-setting bodies.

[23] KPMG (n 9) 28. A total of 63 per cent of N100 (a sample of 4,900 companies, the top 100 companies by revenue in 49 countries) and 75 per cent of G250 (the 250 largest companies by revenue based on Fortune 500 rankings for 2016) reported under the GRI, while the GRI reports that 315 of the FT Europe 500 companies use the GRI to report (GRI, 'Annual Report', 2016/17, 23).

Declaration of Human Rights, the International Labour Organization's Declaration on Fundamental Principles and Rights at Work, the Rio Declaration on Environment and Development and the UN Convention Against Corruption. Described by the UN as 'the world's largest corporate sustainability initiative', the UNGC claims participation by more than 9500 companies in 160 countries, representing every sector and size of business. The UN sees compliance by business with the UNGC as a leading catalyst to achieving the 17 SDGs by the deadline of 2030. Participating UNGC companies must produce an annual Communication on Progress (COP) that details their work to embed the Ten Principles into their strategies and operations, and a key component of being a signatory to the UNGC is increased reporting on sustainability.[24] This reporting can be under any number of frameworks, including GRI Standards, and UNGC companies are also encouraged to use the new integrated reporting (IR) framework (2013) – another important approach in this area.[25] The IR framework has been developed by the International Integrated Reporting Council (IIRC), a global coalition of regulators, investors, companies, standard setters, the accounting profession and non-governmental organisations (NGOs). It provides principles-based guidance for companies wishing to provide an integrated report that shows 'a holistic picture of the combination, interrelatedness and dependencies between the full range of factors that materially affect the ability of an organisation to create value over time' (IR Guiding Principles, 2013). The primary purpose of an integrated report is to explain value creation 'to providers of financial capital', but it also 'benefits all stakeholders with an interest in the ability to create value such as employees, customers, suppliers, business partners, local communities, legislators, regulators and policymakers'.[26] In addition to these international framework initiatives, narrative non-financial reporting is the key mechanism for corporate governance codes, such as the UK Corporate Governance Code (July 2018) or the French AFEP/MEDEF Code (June 2018), which require boards to articulate their strategy, business model, risk appetite and risk management processes.[27] More recently, corporate governance codes have begun to require additional reporting on board composition and diversity.[28] Hence, Article 20 of the Accounting Directive 2013/34,[29] as amended by the NFRD, now requires quoted companies to provide further diversity information[30] – the rationale

[24] UN, 'UN Global Compact Progress Report 2018' 19.

[25] For differing views on this initiative, see C Adams, 'The International Integrated Reporting Council: A Call to Action' (2015) 27 *Critical Perspectives on Accounting* 23; J Flower, 'The International Integrated Reporting Council: A Story of Failure' (2015) 27 *Critical Perspectives on Accounting* 1. See generally de C Villiers, E Venter and P Hsiao, 'Integrated Reporting: Background, Measurement Issues, Approaches and an Agenda for Future Research' (2017) 57 *Accounting & Finance* 937.

[26] IR Framework (2013) paras 1.7, 1.8. KPMG (n 9) 24 reports only modest progress on reports being labelled as integrated, with 14 per cent of the global 250 companies so reporting in 2017 compared to 15 per cent in 2018.

[27] See UK Corporate Governance Code (July 2018) Provision 28 and 31; AFEP/MEDEF Code (June 2018) paras 1.2–1.5.

[28] See UK Corporate Governance Code (n 27) Principle L, Provision 23.

[29] Directive 2013/34/EU of the European Parliament and of the Council of 26 June 2013 on the annual financial statements, consolidated financial statements and related reports of certain types of undertakings, amending Directive 2006/43/EC of the European Parliament and of the Council and repealing Council Directives 78/660/EEC and 83/349/EEC [2013] OJ L182/19.

[30] The corporate governance statement must include a description of: (a) the diversity policy applied to the board with regard to aspects such as age, gender or educational and professional backgrounds; (b) the objectives of that diversity policy; (c) how the diversity policy has been implemented; and (d) the results in the reporting period. If the company has no diversity policy, it must include an explanation as to why this is the case.

being that effective boards are determined by board composition and the evidence is that a diverse board will offer governance benefits, reducing group-think etc.[31] The UK has extended the requirement in Article 20 to publish a corporate governance statement to private and public companies with either 2,000 or more global employees or a turnover over £200 million globally and a balance sheet over £2 billion globally, with effect for financial years commencing on or after 1 January 2019.[32]

Many of the initiatives above are directed at issuers. From the investor side of the equation, the UN-supported PRI initiative is a network of international investors launched in 2006 which identified six Principles for Responsible Investment, which promote the integration of ESG issues into investment decision making and ownership practices and policies. PRI signatories (about 1,500) are asset owners and (mainly) investment managers. Stewardships codes, which have been in vogue since 2012, support the inclusion of ESG factors in investor decision making. The International Corporate Governance Network (ICGN) Global Stewardship Code (2016) includes, as Principle 6, that investors should promote the long-term performance and sustainable success of companies, and should integrate material ESG factors in stewardship activities. The speed of change is evident if it is considered that the UK Stewardship Code 2012 does not have such an explicit focus on ESG, whereas, for example, the Dutch Stewardship Code 2018 provides, in Principle 2, that asset owners and asset managers should monitor the Dutch listed investee companies on material issues including, inter alia, the business model, social and environmental impact, and corporate governance.[33] In assessing the investee companies' long-term value creation opportunities, risks, strategy and performance, Guidance Principle 2 states that 'it is critical to consider environmental (including climate change risks and opportunities), social and governance information (including board composition and diversity) besides financial information'.

On one level, this explosion of transparency and compliance with (mainly) voluntary standards is welcome. Clearly, businesses have identified benefits in making disclosures to date, even if sometimes reluctantly and in response, perhaps, to actual or perceived stakeholder pressure. It is not all disinterested altruism, of course. The impact assessment behind the NFRD noted a detailed study by Deutsche Bank, in 2012,[34] which concluded that the weight of academic research does indicate a positive correlation between better non-financial reporting and financial performance, and that front-running companies on sustainability issues outperform their competitors in financial terms, particularly over the medium to long term.[35] The key benefits obtained from non-financial reporting, as suggested by the impact assessment, include a lower cost of capital in terms of debt and equity, that companies which disclose are generally considered as lower

[31] European Commission (n 18) 5, 12–17. See DG Szabó and KE Sørensen, 'New EU Directive on the Disclosure of Non-financial Information (CSR)' (2015) 12 *European Company and Financial Law Review* 310, who comment on the lack of any 'logical connection' between sustainability and boardroom diversity.

[32] Companies (Miscellaneous Reporting) Regulations 2018, SI 2018/860.

[33] Dutch Stewardship Code (20 June 2018).

[34] See Deutsche Bank, 'Sustainable Investing: Establishing Long-Term Value and Performance' (June 2012), available at https://www.db.com/cr/en/docs/Sustainable_Investing_2012.pdf. This review looked at more than 100 academic studies of sustainable investing, closely examined 56 research papers, and conducted two literature reviews and four meta-studies.

[35] European Commission (n 18) 18.

risk than competitors and that disclosure gives a competitive advantage in attracting, motivating and retaining talented employees and consumer loyalty.[36] On the other hand, a failure to manage ESG factors can result in 'operational delays', 'problematic relations with government and communities, and reputational damage'.[37] An influential study by Harvard Business School in 2015 found that firms with good performance on material sustainability issues significantly outperform firms with poorer performance on these issues, suggesting that investments in sustainability issues are shareholder value-enhancing.[38] The European Commission has noted a review by the University of Oxford and Arabesque Partners of over 190 academic studies and sources on sustainability, which concluded that 80 per cent of the studies demonstrate that the stock price performance of companies is positively influenced by prudent sustainability practices.[39] The benefit for investors of integrating ESG factors into their decision making and doing due diligence on their impact is that, as the OECD noted, by acting with respect to adverse impacts on society and the environment, 'institutional investors can avoid financial and reputational risks, respond to the expectations of the client's beneficiaries and contribute to global goals in climate and sustainable development'.[40] In his annual influential letter to investee companies in January 2018, Larry Fink of investment giants BlackRock, noted that 'a company's ability to manage environmental, social, and governance matters demonstrates the leadership and good governance that is so essential to sustainable growth'.

Welcome though it is to see increased transparency and business support for these various initiatives, haphazard compliance of this nature may generate unnecessary costs as companies comply with similar but overlapping requirements, there may be over-inclusion of (smaller) entities and elements of the supply chain, while multiple obligations mean that it is difficult to secure consistent and comparable information. Differing thresholds of materiality coupled with disclosures in different locations (public registries, NGO websites and corporate websites) mean that information is available, but nonetheless difficult to access. The reliability of the information may be difficult to assess, given varying levels of verification. These can range from a review of provision,[41] to audit assurance, to assurance by external service providers through adherence to

[36] See ibid.

[37] See ibid.

[38] M Khan, G Serafein and A Yoon, 'Corporate Sustainability: First Evidence on Materiality' (2016) 91 *Accounting Review* 1697–1724.

[39] See European Commission, 'Feedback Statement, Public Consultation on Institutional Investors and Asset Managers Duties Regarding Sustainability' (24 May 2018) 5; University of Oxford, Arabesque Partners, 'From the Stockholder to the Stakeholder, How Sustainability Can Drive Financial Outperformance' (March 2015).

[40] OECD, *Responsible Business Conduct for Institutional Investors* (2017) Foreword.

[41] NFRD 2014/95/EU (n 2) provides for the lowest level of verification limited to the auditor ensuring that the non-financial statement has been provided (art 19a(5)); Member States may require that the information provided be verified by an independent assurance services provider (art 19a(6)). B Ballou, PC Chen, JH Grenier and DL Heitger, 'Corporate Social Responsibility Assurance and Reporting Quality' (2018) 37 *Journal of Accounting and Public Policy* 167 found that the quality of Corporate Social Responsibility (CSR) reporting improved if the GRI standard was used coupled with assurance. Szabó and Sørensen (n 31) 337 f note that provision could have been made in the NFRD for the auditor to check the consistency of the representations in the non-financial report with the data in the financial statements, but they concede that it is not clear if a consistency check improves the quality of the reporting substantially.

an external framework.[42] What is needed now is for policy makers to work to achieve internationally accepted frameworks that facilitate the efficient production of consistent and comparable information of real, decision-influencing, value to users. Here, the EU seems well positioned to be a frontrunner.

III. Rapid Evolution: Step Changes in the NFR Directive, the TCFD and the HLEG Report

The EU reporting position has evolved in stages[43] from the original Fourth Company Law Directive 78/660/EEC[44] and the Seventh Company Law Directive 83/349/EEC,[45] to the Accounting Directive 2013/34/EU[46] as amended by NFRD 2014/95/EU,[47] specifically Articles 19, 19a and 20 (Article 20 on corporate governance statements was discussed above).

The foundation of narrative reporting is found in Article 19 of the Accounting Directive which originated in a requirement in Article 46(1) of the Fourth Company Law Directive 78/660/EEC that the annual report should include at least a fair review of the development of the company's business and its position. Initially, only a few limited items were identified for inclusion: an indication of important events since the end of the financial year; the company's likely future development; activities in the field of research and development; and acquisition of its own shares.[48] A step change in approach came with the adoption of a new Article 46(1), inserted by Article 1(14) of the Accounts Modernisation Directive 2003/51/EC,[49] which required the inclusion by a company in

[42] Two-thirds of the largest 250 global companies do have their ESG reports independently assured as standard practice (KPMG (n 9) 26) and there is some evidence that assurance by auditors does improve the quality of the ESG reporting and with it the access to capital etc. As such, it has been suggested that assurance should be mandated by regulators: see Ballou et al (n 41).

[43] For the background to the EU approach to what was then described as CSR reporting, see 'Green Paper – Promoting a European Framework for Corporate Social Responsibility' COM(2001) 366 final, 18 July 2001; 'Communication from the Commission Concerning Corporate Social Responsibility: A Business Contribution to Sustainable Development', COM(2002) 347 final, 2 July 2002; 'Modernising Company Law and Enhancing Corporate Governance in the European Union: A Plan to Move Forward' COM(2003) 284 final, 21 May 2003; 'A Renewed EU Strategy 2011–14 for Corporate Social Responsibility', COM(2011) 681 final, 25 October 2011.

[44] Fourth Council Directive 78/660/EEC of 25 July 1978 based on Article 54(3) g of the Treaty on the annual accounts of certain types of companies [1978] OJ L222/11.

[45] Seventh Council Directive 83/349/EEC of 13 June 1983 based on the Article 54 (3) (g) of the Treaty on consolidated accounts [1983] OJ L193/1.

[46] Directive 2013/34/EU of the European Parliament and of the Council of 26 June 2013 on the annual financial statements, consolidated financial statements and related reports of certain types of undertakings, amending Directive 2006/43/EC of the European Parliament and of the Council and repealing Council Directives 78/660/EEC and 83/349/EEC Text with EEA relevance [2013] OJ L182/19.

[47] See NFRD 2014/95/EU (n 2).

[48] The list was amended by Directive 2001/65/EC of the European Parliament and of the Council of 27 September 2001 amending Directives 78/660/EEC, 83/349/EEC and 86/635/EEC as regards the valuation rules for the annual and consolidated accounts of certain types of companies as well as of banks and other financial institutions [2001] OJ L283/28, to include a requirement to give an indication of the company's risk management objectives and policies in relation to its use of financial instruments.

[49] Directive 2003/51/EC of the European Parliament and of the Council of 18 June 2003 amending Directives 78/660/EEC, 83/349/EEC, 86/635/EEC and 91/674/EEC on the annual and consolidated accounts of certain types of companies, banks and other financial institutions and insurance undertakings [2003] OJ L178/16.

the annual report of 'at least a fair review of the development and performance of the company's business and of its position, together with a description of the principal risks and uncertainties that it faces'. Further, to the extent necessary for the understanding of the company's development, performance or position, the analysis was to include both financial and, where appropriate, non-financial key performance indicators relevant to the particular business, including information relating to environmental and employee matters. Article 46(1) of Directive 78/660, as amended by Directive 2003/51, was replaced by Article 19 of the Accounting Directive 2013/34, which is not amended by the NFRD, so it reflects requirements which have been settled since 2003. The UK chose to rebrand the business review as a 'Strategic Report' in October 2013.

The significant development is the amendment of the Accounting Directive 2013/34 by NFRD 2014/95,[50] inserting Article 19a, requiring public-interest entities (PIEs)[51] with more than 500 employees to provide a non-financial information statement,[52] essentially an enhanced version of Article 19(1), noted above, and hence a PIE that complies with Article 19a is exempt from the requirements of Article 19(1). Article 29a requires a consolidated non-financial reporting statement from the parent undertaking of a group where the group has more than 500 employees and the parent undertaking is a PIE.[53] The focus of discussion here is Article 19a, which is a step change because of the breadth of the matters which must be addressed (reflecting the many voluntary frameworks noted above),[54] extending, as a minimum, from environmental and employee matters (which had been included in the review since 2003) to social matters, human rights, anti-corruption and bribery. The non-financial reporting statement must briefly

[50] Directive 2014/95/EU of the European Parliament and of the Council of 22 October 2014 amending Directive 2013/34/EU as regards disclosure of non-financial and diversity information by certain large undertakings and groups [2014] OJ L 330/1; see Szabó and Sørensen (n 31) 307.

[51] Essentially, a PIE is a traded company (admitted to trading on a regulated market in any Member State), any banking or insurance undertaking and any undertaking designated as a PIE by a Member State (the UK has not designated any entities as PIEs). It must be a large company for accounting purposes. The European Commission considers that the NFRD applies to around 6,000 large companies; see European Commission, 'Consultation Document, Fitness Check on the EU Framework for Public Reporting by Companies' (March 2018), Part V, 29.

[52] The non-financial reporting statement may be included in the management report or it can be published on a stand-alone basis. There is an exemption if the information is contained in another separate report, provided that separate report: (a) is published together with the management report; or (b) is made publicly available within a reasonable period of time, not exceeding six months after the balance sheet date, on the undertaking's website, and is referred to in the management report: NFRD 2014/95, art 19a(4). If information required to be included in the statement is published by the company by means of a national, EU-based or international reporting framework, the statement must specify the framework or frameworks used, instead of including that information: Article 19a(1). The provision applies to financial years commencing on or after 1 January 2017.

[53] Subsidiaries need not provide a statement if there is a consolidated statement and a parent undertaking which provides this information in relation to the group in some other report can rely on that other report provided it is published with the management report or is publicly available on the parent undertaking's website: NFRD 2014/ 95/EU, art 29a(4). As to whether the approach adopted by the NFRD towards group compliance works as an incentive for groups to integrate, see DG Szabó and KE Sørensen, 'Non-financial Reporting, CSR Frameworks and Groups of Undertakings: Application and Consequences' (2017) 17(1) *Journal of Corporate Law Studies* 137, 141.

[54] Likewise, the many categories of additional reporting required of UK companies on matters such as human trafficking, the payment policies of large companies, carbon emissions and gender pay disclosure, though often not effected via the companies legislation, would be social matters which could fall within the NFRD, but specific legislation allows for differing materiality thresholds to be set and allows for greater prescription as to the content disclosed.

describe the undertaking's business model; the policies pursued by the undertaking in relation to those matters (environmental, employee, social etc), including due diligence processes with respect to them; the outcome of those policies; the principal risks (and management of those risks) related to those matters linked to the undertaking's operations including, where relevant and proportionate, its business relationships, products or services which are likely to cause adverse impacts in those areas; and non-financial key performance indicators relevant to the particular business. Where the undertaking does not pursue policies in relation to one or more of those matters, the non-financial statement must provide a clear and reasoned explanation for not doing so.[55] Member States may allow the exclusion of information where the disclosure of such information would be seriously prejudicial to the commercial position of the undertaking, provided that such omission does not prevent a fair and balanced understanding of the undertaking's development, performance, position and impact of its activity (Article 19a(1)).

The NFRD is not prescriptive as to the content of the non-financial reporting statement (beyond that outlined above), so there is the risk of box-ticking compliance and boilerplate explanations; certainly, it will be difficult to maintain consistent and comparable disclosures.[56] In response to a subsequent consultation by the European Commission on institutional investors and asset managers' duties regarding sustainability, respondents commented on the absence of 'common or consistent disclosure standards and aligned metrics on sustainability information which is therefore hardly comparable'.[57] They also complained of a lack of forward-looking analysis and high-quality data from companies, noting that the available level of corporate sustainability disclosure does not necessarily match the risk assessment needs of investors.[58] Equally, the Commission found that the investment industry was very split about a proposal to develop uniform criteria to perform sustainability risks assessments at the EU level.[59] To assist companies in complying with Article 19a NFRD, the European Commission has issued reporting guidelines[60] (hereinafter the Commission NFRD Guidelines), but equally companies reporting under the NFRD may use widely accepted, high-quality reporting frameworks, such as the GRI Standards, discussed above.

The breadth of the reporting required is emphasised by the extension of reporting requirements to business impacts, a central requirement of voluntary sustainability

[55] NFRD 2014/95, art 19a(1). Szabó and Sørensen (n 31) 332 make the point that this approach encourages the adoption of 'hollow' policies on all the matters specified in order to avoid the need to provide an explanation.

[56] The FRC has produced a number of valuable reports from its Financial Reporting Lab on 'Business Model Reporting' (2016); 'Risk and Viability Reporting' (November 2017) and 'Performance Metrics' (2018). These reports are all available at www.frc.org.uk/investors/financial-reporting-lab. In essence, the Lab found that investors want entity specific information which avoids boilerplate and jargon, is linked to strategy and long-term value creation with performance metrics that are transparent, placed in context, are reliable and consistent, and aligned to strategy. See also FRC, 'Performance Metrics – Principles and Practice' (November 2018).

[57] See European Commission (n 39) 14.

[58] See ibid.

[59] See ibid 15.

[60] Communication of the Commission – Guidelines on non-financial reporting [2017] OJ C215/01; see Szabó and Sørensen (n 31) 330, who note that flexible reporting requirements coupled with non-binding guidelines may increase the quantity of information disclosed without an increase in the consistency and comparability of the information.

reporting, and now a mandatory requirement of the NFRD. The Commission NFRD Guidelines advise that when entities are considering the impact of their activities, they should look at the impacts *of* their products, services and business relationships (including supply chain aspects).[61] Of course, as the guidelines make clear, the impacts of ESG factors and climate change *on* the business would have to be disclosed as a principal risk if that was in fact the case.[62] The Financial Reporting Council (FRC) guidance on the Strategic Report is clearer and specifies that companies should report in a way that enables a user 'to understand the impact of these factors on the business of the entity and the impact of the business of the entity on stakeholders and society'.[63] For its part, the Task Force on Climate-Related Financial Disclosures (TCFD) (for more on which, see below) explicitly limits its focus to the financial impact of climate-related risks and opportunities on the organisation – this in itself is a materiality choice. Vice versa, the OECD guidelines focus on the impact of the enterprise's activities and the consequences for society, which is an outward-looking approach.[64]

The TCFD was set up by the Financial Stability Board (FSB) in 2016 with 32 members chosen by the FSB to 'include both users and preparers of disclosures from across the G20 constituency', with a mission 'to develop voluntary, consistent climate-related financial risk disclosures for use by companies in providing information to investors, lenders, insurers, and other stakeholders'. The French government had already given a lead with Article 173-vi of the French 'Energy Transition for Green Growth' law of 17 August 2015, which, as the HLEG report noted, 'has proved to be a powerful tool for bringing disclosure onto the agenda of financial institutions'[65] and which requires all listed firms to evaluate, report and address their exposure to long-term climate-related financial risk. In its final report in June 2017, the TCFD recommended that organisations make disclosures on climate-related risks and opportunities. Disclosure should be of decision-useful, forward-looking information. Disclosures should be grouped into four thematic areas, namely governance, strategy, risk management, and metrics and targets, and the report identifies 11 specific recommended disclosures that organisations should include in their reporting. For example, with respect to governance, companies should describe how the board has oversight of climate-related risks and opportunities, and how management assesses and manages those risks. With respect to strategy, companies should disclose the actual and potential impact of climate-related risks and opportunity on the organisation's businesses, strategy and financial planning where such information is material, and should disclose the metrics and targets used to assess and manage relevant climate-related risks and opportunities where such information is material. The report also includes supplemental guidance for the financial sector (banks, insurers, asset owners and managers) and for those non-financial sectors most affected by climate-related financial impacts (energy, materials and building, transport, agriculture, food and forest products). The TCFD stressed the importance of using and disclosing the results of scenario analysis, and its report includes a technical supplement

[61] Commission Guidelines (n 60) C215/6.
[62] ibid C215/2 and C215/12.
[63] FRC, Guidance on the Strategic Report (2018) para 7B.43.
[64] OECD, Guidelines on Multinational Enterprises (2011) para 1.1, box 2.
[65] HLEG (n 4) 24.

to guide issuers in preparing scenario disclosure.[66] The recommendations are directed to all organisations with public debt or equity and the Task Force recommends that the disclosures be provided by companies in their public annual financial statements.[67] Given that such organisations are required in any event to disclose material information, the Task Force considered that its recommendations will help companies meet existing disclosure obligations more effectively.

Considerable impetus has developed around the TCFD framework, with the recommendations being welcomed, variously, for being innovative, clear, comprehensive and workable.[68] At the One Planet Summit in 2018, a meeting of global leaders to review and progress the implementation of the Paris Agreement, the TCFD reported a growing list of 513 TCFD supporters, including 287 financial and 170 non-financial companies, with a combined market capitalization of $7.9 trillion, and where the supporting financial firms are responsible for managing almost $100 trillion of assets.[69] KPMG in its annual survey of corporate responsibility reporting for 2017 noted that 48 per cent of the 250 largest global companies acknowledge the financial risk of climate change with significantly higher figures depending on where the company is headquartered (90 per cent in France, 60 per cent in the UK and 61 per cent in Germany).[70] The Investor Agenda, an important investor network, reports that in 2018, nearly 500 PRI signatories have piloted climate reporting based on the TCFD recommendations through the PRI Reporting Framework.[71] A key development is that the European High-Level Expert Group on Sustainable Finance (HLEG) has recommended that the EU Commission integrates the requirements of the TCFD into the NFRD, thus unifying these important developments.

The HLEG was established by the European Commission in late 2016 to help 'to develop an overarching comprehensive EU roadmap on sustainable finance', which was defined in the report as a 'joined-up approach to the development of financial services that integrates the ESG dimensions across market practices, products and policy frameworks'.[72] The HLEG considers that the European Commission should better align the NFRD requirements with the TCFD, given the very rapid acceptance of businesses

[66] TCFD, 'Technical Supplement: The Use of Scenario Analysis in Disclosure of Climate-Related Risks and Opportunities' (June 2017).

[67] In keeping with this approach, the UK is adopting a Streamlined Energy and Carbon Reporting Framework (SECR) and will require companies to report under that framework in their annual reports, as recommended by the TCFD. The SECR applies to all quoted companies and to large private companies, which is an extension of the current reporting requirement on greenhouse gas emissions, which is only required of quoted companies. See Department for Business, Energy & Industrial Strategy (n 14).

[68] See, eg, C Williams, 'Disclosure of Information Concerning Climate Change: Liability Risks and Opportunities' (2018) *Commonwealth Climate and Law Initiative* 10; R Bishop, 'Investing in the Future: Why the SEC Should Require a Uniform Climate Change Disclosure Framework to Protect Investors and Mitigate US Financial Instability' (2018) 48 *Environmental Law* 491; N Nowiski, 'Rising above the Storm: Climate Risk Disclosure and its Current and Future Relevance to the Energy Sector' (2018) 39 *Energy Law Journal* 1.

[69] TCFD Press Release, 27 September 2018; TCFD, 'Status Report 2018'. A further TCFD status report is expected in mid-2019; see also n 67.

[70] KPMG (n 9) 34.

[71] See https://theinvestoragenda.org/about-the-agenda. The Investor Agenda was set up in 2018 to bring together the collective reach and influence of key investor networks in Asia, Australia, Europe and North America. Its focus is on investor action on climate change in four respects: investment; corporate engagement; investor disclosure; and policy advocacy.

[72] HLEG (n 4) 9.

of the approach recommended by the TCFD[73] and noting the 'concerns on the part of regulators, investors and civil society that voluntary reporting can be slow and uneven'.[74] The HLEG Report also recommends that work be done to identify the type of climate and ESG disclosures which provide strategic information useful for investors' decision making.[75]

The UK government has endorsed the TCFD recommendations and encouraged all listed companies to implement them,[76] with the House of Commons Environmental Audit Committee recommending that implementation be required on a 'comply or explain' basis by 2022.[77] The UK government considers that it is too early to mandate the TCFD recommendations,[78] though this decision may mainly be seen in political terms – the government would prefer industry to lead rather than legislate on this matter.[79] An industry-led Green Finance Taskforce, formed at the invitation of the government[80] and joined by the City of London Green Finance Initiative, has also recommended that the TCFD recommendations be embedded in all UK corporate governance and reporting frameworks, and be supported in due course by additional guidance.[81] A further recommendation is that new and voluntary UK sustainability-related financial disclosures (SFD), introducing additional elements not fully covered by the TCFD recommendations or beyond the scope of the TCFD process, should be created. For example, a new framework should be developed for measuring and reporting on impacts related to climate change, the environment and the SDGs, and the reporting processes and standards for disclosing green revenues should be clarified.[82] Meanwhile, the Financial Conduct Authority (FCA), the supervisory body with responsibility for the UK's financial markets, has started a public discussion about the effect that the risks posed by climate change will have on the financial services sector.[83] As part of this discussion, the FCA has posed the question whether regulatory encouragement is needed, for example, by requiring premium-listed issuers to provide a statement to investors explaining whether or not they have followed the TCFD recommendations in preparing their annual disclosures and, if not, issuers could be required to explain why not.[84] The FCA notes that the TCFD framework is relatively new and companies may still

[73] ibid 24.
[74] ibid 25.
[75] ibid 26.
[76] See Press Statement by UK Department of Business, Energy & Industrial Strategy, 19 September 2017, 'UK Government Launches Plan to Accelerate Growth of Green Finance', www.gov.uk/government/news/uk-government-launches-plan-to-accelerate-growth-of-green-finance.
[77] House of Commons Environmental Audit Committee (n 5).
[78] Department of Business, Energy & Industrial Strategy (n 14) Consultation Question 13B, pp 26–29, also para 100.
[79] See B Choudhury and M Petrin, 'Corporate Governance that "Works for Everyone": Promoting Public Policies through Corporate Governance Mechanisms' (2018) 18 *Journal of Corporate Law Studies* 381, which discusses governments' preference for using indirect regulation over direct regulation in this area, even though there are question marks about the effectiveness of disclosure in altering corporate behaviour.
[80] See BEIS Press Statement (n 76).
[81] See Green Finance Task Force, 'Accelerating Green Finance' (March 2018); City of London Green Finance Initiative, 'Working Group Report on Data, Disclosure and Risk' (March 2018).
[82] City of London Green Finance Initiative (n 81) 81.
[83] FCA, 'Climate Change and Green Finance', Discussion Paper, DP18/8, October 2018.
[84] See ibid paras 5.18–5.22.

be adapting their reporting mechanisms to meet its requirements.[85] The TCFD Status Report 2018 found that, in terms of current disclosure practice, some climate-related information is being disclosed, but it is often located in multiple reports, the financial implications of climate change on the company are not being discussed, and the quality of disclosure is variable across sectors and regions – in particular, there is limited use of climate-related scenario analysis.

In 2019, the European Commission expects to reissue the Commission NFRD Guidelines, having updated them to take account of, inter alia, the TCFD recommendations. It also intends to establish a European Corporate Reporting Lab to promote best reporting practice, which is an important innovation, given the need quickly to develop consistent, coherent and comparable disclosure frameworks. Meanwhile, the Corporate Reporting Dialogue, an initiative set up in 2014 by the International Integrated Reporting Council, has announced a two-year project focusing on driving better alignment of sustainability reporting frameworks and promoting further integration between non-financial and financial reporting. This project will work on aligning standards with the TCFD recommendations. Given the participants in the Corporate Reporting Dialogue (the eight principal organisations charged with establishing standards and guidance on reporting),[86] this project should see a significant alignment of standards going forward.

A. Materiality

Given the range of matters within the scope of the NFRD non-financial reporting statement and the TCFD recommendations, a key issue is the materiality threshold which delimits the reporting obligations which would otherwise be entirely open-ended. In the context of financial statements, materiality has always been closely linked to the investor need to make rational allocations of capital. Hence, in Article 2(16) of the Accounting Directive 2013/34, information is material information where its omission or misstatements could reasonably be expected to influence decisions that users make on the basis of the financial statements. However, the whole purpose of sustainability reporting is to address a wider dimension than investor decision making.[87] Article 19a NFRD itself contains some identifiable determinants of materiality, as the FRC has pointed out, in the form of filters with its reference to 'principal' risks and 'key' performance indicators, and requiring information to be disclosed 'to the extent necessary' for an understanding of the undertaking's development, performance, 'where relevant and proportionate' etc.[88]

[85] See ibid para 5.21.

[86] The participants in Corporate Reporting Dialogue include the Global Reporting Initiative (GRI); the International Accounting Standards Board (IASB); the International Integrated Reporting Council (IIRC); the International Organisation for Standardisation (ISO); the Sustainability Accounting Standards Board (SASB); the Climate Disclosure Standards Board (CDSB); and the CDP (an international NGO focused on environmental impacts). The Financial Accounting Standards Board (FASB) participates as an observer; see https://corporatereportingdialogue.com.

[87] See GRI 101 Foundation (2016), Guidance, para 1.3.

[88] FRC (n 63) para 5.7.

Materiality is always entity-specific; as such, the Commission NFRD Guidelines state[89] that the non-financial reporting statement is expected to reflect a company's fair view (subjective) of the information needed by relevant stakeholders, Material information must be assessed in the context specific to the company circumstances and the company's assessment of the importance of that information in understanding the company's development, performance, position and impact.[90] There are a number of factors which may be taken into account when assessing the materiality of information, including: the business model, strategy and principle risk; the main sectoral issues; the interests and expectations of relevant stakeholders; the impact of the activity; and public policy and regulatory drivers.[91] Of course, materiality is reflected indirectly in the thresholds for the application of these provisions. The NFRD applies to large undertakings (as determined by the Accounting Directive thresholds), which are public-interest entities with more than 500 employees.[92] The TCFD (voluntary) recommendations are directed at all entities with public equity or debt. While the TCFD recommendations extend to four specific areas of disclosure – governance, strategy, risk management, and metrics and targets – it is only with respect to strategy and metrics and targets that there is a (undefined) materiality constraint. Disclosure is required of the actual and potential impacts of climate-related risks and opportunities on the organisation's businesses, strategy and financial planning where such information is material. Likewise, organisations should disclose the metrics and targets used to assess and manage relevant climate-related risks and opportunities where such information is material. It was not necessary for the TCFD to define materiality more specifically as the disclosures they advocate are to be made within an organisation's annual filings and so materiality will be determined by the relevant framework.

A key determinant of materiality is the intended audience for the disclosures with a horizon that extends from current and prospective shareholders all the way to the public. The Commission NFRD Guidelines make clear that stakeholders, not investors, are the NFRD audience, defined in the broadest of terms as possibly including, as appropriate, 'investors, workers, consumers, suppliers, customers, local communities, public authorities, vulnerable groups, social partners and civil society'.[93] The Guidelines note that companies are expected to consider the information needs of all relevant stakeholders as a collective group. The FRC for its part emphasises that the strategic report is a 'medium of communication between a company's board and its shareholders'[94] and information is material if 'its omission or misrepresentation could reasonably be expected to influence the economic decisions shareholders take on the basis of the annual report as a whole'.[95] The UK is different in that a statutory purpose is ascribed to the strategic report, which is stated as being to provide shareholders of the company

[89] Commission Guidelines (n 60) C215/1, para 3.1.

[90] ibid C215/5; see also FRC Guidance (n 63) para 5.3. Because it is entity-specific and an subjective assessment, the assessment of materiality should be reviewed at regular intervals to ensure that matters reported continue to be material: Commission Guidelines (n 60) C215/6; FRC Guidance (n 63) para 5.6.

[91] Commission Guidelines (n 60) C215/6; FRC (n 63) para 5.5.

[92] See European Commission (n 51).

[93] Commission Guidelines (n 60) C215/5, para 3.5.

[94] FRC (n 63) 4.

[95] ibid para 5.1.

with information that will enable them to assess how the directors have performed their duty to promote the success of the company for the benefit of the members as a whole, while having regard to the (generally stakeholder) matters set out in the statute in section 172 of the UK Companies Act 2006.[96] The FRC attempts to square the circle by acknowledging that information in the annual report may be of interest to other investors (such as debt investors and potential investors) and creditors, and that other stakeholders such as customers, employees and members of society more widely may also wish to use the information contained within it.[97] It notes that the annual report should address issues relevant to these other users where, because of the influence of those issues on the development, performance, position and future prospects of the entity's business, they are also material to shareholders.[98] The FRC does note that when determining whether information is material, an entity should consider whether the fact or circumstance would affect the ability of the entity to generate or preserve value in the long term,[99] which would include matters relevant to stakeholders.

By way of contrast, the audience for the TCFD disclosures is specifically expressed to be investors, lenders and insurers, so materiality should be determined by their (essentially financial) needs and the efficient allocation of capital and risk. Regulators are also part of the TCFD target audience 'to understand risks that may be building in the financial system'. Interestingly, the GRI Standards define materiality in two ways: either as matters that reflect the reporting organisation's significant economic, environmental and social impacts (which they therefore would wish and need to report upon); or matters that substantively influence the assessment and decisions of stakeholders.[100] Under the GRI Standards, it is for the reporting organisations to identify their stakeholders, defined as those that can reasonably be expected to be significantly affected by the reporting organisation's activities, products or services.[101]

Ultimately, as the FRC notes, it is for directors to apply judgement in determining materiality,[102] and this raises a problem in ensuring consistent and comparable information if materiality is determined both on the basis of entity specific considerations and the directors' judgement. The UK's Financial Conduct Authority recognises that it may be difficult for issuers to decide whether a materiality threshold is reached in a specific scenario.[103] It intends to highlight to issuers the need to make adequate disclosures regarding materially important information, including information that allows investors to understand how ESG matters affect the valuation of a listed company's securities and how these matters are managed by the company.[104] The European Commission has already indicated that 'an appropriate balance' needs to be struck between flexibility (as currently provided for by the NFRD) and 'the standardisation of disclosure necessary to generate the data needed for investment decisions'.[105] In that regard, it is more likely

[96] UK Companies Act 2006, s 414C(1).
[97] FRC (n 63) para 3.4.
[98] ibid.
[99] ibid paras 5.2, 7B.36.
[100] See GRI 101, para 1.3 (2016).
[101] See ibid para 1.1.
[102] FRC (n 63) para 4.1.
[103] FCA (n 83) para 5.16.
[104] FCA letter of response (dated 6 July 2018) to HC Environmental Audit Committee Report; see n 5.
[105] See European Commission (n 8) 10.

that quantitative climate-related disclosures will be prescribed rather than with respect to more broadly framed ESG factors. In any revised guidelines, the Commission may wish to look again at the audience issue. It is difficult to exclude stakeholders, given that the whole point of the inclusion of ESG factors and climate-related financial risk is due to the impact on stakeholders, but materiality cannot easily be determined if the audience is without limit. Valuable guidance on materiality can be found in the Statement of Common Principles of Materiality of the Corporate Reporting Dialogue (March 2016), which is intended to represent common foundational principles. The Statement makes clear that:

- the definition of materiality focuses on the material information needs of the primary stakeholders for the report being issued, so the focus of reporting should be on primary stakeholders as a group;
- material information is that which is reasonably capable of making a difference to the proper evaluation of the issue in hand;
- assessment of what is or is not material is primarily qualitative and therefore judgement is both critical and necessary;
- business management is ultimately responsible for determining which information is material, ie, relevant to the purposes of its primary stakeholders.

The key then is to identify the primary stakeholders for this purpose, ie, for sustainability reporting, and the Commission Guidelines, as currently drafted, do not define that group in any meaningful way.

B. The Investor Perspective

In addition to recommending the adoption of the TCFD recommendations, the HLEG Report identified, as an imperative, the need to strengthen financial stability by incorporating ESG factors into investment decision making.[106] This shift to the integration of ESG factors into investment decisions, while it has been evolutionary over many decades, has gained traction over the past 20 years. Just as with issuer reporting, it is hard to determine a single defining initiative; rather, some key levers can be identified, including the 2006 UN-backed PRI and the growth in stewardship codes since 2012, practically all of which adopt this approach with varying levels of transparency and compulsion.

The HLEG Report recommends that asset owners and investment intermediaries should examine the materiality of risks and value drivers, including ESG factors, consistent with the timeframe of the obligations of their clients and beneficiaries and members, and should incorporate them into their investment strategies and mandates as well as reflect them in their expectations about stewardship.[107] The HLEG recommends, for example, the adoption of minimum stewardship standards for investment mandates.[108] Proceeding in this way would have the advantage of driving sustainability across the investment chain.[109] Asset managers should give effect, the report states, to those sustainability

[106] HLEG (n 4) 20–23.
[107] ibid 21.
[108] ibid 38.
[109] ibid 21.

considerations identified in the mandates and should engage with investee companies with the aim of preserving or enhancing long-term value.[110] The goal is a position where investors will bring fully integrated ESG considerations to bear on the allocation of capital and carry through that consideration of ESG factors to engagement with the investee companies. In effect, both sides of the equation are aligned – companies engage with and report on ESG considerations and climate-related financial risk and their management thereof, and these HLEG recommendations, if adopted, will bring investors to the table from the same perspective, having integrated ESG matters into their capital decisions and stewardship activities. To further drive home the point, the HLEG recommends that a clear commitment to sustainability be embedded in the duties of company directors and in the governance rules related to company management, supervision and incentive structures.[111] We will return to this point below.

The stewardship approach favoured by the HLEG is already present in an embryonic state in the Shareholder Rights Directive 2007/36[112] as amended by Directive 2017/828,[113] Article 3g of which requires (on a comply or explain basis) institutional investors to publicly disclose an engagement policy that describes how they integrate engagement in their investment strategy and describes how they monitor companies and include ESG factors in that monitoring, and how they conduct dialogue, exercise voting rights etc. Article 3h requires disclosure on a 'comply or explain' basis by institutional investors of the main elements of their investment strategy and key information regarding their mandates to asset managers. Article 3i requires asset managers to disclose information regarding their investment approach and the execution by them of the investment mandate. Nevertheless, the European Commission considers that 'there is still a lack of transparency in how institutional investors, asset managers and financial advisers consider sustainability risks in their investment decision-making or advisory processes. As a result, their clients do not get the full information they need to inform their investment decisions or recommendations'.[114] Indeed, the Shareholder Rights Directive (SRD) provisions do reflect a weak form of stewardship code, so it is unsurprising that the HLEG considers that in order to achieve these goals, it will be necessary to amend multiple EU directives, including the Shareholder Rights Directive 2007/36 and the NFRD, to link investor duties to the investment horizon of the individual or institution they serve and to the ethical preferences on sustainability of members, clients and beneficiaries.[115] In this regard, the HLEG recommendations with respect to the stewardship obligations of institutional investors and asset managers[116]

[110] ibid 40.

[111] ibid 39.

[112] Directive 2007/36/EC of the European Parliament and of the Council of 11 July 2007 on the exercise of certain rights of shareholders in listed companies [2007] OJ L184/17.

[113] Directive (EU) 2017/828 of the European Parliament and of the Council of 17 May 2017 amending Directive 2007/36/EC as regards the encouragement of long-term shareholder engagement [2017] OJ L132/1.

[114] See the Explanatory Memorandum (p 3) to a Proposal for a Regulation on disclosures relating to sustainable investments and sustainability risks, COM (2018) 354 final, 24 May.

[115] HLEG (n 4) 20–23.

[116] See ibid 40. The HLEG recommends that institutional investors should have regard to the following stewardship principles: investors should report on their stewardship activities to clients and beneficiaries; asset owners should incorporate expectations about stewardship in the awarding of investment management mandates; investors should continuously analyse portfolio holdings with respect to sustainability risks;

become in effect a proposal for a stewardship code across the EU, but a mandatory one enshrined in a directive. This approach would bring some welcome consistency, coherence and legal authority to what is currently a mishmash of differing stewardship obligations of varying significance across some but not all Member States.[117] The European Commission has already issued an Action Plan on sustainable finance as a follow-up to the HLEG report,[118] and it has brought forward a proposal for a regulation on disclosures relating to sustainable investments and sustainability risks which will require financial market participants and financial advisers to provide information as to how sustainability risks are integrated by financial market participants in the investment decision-making processes and advisory processes.[119] In bringing forward a proposal for mandatory disclosures, the Commission notes that the benefits include an increase in overall transparency, reduced asymmetry of information, increased granularity of information, a better-informed market and reduced search costs for end-investors.[120]

The significant factor here is not just that the two sides of the equation are aligned (investors factoring ESG considerations into capital allocation and stewardship, boards factoring ESG considerations into strategy and risk management), but that ESG and climate-related financial disclosures typically relate to longer rather than shorter timeframes. As the European Commission has noted, 'sustainability and long termism go hand in hand'.[121] Hence, out of disclosure may have come a mechanism whereby boards and investors together come to take a longer-term perspective, which is often considered to be the holy grail of corporate governance.[122] If so, this would be the defining benefit of successful non-financial reporting.

IV. Financial Reporting: Three Stages to Public Interest

The evolving legal framework is likely to involve, it is suggested, in three stages: stage 1, in which we are currently engaged, is focused on developing the reporting framework; stage 2 is the corporate governance stage; and stage 3 is the acknowledgement that large businesses are public-interest entities.

investors should engage with investee companies with the aim of preserving or enhancing long-term value on behalf of clients; as is appropriate and feasible; investors should in their voting processes address concerns over investee companies sustainability performance; and investors should promote the long-term performance and sustainable success of companies.

[117] There are stewardship codes or principles in Italy (2016), the Netherlands (2018), Denmark (2016) and the UK (2012, with a new version promised for 2019), and cross-EU stewardship codes such as that of the European Fund and Asset Management Association (EFAMA) (2011, revised 2017–18). See generally B Hannigan, 'The Rise of Stewardship: "Smoke and Mirrors" or Governance Realignment?' in H Siekmann (ed), *Festschrift fuer Theodor Baums zum siebzigsten Geburtstag* (Tübingen, Mohr Siebeck, 2017) 561–78.

[118] See European Commission (n 8).

[119] Proposal for a Regulation on disclosures relating to sustainable investments and sustainability risks and amending Directive (EU) 2016/2341, COM(2018) 354 final, 24 May 2018.

[120] See the Explanatory Memorandum (p 10) to the Proposal for a Regulation on disclosures relating to sustainable investments and sustainability risks and amending Directive 2016/2341, COM(2018) 354 final, 24 May 2018.

[121] See European Commission (n 8) para 1.3.

[122] See European Commission (n 18) para 4, p 23.

Stage 1 is well underway with the immediate next steps in non-financial reporting focused on ensuring that the frameworks ultimately agreed upon deliver high-quality, comparable, reliable information. The NFRD and related guidelines will be amended soon to capture the TCFD recommendations; the international frameworks will be more closely aligned (driven in part by the Corporate Reporting Dialogue project noted above), again with the TCFD recommendations in mind; and regulators especially will increase their pressure on financial institutions to address climate-related financial impacts.[123] In mid-2018, the European Commission undertook a review of EU legislation on corporate reporting to assess, inter alia, whether the EU framework is 'fit for new challenges (such as sustainability and digitalisation)' and it will report back in mid-2019.[124] Likewise, the FRC intends in the second half of 2019 to publish a paper on the outcomes of a major UK project plan on the future of corporate reporting noting that 'recent developments and narrative reporting are raising some fundamental questions relating to the purpose of the annual report, and company accountability to a wider group of stakeholders'.[125] Cumulatively, there will be more non-financial information, much of it forward-looking, and stakeholders will be better informed, but the evidence suggests that disclosure requirements alone do not change corporate behaviour or at least do so only incrementally over an extended period of time,[126] the classic example being with respect to directors' remuneration, where extensive disclosures have been provided in the UK for more than a decade with minimal impact on the setting of directors' remuneration.[127] Beyond disclosure, further measures are needed to drive behaviour; on directors' remuneration, further measures have included statutory rights for shareholders to have binding votes on directors' remuneration policy. On financial reporting, we need to move to improvements in corporate governance.

Stage 2 is the corporate governance stage, where the focus turns to the integration of the ESG factors and climate-related financial risk into the business model, strategy and risk management of the enterprise to ensure that boards address the impact of these risks on long-term sustainability and value creation, ie, that the disclosures are not 'in a vacuum'.[128] The European Commission in its Action Plan in response to the HLEG Report has indicated, tentatively, that it will work with the relevant stakeholders to assess 'the possible need to require corporate boards to develop and disclose a sustainability strategy, including appropriate due diligence throughout the supply chain, and measurable sustainability targets'.[129] It is curious that the suggestion is so tentative. We have since the first Cadbury ('comply or explain') Code of Corporate Governance in 1992[130] used corporate governance codes to drive boardroom behaviour and so it

[123] The UK's Prudential Regulation Authority is already consulting on how banking and insurance firms should address financial risks arising from climate change: see Prudential Regulation Authority, 'Enhancing Banks' and Insurers' Approaches to Managing the Financial Risks from Climate Change', Consultation Paper 23/18 (October 2018).

[124] European Commission (n 51). The intention is to publish a Staff Working Document on the fitness of the EU framework for public reporting by companies in 2019.

[125] FRC, 'Annual Review of Corporate Governance and Reporting 2017/2018' (October 2018) 48.

[126] See, eg, Choudhury and Petrin (n 79).

[127] See ibid; Hannigan (n 1) 65–66.

[128] See HLEG (n 4) 26.

[129] European Commission (n 8) action 10, p 11.

[130] See the report of the Committee on the Financial Aspects of Corporate Governance (1992) known as the Cadbury Committee.

might be expected that codes would be strengthened to reflect the need for a greater board focus on ESG and climate-related risks. The HLEG Report, for example, noted the importance of executive and non-executive supervisory directors 'understanding sustainability drivers and being able to translate the risks and opportunities into their business models'.[131] The most recent iteration of the UK Corporate Governance Code, in 2018, strangely makes only minimal reference to sustainability and does not capture the developing dynamic around the integration of ESG and climate-related financial risks into business models and strategies, merely stating that the board must promote the long-term sustainable success of the company (Principle A) and requiring that the board describe the sustainability of the company's business model in the annual report (Provision 1).[132] By way of contrast, changes have been proposed to the German Corporate Governance Code for 2019 which include the addition of the following to the Foreword to the Code: 'With their actions, the enterprise and its governing bodies must be aware of the enterprise's role in the community and its responsibility vis-à-vis society. Social and environmental factors influence the enterprise's success. In the enterprise's best interests, [the] Management Board and Supervisory Board ensure that the potential impact from these factors on company strategy and operating decisions is identified and addressed.'[133] The French Corporate Governance Code, amended in June 2018, requires a board to regularly review, 'in relation to the strategy it has defined, the opportunities and risks, such as financial, legal, operational, social and environmental risks, as well as the measures taken accordingly'.[134] The Dutch Corporate Governance Code of 2016 requires boards, when developing strategy, to pay attention, inter alia, to 'any other aspects relevant to the company and its affiliated enterprise, such as the environment, social and employee-related matters, the chain within which the enterprise operates, respect for human rights, and fighting corruption and bribery'.[135] Rather than have a piecemeal approach across Europe, it would be preferable for the European Commission to take the lead on the need for boards to have a sustainability strategy and to invite Member States to amend their corporate governance codes to reflect that requirement. Having such a strategy would merely be a logical next step, following on from reporting obligations which have identified risks to sustainability and value creation.

The European Commission in its Action Plan on sustainable finance did note that it is also considering the possible need to 'clarify the rules according to which directors are expected to act in the company's long-term interest',[136] which also follows from the recommendation of the HLEG report that the Commission explore the option of adopting a provision along the lines of section 172 of the UK Companies Act 2006 'to enhance directors duties and corporate governance by explicitly incorporating sustainability'.[137] Under section 172(1), a director of a company must act in the way he considers, in good

[131] HLEG (n 4) 38.
[132] FRC, UK Corporate Governance Code (July 2018).
[133] See German Corporate Governance Commission, Draft of an Amended German Corporate Governance Code, Consultation on amended draft (25 October 2018), available at https://dcgk.de/en/consultations/current-consultations.html.
[134] See AFEP/MEDEF French Corporate Governance Code (June 2018) para 1.5.
[135] See Dutch Corporate Governance Code (8 December 2016) para 1.1.1.
[136] See European Commission (n 8) 129.
[137] HLEG (n 4) 40.

faith, would be most likely to promote the success of the company for the benefit of its members as a whole, and in doing so have regard (amongst other matters) to various (generally stakeholder) factors, including the likely consequences of any decision in the long term, the interests of the company's employees, the need to foster the company's business relationships with suppliers, customers and others, and the impact of the company's operations on the community and the environment. As noted above, the section is explicitly linked to the strategic report which is intended to inform and help members assess how the directors have performed their duty under section 172.[138] In this way, the reporting obligation is meant to act as a mechanism for reinforcing directors' duties and for facilitating shareholder engagement. However, it would be somewhat surprising if the European Commission was tempted to follow this section 172 route, not least because there are doubts in the UK about the effectiveness of section 172,[139] so much so that, ironically, the government has recently increased the reporting obligations with respect thereto. With effect for financial years starting on or after 1 January 2019, all large companies, both private and public, will be required to explain how their directors comply with their duties under section 172 and how they engage with stakeholders, and any company with more than 250 UK employees has to provide additional information on employee engagement.[140] Overall, the route to changing boardroom behaviour to reflect ESG risks probably lies more directly through the corporate governance codes than it does through a statutory provision such as section 172. The issue is the directors' business judgement in recognising and reflecting on the risks posed by ESG factors to their business model, strategy and risk management with consequent risk to the viability and sustainability of the enterprise. As the reporting elements in stage 1 crystallise, we might expect to see governance bodies reflect these obligations in corporate governance codes over the next few years, probably by 2020.

Stage 3, recognising that large businesses are public-interest entities, is coming, gradually, but possibly not until 2030. This topic of the corporation as a public interest entity is one of intense debate that is beyond the scope of this chapter. I have discussed elsewhere that these mandatory disclosure requirements are being used to establish a framework of corporate responsibility as to how business should be conducted.[141] The need for such a framework has intensified since the financial crisis of 2007–08, which starkly illustrated the importance of ensuring sustainable, value-creating enterprises. The debate on corporate purpose has shifted again with the growing climate-change risks and the political risks from the rise of populism. A mechanism must be found

[138] See generally, J Lowry, 'The Duty of Loyalty of Company Directors: Bridging the Accountability Gap through Efficient Disclosure' (2009) 68 *Cambridge Law Journal* 607.

[139] See Government Response to the 'Corporate Governance Reform Green Paper' (August 2017) paras 2.22–2.24; HC BEIS Committee, Third Report of Session 2016–17, *Corporate Governance* (April 2017) HC 702, paras 31–35.

[140] Companies (Miscellaneous Reporting) Regulations 2018, SI 2018/860. The new obligations are explained in a Q&A document produced by the Department for Business, Energy and Industrial Strategy; see Corporate Governance, Companies (Miscellaneous Reporting) Regulations 2018 Q&A (November 2018). See also GC100, 'Guidance on Directors Duties, Section 172 and Stakeholder Considerations' (2018).

[141] See Hannigan (n 1); see also Hannigan, 'Board Failures in the Financial Crisis: Tinkering with Codes and the Need for Wider Corporate Governance Reforms (Part 2)' (2012) 32 *The Company Lawyer* 35, 39f.

to restore trust in business[142] and a first step in that regard is building transparency, followed by a recognised and clearly identified corporate contribution to advancing the interests of wider society. Governments have promised to deliver on the SDGs by 2030 and they will need the help of the largest businesses to do so, which means acknowledging that businesses serve wider purposes than the (sole) pursuit of investor returns. The clock is ticking.

[142] See Hannigan (n 1) 68.

11

Ownership Disclosure in Anti-money Laundering Law

KONSTANTINOS SERGAKIS

I. Introduction

In their efforts to safeguard the integrity of the EU financial system and broader corporate sector, policy makers and law makers have placed great emphasis on the issue of transparency in the beneficial ownership of corporations. When the beneficial owner is opaque and dissociated from the formal owner, illegal activities such as money laundering can easily be carried out, as criminals can hide their identities by misusing corporate entities and misrepresenting other entities or other natural persons as their beneficial owners. The Fourth Anti-Money Laundering Directive (EU 2015/849)[1] made a decisive step towards increased transparency of beneficial ownership with a series of amendments and improvements in terms of both disclosure (applicable to credit and financial institutions via the obligation of customer due diligence, as well as to the owned entities via beneficial ownership disclosure obligations) and supervision structures (cooperation amongst national competent authorities (NCAs, Financial Intelligence Units (FIUs) and the European Commission). Media coverage of high-profile scandals (such as the Panama Papers and the Paradise Papers) has nevertheless exposed the difficulty for legal norms to keep pace with new and very complex techniques that exacerbate opacity in ownership structures, while allowing for money laundering practices to proliferate.

Thus, the Fifth Anti-Money Laundering Directive (hereinafter the 'AML Directive')[2] was adopted in 2018 by bolstering certain restrictive provisions so as to better detect,

[1] Directive (EU) 2015/849 of the European Parliament and of the Council of 20 May 2015 on the prevention of the use of the financial system for the purposes of money laundering or terrorist financing, amending Regulation (EU) No 648/2012 of the European Parliament and of the Council, and repealing Directive 2005/60/EC of the European Parliament and of the Council and Commission Directive 2006/70/EC (Text with EEA relevance) [2015] OJ L141/73.

[2] Directive (EU) 2018/843 of the European Parliament and of the Council of 30 May 2018 amending Directive (EU) 2015/849 on the prevention of the use of the financial system for the purposes of money laundering or terrorist financing, and amending Directives 2009/138/EC and 2013/36/EU [2018] OJ L156/43 (hereinafter 'AML Directive'). Member States must implement the Directive by 10 January 2020.

analyse and enforce various violations in this area. Problems nevertheless remain at various levels, given the lack of a commonly shared vision in the perception, use and implementation of rigorous transparency standards of beneficial ownership information. The succession of money laundering scandals, with the latest example being the largest money laundering scandal in Europe that came to light in 2018 (Danske Bank),[3] highlight long-standing institutional and market pathologies that require a bolder stance at the national and EU levels, inter alia, in the area of beneficial ownership transparency.

This chapter will analyse the current revision efforts of the AML Directive and will address the efficiency of the main regulatory tools (enhancement of disclosure, increased cooperation mechanisms and enforcement mechanisms), as well as the challenges ahead in combating money laundering through opaque ownership structures. It will also touch on some national laws that show variations in the way they face these challenges and will seek to formulate proposals with regard to further harmonisation and future reforms in this area.

II. The AML Beneficial Ownership Transparency Framework

A. The Notion of Beneficial Ownership

Money laundering consists of a series of intentionally committed acts, such as the conversion or transfer of property for the purpose of concealing or disguising its illicit origin, the concealment or disguise of its characteristics, its acquisition, possession or use and, more generally, participation in any way in the above-mentioned activities.[4] The property must be derived from criminal activity.[5] Beneficial ownership is crucial to the detection of money laundering activities as it offers insight into the identity of the natural persons who ultimately own or control a corporate entity. In the absence of such insight, corporate entities may easily be used for money laundering purposes without the risk of such illegal practices being detected. The effects are harmful not only to the entire reliability of markets, but also to a series of actors who deal with or have an interest in such entities.

The AML Directive aims to ensure transparency of beneficial ownership in private companies.[6] This type of (direct or indirect) ownership relates at least to the percentage of shares of the entity or voting rights or ownership interest in that entity, including

[3] For a complete overview up to this date, see Bruun Hjehle, 'Report on the Non-resident Portfolio at Danske Bank's Estonian Branch' (2018), available at https://danskebank.com/-/media/danske-bank-com/file-cloud/2018/9/report-on-the-non-resident-portfolio-at-danske-banks-estonian-branch-.-la=en.pdf.

[4] AML Directive, art 1(3).

[5] For the various types of such activity, see ibid art 3(4).

[6] Ownership information in listed companies is dealt with by art 12(1) of the Transparency Directive via the notification of major shareholdings: Directive 2013/50/EU of the European Parliament and of the Council of 22 October 2013 amending Directive 2004/109/EC of the European Parliament and of the Council on the harmonisation of transparency requirements in relation to information about issuers whose securities are admitted to trading on a regulated market, Directive 2003/71/EC of the European Parliament and of the

through bearer shareholdings or through control via other means.[7] Direct ownership is indicated by a shareholding of 25 per cent plus one share or an ownership interest of more than 25 per cent in the company held by a natural person. Indirect ownership is indicated by the holding of the above-mentioned shares or interests by a corporate entity (or by multiple corporate entities) that is under the control of a natural person(s). Member States can decide to adopt a lower percentage for the indication of ownership or control so as to enlarge the spectrum of transparency in this area.[8] For example, Portugal has no fixed threshold for determining beneficial ownership,[9] so it could be assumed that any person holding one share or more should be considered a beneficial owner.[10]

The European Parliament has also called, unsuccessfully, for the beneficial ownership threshold to be lowered to address the current concerns of deficient levels of detection.[11] Another very interesting proposal was put forward more recently (during the revision of the AML Directive), but was ultimately not adopted: for non-financial passive entities, the threshold determining beneficial ownership would be 10 per cent so as to capture a wider range of beneficial owners of entities that simply exist as intermediary structures and do not create income on their own.[12] Had this proposal been adopted, the means by which entities are misused so as to distance beneficial owners from their assets would have been considerably reduced. It therefore becomes evident that the political resistance to more transparency in this area is persistent and more decisive efforts are required to achieve a better overall result at the EU level.

Although the current 25 per cent of beneficial ownership may appear straightforward and convey an impression of harmonisation of standards across the EU, the reality is quite different and has serious implications for the detection of beneficial owners and the ensuing transparency issues. Indeed, as highlighted in 2012 during a study conducted by the European Supervisory Authorities,[13] Member States have different methods for interpreting the 25 per cent threshold:

a) Some of them adopt a 'top-down' approach, whereby they consider the indirect beneficial owner to be the natural person who owns or controls this percentage

Council on the prospectus to be published when securities are offered to the public or admitted to trading, and Commission Directive 2007/14/EC laying down detailed rules for the implementation of certain provisions of Directive 2004/109/EC [2013] OJ L294/13. On this topic, see K Sergakis, *The Law of Capital Markets in the EU* (London, Palgrave Macmillan, 2018) 119.

[7] AML Directive, art 3(6)(a)(i).

[8] ibid.

[9] Law 89/2017.

[10] Financial Secrecy Index, 'Portugal Report' (2018), available at financialsecrecyindex.com/database/Portugal_Madeira.xml#b137.

[11] European Parliament, 'Recommendation of 13 December 2017 to the Council and the Commission Following the Inquiry into Money Laundering, Tax Avoidance and Tax Evasion' (2016/3044(RSP)) 13, available at www.europarl.europa.eu/cmsdata/135340/P8_TA-PROV(2017)0491_EN.pdf.

[12] Proposal for a Directive of the European Parliament and of the Council amending Directive (EU) 2015/849 on the prevention of the use of the financial system for the purposes of money laundering or terrorist financing and amending Directive 2009/101/EC, COM(2016) 450 final, 2016/0208 (COD) 30, available at eur-lex.europa.eu/legal-content/en/TXT/?uri=CELEX:52016PC0450.

[13] EBA, ESMA and EIOPA, 'Report on the Legal, Regulatory and Supervisory Implementation Across EU Member States in Relation to the Beneficial Owners Customer Due Diligence Requirements under the Third Money Laundering Directive' (2012) AMLTF/2011/05, available at https://eiopa.europa.eu/Publications/

of the concerned corporate entity. Further differences have also been noted under this approach that make convergence in this area quite unlikely.[14]

b) Others adopt a 'bottom-up' approach by acknowledging as beneficial owners also natural persons who not only own 25 per cent in the concerned corporate entity but also own 25 per cent in any other entity that owns at least 25 per cent of the concerned entity.[15]

Such differences in national laws may appear to be less significant compared to other problems in this area (which we will examine below), since they refer to some minor details in characterising who can be considered a beneficial owner under the national provisions. Nevertheless, it is crucial to understand that natural persons will seek to exploit minor details in order to avoid being transparent in these types of scenarios. It is therefore vital to focus on and critically challenge such differences, since they can pave the way for abuse.

Another important feature of the AML Directive is the provision that the natural person(s) who hold the position of senior managing official(s) can also be considered beneficial owners if it is impossible to identify such owner(s) following the above-mentioned criteria or if there is any doubt that the person(s) identified is (are) the beneficial owner(s).[16] This provision allows for an even more intrusive legal stance as to the identification of beneficial owners and should be a valuable tool in the hands of the 'obliged entities'[17] who need to keep ownership identification records. The AML Directive also provides that if such officials have only been designated as beneficial owners *ex officio* and not because they have an ownership interest or control, this information should be clearly mentioned in the registers so as to give a more complete image of the ownership structure.[18] Obliged entities must, according to the AML Directive, take all necessary measures to verify the identity of these persons by keeping records of the actions taken and of the difficulties met during the verification process.[19]

Reports/JC_2011_096__AMLTF_2011_05_-_UBO_Report_.pdf. See also the Commission's acknowledgement of these issues, Commission, 'Impact Assessment' SWD(2013) 21, available at: eur-lex.europa.eu/LexUriServ/LexUriServ.do?uri=SWD:2013:0021:FIN:EN:PDF.

[14] As the Commission (ibid 22) notes, 'some MS require institutions to determine whether a natural person at grandparent level (or beyond) holds 25% plus one share of the customer or more, eg a 30% share (grandparent level) of a 60% share (parent level) in the customer is considered an indirect 18% share in the customer and is not normally considered an ultimate beneficial owner. Other MS following the "top-down" approach, seeking to determine whether a natural person at grandparent level (or beyond) exercises control or owns at least 25% plus one share of the customer (de jure or de facto)'. See also the analysis in R Nowinski, 'The Importance of Beneficial Ownership' (2016) 6 (362A) *Butterworths Journal of International Banking and Financial Law* 1.

[15] As the Commission (ibid 22) observes, 'ownership at any layer has to be counted in full, eg a 30% share (grandparent level) of a 60% share (parent level) in the customer is considered an indirect 30% share in the customer and thus a person who owns more than 25% of such entity is considered the ultimate beneficial owner'.

[16] AML Directive, art 3(6)(a)(ii).

[17] Analysed in detail in section II.B.iv below.

[18] AML Directive, Recital 34.

[19] ibid art 13(1)(b). The inevitable interpretation problem in relation to the notion of 'necessary steps' is that companies and national laws will inevitably conceive and apply these steps in a different way, therefore allowing different implementation standards to emerge at the expense of this requirements' efficiency.

At the international level,[20] the Financial Task Force Guidance[21] and the G20 Principles on beneficial ownership transparency were put forward in 2014 to offer broadly formulated provisions and a flexible framework adaptable to different national laws, and to enhance common understanding of the benefits of transparent beneficial ownership.[22] These principles have traditionally been nurtured within a soft law framework and they consist of recommendations to national law makers in order to achieve gradual convergence towards higher transparency and operational standards in this area. Of particular importance to our study are the following provisions of the G20 Principles:

- the definition of beneficial owner should capture the natural person(s) who ultimately owns or controls the legal person;
- the maintenance of beneficial ownership information onshore as well as the adequacy, accuracy and updated version of such information;
- the potential misuse of legal persons via the ongoing use of bearer shares or the allowance for nominee shareholders or nominee directors.

These principles aim to increase awareness of the risks associated with beneficial ownership information at the international level. However, real concerns remain, including within the EU, in relation to companies' overall compliance with these principles. In various cases, other companies' names are provided as ultimate beneficial owners, most of which are offshore, and the information is rarely updated or even contains blatantly erroneous information.[23] The issue of keeping beneficial ownership information constantly updated is of the upmost importance as it may prove to be incorrect after the composition of the shareholding structure changes. Several studies have highlighted a series of deficiencies in this area, criticising the fact that some jurisdictions have complicated systems or (mentioning countries outside the European Economic Area (EEA)) do not require updating at all.[24] Concerning jurisdictions covered by EU law provisions, which is the focus of our study, the most common problem relates to the fact that although a regular update of beneficial ownership information is required, the monitoring of such updates is insufficient, with the inevitable result of constantly inaccurate registration records, as we will analyse in the following section.

[20] For a complete overview, see JP Owens and R McDonell, 'Creating Mechanisms to Get Good Access to Beneficial Ownership Information in International Context' (2018) 2nd High-Level Conference on High Net-Worth Individuals: The Challenge They Pose for Tax Administrations, FIUs and Law Enforcement Agencies, available at ssrn.com/abstract=3161723.

[21] FATF, 'Guidance Transparency and Beneficial Ownership' (2014), www.fatf-gafi.org/media/fatf/documents/reports/Guidance-transparency-beneficial-ownership.pdf.

[22] G20 High-Level Principles on Beneficial Ownership Transparency, Australia (2014), star.worldbank.org/sites/star/files/g20_high-level_principles_beneficial_ownership_transparency.pdf.

[23] Amongst various studies, see some interesting examples at Open Ownership & Global Witness, 'Learning the Lessons from the UK's Public Beneficial Ownership Register' (2017), available at globalwitness.org/documents/19250/Learning_the_Lessons_from_the_UKs_public_Beneficial_Ownership_register.pdf.

[24] For a series of interesting data, see A Knobel, M Harari and M Meinzer, 'The State of Play of Beneficial Ownership Registration: A Visual Overview' (2018), available at ssrn.com/abstract=3204532.

B. Information Provided by Corporate Entities

i. Central Registers

Information relating to beneficial ownership must be held in a central (commercial, companies or public) register in each Member State. The information must be adequate, accurate and current. Access to such information varies according to the potentially interested parties, falling into these three categories:

a) competent authorities and FIUs have unrestricted access;
b) obliged entities have access within the customer due diligence framework;
c) any member of the general public.[25]

Beneficial ownership information must be accessible in a timely manner by competent authorities and FIUs.[26] As a general principle, corporate entities are obliged to obtain and hold adequate, accurate and current information on their beneficial ownership, including the details of the beneficial interests held.[27] Compared to the beneficial ownership disclosure obligations in the case of listed companies applicable to shareholders, the onus of disclosure of such information in private companies falls on the *companies*, not on the beneficial owners. This differentiation can be explained not only by some features that do not exist outside regulated markets (for example, the constant need for listed companies to have access to the identity of major shareholdings for control purposes and for the public to have the same access for market efficiency purposes), but also by the necessity for centralising this internal transparency function around the corporate entity and not its shareholders.

Nevertheless, in light of continuous difficulties in identifying beneficial owners in various national contexts, the AML Directive now provides that beneficial owners (including through shares, voting rights, ownership interest, bearer shareholdings or control via other means) of certain entities shall provide those entities with all the information that is necessary so as to enable them to comply with their own obligations of updating and keeping records of beneficial ownership.[28] The Directive therefore seeks to engage more actively with the shareholders that fall under this category to make them an integral part of the disclosure framework. It will be particularly interesting to see how this provision will be enforced at the national level after the Directive is enacted by Member States.

Focusing on the function and efficiency of central registers, various concerns and criticisms have been raised throughout the years due to allegations of passive registration methods of beneficial ownership information and of a lack of ongoing monitoring of the accuracy of the information provided by companies.[29] Most frequently, the information held by these registers is outdated or simply incorrect, since from the beginning it has not been detected as such by registers during the registration process. Companies

[25] AML Directive, art 30(5).
[26] ibid art 30(2).
[27] ibid art 30(1).
[28] ibid.
[29] Brooke Masters, 'Danske Money Laundering Details are Shocking But Sadly Familiar' *Financial Times* (21 September 2018).

usually claim that they have difficulties understanding the registration requirements, and central registers can hardly distinguish between such companies and others that deliberately mislead them when providing beneficial ownership information.[30]

Reinforcement of central registers by dedicating greater resources and more powers is therefore essential as it is at the registration entry stage that beneficial ownership information needs to be verified as accurate.

ii. The Shift to Public Access to Beneficial Ownership Information

According to the Fourth AML Directive, the third category eligible to access beneficial ownership information found in central registers included any person or organisation with a 'demonstrable legitimate interest' in such information.[31] The AML Directive thus considerably enlarges the spectrum of parties eligible to access such information without the need to demonstrate a legitimate interest, since it now refers to 'any member of the general public', as seen above.[32]

By looking at this decision in a critical and highly politicised perspective, there can be no doubt that the Commission's aspirations relate to maintaining third parties' trust in business transactions, combating the misuse of corporate structures by increasing the visibility of beneficial owners, the need to convey the message of greater accountability to civil society and, more generally, subjecting companies increased scrutiny by the press. More generally, one can argue that this level of public exposure will also benefit other companies that want to know the identity of beneficial owners of the entities they do business with. This will allow them to reduce their risk and also the costs of due diligence, as well as benefit from a more competitive negotiation environment that creates an informational level playing field amongst companies. Investors can also benefit since they will be in a position to make more informed investment decisions, thus – at least in theory – favouring the overall market thanks to better allocation of capital. In parallel, allowing the public to function as an auxiliary pressure for compliance will inevitably

[30] For these and similar problems, see ED Willebois, EM Halter, RA Harrison, JW Park and JC Sharman, *The Puppet Masters: How the Corrupt Use Legal Structures to Hide Stolen Assets and What to Do About it* (Washington DC, Stolen Asset Recovery Initiative/The World Bank/UNODC, 2011) 69, available at https://star.worldbank.org/sites/star/files/puppetmastersv1.pdf.

[31] The definition of 'legitimate interest' is left up to national laws, both as a general concept and as a criterion for accessing beneficial ownership information. It is obviously a problem of having different interpretations of such concepts across the EU, since this can render access to beneficial ownership information even more complicated and dependent on national specificities. The EU Parliament has merely touched on the topic by mentioning that access should be allowed to 'any person or organisation who can demonstrate a "legitimate interest", such as investigative journalists and other concerned citizens', by avoiding therefore to provide more details on the range of parties eligible to demonstrate such interest: European Parliament, 'Money Laundering: Parliament and Council Negotiators Agree on Central Registers', press release (2014), available at europarl.europa.eu/news/en/press-room/20141216IPR02043/money-laundering-parliament-and-council-negotiators-agree-on-central-registers. The AML Directive specifies that national definitions of 'legitimate interest' should not restrict this concept to cases of pending administrative or legal proceedings and that they should allow for inclusion under this category the preventative role that investigating journalists and NGOs may play in the area of anti-money-laundering: Recital 42.

[32] Denmark, Estonia, Finland, Lithuania, the Netherlands, Poland, Portugal, Slovakia, Slovenia and Sweden had already shown this type of openness to public scrutiny of the beneficial ownership information. Such a requirement is nevertheless kept for access to beneficial ownership of trusts.

help the law enforcement, both in terms of efficiency and in terms of resources, to perform its monitoring role in this area.

On an even larger scale, all types of stakeholders benefit from such disclosure. Employee, consumer, civil and environmental rights can be protected more efficiently if beneficial owners are known to the public, since various groups interested in a company's activities will – in theory – be able to exert social pressure in relation to suspicious corporate strategies if they have access to beneficial ownership information.

Notwithstanding the obvious merits of such an approach, reservations may be formulated in relation to the considerable openness of this informational spectrum to the public at large, since increased transparency in this area may also be instrumentalised for various purposes and not necessarily for combating money laundering. Other concerns related to the disproportionality of such measures have been put forward, including rights to privacy and data protection, as well as the risks encountered by the beneficial owners.[33] The Directive endeavours to address some of these concerns by allowing for an exception from access to all or part of the information on the beneficial ownership on a case-by-case basis. Exceptional circumstances that justify restricted access include exposing the beneficial owner to disproportionate risk, risk of fraud, kidnapping, blackmail, extortion, harassment and violence or intimidation. Exceptions can also be applied when the beneficial owner is a minor or otherwise legally incapable.[34] Such exceptions are welcome, but do not fully address the concerns raised above in relation to any other instrumentalisation of such information by the public.

Moreover, for such access to be beneficial to society, interested parties should be adequately informed and prepared to make the best use of such information. In the absence of such preparation, concerns may be expressed in relation to the realistic benefits of transparency in the public sphere as well as to the underlying regulatory rationales for this reform. There is no doubt that non-governmental organisations (NGOs) and journalists would be prepared to properly analyse and use the available information, but the same cannot always be said for all types of stakeholders who could function as a social enforcement mechanism in the presence of suspicious strategies and opaque ownership structures. The multiplication of educational efforts to better prepare the recipients of this publicly available information is therefore vital to creating a truly meaningful informational spectrum at the service of society. In the absence of such efforts, the current regulatory choice does not adequately address the use of disclosure as a regulatory tool for combating opacity in ownership structures. Under an even more critical perspective, it could be seen as a populist approach aiming to convey an impression of transparency and accessibility of such information without a concrete strategy for increasing social and media pressure against money laundering.

[33] EDPS, 'Opinion on a Commission Proposal Amending Directive (EU) 2015/849 and Directive 2009/101/EC: Access to Beneficial Ownership Information and Data Protection Implications' (2017), available at edps.europa.eu/sites/edp/files/publication/17-02-02_opinion_aml_en.pdf.

[34] AML Directive, art 30(9).

iii. The European Central Platform

Another significant step forward in improving the current disclosure framework is the establishment of the European Central Platform,[35] which allows for the interconnection of the national central registers that hold beneficial ownership information.[36] This new framework will allow for an easier and more efficient identification of beneficial owners by NCAs, FIUs and obliged entities, and will increase transparency across the EU. It is hoped that this new platform will also assist in the detection of money laundering activities in relation to potentially opaque ownership structures and will also assist the general public to access such information on an EU-wide basis.

Nevertheless, technical and operational issues persist at the national level and the coordination of convergence efforts in this area is strongly needed. The Commission will further enrich this framework by adopting implementing acts, technical specifications and procedures that will enable the interconnection of national central registers.[37]

iv. Customer Due Diligence by Obliged Entities

Obliged entities are, according to the AML Directive, credit institutions, financial institutions, natural or legal persons acting within their professional activities (auditors, external accountants, tax advisers, notaries and other independent legal professionals involved in various transactions specified in the Directive), trust or company service providers, estate agents, persons trading in goods with cash payments of €10,000 or more, and providers of gambling services.[38] These entities must conduct customer due diligence by identifying the customer and verifying the customer's identity on the basis of documents, data or information obtained from a reliable and independent source, by identifying the beneficial owner and by taking measures to verify the person's identity and to understand the ownership and control structure of the company, by assessing and obtaining information on the purpose and nature of the business relationship, as well as conducting ongoing monitoring of such a relationship.[39]

National laws must provide rules for the corporate entities' obligation to provide information about their legal and beneficial owner to obliged entities within the framework of customer due diligence.[40] Obliged entities are also required, under the AML Directive, to report any discrepancies they may find between the beneficial ownership information held in the central registers and that provided to them by companies.[41]

[35] Article (4)(a)(1) of the Directive 2012/17/EU of the European Parliament and of the Council of 13 June 2012 amending Council Directive 89/666/EEC and Directives 2005/56/EC and 2009/101/EC of the European Parliament and of the Council as regards the interconnection of central, commercial and companies registers [2012] OJ L156/1. See also Directive (EU) 2017/1132 of the European Parliament and of the Council of 14 June 2017 relating to certain aspects of company law [2017] OJ L169/46.

[36] Such interconnection via the EU Platform needs to take place by 10 January 2021.

[37] AML Directive, art 31(a).

[38] ibid art 2.

[39] ibid art 13(1).

[40] ibid art 30(1).

[41] ibid art 30(4).

This provision will allow for better coordination across various sources of such information and an overall efficient monitoring mechanism, since it is a common phenomenon to observe discrepancies between the information provided to the central register and that provided to obliged entities.

III. Supervision

A. Financial Intelligence Units

FIUs were introduced by the Third Anti-Money Laundering Directive as central national units in charge of the receipt, analysis and dissemination to the NCAs of information that may be relevant to money laundering activities.[42] FIUs have a valuable role in the prevention, detection and combat of money laundering. They are operationally independent and autonomous, having the authority to carry out their functions without restrictions, and able to take autonomous steps for the analysis, request and dissemination of specific information. They are also responsible for the receipt and analysis of suspicious transaction reports and other information related to money laundering, as well as for the dissemination of the results of their analysis and of any additional information to the competent authorities in the presence of suspicion of money laundering.[43]

The status of FIUs varies across the EU, since they can belong to different typologies: administrative, law enforcement, judicial and hybrid.[44] In the EU,[45] most FIUs belong to the two first typologies (administrative[46] and law enforcement),[47] with two judicial[48] and two hybrid ones.[49] As has been correctly mentioned, the typology of FIUs can present different merits and shortfalls. For example, administrative FIUs can function as an interlocutor between reporting entities and law enforcement agencies, but without having the investigation powers that are awarded to law enforcement FIUs in other countries. The judicial FIUs have the advantage of political independence, but they do not develop any dialogue with obliged entities. The hybrid model has the advantage of combining different powers from different models, but it has only been used in two countries so far.[50]

[42] Directive 2005/60/EC of the European Parliament and of the Council of 26 October 2005 on the prevention of the use of the financial system for the purpose of money laundering and terrorist financing [2005] OJ L309/15, article 21.

[43] ibid art 32(3); see also Recital 17.

[44] I Deleanu, 'FIUs in the European Union – Facts and Figures, Functions and Facilities' in B Unger, J Ferwerda, M van der Broek and O Deleanu (eds), *The Economic and Legal Effectiveness of the European Union's Anti-money Laundering Policy* (Cheltenham, Edward Elgar, 2014) 97.

[45] ibid 101.

[46] Most notably, Belgium, Greece, Spain, France and Italy.

[47] Most notably, Denmark, Germany and the UK.

[48] Luxembourg and Cyprus.

[49] Hungary and the Netherlands.

[50] Deleanu (n 44) 97.

FIUs have reported difficulties in relation to the exchange of information with their national counterparts for a series of reasons, notably different interpretations of certain offences at the national level. These difficulties persist notwithstanding the creation of an EU FIUs Platform since 2006, which is an informal group composed of representatives from national FIUs and purports to facilitate the exchange of views on cooperation matters, most notably on the joint analysis of cross-border cases and of trends and factors in relation to assessing the risks of money laundering at both the national and international levels. Another very important initiative is the decentralised and sophisticated computer network 'FIU.net' (incorporated into Europol as of 2016) that enables a more secure and efficient exchange of information amongst FIUs in combating money laundering while making use of Europol's services. It is apparent that the different status that FIUs have (including staff and resources) renders the overall supervision framework quite complex and difficult to coordinate so as to ensure convergence of practices at the EU level.

B. National Competent Authorities

Under the AML Directive, Member States must provide the Commission with a list of NCAs and obliged entities, and must keep this list updated. Obliged entities are subject to supervision, and NCAs have the power to conduct on-site and off-site audits and to take appropriate and proportionate administrative measures in the presence of breaches.[51] NCAs must be given adequate powers, including the power to compel the production of any information that is relevant to monitoring compliance. They must also report any discrepancies that may exist between the beneficial ownership information held in the central registers and the one that is available to them.[52] This will ensure a better overview of such information for consistency and monitoring purposes.

C. Cooperation at the National and EU Levels

Cooperation should be viewed under two different angles: the national angles and the EU angles. At the national level, FIUs, law enforcement authorities and NCAs involved in anti-money laundering need to cooperate efficiently so as to ensure that anti-money laundering efforts are well organised and run efficiently. At the EU level, all the above-mentioned organisations need to cooperate efficiently with their national counterparts on an ongoing basis. More specifically, the Commission may provide assistance to facilitate coordination and the exchange of information between FIUs across the EU via a series of measures, such as meetings amongst national FIU representatives with the aim of standardising reporting formats, jointly analysing cross-border cases, and identifying trends and factors in relation to money laundering risk assessment.[53]

[51] Directive 2005/60/EC (n 42) art 48(1)(a).
[52] ibid art 30(4).
[53] ibid art 51.

FIUs must exchange, spontaneously or upon request, any information that may be relevant to AML efforts, regardless of the type of the associated predicate offences and even if the type of such offences is not identified at the time of the exchange.[54] This is to ensure cooperation even at the early stages of investigations conducted by other FIUs.

NCAs are expected to cooperate with their national counterparts to ensure effective supervision across countries. However, problems may arise in relation to the exchange of information or assistance due to various reasons pertaining to national issues, such as tax matters, secrecy or confidentiality, and pending proceedings, amongst other things. The AML Directive provides that such matters cannot be resolved by NCAs so as to facilitate the exchange of information or assistance in this area by also mentioning that Member States should refrain from prohibiting or placing unreasonable or unduly restrictive conditions on such exchanges.[55]

More generally, the AML Directive strengthens the cooperation between the NCAs that supervise credit and financial institutions and other authorities bound by professional secrecy so as to exhaust all possible means of exchanging information and cooperation between such authorities in combating money-laundering. Cooperation is also provided between NCAs that supervise credit and financial institutions and the European Central Bank (ECB).[56]

Anti-money laundering cooperation aspects can be further enriched with the assistance of other parties. For example, in the Netherlands, Portugal and Sweden, a reporting obligation applies to certain institutions and professional advisers (eg, banks and notaries) that consult the register. If any of these parties encounters incorrect information in the register, it must be reported to the authority in charge of maintaining the register. This is a very welcome framework upon which a multi-layered cooperation will be able to bring more benefits to the overall supervisory framework. The discrepancy across the EU is nonetheless flagrant since most countries do not have such an obligation. Other countries have made some progress in this respect. For example, Romania applies the obligation to report incorrect information to authorities responsible for supervision and compliance, and in Austria, the reporting of incorrect information is possible but not mandatory. As we can see, considerable progress still to be made in terms of convergence of cooperation methods – in the absence of such progress, money laundering continues to proliferate.[57]

D. Reinforcement of Supervision: The 2018 Proposals

On 12 September 2018, only some months after the adoption of the Fifth AML Directive and after some highly publicised money laundering scandals across the EU, the

[54] ibid art 53(1).
[55] ibid art 50(a).
[56] ibid art 57(a).
[57] T Keatinge, 'We Cannot Fight Cross-border Money Laundering with Local Tools' *Financial Times* (9 September 2018).

Commission put forth further proposals to strengthen the oversight of EU institutions responsible for combating money laundering.[58] The main focus is in relation to the strengthening of supervisory and enforcement mechanisms that still seem to be lagging behind. The Commission has noted three main problematic areas that require particular attention:

a) delayed and insufficient supervisory actions in targeting and resolving weaknesses in financial institutions' anti-money laundering risk management;
b) deficiencies in relation to cooperation and information sharing between prudential and anti-money laundering authorities, at both the national and EU levels;
c) a lack of common cooperation arrangements with third countries in relation to the anti-money laundering supervision of financial institutions.

More specifically, the Commission has proposed strengthening the European Banking Authority's (EBA) role to ensure effective cooperation and convergence of supervisory standards by bestowing it with anti-money laundering responsibilities in the financial sector. The EBA will therefore have a more explicit and comprehensive mandate via, inter alia, the following ways: the consistent investigation of anti-money laundering breaches by requesting that national anti-money laundering supervisors investigate potential breaches and consider targeted actions, direct power to address decisions to individual financial sector operators if national supervisors do not cooperate properly with prudential supervisors to act accordingly, enhancement of the quality supervision and, lastly, establishment of a new standing committee made up of by national anti-money laundering supervisory authorities.

The emphasis placed on the EBA, as well as the proposal for the attribution of direct intervention rights in the absence of actions by national authorities, may be the first sign of further centralisation of supervisory powers at the EU level in light of the recent money laundering scandals. These recent developments may therefore trigger further action at the EU level in relation to the monitoring of beneficial ownership information that remains, at least for the time being, a national affair, notwithstanding the well-known problems in terms of cooperation and convergence of supervisory practices.

IV. Sanctions

A. The Preponderance of Administrative Sanctions and Measures

Sanctions for breaches of beneficial ownership disclosure duties have been marginalised, notwithstanding the well-known problems in detecting and enforcing such breaches. The revised Article 30(1)(i) provides for effective, proportionate and dissuasive measures or sanctions at the national level in this area of disclosure obligations, alongside a more general provision, applicable to all types of breaches of the

[58] Commission, 'State of the Union 2018: Stronger Anti-money Laundering Supervision for a Stable Banking and Financial Sector – Questions and Answers', europa.eu/rapid/press-release_MEMO-18-5725_en.htm.

AML Directive's provisions, that imposes administrative sanctions and measures while allowing Member States to also provide for and impose criminal sanctions.[59]

The sanctions framework is a matter of utmost priority for the EU as the discrepancy between national provisions is striking. Fines for non-compliance with the registration requirements vary substantially across the EU:[60] from €103 to €1,032,[61] €30 to €1,450,[62] up to €20,000[63] or up to €1,000,000 or twice the amount of the economic advantage gained by repeated or systematic non-compliance,[64] or as high as €5,000,000.[65] It therefore becomes clear that disclosure duties of beneficial ownership information have not yet been perceived as a real threat to the integrity and reliability of markets in the EU and are mostly seen as a matter of national law. Moreover, the perception of the severity of such violations varies dramatically from one Member State to the next, based on the range of sanctions.

What is even more surprising is that the minimum harmonisation of pecuniary administrative sanctions via the introduction of 'minimum maximums', namely the obligation for national laws to set a maximum at least at a certain amount that they can also raise at their discretion, is not provided for this type of breaches. Indeed, the only categories that have been subject to such minimum harmonisation relate to breaches by obliged entities (customer due diligence, suspicious transaction reporting, record keeping and internal controls).[66] Moreover, such breaches must be serious, repeated and systematic. The exclusion of beneficial ownership disclosure breaches from this framework needs to be reconsidered as any type of violation is equally harmful to the integrity of markets and to the third parties' continued trust in corporate entities.

The range of administrative measures provided in the Directive is also applicable to the above-mentioned categories by excluding and thus leaving it entirely up to national laws to provide sanctions and measures for the breach of disclosure duties in relation to beneficial ownership. Administrative measures refer to public statements that identify the natural or legal person and the nature of the breach, orders that require such persons to seize the conduct and to desist from repetition of such conduct, withdrawal for suspension of authorisation for obliged to entities and temporary bans against any person discharging managerial responsibilities in an obliged entity.[67] The inclusion of beneficial ownership breaches in minimum harmonisation would be a first step towards conveying the message to companies and beneficial owners of the importance of such information and of compliance with the existing rules. In the absence of a dissuasive sanctions framework, real concerns must be formulated for the efficiency of the overall disclosure spectrum and the expected results of such a 'light touch' regulatory approach.

[59] AML Directive, art 58.

[60] For all national data present in this study, see NautaDutilh, 'Status Overview UBO Register Europe' (2017), available at https://www.cobalt.legal/files/bundleNewsPost/2990/Overview_status_implementation_UBO_register_-_survey_NautaDutilh_31_August_2017.PDF.

[61] Italy.

[62] Lithuania.

[63] The Netherlands.

[64] Germany.

[65] Slovakia.

[66] AML Directive, art 59.

[67] ibid art 59(2).

The AML Directive also requires NCAs to take into account certain circumstances when determining the type and level of administrative sanctions and measures. These circumstances refer to the gravity and the duration of the infringement, the degree of responsibility and the financial strength of the person subject to the sanction or measure, the impact of the infringement on retail investors' interests, the magnitude of the profits gained or losses avoided, the degree of cooperation of the concerned person with the NCA, previous infringements by that person, and the measures taken after the infringement by the person to prevent a recurrence of such infringements.[68] This requirement is undoubtedly a useful driver for an indirect harmonisation trend that may occur through gradual convergence amongst NCAs in this area, functioning with the same rationales, notwithstanding the wide discrepancy between national laws in relation to the administrative sanctions and measures (as previously mentioned).

Alongside administrative sanctions, NCAs can also take administrative measures to enforce beneficial ownership disclosure obligations. Once again, practices vary considerably amongst national laws. NCAs can, in the first instance, issue an order for the company to correct the beneficial ownership information or provide evidence of its accuracy.[69] More dissuasive measures include disqualification from public tenders,[70] suspension of licences, freezing of assets[71] and issuance of public statements in relation to the violation and the identity of the concerned person,[72] which can also have a dissuasive effect. Natural persons may also face bans from directing, managing or administering businesses, and may be deprived of their civil and civic rights.[73]

B. The Rarity of Criminal Sanctions

Nor are criminal sanctions harmonised at the EU level. They tend to be rare as many national laws focus instead on administrative sanctions and measures. Member States that have criminal sanctions in place provide for fines and imprisonment up to two years[74] or up to six months.[75] In practice, sanctions have rarely been levied. The only UK case of prosecution for disclosure of false beneficial ownership information took place in 2018. A businessman seeking to shed light on how easy it is to violate this framework decided to name politicians as beneficial owners of various corporate entities that he incorporated himself. He then pleaded guilty to filing false information on the company register and was ordered to pay a fine of approximately £12,000.[76] This case denotes the seriousness of the overall lack of meaningful enforcement mechanisms

[68] ibid art 60(4).
[69] Sweden.
[70] The Czech Republic.
[71] Romania.
[72] Finland and Germany.
[73] France.
[74] Malta, the Netherlands and the UK: NautaDutilh (n 60).
[75] France, ibid.
[76] For more details, see https://www.gov.uk/government/news/uks-first-ever-successful-prosecution-for-false-company-information.

in the UK, especially considering the myriad potential violations in the area of beneficial ownership information not currently detected and sanctioned.

These reservations are also highlighted in a report drafted by Global Witness,[77] which found that more than one in 10 companies had failed to name their controlling shareholders and that thousands of businesses have disclosed as shareholders offshore corporations instead of natural persons as required. In the majority of cases, businesses say that they are in the process of identifying persons with significant control, a strategy that allows them to avoid temporarily non-compliance allegations.

C. The Lack of Private Enforcement

Private enforcement is non-existent in this area since the regulatory focus has been expressed in relation to public enforcement only. Nevertheless, some organisations have put forward interesting proposals for triggering dissuasive private enforcement mechanisms. For example, it has been proposed that registered information denoting the beneficial owner should prevail over secret (unregistered) agreements with the real beneficial owner. This would result in declaring void all corporate decisions taken by the latter and would enable the declared owner to enjoy the full range of benefits of shareholder status (voting rights, control rights and rights to receive dividends), even if this would result in violating the secret agreement between the two parties. An even bolder proposal would be to consider the beneficial ownership registration as a precondition for the validity of the legal vehicle[78] and the rights that it may enjoy (holding assets, engaging in business transactions etc). National laws that have dealt with private enforcement mechanisms are rare. Although these proposals are quite revolutionary, they denote the potential importance that private enforcement may gain in this area of anti-money laundering.[79]

V. Conclusion

Beneficial ownership information is crucial for combating money laundering and ensuring the reliability of corporations across the EU. Individuals and other entities continue to abusively use corporate entities with the purpose of making ownership structures opaque. These practices impact a series of stakeholders and threaten the integrity of markets at large. EU law continues to address these concerns with an increased focus on disclosure tools, with the most recent example of making beneficial ownership information accessible to the general public. It is expected that this new era of public exposure will enable stakeholders (apart from journalists and NGOs that have

[77] Open Ownership & Global Witness (n 23) 3.

[78] Nevertheless, such a proposal would be incompatible, under the current legal framework, with the specific conditions for nullity of a company that regard a finite number of cases under which such nullity can be imposed: see Directive (EU) 2017/1132 of the European Parliament and of the Council of 14 June 2017 relating to certain aspects of company law [2017] OJ L169/46, art 11(b).

[79] Knobel, Harari and Meinzer (n 24) 9.

been active in this area) to exert an additional layer of social pressure against the opacity of ownership structures for money laundering purposes.

In this chapter, attention was given to the recent EU efforts to consolidate the storage of this type of information via a new European Central Platform that enable interconnection between central national registers. These initiatives will enable FIUs and NCAs to better exercise their role given the wide range of powers and regulatory tools at their disposal for the monitoring and enforcement of beneficial ownership disclosure obligations that have not shown positive signs to date. This is due to cooperation problems and to inconsistencies in the exercise of monitoring tasks. Our analysis emphasised the full range of regulatory powers and the need to coordinate the respective efforts of these organisations and to promote convergence of practices at both the national and EU levels.

Another major challenge that this study aimed to highlight relates to the lack of a reinforced and harmonised sanctioning power regime for violations in this area. Persistent differences and discrepancies in the way in which these powers are conceived, evaluated and ultimately exercised at the national level by NCAs continue to impede convergence in the public enforcement of beneficial ownership disclosure violations and the creation of a meaningful sanction spectrum that could safeguard market integrity. The crucial question is for NCAs to be given more resources and guidance so as to have further incentives and tools to converge with other NCAs. In parallel, minimum harmonisation of administrative sanctions and measures, as the AML Directive currently lays out for other violations, is absolutely necessary.

Other sanctioning regimes, such as criminal sanctions, have received varying levels of attention from national legislatures. The overall conclusion is therefore not particularly optimistic with regard to the dissuasive force and efficiency of sanction regimes. Thus, there is a legitimate and realistic concern that lax and rare enforcement will enable opaque ownership structures to persist, notably in furtherance of money laundering activities.

Although the centralisation of monitoring and enforcement tasks at the EU level currently looks too ambitious, it is certain that such a scenario should not be ruled out given the repeated scandals that harm financial stability and confidence in business. Judging from the Commission's plans announced in September 2018, the EBA's role is also crucial in this area as it disposes of a series of convergence tools and can provide invaluable and ongoing support to NCAs. If current efforts prove to be unsuccessful in warding off frequent money laundering scandals, the EBA may be called upon to assume direct supervisory and enforcement mechanisms while maintaining cooperation with NCAs and benefiting from their assistance at the national level.

PART IV

The Limits of Transparency

12

Transparency of Stock Corporations and Personal Data Protection

Access to the Shareholder Register

VASSILIOS TOUNTOPOULOS

I. Introduction

The protection of natural persons in relation to the processing of their personal data is recognised at the European level as a fundamental right.[1] Nonetheless, this right is not absolute.[2] It must be weighed against other fundamental rights in accordance with the principle of proportionality.[3] In the field of company and capital market law, disclosure of directors' remuneration,[4] directors' dealings[5] and ad hoc disclosure requirements of price-sensitive information[6] are characteristic examples of the interplay between personal data protection and the smooth functioning of the market. In this chapter, we will focus on the shareholder register, ie, the list on which owners of the company

[1] See Recital 1 to Regulation (EU) 2016/679 of the European Parliament and of the Council of 27 April 2016 on the protection of natural persons with regard to the processing of personal data and on the free movement of such data, and repealing Directive 95/46/EC (hereinafter GDPR), Moreover, Art 8(1) of the Charter of Fundamental Rights of the European Union (the 'Charter') and Art 16(1) of the Treaty on the Functioning of the European Union (TFEU) provide that everyone has the right to the protection of personal data concerning him or her.

[2] Recital 4 to Regulation (EU) 2016/679 of the European Parliament and of the Council of 27 April 2016 on the protection of natural persons with regard to the processing of personal data and on the free movement of such data, and repealing Directive 95/46/EC (General Data Protection Regulation) (hereinafter GDPR).

[3] See generally on the principle of proportionality Case C-73/07, *Satakunnan Markkinapörssi and Satamedia*, EU:C:2008:727, para 56; Case C-92/09 and C-93/09, *Volker und Markus Schecke and Eifert*, EU:C:2010:662, para 77; Case C-293/12 and C-594/12, *Digital Rights*, EU:C:2014:238, para 52; Case 362/14, *Schrems*, EU:C:2015:650 para 92.

[4] See on this issue the Opinion of the European Data Protection Supervisor on the Commission Proposal for a Directive of the European Parliament and of the Council amending Directive 2007/36/EC as regards the encouragement of long-term shareholder engagement and Directive 2013/34/EU as regards certain elements of the corporate governance statement dated 28 October 2014.

[5] Hessischer Verwaltungsgerichtshof (Germany) (2006) *BKR* 288.

[6] M Pfüller, 'Mitteilung, Veröffentlichung und Übermittlung von Insiderinformationen an das Unternehmensregister' in A Fuchs (ed), *WpHG*, 2nd edn (Munich, CH Beck, 2016) § 15 no 275.

(registered) shares are entered. We will not address the nature of the shareholder register keeper.[7] Emphasis will be placed on the question of who has access to the shareholder register.[8]

For systemic reasons, we can classify persons asking for identification of shareholders and access to the shareholder register into the following categories: a) the company (ie, the issuer); b) members of the company; and c) third parties. In an interesting case, recently decided by the courts of South Africa, a journalist requested access to the shareholder register.[9] Moreover, the interests of the issuer, shareholders and third parties are clearly not necessarily identical and can diverge. Accordingly, we will initially examine the right of issuers to identify their shareholders.[10] Then we will address the question of whether a member of the company or a third individual has the right to have access to the shareholder list.[11] Finally, we will address the issue of access to the shareholder register from the perspective of European data protection law.[12]

II. Identification of Shareholders by the Issuer

Shares can theoretically be held in two forms: registered and bearer shares. Traditionally, the shareholder register refers to registered shares (name shares) because with bearer shares, the name of the shareholder does not appear on the share certificate; hence, the name of the shareholder is unknown to the company and its registration in the shareholder list is not possible. Nonetheless, the pace of technological development in recent decades has brought about a change of paradigm. Share certificates in almost all Member States are dematerialised, ie, they are converted into electronic securities, which are registered in electronic records. This process leads to de facto identification of shareholders by the corporation and makes the basic characteristic of bearer shares (ie, anonymity) obsolete. Moreover, at the European level, there is a trend to convert bearer shares to registered shares[13] for both corporate governance and tax/anti-money-laundering reasons. This trend is reflected in the following legislation:

(a) *The Shareholder Directive*. The holding of listed shares through complex chains of intermediaries is currently a very common phenomenon, particularly in cross-border situations.[14] This phenomenon complicates the direct communication between a company and its shareholders, and renders the exercise of shareholder

[7] The register keeper can be the company itself or a person authorised by the company (governed by public or private law).

[8] It should be pointed out that access is also considered the making of copies of the shareholders' register. See on this issue *State ex rel Healy v Superior Oil Corporation*, 40 Del 460, 13 A.2d 453 (Del Super Ct 1940); *Shea v Parker*, 234 Mass 592, 126 NE 47 (1920).

[9] *Nova Property Group Holdings v Cobbett* (20815/2014) [2016] ZASCA 63.

[10] See below, section II.

[11] See below, sections III and IV.

[12] See below, section V.

[13] See generally U Noack, 'Die Umstellung von Inhaber- auf Namensaktien' in HP Westermann and K Mock (eds), *Festschrift für Bezzenberger* (Berlin, De Gruyter, 2000) 291.

[14] See generally S Schwarz, *Globaler Effektenhandel* (Tübingen, Mohr Siebeck, 2016) 78 ff; M Born, *Europäisches Kollisionsrecht des Effektengiros* (Tübingen, Mohr Siebeck, 2014) 28 ff; U Schneider, 'Die reformierte Namensaktie' in S Grundmann et al (eds), *Festschrift für Hopt* (Berlin, De Gruyter, 2010) 1327.

rights and the engagement of shareholders more difficult. To address this issue, the European legislature recently recognised the right of a listed company to identify its shareholders.[15] The goal of this right, as stated in the preamble to Directive 2017/828, is to enable the communication between the company and its shareholders, resulting in facilitating the exercise of shareholder rights and shareholder engagement.[16] Thus, the company is allowed to process the personal data of its shareholders for the above-mentioned goals, and Member States shall ensure that intermediaries communicate to the company information concerning shareholder identity without delay.[17]

(b) *Anti-money-laundering (AML) legislation.* AML legislation results in a similar outcome, but is based on a different rationale, namely the prevention of the use of the financial system for money laundering or terrorism financing. According to Article 30 of Directive 2015/849, corporate and other legal entities incorporated within the Member States are required to obtain and hold adequate, accurate and current information on their beneficial ownership, including the details of the beneficial interests held.[18] Moreover, Member States shall ensure that the information on the beneficial ownership is accessible in all cases to any member of the general public.[19] The difference between this obligation and the obligations laid down in Directive 2017/828 is obvious. Nonetheless, both Directives focus on the owners of a corporation and foster transparency, at least in listed companies.

III. Shareholder Access to the Shareholder List

Shareholder access to the shareholder list is a necessary tool for a) communication between shareholders in anticipation of shareholder meetings (general assemblies) to vote in favour of or against a specific topic (eg, amend the company's bylaws[20] or appoint directors);[21] b) proxy solicitation;[22] and c) solicitation of shareholders to exercise a minority right, particularly to join a derivative suit against directors.[23]

[15] See Directive (EU) 2017/828 of the European Parliament and of the Council of 17 May 2017 amending Directive 2007/36/EC as regards the encouragement of long-term shareholder engagement [2017] OJ L 132/1.

[16] Recital 4 to Directive (EU) 2017/828.

[17] Article 3a of Directive 2007/36 as amended.

[18] Article 30 of Directive (EU) 2015/849 of the European Parliament and of the Council of 20 May 2015 on the prevention of the use of the financial system for the purposes of money laundering or terrorist financing, amending Regulation (EU) No 648/2012 of the European Parliament and of the Council, and repealing Directive 2005/60/EC of the European Parliament and of the Council and Commission Directive 2006/70/EC (hereinafter the 'AML Directive').

[19] ibid art 30(5), as modified.

[20] *Kaplan v First Hartford Corp*, 2005 Me. Super. LEXIS 8, 2005 WL 2727062 No. Civ. 04-275.

[21] *Donaldson v Boston Herald-Traveler Corporation*, 197 NE 2d 671, 676 (Mass 1964). See also J Watson, 'Protecting the Shareholders' Right to Inspect the Share Register in Corporate Proxy Contest for the Election of Directors' (1978)50 *Southern California Law Review* 1273; F Newman, 'Inspection of Stock Ledger and Voting Lists' (1962) 16 *Southwestern Law Journal* 439, 440.

[22] *EL Bruce Co v State ex rel Gilbert*, 144 A 2d 533, 534 (1958); *General Time Corporation v Talley Industries, Inc*, 240 A 2d 755 (1968); *Schnell v Chris-Craft Indus, Inc*, 283 A 2d 852 (1971).

[23] *Weisfeld v Spartans Industries, Inc*, 58 FRD 570, 579 (SDNY 1971); *State ex rel Foster v Standard Oil Co*, 41 Del. 172, 18 A 2d 235 (1941).

Nonetheless, at the European level, there is no general provision referring to a shareholder's full access to shareholders lists. Access to shareholder lists is non-harmonised EU law.[24] It remains at the discretion of national legislators to adopt relevant provisions, always considering the European data protection regime. In the preamble to Directive 2017/828, it is expressly stated that:

> This is without prejudice to Member State law providing for processing of the personal data of shareholders for other purposes, such as to enable shareholders to cooperate with each other.[25]

Accordingly, there is a plethora of different legislative approaches and regulatory mechanisms across Europe. For systemic reasons, we can distinguish these approaches into two categories. In the first category, the issue is resolved by the adoption of special provisions regulating with details who has access to the shareholder list, for what reason and under what terms and conditions. In the second category, there is no special provision regulating the access right to the shareholder list. This issue is approached and resolved by the general principles of corporate and civil law. These different legislative approaches do not address the issue similarly. In the same category, we can find diametrically opposed solutions. Again, the above-mentioned categorisation is useful only for systemic reasons.

A. Corporate Law

Special corporate provisions exist in Germany,[26] Italy,[27] Cyprus[28] and the UK, among others. In common law countries, a liberal approach is endorsed.[29] Common law jurisdictions have generally vested a statutory right to inspect shareholder lists in shareholders, particularly if they have held corporate securities for a specific period or have a specific percentage of shares.[30] In the UK, the right to inspect the shareholder register is linked only to the proper purpose of the inspection.

More specifically, according to section 116 of the Companies Act 2006, the index of member names of a company must be open to inspection, provided that a proper purpose can be established.[31] The dogmatic background on this provision is that

[24] On the AML Directive see above, section II.

[25] Recital 6 to Directive (EU) 2017/828.

[26] See § 67 AktG.

[27] See art 2422 of the Civil Code.

[28] See art 108 of the Cyprus Company Act.

[29] See, eg, *MMI Investments LLC v Eastern Co*, 701 A 2d 50 (1996): 'The right of a shareholder to examine the corporation's list of shareholders for a proper purpose is to be liberally construed.'

[30] See, eg, *Caspary v Louisiana Land and Exploration Co*, 707 F 2d 785, 793 (4th Cir 1983). See also J Pimentel, 'Tender Offers and Bidder Access to Target Company Shareholders List' (1978) *Brigham Young University Law Review* 436, 444.

[31] See Companies Act 2006, s 116: 'Rights to inspect and require copies (1) The register and the index of members' names must be open to the inspection – (a) of any member of the company without charge, and (b) of any other person on payment of such fee as may be prescribed. (2) Any person may require a copy of a company's register of members, or of any part of it, on payment of such fee as may be prescribed. (3) A person seeking to exercise either of the rights conferred by this section must make a request to the company to that effect. (4) The request must contain the following information – (a) in the case of an individual, his name and

access to a shareholder's list is linked to the shareholder's ownership of the corporate assets.[32] Nonetheless, it is not clear in all jurisdictions whether the onus of proof of the (improper) purpose is on the company[33] or the shareholder.[34] The majority of common law jurisdictions have interpreted the relevant provisions as placing the burden of proof on the defendant corporation.[35]

In the same vein (but not necessarily with the same rationale), the Italian Civil Code (Article 2422) and the Spanish Company Act (Article 116)[36] provide that shareholders have the right to examine company registers, among them the shareholder register, and obtain abstracts at their own expense.[37] Similar rights are also provided in Lithuanian company law.[38]

In Germany, the approach is very different. According to § 67(6) of the German Company Act (AktG), each shareholder can demand from the company information about the data relating to him entered in the share register. In the case of unlisted companies, the articles can further provide for this disclosure.[39] Based on the wording of this provision, for listed companies, the articles of a company cannot widen the inspection right of shareholders to the detriment of other shareholders' rights.[40] The relevant rationale is the data protection of other shareholders. It should be noted that the predecessor of § 67 AktG provided for a general right of shareholders to inspect the

address; (b) in the case of an organisation, the name and address of an individual responsible for making the request on behalf of the organisation; (c) the purpose for which the information is to be used; and (d) whether the information will be disclosed to any other person, and if so – (i) where that person is an individual, his name and address, (ii) where that person is an organisation, the name and address of an individual responsible for receiving the information on its behalf, and (iii) the purpose for which the information is to be used by that person.'

[32] See generally B Griffin, 'Shareholders' Inspection Rights' (1977) 30 *Oklahoma Law Review* 616; M Baylson and J Gailey, 'Who Has the Right to the Shareholder Lists of National Banks during Tender Offers?' (1987) 104 *Banking Law Journal* 447, 455; R Thomas, 'Improving Shareholders' Monitoring of Corporate Management by Expanding Statutory Access to Information' (1996) 38 *Arizona Law Review* 331; B Jeffries, 'Shareholders' Access to Corporate Books and Records' (2011) 59 *Drake Law Review* 1087, 1099. See also *Guthrie v Harkness*, 199 US 148 (1905), according to which 'the right of inspection rests upon the proposition that those in charge of the corporation are merely the agents of the stockholders who are the real owners of the property'.

[33] *Stone v Kellogg*, 165 III 192 (1897).

[34] *Morris v Broadview, Inc*, 52 NE 2d 769 (1944).

[35] Griffin (n 32), 619.

[36] Article 116 of the Spanish Company Act: 'Cualquier accionista que lo solicite podrá examinar el libro registro de acciones nominativas.' See also Agencia Española De Protección De Datos, Informe 0338/2012.

[37] Article 2422 of the Civil Code: 'I soci hanno diritto di esaminare i libri indicati nel primo comma, numeri 1) e 3) dell' articolo 2421 e di ottenerne estratti a proprie spese'. See also art 2421, according to which 'la società deve tenere: 1) il libro dei soci [2346, 2478], nel quale devono essere indicati distintamente per ogni categoria il numero delle azioni, il cognome e il nome dei titolari delle azioni nominative, i trasferimenti e i vincoli ad esse relativi e i versamenti eseguiti'.

[38] Article 18 of the Lithuanian Company Act.

[39] AktG, § 67(6): '1. Der Aktionär kann von der Gesellschaft Auskunft über die zu seiner Person in das Aktienregister eingetragenen Daten verlangen. 2. Bei nichtbörsennotierten Gesellschaften kann die Satzung Weiteres bestimmen. 3. Die Gesellschaft darf die Registerdaten sowie die nach Absatz 4 Satz 2 und 3 mitgeteilten Daten für ihre Aufgaben im Verhältnis zu den Aktionären verwenden. 4. Zur Werbung für das Unternehmen darf sie die Daten nur verwenden, soweit der Aktionär nicht widerspricht. 5. Die Aktionäre sind in angemessener Weise über ihr Widerspruchsrecht zu informieren.'

[40] Bundesgerichtshof (Germany) (2008) *NZG* 149, 150: 'Das Auskunftsbegehren ist jedenfalls unbegründet, weil ihm die in § 67 VI 3 AktG berücksichtigten Geheimhaltungsinteressen der Aktionäre entgegenstehen, wie das Berufungsgericht zutreffend ausführt.'

shareholder register.[41] This provision was amended in 2001[42] to make the German legal standards compliant with European legal standards on data protection.[43]

B. General Principles

Many other jurisdictions have chosen to address the issue of access to shareholder lists by applying general principles of corporate and civil law, which often results in contradictory judgments. Hence, in Austria, special emphasis is placed on the argument that shareholders have a vested right to know the names of other corporate members, particularly if the corporation has issued name shares. Based on this argument, the Austrian Supreme Court ruled in a landmark decision that a shareholder of a stock corporation has the right to be informed of the names of other shareholders registered in the shareholder list.[44] A similar view was also endorsed in Greece.[45] In contrast with this view and in the absence of a special provision, in Switzerland, the interest of a shareholder to have access to the shareholder list does not prevail over the interests of other shareholders to keep their privacy.[46]

IV. Third Party Access to the Shareholder List

Third parties usually lack legal standing to require access to the shareholder list if access is also denied to shareholders (*argumentum de majore ad minus*). However, the granting

[41] AktG, § 67 V: 'Jedem Aktionär ist auf Verlangen Einsicht in das Aktienbuch zu gewähren.'

[42] Gesetz zur Namensaktie und zur Erleichterung der Stimmrechtsausübung – Namensaktiengesetz (NaStraG) from 18 January 2001.

[43] A Cahn in G Spindler and E Stilz (eds), *Kommentar zum Aktiengesetz* (Munich, CH Beck, 2015) § 67 no 108; W Bayer in W Goette et al (eds), *MüKo AktG* (Munich, C.H. Beck, 2016) § 67 no 15; J Koch in U Hüffer and J Koch (eds), *AktG* (Munich, CH Beck, 2016) § 67 no 28.

[44] Oberster Gerichtshof (Austria) 8Ob260/65: 'Doch hat das Interesse des Aktionärs an dem Inhalt des Aktienbuches besonders bei Namensaktien nicht unbeachtet zu bleiben, weil gerade bei Namensaktien die Persönlichkeit des Aktionärs im Vordergrund steht und sowohl der Gesellschaft als auch den Mitaktionären das Recht einzuräumen ist, zu erfahren, mit wem sie es zu tun haben (Godin – Wilhelmi, Aktiengesetz[2], S. 249, zu § 61 Anm. A 1, Gadow, Aktiengesetz[2], 1961, S. 379, Anm. 6 zu § 61, Baumbach – Hueck, Aktiengesetz[11], S. 196 f, zu § 61, Anm. 2).' See also N Aburumieh and H Foglar-Deinhardstein, 'Neues im Recht der (Namens-) Aktien' (2011) *Aufsichtsrat aktuell* 5, 7.

[45] ΜονΠρωτΚαβ 738/07 (2007) *ΕπισκΕΔ* 943; V Antonopoulos, *Δίκαιο ΑΕ & ΕΠΕ* (Athens, Sakkoulas, 2009) 278, fn 25; N Vervessos in E Perrakis (ed), *ΔικΑΕ*, vol 2A (Athens, NB, 2003) art 8β no 53; K Pamboukis, 'Κάλυψη του μετοχικού κεφαλαίου με δημόσια εγγραφή' (1979) *Αρμ* 836; I Varvitsiotis, *Η ονομαστική μετοχή* (Athens, Sakkoulas, 1961) 43; C Chrysanthis in B Antonopoulos and S Mouzoulas (eds), *Ανώνυμες Εταιρίες*, vol I (Athens, Sakkoulas, 2013) art 8β no 31. See, however, art 141(11) of the newly adopted Law 4548/2018, which provides that a shareholder has access to the shareholders list if the articles of association so provide. Nonetheless, the issuer is not obliged to disclose information for shareholdings less than one per cent of the capital.

[46] P Forstmoser, A Meier-Hayoz and P Nobel, *Schweizerisches Aktienrecht* (Bern, Stämpfli, 1996) 556: 'Zusätzlich ist jedoch … auch das Diskretionsinteresse der betroffenen Mitaktionäre zu berücksichtigen …'; C Lambert and P Schleiffer, 'Auskunfts- und Einsichtsrecht' (2008) *GesKR* 98, 101; R Watter and C Rampini, 'Proxy Fights' in R Tschäni (ed) *Mergers & Acquisitions* III (Zürich, Schulthess, 2001) 14; P Forstmoser, 'Informations- und Meinungsäusserungsrechte des Aktionärs' in *Rechtsfragen um die Generalversammlung* (Zürich, Schulthess, 1997) 85, 104: 'Ein Auskunft oder Einsicht zwecks Kontaktnahme mit anderen Aktionären wird von der Lehre abgelehnt.'

of access to shareholders does not automatically mean that third parties have the same rights as shareholders have. Third parties are not members of the company and cannot be treated as members of the company.

Nonetheless, in some (common law) jurisdictions, access is explicitly recognised for third parties (anyone) under the same conditions as shareholders upon the payment of a fee.[47] Emphasis is placed again on establishing a proper purpose. Hence, the establishment of a proper purpose makes the shareholder list accessible to both shareholders and third parties.

In other jurisdictions, third parties have access to the shareholder register only in specific cases. A characteristic example refers to tender offers.[48] Tender offers are usually considered a proper corporate purpose.[49] Consequently, a bidder, who is already a shareholder, enjoys the right to communicate with the target company's shareholders.[50] Nonetheless, there is no reason a tender offer by a shareholder should be treated differently from a tender offer by a third party. If the third party is treated differently, that third party need only purchase a few shares to have access to the shareholder list.[51] Therefore, case law in the US has long recognised the right of a third party to have access to shareholder lists to explore the interest of target company shareholders in selling their shares and to inform shareholders of the tender offer.[52]

In a recent decision, the Supreme Court of Appeal of South Africa extensively widened the notion of proper purpose in relation to third party access, holding that journalists enjoy an access right to shareholder lists. According to the Court, 'the unqualified right of access to a company's register is an essential component of effective journalism and informed citizenry'.[53] The argument of the company that the right to privacy of shareholders would be violated was dismissed because, according to the Court, interference with the ability to access such information would impede the freedom of the press and the concomitant freedom of expression.[54]

V. Comparative Remarks

Based on the above-mentioned analysis, we can easily conclude that the legislative approaches in different jurisdictions vary significantly and result in completely different conditions with respect to access to shareholder lists. Nonetheless, a minimum prerequisite for access to shareholder lists can be established, which is

[47] On English law, see above, section III.A. See also s 173 of the Australian Corporations Act 2001.

[48] Pimentel (n 30) 436; Baylson and Galley (n 32); D Bradshaw, 'Defensive Tactics Employed by Incumbent Managements in Contesting Tender Offers' (1968–69) 21 *Stanford Law Review* 1104.

[49] *Mite Corporation v Heli Coil Corporation*, 256 A 2d 855 (Del Ch 1969); *Crane Co v Anaconda Co*, 39 NY 2d 14 (1976).

[50] Pimentel (n 30) 436.

[51] See the facts on *Mite Corporation v Heli Coil Corporation*,(n 49).

[52] *Mesa Petroleum Co v Aztec Oil & Gas Co*, 406 F Supp 910 (1976); *Applied Digital Data Systems Inc. v Milgo Electronic Corporation* 425 F Supp 1163, 1165 (1977).

[53] *Nova Property Group Holdings v Cobbett* (20815/2014) [2016] ZASCA 63, para 39.

[54] ibid paras 38, 39.

proper purpose.[55] Proper purpose has generally been defined as including purpose reasonably related to the interest of a person as shareholder.[56] In other words, a proper purpose must be lawful and related to the petitioner's status as a shareholder.[57] '[A]nything which may properly come before a stockholders' meeting for deliberation or vote is a proper purpose for seeking a stockholders' list.'[58] Curiosity,[59] harassment, haranguing[60] and selling of shareholder lists[61] are generally considered improper use. Beyond this, there is a plethora of remaining unanswered issues.

More specifically, consensus has not been established on whether the intent to find sellers or buyers for a corporation's shares constitutes an (im)proper use.[62] Moreover, it also remains unclear whether an improper purpose behind a proper one can affect the right of a shareholder to have access to the shareholder list.[63] There is also controversial case law on whether a negative outcome for the corporation should also be considered. An Australian court answered this question positively, holding that the invitation to shareholders to participate in a collective recovery action against the company could not be considered proper purpose.[64] However and despite interpretational difficulties, the proper purpose criterion can be useful for our analysis based on the new data protection regime.

Nonetheless, before analysing the new data protection regime, we must note that the data protection dimension is not always considered, and when it is, legal conclusions are not always the same.[65] However, at the European level, the right to respect for private life with regard to the processing of personal data concerns any information relating to

[55] See F McChesney, 'Proper Purpose, Fiduciary Duties and Shareholder-Raider Access to Corporate Information' (2000) 68 *University of Cincinnati Law Review* 1199, 1203: 'Whatever the variations in statutory procedure, proper purpose has become the substantive touchstone in most jurisdictions', citing R Clark, *Corporate Law*, 2nd edn (New York, Aspen Publishers, 1986) 100; L Metcalf, 'The Secrecy of Corporate Ownership' (1973) 6 *Indiana Law Review* 645, 651.

[56] *General Time Corporation v Talley Industries, Inc* (n 22). See also *Wolozyn v Begarek* 378 P 2d 1007, 1010 (1963), defining proper purpose as 'a purpose lawful in character, wherein a stockholder in good faith seeks information bearing upon the protection of his interest and that of other stockholders in the corporation, and not in contrary to the interests of the corporation, as distinguished from one seeking to gratify his curiosity or proceeding for speculative or vexatious purposes'.

[57] *Pagett v Westport Precision, Inc*, 845 A 2d 455 (2004).

[58] *NVF Co v Sharon Steel Corporation*, 294 F Supp 1091, 1094 (1969).

[59] *Guthrie v Harkness*, 199 US 148, 156 (1905); *Steinberg v American Bantam Car Co*, 76 F Supp 426, 436 (1948); *Sawers v American Phenolic Corporation*, 404 III 440, 89 NE 2d 374 (1949).

[60] *Burry & Knight Ltd v Knight* [2014] WLR 4046.

[61] *Theile v Cities Service Co*, 31 Del 514, 115 A 773 (1922).

[62] *Shabshelowitz v Fall River Gas Company*, 30 Mass App Ct 769 (1990): 'Here, the plaintiff's sole purpose for inspecting and copying the defendant's stockholders list, as framed by the reported question, is to identify "current stockholders whom he can contact in order to determine whether they are willing to sell their shares of Company stock to him for his own investment portfolio". That purpose, it is clear, was solely for the benefit of the plaintiff and is not, as required by G.L.c. 156B, § 32, "in the interest of the [plaintiff], as a stockholder, relative to the affairs of the corporation," and, in deciding the narrow issue before us, we hold that a stockholder in a company does not have the right to inspect stockholders lists where his sole purpose is to obtain information that might result in acquiring additional company stock for his investment portfolio.' However, see *Western Pac. Indus, Inc v Liggett & Myers, Inc*, 310 A 2d 669 (Del Ch 1973).

[63] *General Time Corporation v Talley Industries, Inc* (n 22); *EL Bruce Co v State ex rel Gilbert* (n 22).

[64] *IMF (Australia) Ltd v Sons Of Gwalia Ltd* (Administrator Appointed) [2004] FCA 1390.

[65] Recitals 7 and 8 in the preamble to Directive 95/46.

an identified or identifiable individual.[66] Accordingly, acquisitions of shares and registrations in shareholder lists are personal data. In the same vein, shareholder lists are considered filing systems according to data protection law.[67] It follows that any form of disclosure, dissemination or making available of information contained in shareholder lists is a processing of personal data. The lawfulness of this processing can be accepted only if and to the extent that the conditions laid down in General Data Protection Regulation (GDPR) are fulfilled.[68]

VI. The New Data Protection Regime

At the European level, the data protection regime is governed by the newly effective GDPR. The goal of the GDPR is to strengthen and unify data protection for all individuals in the EU.[69] Due to its nature, the GDPR is directly applicable in all Member States.[70] Moreover, it is linked to major functional and procedural changes to data processing. Nonetheless, the new data protection regime essentially replicates the general principles of data processing endorsed in Directive 95/46. Referring to access to shareholder lists, the following two conditions are the most relevant in order for the processing of personal data to be lawful: (a) processing is necessary for compliance with a legal obligation to which the controller is subject; and (b) processing is necessary for the purposes of the legitimate interests pursued by a third party. These conditions will be discussed below.

A. Processing is Necessary for Compliance with a Legal Obligation to Which the Controller is Subject

Compliance with a legal obligation, for which processing is needed and the controller is subject, as legal grounds for the lawfulness of personal data processing is laid down in Article 6(1)(c) GDPR. As already mentioned, this provision is not a novelty. Article 6(1)(c) GDPR mirrors Article 7c of the Data Protection Directive. Article 6(1)(c) GDPR explicitly provides that the legal obligation in question must be an obligation of

[66] Case C-101/01, *Lindquist*, ECLI:EU:C:2003:596, para 24; Joined Cases C-92/09 and C-93/09, *Volker und Markus Schecke and Eifert*, ECLI:EU:C:2010:662, para 52; Case C 468/10, *Asociación Nacional de Establecimientos Financieros de Crédito (ASNEF)*, ECLI:EU:C:2011:777, para 42.

[67] See also ECtHR, *MN and Others v San Marino*, App No 28005/12, 7 July 2015, § 51, referring to banking documents.

[68] GDPR (n 2).

[69] ibid Recital 10.

[70] As art 288 of the Treaty on the Functioning of the European Union (TFEU) explicitly provides, a regulation '[s]hall be binding in its entirety and directly applicable in all Member States'. Direct applicability of a regulation means that its entry into force and its application to the persons subject to it are independent of any measure of reception into national law. See Case 34/73, *Variola Spa v Amministrazione delle finanze dello Stato*, ECLI:EU:1973:101, para 10; Case C-606/10, *ANAFE v Ministre de l'Intérieur*, ECLI:EU:C:2012:348, para 72; Joined Cases C-4/10 and C-27/10, *Bureau national interprofessionnel du Cognac v Gust Ranin Oy*, ECLI:EU:C:2011:484, para 66.

the Member State or EU law to which the controller is subject. There is a wide consensus that the aim of the processing shall be determined by law and shall be necessary for the performance of a task performed in the public interest.[71] Other types of obligations such as contractual obligations (including obligations deriving from articles of associations) are not covered by this provision.[72]

The dogmatic background of Article 6(1)(c) GDPR is that an interference with the right to respect for private life should be based on a legal provision.[73] This principle is also laid down in Article 8(2) of the European Convention on Human Rights (ECHR).[74] The latter states that an interference with the right to respect for private life is possible when that interference is 'in accordance with the law and is necessary in a democratic society in the interests of national security, public safety or the economic well-being of the country, for the prevention of disorder or crime, for the protection of health or morals, or for the protection of the rights and freedoms of others'.[75] To this end, it is generally accepted that the legal obligation must be accessible, clear and precise.[76] Additionally, its application must be foreseeable for those subject to it.[77] Attention must also be given to the fair balance that must be struck between the competing interests of the data subject and the community.[78] Moreover, the legal obligation should refer to the specific processing form.[79] Hence, the obligation to collect data does not necessarily allow the transmission or dissemination of this information. Furthermore, the concept of necessity as a precondition for the data processing cannot have a meaning that varies among Member States.[80]

Nonetheless, as stated in the preamble to the GDPR:

> [R]egarding the processing of personal data for compliance with a legal obligation, for the performance of a task carried out in the public interest or in the exercise of official authority vested in the controller, Member States should be allowed to maintain or introduce national provisions to further specify the application of the rules of this Regulation.[81]

[71] H Heberlein in E Ehmann and M Selmayr (eds), *Datenschutz-Grundverordnung* (Munich, CH Beck, 2017) art 6 no 15.

[72] B Buchner and T Petri in J Kühling and B Buchner (eds), *DS-GVO* (Munich, CH Beck, 2017) art 6 no 77. Contractual obligations are covered in art 6(1)(b) GDPR.

[73] Buchner and Petri (n 72) art 6 no 78.

[74] On the application of art 8 ECHR in the sphere of the relations of individuals between themselves, see ECtHR, *Evans v United Kingdom*, App No 6339/05, ECHR 2007-I, § 75.

[75] Joined Cases C-465/00, C-138/01 and C-139/01, *Österreichischer Rundfunk*, ECLI:EU:C:2003:294, para 71.

[76] GDPR, Recitals 41 and 45. See also ECtHR, *Silver and Others v United Kingdom*, 25 March 1983, Series A No 61, § 87.

[77] GDPR, Recital 41.

[78] ECtHR, *Hämäläinen v Finland*, App No 37359/09, ECHR 2014, § 65; ECtHR, *Gaskin v United Kingdom*, 7 July 1989, Series A No 160, § 42; ECtHR, *Roche v United Kingdom*, App No 32555/96, ECHR 2005-X, § 157.

[79] Bundesverfassungsgericht (Germany), Judgement of 20 April 2016 (2016) *NJW* 1781, 1803.

[80] See in this direction Case C-524/06, *Huber*, EU:C:2008:724, no 52, referring to the Data Protection Directive: 'the concept of necessity laid down by Article 7(e) of Directive 95/46, the purpose of which is to delimit precisely one of the situations in which the processing of personal data is lawful, cannot have a meaning which varies between the Member States'.

[81] GDPR, Recital 10. See also *Lindquist* (n 66) para 83, referring to the Data Protection Directive: 'the directive quite properly includes rules with a degree of flexibility and, in many instances, leaves to the Member States the task of deciding the details or choosing between options'.

In the same vein, the European Court of Human Rights (ECtHR) recognises a certain margin of discretion for Member States in implementing their obligations according to Article 8 ECHR, particularly if competing private and public interests are at stake.[82]

Considering the margin of discretion given to the national legislator, we can now turn to the national provisions referring to the keeping of shareholder registries and access to them. The keeping of shareholder lists and access to them is clearly an interference with the private life of the shareholders registered therein.[83] Nonetheless, this interference can be justified with reference to the national economic well-being. As mentioned previously, the direct communication between the company and its shareholders facilitates the exercise of shareholder rights and the engagement of shareholders.[84] Moreover, the communication between shareholders can foster shareholder cooperation and engagement. At the same time, shareholder transparency can strengthen confidence in the function of corporations and enhance investments. Moreover, in Directive 2017/828, it is foreseen that Member States can provide by law for the processing of the personal data of shareholders for other purposes than the identification of shareholders by the company itself.[85] Again, the preamble to Directive 2017/828 explicitly states:

> This is without prejudice to Member State law providing for [the] processing of the personal data of shareholders for other purposes, such as to enable shareholders to cooperate with each other.

However, it is questionable whether a shareholder access right to the member registry of a listed company with widely dispersed shares can be compatible with the right to respect for private life, considering always the principle of proportionality. This question exists because for small shareholdings, the acquisition of shares in listed companies is largely a means of investment and only incidentally and reflectively an expression of the will of the shareholder to be a member of the corporation. Moreover, anonymity and discretion are essential motives for the realisation of the investment, whereas major shareholdings in listed companies are disclosed in accordance with special provisions of capital market and AML law. Additionally, as will be discussed below, there are other, less intrusive means to achieve the same goal, ie, the cooperation and engagement of shareholders.[86]

B. Processing is Necessary for the Purposes of the Legitimate Interests Pursued by a Third Party

Much of the processing of personal data that occurs today at the European level relies on the 'legitimate interests' grounds.[87] On this basis, the processing of data is lawful insofar

[82] ECtHR, *Evans v United Kingdom*, App No 6339/05, ECHR 2007-I, § 77; ECtHR, *Dickson v United Kingdom*, App No 44362/04, ECHR 2007-V, § 78. See also *Österreichischer Rundfunk* (n 75) para 83; *Lindquist* (n 66) para 84.

[83] See however *Bernstein and Others v Bester NO and Others* [1996] ZACC 2; 1996 (2) SA 751 (CC), para 85.

[84] See above, section II.

[85] See art 3a (4) of Directive 2007/36 as amended by Directive 2017/828.

[86] See below, section VI.B and VI.C.

[87] Article 7(f) of Directive 95/46 and art 6(1)(f) GDPR. See generally Opinion 06/2014 on the notion of legitimate interests of the data controller under art 7 of Directive 95/46/EC, 844/14/EN, WP 217.

as it is necessary for the purposes of the legitimate interests pursued by a third party. Nonetheless, to date, the 'legitimate interest' grounds as set out in the Data Protection Directive have not been interpreted uniformly by the national authorities.[88] This situation has resulted in divergent applications across the EU and created a lack of legal clarity and predictability, particularly in cross-border situations. This problem appears to have been partially resolved by the introduction of the GDPR. Due to the legal nature of the new legal framework, there is no discretion left to the national legislator when referring to the interpretation and application of the provision.[89] The new legal framework presupposes a common interpretation of the relevant provisions by the national authorities, enhancing legal certainty and clarity.[90] However, the 'legitimate interests' are not defined in the GDPR. Hence, an overall assessment on an ad hoc basis is always required.[91]

In legal theory, there is a consensus that the following conditions must be met in order for the processing to be lawful according to the 'legitimate interests' grounds. More specifically: (a) the interest must be legitimate (any type of interest, eg, legal, financial and social interests can be legitimate);[92] (b) yhe interest must be concrete, real and present; (c) the processing must be in accordance with the interest pursued; (d) the processing must be necessary and the data controller cannot achieve the same result with another, less intrusive approach;[93] and, finally, (e) the data controller's interests must be balanced against the interests of the individual concerned.[94] The legitimate interest grounds will not apply when such interests are overridden by the interests or fundamental rights and freedoms of the data subject that require the protection of personal data,[95] particularly when the data subject is a child. As stated in the preamble to the GDPR, the existence of a legitimate interest would need careful assessment, including whether a data subject can reasonably expect at the time and in the context of the collection of the personal data that processing for that purpose might occur.[96]

[88] See art 5 of the Data Protection Directive. See also *Asociación Nacional de Establecimientos Financieros de Crédito (ASNEF)* (n 66) para 46.

[89] Buchner and Petri (n 72) Art 6 no 143; Heberlein (n 71) Art 6 no 28.

[90] Recital 10 to GDPR 'Consistent and homogenous application of the rules for the protection of the fundamental rights and freedoms of natural persons with regard to the processing of personal data should be ensured throughout the Union'.

[91] See also Bundesgerichtshof (Germany) (2010) *NZG* 1430, 1431: 'Unter welchen Voraussetzungen ein berechtigtes Interesse des einzelnen Vereinsmitglieds anzunehmen ist, Kenntnis von Namen und Anschriften der anderen Vereinsmitglieder zu erhalten, ist keiner abstrakt generellen Klärung zugänglich, sondern auf Grund der konkreten Umstände des einzelnen Falls zu beurteilen'. See in this direction *Burry & Knight Ltd v Knight* [2014] WLR 4046: 'Thus it has left the words "proper purpose" at large for the courts to work out in the conventional way, using the context and on a case by case basis.'.

[92] Buchner and Petri (n 72) Art 6 no 146.

[93] See *Österreichischer Rundfunk* (n 75) paras 86, 88; Case C-92/09 and C-93/09, *Volker und Markus Schecke and Eifert*, EU:C:2010:662, paras 65, 74; Case C-73/07, *Satakunnan Markkinapörssi Oy*, ECLI:EU:C:2008:727, para 56: 'the protection of the fundamental right to privacy requires that the derogations and limitations in relation to the protection of data provided for in the chapters of the directive referred to above must apply only in so far as is strictly necessary'.

[94] Heberlein (n 71) Art 6 no 22.

[95] *Asociación Nacional de Establecimientos Financieros de Crédito (ASNEF)* (n 66) para 38.

[96] GDPR, Recital 47.

If we now try to apply the above-mentioned conditions to the processing of data included in the shareholder list, we must make the following remarks:

(i) In the absence of a legal provision governing access to the shareholder list, we must ask whether the third party (including the shareholder of the company) has a legitimate interest in requiring access to the shareholder list and whether the access is necessary and in accordance with the aim pursued. It follows that an ad hoc analysis is necessary. Curiosity, harassment and haranguing clearly cannot establish a legitimate interest for the data access.[97] The ECHR requires that Member States ensure that private data are protected from misuse and abuse.[98]

(ii) The status of a shareholder as such cannot establish a legitimate interest. Although it is a widespread opinion in common law countries,[99] we cannot share the view that in a stock corporation, each shareholder in the capacity as 'owner of the assets of the company' has an implied right to know all the other members of the company. Nor can we share the view that a shareholder has the right to know all other shareholders due to their contractual company relationship.[100] Currently, the acquisition of shares in stock corporations (particularly in listed corporations with widely dispersed shares) is usually an investment of personal wealth. The investment is the motive and the predominant element of the underlying transaction. The investment of personal wealth of minor shareholders clearly cannot be considered a professional activity.[101] Accordingly, it is not appropriate to apply the general contractual principle, according to which one party to the agreement must know its counterparty. This point is particularly true for listed stock corporations. Moreover, in listed stock corporations, the small shareholdings are of minor importance for the functioning of the company, whereas for major shareholdings, the law specifically provides for a disclosure.

(iii) The privacy rights of investors and shareholders should be respected. A person has the right to keep investments secret. The reason for this is twofold; first, the disclosure of the personal investments of a person can have severe and adverse consequences for his safety, particularly if these data are accessed by criminals; second, corporate democracy and dialogue cannot be enforced on shareholders against their will to maintain their privacy and anonymity. Moreover, the aim of the GDPR is specifically to protect data subjects from the processing of their personal data. In other words, the aim of the data protection law is to set limits on the processing of data in favour of data subjects.[102] Accordingly, the relevant provisions must necessarily be interpreted in the light of fundamental rights, which form an integral part of the general principles of law.[103] From this point of view,

[97] See above, section V.

[98] ECtHR, *Gardel v France*, App No 16428/05, ECHR 2009, § 62.

[99] See above, section III.A.

[100] See, however, the case law in Germany referring to association (Bundesgerichtshof (2010) *NZG* 1430), partnership (Bundesgerichtshof (2010) *NZG* 61) and atypischen Treuhand-Publikums-KG (Bundesgerichtshof (2011) *ZIP* 322).

[101] See for professional activities Oberlandesgericht Stuttgart (Germany) (2003) *NJW RR* 1410, 1412.

[102] Bundesgerichtshof (Germany), 17 December 1985 – VI ZR 244/84 (1986) *NJW* 2505, 2506.

[103] See *Österreichischer Rundfunk* (n 75) para 68.

it is irrelevant that shareholders not wishing to have their private information made available to third parties could eventually hold their shares through an intermediary (bank or broker) and thus avoid direct communication with other shareholders (shares held in street names). The obligation of the issuer/data controller to process personal data lawfully remains.

(iv) Moreover, even when a legitimate interest of a shareholder can be established (ie, communication with other shareholders in anticipation of a general meeting (GM)), it must be: (a) balanced against the interests of both the company to protect itself and other shareholders from infringement of their privacy rights; and (b) examined under the principle of proportionality. This principle is laid down in Article 5(1)(c) GDPR. According to this principle, personal data shall be adequate, relevant and limited to what is necessary in relation to the purposes for which they are processed ('data minimisation'). Under this principle, special emphasis should be placed on when there is a possibility that the legal interest of the shareholder can be achieved less intrusively.

C. Communication between Shareholders through the Company and Online Forums as an Alternative

It is settled case law that when there is a choice between several appropriate measures that are prone to limit a fundamental right, recourse must be had to the least onerous, and the disadvantages caused must not be disproportionate to the aims pursued.[104] Consequently, the question is whether other appropriate means exist that allow communication between shareholders without jeopardising their privacy rights. The answer to this question appears to be positive. A less intrusive and appropriate means could be considered, for example: (a) the compilation of voting lists; (b) communication through the company; and (c) a Web-based shareholder forum:[105]

(i) *Compilation of voting lists*: many jurisdictions require management to compile a list of shareholders qualified to vote in an upcoming general meeting.[106] The disclosure of voting lists before the general meeting allows shareholders to communicate with one another. Nonetheless: (a) the voting list does not always contain the contact details of *all* shareholders (in some legal orders, only the shareholders who will participate in the general meeting are registered); and (b) the time it provides (usually a few days) for inspection prior to the general meeting is usually insufficient.[107] The time needed for optimal use of the shareholder list is at least one

[104] Case C-331/88, *R v Minister of Agriculture, Fisheries and Food ex parte Fedesa*, EU:C:1990:391, para 13.

[105] See on public advertisement *IMF (Australia) Ltd v Sons Of Gwalia Ltd* (n 64): 'This does not prevent IMF from publicly advertising its proposal to present and former shareholders of Sons of Gwalia provided it does not use Register information in so doing.' See also Forstmoser, Meier-Hayoz and Nobel (n 46) 556: 'Aus einer Interessenabwägung kann sich daher im Einzelfall ein Recht auf eine beschränkte Einsicht ergeben.'

[106] Newman (n 21) 446; Watson (n 21) 1286. On French law, see M Germain, *Les sociétés commerciales* (2009) *LGDJ* 382.

[107] Watson (n 21) 1295.

month before the general meeting. Consequently, the value of the voting list as a means to facilitate communication between shareholders is limited.

(ii) *Communication through the company*: a more efficient means in relation to voting lists appears to be to use the company as a communication tool between shareholders. More specifically, the shareholder's communication can be sent to other shareholders through the company without the disclosure of the names of other members of the company being necessary. This approach, eg, exists in US legislation, in which the relevant rules (Article 14a-7of the Securities and Exchange Commission (SEC) Rules) give the corporation the option of mailing at the expense of the shareholder the communication furnished by him. The problem with this communication method is that the directors of the company have a temporal advantage to the detriment of the applicants. Moreover, interaction between shareholders through the company is inconvenient, and it is difficult for the shareholder requesting the communication to confirm that the company sent the communication to other shareholders.

(iii) *Web-based shareholder forum*: the use of Web-based technology can resolve many contentious issues concerning shareholder communication and improve corporate governance by protecting the privacy of shareholders.[108] More specifically, it can provide an unimpeded and inexpensive communication tool between shareholders and the company, and among shareholders themselves. This tool is the online forum for shareholders.[109] There are of course different forms of shareholder forums. For example, the online forum can be hosted either outside the company or on the website of the company.[110] In both cases, shareholders can be registered in the forum and informed by other shareholders (without being obliged to disclose their personal data to other participants). Consequently, the online forum can effectively facilitate communication between shareholders by protecting their privacy. This ability is exactly the advantage of the shareholder forum as a communication tool in comparison with other communication tools.

VII. Conclusion

Access to the shareholder list is an issue closely connected to protecting the data of the members of the company. Nonetheless, the data protection dimension is not widely discussed and, when it is discussed, the conclusions are very often contradictory. The new data protection regime, although in the form of a regulation, does not establish a fully harmonised environment with respect to data protection. Accordingly, it remains at the discretion of the national legislator to widen the inspection right of shareholders

[108] See generally B Smith, 'Proxy Access and the Internet Age: Using Electronic Shareholders Forums to Improve Corporate Governance' (2008) *Columbia Business Law Review* 1111.

[109] On the shareholders' forum in Germany, see D Kubis in Goette et al (n 43) § 127a no 1; Koch (n 43) § 127a no 1.

[110] In such a case, it must be ascertained that the company will not be held liable for comments posted by participants in the forum.

by issuing special provisions always taking into consideration the principle of proportionality. Nonetheless, in the absence of such national provisions, a balance of interests based on the general principles of European data protection law is necessary. This balance of interests must lead to common results in the European legal orders. As stated in the preamble to the GDPR: 'Consistent and homogenous application of the rules for the protection of the fundamental rights and freedoms of natural persons with regard to the processing of personal data should be ensured throughout the Union.'[111]

[111] GDPR, Recital 10.

13

The Trade Secrets Directive and Transparency Obligations in Company and Capital Market Law

An Initial Approach

MICHAIL-THEODOROS MARINOS

I. Introduction

Mandatory disclosure is an established mechanism employed by the European legislator in the field of company and capital market law. From a regulatory perspective, transparency rules as well as mandatory information obligations can refer to products, services, product/service distribution activities or producers. It is self-evident that there is an inherent conflict between trade secrets and mandatory disclosure provisions.[1]

The crucial question in the context of Directive (EU) 2016/943 (hereinafter 'the Directive') about the protection of trade secrets is whether this Directive can act as a barrier to the extension of mandatory disclosure regulation in company and capital market law.

A 'trade secret' is nothing more than (technological or business) secret information. It may therefore be considered to be 'qualified information' (secret information). It is also worth mentioning that every system of intellectual property (IP) protection establishes the notion of the privatisation of information, which must meet some objective criteria (qualified information, such as substantive requirements of patentability, distinctiveness, originality of works within the meaning of copyright law etc). The same applies to trade secrets as a quasi-IP right (Article 2 of the Directive).[2] It is referred to 'as a proprietary right' of the trade secret holder, who is defined as the person lawfully controlling a trade secret (Article 2(3) of the Directive). So, in fact, the process of attributing information to a holder/undertaking is nothing more than the privatisation

[1] This is reflected in decisions of the European Court of Justice. See Order of the Court of 3 September 2004 in Joined Cases C-435/02 and C-103/03, *Axel Springer AG*, ECLI:EU:C:2004:552 paras 43 ff; Judgment of 21 June 2006, *Danzer*, Case T-47/02, ECLI:EU:T:2006:167, paras 41 ff.

[2] M McGuire, 'Der Schutz von know-how im System der Immaterialgüterrechte' (2016) 118 *Gewerblicher Rechtsschutz und Urheberrecht* 1006: 'schutzrechtähnlicher Ansatz'.

of information, which according to the prevailing view does not create a de jure but only 'de facto exclusivity'. Mandatory disclosure 'deprivatises' this information, if it is disseminated to the public, via the press, for example, or in the implementation of environmental or capital market provisions.

II. Directive (EU) 2016/943 on the Protection of Undisclosed Know-How and Business Information (Trade Secrets)

The Directive protects 'undisclosed know-how and business information (trade secret)'. According to the Directive, trade secrets have an immaterial character and function 'as a complement or as an alternative to intellectual property rights'.[3] Trade secret protection is a key factor in competition and investment.[4]

The Directive harmonises the notion of 'trade secret' as qualified secret information (Article 2). It also harmonises the civil law protection of trade secrets (Articles 3–4, 14–15) and contains provisions which affect the treatment of secret information under civil procedure (Articles 9–13).

The Directive itself is intended to create a 'sufficient and consistent level of civil redress',[5] consisting of protection against the 'unlawful' acquisition, use or disclosure of trade secrets to third parties. The issue of what is unlawful acquisition (unauthorised access), use (without the consent of trade secret holder) or disclosure (without the consent of trade secret holder) is defined in Article 4, a provision which mainly reflects aspects of the law of unfair competition. The concept in the Directive follows the Directive on the enforcement of intellectual property (IP) rights (Directive 2004/48/EC). The aim of both Directives is the effective protection of trade secrets, which – together with the effective protection of IP rights – effectively protects the knowledge-based economy and fosters competition.

The Directive establishes a system of protection based exclusively on tort law, especially unfair competition law.[6] A trade secret in the technological field is not protected as a genuine IP right, although its protection gives the impression that a

[3] Directive EU 2016/943 of the European Parliament and the Council of 8 June 2016 on the protection of undisclosed know-how and business information (trade secrets) against their unlawful acquisition, use and disclosure, [2016] OJ L157/1 ("Trade Secrets Directive"), Recital 2.

[4] *cf* ibid, Recitals 1–2, 4.

[5] ibid Recital 10.

[6] See ibid, Recital 2, 16: 'In the interest of innovation and to foster competition, the provisions of this Directive should not create any exclusive right to know-how or information protected as trade secrets.' For the prevailing view in legal literature, *cf* N Sousa e Silva, 'What Exactly is a Trade Secret under the Proposed Directive?' (2014) 9 *Journal of Intellectual Property Law & Practice* 927; McGuire (n 2) 1002 ff. Recital 39 asserts that the application of any other relevant law in other areas, particularly IP rights, shall not be affected. As such, the sentence can be viewed as supporting the clear distinction between trade secrets, as part of unfair competition law, and IP rights. *cf* European Commission, Impact Assessment accompanying the Proposal for a Directive of the European Parliament and of the Council on the protection of undisclosed know-how and business information (trade secrets) against their unlawful acquisition, use and disclosure, SWD(2013) 471 final, 267; M Marinos, 'The Draft Directive on the Protection of Trade Secrets' (2015) *Commercial Law Review* 5 ff (in Greek); McGuire (n 2) 1004: 'Protection object is not the information as such but the secret information.'

'quasi'-absolute IP right is being protected. The protection confines itself to the 'unlawful' access to, use or disclosure of the trade secret. By implication, this means that the Trade Secrets Directive is intended to ensure de facto harmonisation of unfair competition law in relation to trade secrets. In this context, it is evident that the aim of the Directive is to protect an undertaking's competitive position in the marketplace.

The Directive has two aspects:

(i) It may be perceived as a step towards protecting a firm's private sphere against disclosure.[7]
(ii) It can also be partially perceived as a European step towards harmonisation through tort law (ie, unfair competition) designed to prevent the 'misappropriation of secret, valuable technological or business information'.

III. Basic Issues in the Context of the Mandatory Disclosure of Business Information

A. Disclosure as Public Policy and Trade Secret Protection

The concept of the privatisation of information, which also covers the secrecy of trade secrets, collides with the public interest in transparency and notification requirements imposed by company and capital market law, as well as antitrust law. The same collision exists in other fields, for example, product safety regulations[8] and environmental regulation. In this context, two interrelated questions may arise:

(i) Can public policy considerations, especially transparency rules in the field of company and capital market law, override trade secret protection?
(ii) Does the Directive have a 'transparency-proof' hard core?

Public law offers two basic options:

(1) To order disclosure of secret information (transparency) without leaving any exception for business secrets. In this case the public authority is bound by professional secrecy.[9] Professional secrecy is seen as a countervailing measure to

[7] M Marinos, 'Members of the Board of Directors: Duty of Confidentiality' (2016) *Commercial Law Review* 788 (in Greek); Marinos (n 6); McGuire (n 2) 1006; *cf* in this direction V Pfisterer, *Unternehmensprivatsphäre* (Tübingen, Mohr Siebeck, 2014) passim, with analysis of various decisions of the European Court of Human Rights and the European Court of Justice; F Schweyer, *Die rechtliche Bewertung des Reverse Engineering in Deutschland und den USA* (Tübingen, Mohr Siebeck, 2012) 399 ff. See also on the conflict between secrecy and mandatory disclosure requirements H Beyerbach, *Die geheime Unternehmensinformation* (Tübingen, Mohr Siebeck, 2011) 70 ff.

[8] See, for example, art 73(3) of Regulation (EU) No 2017/745 on medical devices: 'The information referred to in the other points of that paragraph shall be accessible to the public, unless, for all or parts of that information, confidentiality of the information is justified on any of the following grounds: b) protection of commercially confidential information, especially in the investigators brochure, in particular through taking into account the status of the conformity assessment for the device, unless there is an overriding public interest in disclosure.'

[9] *cf* as an example art 27 of Regulation (EU) No 596/2014 (Market Abuse Regulation (MAR)); art 64 of Directive 2009/138/EC on the taking-up and pursuit of the business of Insurance and Reinsurance

such extensive mandatory disclosure or as an insubordinate follower of mandatory disclosure results. Its violation is subject to penal, administrative and even civil law sanctions.

As pointed out, this ensures that there is no core of business information which is 'transparency-proof'.[10] The ultimate limit continues to be that the authority cannot ask for information which is not related to its regulatory function, as established by law.[11]

(2) To reach a compromise by balancing interests, thus transferring a feature which does not exist in the trade secret definition (namely a justified interest in keeping privileged secret information secret) into the balancing of interests. A central point in weighing up interests is the anticipated competitive disadvantage and the extent to which investment will become devalued through transparency. This includes cases of disclosure of business information to the public. Such cases create the interface between trade secret protection and company and capital market law.

One example is Article 17(5) of the Market Abuse Regulation and many other provisions in various directives and regulations.[12] They show that in exceptional cases, trade secrets can be a barrier to disclosure requirements.[13]

(Solvency II); art 28 of Regulation (EC) No 1/2003 on the implementation of the rules on competition laid down in arts 81 and 82 of the Treaty.

[10] L Rudkowski, *Transparenzpflichten zur Kontrolle von Finanzdienstleistungsunternehmen, unter besonderer Berücksichtigung des Schutzes von Geschäftsgeheimnissen* (Tübingen, Mohr Siebeck, 2015) 145.

[11] See, for example, art 12 of Regulation (EC) No 1/2003; Rudkowski (n 10) 164.

[12] In order to preserve the stability of the financial system, an issuer that is a credit institution or a financial institution may, on its own responsibility, delay the public disclosure of inside information, including information which is related to a temporary liquidity problem and, in particular, the need to receive temporary liquidity assistance from a central bank or lender of last resort, provided that the following condition is met: the disclosure of the inside information entails a risk of undermining the financial stability of the issuer and of the financial system. See also art 19a(1) of Directive 2014/95/EU (Corporate Social Responsibility Directive): 'Member States may allow information relating to impending developments or matters in the course of negotiation to be omitted in exceptional cases where, in the duly justified opinion of the members of the administrative, management and supervisory bodies, acting within the competences assigned to them by national law and having collective responsibility for that opinion, the disclosure of such information would be seriously prejudicial to the commercial position of the group, provided that such omission does not prevent a fair and balanced understanding of the group's development, performance, position and impact of its activity, Recital 25: Exemption from certain disclosure obligations is justified where such disclosure would be prejudicial to certain persons or to the undertaking.' Article 4(2)(2) of Directive 2003/4/EC on public access to environmental information and repealing Council Directive 90/313/EEC: 'Member States may provide for a request for environmental information to be refused if disclosure of the information would adversely affect: (d) the confidentiality of commercial or industrial information where such confidentiality is provided for by national or Community law to protect a legitimate economic interest, including the public interest in maintaining statistical confidentiality and tax secrecy.' See also art 4(2) of Regulation (EC) No 1049/2001 regarding public access to European Parliament, Council and Commission Documents: 'The institutions shall refuse access to a document where disclosure would undermine the protection of: – commercial interests of a natural or legal person, including intellectual property.' See also the General Court judgments in Case T-235/15, *Pari Pharma v EMA*, ECLI:EU:T:2018:65; Case T-718/15, *PTC Therapeutics International v EMA*, ECLI:EU:T:2018:66; and Case T-729/15, *MSD Animal Health Innovation and Intervet international*, ECLI:EU:T:2018:67. Article 53(1) of the Solvency II Directive states that: 'Supervisory authorities shall permit insurance and reinsurance undertakings not to disclose information where: (a) by disclosing such information, the competitors of the undertaking would gain significant undue advantage;(b) there are obligations to policy holders or other counterparty relationships binding an undertaking to secrecy or confidentiality.'

[13] M Goldhammer, 'Geschäftsgeheimnis-Richtlinie und Informationsfreiheit' (2017) 26 *Neue Zeitschrift für Verwaltungsrecht* 1810. *cf* also art 41(2)(b) of the Charter of Fundamental Rights of the European Union: 'the

This balancing of interests can be found inherently 'plugged into' the notion of lawful interest (*berechtigtes Interesse*). It takes place under the notion of lawful interest[14] and it seems to fulfil the proportionality principle found in the Directive.[15]

In those cases, the aspect of protection of trade secrets under the Charter of Fundamental Rights of the European Union has a crucial impact (see section VII below).

B. Trade Secrets as a Possible Exception to Disclosure Obligations in Company and Capital Market Law

Taking into account that in some cases, trade secrets by virtue of special provisions could justify an exception to mandatory disclosure, the following questions could arise in this context:

(1) What is the notion of 'trade secret' which should be balanced with the public interest of mandatory disclosure to the public? Two issues in particular are crucial in this context:
   (i) Does the notion of 'trade secret' also cover 'illegal' technological know-how or business information (see section VI.A below)?
   (ii) Does the notion of 'trade secret' also include the 'damage to image' caused by secret business information which itself has no commercial value, but if disclosed could be detrimental to the undertaking, also resulting in competitive disadvantage (see section VI below)?

(2) How will this happen, given that trade secrets might be protected by fundamental rights (see section VII below)?

(3) Does the notion of trade secret established by the Directive have a de facto impact on public law (see section VIII below)?

IV. Collision between Undisclosed Information and a Public Law Obligation to Disclose Business Information

The Directive addresses the collision between undisclosed information and a public law obligation to disclose business information in a negative way. Because its scope is broad due to the open definition of 'trade secret', the legislator has provided exceptions and

right of every person to have access to his or her file, while respecting the legitimate interests of confidentiality and of professional and business secrecy'.

[14] Goldhammer (n 13) 1812.

[15] *cf* Trade Secrets Directive, Recital 21.

limitations to its protection in an equally broad sense. Thus Article 2(2) clearly states that the Directive shall not affect:

(a) the exercise of the right to freedom of expression and information as set out in the Charter (meaning Article 11 of the Charter of Fundamental Rights of the European Union), including respect for the freedom and pluralism of the media (see also Article 5(a));
(b) the application of EU or national rules requiring trade secret holders to disclose, for reasons of public interest, information, including trade secrets, to the public or to administrative or judicial authorities for the performance of the duties of those authorities.[16] This provision guarantees, in particular, the enforcement of overriding 'public interest';
(c) the application of EU or national rules requiring or allowing EU institutions and bodies or national public authorities to disclose information submitted by businesses which those institutions, bodies or authorities hold pursuant to, and in compliance with, the obligations and prerogatives set out in EU or national law.

Furthermore, Article 3(2) states that: 'The acquisition, use or disclosure of a trade secret shall be considered lawful to the extent that such acquisition, use or disclosure is required or allowed by Union or national law.'

Finally, the Directive contains a general 'catch-all' clause in Article 5(d). It provides that the alleged acquisition, use or disclosure of the trade secret is permitted if it was done, inter alia, 'for the purpose of protecting a legitimate interest recognised by Union or national law'.

The list of grounds in Article 5 justifying the acquisition, use and disclosure of trade secrets allows for the interests of trade secret holders to protect their secrets to be balanced against the interests of third parties, also including the general public interest.[17] It clarifies that this provision is not subject to a narrow interpretation, in the sense that it establishes an exception to the rule ('singularia non extendenda').[18] Based on the general public interest, third parties may be entitled to access, use and disclose them on a case-by-case basis.[19]

[16] Recital 11 also remarks that: 'This Directive should not affect the application of Union or national rules that require the disclosure of information, including trade secrets, to the public or to public authorities. Nor should it affect the application of rules that allow public authorities to collect information for the performance of their duties, or rules that allow or require any subsequent disclosure by those public authorities of relevant information to the public.' It is interesting in this context to take into account art 23(4) MAR: 'A person making information available to the competent authority in accordance with this Regulation shall not be considered to be infringing any restriction on disclosure of information imposed by contract or by any legislative, regulatory or administrative provision, and shall not involve the person notifying in liability of any kind related to such notification.'

[17] *cf* C Alexander, 'Das Spannungsfeld zwischen investigativen Journalismus und dem Schutz von Geschäftsgeheimnissen' (2017) 48 *Zeitschrift für das Medien- und Kommunikationsrecht* 373.

[18] Marinos (n 7) 19.

[19] R Knaak, A Kur and R Hilty, Comments of the Max Planck Institute for Innovation and Competition of 3 June 2014 on the Proposal of the European Commission for a Directive on the Protection of Undisclosed Know-How and Business Information (Trade Secrets) Against Their Unlawful Acquisition, Use and Disclosure of 28 November 2013 (2013) COM 813 Final, IIC 2014, 956 No 38; Marinos (n 7) 19.

So the first dilemma of 'undisclosed secret business information' versus 'disclosure of information' based on public law obligations is prima facie solved. The public interest can override trade secret protection.[20] There is no general presumption of confidentiality. In taking this basic approach, the Directive is but one of many other EU directives or regulations.[21] But the public interest is also reflected in the litigation procedure itself (provisional and precautionary matters). The court must decide taking into account, inter alia and where appropriate, the interests of third parties, the 'public interest' and the 'safeguarding of fundamental rights' (Article 11(2)(f), (g) and (h)). The same applies to adopting of injunctions and corrective measures (Article 13(1)(f)–(h)). It seems that the protection of trade secrets is as shaped by private autonomy considerations (undertaking/trade secret holder) as by public law.

V. Fundamental Rights and the General Interest Dimensions of the Directive

A. Fundamental Rights in Potential Conflict with Trade Secret Protection

If we look more carefully at the Directive, we see that its rules are not strictly confined to private law matters. It seems that trade secret protection covers a very wide interface between private and public law, whereas fundamental rights are used to limit the protection of trade secrets against disclosure. The Directive manifests a fundamental rights sensibility (Article 5)[22] and refers constantly to the public interest. This is understandable, since it refers to qualified information (secret information under the definition in Article 2 of the Directive).

The provisions of the Directive go beyond the balancing of private interests, which is the norm in IP rights. However, even genuine IP rights are not acquired or exercised in a general interest 'vacuum'.

[20] See also General Court Case T-729/15, *MSD Animal Health Innovation GmbH*, ECLI:EU:T:2018:67 para 50: 'Article 39(2) and (3) of the TRIPS Agreement cannot mean, however, that protection granted to intellectual property rights must be given absolute precedence over the presumption in favour of disclosure of the information submitted in the context of an application for derogation from the market exclusivity of an orphan medicinal product.'

[21] See, for example, art 102 of Regulation (EU) No 2017/746 on in vitro diagnostic medical devices: '1. Unless otherwise provided for in this Regulation and without prejudice to existing national provisions and practices in the Member States on confidentiality, all parties involved in the application of this Regulation shall respect the confidentiality of information and data obtained in carrying out their tasks in order to protect the following: b) commercially confidential information and trade secrets of a natural or legal person, including intellectual property rights unless disclosure is in the public interest.'

[22] Recital 22: 'This Directive respects the fundamental rights and observes the principles recognised in particular by the Charter of Fundamental Rights of the European Union, including freedom to conduct a business, respect for private life and the protection of personal data. This Directive must be implemented in accordance with those rights and principles'; *cf* Goldhammer (n 13) 809.

As mentioned above, the Directive contains provisions which create 'free space' for third parties and for the 'general public interest' or 'legitimate interests' recognised by EU or national law (Article 5(b) and (d)):

(i) for third parties (undertakings), ie, reverse engineering, independent discovery or creation (Article 3(a) and (b));
(ii) for the exercise of fundamental rights, Article 5 of the Directive (exercising the right to freedom of expression and information as set out in the Charter of Fundamental Rights (Article 11),[23] including respect for the freedom and pluralism of the media; and
(iii) for revealing misconduct, wrongdoing or illegal activity, provided that the respondent acted to protect the 'general public interest' (enforcement of general public interest (whistleblowing), a kind of hybrid protection),[24] for example, in the area public safety, consumer protection, public health and environmental protection.[25] In essence, it makes clear that public law, which incorporates aims of general interest, cannot overrule obligations of confidentiality (whistleblowing). Whistleblowing (internal or external) is a means to enforce the public interest and a tool to ensure company compliance. This provision has a wide scope. There is no limitation on the persons who can be whistleblowers: employees or members of management.[26]

Finally, the provisions on the scope of trade secret protection in litigation reflect the fundamental rights sensibility of the Directive (Articles 11(2)(f)–(h) and 13(1)(f)–(h)). The judicial protection of trade secrets entails a balancing of interests.

B. Absence of a Fundamental Rights Dimension for Trade Secrets in the Directive

However, one question related to the protection of trade secrets under the Charter of Fundamental Rights remains unanswered by the Directive. Curiously, no recital or provision is dedicated to this issue, although the protection of trade secrets under the Charter of Fundamental Rights is an important issue in the protection of trade secrets (see section VII below).

[23] See also Trade Secrets Directive, Recital 19.
[24] *cf* ibid, Recital 20, 21. In this regard, the Directive follows many other EU directives or regulations, which establish sectoral whistleblowing rules. *cf* art 11 of Directive 2000/78/EC (Equal Treatment in Employment and Occupation Directive); art 21 of Directive 2005/60/EC (Money Laundering Directive); art 71 of Directive 2013/36/EU (activity of credit institutions and the prudential supervision of credit institutions and investment firm); art 32(1) and (2) MAR; *cf* V Abazi, 'Trade Secrets and Whistleblowing Protection in the European Union', (2016) 1 *European Paper* 1061 ff. See also from the point of labour law S Kreis, *Whistleblowing als Beitrag zur Rechtsdurchsetzung* (Tübingen, Mohr Siebeck, 2017).
[25] *cf* Trade Secrets Directive, Recital 21.
[26] Marinos (n 7) 7.

VI. The Definition of 'Trade Secret' under the Directive and the Possible Reception of its Definition in Public Law

A. Definition

A comparison of the American Defend Trade Secrets Act (DTSA), the Directive and Article 39(1) of the TRIPS Agreement shows that all three contain the same broad definition (18 USC; Article 2(1) of the Directive).[27] The concept of trade secret includes technological information and business information with 'commercial value'.

For the purposes of this Directive, the following definitions apply: the information must be secret ('undisclosed information' according to Article 39(1) of the TRIPS Agreement) and therefore, has commercial value.[28]

By connecting the commercial value to the information's secrecy, the criterion is broadened to the extent that information must not be objectively valuable, but instead its value depends on whether:

(i) the confidential information is potentially able to be commercialised by the information holder;
(ii) it confers a competitive advantage (competition sensibility of the secret information, which also includes the potential commercial value of information for trade secret holders);
(iii) reasonable steps under the circumstances have been taken by the person lawfully in control of the information, to keep it secret.

It is a descriptive definition composed of these three parts. The Directive departs from a definition, which contains a normative dimension, ie, the justified interest to keep the information secret as well as the intention to keep the information secret. The definition of trade secret in the Directive is also neutral. It seems to be in accordance with the view prevailing in legal theory, which also includes 'illegal' trade secrets, for example, violation of transparency requirements, antitrust violations or tax evasion. The problem of illegal trade secrets is thus shifted to the legal consequences entailed (*Rechtsfolgen*, legal consequences),[29] as the provision about whistleblowing demonstrates (Article 5(d)).

[27] A Patel, J Pade, V Cundiff and B Newmann, 'The Global Harmonization of Trade Secret Law: The Convergence of Protections for Trade Secret Information in the United States and European Union' (2016) 83 *Defence Counsel Journal* 472 ff; Sousa e Silva (n 6) 923 ff.

[28] Article 2(1)(b): 'It has commercial value because it is secret.' It appears that the Directive establishes causality between secrecy and commercial value; Marinos (n 7) 11.

[29] Rudkowski (n 10) 22; A Götz, *Der Schutz von Betriebs- und Geschäftsgeheimnissen im Zivilverfahren* (Tübingen, Mohr Siebeck, 2014) 21 ff; H Köhler in H Köhler, J Bornkamm and J Feddersen (eds), *Gesetz gegen den unlauteren Wettbewerb*, 36th edn (Munich, CH Beck, 2018) vor § 17, no 16; H Harte-Bavedamm in H Harte-Bavedamm and F Henning-Bodewig (eds), *Gesetz gegen den unlauteren Wettbewerb*, 4th edn (Munich, CH Beck, 2016) § 17, no 6; *cf* also before the Directive J Brammsen in W Heermann and J Schlinghoff (eds), *Münchener Kommentar zum Lauterkeitsrecht*, 2nd edn (Munich, CH Beck, 2014) § 17, no 24 with further references.

It is the aim of norms which impose sanctions to oppress or sanction illegal behaviour or acts. In such a situation, the undertaking would suffer a double sanction.[30]

However, the illegal nature of the trade secret has an impact: according to Article 5, secrecy gives way if the requirements laid out by Article 5 ('exceptions') are fulfilled.[31]

The definition does not contain the inherent characteristic of the 'legitimate interest' (*berechtigtes Interesse*) to keep the information secret. This is examined in a further step. If there is a justified interest, then a notification or disclosure exception may be granted. In particular, the simplicity of the definition and its descriptive, non-normative dimension guarantees that it can have access to public law transparency provisions.[32]

The Directive aims at private law enforcement. Thus, a first open question is whether public law, which uses the term 'secret know-how', can adopt the definition. One would expect that the simple, descriptive definition of trade secret adopted by the Directive will cause de facto harmonisation in this context.

B. Forms of Trade Secret

What does the commercial value of a trade secret mean? This is an important question in order to 'distil' the core of what a trade secret is. According the Directive, it seems that the protection is 'tailor-made' for a 'quasi IP right', but its definition of trade secret is much broader.

In the Directive, we can distinguish three groups of trade secrets. Two of them are without doubt contained in the definition of trade secret,[33] and for the other, it is still uncertain whether it is covered by the admittedly very broad definition in Article 2(1).

i. Technical Information

This comprises the hard core of trade secret protection under the Directive. It is protected as if it were an absolute *erga omnes* quasi-IP right,[34] although the protection granted is clearly tortious protection (unfair competition). It sanctions a form of behaviour, ie, the unlawful 'acquisition, use or disclosure of a trade secret'. Without doubt, it has commercial and competitive value.

[30] Götz (n 29) 21.

[31] Harte-Bavedamm (n 29) §17, no 6.

[32] As pointed out by Goldhammer (n 13) 1812 ff, the definition of 'trade secret' may have a hidden, indirect influence in company and capital market law. It has all the elements to also prevail in public law, de facto harmonising the notion of 'business secret', proprietary or confidential information. This might be an additional side-effect of the Directive on mandatory transparency requirements.

[33] It is an ongoing discussion under the Technology Transfer Regulation (Regulation (EU) No 316/2014) as to whether know-how includes only technical information or also business information; for both options, see C Ann, M Loschelder and M Grosch, *Praxishandbuch Know-how-Schutz* (Cologne, Carl Heymanns, 2010) 9 with further references. For a narrower understanding, see C Klawitter, *Lizenzverträge und Kartellrecht* (Baden-Baden, Nomos, 2015) nos 46 ff.

[34] See McGuire (n 2) 1005.

However, to a great extent, the Directive also transfers the protection afforded to IP rights by the Enforcement Directive (Directive 2004/48/EC) to any trade secret, which embodies a technical or commercial innovation.[35] This is manifested in various provisions. Infringing goods are defined as 'goods, designs, characteristics, the functioning, production process or marketing of which significantly benefits from trade secrets unlawfully acquired, used or disclosed' (Article 2(4)). Technological know-how may be disclosed by virtue of public law requirements governing the safety of products and environmental protection.

ii. Business Information or Business Know-How

This is protected under the Directive. According to Recital 14: 'Furthermore, such (business) know-how or information should have a commercial value, whether actual or potential.' Transparency requirements focus on this notion of 'trade secret'. If it is disclosed, there can be a negative effect (effect on competition, *Wettwerbsrelevanz*)[36] on the competitive position or ability of the trade secret holder.

This distinction also reflects the attitude of legal experts. Experts from the fields of IP and competition law tend to downplay the second aspect and over-estimate the 'quasi-IP dimension' of trade secrets.

It is evident that such information – and not technological information/innovation – creates exactly the conflict with transparency requirements or may be the target of these requirements.

iii. Does the Notion of Know-How Cover Information Whose Disclosure Results in Image or Reputation Damages?

There is secret business information, which itself has no commercial value; however, its disclosure could cause major damage to an undertaking. Take, for example, information which harms the image of a company or information about antitrust violations. Such information which causes harm to reputation or image undoubtedly has an impact on a firm's ability to compete.[37] It is highly controversial whether this kind of information is covered by the concept of trade secret in the Directive. The answer could be negative,

[35] If the Directive has gaps, the Enforcement Directive may be applied to fill them, if one considers Directive (EU) 2016/943 as a *lex specialis* to the Enforcement Directive (2004/48/EC), as per Knaak, Kur and Hilty (n 19) No 12. For an application by analogy, see Marinos (n 7) 29.

[36] Rudkowski (n 10) 19.

[37] As Recital 14 states: 'Such know-how or information should be considered to have a commercial value, for example, where its unlawful acquisition, use or disclosure is likely to harm the interests of the person lawfully controlling it, in that it undermines that person's scientific and technical potential, business or financial interests, strategic positions or ability to compete.' Regulation (EU) No 575/2013 on prudential requirements for credit institutions and investment firms and amending Regulation (EU) No 648/2012 provides in art 432(2) that: 'Information shall be regarded as proprietary to an institution if disclosing it publicly would undermine its competitive position. It may include information on products or systems which, if shared with competitors, would render an institution's investments therein less valuable. Information shall be regarded as confidential if there are obligations to customers or other counterparty relationships binding an institution to confidentiality.'

based on Recital 14, which remarks that 'such know-how or information should have a commercial value whether actual or potential'.[38]

Again, the same Recital refers to business or financial interests, strategic position or ability to compete, which might also include damage to image which weakens the competitive advantage of the trade secret holder or strengthens the competitor's hand. That is the reason why the voices in the legal literature hold the view that every undertaking's secret information is included in the notion of trade secret,[39] with the exception of trivial information and the experience and skills gained by employees in the normal course of their employment, but also excluding information which is generally known (Recital 14). The potential value of secret information could therefore cover 'negative' know-how. This contains negative data, like withdrawal of credit by a bank, a reduction in the volume of credit, liquidity problems faced by the company as well as 'illegal' data.

Again, there is a counter-argument. Taking an expansionist approach, every piece of information – for example, a CEO's affiliation to a political party – could be commercial information, although it apparently does not have 'commercial value, because it is secret' (Article 2(1) of the Directive).

VII. Is There Room for a Balancing of Interests?

This question ostensibly relates to the fundamental rights dimension of trade secrets themselves, which is still a very controversial topic.[40] This is not mentioned in the Directive itself. In the Charter of Fundamental Rights of the European Union (2000/C 364/01), IP is covered by the right to property (Article 17(2): 'Intellectual property shall be protected').

Despite its fundamental rights sensibility, this issue is left unanswered by the Directive. However, this issue has an imminent practical impact. If a trade secret can be protected by a fundamental right such as the right to property (Article 17 of the Charter of Fundamental Rights of the European Union (2000/C 364/01))[41] or the right to conduct business (Article 16), then there can be a balancing of interests regarding the transparency obligations imposed by environmental or capital market law, for example. As pointed out, in the 'catch-all provision' of Article 5(d), the Directive itself accepts the balancing of interests. The same applies when it comes to the scope of protection

[38] In favour of a narrow interpretation, see B Kalbfus, 'Die EU-Geschäftsgeheimnis-Richtlinie. Welcher Umsetzungsbedarf besteht in Deutschland' (2016) 118 *Gewerblicher Rechtsschutz und Urheberrecht* 1011; Goldhammer (n 13) 1813, pleading for a wide interpretation; Marinos (n 6); Marinos (n 7) 770; S Redeker, S Pres and C Gittinger, 'Einheitlicher Geheimnisschutz in Europa (Teil 1)' (2015) 61 *Wettbewerb in Recht und Praxis* 683.

[39] Brammsen in Heermann and Schlinghoff (eds) (n 29) § 17, no 13 ff.

[40] Beyerbach (n 7) 285 ff; Pfisterer (n 7) 165 ff; Rudkowski (n 10) 23 ff; J Brammsen in Heermann and Schlinghoff (eds) (n 29) §17, no 6.

[41] A Papadopoulou, 'The Proposal of a Directive on the Protection of Trade Secrets' (2015) *NoB* 685 (in Greek); Brammsen in Hermann and Schlinghoff (eds) (n 29) § 17, no 6; Rudkowski (n 10) 28 ff; contra Beyerbach (n 7) 222 ff.

of trade secrets.[42] All the provisions of the Directive related to the protection of trade secrets in litigation seek to reconcile the principle of fair litigation with the inherent confidentiality of the secret information. This aim has a stronger impact in this Directive compared to other directives (the Enforcement Directive (2004/48/EC) and the Antitrust Private Enforcement Directive (2014/104/EC)).

In his opinion of 8 December 2011 in *Interseroh*, Advocate General Bot left the question unanswered, but pointed out two legal grounds: the right to property and the freedom to conduct business.[43] In the judgments in *AKZO* and *SEP*, the European Court referred to 'the general principle of the right of undertakings to the protection of their business secrets'.[44]

Moreover, some voices in legal theory seem to assign the protection of trade secrets to the right to property (Article 17 of the Charter of Fundamental Rights of the European Union), where IP rights are also explicitly mentioned (Article 17(2)). This provision does not require exclusive rights with an *erga omnes* character. It seems that secret innovation – as the hard core of a trade secret – could also be covered by this fundamental right as a quasi-IP right[45] (a transferrable, proprietary, pecuniary right). This may be true for technological know-how which can be freely transferred or licensed. This fundamental right to property may be weighed up against disclosure requirements related to product safety and environmental issues.

The freedom to conduct business (Article 16 of the Charter of Fundamental Rights of the European Union) seems to be the most promising candidate[46] in transparency and information issues connected to secret business data. Business secrets cover every economic and business activity of a firm and are closely related to its standing in competition.[47] Undoubtedly, mandatory disclosure/information requirements regulate how an undertaking should conduct its business. The disclosure of trade secrets affects the undertaking's chances of conducting its business successfully in a competitive environment. It would be a paradox to qualify mandatory disclosure requirements as regulations to conduct business, but to reject protection for a trade secret under this fundamental right.[48]

[42] Article 13(1)(f)–(h) of the Directive.

[43] Case C-1/11, *Interseroh*, ECLI:EU:C:2011:821, para 83: 'Since the protection of business secrecy has been directly enshrined as a general principle, it does not appear to me to be necessary to ascertain whether it must be protected as a component of the right to property or of the freedom to pursue an economic activity.' See also para 84: 'In any event, that principle is not absolute, but must be viewed in relation to its function in society. Consequently, it may be restricted, provided the restrictions are justified by overriding requirements relating to the general interest, are appropriate for securing attainment of the objective pursued and do not go beyond what is necessary for attaining that objective.'

[44] Judgment in Case 53/85, *AKZO Chemie v Commission*, ECLI:EU:C:1986:256, para 28; and the judgment in Case C-36/92 P, *SEP*, ECLI:EU:C:1994:205, para 36.

[45] T Hoeren and R Münker, 'Die EU Richtlinie für den Schutz von Geschäftsgeheimnissen und ihre Umsetzung- unter besonderer Berücksichtigung für Produzentenhaftung' (2018) 73 *Betriebs-Berater* 152: 'minor intellectual property right'; N Gajeck, *Das Wirtschaftgeheimnis in der Verfassung* (Baden-Baden, Nomos, 2018) 158, 199 ff. See also Recitals 2 and 3 of the Directive; contra Beyerbach (n 7) 208 ff.

[46] German Constitutional Court, BVerfGE 115, 2005, no 81.

[47] Beyerbach (n 7) 305 with further references.

[48] Rudkowski (n 10) 25.

In any case, there is room for the balancing of interests[49] laid down by the Directive itself (Articles 1(2) and 3), bearing in mind that the protection of confidential business information is not absolute. This leaves space for such a balancing of interests under the principle of proportionality.

However, the Directive is one-sided. Fundamental rights are used only to limit trade secret protection and not to override transparency requirement imposed by public law. It does not address the opposite situation, which leads to a fundamental question: should mandatory transparency requirements be limited by weighing up the conflicting interests? Mandatory disclosure obligations not covered by the public interest, and in particular the extension of already-existing obligations, must be weighed up against the secrecy of the business secrets, ie, whether they impose 'disproportionate' restrictions on the right to conduct business.[50] Thus, the Directive could contribute to building the undertaking's private sphere as a countermeasure to mandatory transparency requirement.[51]

VIII. Concluding Remarks

The Directive seems to be a step towards safeguarding an undertaking's private sphere, protecting its secret business information and standing in competition. However, the Directive does not provide any help 'as a shield' against information and mandatory disclosure requirements. It cannot contribute to 'transparency-proof business information' and it cannot override public interest requirements in disclosure; in fact, it does exactly the opposite. Public law possesses a 'strong entrance-ticket' to protected trade secrets.

But there may be another aspect worth mentioning. It seems that despite its wording, the Directive may leave room for a case-by-case balancing of 'legitimate interests recognised by Union or national law' as laid down in the catch-all limitation in

[49] It follows the European Court of Justice, which stated in the *Varec* judgment (Case C-450/06, ECLI:EU:C:2008:91, para 52) that: 'The principle of the protection of confidential information and of business secrets must be observed in such a way as to reconcile it with the requirements of effective legal protection and the rights of defence of the parties to the dispute (see, by analogy, Case C-438/04 *Mobistar* [2006] ECR I-6675, paragraph 40) and, in the case of judicial review or a review by another body which is a court or tribunal within the meaning of Article 234 EC, in such a way as to ensure that the proceedings as a whole accord with the right to a fair trial.' See also Advocate General Sharpston's opinion in the *Varec* case (at para 49): 'Where rights are not absolute, they must be considered in relation to their function. Restrictions may be imposed, provided that they meet objectives of general interest and do not constitute a disproportionate and intolerable interference impairing the very substance of the rights.' *cf* also Advocate General Bot in his opinion of 8 December 2011 in *Interseroh* (n 43) para 83; and Order of the Court in Joined Cases C-435/02 and C-103/03, *Axel Springer AG*, ECLI:EU:C:2004:552, paras 43 ff; and the judgment in Case T-47/102, *Danzer*, ECLI:EU:T:2006:167.

[50] See, for example, Order of the Court in Joined Cases C-435/02 and C-103/03, *Axel Springer AG*, ECLI:EU:C:2004:552, paras 43 ff; and judgment of 21 June 2006 in Case T-47/102, *Danzer*, ECLI:EU:T:2006:167, paras 41 ff.

[51] See Pfisterer (n 7) 209 ff before the adoption of Trade Secrets Directive.

Article 5 and trade secret protection as far as information provided to the public is concerned.

Furthermore, the balancing of interests depends on the fundamental rights dimension of the trade secret in question. If information is a trade secret, there will be strong public interest in protecting it because of the level of investment involved and the extent to which disclosure would undermine the relevant party's competitive advantage.[52]

[52] Trade Secrets Directive, Recitals 1–3.

14

Transparency and its Limits under EU Competition Law

ALEXANDRA P MIKROULEA

I. Introduction

In corporate and securities law, it is generally accepted that transparency positively affects the corporate governance of companies – by enabling and making it easier for shareholders to exercise their rights – as well as the pricing mechanisms, by ensuring the rational pricing fluctuation of securities. However, for the purposes of competition law, information exchange, whether horizontal (between competitors) or vertical (between undertakings operating in different levels of the market), can be harmful to competition by leading to coordination and collusive behaviour in the market. This is especially the case when information exchange creates transparency in commercially sensitive information, ie, future pricing policies, quantities, capacity, costs and demand. This kind of transparency is likely to lead to collusive behaviour even in the absence of an explicit anti-competitive agreement. Besides, the existence of an agreement is not necessary in an oligopolistic market structure, where it is easier to monitor the behaviour of rival companies and adjust one's commercial practices to the competitors' commercial conduct. The overarching objective of this chapter is to analyse the interrelation between transparency and competition, taking into account both the case law of the European Court of Justice (ECJ) and the Commission's Guidelines and Notices. Particular reference will be made to signalling practices and their potential anti-competitive effects, to information sharing within the context of due diligence and merger negotiations, as well as to algorithmic collusion, so as to reflect on the role of transparency and its effects on competition. Finally, emphasis will be placed on the potential restriction of competition that an information exchange among banks may cause in the case of non-performing loans negotiations.

II. Information Exchange and Competition Law

A. Arguments in Favour of and against Exchanges of Information

The exchange of commercially sensitive information between competitors is a very complex and controversial subject within European competition law.[1] This is largely because this type of practice can produce not only anti-competitive but also pro-competitive effects vis-a-vis the consumers and the market itself.

Information exchange can indeed be beneficial to the competitive structure of the market, to competitors and to consumers. The Commission's Guidelines recognise the fact that information sharing is an element found in many competitive markets.[2] Transparency can create efficiencies and benefits to both consumers and suppliers.[3] It allows suppliers to improve their commercial strategies, produce different kinds of efficiencies and promote innovation. On the consumers' side, transparency can lead to the reduction of search costs and time wasted, and can provide them with better knowledge to make the right choices.[4] It should also be pointed out that transparency is enhanced through trade associations, which collect market data and help their members plan their business strategies, by making this data available to them through their publicly available websites and resources. Information exchange may also be a part of a research and development (R&D) horizontal agreement or a standardisation agreement or a standalone practice not related to a cartel.

On the other hand, increased market transparency and access to *sensitive* commercial information can produce significant anti-competitive effects in certain market conditions. There are various ways in which competition can be distorted as a consequence of information sharing among competitors. The theories of harm are principally based on coordinated effects and to a lesser extent on non-coordinated effects of information exchanges. With regard to coordinated effects, exchange of information can facilitate collusion among competitors by allowing them to follow a coordinated behaviour in the

[1] See among others, E Langen and HJ Bunte (eds), *Kartellrecht, Band II, Europäisches Kartellrecht*, 13th edn (Munich, CH Beck, 2018); V Emmerich and KW Lange, *Kartellrecht*, 14th edn (Munich, CH Beck, 2018); W Berg and G Mäsch, *Deutsches und Europäisches Kartellrecht. Kommentar*, 3rd edn (Munich, CH Beck, 2018); R Bechtold and W Bosch, *Gesetz gegen Wettbewerbsbeschränkungen*, 9th edn (Munich, CH Beck, 2018). See also R Whish and D Bailey, *Competition Law*, 9th edn (Oxford, Oxford University Press, 2018) 581, D Bailey and LE John (eds), *Bellamy & Child, EU Law of Competition*, 8th edn (Oxford, Oxford University Press, 2018); J Faull and A Nikpay (eds), *The EU Law of Competition*, 3rd edn (Oxford, Oxford University Press, 2014).

[2] Guidelines on Horizontal Cooperation Agreements, para 57. See also F Wagner von Papp, 'Information Exchange Agreements' in I Lianos and D Geradin (eds), *Handbook on EU Competition Law* (Cheltenham, Edward Elgar, 2013).

[3] M Bennett and P Collins, 'The Law and Economics of Information Sharing: The Good, the Bad and the Ugly' (2010) 6 *European Competition Law Journal* 311. See also Whish and Bailey (n 1) 581; Bailey and John (n 1) § 5.093; Emmerich and Lange (n 1) 66.

[4] Asymmetry of information is one of the reasons why imperfect competition exists in the market. Therefore, transparency helps to address this issue and render information available to consumers in order to make more beneficial choices in terms of quality and price.

market, for instance, by raising their prices simultaneously, monitoring compliance to the commonly agreed behaviour and effectively punishing any deviations. With respect to theories of harm based on non-coordinated effects, information exchanges may lead to anti-competitive foreclosure of the market where the information sharing takes place or of a related market. These concerns are not exhaustive.[5]

As far as the European Commission's stance towards this matter is concerned, in 1968, the Commission published the first Notice on Cooperation Agreements.[6] After that, it adopted Guidelines on Horizontal Cooperation Agreements on 2001[7] and at the end of 2010, it adopted new Guidelines on the applicability of Article 101 of the Treaty on the Functioning of the European Union (TFEU) to horizontal cooperation agreements.[8] The Guidelines were intended to provide helpful guidance on lawful exchanges of information under EU competition law and enhance legal certainty, so that undertakings would escape falling within the prohibition of Article 101(1) TFEU. The first guidance on information exchange was included in the EU Commission 2008 Guidelines 'on the application of Article 81 of the EC Treaty to maritime transport services'.[9] General guidance applicable to all sectors followed in the 2010 Guidelines. The real issue here for competition law is to clearly distinguish between harmful and beneficial exchanges of information and, eventually, avoid collusive behaviours.[10]

B. Types of Exchange of Information

Information exchanges can be horizontal (between actual or potential competitors or through a third-party facilitator) or vertical (for example, between suppliers and retailers or between retailers and customers). Horizontal information exchanges can take place directly between competitors or through third parties (such as a trade association or a market consultancy company) or even be published (for example, on a website that deals with collecting and processing market data). This kind of information sharing carries a significantly higher risk of restricting competition, as the companies involved aim at lessening the level of competitive risk, which is inherent in free competition. The Commission assesses the types of information exchange on a case-by-case analysis according to the Horizontal Guidelines. However, certain types of information exchange, ie, on future quantities and pricing strategies, will always be prohibited under Article 101(1) TFEU and will be treated as cartels.

[5] Guidelines on Horizontal Cooperation Agreements, para 57.

[6] Commission, Notice concerning agreements, decisions and concerted practices relating to cooperation between enterprises of 29 July 1968 [1968] OJ C75.

[7] Commission, Guidelines on the applicability of Article 81 of the EC Treaty to horizontal cooperation agreements of 6 January 2011 [2011] OJ C003.

[8] Commission, Guidelines on the applicability of Article 101 of the Treaty on the Functioning of the European Union to horizontal co-operation agreements of 14 January 2011 [2011] OJ C11.

[9] Commission, Guidelines on the application of Article 81 of the EC Treaty to maritime transport services of 26 July 2008 [2008] OJ C245/2.

[10] Whish and Bailey (n 1) 552; Bechtold and Bosch (n 1) paras 101, 102.

C. Assessment under Article 101(1) TFEU

The Commission's Horizontal Guidelines set out a general framework for the assessment of information exchange cases, according to which the Commission takes into account the type of information exchanged (eg, information exchange in support of a horizontal cooperation agreement or in support of a cartel), as well as the market characteristics. The more strategic the data (that reduce the uncertainty in the market), the more likely it is that the Commission finds the exchange of information to be detrimental to competition. The Commission's scrutiny of information sharing includes the consideration of different factors, such as the age and type of data exchanged. Market-related data that are genuinely historical is less likely to restrict competition.[11] In addition, the Commission regards individualised data as more likely to restrict competition because this facilitates a common understanding of the market and allows the involved parties to single out a company which deviates from a commonly agreed behaviour or even to foreclose a potential market entrance. By contrast, the more aggregated the data, the less likely that competition will be restricted. The Commission may also take into account the extent of the market coverage of the information exchange (whether it covers a 'sufficiently large part of the market' or not) in order to conclude whether the conduct can be constrained by market players not participating in the information exchange.[12] This is particularly relevant to information research companies, where it is accepted that the more frequent the information exchange, the more likely it is to lead to a better common understanding of the market and for allowed participants to monitor deviations.[13] Note, however, that in some circumstances, depending on the structure of the market and the overall context of the exchange, an isolated and circumstantial exchange or disclosure may be sufficient as such.[14] To elaborate on this further, in the case of independent schools,[15] the UK Office of Fair Trading (OFT) concluded that the fact that the exchange took place on a regular and highly systematic basis was relevant to the assessment of the infringement as a restriction of competition by object. However, the *T-Mobile Netherlands* case[16] suggests that even if the exchange is not systemic or regular, this does not exclude the possibility of a restriction of competition finding. It should be noted that sometimes even a single meeting between competitors can be viewed as a sufficient basis for the undertakings to be involved in collusive behaviour.

The Commission opines that certain market conditions render it easier to develop and help sustain coordination because it becomes easier to monitor and punish

[11] For example, historical data is unlikely to facilitate the monitoring of deviations from normal competitive conditions. What is historical is decided on a case-by-case basis and will depend on the relevant market. In the past, the Commission has considered data exceeding one year to be historical (see *UK Agricultural Tractor Registration Exchange* (Case IV/31.370) Commission Decision 92/157/EEC [1992] OJ L68/19, para 50).

[12] See Horizontal Guidelines, paras 87–89.

[13] ibid para 91.

[14] See Case C-8/08, *T-Mobile Netherlands BV and Others v Raad van bestuur van de Nederlandse Mededingingsautoriteit*, ECLI:EU:C:2009:343; and Case C-74/14, *Eturas and Others v Lietuvos Respublikos*, ECLI:EU:C:2016:42.

[15] Office of Fair Trading, 20 November 2006, Decision No CA98/05/2006, Exchange of information on future fees by certain independent fee-paying schools, Case CE/2890-03.

[16] Case C-8/08, *T-Mobile Netherlands BV and Others v Raad van bestuur van de Nederlandse Mededingingsautoriteit*, ECLI:EU:C:2009:343.

deviations. In particular, the Commission considers an information exchange to be more likely to restrict competition where markets are characterised by high levels of concentration, high barriers to entry and have a non-complex and quite stable structure. In particular, it considers that tight oligopolies[17] can facilitate a collusive outcome on the market as it can be easier for a small number of market players to reach a common understanding on the terms of coordination.[18]

Information exchange outside a cartel context refers to information exchanges which are ancillary to legitimate 'horizontal cooperation agreements' (such as R&D agreements, joint production agreements, joint purchasing arrangements and joint commercialisation agreements).[19] These are assessed as part of the entire cooperation agreement and are not likely to carry additional competition risks, so long as they are strictly limited to the information objectively necessary for the completion of the transaction.[20]

The Commission typically applies the general framework described above to assess the extent to which these types of information exchanges are capable of restricting competition. In doing so, the Commission considers the extent to which the information exchange results in a collusive outcome (whether it can facilitate[21] coordination (alignment), increasing transparency in the market as regards companies' competitive behaviour) and/or the extent to which the information exchange may result in anti-competitive foreclosure in the market where the exchange takes place and/or in the downstream market.

i. Restriction of Competition by Object

Information exchange on individualised future pricing strategies and/or quantities are normally treated as hardcore cartels pursuant to Article 101(1), which expressly prohibits restrictions on competition which 'directly or indirectly fix purchase or selling prices or any other trading conditions'. The Commission regards and fines information exchanges between competitors as cartels:[22] (a) where the information exchange has the object of fixing prices or quantities;[23] and (b) where an information exchange forms part of the monitoring or the implementation mechanism of an existing cartel.[24]

[17] An oligopoly exists when a certain number of firms supply all or most of the goods or services in a market without any of them having a clear ascendancy over the others; see in this regard Whish and Bailey (n 1) 570.

[18] See Horizontal Guidelines, paras 77–85; Bailey and John (n 1) § 6.023.

[19] See Horizontal Guidelines, paras 111–49, 150–93, 194–224 and 225–56, respectively.

[20] ibid para 56.

[21] ibid paras 64–71.

[22] ibid para 59; and the famous Case COMP/39188 – *Bananas*.

[23] Especially where the information relates to: quotation prices (Case COMP/39188 – *Bananas*); future interbank offered rate submissions (Case AT.39914 – *EIRD*), price forecasts and prices charged to specific customers (Case AT.39574 – *Smart Card Chips*); information on sales volumes and orders received and at what price (Case COMP/39406 – *Marine Hoses*); pricing policies, production capacities and sales to individual customers (Case AT.38589 – *Heat Stabilizers*).

[24] Exchange of information intended to facilitate constant monitoring on current deliveries in order to ensure that a price-fixing and quota allocation cartel was effective was found to constitute, in and of itself, a concerted practice (Case T-148/89, *Tréfilunion SA v Commission*, ECLI:EU:T:1995:68). In a different context, information on sales and exports data formed part of a monitoring system allowing cartel participants to verify that the price increases decided in earlier meetings were in fact being implemented (Joined Cases T-379/10

Exchange of information on the future pricing policy and quantities is envisaged as a restriction of competition by object. In *Castle Round*,[25] the Bundeskartellamt imposed fines on manufacturers of high-quality cosmetic products on the grounds that nine involved companies exchanged individualised information regarding advertising expenditure, returned goods, planned product launches and price increases. The German Competition Authority concluded that while there was no evidence of an existing cartel, the exchange of information constituted an infringement of Article 101(1) both by object and by effect. In Denmark, the *Local Banks* case[26] involved seven local banks which directly exchanged information about the individual fees, interest rates and interest margins amongst each other.[27] The Danish Competition Authority and the Competition Appeals Tribunal found that the exchange of information among the associations' members had the object and the effect of restricting competition. In the *Euribor* and *Yen Libor* cases,[28] several banks admitted that they had infringed Article 101(1) by informing each other of their strategies and submissions for the calculation of benchmark interest rates.[29]

However, the above does not apply to all forms of information exchange. If information exchange has a positive impact on the market in view of the specific circumstances of the case, it does not constitute a restriction by object.[30]

ii. Restriction of Competition by Effect

In *Asnef-Equifax*,[31] the question arose as to whether agreements between credit institutions in Spain regarding the exchange of information for the creditworthiness of borrowers were restrictive of competition. The court said that agreements of that type do not have as their object the restriction of competition.[32] The agreements had to be considered in the economic context in which they occurred.

iii. Third Parties Acting as Cartel Facilitators

Although cartels traditionally take place directly between competitors, this does not preclude a third party that is inactive in the alleged cartelised market (for example,

and T-381/10, *Keramag Keramische Werke AG and Others v Commission*, ECLI:EU:T:2018:400 (appeal of Case COMP/39092 – *Bathroom Fittings and Fixtures*).

[25] See Bundeskartellamt, press release dated 10 July, 2008 (available at http://www.bundeskartellamt.de/wEnglisch/News/Archiv/ArchivNews2008/2008_07_10.php).

[26] Danish Competition Authority (Konkurrencerådet), 28 March 2007, Lokalbanksamarbejdet (Cooperation between local bank), Journal n° 4/0120-0204-0040/ISAFAB, JKM, KLC.

[27] Information and communication such as 'today we do not charge anything to provide a guarantee but we are considering doing so. Are you charging such a fee and if you are, how much do you charge?'.

[28] 39914 Euro Interest Rate Derivatives, 39861 Yen Interest Rate Derivatives (YIRD), http://europa.eu/rapid/press-release_IP-13-1208_en.htm.

[29] Commission decision of 4 December 2013 – *Settlement Procedure*. See further the case with three other banks that participated in the EURIBOR cartel and they do not choose to settle; Commission decision of 7 December 2016, on appeal cases T-105/17HSCS *Holdings v Commission*.

[30] Case C-238/05, *Asnef-Equifax*, ECLI:EU:C:2006:734, paras 46–48 (concerning the exchange of information on customer creditworthiness).

[31] ibid.

[32] ibid para 48.

a consultancy, market research company, administrator of an online booking system[33] or industry association) from being held liable as a cartel facilitator.[34] In *Icap*, the General Court upheld the finding that Icap, a broker, had facilitated the manipulation of a benchmark used in the trading of yen interest rate derivatives.[35] This will be the case where the third party actively and intentionally contributes to the cartel. In finding a third party liable, the Commission applies certain criteria which can be summarised as follows: the third party, through its own conduct, must have contributed to the common objectives pursued by the cartel participants, and it must have been aware of the substantive conduct planned or implemented by other undertakings while pursuing those objectives, or it could reasonably have foreseen the unlawful conduct, but was willing to accept the risk.[36]

iv. Burden of Proof and Evidence

The burden of proof is on the Commission to substantially demonstrate a restriction on competition premise and back up this argument with sufficient evidence. The Commission must adduce evidence to the 'requisite legal standard' (sufficiently precise and consistent) to support the finding that the alleged infringement took place.[37] It is not necessary for the Commission to show that every piece of evidence is sufficiently precise and consistent; in fact, it is entitled to rely on a body of evidence and to infer an infringement from a number of indicia and coincidences, which, considered altogether, in the absence of any plausible explanation, lead to the conclusion that there is an infringement.[38]

When evaluating an information exchange in the context of a concerted practice, it may be sufficient for an infringement finding simply to disclose commercially sensitive information to a competitor and for the latter not to reject the information. This is because there is a rebuttable presumption that an undertaking that took part in a concerted practice and remained active in the market took the information into account when determining its conduct in the market. However, the Commission cannot expect undertakings to take excessive or unrealistic steps to rebut; it may be sufficient to prove that the undertaking did not receive the information or did not look at it until time had passed.[39] It should be noted that the burden lies with the defendant to demonstrate other plausible explanations.

Where the Commission relies solely on the commercial conduct of the undertakings in the market (for instance, uniformity of prices) and not on substantial evidence to prove collusion, it is possible to rebut the finding of an infringement by proving the existence of circumstances which cast the facts established by the Commission in

[33] See Case 74/14, *'Eturas' UAB and Others*, ECLI:EU:C:2016:42.

[34] See further Bailey and John (n 1) § 5.012.

[35] Case T-180/15, *Icap plc and Others v European Commission*, EU:T:2017:795.

[36] See Case AT.38589 *Heat Stabilisers*, para 382; and Case T-99/04, *AC Treuhand v Commission*, ECLI:EU:T:2008:256, para 122.

[37] See Case C-49/92, *Commission v Anic Partecipazioni*, ECLI:EU:C:1999:356, at para 86.

[38] See *'Eturas' UAB and Others* (n 30) para 36.

[39] ibid paras 33–41.

a different light, allowing for another 'plausible explanation'.[40] For example, parallel conduct established by the Commission did not constitute evidence of concerted practice because the price parallelism and pricing trends could be satisfactorily explained by the oligopolistic tendencies of the market and by the specific circumstances prevailing in certain periods.[41] In fact, it is often the case that undertakings in an oligopolistic market benefit from a higher level of transparency and can easily adapt their commercial conduct to the policy that rival companies follow so as not to lose consumers and remain in market play.

Consequently, it becomes apparent that it is difficult to draw a clear distinction between a cartel agreement and an exchange of information as such. In the *Banana* decision,[42] the Commission found that the weekly bilateral telephone calls between the parties involved were aimed at disclosing their weekly initial pricing and sales expectations for bananas, and this constituted a coordination of their price-setting behaviour, and, as such, was assessed as a cartel. In *Tate & Lyle*,[43] the General Court held that the fact that only one of the participants at the meetings revealed its intentions was not sufficient to exclude the possibility of an agreement or concerted practice. In *Hüls*,[44] the Court held that unless the company publicly distances itself from the meeting that has taken place and unless it reports it to the competent administrative authority, it is passively engaging in the infringement and hence is a party to the concerted practice. Finally, in *Loan Products to Professional Services*,[45] the OFT found that while Barclays did not itself provide pricing data to RBS, the fact that Barclays did not actively distance itself from the pricing data received from RBS indicated that it was party to either an agreement or a concerted practice.

D. Assessment under Article 101(3) TFEU

An information exchange may satisfy the criteria of Article 101(3) because of its beneficial effects. The Commission's Guidelines on Horizontal Cooperation Agreements[46] provide helpful guidance.

Regulations have been enacted pursuant to Article 101(3) TFEU providing special conditions according to which certain types of agreements are exempted from Article 101(1). When the conditions of the Block Exemption Regulation (BER)

[40] See Case T-112/07, *Hitachi Ltd and Others v Commission*, ECLI:EU:T:2011:342, paras 60–99.

[41] See Joined Cases 89/85, C-104/85 et al, *Woodpulp II*, ECLI:EU:C:1993:120.

[42] Information exchange between competitors is a very significant issue under EU competition law. The judgment of the ECJ confirmed its significance when it ruled that a bilateral exchange between banana importers of pre-pricing information relating to the weekly quotation prices for bananas amounted to a concerted practice with the object of restricting competition under art 101 TFEU (Case C-286/13P, *Dole v Commission*, ECLI:EU:C:2015:184).

[43] See Case T-202/98, *Tate & Lyle plc and Others v Commission*, ECLI:EU:T:2001:185.

[44] See Case C-199/92P, *Hüls v Commission* [1999] ECR I-4287.

[45] See Case CE/8950/08 and Decision No CA98/01/2011 of the UK Office of Fair Trading.

[46] See Horizontal Guidelines, paras 39, 95.

are fulfilled, the agreement is automatically valid and enforceable. In this context, information exchange was explicitly allowed in the insurance sector under Regulation 267/2010 (the Insurance Block Exemption Regulation), which, however, expired in 2017.[47] The Commission did not renew the BER, considering that the Horizontal Cooperation Guidelines, which apply to all sectors, offer adequate guidance on lawful cooperation to the undertakings.[48] Also, Article 101(1) does not apply to agreements where carriers enter into a liner shipping consortia and have combined market shares not exceeding 30 per cent according to Regulation 906/2009.[49] It will be permissible to exchange information necessary for the functioning of the consortia (such as on vessel slots, ports installations, sailing times, capacity and to use a computerised data exchange system). It should be noted that subject to certain conditions, agreements between competitors or non-competitors for the licensing of know-how (a package of secret, substantial and identified information resulting from experience and testing) are exempt from Article 101(1) where their combined market share does not exceed 20 per cent for agreements between competitors and 30 per cent for agreements between non-competitors.

III. Information Exchange and Transparency

A. Public Announcement/Signalling

Public announcements with regard to sensitive information can be alarming and harmful to competition.[50] Price signalling refers to a situation where there is no direct agreement or concerted practice between undertakings, but the firms send signals to one another through interviews, speeches at conferences and discussions with customers about their commercial intentions.[51] The signals may facilitate parallel behaviour. The Commission's Guidelines on Horizontal Cooperation Agreements say that price announcements can amount to a concerted practice if they reduce strategic uncertainty.[52] There have been cases where a whole sector was publicly exchanging information and this transparency in the market led to collusion without any explicit communication among the companies involved in the case.

[47] Whish and Bailey (n 1) 625. The Commission concluded that a block exemption is no longer required; Commission MEX/16/4369, 13 December 2016.

[48] Bailey and John (n 1) § 12.134.

[49] [2009] OJ L256/31, 29 September. *cf* Bailey and John (n 1) § 12.205.

[50] OECD, 'Algorithms and Collusion: Competition Policy in the Digital Age' (2017), oecd.org/competition/algorithms-collusion-competition-policy-in-the-digital-age.htm, 30. See also L Maritzen in J Busche and A Röhling (eds), *Kölner Kommentar zum Kartellrecht* (Cologne, Carl Heymanns, 2017) § 1 GWB para 181; WH Roth and T Ackermann in W Jaeger, J Kokott, P Pohlmann and D Schroeder (eds), *Frankfurter Kommentar GWB* (Cologne, Otto Schmidt, 2019) art 81, para 206; Whish and Bailey (n 1) 535.

[51] OECD, 'Roundtable Unilateral Disclosure of Information with Anticompetitive Effects', DAF/COMP(2012)17, oecd.org/daf/competition/Unilateraldisclosureofinformation2012.pdf.

[52] Horizontal Guidelines, para 63.

i. The Airline Tariff Publishing Company Case[53]

During the early 1990s, the US Department of Justice (DOJ) investigated tariff-fixing activities in the airline industry where the cartel members were able to implicitly coordinate tariffs using a third-party centre and sophisticated signalling mechanisms.[54]

In the US airline industry, airline companies send fare information on a daily basis to the Airline Tariff Publishing Company (ATPCO), a central clearing house that compiles all the data received and shares it in real time with travel agents, computer reservations systems, consumers and even the airline companies themselves. The database published by ATPCO includes information about prices, travel dates, origin and destination airports, ticket restrictions as well as first and last ticket dates, which indicate the time range when the tickets at a particular fare are sold.

Airline companies were using first ticket dates to announce tariff increases many weeks in advance. If the announcements were matched by the rivals, when the first ticket date arrived, all companies would simultaneously raise the tariff. Some of the coordination strategies were more complex, involving the use of fare code numbers and ticket date footnotes to send signals or negotiate multimarket coordination.

According to the US DOJ, it was the existence of a fast date exchange mechanism to monitor tariffs and react rapidly to price changes that enabled companies to collude without explicitly communicating. As tacit collusion is not forbidden and any explicit coordination was very hard to prove, the DOJ reached a settlement agreement with the airline companies under which the latter agreed to stop announcing most price increases in advance, with the exception of a few circumstances where early announcements could enhance consumer welfare.[55]

All the airline fares had to be concurrently available for sale to consumers. As this case shows, signalling can be very effective in establishing an informal cartel. Finally, companies may use algorithms to publicly disclose data and use codes in order to propose and negotiate price increases. Companies may use algorithms to publicly disclose detailed data that is used to propose and negotiate price increases.[56]

ii. Price Announcements in the Liner Shipping Industry/General Rate Increase Announcements[57]

Public announcements of future prices may provide efficiencies but would also be a focal point at which competitors align their behaviour. It is a grey zone and an uncertain

[53] See *United States v Airline Tariff Publishing Company, Alaska Airlines, Inc, American Airlines, Inc, Continental Airlines, Inc, Delta Air Lines, Inc, Northwest Airlines, Inc, Trans World Airlines, Inc, United Air Lines, Inc*, and *USAir, Inc*, https://www.justice.gov/atr/case/us-v-american-airlines-2004; see also OECD, Algorithms and Collusion – Background Note by the Secretariat of 9 June 2017, DAF/COMP(2017)4, 29 Box 10.

[54] The case is described in S Borenstein, 'Rapid Price Communication and Coordination: The Airline Tariff Publishing Case' in JE Kwoka and LJ White (eds), *The Antitrust Revolution*, 3rd edn (New York, HarperCollins, 1999) 310.

[55] *United States v Airline Tariff Publishing Co*, 1994-2 Trade Cas.

[56] OECD (n 50) para 73.

[57] See Case COMP/39850 *Container Shipping*. See further I Rabinovici, 'Public Exchange of information after Container Shipping' (2017) 8 *Journal of European Competition Law & Practice* 149.

area because it is not clear enough how the antitrust authorities and the courts are going to decide upon infringement or not.

The Commission opened formal antitrust proceedings on its own initiative (*ex officio*) to investigate the practice of publishing General Rate Increase (GRI) announcements in the liner shipping market in November 2013.

Container liner shipping is the transport of containers by ships according to a fixed time schedule on a specific route between a range of ports at one end (eg, Shanghai – Hong Kong – Singapore) and another range of ports at the other end (eg, Rotterdam – Hamburg – Southampton). More than half of EU imports and exports are carried by sea and around 40 per cent are shipped in containers.

Fourteen container liner shipping companies ('carriers') were regularly announcing their intended future increases of freight prices on their websites, via the press or in other ways.[58] These price announcements, known as GRI announcements, did not indicate the fixed final price for the service concerned, but only the amount of the increase in US dollars per transported container unit (20-foot equivalent unit (TEU)), the affected trade route and the planned date of implementation. They generally concerned sizable increases of several hundred US dollars per TEU.

GRI announcements were made typically three to five weeks before their intended implementation date, and during that time some or all of the other carriers announced similar intended rate increases for the same or similar route and same or similar implementation dates. Carriers were not bound by the announced increases and some carriers had indeed postponed or modified announced general rate increases, possibly aligning them with those announced by other carriers.

The Commission had concerns that GRI announcements did not provide full information on new prices to customers, but merely allowed carriers to be aware of each other's pricing intentions and might make it possible for them to coordinate their behaviour.

Announcing future price increases may signal the intended market conduct of carriers and by reducing the level of uncertainty about their pricing behaviour, decrease their incentives to compete against each other. Because the announcements provide only partial information to customers and may not be binding on the carriers, customers may not be able to rely on them and therefore carriers may be able to adjust prices without the risk of losing customers.

In order to address the Commission's concerns, the carriers proposed commitments. The carriers would stop publishing and communicating GRI announcements, ie, changes to prices expressed solely as an amount or percentage of the change. The commitments addressed the Commission's concerns that the companies' practice of publishing their intentions on future price increases may have harmed competition and customers. This practice may have raised prices on the market for container liner shipping services on routes to and from Europe, in breach of EU antitrust rules.

[58] The carriers were CMA CGM (France), COSCO (China), Evergreen (Taiwan), Hamburg Süd (Germany), Hanjin (South Korea), Hapag Lloyd (Germany), HMM (South Korea), Maersk (Denmark), MOL (Japan), MSC (Switzerland), NYK (Japan), OOCL (Hong Kong), UASC (United Arab Emirates) and ZIM (Israel).

The commitments will increase price transparency for customers and reduce the likelihood of concerted price signalling by binding the carriers to the prices announced.[59]

Since the case was brought to an end by an Article 9 decision,[60] the Commission's decision did not address whether there was another plausible explanation for the announcements. It therefore remains unclear whether such announcements would have been held to be in breach of Article 101(1). Given the uncertainty in this area, some academics support the idea that the Commission should have adopted an infringement decision.[61]

B. Information Exchange and Mergers/Due Diligence and Gun Jumping

Another example of information sharing that can pose a great threat to the competitive process in the market is the exchange of information that takes place for the purposes of merger negotiations between the interested parties. Although this situation may cause several issues, it is accepted that if the parties involved in a transaction take all the necessary measures in order to avoid potential anti-competitive effects, then the risks to competition are limited to a great extent.

Companies interested in acquisitions, mergers or joint ventures typically have a legitimate request to access detailed information about the other party's business in order to negotiate the deal and implement the merger. But some information of interest may be commercially sensitive, such as current and future price information, strategic plans and costs. This is especially true when the companies compete with each other.

The antitrust agencies and competition authorities have taken action against companies for unreasonable information sharing, whether as standalone conduct or during mergers and acquisitions (M&A) proceedings.[62] The Federal Trade Commission (FTC) charged a hair transplant services company with violating the FTC Act after it was discovered during the FTC's review of a proposed merger that the merging firms' CEOs repeatedly exchanged company-specific information about future product offerings, price ranges, discounting practices, expansion plans, operations and performance.[63] Even though the FTC did not challenge the merger, it concluded that the exchange of information facilitated coordination and endangered competition by reducing the

[59] The Commission has therefore made the commitments legally binding on the carriers for a period of three years starting from 7 December 2016.

[60] Article 9 provides that when the Commission intends to adopt a decision requiring that an infringement of art 101 or 102 be brought to an end, but where the undertakings concerned offer commitments to meet the concerns articulated by the Commission, the Commission may by decision make those commitments legally binding on the businesses concerned. When adopting such a decision, the Commission does not take a final position on whether there has been an infringement, whether the companies involved could satisfy the four conditions of art 101(3) or whether a firm is dominant in any defined market and whether it had an objective justification for its conduct.

[61] Whish and Bailey (n 1) 583.

[62] Maritzen (n 47) § 1 GWB para 506.

[63] R Liebeskind, 'Gun-Jumping: Antitrust Issues before Closing the Merger' (8 August 2003), pillsburylaw.com/images/content/1/8/v2/1842/16ADC9E2C53CF6E9F97E3F0A3F6F3242.pdf.

firm's uncertainty about its rival's specific product offerings, prices and plans. The FTC also opined that the exchange served no legitimate business purpose. In another case, it challenged both the merger and the exchange of competitively sensitive information between two welded-seam aluminium tube manufacturers. The FTC found the sharing of non-aggregated, customer-specific information, including current and future pricing plans, particularly harmful to competition because the two companies competed against each other in two highly concentrated markets. According to the Commission: 'This transfer had the potential to harm competition in the interim pre-consummation period and in the event the acquisitions were delayed, modified, or abandoned, may have led to even greater and more long-lasting harm.'

The reason for concern is simple: competitive harm from illegal information sharing can inflict harm to competition similar to the harm caused by an anti-competitive merger. Exchanging information about competitive plans, strategies and crucial data such as prices and costs can facilitate coordination between firms (and, if accompanied by accommodating actions, could constitute an unlawful agreement). The merger parties are still independent businesses and they must continue to operate independently – including safeguarding their competitively sensitive information – to ensure competitive vigour in the short term and also in the event that the merger does not happen. The FTC therefore looks carefully at pre-merger information sharing to make sure that there has been no inappropriate dissemination of or misuse of competitively sensitive information for anti-competitive purposes. It should be noted that pre-merger information sharing may contribute to unlawful 'gun jumping' in violation of the Hart-Scott-Rodino (HSR) Act and Rules if it results in the buyer effectively gaining beneficial ownership of the seller prior to the close of the transaction.[64]

Unlawful gun jumping may include the exchange of competitively sensitive information, but it typically also involves the actual coordination of business activities during the HSR pre-merger review period.[65] Such conduct could also constitute evidence of a standalone illegal agreement that violates section 1 of the Sherman Act.[66]

In the European context, gun-jumping violations may be sanctioned in two different ways: as violations of the EU Merger Regulation (EUMR) requirement that reportable transactions 'shall not be put into effect" before approval, or as infringements of the Article 101(1) TFEU prohibition of restrictive agreements, decisions or concerted practices.[67]

[64] See *United States v Computer Associates International, Inc* (2002) (merger agreement required buyer pre-approval for the seller to offer customers discounts greater than 20 per cent off the list price).

[65] The Hart-Scott-Rodino ('HSR') Act and s 7A of the Clayton Act, 15 USC § 18a, which require merging parties to abide by waiting periods following notification to the government of certain stock or asset acquisitions The HSR Act has been interpreted by the Antitrust Division to prohibit an acquirer from exercising 'substantial operational control' over an acquired firm prior to the expiration of the HSR waiting period, typically 30 days after filing the HSR, unless the government requests additional information. See also Bailey and John (n 1) § 8.138.

[66] See *United States v Gemstar-TV Guide International, Inc* (2003), https://www.justice.gov/atr/case/us-v-gemstar-tv-guide-international-inc-and-tv-guide-inc.

[67] Council Regulation (EC) No 139/2004 of 20 January 2004 on the control of concentrations between undertakings ('EC Merger Regulation') [2004] OJ L24.

In her May 2017 speech on 'Competition and the Rule of Law', Commissioner Vestager said that if merging parties 'jump the gun, we take that very seriously indeed' because 'otherwise, the harm to competition could already be done, before we have the chance to intervene'.[68] Also in May, the Commission announced gun-jumping proceedings against the French company Altice,[69] which recently received a gun-jumping fine from the French authority in connection with two other transactions. Two months later, the Commission opened another gun-jumping case against Canon.[70]

More specifically, in her May 2017 speech, Vestager announced that 'we found that [under] Altice's agreement to buy PT Portugal … Altice had already been acting as if it owned PT Portugal giving instructions on how to handle commercial issues, such as contract negotiations. And it also seems to have given sensitive information. Information that only PT Portugal's owner should have had – and without any safeguards to stop it misusing that information'.[71] The Commission has not yet elaborated on the specific contractual provisions in question or the nature of the information disclosed. It has also not yet clarified whether its investigation is limited to a potential violation of the EUMR's suspensory obligation or to a potential violation of Article 101. Interestingly, the Commission's Altice investigation followed close on the heels of a November 2016 decision by the French competition authority imposing an €80 million fine against Altice and SFR Group for gun jumping in two other transactions notified in 2014, Altice-SFR and Altice-OTL. The French Altice case, the first of its kind in France, illustrates that the Commission is not the only European authority taking a harder line on gun jumping.

On 24 April 2018 the European Commission imposed a €124.5 million fine on Altice,[72] the multinational cable and telecommunications company based in the Netherlands, for implementing its acquisition of the Portuguese telecommunications operator PT Portugal before notification or approval by the Commission.[73] In particular, the Commission concluded that certain provisions of the purchase agreement resulted in Altice acquiring the legal right to exercise decisive influence over PT Portugal, for

[68] M Vestager, 'Competition and the Rule of Law' (18 May 2017), ec.europa.eu/commission/commissioners/2014-2019/vestager/announcements/competition-and-rule-law_en.

[69] See the European Commission's press release dated 24 April 2018, where it was announced that the Commission fined Altice €125 million for infringing the EU competition rules. See also R Hoffer, 'Gun Jumping in Europa, endlich Klarheit?' (2018) 7 *NZKart* 300, 301.

[70] See the European Commission's press release dated 6 July 2017, where it was announced that Canon was in breach of EU merger procedural rules.

[71] Vestager (n 65).

[72] In February 2015, Altice notified the Commission of its plans to acquire PT Portugal. The transaction was conditionally cleared by the Commission on 20 April 2015, subject to the divestment of Altice's businesses in Portugal at the time, Oni and Cabovisão. In May 2017, the Commission addressed a Statement of Objections to Altice detailing its concerns that Altice implemented its acquisition of PT Portugal before obtaining the Commission's clearance and, in some instances, even before its notification of the merger. In this decision, the Commission confirmed its preliminary view that Altice breached the EU Merger Regulation and imposed a fine of €124.5 million on Altice.

[73] See the European Commission's press release dated 24 April 2018, where a part of Commissioner Vestager's speech is included. In particular, Commissioner Vestager, who was in charge of competition policy, said: 'Companies that jump the gun and implement mergers before notification or clearance undermine the effectiveness of our merger control system. This is the system that protects European consumers from any merger that would lead to higher prices or reduced choice. The fine imposed by the Commission on Altice today reflects the seriousness of the infringement and should deter other firms from breaking EU merger control rules.'

example, by granting Altice veto rights over decisions concerning PT Portugal's ordinary business and in certain cases, Altice actually exercised decisive influence over aspects of PT Portugal's business, for example, by giving PT Portugal instructions on how to carry out a marketing campaign and by seeking and receiving detailed commercially sensitive information about PT Portugal outside the framework of any confidentiality agreement. The aforementioned decision had no impact on the Commission's April 2015 decision to authorise the transaction under the EUMR. The assessment of the Commission at the time was independent of the facts assessed by the Commission in relation to Altice in the above decision.[74]

In July 2017, the Commission opened proceedings against Canon in connection with its acquisition of Toshiba Medical Systems, in which Canon paid the full price for non-voting shares in Toshiba Medical Systems and options for voting shares that were held by an interim buyer.[75] Although Canon only exercised these options after clearance was obtained, the Commission considered that the combination of Canon's ownership of 100 per cent of the target's non-voting shares and options to acquire the voting shares allowed Canon to effectively acquire Toshiba Medical Systems before the transaction was even notified.

In this regard, it should be said that parties to a prospective transaction have rational and legitimate interests to share information, eg, for due diligence purposes, to identify possible synergies or to prepare for integration. However, the rule is that competitors must not have access to commercially sensitive information (such as prices, costs, R&D projects or other strategic plans) before closing the deal. In the Altice case, the French authority did not deem it sufficient that the exchange of certain sensitive information had been restricted to in-house counsel.[76] The FTC Antitrust Division handled the issue in its Computer Associates and Gemstar consent orders by requiring the following conditions to disclosure of current or future prices or pending bids: (1) the information is reasonably related to a party's understanding of future earnings and prospects; and (2) the disclosure occurs pursuant to a non-disclosure agreement that (a) limits the use of the information for conducting due diligence, and (b) prohibits the disclosure of any such information to any employee of the person receiving the information who is directly responsible for the marketing, pricing or sales of the competing products.[77]

Another way to protect client confidentiality and prevent information from being circulated among unauthorised companies is introduced by the so-called Chinese walls. Information should be exchanged through virtual exchange rooms (VDRs) or yellow/green/red data rooms. A 'clean team' should also be appointed, which is an impartial third party that removes some of the competition risks by guaranteeing strong confidentiality and facilitating the process of exchanging sensitive information between the

[74] See the European Commission's press release dated 24 April 2018.

[75] Norton Rose Fulbright, 'The EU Gets Tough on Gun Jumping' (November 2017), https://www.nortonrosefulbright.com/en/knowledge/publications/de169d97/the-eu-gets-tough-on-gun-jumping.

[76] Dentons, '"Gun-Jumping": Antitrust Pre-closing Risks and How to Avoid Them' (28 December 2017), dentons.com/en/insights/alerts/2017/december/28/gun-jumping.

[77] Computer Associates, Competitive Impact Statement at 3 (filed 23 April 2002); *US v Gemstar-TV Guide International, Inc*, complaint 56 (DDC filed 6 February 2003) (No 03 CV 000198).

vendor and the existing bidders.[78] Therefore, some care should be taken with information exchanges, especially regarding current or future prices. It is preferable that sensitive information be shared on a need-to-know basis and ideally kept away from line business people who could use the information competitively. In many situations, an outside auditor may be able to confirm facts without businesspeople seeing (and having an opportunity to use) sensitive information.

C. Transparency, Information Exchange and Algorithmic Collusion

Another very interesting example of transparency in the market that can prove to be harmful to competition is the use of algorithms, which improve market transparency and enable high-frequency trading.[79]

In the European Commission's sector inquiry on e-commerce, it is stated that increased price transparency allows retailers to monitor their competitors' prices and, in some cases, even adapt their prices automatically by using software programs based on the prices prevailing in the market. Because of the possibility that this facilitates price setting and price coordination, the use of this special software might sometimes be in need of scrutiny so as to prevent competition problems.[80] Humans may use technology and algorithms to support traditional forms of collusion, that is, the collusion agreed by humans and subsequently executed by algorithms. When transparency increases in concentrated markets with substitutable products, so does the risk of tacit collusion.[81]

As a clear illustration of the above competition risks, the German Competition Authority suspected that an oligopoly of five firms – BP (Aral), ConocoPhilips (Jet), ExxonMobil (Esso), Shell and Total – dominated the off-motorway petrol station business.[82] In order to monitor pricing, the petrol station owners would drive past specified competitor petrol stations several times a day and note their prices. The monitored prices were then fed into the respective oil company's electronic system. Generally, when one competitor increased its petrol price, its rivals generally responded three to six hours later.

[78] See Maritzen (n 47) § 1 GWB, para 512.

[79] See, among others, SK Mehra, 'Robo-seller Prosecutions and Antitrust's Error-Cost Framework' (Spring 2017) 2 *CPI Antitrust Chronicle May*; SK Mehra, 'De-humanizing Antitrust: The Rise of the Machines and the Regulation of Competition' (2014) *Temple University Legal Studies Research Paper No 2014-43*; A Ezrachi and ME Stucke, *Virtual Competition: The Promise and Perils of the Algorithm-Driven Economy* (Cambridge, MA, Harvard University Press, 2016).

[80] Report from the Commission to the Council and the European Parliament, Final report on the E-commerce Sector Inquiry, para 13.

[81] A Ezrachi and ME Stucke, 'Algorithmic Collusion: Problems and Counter-measures', OECD Roundtable on Algorithms and Collusion of 31 May 2017, DAF/COMP/WD(2017)25.

[82] Bundeskartellamt, Fuel Sector Inquiry, Final Report (May 2011), bundeskartellamt.de/SharedDocs/Publikation/EN/Sector%20Inquiries/Fuel%20Sector%20Inquiry%20-%20Final%20Report.pdf?__blob=publicationFile&v=14.

With view to promoting competition, the German government required the petrol stations to report to the government's transparency unit any price changes for gasoline or diesel fuel in real time. The unit then transmitted the price data to consumers so as to find the cheapest petrol nearby. Instead of lowering the prices, the enhanced market transparency led to further price increases. Compared to the control group, retail petrol prices increased by about 1.2–3.3 euro cents and diesel increased by about 2 euro cents.[83]

This case study shows that a mechanism meant to promote price competition could easily end up undermining it. No petrol station wants a reputation as a price discounter and there are no big profits to be made by discounting. Companies may now need only seconds rather than days to signal price increases and foster collusion.

In another interesting case, four major oil firms (BP, Caltex, Mobil and Shell) and two supermarket chains (Coles and Woolworths) dominated Australian Perth's concentrated retail petrol market.[84,85] In 2001, the government introduced a petrol price transparency program called 'Fuelwatch'. Each firm had to submit before 2 pm its next day's station-level prices. Retail prices were fixed at these posted levels for 24 hours. Fuelwatch was proved to be very useful in promoting tacit collusion. Rivals could see the prices for every petrol station online and after 2.30 pm each day they could also know tomorrow's prices. The economic study found that the market leader BP facilitated tacit collusion which substantially improved retail margins, created price stability in the presence of aggregated shocks and enabled firms to resolve conflicts quickly. According to the study, it took 12 years in Perth from the start of the government's price transparency policy for the six competitors to develop a stable collusive pricing structure.

i. Algorithms

By improving market transparency and enabling high-frequency trading, algorithms increase the likelihood of collusion in market structures that would traditionally face fierce competition.[86] Algorithms might facilitate tacit coordination by providing companies with automated mechanisms to signal and implement common policies as well as monitor and punish deviations. The algorithms can make tacit collusion more likely both in oligopolistic markets with high barriers to entry and a high degree of transparency, and in markets when traditionally tacit collusion would be difficult to achieve.

On the supply side, algorithms can help to increase transparency, improve existing products or develop new ones.[87] The work of the Organisation for Economic

[83] R Dewenter, U Heimeshoff and H Lueth, 'The Impact of Market Transparency Unit for Fuels on Gasoline Prices in Germany' (May 2016), uni-duesseldorf.de/home/fileadmin/redaktion/DUP/Info_PDFs/Reihen/Wirtschaftswissenschaften/DICE_DP/220_Dewenter_Heimeshoff_Lueth.pdf.

[84] Ezrachi and Stucke (n 78).

[85] D Byrne and N de Roos, 'Learning to Coordinate: A Study in Retail Gasoline' (19 January 2017), ssrn.com/abstract=2570637.

[86] OECD, Algorithms and Collusion in the Digital Age, Background Note from Capobianco, Gonzaga and Nyeson at the OECD Competition Committee Roundtable on Algorithms and Collusion, DAF/COMP(2017)4, one.oecd.org/document/DAF/COMP(2017)4/en/pdf.

[87] See M Gal and N Elkin-Koren, 'Algorithmic Consumers' (2017) 30 *Harvard Journal of Law and Technology* 309, where it is stated that 'on the demand side, algorithms may affect the dynamics of the market by supporting consumer decisions. They do not only help companies improve their business processes, but they also assist consumers in their purchasing decisions and demand side efficiencies'. In addition, algorithms can be

Co-operation and Development (OECD) on disruptive innovation has shown how market entry has been promoted by the ability of firms to develop new offerings based on algorithms.[88] On the other hand, as was clearly illustrated above, algorithms may work as a facilitating factor for collusion and may enable new forms of coordination.[89]

Algorithms are without any doubt affecting market conditions, resulting in price transparency and high-frequency trading that allows companies to react quickly and aggressively. Changes in digital markets could make collusive strategies stable in virtually any market structure. This is because by providing companies with powerful automated mechanisms to monitor prices, implement common policies, send market signals or optimise joint profits with deep learning techniques, algorithms might enable firms to achieve the same outcomes of traditional hardcore cartels through tacit collusion. Michal Gal supports the idea of coordination by design. Suppliers consciously use similar algorithms even when better algorithms are available to them. The algorithms need not be identical, but their operative part – which calculates the trade conditions – should generate relatively similar outcomes.[90]

Pricing algorithms are used to a large extent in today's economy as they enable firms to gather intelligence about the market in which they operate. It is apparent that such mechanisms confer multiple efficiencies and reduce the costs. For instance, algorithms are used in the air transport and insurance sectors to solve problems such as clearing markets and ensuring that risk is evaluated and priced effectively. Nevertheless, pricing algorithms can contribute to concerted outcomes.

An agreement between rivals to use a common algorithm in order to coordinate their prices fits the criteria for a standard cartel. The situation arose in a recent investigation by the UK's Competition and Markets Authority (CMA) where firms selling posters and frames on Amazon agreed with each other what their algorithms should look like.[91] Trod Limited admitted agreeing with one of its competing online sellers, GB eye Ltd (trading as 'GB Posters'), that they would not undercut each other's prices for posters and frames sold on Amazon's UK website. The agreement was implemented by using automated repricing software which the parties each configured to give effect

used to compare prices and quality, predict market trends and make fast decisions; they can also reduce search costs, transaction costs, help consumers overcome bias and make rational choices, strengthening buyer power.

88 OECD, 'Big Data: Bringing Competition Policy to the Digital Era', DAF/COMP(2016)14, one.oecd.org/document/DAF/COMP(2016)14/en/pdf.

89 See in this regard Commissioner M Vestager's speech at the Bundeskartellamt 18th Conference on Algorithms and Competition, in Berlin, 16 March 2017: 'What businesses can and must do is to ensure antitrust compliance by design. That means that pricing algorithms need to be built in a way that does not allow them to collude. Like a more honourable version of the computer HAL in the film 2001, they need to respond to an offer of collusion by saying, I am sorry, I am afraid I can't do that.' See ec.europa.eu/commission/commissioners/2014-2019/vestager/announcements/bundeskartellamt-18th-conference-competition-berlin-16-march-2017_en.

90 Ezrachi and Stucke (n 78) 83; M Gal, 'Algorithms as Illegal Agreements' (forthcoming) *Berkeley Technology Law Journal*, available at ssrn.com/abstract=3171977; see also Laitenberger, 'Developments in EU Competition Control in the Global and Digital Age' (6 September 2018), http://ec.europa.eu/competition/speeches/text/sp2018_12_en.pdf; EJ Green et al, 'Tacit Collusion in Oligopoly' in RD Blair and DD Sokol (eds), *Oxford Handbook of International Antitrust Economics* (Oxford, Oxford University Press, 2015).

91 Competition and Markets Authority, Online Pricing of Posters and Frames of 4 December 2015, 'Online Seller Admits Breaking Competition Law' (21 July 2016), gov.uk/government/news/online-seller-admits-breaking-competition-law.

to the illegal cartel. Trod, based in Birmingham, and GB eye, based in Sheffield, sold licensed sport and entertainment merchandise and related products, including posters, frames, badges, stickers and mugs, with popular images from the sport and entertainment world, such as One Direction and Justin Bieber.[92] The CMA coordinated its investigation with that of the US DOJ into conduct involving the use of algorithms to facilitate price fixing in the online sale of wall décor in the US.[93]

In a previous similar case in 2015, the US DOJ charged a seller on Amazon marketplace, David Topkins, for coordinating with other sellers the prices of posters sold online between September 2013 and January 2014. David Topkins and the other conspirators designed and shared among each other dynamic pricing algorithms which they programmed to act in conformity with their agreement.[94] Although algorithmic pricing is not illegal, it was the existence of an agreement to jointly implement the algorithm that made the case for the DOJ.

However, other uses of pricing algorithms appear not to meet the criteria of an unlawful anti-competitive agreement. For example, the parallel but uncoordinated adoption of pricing algorithms that incorporate price matching clauses appears to be a parallel oligopoly that it is not condemned by competition law. Concerns of coordination could possibly arise if firms outsourced the creation of algorithms to the same IT companies and programmers. This might create a hub and spoke scenario where coordination is caused by competitors using the same hub for developing their pricing algorithms and they end up relying on the same algorithms to develop their pricing strategies.

Collusive behaviour could be achieved if many companies were using pricing algorithms to follow in real time a market leader (tit for tat strategy), who in turn would be responsible for programming the pricing algorithm that fixes prices above the competitive level.

ii. Explicit and Tacit Collusion

As is apparent from the above discussion, a transparent environment is more prone to collusion.[95] In fact, transparency in the relevant markets combined with frequency of interaction make several industries prone to collusion. One of the main risks of algorithms is that they expand the grey area between unlawful explicit collusion and

[92] Trod has agreed to accept a fine of £163,371 for taking part in the cartel. This is after deducting a 20 per cent discount to reflect the resource savings to the CMA as a result of Trod's admission and cooperation with the CMA's investigation. Provided it continues to cooperate and comply with the other conditions of the CMA's leniency policy, GB eye will not receive a fine, having reported the cartel to the CMA and cooperated with the investigation, in accordance with the CMA's leniency policy.

[93] Algorithms and Collusion, Note from the United Kingdom, DAF/COMP/WD (2017) 19, para 48.

[94] OECD (n 50) 27 Box 9.

[95] See in this regard l'Autorité de la Concurrence and Bundeskartellamt, 2016, where it was said that 'even though market transparency as a facilitating factor for collusion has been debated for several decades now, it gains new relevance due to technical developments such as sophisticated computer algorithms. For example, by processing all available information and thus monitoring and analysing or anticipating their competitors' responses to current and future prices, competitors may easier be able to find a sustainable supra-competitive price equilibrium which they can agree on'. See A Ezrachi and ME Stucke, 'Artificial Intelligence and Collusion: When Computers Inhibit Competition' (2015) 7, law.ox.ac.uk/sites/files/oxlaw/cclpl40.pdf.

lawful tacit collusion, allowing firms to sustain profits above the competitive level more easily without necessarily having to enter into an agreement. In economic literature, reaching an agreement captures both explicit agreements and conscious parallelism. The former refers to cases where the parties exchange mutual assurances prior to their actions to act in a coordinated manner. The latter, sometimes called oligopolistic coordination or tacit collusion, occurs when firms independently set their trade terms while taking into account their competitors' probable reactions to their actions. As Kaplow claims, 'distinction between express collusion and conscious parallelism is blurry' and 'the definition of 'agreement' can include both'. In legal literature, only the former are considered to constitute 'agreements' in the legal sense and are therefore potentially illegal; instances of conscious parallelism are not. According to Posner, conscious parallelism involves the making and acceptance of an offer through conduct, and therefore literally and materially fulfils the conditions for an agreement.[96] More recently, Posner has repudiated his view on this.[97]

There is no doubt that algorithms are changing the competitive landscape. By improving the market transparency and enabling high-frequency trading, the likelihood of collusion is increased.[98] Therefore, algorithms may enable firms to replace explicit collusion with tacit coordination. Although this can easily be the case, we ought to be extremely careful because in the real world, where there is no perfect competition, it takes a lot of effort to distinguish between coordinated and non-coordinated outcomes. It is a very complex assessment that requires the proper expertise and taking into account previous experiences. Attempts to intervene against such contact carry a clear risk of false convictions. It would create regulatory uncertainty if the firms were condemned for adapting intelligently to the oligopolistic markets in which they find themselves competing. A solution could be to engage in market studies and market investigations in order for the competition authorities to understand the dynamic of the market or the market failure.[99] Another possible remedy could be the introduction of auditing mechanisms for algorithms.[100] But as Ezrachi and Stucke say, this is not possible, since algorithms do not include instructions to collude, but rather to maximise profits.[101]

[96] RA Posner, *Antitrust Law: An Economic Perspective* (Chicago, University of Chicago Press, 1976) 146.

[97] RA Posner, 'Review of Kaplow, Competition Policy and Price Fixing' (2014) 79 *Antitrust Law Journal* 761, 765. See also N Petit, 'The Oligopoly Problem in EU Competition Law' in I Liannos and D Geradin (eds), *Research Handbook in European Competition Law* (Cheltenham, Edward Elgar, 2013) 259.

[98] Ariel Ezrachi and Maurice E Stucke, 'Is Your Digital Assistant Devious?' (2016) *Oxford Legal Studies Research Paper No 32/2016*, *University of Tennessee Legal Studies Research Paper No 304*; Gal and Elkin-Koren (n 84).

[99] OECD (n 47) 40. See also Gal (n 87) 42, who describes five algorithms cases which should alert the competition authorities, red flags as the author says.

[100] OECD (n 47) 42. See also the remedies that Google offered to the European Commission regarding the Android case and Google Search (2018).

[101] Ezrachi and Stucke (n 78) 30; Ariel Ezrachi and Maurice E Stucke, 'How Pricing Bots Could Form Cartels and Make Things More Expensive' (2016), hbr.org/2016/10/how-pricing-bots-could-form-cartels-and-make-things-more-expensive. See also FTC Commissioner McSweeny, who recognised the increased detection challenges created by algorithms: T McSweeny, 'Algorithms and Coordinated Effects' (22 May 2017), ftc.gov/public-statements/2017/05/algorithms-coordinated-effects.

Thus, the crucial question that arises is if we need to regulate the algorithms *ex ante* rather than *ex post*.[102] In the scope of state intervention, some academics suggest the establishment of a global digital regulator to handle the problem of digital economy and algorithms.[103] In the words of Commissioner Vestager, antitrust compliance by design should be established. Businesses have the obligation of programing algorithms to deliberately comply with data protection and antitrust laws.[104] Should the algorithms be programmed not to react to most recent changes in prices or to ignore price variations of individuals companies while still accounting for average prices?[105] The problem and the challenges that arise are that the markets are less transparent and thus the answers are not clear-cut. Therefore, there are real challenges for the enforcers to devise proportionate policy responses to address the concerns raised by algorithms.[106]

IV. Information Exchange, Non-performing Loans and Competition Law

A. Introductory Remarks

Exchanges of information (including commercially sensitive information) between credit institutions (eg, among the four systemic Greek banks)[107] about the financial status of specific borrowers, with the intention of adopting a uniform policy per borrower by the banks, is likely to infringe Article 101 TFEU. However, the answer would be different if such an exchange was taking place in the context of the non-performing loans (NPLs) negotiations, aiming at their restructuring within an electronic platform framework between banks.

Pursuant to section 3 (Safeguarding of financial stability) of the Memorandum of Understanding, which was attached to the Financial Assistance Facility Agreement entered into, among others, by the Hellenic Republic, the European Commission and the Bank of Greece on 19 August 2015, the Hellenic Republic undertook the commitment, among other things, to develop a credible strategy for addressing the issue of

[102] See, among others, Gal (n 87) 44; M Perel, 'Digital Remedies' (2019, forthcoming) *Berkeley Technology Law Journal*, available at ssrn.com/abstract=3143039.

[103] A Gawer, 'Competition Policy and Regulatory Reforms for Big Data' (2016), note submitted to the Hearing on Big Data of the 126th Meeting of the OECD Competition Committee, DAF/COMP/WD(2016)74, one.oecd.org/document/DAF/COMP/WD(2016)74/en/pdf.

[104] See n 86.

[105] Reduce the high frequency of interaction, enforce lags on price adjustments or compromise to any new offer for a minimum time period (A Ezrachi and ME Stucke, 'Two Artificial Neural Networks Meet in an Online Hub and Change the Future of Competition' (2017), papers.ssrn.com/sol3/papers.cfm?abstract_id=2949434.

[106] See measures on algorithmic transparency and accountability. In the US, the FTC's Bureau of Consumer Protection established the Office of Technology Research and Investigation, which is responsible, among other things, for conducting studies and providing guidance for the transparency of algorithms; see Algorithms and Collusion, Note by the Secretariat, DAF/COMP(2017)4, 45, 46.

[107] These are the National Bank of Greece (NBG), Alpha Bank, Eurobank and Piraeus Bank – and a few non-systemic banks, the biggest being Attica Bank.

non-performing exposures that aims at minimising the implementation time and the use of capital resources, and drawing on the expertise of external consultants for both strategy development and implementation.

In line with this commitment, Law 4354/2015 on the management of non-performing loans was enacted as subsequently amended and is currently in force, liberalising the servicing of NPLs and providing for a legal framework for the assignment of management to licensed servicers and the sale of NPLs to potential investors, as well as allowing the establishment of a strictly regulated secondary NPLs market.

Several alternatives are being considered in order to avoid the negative effects of NPLs. Managing NPLs is the most important challenge that the Greek banking system faces nowadays. The reduction of the high NPE ratio of the Greek banks is a key requirement for gradually restoring an adequate and efficient supply of credit to the Greek economy and for achieving sustained growth.

With this aim in mind, the commitments of the Greek banks vis-a-vis the prudential regulator were introduced to meet specific operational targets with regard to NPLs. In this context, the Greek banks have set up comprehensive strategies, including detailed operational measures and actions, prioritised and scheduled, as well as numerical targets to significantly reduce their NPLs over the coming years.

The banks decided, among other things, to manage a selected pool of common NPLs of the four systemic Greek banks under a common management and servicing framework. The objective of such collaboration was to maximise recoveries of the portfolio, reduce NPLs exposure, facilitate the sustainability of Greek undertakings and enable asset deconsolidation. In order to achieve such objectives, the initiative relied on selecting a third-party servicer capable of managing the portfolio on an independent basis, through a pre-defined set of rules that was fair to all banks. A fair treatment of each bank would be assured (each bank would gain at least what it could have obtained in the liquidation scenario), while maximising recoveries of NPLs at the portfolio level.

B. Merger Control Aspects

The first question to be answered is whether the management and restructuring of NPLs constitutes a concentration of undertakings. It should be pointed out that the Servicer-Electronic Platform would only take over the oversight, management and restructuring of the participating banks' NPLs and would not acquire the associated assets, eg, the NPLs and/or personnel from the banks. The NPLs would stay with the respective accounts of the banks. As such, the platform would not constitute a concentration under the EU and Greek merger control rules.

The above is consistent with the European Commission Consolidated Jurisdictional Notice on the control of concentrations between undertakings (paragraphs 25 and 26). Although, in the event that NPLs are bought by a third party, such a distinct transaction shall qualify as a concentration and shall be scrutinised accordingly.

Another question to be answered is whether the management and restructuring of NPLs entails any pooling agreement, ie, the joint exercise of voting rights in any of the undertakings included in the assigned portfolio.[108] The whole management of NPLs is inconsistent with any sort of agreement to jointly exercise their voting rights (if any) in the undertakings concerned.

C. Antitrust Issues and Exchange of Information

i. The Necessary Synergy

The illegal character of the trade and strategic information exchange system at issue between the credit institutions involved, with regard to the financial status of certain borrowers, in order for a specific borrower to be treated under a uniform trade policy is applied under normal operational conditions in the relevant market. Therefore, by definition, competition requires more than one party claiming business success. In this context, the European Commission outlines the target of Article 101 TFEU as the 'protection of competition in the market so as to increase the consumer's prosperity and ensure an effective allocation of resources. Competition and market integration serve such goals, given that the creation and preservation of a unified open market favours the effective allocation of resources throughout the entire Community for the consumers' benefit'.[109]

The aforementioned fundamental function of competition, aiming at gaining market shares and business profits, is challenged in the case of insolvency and NPL management procedures. More specifically, the common ground amongst all the relevant legislative rules and regulations of the bankruptcy law field is the optimum exploitation for the creditors of the existing assets and, in addition, the safeguarding of (any ascertained) viability of the relevant business undertaking. In view of this, it is effortlessly concluded that corporate creditors suffering minor or more considerable property loss due to the debtor's subjection to one of the above-mentioned procedures (*par condicio creditorum*) is counterbalanced and compensated for by their increased potential to intervene and affect the development of procedures each time this is at issue. A reasonable requirement for this is the creditors' gathering of valid and credible information concerning the debtor's financial situation, a fact that facilitates the creditors' coordinated action within the framework of bodies and procedures provided by the insolvency or NPLs management legislation. Thus, the coordinated action of creditors and especially of credit institutions constitutes a legitimate implementation method of the legislation and so prevents the rise of compatibility issues with Greek or EU antitrust legislation. More specifically, the creditors' coordinated action provided as compulsory, either due to their organising in collective bodies or due to their need for prior mutual agreement as regards their steps of action to be followed, does not entail the competition's restriction in some relevant

[108] European Commission Consolidated Jurisdictional Notice on the control of concentrations between undertakings, para 75.

[109] See the BEUC Discussion Paper on 'The Goals of EU Competition Law and the Digital Economy', report commissioned by BEUC Professor A Ezrachi (University of Oxford).

market, given that the corporate creditors participate exclusively and only in sharing the damage of the above procedures, which negates the basic and reasonable pre-requisites of the antitrust legislation.

As evidenced by the overview of the particular provisions, it is a 'necessary synergy of the credit institutions involved', which is compulsory, given the form and context of the insolvency or workout procedures, under the meaning of management and restructuring of NPLs.[110] Moreover, in view of the nature of the NPLs at stake – where the same debtor has significant exposure to multiple banks – it is rather meaningless or inapplicable to ask whether 'each operator – here each Bank – could be expected to act independently and autonomously when adopting a given course of conduct'. The aim of the creditors here is not how to generate business in a less risky environment, but to minimise losses and keep the banking system afloat (including meeting prudential control/capital requirements etc).

Besides bankruptcy law provisions (including pre-bankruptcy proceedings) and Law 3869/2010 (Forbearance of over-indebted natural persons' debt and other provisions) as amended, other recent developments in Greek legislation and implementing regulation also dictate the need for close cooperation of banks as well as the minimum necessary exchange of sensitive information. According to Law 4469/2017 on Out of Court Workouts (OCWs), a new process of extrajudicial settlement of debts is introduced in Article 17, which reads as follows:

> When more than one credit institutions, financial institutions or companies active in the management and transfer of bank exposures of Law 4354/2015, own or manage claims against the same debtor, in relation to whom there are sufficient indications of the current or future inability to meet his financial obligations, these institutions can cooperate, in order to work on and submit, to the debtor, a joint proposal with the aim of finding a sustainable solution. To that end, the aforementioned institutions can exchange the information required to assess the viability of the debtor's company and draft the terms and conditions of the joint proposal, which they will submit in the context of the current regulatory framework.

According to Annex III bearing the title 'Approach of the International Association of Restructuring, Insolvency & Bankruptcy Professionals (INSOL) in Cases of Multiple

[110] In the US, the antitrust issue was raised in the context of a restructuring. In a case called *CompuCredit Holdings Corporation v Akanthos Capital Management, LLC*, CompuCredit, a provider of credit and other financial services, initiated a tender offer for up to $160 million of its bonds at a price purportedly at market. Seventy per cent of the notes were held by 21 hedge funds and none of them were tendered. CompuCredit filed suit, alleging that the hedge funds had engaged in an unlawful conspiracy to boycott the tender offer to inflate the tender price. In June, 2011, the district court granted the funds' motion to dismiss and, on appeal, a panel of judges on the US Court of Appeals for the 11th Circuit affirmed, holding that a violation of the Sherman Anti-Trust Act does not occur when creditors act collaboratively to collect pre-existing debts. The 11th Circuit then granted CompuCredit's petition for 'rehearing en banc' (by the entire court), which alleged that the panel's ruling resulted in an 'implied exemption' to the Sherman Act, something forbidden by Supreme Court precedent. The Loan Syndications and Trading Association (LSTA) filed an amicus brief arguing that were the 11th Circuit to adopt CompuCredit's proposed rule, it would threaten to freeze all pre-bankruptcy coordination among creditors for existing debt (including both bonds and loans) forbidding 'as per se illegal a long-established, near universal creditor behavior that benefits not only creditors but also borrowers, businesses and the economy as a whole'. The 10 judges from the 11th Circuit heard oral arguments in Atlanta and two days later issued a one-page decision affirming the district court's decision. United States Court of Appeals for the 11th Circuit, No 11-13254 Non-Argument Calendar DC Docket No 1:11-cv-00117-TCB COMPUTERCREDIT.

Creditors' the following are crucial: (a) all involved creditors must be willing to cooperate in order to ensure enough time (standstill period), in order to gather and evaluate information on the debtor's financial status; (b) during the standstill period, all involved creditors must agree to abstain from taking any measures aiming at reducing their claim against the debtor; (c) the involved creditors' interests are much better served when creditors are coordinated as to the manner in which they treat the debtor. Such coordination may be facilitated, when coordination committees, composed of the involved creditors' representatives, are established, also receiving support from experts; and (d) information gathered for the purposes of the present procedure, as well as any suggestions on the debt workout, should be available to all creditors involved, who should treat them as confidential, unless they are information already publicly available.

In light of the above, it becomes apparent that the statutory framework governing the management of NPLs by credit institutions not only allows but in fact also imposes the exchange of information concerning every debtor examined from time to time, in order for a joint proposal to be adopted, namely a common strategy as regards the restructuring of their debts. All these developments are a sound argument for the pro-competitive effects of management of NPLs. The legislative framework for NPLs, the current Financial Adjustment Programme for Greece and its commitments, and the stakes at risk for the banks are more than sufficient to exclude any allegation that the management and restructuring of NPLs through a third-party servicer has an object of restricting or distorting competition.

The above conclusions are also reinforced by reference to the rule of reason, also referred to as the 'rule of reasonable cause', which has been developed in antitrust law. First of all, it should be noted that the concept of ancillary restraints covers every assumed competition restraint, which is directly linked and is necessary for the realisation of a main non-restrictive transaction. Consequently, if the basic parameters of a main agreement do not contain or result in competition restriction, then the restraints which are directly linked and are necessary for the execution of the main transaction also do not fall within the scope of application of the above prohibitive provisions.[111] As clearly defined by the European Commission,[112] a restraint is directly associated with the main transaction, if it depends on the latter's realisation and is inextricably connected thereto. The necessity criterion means that the restraint must be objectively necessary for the main transaction's realisation and proportionate/corresponding to the same. In this context, each restraint, even if it is to be considered necessary for the agreement's conclusion, must be reviewed in its particular parameters, namely its duration, scope of application in terms of object and place, and finally it must be ascertained whether it exceeds the necessary degree.[113]

It should be pointed out that the close interaction between the information exchange at issue and the structure and functionality of the insolvency and non-performing

[111] See General Court, judgment of 18 September 2001, Case T-112/99, *Métropole télévision (M6) and others v Committee*, para 104.

[112] Guidelines on the application of Article 81 paragraph 3 of the Treaty, EE C 101 (27 April 2004), para 29 with further references.

[113] See Case C-309/99, *Wouters*, EU:C:2002:98, para 109. Likewise see ECJ, judgment dated 15 December 1994, Case C-250/92, *Goettrup-Klim Grovvareforening*, para 35.

exposures' management procedures in general does not fall under the prohibition rule, concerning the rules of regulatory nature which, in the light of overriding reasons of public interest, relate to the general regulation of specific procedures (regulatory rules).[114] From the case law in *Wouters*, *Arduino* and *Meca Medina*[115] arises the conclusion that the court – by means of a 'competition balance sheet' – proceeds with an ad hoc examination of a probable restrictive effect of competition, assessing the latter based on the diagnosis of another purpose which promotes competition, as well as by virtue of the proportionality principle.

Consequently, the need for effective structuring of the insolvency and NPLs management procedures in general should be deemed as promoting the competition between credit institutions within the loan market. These assumptions are effortlessly concluded from the relevant recommendations and obligations set forth by the competent supervisory authority, namely the Bank of Greece, in the specific regulations that are applicable pursuant to the above.

In any case, if the specific policy targeting is considered as neutral from the perspective of antitrust legislation, the public interest objective cannot be ignored, an objective aiming at the effectiveness of the aforementioned procedures. In view of these assumptions, any competition restraints imposed contrary to expectations constitute an essential means for the achievement of the above purposes of public interest and in all cases are subject to the proportionality test.

ii. On the Application of Exemption Rules (Article 101(3) TFEU)

In general, an information exchange may satisfy the Article 101(3) criteria when there are beneficial effects. The European Commission discusses the Article 101(3) criteria and its application to information sharing in paragraphs 95–104 of its Guidelines. The Commission also refers at benchmarking in paragraph 95 and explains that this helps undertakings be more efficient and compare themselves to the best example in their respective industry.[116] In certain circumstances, information might be shared in order to provide an optimal allocation of resources and reduce any mismatch between supply and demand. In addition, information sharing can produce multiple efficiencies, eg, in markets where there is asymmetric information. A final and very helpful example in our case is the exchange of information between credit institutions about the solvency of their customers.[117]

However, even in the unlikely scenario that the banks were accused on the grounds that the management of NPLs entails anti-competitive effects, they could invoke the exemption of Article 101(3) TFEU. The application of the exemption provided

[114] 'Regulatory Ancillarity', Whish and Bailey (n 1) 138.

[115] ECJ, judgment dated 18 July 2006, Case C-519/04 P, *Meca Medina*, C-35/99 EU:C:2002:97, para 42.

[116] Guidelines on Horizontal Cooperation Agreements, para 95; see BR Henry, 'Benchmarking and Antitrust' (1993) 62 *Antitrust Law Journal* 483. On benchmarking and EU law, see J Carle and M Johnsson, 'Benchmarking and EC Competition Law' (1998) 19 *European Competition Law Review* 74; L Boulter 'Competition Risks in Benchmarking' (1999) 20 *European Competition Law Review* 434.

[117] In *Asnef-Equifax* (n 27), the Court of Justice suggested that such an exchange of information might satisfy the criteria of art 101(3).

in Article 101(3) TFEU is subject to four cumulative conditions laid down in that provision.[118]

The fulfilment of the above requirements in a way that justifies any competition restraints deriving from the information exchange at issue is demonstrated by the analysis of the macro-economic benefits from the specific procedural framework's function, having an impact on both the financial stability as well as on the soundness of the Greek banking system. This fact entails lower risk for the Greek credit institutions and higher predictability as regards the management of NPLs, and so the risks assumed from banking loans are limited, credit availability is increased and loan interest rates are decreased to the benefit of consumer welfare and especially the reliable debtors. In this context, special mention should be made of the significant cost and human resources efficiencies regarding the procedures at issue. As the court explained in the *Asnef-Equifax* case, 'in order for the condition that consumers be allowed a fair share of the benefit to be satisfied, it is not necessary, in principle, for each consumer individually to derive a benefit from an agreement, a decision or a concerted practice. However, the overall effect on consumers in the relevant markets must be favourable'.[119]

As stated in the European Commission's Guidelines, the following are fulfilled in the present case:

a. *Efficiencies*: the information exchange at issue accelerates the effective execution of the NPLs management procedure, achieves legal certainty and reduces the courts' huge workload. Finally, both the debtors and the involved credit institutions are released from long-term and arduous litigation. Similarly, there is significant efficiency in terms of the operational cost of the credit and financial institutions, as well as in the expenses burdening the debtors upon the commencement and carrying-out of the relevant procedures. In addition, the viable and constant performance of due and payable loan obligations increases the cash-flows of the specific credit institutions, decreasing the amount of NPLs and improving their capital adequacy. The legal policy targets of public interest have a beneficial effect on competition between credit and financial institutions, since they create clarity regarding the amount of the required provisions and the calculation of exposures, while they also contribute drastically to the effective management of NPLs.
b. *Necessity of competition restraints imposed contrary to expectations*: as mentioned above, the creditors' coordinated action constitutes a necessary and integral parameter of bankruptcy and resolution legislation, without which the latter cannot function. On the contrary, uncoordinated action would cause debt forbearance and especially refunding of a certain undertaking to operate for the benefit of the

[118] In particular, art 101(3) provides that: 'The provisions of paragraph 1 may, however, be declared inapplicable in the case of any agreement or category of agreements between undertakings, any decision or category of decisions by associations of undertakings, any concerted practice or category of concerted practices, which contributes to improving the production or distribution of goods or to promoting technical or economic progress, while allowing consumers a fair share of the resulting benefit, and which does not: (a) impose on the undertakings concerned restrictions which are not indispensable to the attainment of these objectives; (b) afford such undertakings the possibility of eliminating competition in respect of a substantial part of the products in question.'

[119] *Asnef-Equifax* (n 27) para 72.

particular credit institution which has not consented to a specific solution, seeking to be satisfied exclusively and preferentially by means of law enforcement measures, consequently to the expense of the borrower and the other involved credit institutions. To this end, Article 106e(1) indent c of the Greek Bankruptcy Code (BC) regulates, among other things, the relationship between creditors following the agreement ratification, either in their capacity as creditors or, in the case of capitalisation, in their capacity as shareholders or partners. In this context, the resolution agreement may provide that a certain category of creditors cannot demand the repayment of claims to the same prior to the full satisfaction of another category.

c. *Consumers' benefit*: as was previously mentioned, both the stability of the national financial system and the increase of available credit at significantly lower rates of interest are achieved. This particular macro-economic parameter, consisting of the allocative efficiency and consumers' prosperity (allocative efficiency), is accompanied by the macro-economic dimension of legal certainty for the benefit of both debtors and the involved credit and financial institutions.
d. *Non-elimination of competition*: first of all, none of the credit institutions involved is obliged to proceed with a specific debt forbearance action proposed by the others. It should be noted that the same also applies to the debtor, who reserves their intact right not to concede to the proposed forbearance measures and recourse to judicial proceedings. Second, credit institutions participating in the considered information exchange procedure do not gain any commercial or other business advantage in relation to their other competitors from the coordination at issue. The non-functionality of the statutory framework in force proves the fact that without any regulatory intervention regarding the behaviour of the involved credit institutions, the management of NPLs will remain obsolete and will not fulfil its purpose. The provision for an option of mutual understanding and cooperation subject to certain safeguards concerning the due and proper actions by no means eliminates competition, but instead allows the effective operation of the market, even at the ultimate stage of forbearance of the due and payable loan obligations.

The assumptions at issue here are upheld by the European Commission in the Guidelines on horizontal cooperation agreements.[120] These assumptions not only concern the databases but also reflect the general legal policy goals of the EU competition legislation with regard to the exchange of commercially strategic information. In light of the above, it is concluded that the information exchange at issue meets all four cumulative conditions set forth by Article 101(3) TFEU.

[120] Guidelines on horizontal cooperation agreements, para 97: 'Exchange of consumer data between companies in markets with asymmetric information about consumers can also give rise to efficiencies. For instance, keeping track of the past behaviour of customers in terms of accidents or credit default provides an incentive for consumers to limit their risk exposure. It also makes it possible to detect which consumers carry a lower risk and should benefit from lower prices. In this context, information exchange can also reduce consumer lock-in, thereby inducing stronger competition. This is because information is generally specific to a relationship and consumers would otherwise lose the benefit from that information when switching to another company. Examples of such efficiencies are found in the banking and insurance sectors, which are characterised by frequent exchanges of information about consumer defaults and risk characteristics.'

iii. Safeguards and the Role of Clean Teams

While the information exchange in the management and restructuring of NPLs is producing benefits and efficiencies, it can also raise concerns of possible anti-competitive behaviour. Thus, it is of paramount importance that the information exchange does not exceed the sharing of data necessary for the objectives that need to be achieved within the framework of the management and restructuring of NPLs. Thus, the information exchange should not be extended to other non-performing or performing loans, neighbouring products, price-setting issues or even other commercial policy matters. In line with New Credit Line, no information should be exchanged with regard to terms and conditions of loans refinancing by the banks (except of syndicated loans). Possible spillover effects should be avoided through so-called 'clean teams'.[121]

It is evident that the banks will need access to confidential information, including competitively sensitive information. The Banks must only share information that is reasonably necessary to implement the Management and Restructuring of NPLs. Unnecessary information must not be sought from or shared with other Banks as they continue to be competitors in the relevant market. Information received must only be used for the specifically described purpose. Access to competitively sensitive information shall be limited to a team of pre-approved employees by each bank (the 'Clean Team'). The purpose of the Clean Team is to collect, share and process the collected competitively sensitive information that will be used solely for the purposes of implementing the special purpose and will be undertaken in a manner that is fully consistent with and in compliance with all relevant antitrust laws and regulations. Last but not least, the banks must also enter into a non-disclosure agreement (NDA).

Clean Team members should not be involved in performing loans either for small or for big corporations. The establishment of a Clean Team does not allow for the exchange between the banks of the terms and conditions of NPLs other than syndicated loans offered by the banks for a single borrower; information regarding competitors' commercial behaviour and strategy in the markets in which they are active (ie, all information that is capable of removing uncertainties concerning the intended commercial conduct of the banks); current or future business plans, strategies, marketing plans, pipeline projects, budgets or any other non-public information about current or future operations of competitors; current or future information on prices, lending rates, deposit amounts, loan amounts, mortgage rates, pricing formulas, costs, margins or credit terms; or customer-specific information (contracts, customer lists, financial data) or customer-related strategies.

Furthermore, each bank should include in its Clean Team either the in-house lawyers of the banks or an external lawyer in order to prevent any exchange of confidential information. Prior to any meeting or conference call, an agenda must be circulated to all those attending the meeting; the agenda for these meetings will be prepared and circulated by the servicer after having been pre-approved by (preferably external) legal counsel and/or in-house counsel of each bank. In addition and most importantly, minutes must be kept and signed off by all banks and the legal counsel present in the meeting.

[121] See Maritzen (n 47) § 1 GWB, para 512.

It should be noted that a clear and distinct classification must be kept for this information (Clean Team material) eg, in the subject matter of emails, special Outlook subfolders etc, and that certain documents/Clean Team material may be locked with passcodes attributed to the members of the Clean Team. The Clean Team may share competitively sensitive information with each respective bank only upon necessary sanitisation (ie, in a non-sensitive summary, a format that sufficiently aggregates and anonymises the competitively sensitive information including without limitation through the removal of specific information).

V. Conclusion

In summary, it should be highlighted that information exchange can be beneficial to the competitive structure of the market, but can also result in anti-competitive effects. Information exchange, either horizontal or vertical, can be destructive to competition by leading to coordination and collusive conduct. However, parties to different kinds of agreements, such as a merger agreement or an information sharing agreement in light of NPLs, can use a wide range of measures to ensure that competition issues are not likely to arise. For instance, they must enter into an NDA and exchange information through VDRs or appoint a 'Clean Team', which is an impartial third party in charge of managing a standalone VDRs, often called 'the clean room'. The Clean Team removes some of the competition risks by guaranteeing strong confidentiality and facilitating the process of exchanging sensitive information between the vendor and the existing bidders, for example, in the context of a due diligence process. In the event that the deal does not go through, there is no possibility that sensitive information disclosed by either party during due diligence will be transmitted to the marketplace.

Despite the measures that the parties to a transaction or business relationship can adopt with a view to preventing competition concerns, there are still multiple challenges to be addressed and problems to be tackled by the competent competition authorities. It is their job to balance the pros and cons of information sharing and decide upon such critical issues. Thus, a thorough assessment of an information exchange that is restrictive on competition requires a case-by-case examination. Things to be considered may include the characteristics of the market, the nature of the information and the manner in which it is exchanged within the specific market context, as well as its potential beneficial effects. In addition, any claim on the existence of a negative harmful impact on the market should be tested against empirical evidence and be properly counterbalanced against the positive aspects of the conduct under assessment.

However, the authorities should be vigilant enough in order to avoid legal uncertainty and findings that condemn undertakings for simply adapting intelligently in the market. All businesses should be able to adapt intelligently to the market conduct of their rival companies. In this regard, price signalling, which signifies the unilateral public announcement of prospective strategic information, is a highly complex issue in the antitrust world with both positive and negative effects. It is extremely important for undertakings to be aware in advance of what is considered to be lawful and what is considered to cross the line and thus must be criticised. Unfortunately, the law in the EU regarding price signalling is still obscure, with only limited case law and guidance. As such, it is crucial that competition authorities recognise this and try to help companies not cross this fine line.

Finally, it remains to be seen whether we need rules on algorithmic design. Algorithms can pose a threat nowadays and can be used to facilitate collusion. The increasing flow of data and technologically advanced tools such as pricing algorithms are affecting the competitive landscape in the digital world. There are a large number of companies that use computer algorithms to improve pricing models, customise services and also foresee market trends. This can certainly generate efficiencies, but at the same time, the increased use of algorithms can also produce negative effects by facilitating collusion without any explicit agreement or human communication. Do algorithms cause automatic harm to competition? It remains to be seen, but the competition law enforcers must be cautious and not overreact by adopting measures against innovation.

To sum up, although nowadays the competition challenges are even bigger, there are still several measures that undertakings can adopt so as to avoid being considered liable for engaging in anti-competitive conduct. It is also up to the EU and the competition authorities to offer the proper guidance and indicate the boundaries of the legal provisions by conducting market studies and sector inquiries to address the challenges in the current legal and economic framework. In a nutshell, one could say that the most important thing would be to properly conduct the balancing exercise between the pro-competitive and anti-competitive effects of commercial conduct in the market.

PART V

Enforcement

15

Transparency

Public Enforcement Strategies

JÖRN AXEL KÄMMERER

I. Introduction

Public enforcement of the transparency regime in EU capital markets law is crucial for its success. Yet, the blurriness, lack of rigour and deficient sophistication in EU legislation hampers coherent national enforcement strategies. It affects not only the transposition of the Transparency Directive (TD) into national law – as the first step of public enforcement – but also for its second step, which consists of the application of the national provisions thus adopted by the national competent authorities. This causes a plethora of problems, of which the most important will be addressed in this chapter – such as the difficulty of distinguishing between 'administrative powers' and 'administrative sanctions', and uncertainties in the determination and calculation of pecuniary sanctions.

II. Public Enforcement Strategies in EU Capital Markets Law

A. Enforcement

Traditionally, enforcement may be defined as the ensemble of measures that are directed at ensuring compliance with the regulatory goals and standards enshrined in the law. Thus, enforcement is usually perceived as measures (including foreclosure) that administrative bodies take vis-a-vis non-state actors. This perception is put to the test – and may appear too narrow – wherever regulatory standards are determined by EU law, which in financial markets regulation is generally the case and which is also true of the EU transparency regimes applying to stock corporations and the trading of their shares, on the following two grounds:

- Where law emanates from the EU, especially where a directive such as the TD[1] has been adopted, enforcement is not confined to the execution of norms (by public authorities), but includes the transposition of EU law into national law.[2] In other words, as far as public enforcement is concerned, legislative enforcement by national parliaments must be distinguished here from the subsequent administrative enforcement, which normally is laid into the hands of the National Competent Authority (NCA). This must be given due account by whoever sets up an 'enforcement strategy' at the European level since friction can occur on both the legislative and the executive level of enforcement.
- The increasing sophistication of EU legislation on financial markets has brought about a complex mechanism of EU standard setting involving various steps ('levels 1 to 3' – the so-called *Lamfalussy* process),[3] in which the dividing line between 'enactment' and 'enforcement' (just like the one between EU and national enforcement) has become blurry. European supervisory bodies – ESMA,[4] EIOPA[5] and EBA[6] – are also involved in the adoption of delegated[7] and implementing acts,[8] the latter addressing national authorities, which also receive guidelines from ESMA relating to their administrative practice.[9] ESMA takes part in the making of regulatory

[1] Directive 2004/109/EC of the European Parliament and of the Council of 15 December 2004 on the harmonisation of transparency requirements in relation to information about issuers whose securities are admitted to trading on a regulated market and amending Directive 2001/34/EC [2004] OJ L390/38; amended by Directive 2013/50/EU of the European Parliament and of the Council of 22 October 2013 amending Directive 2004/109/EC of the European Parliament and of the Council on the harmonisation of transparency requirements in relation to information about issuers whose securities are admitted to trading on a regulated market; Directive 2003/71/EC of the European Parliament and of the Council on the prospectus to be published when securities are offered to the public or admitted to trading and Commission Directive 2007/14/EC laying down detailed rules for the implementation of certain provisions of Directive 2004/109/EC [2013] OJ L294/13.

[2] Article 288(3) of the Treaty on the Functioning of the European Union (TFEU). On the transposition of EU directives by national legislators in detail, see R Král, 'On the Choice of Methods of Transposition of EU Directives' (2016) 41 *European Law Review* 220.

[3] See D Chatzimanoli, 'A Crisis of Governance? From Lamfalussy to de Larosière or Bridging the Gap between Law and New Governance in the EU Financial Services Sector' (2011) 2 *European Journal of Risk Regulation* 322.

[4] European Securities and Markets Authority, established by Regulation (EU) No 1095/2010 of the European Parliament and of the Council of 24 November 2010 establishing a European Supervisory Authority (European Securities and Markets Authority), amending Decision No 716/2009/EC and repealing Commission Decision 2009/77/EC [2010] OJ L331/84.

[5] European Insurance and Occupational Pensions Authority, established by Regulation (EU) No 1094/2010 of the European Parliament and of the Council of 24 November 2010 establishing a European Supervisory Authority (European Insurance and Occupational Pensions Authority), amending Decision No 716/2009/EC and repealing Commission Decision 2009/79/EC [2010] OJ L331/48.

[6] European Banking Authority, established by Regulation (EU) No 1093/2010 of the European Parliament and of the Council of 24 November 2010 establishing a European Supervisory Authority (European Banking Authority), amending Decision No 716/2009/EC and repealing Commission Decision 2009/78/EC [2010] OJ L331/12.

[7] Based on art 290 TFEU.

[8] Based on ibid art 291.

[9] See Niamh Moloney, *The European Securities and Markets Authority and institutional design for the EU financial market – a tale of two competences: Part 1: rule-making*, European Business Organization Law Review 12 (2011), 41, 66 et seq.

provisions and imposes Implementing Technical Standards (ITS) on the NCAs. Yet, it holds no major stake in the determination of enforcement mechanisms, which remains mainly in the hands of the legislative bodies of the EU and the Member States, as will be shown below.

B. Enforcement Strategies

This chapter focuses on the TD, which accommodates the most elaborate enforcement system of all transparency-related legislative acts in European capital markets law. Enforcement of directives always is two-tiered – legislative as well as administrative – by nature. Hence, strategies of enforcement must be pursued not only by the (law-making or administrative) national entities declared competent for it, but also by the law-making bodies of the EU (and, to a lesser degree, national parliaments). Adopting rules that require enforcement involves a concept as to how, why and where to enforce them.[10] One tier below, upon transposing them, the national legislator will have to adopt its own enforcement strategy insofar as, and to the extent that, the directive leaves sufficient room for legislative discretion, and so will an NCA – usually a large and powerful body – where the rules it needs to (administratively) enforce require a discretionary decision.

C. Public Enforcement

The subject of this chapter is *public* enforcement, whereas private enforcement is dealt with elsewhere in this volume.[11] We may define public enforcement broadly as all steps taken by a public body (usually an authority) to ensure that the addressee of a legal provision complies with it. (As a matter of evidence, where enforcement also extends to the adoption of legislative acts, as in the transposition of directives, the latter also counts as public enforcement.) The emanations of public enforcement are manifold: its bias can be preventive or repressive, even punitive, it may address a larger audience (as in public warnings) or individuals because of an infringement committed or simply in order to ascertain that they comply with their legal obligations. Public enforcement of capital markets law also is not confined to measures that – in the traditional sense – aim to counter certain risks.

Whether and to what extent enforcement by private actors – who pursue their respective individual interest, governed by constitutional rights and are unlikely to assent to being instrumentalised by the state or the EU – is a valid category at all has long been a controversial matter.[12] The EU has become increasingly receptive to the

[10] Traditionally, EU directives did not fully outline their enforcement. See JA Kämmerer, 'Bemessung von Geldbußen im Wettbewerbs- und Kapitalmarktrecht: Eine komparative Betrachtung' in S Grundmann, B Haar and H Merkt et al (eds), *Festschrift für Klaus J Hopt, II* (Berlin, De Gruyter, 2010) 2043, 2049.

[11] See Paolo Giudici, ch 16 in this volume.

[12] See, inter alia, KU Schmolke, 'Private Enforcement und institutionelle Balance' (2016) *Neue Zeitschrift für Gesellschaftsrecht* 721. Historically, private enforcement played a greater role until legislators and regulators fostered public enforcement because of the cost for private litigation; see OH Dombalagian, 'Regulating Information Flows in Capital Markets' (2015) 68 *SMU Law Review* 727, 733.

idea of private supplementing public enforcement, especially in EU competition law.[13] For some areas of capital markets law, it has outlined a duty of Member States to establish civil liabilities for infringements of EU law or has fostered the establishment of specialised non-public bodies for consumer complaints.[14] Even so, we find that private enforcement is virtually never purely private, but that it happens within the confines of public legislation (for example, on class actions) or even emulates it, as in the establishment of compliance mechanisms. With public enforcement elements (and strategies) inherent in private enforcement, both categories not only supplement each other but are also intertwined.

III. Enforcement According to the TD

A. The TD 'Toolkit' of Public Enforcement

As regards public enforcement, the TD and the Markets Abuse Regulation (MAR)[15] list various categories of measures. However, due to the absence of precise definitions, they fail to provide sufficient guidance on their nature and any differences that may exist between 'administrative sanctions', 'administrative powers' (as in Articles 28 ff TD) and 'necessary powers' (enumerated in Article 24(4) TD). If the legal consequences triggered were the same, categorisation and definition would not be relevant here, but, as will be shown below, we have reason to believe that differences indeed exist. This is why, in the end, the lack of rigour and conceptualisation appear to unduly complicate the enforcement of the Directive.

Evidently, the EU seeks to draw a clear distinction between administrative measures/sanctions on the one hand and criminal sanctions on the other hand. The MAR allows Member States to supplant the former by criminal sanctions insofar as the infringement is punishable as a criminal offence on 3 July 2016 (see Article 30(1)(2), sentence 1). Member States then need to observe the standards set out by the second Market Abuse Directive (MAD II),[16] which supplements the MAR. This raises problems as the criminal law of some Member States does not provide for equivalents of the minimum standard under the MAR.[17] The TD, unlike the MAR, permits no waiver of the aforementioned kind, but its wording seems to corroborate the idea that the EU perceives

[13] See, for example, Communication from the Commission to the European Parliament and the Council: Ten Years of Antitrust Enforcement under Regulation 1/2003: Achievements and Future Perspectives, COM(2014) 453, at no 7.

[14] K Sergakis, *The Law of Capital Markets in the EU* (Oxford, Macmillan Education, 2018) 41 ff.

[15] Regulation (EU) No 596/2014 of the European Parliament and of the Council of 16 April 2014 on market abuse (Market Abuse Regulation) and repealing Directive 2003/6/EC of the European Parliament and of the Council and Commission Directives 2003/124/EC, 2003/125/EC and 2004/72/EC [2014] OJ L173/1.

[16] Directive 2014/57/EU of the European Parliament and of the Council of 16 April 2014 on criminal sanctions for market abuse [2014] OJ L173/179.

[17] See in detail JA Kämmerer, in C Kumpan and M Lehman (eds), *Financial Services Law (Commentary)* (Oxford, Hart Publishing, 2019); Art. 30 MAR para 16.

criminal sanctions as a category of its own. It is needless to stress that criminal sanctions involve enforcement and that this kind of enforcement is genuinely public. While we have no reasonable doubt that public criminal enforcement is distinct from public administrative enforcement (considering, inter alia, principles such as *ne bis in idem*, *nulla poena sine lege* or *habeas corpus* rights, which apply only to the persecution for criminal offences), we have reason to question, from the perspective of EU primary and national constitutional law, that the dividing line between both categories really runs where the EU wants to map it – if mapping matters to it at all. The European Court of Human Rights (ECtHR)[18] and some national courts[19] have repeatedly qualified measures as penal that were not explicitly designated as criminal law. To the extent that this would include those measures enumerated in Article 28b(1) and possibly even Article 24(4) TD, and provided that the aforementioned jurisprudence binds the EU and/or the national legislature and the NCAs, measures with a 'criminal bias' would have to be factored into the criminal sanctions imposed.[20]

Even more unclear is what distinguishes administrative measures from administrative sanctions. At first glance, an understanding of a sanction would be that of a measure taken against persons who have breached a duty. As this is true for Article 28b, points (a)–(c) TD, its heading ('sanctioning powers') seems to be consequential, but its wording, referring to 'measures and sanctions', dispels the categorical certitude one may have hoped for. If everything encompassed by Article 28b TD is a sanction, must 'measures and sanctions' then be understood as an oxymoron? And why is the conglomeration of 'necessary powers' that Article 24(4) TD requires the NCAs to be endowed with under all circumstances (in addition to those listed in Article 28b(1)) branded as neither administrative measures nor as administrative sanctions, although at least some of them are imposed for the non-compliance with regulatory standards (such as Article 24(4), points (d) or (g))? Moreover, upon a closer look, the target of an order requiring the infringer to cease the breach and to desist from its repetition (Article 28(1), point (b) TD) is much more akin to 'powers necessary for the performance' of the NCA's function than to pecuniary sanctions, as provided for in point (c) of the same paragraph.

As indicated further above,[21] arbitrariness in the choice of the legal terminology – this at least is the impression one is left with by the TD (and the MAR) – does not necessarily pose a threat to legal certainty, provided the legal consequences are obviously identical. But this remains unclear, considering the uncertainty about how, and where, to trace the dividing line between criminal and non-criminal sanctions and between sanctions and non-sanctioning measures – and, hence, the intra- and inter-categorical parameters of discretion.

[18] *Dubus SA v France*, App No 5242/04 (ECtHR, 11 June 2009) para 37; *Grande Stevens and Others v Italy*, App Nos 18640/10, 18647/10, 18663/10, 18668/10 and 18698/10 (ECtHR, 7 July 2014) paras 94–101.

[19] BVerfG (Germany) of 17 November 2009 – 1 BvR 2717/08.

[20] For more on this, see section III.C below.

[21] See section III.A above.

B. Legislative Enforcement of the TD

The sanctions regime of the TD lags behind that of the more recent (and, in this respect, more sophisticated) MAR insofar as it is less comprehensive and elaborate. This is not surprising, considering that directly applicable regulations tend to be more detailed than directives. However, despite being adopted as a regulation, the MAR gives the Member States broader room for legislative discretion than the TD, as will be shown below. The 2013 amendment of the TD[22] sought to approximate the terminology of both legislative acts and has facilitated a comparison of their enforcement mechanisms, but apart from the wording, not much else has been approximated.

The TD requires Member States to lay down rules for what the directive refers to as 'administrative measures and sanctions' (Article 28(1)). The prerogative of the Member States to impose 'criminal sanctions' is declared to be unaffected, which implies that a legislative right of choice between criminal and non-criminal enforcement measures, as in the MAR (Article 30(1)), does not exist here. In other terms, a Member State cannot waive administrative measures or sanctions but may discretionally decide to add criminal measures to the toolkit. Any legislative act that allows to substitute them for administrative sanctions, such as the MAR, gives rise to the assumption that the EU holds them to be different categories. Indeed, both the MAR and the TD view especially pecuniary sanctions (fines, penalties)[23] as a category that is distinct from, and does not intersect with, criminal sanctions. This is not necessarily the final determination where provisions must meet the standards of national constitutional law and of the European Convention on Human Rights (ECHR), which both extend the reach of 'criminal law' and its general principles well beyond its nominal scope. National legislation transposing the TD is likely to be subject to these standards, but even national enforcement provisions on the enforcement of MAR rules might not be spared here.[24]

Article 28a TD stipulates that the Member States must in any case provide for sanctioning powers in terms of Article 28b TD for: (a) breaches of duties to publicise information (*cf* Articles 4–6, 14 and 16 TD); and (b) the failure to notify the acquisition or the disposal of a holding (*cf* Articles 9, 10, 12 and 12a TD).[25] To these breaches, the following 'administrative measures and sanctions' (Article 28b TD) shall 'at least' apply:

- a public statement indicating the perpetrator and the breach (point (a));
- an order requiring the cessation of that conduct (point (b)); and
- administrative and pecuniary sanctions, as set out in point (c).

This catalogue was introduced, along with Articles 28 and 28c TD, in the 2013 amendment of the TD. Before this, the TD had not specified the nature of the measures to be taken, nor had it determined the amount of the pecuniary sanctions, then referred to

[22] Member States were obliged to transpose the amended provisions into national law by 26 November 2015.

[23] Art 30 MAR; art 28b TD.

[24] See in detail Kämmerer (n 16), Art. 30 MAR para 7.

[25] An outline of the 'toolkit' of the TD can be found in HP Roth, 'Das Gesetz zur Umsetzung der Transparenzrichtlinie-Änderungsrichtlinie' (2015) *Gesellschaft und Wirtschaftsrecht* 485, 486.

as 'penalties'. It must be stressed that the brief catalogue is not exhaustive: as reflected by the term 'at least', which appears in both Article 28a and Article 28b TD, the Directive provides for minimum harmonisation with respect to: (a) the breaches eligible for the toolkit of sanctions composed by Article 28b; and (b) the sanctions (categories) available in a Member State. The latter may go beyond that compulsory minimum – on the condition that their constitutional order and the ECHR pose no obstacle, as mentioned above. Even if they do not, the potential qualification of pecuniary sanction as penal, or simply the principle of legal certainty, may have an influence on the interpretation and hence the handling of the sanction provisions. This touches upon the question as to whether benchmarks may (or must) be interpreted as caps or upper limits.

C. Administrative Enforcement of the Transparency Directive

The Member States 'obligation' to activate the sanctions mechanisms and toolkit set out by Articles 28a and 28b TD when transposing the Directive does not mean that their NCAs need to apply them all in each individual case. As long as it does not hamper the effectiveness of EU law (Article 4(3) of the Treaty on European Union (TEU) – 'effet utile'),[26] the NCAs may decide discretionarily on the nature, scope and dimension of their measures. However, their administrative discretion is confined by the principle of proportionality and, more specifically, by the parameters listed in Article 28c TD, all of which are nothing but concretisations of the aforementioned general principles. In many cases, the room for discretion will shrink to zero – or, in other words, will be exhausted – anyway. Where a breach is minor and merely accidental, imposing a pecuniary sanction is normally excessive and hence unlawful. But the contrary may also be the case: where an infraction, like the damage inflicted, is serious, where the infringer is financially powerful and where the profit yielded, or loss avoided, is known (Article 28, points (a), (c), (d) and (e)), there is no alternative for the NCA other than to skim that profit off and impose a sufficiently deterrent pecuniary sanction so as not to undermine the objective of the TD. Its amount cannot be forecast with precision as multiple aspects have to be taken into account by the authority when exercising its discretion.

Considering that discretion involves a choice of measures, Article 28c TD fails to specify whether this choice is confined to the measures listed in Article 28b TD or extends to Article 24 TD and its list of 'powers' to be given to the NCAs as well. Could an NCA be obliged to desist from an Article 28b measure where the exercise of one of the powers conferred upon it under Article 24(4) TD could suffice to protect the market? What appears to speak in favour of 'factoring Article 24 TD in' is the 'punitive bias' inherent in more than just one of the measures listed therein. This is particularly true of those powers that are endowed with a repressive effect, such as suspension of trading (point (d)), prohibition of trading on a regulated market (point (e)), making a person's non-compliance public (point (g)) and, to a lesser extent, the publication of the information by the NCA where an issuer fails to comply with its order to do so

[26] On the 'twin article' art 31 MAR, see in detail Kämmerer (n 16), Art. 31 MAR paras 3 ff.

(point (b), sentence 2), and the taking of appropriate measures against the breach of the duty to draw up information (point (h)). Other measures listed in Article 24(4) TD clearly aim not to penalise past infractions but to detect them and to prevent future ones, and may therefore qualify as mere 'intelligence measures': order to provide information and documents (point (a)), order against the issuer to disclose information (point (b), sentence 1), order against managers to notify or provide information (point (c)), monitoring of timely disclosure of information (point (f)), examination of duly drawn-up information (point (h)) and on-site inspections (point (i)). In addition, precautionary measures may be taken pursuant to Article 26 TD. When a violation is serious (Article 28a TD), resorting to the powers listed in Article 24 TD potentially eliminates a hazard arising from the unlawful behaviour. However, these measures usually lack a potential to punish and to ostracise the infringer and to deter others; only the measures mentioned in Article 28b TD would really suit this purpose.

The complex reasoning which all this requires is virtually sourced out to the NCAs insofar as the EU, in its legislative acts, abstains from defining sanctions and their purpose. If it had done so, it would have provided the NCAs and the national legislators with valuable guidance and fostered the coherence of administrative practice throughout the EU. An explanation for why it shuns drawing a clear line between administrative measures and sanctions might be a desire to avoid conflicts with Member States that could arise from the EU's encroachment on matters that Member States regard as their regulatory domain.[27] It will ultimately be on the judiciary to address the unanswered questions. Until then, the depicted uncertainties persist.

D. Pecuniary Sanctions

The parameters of discretion are not confined to the choice of measure, but include, inter alia, the person(s) that the measures shall be directed at and, where a pecuniary sanction is appropriate, its amount. As will be shown, the EU sets standards for these decisions but fails to clarify the basis of calculation and to answer the tricky question how pecuniary sanctions are expected to relate with other sanctions and measures. This challenges not only the national legislative bodies, which will have to determine what EU law requires from them while respective constitutional limits may apply at the same time, but also the NCAs when they must decide upon the sanctions to be imposed and on whom on the basis of the yardstick set by the national legislators.

Member States must provide for pecuniary sanctions[28] against *natural persons* of up to €2 million and up to two times the amount of the profits gained or the losses avoided. The TD deviates from the MAR[29] insofar as the highest amounts are 'minimum maximums' and Member States are therefore not allowed to exceed them when

[27] See H Fleischer and KU Schmolke, 'The Reform of the Transparency Directive: Minimum or Full Harmonisation of Ownership Disclosure?' (2011) 12 *European Business Organization Law Review* 121, 142.

[28] For a brief overview of the sanctions regime, see CH Seibt and B Wollenschläger, 'Revision des Europäischen Transparenzregimes: Regelungsinhalte der TRL 2013 und Umsetzungsbedarf' (2014) *Zeitschrift für Wirtschaftsrecht* 545, 551 ff.

[29] See in detail Kämmerer (n 16), Art. 30 MAR paras 19 ff.

transposing the Directive. A laconic 'whichever is higher' links these two standards. This addendum seems to address the NCAs only, but above all, it binds the national legislator, which must set up a dual standard upon transposing the Directive into national law and prescribe that, where gains or avoided losses can be determined, the higher of the two amounts is decisive.

As for *legal persons*, the triple benchmarks prescribed by the TD appear to further complicate its transposition, considering that the relation between the three standards requires clarification and that the Directive does not specify if the first two of them shall be regarded as caps or upper limits. Against legal persons, Member States must make sure that – as an alternative to the disgorgement of profits (or avoided losses) – pecuniary sanctions of up to €10 million *or* of up to five per cent of their annual turnover can be imposed.[30] The phrase 'whichever is higher' figures here too, but its point of reference is unclear, as is the meaning of the conjunctions 'or' and 'and'. The provision is structured in a way that the required comparison ('higher or lower') must be made between the profit-related benchmark and the other benchmarks – which are covered by the same dash and would then be dealt with in compounds. However, this interpretation, albeit close to the wording, would not meet the aim and purpose of the TD. It would be inconsistent with that aim and purpose to read the conjunction 'or' as a prerogative of legislative choice between an amount-based and a turnover-based standard: both need to be implemented. We must then ask whether the NCA, upon applying the national sanctions provisions where they exactly follow this pattern, has that discretionary right of choice or whether 'whatever is higher' covers all three benchmarks in the same manner. Irrespective of the wording, which speaks against it (because 'whichever is higher' stands on the same level as both dashes), this must be answered in the positive. It would defy the logic of the provision to give the authority the right to resort to either the amount-based or the turnover-based standard and thus to confer upon it a prerogative to disregard what might turn out to be the highest of all three figures. The German legislator adopted this pattern upon transposing the Directive in at least one provision[31] but left the question open in others.[32]

Another, but related, question is how to calculate the amounts referred to in the first dash: must the ceilings – €10 million (€2 million for natural persons) and five per cent of the turnover, respectively – be interpreted as upper limits or as caps? In the first case, the ceiling applies to the severest infringement imaginable, which implies that amount-based or turnover-based sanctions are almost always lower. In the second case, the 'deserved' sanction may be well above €10 million or five per cent, but the sanctions amount is truncated at these ceilings. Capped sanctions would thus tend to be higher than limited ones. Article 28b(1), point (c)(i) TD differs from Article 30(2) MAR, which provides for 'maximum administrative pecuniary sanctions of at least'

[30] For a critical perspective on the introduction of a turnover-based sanction in the TD, see Seibt and Wollenschläger (n 27) 552.

[31] See art 8 Gesetz zur Umsetzung der Transparenzrichtlinie-Änderungsrichtlinie v 20 November 2015, BGBl I, 2029 (§ 335(1a) HGB).

[32] Such as § 39(4) WpHG = art 1 nr 30 point (c) Gesetz zur Umsetzung der Transparenzrichtlinie-Änderungsrichtlinie.

the dimensions mentioned there, that is, for 'minimum maximums'.[33] The interpretation of the latter as a capping provision would be consistent with EU competition law (Article 23 of Regulation 1/2003), where the capping of penalties is commonplace,[34] and with the perspective of the Commission, shared by the European Court of Justice (ECJ),[35] that pecuniary sanctions do not pertain to criminal law and that the principle of legal certainty does not prevent the EU from imposing truncated fines.[36] An open question is what capping entails in the event of multiple benchmarks: does it require the capped figures to be recapped at the other benchmarks (which would at least be consistent with the logic of capping)? Hence, the capping regime has problems in coping with multiple benchmarks and may result in lower fines than upper limits. The sanction amounts thus determined could impede the effectiveness of the sanctions provisions. Here, the TD deviates from MAR in several respects. First, Article 28b(1), point (c) does not provide for 'minimum maximums', but simply for maximums ('up to'). This does not only imply that the Member States must not set the ceilings any higher, but it also corroborates – alongside the decisiveness of the relatively higher amount ('whichever is higher') – that the provision does not aim at capping. A second difference is that the profit/avoided loss-based sanction is formally declared to be a subsection of financial sanctions and hence is not a distinct category of sanction, as is the case in the MAR. The Directive clearly stipulates that the profit/avoided loss-based sanction shall be factored into the (comparative) approach to the determination of the financial sanction. Third, no discretion applies to the choice of sanction and the determination of its amount. If the profit can be determined and if, multiplied by two (not tripled, as in Article 30(2), point (h) MAR), it proves to be the highest benchmark, the amount thus determined invariably becomes that of the pecuniary sanction.

Concerns about legal certainty, as raised against Article 30(2) MAR,[37] are unfounded in the case of Article 28b(1), point (c) TD because capping certainly does not apply here. However, this does not mean that the Directive is entirely uncritical in the light of the rule of law and the principles of criminal law as the ECtHR and national constitutional courts understand them. As mentioned above,[38] the ECtHR and national constitutional courts would consider the principles governing criminal law to be applicable to some of the measures provided for in Articles 24(4) and 28 ff TD. Considering the leeway Member States are given in their decision making, we cannot rule out that a constitutional court will declare itself competent (insofar as it finds that the act no longer enforces EU law in terms of Article 51(1) of the Charter of Fundamental Rights of the European Union (CFR)) and adopt the stricter national approach.

[33] See in detail Kämmerer (n 16), Art. 30 MAR para 19.

[34] See the overview given in G Dannecker and J Biermann, in U Immenga and EJ Mestmäcker (eds), *EU-Wettbewerbsrecht*, 5th edn (Munich, CH Beck, 2012) art 23 of Regulation (EU) No 1/2003, paras 114 ff.

[35] ECJ Case C- 266/06 P, *Evonik Degussa*, ECLI:EU:C:2008:295, paras 50 ff; see also ECJ Case C-501/11 P, *Schindler*, ECLI:EU:C:2013:522.

[36] However, the Federal Supreme Court of Germany interprets the turnover-based sanction pursuant to the (corresponding) section of the Act against Restrictions of Competition (Gesetz gegen Wettbewerbsbeschränkungen) as an upper limit. See *BGHSt* 58, 158.

[37] See Kämmerer (n 16), Art. 30 MAR paras 21 ff.

[38] See section III.A above.

The ECHR does not apply to legislative acts of the EU,[39] but it does apply to national law transposing it,[40] although the ECtHR is self-restrictive in its scrutiny in these cases[41] because it (still) seeks to avoid judicial clashes with the ECJ. To the extent that measures qualify as criminal sanctions – not in terms of the TD, but of the ECHR and constitutional law – principles such as *ne bis in idem* and *nemo tenetur se ipsum accusare* must apply. A problem arises where two or several NCAs wish to impose pecuniary sanctions for the same infringement(s). Whilst the TD enunciates a duty of NCAs to cooperate with other NCAs (*cf* Article 24(4b) and Article 25(2)), it fails to determine the competent authority where the breach has a transborder effect and where more than one NCA is thus involved, and where each of them intends to sanction the unlawful behaviour. Although this may result in double jeopardy, no mechanism is in place to prevent it. NCAs are left alone with the difficult task of assessing: (a) whether a measure has a criminal bias (since the EU does not draw a clear distinction); (b) whether it is also inherent in other sanctions and measures the same NCA intends to impose – and if the aggregate result is still proportional; and, ultimately, (c) whether other NCAs have already sanctioned, or are about to sanction, that behaviour in a similar way.

E. Administrative Enforcement Practice at the Example of the BaFin

The implementation of the TD by the individual Member States varies considerably. This must be attributed not only to the relatively broad margin of discretion they enjoy when transposing the sanction provisions and of course to the inherited differences between the national sanction regimes, but also to divergent administrative practice and cultures. Assessing and analysing all these differences would be the matter for a rather extensive research project. This chapter is confined to the administrative practice of the BaFin as the German NCA. The 2013 amendment of the TD was cast into a national statute amending extant legislative provisions in November 2015, of which numerous provisions deal with financial sanctions.[42]

The sanctioning practice of the BaFin is two-tiered.[43] The authority first determines the general scope of the sanction it intends to impose by fixing the respective maxima according to the three benchmarks (amount, turnover and profit/avoided loss). In a second step, the individual sanction is determined. To this end, the BaFin takes a

[39] ECtHR, Decision of 31 March 2015, Application No 28827/11, paras 58 ff – *Andreasen/United Kingdom and 26 Other Member States of the European Union.*

[40] See W Frenz, *Handbuch Europarecht, IV* (Berlin, Springer, 2009) para 115.

[41] See ECtHR, Judgment of 30 June 2005, Application No 45036/98, paras 160 ff – *Bosphorus*; Judgment of 23 May 2016, Application No 17502/07, paras 101 ff – *Avotiņš/Latvia.*

[42] Gesetz zur Umsetzung der Transparenzrichtlinie-Änderungsrichtlinie v 20 November 2015, BGBl I, 2029.

[43] See BaFin, 'WpHG-Bußgeldleitlinien' (November 2013), available at: bafin.de/SharedDocs/Downloads/DE/Leitfaden/WA/dl_bussgeldleitlinien_2013.pdf?__blob=publicationFile&v=14; BaFin, 'WpHG-Bußgel dleitlinien II' (February 2017), available at: bafin.de/SharedDocs/Downloads/DE/Leitfaden/WA/dl_bussgel dleitlinien_2016.html?nn=7845970; and BaFin, 'WpHG-Bußgeldleitlinien II update' (January 2018), available at: bafin.de/SharedDocs/Downloads/DE/Leitfaden/WA/dl_aktualisierung_bussgeldleitlinien_2018.pdf?__blob=publicationFile&v=6.

subset of steps. First, a basic amount is determined, having regard to the circumstances of the case and the categories in which the issuers belong. After this, attenuating or aggravating circumstances are considered; this may entail an adjustment of the basic amount. For example, a settlement with the BaFin can yield the infringer a discount on the penalty of up to 30 per cent. Ultimately, the BaFin considers the economic situation of the infringer, who or which will be requested to give a statement on the individual financial situation. All in all, the BaFin distinguishes six categories of issuers (staggered according to their market capitalisation) and five classes of severity of the infringement. This leads to 30 distinctive 'basic amounts' to be perceived as thresholds or minimum standards. If, for example, both the issuer and the infraction rank within the highest categories, the basic amount is €800 million. This will become the amount of the imposed penalty – unless adjusted in the next substeps – although it may be above the turnover-based maximum. The truth about the pecuniary sanctions imposed by the BaFin is that most of the fines imposed between July 2015 and the end of December 2016 – the first year of the new sanctions regime – remained well below €100,000, with the highest one (of €1,100,000) sanctioning the breach of various notification duties.[44] This means that the discussion on the relationship between the various benchmarks and the upper limits set for each of them has had very little relevance to the administrative sanctioning practice until now – but this could change.

IV. Conclusions

The TD offers an extensive 'toolkit' for public enforcement, composed of what it refers to as administrative powers, measures and sanctions, but lacking clear criteria of distinction between these categories. The character of the sanctions (and measures) listed in Article 28b TD is obviously repressive, while in Article 24(4), a repressive bias alternates with a preventive one. The parameters underlying the use of (both legislative and administrative) discretion are blurry and incomplete, insofar as the delineation between the above categories remains unclear and no guidance is given in the TD on the choice of measure.

Pecuniary sanctions are a core instrument of the TD, but as the Directive does not aim to harmonise the national sanction regimes, its transposition takes place within the confines of the latter. Against the backdrop of a lack of EU competency on the fundamentals of criminal law, this given range of variation must be accepted; however, more legislative clarity about the categorisation of standards and the parameters of discretion would have fostered the consistency of public enforcement throughout the EU. The same is true for the hierarchy of benchmarks. Member States tend to apply 'whichever is higher' to them as a triad of standards, but we cannot be sure that this interpretation is shared by them all. Strikingly, the approach of the TD markedly deviates from the MAR regarding pecuniary sanctions, their spectrum and scope. What accounts for this difference is by no means clear, but it is obvious that the nascent Capital Markets Union is still far from setting up a coherent and consistent sanctions regime.

[44] BaFin, 'BaFin Journal, November 2017' (Bonn, BaFin, 2017) 27 et seq, available at: bafin.de/SharedDocs/Downloads/DE/BaFinJournal/2017/bj_1711.pdf?__blob=publicationFile&v=3.

16

Private Enforcement of Transparency

PAOLO GIUDICI

I. Introduction

This chapter is about the private enforcement of European transparency rules. Reference is made to transparency in general terms, meaning mainly issuers' information to the market (mandatory information) with specific regard to the secondary market. The main issues covered are fourfold. The first is whether private enforcement is really important, and therefore if it is worth spending time and resources on this issue. The second is whether we have a clear theory of how civil liability should work with reference to liability for misstatements to the market. The third is whether Europe should follow the US securities class actions experience, or how the warnings that come from the other side of the Atlantic Ocean, which invites Europe not to adopt the US private enforcement system, are to be considered. The fourth one is whether a harmonised approach is advisable and how it can be implemented.

In order to deal with these points, the chapter proceeds as follows. Section II deals with the rules on civil liability contained in the EU 'Transparency' Rulebook, where I initially consider both primary market (prospectus liability) and secondary market liability, as well as rules concerning auditors' and rating agencies' liability. Section III deals with the debate on the importance of private enforcement in financial markets law. Section IV investigates the theory of civil liability for misstatements to the market, with particular regard to aftermarket liability. This section covers the issue from the standpoint of the US debate on securities class actions, which is certainly the most important forum where the topic has been addressed and extensively covered. Section V discusses how the US warnings against US securities class actions are to be considered, and why some form of harmonisation in the private enforcement infrastructure is needed in order to improve the quality of the harmonised regulation of capital markets, and how it can be achieved, taking the European Directive on antitrust damages as a reference point.

II. Civil Liability in the EU 'Transparency' Rulebook

A. Prospectus Liability

Under Article 6(1) of the Prospectus Directive (PD): 'Member States shall ensure that responsibility for the information given in a prospectus attaches at least to the issuer or its administrative, management or supervisory bodies, the offeror, the person asking for the admission to trading on a regulated market or the guarantor, as the case may be.' Article 6(2) provides that Member States ensure that their laws, regulation and administrative provisions on civil liability apply to those persons responsible for the information given in a prospectus. The same provisions are now contained in Article 11 of the Prospectus Regulation.

Accordingly, European law prescribes that Member States put in place a prospectus liability regime, but does not say anything specific about it. The majority of Member States already had some form of prospectus liability in place when the Directive was adopted and simply re-adjusted it in the light of the European rules. Others introduced specific provisions.[1] One of the issues to be addressed was whether directors and managers should be jointly and severally liable with the issuer, and whether underwriters should generally liable as well, following the US model, or whether they should be considered liable under certain very specific circumstances only, such as the participation in the drafting of the prospectus.

B. The Transparency Directive

The Transparency Directive requires issuers of securities traded on regulated markets to publish information concerning yearly (Article 4) and half-yearly financial reports (Article 5), and to inform the market about any change in the rights attaching to the various classes of shares and securities it issued (Article 16). Under Article 7, Member States shall ensure that responsibility for that information lies at least with the issuer or its administrative, management or supervisory bodies and shall ensure that their laws, regulations and administrative provisions on liability apply to the issuers, the bodies referred to or the persons responsible within the issuers. Accordingly, there must be a liability regime, but once again it is not regulated in detail. Member States are free to choose among possible liable parties and to exclude from liability other parties. Therefore, the framework is the same as that of the PD/PR.

C. Market Abuse

Another very important set of rules comes from the market abuse regime. The European market abuse rulebook is composed by Directive 2014/57/EU (Market Abuse

[1] For a recent paper on the issue, see D Boreiko and S Lombardo 'Prospectus Liability and the Role of Gatekeepers as Informational Intermediaries: An Empirical Analysis of the Impact of the Statutory Provisions on Italian IPOs' (2019, forthcoming) *European Business Organization Law Review*.

Directive (MAD)), mainly concerning criminal sanctions, and by Regulation 596/2014 (Market Abuse Regulation (MAR)). The MAR covers one of the most important issues concerning civil liability in financial markets, namely the public disclosure of privileged inside information. Under Article 17 MAR, issuers have a duty to inform the public as soon as possible of inside information which directly concerns the issuer (Article 17). However, unlike the PD and the Transparency Directive, the MAR does not even mention civil liability; it is entirely focused on public enforcement (see Article 30).[2]

Yet, a significant part of current European securities litigation concerns violations of MAD/MAR duties, and we have at least one interesting decision by the European Court of Justice (ECJ) on private actions based on the violation of the market abuse rulebook.[3] The typical scenario is an issuer that does not release privileged information or that has released the information with delay and is then sued by investors that bought in the period of time which spans from the moment the information should have been released and the time it was actually made public.

Special rules may affect forward-looking statements, whereas general principles of civil law usually cover voluntary information disclosed by the issuer, by which the issuer informs the market, outside of any MAR obligation to do so, about facts, figures and topics that it wants to disclose and that are not correct.

D. Financial and Non-financial Statements

Under the EU legislation, all listed EU companies must prepare their consolidated accounts in accordance with a single set of global standards – the International Financial Reporting Standards (IFRS). According to Article 33(2) Directive 2013/34/EU, Member States shall ensure that 'their laws, regulations and administrative provisions on liability, at least towards the undertaking, apply to the members of the administrative, management and supervisory bodies of the undertakings for breach of the duties referred to in paragraph 1', among which is the duty to draw up the financial statements in accordance with Regulation (EC) No 1606/2002 on: International Financial Reporting Standards (IFRS). Accordingly, liability should be at least towards the undertaking, even though it is not specified in European law what the specific form of this liability is or should be. However, under national laws, misstatements and violations of accounting rules can expose the issuer and the administrative, management and supervisory bodies to securities actions by investors that have bought the issuer's financial instruments relying on information contained in the financial and non-financial statements. This is the typical area where auditors' liability also comes into play.

E. Auditors

According to Directive 2006/43/EC, the financial statements and accounts of listed companies are audited by an audit firm. The Directive does not contain any specific

[2] V Tountopoulos, 'Market Abuse and Private Enforcement' (2014) 11 *European Company and Financial Law Review* 36.

[3] Judgement of the Court of 28 June 2012, *Geltl*, C-19/11, EU:C:2012:397.

rule on auditors' liability, but talks about civil liability when it reads, at Recital 19, that statutory auditors and audit firms are responsible for carrying out their work with due care and thus should be liable for the financial damage caused by a lack of the care owed (an assertion which is not followed by any subsequent provision in the Directive's rules), adding that 'however, the auditors' and audit firms' ability to obtain professional indemnity insurance cover may be affected by whether they are subject to unlimited financial liability'.

The idea of limiting auditors' liability was hotly discussed in the aftermath of the auditing crisis of 2001–02 and then in the wake of the financial crisis. Since then, however, the issue has been abandoned, also after fierce criticism by academics.[4]

Audit firms are usual defendants in proceedings where investors allege losses caused by incorrect information contained in financial statements, especially when the company has gone bankrupt and the audit firm is the only solvent defendant that can redress, at least partially, the plaintiffs. The literature on the issue is immense.

F. Rating Agencies

Regulation 1060/2009 (CRA I), as amended by Regulation 462/2013 EU (CRA III), covers in a very detailed way, under Article 35a, the civil liability of rating agencies. This is the only common European private law rule in the field of securities regulation and it works as a reference point in discussions concerning the harmonisation of civil liability rules in the area of market information across Europe.[5] However, it should be noted that Article 35(a)(4) enables national law to determine many significant issues of credit rating (CR) liability that influence the effectiveness of the liability provision on rating agencies, thereby somehow reducing the impact of this important first European foray into the regulation of civil liability.

III. The Regulatory Role of Private Enforcement

European transparency law considers civil liability and requires in some instances the presence, in Member States, of liability rules, even though the specific content is never spelled out and it is left to the autonomy of Member States. The general framework of the European rulebook is set down with public enforcement in mind. Civil liability, which means private enforcement, has a role, but it is not stated how it should work in detail; the issue is left in the hands of Member States. The only exception is the one concerning rating agencies, whose civil liability is governed by a specific provision contained in a regulation and therefore applicable across the EU, even though, as was

[4] *cf* W Doralt, A Hellgardt, KJ Hopt, PC Leyens, M Roth and R Zimmermann, 'Auditor's Liability and its Impact on the European Financial Markets' (2008) 67 *CLJ* 68; P Giudici, 'Auditors' Multi-layered Liability Regime' (2012) 13 *European Business Organization Law Review* 501.

[5] G Risso, 'Investor Protection in Credit Rating Agencies' Non-contractual Liability: The Need for a Fully Harmonised Regime' (2015) 40 *European Law Review* 706; M Lehmann, 'Civil Liability of Rating Agencies: An Insipid Sprout from Brussels' (2016) 11 *Capital Markets Law Journal* 60.

mentioned, specific rules posed at the Member State level are still important to determine the effectiveness of rating agencies' exposure to liability.

In order to understand whether this 'leave it to Member States' approach still makes sense or should be revisited, the preliminary question to be addressed is whether civil liability is really an important regulatory tool. This question considers liability for misstatements to the market, which is generally qualified as a form of tort liability, as an instrument for controlling social activities that create risks of harm to others and therefore an alternative (or at least a complementary regulatory tool) to public regulation and enforcement.[6] If private enforcement is not an important regulatory tool, the current European approach would be justified or, to put it in a slightly different way, it would not be worth to investigate whether to harmonise private enforcement or not.

According to some famous studies, private enforcement is even more important than public enforcement for the efficiency and quality of capital markets. Probably the most influential paper in this area is a 2006 article by la Porta, de Silanes and Shleifer,[7] where the authors analyse the effect of securities laws on financial market development in 49 countries. They find little evidence that public enforcement benefits stock markets and strong evidence, instead, that laws mandating disclosure and facilitating private enforcement through liability mechanisms have a positive effect on the growth of stock markets.

However, these authors' results are contested by other studies and, in particular, by Jackson and Roe in an equally important paper of 2009.[8] The two authors are in agreement with regard to the importance of disclosure regulation, less so with regard to liability rules. They argue that public enforcement is much more important than liability rules in explaining the outcomes of modern financial markets.[9]

If there is no clear agreement on the compared importance of private and public enforcement, it is clear that in capital markets law, there is, in any important jurisdiction, a combined interplay of public and private enforcement, where the two forms of enforcement work more as complements than substitutes. Moreover, there seems to be agreement on the fact that at least some form of private enforcement is important, and the lack of it can create significant underdeterrence. There are many examples of this. With regard to the accounting scandals at the beginning of this century, there is a widespread view that they were favoured, both in Europe and in the US, by the absence or the reduction of private enforcement.[10] As to investment service regulation, the European experience tells us that private enforcement played an

[6] S Shavell, 'Liability for Harm versus Regulation of Safety' (1984) 13 *Journal of Legal Studies* 357.

[7] R la Porta, F Lopez de Silanes and A Shleifer, 'What Works in Securities Laws?' (2006) 61 *Journal of Finance* 1.

[8] HE Jackson and MJ Roe, 'Public and Private Enforcement of Securities Laws: Resource-Based Evidence' (2009) 93 *Journal of Financial Economics* 207.

[9] There is a general agreement, instead, on the fact that actual enforcement is extremely important because, paradoxically, there are situations where 'no law' might be better than a good law on books that is badly enforced: U Bhattacharya and H Daouk, 'When No Law is Better Than a Good Law' (2009) 13 *Review of Finance* 577.

[10] G Ferrarini and P Giudici, 'Financial Scandals and the Role of Private Enforcement: The Parmalat Case' in J Armour and JA McCahery (eds), *After Enron* (Oxford, Hart Publishing, 2006), 159; JC Coffee, Jr, 'Understanding Enron: "It's About the Gatekeepers, Stupid"' (2002) 57 *Business Lawyer* 1403.

unforecasted role in the enforcement of law.[11] In some countries such as Italy, this role was so important that it is now generally agreed that public enforcement played no significant role, whereas private enforcement really had an impact on financial intermediaries' behaviour. Litigation was really intense and there is a large body of cases. Private litigation in the investment service industry was probably the most important event in private litigation in Italy, and probably across other European countries as well, in the last decade. Almost everything has been brought before courts across Europe: portfolio management, broker-dealer services, investment advice and, of course, financial product misselling[12] and issuers' prospectus liability.[13]

Accordingly, the approach in favour of a better mix of public and private enforcement is gaining momentum in Europe. It has been observed that the single most important factor which can explain why in some areas of EU law there is more inclination to seek to encourage and facilitate private enforcement is precisely that in those areas – at least as a matter of EU law – public enforcement is largely or even entirely absent, or it is perceived as not being able to provide deterrence.[14] European competition law is a case in point. This is a field where there has been an intense regulatory effort to promote private enforcement in order to get more 'enforcers' on the ground: private parties who can help in raising the deterrence effect of antitrust regulation through actions for damages.

In sum, it is not important to establish whether public enforcement is more important than private enforcement or vice versa. The issue is that just one of them is almost certainly not enough.[15] Private enforcement is important[16] and therefore it is worth analysing whether we have a theory about how private enforcement should work in order to be efficient and understand whether more harmonisation is needed at the European level.

IV. Do we have a Theory of Private Enforcement Concerning Corporate Transparency? The US Debate on Securities Class Actions

The theoretical analysis of how private enforcement should work in capital markets traditionally makes a distinction between liability in primary markets and liability in

[11] A Perrone and S Valente, 'Against All Odds: Investor Protection in Italy and the Role of Courts' (2012) 13 *European Business Organization Law Review* 31; S Kalss, 'Civil Law Protection of Investors in Austria: A Situation Report from Amidst a Wave of Investor Lawsuits' (2012) 13 *European Business Organization Law Review* 211.

[12] E Ferran, 'Regulatory Lessons from the Payment Protection Insurance Misselling Scandal in the UK' (2012) 13 *European Business Organization Law Review* 247; N Moloney, *How to Protect Investors* (Cambridge, Cambridge University Press, 2010).

[13] E Ferran, 'Are US/Style Investor Suits Coming to the UK?' (2009) 9 *Journal of Corporate Law Studies* 315; P Giudici, 'Representative Litigation in Italian Capital Markets: Italian Derivative Suits and (if Ever) Securities Class Actions' (2009) 2–3 *European Company and Financial Law Review* 246.

[14] F Wilman, 'The End of the Absence? The Growing Body of EU Legislation on Private Enforcement and the Main Remedies it Provides for' (2016) 53 *Common Market Law Review* 887.

[15] Ferrarini and Giudici (n 10).

[16] R Veil, 'Enforcement of Capital Markets Law in Europe: Observations from a Civil Law Country' (2010) 11 *European Business Organization Law Review* 409.

the aftermarket. This analysis is drawn by the US experience in the private enforcement of securities regulation, and it is also framed by the peculiar features of the US class action mechanism.

A. Primary Markets

The primary market setting raises no problems. This is a typical contractual situation, where the issuer (or the offeror) sells financial instruments and needs to convince perspective investors. Since dispersed investors cannot organise a due-diligence review, the issuer instructs a reputational intermediary (an investment bank) which 'certifies' the information contained in the offering memorandum (the prospectus). Accounting information is certified by another reputational intermediary (the audit firm). If the information provided to the buyers was incorrect, the issuer got too much money or money that would have financed different entrepreneurial initiatives. In this standard contract scenario with a seller, many buyers and some certifiers, it is efficient to grant a damage action to buyers in order to redress them and deter the issuer and its reputational intermediary.[17] The disruption of trust in the market by the issuer offers a strong argument for adjunctive public fines and criminal sanctions.

In the primary market scenario, the theoretical issues concern: (i) the liability rule to be applied to the issuer and the reputational intermediaries (strict liability, comparative negligence, contributory negligence, gross negligence, recklessness, wilful misconduct, maliciousness); and (ii) the regime regarding the burden of proof (presumption of negligence with the defendant having the burden to provide contrary evidence versus the burden of proof falling on the plaintiff). These theoretical issues are very difficult to analyse, but at least two millennia of legal experience in sale contracts and pre-sale information distribution have framed an institutional framework that is reasonably stable and well tested. The economic modelling can be very demanding, but it concerns something that works in real life, so any failure can be considered an intellectual problem, but not an institutional one.

B. Open (Secondary) Market Transactions

Open market transactions are very different from a theoretical perspective. Usually the issuer is not a seller or a buyer – the transactions is made by two anonymous parties on the aftermarket and through intermediaries. The omission or the misstatement causes one investor to buy and another to sell at a certain price level. When the misstatement is corrected, the buyer discovers that he has purchased at a price higher than the one he would have chosen, whereas the seller discovers that she was lucky because she sold the shares before the information about the true situation was disclosed. Accordingly, the theoretical problem is to understand whether the purchaser's pure economic loss has to be redressed, by whom and under what circumstances.

[17] For a more developed analysis see especially MB Fox, 'Regulating Public Offerings of Truly New Securities: First Principles' (2016) 66 *Duke Law Journal* 673.

In the US, the topic is fiercely discussed, and the discussion is part of a more general debate about securities class actions and the 'fraud on the market (FOTM)' doctrine. Many European academics and policy makers refer to that discussion, usually to warn against the problems of private enforcement of capital markets law and securities regulation. A short review of the US discussion is therefore helpful in understanding the theoretical framework.

The starting point can be the famous US Supreme Court decision in *Basic v Levinson*, where the court agreed with the presumption, created by the fraud-on-the-market (FOTM) theory and subject to rebuttal by the defendants, that persons who trade shares on the open market do so in reliance on the integrity of the price set by the market and that material misrepresentations by the issuer can artificially increase or depress the share price.[18] This presumption enables courts to conclude that common questions of fact or law are dominant, and to certify class actions, freeing plaintiffs from the obligation to provide evidence of individual reliance on the misrepresented facts. Accordingly, the Supreme Court's support of the presumption made securities class actions possible.

C. The Academic Debate

The FOTM theory had a very strong academic background when the US Supreme Court adopted it in order to support the presumption of reliance. However, academics immediately started to discuss whether the securities class action mechanism was a desirable instrument of enforcement. In an enormously influential paper, Alexander studied computer-related initial public offerings (IPOs) of 1983 and the ensuing litigation. This is a primary market environment, so the paper was not strictly related to open market transactions. However, according to Alexander, settlements in her sample of class actions appear independent from the merits of the case. Her suggestion is that the structure of securities class actions and procedural and settlement mechanisms create incentives to bring actions with no merits.[19]

Alexander's follow-up papers develop an argument raised by Easterbrook and Fischel, according to which in open market actions, damages are not related to the net systemic social cost.[20] For every buyer who pays too much, 'there is a seller – just as innocent of the fraud – who reaps a windfall in an equal amount'.[21] The issuer does not internalise the benefit of its violation. In this situation there is no social loss as there is no wealth destruction (equivalent to social loss). What you see is a mere transfer of

[18] *Basic Inc v Levinson*, 485 US 224 (1988).

[19] JC Alexander, 'Do the Merits Matter? A Study of Settlements in Securities Class Actions' (1991) 43 *Stanford Law Review* 1487.

[20] FH Easterbrook and DR Fischel, 'Optimal Damages in Securities Cases' (1985) 52 *University of Chicago Law Review* 611, 639–44. However, the two authors pointed out that their argument was not equivalent to holding that the optimal damages in the aftermarket are zero because losses and gains net out (at 641). The reasoning is further developed by P Mahoney, 'Precaution Costs and the Law of Fraud in Impersonal Markets' (1992) 78 *Virginia Law Review* 623, 627–35; and by DC Langevoort, 'Capping Damages for Open-Market Securities Fraud' (1996) 38 *Arizona Law Review* 639, 646–48.

[21] JC Alexander, 'Rethinking Damages in Securities Class Actions' (1996) 48 *Stanford Law Review* 1487, 1496.

wealth. If the issuer (or the auditor) were asked to compensate the purchaser for the damages he suffered, the issuer should also be able to get the money back from the seller, who gained because of good luck and not because of some special merits. If the issuer cannot get the money back, the liability system overdeters wrongdoers, and issuers and auditors end up taking too much care when releasing information. Alexander thus proposes, as a better alternative, a regulatory sanction enforceable through the Securities and Exchange Commission (SEC) or private actions (citizen-suits).[22]

In the same direction, Langevoort distinguishes privity cases (primary market) from non-privity cases (open market), where he proposes a civil penalty.[23] Similarly, in order to avoid a zero-sum game among diversified investors and address systemic social cost (loss in liquidity) Pritchard proposes replacing class actions with exchanges as securities fraud enforcers.[24] Arlen and Carney instead distinguish two different situations, proposing that issuers are to be made liable when fraud is a corporate policy designed to benefit shareholders, but should not when fraud was initiated to serve directors and managers' own ends. In the latter situation, directors and managers are to be held liable, not the company.[25]

The diversified investors argument comes from another highly influential paper, written this time by Paul Mahoney. Mahoney observes, as usual, that in primary market frauds, wealth transfer from investors to issuer is a proxy of the net social cost: civil damages are efficient. In secondary markets, instead, the costs are investment in lying by the issuer and precaution costs by investors. Mahoney considers precaution costs and concludes that FOTM theory is inefficient because it induces informed investors to increase research costs, whereas uninformed investors continue to be uninformed and to diversify in order to reduce firm-specific risk.[26] In his analysis, Mahoney rather casually introduces investors' diversification.

The diversification issue will become a reference point in the following literature. It assumes that, from a 'hypothetical bargain' perspective,[27] investors cannot be interested in the legal costs of securities class actions, and cannot be interested in the company spending managerial resources and buying insurance to the benefit of directors and managers, because they hold diversified portfolios and can, with equal probabilities, be on the buy side or on the sell side. In other words, secondary market investors in the aggregate do not care about (socially expensive) liability-based means of protection against wealth transfers, because they can protect themselves through (socially cheap) diversification.[28]

[22] JC Alexander, 'The Value of Bad News in Securities Class Actions' (1994) 41 *UCLA Law Review* 1421; Alexander (n 21).

[23] Langevoort (n 20).

[24] AC Pritchard, 'Markets as Monitors: A Proposal to Replace Class Actions with Exchanges as Securities Fraud Enforcers' (1999) 85 *Virginia Law Review* 925.

[25] JH Arlen and WJ Carney, 'Vicarious Liability for Fraud on Securities Markets: Theory and Evidence' (1992) *University of Illinois Law Review* 691.

[26] Mahoney (n 20).

[27] See D Charny, 'Hypothetical Bargains: The Normative Structure of Contract Interpretation' (1991) 89 *Michigan Law Review* 1815; I Ayres and R Gertner, 'Filling Gaps in Incomplete Contracts: An Economic Theory of Default Rules' (1989) 99 *Yale Law Journal* 87, 89–90, where the authors use the expression 'would have wanted' theory.

[28] The underlying assumption is therefore that primary market investors can only be on the buy side and want protection, whereas secondary market investors do not care, because they do not know where they will be.

The diversification argument is a part of the wider circularity argument, developed by Coffee in another very influential paper. Coffee points out that the securities class actions are also a pocket shifting mechanism where a class of investors (current shareholders) pay another class of investors (generally, investors who purchased at inflated prices). Therefore, securities litigation is a wealth transfer process between two classes of public shareholders: those in the class period and those outside it. In a world of institutional investors who hold diversified portfolios, this process leads the same institution to be in both situations at the same time, at least in the aggregate. Moreover, the class action creates a conflict between 'buy and hold' investors and 'in and out' traders, favouring the latter, and particularly undiversified 'in and out' traders, among which are hedge funds.[29] Coffee therefore proposes not abandoning securities litigation, but putting the incidence of its penalties on the actors who are culpable for the misstatements, namely the directors and the managers.

In the direction of more managerial liability are also the papers of Merritt Fox, who observes that the truly damaged party is the issuer, since the primary role of disclosure is to improve corporate governance and to lower the corporation's cost of capital by increasing the expected level of liquidity. Accordingly, liability should fall on directors, officers and external certifiers, and there should be no insurance. Damages should be proportional to an issuer's annual total investment.[30] In a similar vein, Booth argues that only cases where there is insider extraction of gains should be litigated by the company or for the company in derivative actions.[31]

Further proposals return to Mahoney's insights and suggest applying an actual-reliance standard, basically abolishing securities class actions.[32] But some scholars have more ambitious proposals. In two recent papers, Haeberle and Henderson recommend a full change in the rules of the game. They propose a form of regulation where firms would be allowed to sell early access to their information to anyone who values it, creating a market for corporate information and thus a market-based approach to corporate transparency.[33]

The large consensus among US academics that something is wrong with the securities class action is certainly not undisputed. Many top-level academics defend with various arguments the securities class actions.[34] In a passionate recent paper, Spindler

[29] JC Coffee, Jr, 'Reforming the Securities Class Action: An Essay on Deterrence and Its Implementation' (2006) 106 *Columbia Law Review* 1556.

[30] M Fox, 'Why Civil Liability for Disclosure: Violations When Issuers Do Not Trade' (2009) *Wisconsin Law Review* 297; MB Fox, 'Civil Liability and Mandatory Disclosure' (2009) 109 *Columbia Law Review* 237.

[31] RA Booth, 'The End of the Securities Fraud Class Action as We Know it' (2007) 4 *Berkeley Business Law Journal* 1.

[32] WW Bratton and ML Wachter, 'The Political Economy of Fraud on the Market' (2011) 160 *University of Pennsylvania Law Review* 69. See also, for a very recent article on this specific topic, AM Lipton, 'Reviving Reliance' (2017) 86 *Fordham Law Review* 91.

[33] K Haeberle and T Henderson, 'Making a Market for Corporate Disclosure' (2018) 35 *Yale Journal on Regulation* 383; KS Haeberle and MT Henderson, 'A New Market-Based Approach to Securities Law' (2018) 85 *University of Chicago Law Review* 1313.

[34] Authors in favour of the class actions are, among others: L Georgakopoulos, 'Frauds, Markets, and Fraud-on-the-Market: The Tortured Transition of Justifiable Reliance from Deceit to Securities Fraud' (1995) *49 University of Miami Law Review* 671; JD Cox and RS Thomas, 'Public and Private Enforcement of the Securities Laws: Have Things Changed since Enron?' (2005) 80 *Notre Dame Law Review* 893; Z Goshen and G Parchomovsky, 'The Essential Role of Securities Regulation' (2006) 55 *Duke Law Journal* 711; LE Mitchell,

argues that diversified investors do have expected losses from fraud and have incentives to undertake precaution costs, which are a social cost, and that securities class actions can deter these wasteful costs. Accordingly, all the long list of critiques and proposals for substituting mechanisms would be without foundation.[35] In another paper, Spindler observes that managerial liability is not realistic because of the damages dimension and judgement-proofness, and that securities fraud is not an agency problem within the company, between managers and shareholders, but a problem among current and future shareholders.

V. A European Perspective

A. The US Debate Observed from Europe

It is important to put into context the US debate, or at least the scientific one. Indeed, the US literature is not very interested in comparative analysis. Accordingly, it is not really prepared to use counterfactual arguments drawn from jurisdiction where class actions do not exist or, for whatever reason, are not effective. The many US critics of the securities class actions have not had, for decades, a real counter-example of how their market and their enforcement would work with no securities class actions.

Moreover, Europeans have to remember that all this variety of theories and critiques comes from within a legal system with federal rules of civil procedure, very strong incentives to settle litigation[36] associated to a vibrant Directors and Officers (D&O) insurance policies market,[37] and a very effective weaponry for the plaintiff, such as discovery, which is generally unknown in European jurisdictions. Accordingly, it is not possible disconnect the US literature and the securities class action critique from the specific features of the US enforcement system. When discussing the securities class actions issue, it is important and not always easy to distinguish issues that are not a matter of theory, but concern the way in which the US private enforcement infrastructure is built.

From a theoretical point of view, it can be agreed that damages in secondary market securities class actions can be, at least in some settings, too high in comparison with the real social cost. Accordingly, the securities class action might work as a sort of punitive scheme, where the payment by the issuer or the other liable party is at least partly disconnected from the measurable social cost and contains an implicit punitive component. From this viewpoint, the securities class action has a

'The "Innocent Shareholder": An Essay on Compensation and Deterrence in Securities Class Action Lawsuits' (2009) 2009 *Wisconsin Law Review* 457.

[35] JC Spindler, 'We Have a Consensus on Fraud on the Marke: And it's Wrong' (2017) 7 *Harvard Business Law Review* 67.

[36] LA Bebchuk, 'Suing Solely to Extract a Settlement Offer' (1988) 17 *Journal of Legal Studies* 437; A Katz, 'The Effect of Frivolous Lawsuits on the Settlement of Litigation' (1990) 10 *International Review of Law and Economics* 3.

[37] T Baker and SJ Griffith, 'How the Merits Matter: Directors' and Officers' Insurance and Securities Settlements' (2009) 157 *University of Pennsylvania Law Review* 756.

deterrent component that is, at least in theory, more important than the compensatory component.

However, this theoretical position implies the existence of class actions where all the damaged investors can get the (socially excessive) redress, taking advantage in the course of their action of all the weaponry that the US civil procedure system has to offer to the plaintiff class. In the absence of securities class actions or even one of the many weapons that make the US plaintiff class so effective (for instance, discovery), any general position against securities class actions becomes untenable, and I definitively think that it becomes untenable across Europe, where a common set of harmonised (in the case of directives) or uniform (in the case of regulations) financial market rules sit on top of largely common private law traditions (apart from the probably overrated difference between common and civil law), but very different institutional frameworks concerning civil procedure and the work of courts and administrative authorities. More specifically, in each European jurisdiction, the assumption that private enforcement of corporate transparency rules can lead to overdeterrence cannot hold true when no class actions are available to retail or professional investors, when discovery is prevented or limited, when there is no interplay with public enforcement actions, when courts are not particularly efficient and, generally speaking, when evidence and procedural rules render the exercise of the right to damages excessively difficult. This is, for instance, the case in Italy, where courts as a matter of fact follow the same presumption that the US Supreme Court accepted in *Basic Inc*,[38] namely the FOTM theory. But in an institutional environment where securities class actions are not available, where US-style discovery is not allowed and where there are no incentives to settle, given the length and the very formalistic attitude of Italian courts, the US debate is distant.

B. Harmonisation of the Enforcement Infrastructure Across Europe: The Antitrust Example

The final question is whether some form of harmonisation of the enforcement infrastructure is advisable or whether harmonisation should only concern rules on books, in the form of the CRA III. Some recent indications coming mainly from the accounting literature suggest that enforcement harmonisation by means of harmonised rules far more difficult than is commonly assumed, even in areas where rules are identical, as is the case for IFRS.[39] Paradoxically, some data seem to show that harmonisation can even accentuate differences among countries, instead of leading them towards a common direction, and imposing the same regulation on jurisdictions with very dissimilar initial regulatory conditions can have the unintended consequence of amplifying divergences

[38] *Basic Inc v Levinson*, 485 US 224 (1988).

[39] C Leuz and P Wysocki, 'The Economics of Disclosure and Financial Reporting Regulation: Evidence and Suggestions for Future Research' (2016) 54 *Journal of Accounting Research* 525, noting at 604 that global convergence in accounting standards has not created full harmonisation since 'reporting regulation goes beyond the accounting standards and also comprises the interpretation of the standards, implementation guidance, monitoring of compliance, and enforcement'.

between countries instead of reducing them.[40] Hence, institutional changes that affect the whole enforcement infrastructure are needed in order to make harmonisation truly work.

The problem, of course, is that the harmonisation of the private enforcement infrastructure is a herculean task. There are so many institutional and cultural issues to take into account that it is almost impossible to realistically believe that any form of significant harmonisation can happen, at least in the short to medium term. However, there is a field where issues of harmonisation of the private enforcement infrastructure have been already discussed. Indeed, the problem has been already debated in the area of antitrust law, where Directive 2014/104/EU sets out rules coordinating the enforcement of the competition rules in damages actions before national courts.[41] With regard to procedural rules, the Directive does not touch upon Member States' autonomy in framing their enforcement institutional framework, but simply endorses the principle of effectiveness, stating that Member States shall ensure that all national rules and procedures relating to the exercise of claims for damages are designed and applied in such a way that they do not render practically impossible or excessively difficult the exercise of the EU right to full compensation for harm caused by an infringement of competition law (Article 4). In particular, the Directive does not govern aggregation of claims and therefore stays well away from class actions, and does not address the funding of claims. However, there are two very notable exceptions to this not interventionist approach. The first concerns the rules on disclosure of evidence, which harmonise across Member States rules on access to information held by the defendant or any third party (Article 5) and access and use of evidence held in the file of a competition authority (Articles 6 and 7). The second concerns the effect of the final decision of a national competition authority or by a review court on the establishment, before a national court, of an infringement of competition law (Article 9).[42]

It is probably too early to assess whether this very soft and fragmented level of harmonisation of the Member States' procedural framework will really favour a general improvement of antitrust private enforcement across Europe, and therefore whether it can be the path to follow even with regard to the enforcement of financial markets' transparency rules.[43] The absence of any serious effort concerning the aggregation of claims and funding of actions is certainly worrying. What is clear, in any event, is that the harmonisation of mere substantive rules is not enough to frame a common European level playing field and improve the quality of European financial markets as a whole. Some form of convergence and improvement of private enforcement infrastructures is needed.

[40] HB Christensen, L Hail and C Leuz, 'Capital-Market Effects of Securities Regulation: Prior Conditions, Implementation, and Enforcement' (2016) 29 *Review of Financial Studies* 2885.

[41] D Ashton and D Henry, *Competition Damages Actions in the EU. Law & Practice* (Cheltenham, Edward Elgar, 2013).

[42] For a review of the Directive and an updated assessment of the European literature on the issue, see F Marcos, BJ Rodger and M Sousa Ferro, 'Promotion and Harmonization of Antitrust Damages Claims by Directive EU/2014/10?' in B Rodger, FM Sousa and F Marcos (eds), *The EU Antitrust Damages Directive: Transposition in the Member States* (Oxford, Oxford University Press, 2018).

[43] S Peyer, The Antitrust Damages Directive: Much Ado about Nothing?' in M Marquis and R Cisotta (eds), *Litigation and Arbitration in EU Competition Law* (Cheltenham, Edward Elgar, 2015), 33.

17

Transparency on Stock Corporations through Piercing the Corporate Veil

VICTORIA ATHANASOPOULOU

I. Introduction

The doctrine of piercing the corporate veil is applied by the judge to achieve fairness and justice. By approaching the issue from a comparative law perspective and contrasting Greek law with English, German, French and American law, and considering recent developments in those jurisdictions, this chapter attempts to identify disparate cases, delineate their essential dissimilarities and examine the ideas that underlie these different decisions.

A. The Nature of Legal Personality

The concept of legal personality is the essential foundation of corporate law[1] and a vital element of modern economic life. The legal person – despite being a legal fiction – enjoys a real existence and is capable of being party to different legal relationships.[2] The most salient feature of the corporation is its collective will,[3] which is distinguishable from the will of the individuals pertaining to it and is determined by its specific purpose.[4] Within the legal personality, there is a correlation and interaction between

[1] A Mandaraka-Sheppard, 'New Trends in Piercing the Corporate Veil: The Conservative versus the Liberal Approaches' in L Athanassiou (ed), *8th International Conference of Maritime Law, Shipping in Periods of Economic Distress* (Athens, NB, 2015) 319: 'the unyielding rock of corporate law … is the separate juristic personality of a corporation'.

[2] The legal person has unlimited legal capacity, except for rights and obligations that are specific to natural persons only: A Georgiadis, *General Principles of Civil Law*, 5th edn (Athens, PN Sakkoulas, 2019) (in Greek) 168, 177.

[3] O von Gierke, *Genossenschaftstheorie und die deutsche Rechtsprechung* (Berlin, Weidmann, 1887) 612: 'Die Willens- und Handlungsfähigkeit der Körperschaft gilt uns als eine in und mit ihrer Persönlichkeit gegebene Wirklichkeit.'

[4] F Regelsberger and G Maridakis, *General Principles of Pandects I* (Athens, SN, 1935) (translated into Greek) 353.

the collective will and purpose[5] of the corporation activities towards realising the responsibility[6] arising from the latter.[7]

The concept of legal personality prescribes that a stock corporation is by law an independent, legally separate person with its own uninfringeable rights, liabilities and assets.[8] Even the 'one-man company' is a legal entity distinct from its single owner and controller.[9] Therefore, the company's creditors cannot legally pursue the shareholders for liabilities of the company and, inversely, the shareholder's creditors cannot pursue the company. In the words of Lord Halsbury LC in *Salomon v Salomon*: 'A legally incorporated company must be treated like any other independent person with its rights and liabilities appropriate to itself.'[10]

B. Piercing the Corporate Veil as the Ultimate *Refugium* of the Judge

Through the judicial tool of piercing the corporate veil, in those cases where justice and fairness cannot be awarded, the judge holds liable for the contracting obligations of the company the natural persons, shareholders of the company.[11] The doctrine of piercing the corporate veil is a reversal of the judicial principle of legal personality, which overthrows the effects of company law and therefore is not easily accepted in all jurisdictions.[12] The company as a legal entity is an aggregation of persons and property. The substance of a corporation is therefore stripped and weakened by the attenuation of its essential components: property and human activity. The interaction between these aspects (ie, the corporation's activity and its property) engenders clarity for the stakeholders of the corporate entity. Deficiencies in this dual relationship (subcapitalised companies, business activity of shareholders in their own names, commingling of properties and entrepreneurial activities between the shareholders and the company) create a lack of transparency and therefore damage the corporate interest. In such cases, when the law has no other available recourse,[13] the judge applies the doctrine of piercing the corporate veil.[14]

[5] J von Baltzer, *Der Beschluß als rechtstechnisches Mittel organschaftlicher Funktion im Privatrecht* (Cologne, Grote, 1965) 45, who uses the term 'Wirkungsbereich' (area of influence) instead of 'Zweck' (purpose) of the legal person.

[6] K Roussos, *Law of Legal Persons, Liber Amicorum Filippos Doris* (Athens, PN Sakkoulas, 2010) (in Greek) 142 ff.

[7] L Ennecerus and HC Nipperdey, *Allgemeiner Teil des Bürgerlichen Rechts*, 15th edn (Tübingen, Mohr Siebeck, 1959) § 103, 611.

[8] N Rocas, *Commercial Companies*, 8th edn (Athens-Thessaloniki, Sakkoulas, 2018) (in Greek) 186.

[9] ibid 609, 610. See also Twelfth Directive of 21 December 1989 on single-member private limited liability companies (89/667/EEC) [1989] OJ L395.

[10] *Salomon v Salomon & Co Ltd* [1897] AC 22.

[11] G Dellios in A Georgiadis (ed), *Brief Commentary on Civil Code* (Athens, PN Sakkoulas, 2010) (in Greek), Article 61 CC II, pp 158, 159; Roussos (n 6) 330.

[12] Mandaraka-Sheppard (n 1) 319.

[13] Bundesgerichtshof (Germany) 29 November 1956, *BGHZ* 22, 226, 230: 'wenn die Wirklichkeit des Lebens, die wirtschaftlichen Bedürfnisse und die Macht der Tatsachen es dem Richter gebieten, die personen- und vermögensrechtliche Selbstständigkeit der GmbH und ihres alleinigen Gesellschafters hintanzusetzen'.

[14] The recognition of a limited power to pierce the corporate veil, in carefully defined circumstances, is necessary if the law is not to be disarmed in the face of abuse: *Prest v Petrodel Resources Ltd and Others* [2013] UKSC 34, para 27 (Lord Sumption).

II. Piercing the Corporate Veil Due to Lack of Transparency in Stock Corporations

Groups of companies[15] sometimes function under complex structures that lack transparency to maximise profits, hide assets, and avoid taxation of business and investment income. Furthermore, lack of transparency concerning corporate activities, as well as commingling of private and company funds and gross undercapitalisation, creates an economic climate favourable for the emergence, development and prioritisation of self-interests and threatens market integrity.

To award justice, courts have applied the doctrine of piercing the corporate veil in cases where a natural or legal person is the dominant figure of a corporation or a complex of corporations. The use of the legal entity as a façade by its controllers is a source of conflict for all stakeholders and is generally detrimental to their interests.

A. The Economically Dominant Natural Person

In Greek law, most of the court decisions requiring the application of the doctrine of piercing the corporate veil concern the shipping industry. In the first level of its evolution,[16] the jurisprudence focused on the person who controls or dominates the company in question. In a later development, judges shifted focus to the legal entity and its property. Recently, the essential criterion for the application of the piercing doctrine is the misuse or abuse of the corporate entity by the dominant person.[17] The above three phases of development of the piercing doctrine in Greece reflect at the same time the maturation of the piercing doctrine at an international level. The early phase mirrors the imputation of liability to the natural person who exerts undue influence on the corporation. The second phase corresponds to the commingling of assets and entrepreneurial activities, as well as the devastation of the corporate substance, and the third phase reflects the misuse of corporate entity by its controllers.

In the early phase of the piercing doctrine in Greek jurisprudence, a series of authorities[18] considered as a necessary and only prerequisite for the piercing of corporate veil the existence of a sole shareholder who owns all or most of the shares of the legal person and thus exercises absolute control over it. This view, which was overruled by subsequent authorities,[19] is, as it is rightly written,[20] extremely dangerous because

[15] For comparative analysis of the main conflicts developed in group of companies, see KJ Hopt, 'Group of Companies: A Comparative Study on the Economics, Law and Regulation of Corporate Groups' (2015) *ECGI Working Paper* No 286, 4 f, papers.ssrn.com/sol3/papers.cfm?abstract_id=2560935.

[16] V Athanassopoulou, 'Piercing the Corporate Veil in Maritime Companies', *ΠειρΝ* 2005 (in Greek) 389.

[17] See section II.C below.

[18] Supreme Civil Court of Greece (hereinafter referred to as Areios Pagos) 1058/1987 *ΕΕμπΔ* 1987, 455; Areios Pagos 521/1988, *ΕΕμπΔ* 1988, 593; Areios Pagos 591/1988, *ΕΕμπΔ* 1988, 496; Areios Pagos 1046/1990, *ΕΕμπΔ* 1990, 483. These decisions characterise the early phase of the Greek jurisprudence of the piercing doctrine.

[19] Areios Pagos 17/1994, *ΕΕμπΔ* 1994, 589: 'the criterion of the sole shareholder alone is not enough to declare his responsibility for the debts of the company'.

[20] K Alepakos, *Lifting the Corporate Veil of Stock Corporations in Jurisprudence* (Athens, Foundation for Business Law Studies, 1994) (in Greek) 36; A Kiantou-Pampouki, 'Protection of Creditors of Maritime Companies through Piercing the Corporate Veil', *Αρμενόπουλος*, 1993 (in Greek) 877, 885.

it might shake the precious institution of legal personality and undermine the foundation of the 'one-man' company. Furthermore, it directly disregards the fundamental principle of corporate separateness (eg, the separation of the corporation's and shareholder's assets).

Also, due to the proliferation of offshore companies, which provide a favourable regulatory business environment, a ship can be owned, operated and managed[21] by separate companies[22] controlled by the same natural person who remains at the same time their sole shareholder. This complexity of corporations[23] in the shipping business may cause a lack of transparency concerning the contracting party of a maritime transaction. In particular, in the case where the sole controller is a personal guarantor for loans provided by banks to these companies and also mortgages his personal property as additional security for the loans, the court declares him to be a merchant and direct debtor.[24] The so-called 'control theory' in the Greek doctrine is based on the affirmation that 'the real debtor is the shareholder of the maritime company who holds all or the most of the company's shares so that the continuation of the operational activities or even the existence of the corporation depends on him'.[25]

However, the obiter dictum is not to be conceived as restricted to the economic power of the shareholder. Its real meaning must be perceived in the overall context of the real facts of the case in question, and the most significant of them is the dominant conduct of the shareholder that paralyses the autonomous existence of the corporation. Essentially, the reference to 'the operational activities of the corporation' must be seen as indicating the company as a dynamic organism in a continuous evolutionary path and not as a static economic unit, because its purposes are accomplished through the entrepreneurial proceedings of the shareholder.[26]

B. The Entrepreneurial Activity of the Dominant Person

In the second phase of its evolution, the Greek doctrine of piercing focuses rather on the observation of the legal person, which becomes a 'shell' or a 'façade' due to the entrepreneurial activity of the sole or economically dominant shareholder. Greek courts attributed to the controlling person of the shipowner company personal liability for its debts[27] and held him to be a beneficial owner.[28] Apart from the above-mentioned

[21] Ship Management Agreement (SHIPMAN 2009): 'during the period of this Agreement, the Managers shall carry out the Management Services in respect of the Vessel as agents for and on behalf of the Owners'.

[22] By virtue of a ship management agreement, a maritime company undertakes the management of a ship owned by a second and operated by a third company of the group of companies. The same natural person is the main shareholder and controller of all three legal entities.

[23] '[E]n dehors de tout montage juridique s' efforçant de cacher cette réalité.' *DMF* 1987, 654.

[24] Areios Pagos 1058/1987, *ΕΕμπΔ* 1987, 455.

[25] Kiantou-Pampouki (n 20) 877, 885.

[26] Athanassopoulou (n 16) 389.

[27] Areios Pagos 591/1988, *ΕΕμπΔ* 1988, 496; Areios Pagos 1046/1990, *ΕΝΔ* 1991, 15; Court of Appeal of Athens 8734/1986, *ΕΕμπΔ* 1986, 664; Court of Appeal of Athens 8006/1991, *ΕΕμπΔ* 1993, 286; Court of Appeal of Athens 2620/1993, *ΕΝΔ* 1994, 8; Court of Appeal of Piraeus 1253/1988, *ΕΝΔ* 1991, 106. These authorities point out those maritime operations rendering the shareholder into a ship's operator: conclusion of charter and marine insurance contracts, employment of the master and the crew, mortgages and other commercial activities leading to the exploitation of the ship.

[28] In Greek law, the *efoplistis* (εφοπλιστής) is the person who exploits a ship which is not owned by him. The *efoplistis* concept is taken from German law (*Ausrüster*). According to art 106 of the Greek Code of Private

economic control of the shareholder,[29] his independent entrepreneurial activity is accompanied by the conflation of his private property with the company's property.[30] A key feature of the entrepreneurial activity is the pursuit, on his own, of the maximum possible profit, which is inherent in the economic risk of the corporation. Consequently, the profit arising from the exploitation of the ship is channelled to the private property of the natural person and not of the company, which is the real subject of all transactions and of the total business activity. The legal entity should be an independent economic business unit, which as such has its own business autonomy and self-sufficiency. By the channelling of profits to the natural person and the commingling of assets, the company is weakened and becomes unable to respond to its debtors. By examining this series of cases in depth, we conclude that the proof of the fictitiousness of the company is not easy and is always accomplished by demonstrating the behaviour of another person who weakens both the organisational structure and economic strength of the company in question. A legal entity ends up becoming a shell only when another person acts disastrously with regard to the material substrate of the company[31] as well as to its mercantile activity by undertaking it in his own name and for his own account.

C. The Abuse of the Corporation by the Controlling Person

In the latest phase of its evolution, the piercing theory is applied by the Greek jurisprudence under the requirement of the misuse or abuse of the legal person.[32] Misuse of the legal person occurs when the controlling person uses the legal entity in such a way

Maritime Law, he is personally liable for all debts arising from the exploitation of the ship. In *The Aventicum* [1978] 1 *Lloyd's Rep* 184, 187 Slynn J stated: 'I think that where damages are claimed by cargo-owner and there is a dispute as to the beneficial ownership of the ship the court in all cases can and in some cases should look behind the registered owner to determine the true beneficial ownership … I reject any suggestion that it is impossible to pierce the corporate veil … the court shall not be limited to a consideration of who the registered owner is or who the person having legal ownership of the shares in the ship is: the directions are to look at the beneficial ownership.'

[29] Areios Pagos 1046/1990, *ΕΝΔ* 1991, 15 = *ΕΕμπΔ* 1990, 483. In this case, the controlling shareholder owned 25 per cent of the shares, while the remaining 75 per cent belonged to his spouse and their two children. The following circumstances were considered to be crucial: (a) the operation of the vessels was typically carried out in the name of the companies, but essentially on his own behalf, through other natural or legal persons acting on his behalf and under his instructions; (b) he was guarantor for loans provided by banks to these companies; and (c) he declared his status of beneficial owner by concluding maritime contracts. These companies were considered to belong to the shareholder and constituted a cover of his commercial activities in the name of the companies, but, essentially, on their own personal account.

[30] Cour de Cassation (Commerciale, France), 27 November 1991, *DMF* 1992, 488. The Supreme Court of France hold the natural person personally liable even though he possessed only 35 per cent of the shares of the debtor company.

[31] Court of Appeal of Piraeus 606/2001, *ΕΝΔ* 2002, 108. In this case, the Court examined the economic status of the maritime company and proved that the controlling shareholder systematic and with concrete actions deducted the financial benefits that were destined for the company and transferred them to another company.

[32] Areios Pagos (in plenum) 2/2013, *ΠειρΝ* 2013, 48 = NOMOS. The Court held that the shareholder/natural person had control of the group of shipping companies, which were named after him and had their actual seat in Piraeus. Through these companies, he pursued his business activities and thus he used them as a mechanism to absorb the adverse effects of his business activities. The Court also held that the identification of the interests of the natural person with those of the companies is not an evidence of abuse. All these facts do not prove circumvention of the provisions imposed to the companies or confusion of their properties with his individual property. However, the shareholder had abused the legal personality of the shipowner

to circumvent and slide over prohibitions imposed to him, or intentionally breaches the principles of good faith and causes damage to a third party or avoids individual or corporate obligations.[33] Indicative criteria of the misuse are the inadequate funding of the corporation and the commingling of assets. Thus, the natural person trades under the corporate name for his own benefit, uses the corporate property for his own activities and unfairly transfers to the creditors of the corporation the risks of his own business. In this case, piercing is the sanction imposed by the judge to prevent the misuse of the legal person and to protect the third parties who have been induced to contract with the misuser by misrepresentations made by him.[34] The legal personality is not dismantled or abolished, but suspended from its autonomy only for the particular transaction in question. The company and the main shareholder or partner remain debtors, who are now jointly liable (Articles 481 and 926 of the Greek Civil Code) for the damaging consequences of their transactions. An additional creditor is created, to whom the consequences are spread from the company.[35]

Many objections can be raised against these considerations. It is contestable whether the abuse of the company's institution is the legal basis of the liability of the shareholder.[36] It is also debatable whether the abuse can be seen in relation to a single transaction of the company and not to the whole of its business activity. It is impossible to pinpoint each separate transaction and to trace and quantify the harm caused by such isolated transactions. On the other hand, the abuse of the legal personality from the shareholder is the proof and the affirmation of his intensive mercantile activity against the independent existence of the company. At the same time, the affirmation of the abuse identifies and indicates the person who undertakes the activities in the place of the company.

III. The Entrepreneurial Interest: The Decisive Criterion of Transparency in Stock Corporations

A. Designation of Corporate and Entrepreneurial Interest in Piercing Cases

Piercing theories identify a person (legal or natural) who emerges from the corporation with its entrepreneurial activity. It is not only the person who economically

company since, at the time of the transaction, the company in question, like all other companies in the group, suffered significant financial difficulties (ie, they were underfunding and the critical transaction was drawn up only after the confirmations from the director that the sale price would be paid in due time since the group belonged to Mr P, who also gave similar assurances). In other words, the plaintiff was led to the transaction in question based mainly on the aforementioned assurances, even of the shareholder who thus misled him because of the incomplete financing of the shipowner company. Consequently, this conduct obviously exceeded the limits of the good faith and the economic and social purpose of his respective right.

[33] Single-member Court of First Instance of Piraeus 4996/2017 *ΕΕμπΔ* 2018, 86; K Rigas, Commentary on the decision of Court of First Instance of Athens 4996/2017, *ΕΕμπΔ* 2018, 229; Areios Pagos 537/2016, NOMOS; Areios Pagos 689/2013, *ΔΕΕ* 2014, 65.

[34] Areios Pagos 2/2013. NOMOS.

[35] ibid.

[36] In the German jurisprudence, the shareholder's abusive interference with the company's assets constitutes tortious conduct according to § 826 BGB.

controls the corporation, but also the person who creates – through his factual business behaviour – an aggregate entrepreneurial interest which undermines the corporate interest and, in this way, impoverishes the corporation to such an extent that the latter becomes unable to respond to its debtors. Therefore, it is first necessary to define the concept of corporate interest and then to detect the different ways in which new interests emerge within the company.

i. The Corporate Interest

The key to understanding the function of a corporation lies in the interest of the company. Jehring states: 'The real force which moves man to action is interest.' According to the school of legal positivism,[37] 'we must start from a theory of interests, that is, of the claims or demands or desires which human beings, either individually or in groups or in associations or relations, seek to satisfy, of which therefore the adjustment of relations and ordering of conduct through the forces of politically organized society must take account'.[38] The constituent elements of an interest can be traced to the existence of a person and his profit-aimed activity within a society.[39] The great diversity and plurality of the economic activities and legal relationships aimed towards accomplishing the specific purpose of any given corporation reveal a constellation of competing interests,[40] from which results the ultimate interest of a company: the corporate interest.[41]

Corporate interest is an extensively studied concept. However, it is not legally defined. The company's interest can be defined as the common interest of its shareholders[42] (restrictive definition) or as the interest that reshapes the interests of all stakeholders and contributes to the broader public interest (extensive definition).[43] Stakeholders usually comprise employees, workers, creditors, suppliers and parties

[37] P Heck, *Gesetzesauslegung und Interessenjurisprudenz* (Tübingen, Mohr, 1914); P Heck, *Begriffsbildung und Interessenjurisprudenz* (Tübingen, Mohr, 1932); P Heck, *Das Problem der Rechtsgewinnung*, 2nd edn (Tübingen, Mohr, 1932); P Heck, *Interessenjurisprudenz* (Tübingen, Mohr, 1933); *Die Interessenjurisprudenz und ihre neuen Gegner* (Tübingen, Mohr, 1936); P Heck, 'Rechtsphilosophie und Interessenjurisprudenz' (1937) *AcP* 143, 129 ff. See also M Schoch and L Fuller (eds), *The Jurisprudence of Interests – Twentieth Century Legal Philosophy Series, Volume II* (Cambridge, MA, Harvard University Press, 1948).

[38] R Pound, 'A Survey of Social Interests' (1943) 57 *Harvard Law Review* 1.

[39] The word 'interest' derives from the Latin word 'interesse' and indicates the interaction in relations with others, while it presupposes the existence of a person who acts and is responsible.

[40] There are interests that prevail over others and thus they are recognised and given effect through legal precepts developed and applied in the judicial process (*die Kausalen Interessen*): Heck, *Gesetzesauslegung* (n 38) 7. See also Heck, *Das Problem der Rechtsgewinnung* (n 38) 29: 'Die Rechtsnormen sind ein Resultat miteinander kollidierender menschlicher Interessen.'

[41] Rocas (n 8) 195: 'the company's interest lies in the setting of certain limits that cannot be exceeded by acts or omissions by the company's administration'.

[42] P Mülbert, 'Shareholder Value aus rechtlicher Sicht' (1997) *ZGR* 129, 132 ff; P Mülbert, 'Marktwertmaximierung als Unternehmensziel der Aktiengesellschaft' in G Crezelius, H Hirte and K Vieweg (eds), *Festschrift für Völker Röhricht* (Munich, CH Beck, 2005) 421, 440; WU Schilling, 'Shareholder Value and Aktiengesetz' (1997) *BB* 373, 375; A Rappaport, *Creating Shareholder Value: A Guide for Managers and Interests* (New York, Free Press, 1998) 1 f, 32 f; M Mizruchi and Howard Kimeldorf, 'The Historical Context of Shareholder Value Capitalism' in DE David (ed), *Political Power and Social Theory Vol 17* (Bingley, Emerald Publishing, 2005) 213, 221 f.

[43] G von Bonin, *Die Leitung der Aktiengesellschaft zwischen Shareholder Value and Stakeholder Interessen* (Baden-Baden, Nomos, 2003) 131, 149 f; R Phillips, *Stakeholder Theory and Organizational Ethics* (Oakland, Berrett-Koehler Publishers, 2003).

with heterogeneous interests. In this sense, and to fulfil its social and economic aims, the corporate entity becomes a unit or organism, even an embodiment of functions, rights and duties that can be treated as a legal actor and a complex organisation requiring regulation in many different situations. In my view, the corporate interest represents the aggregate, independent and autonomous interest of the corporation. It results from all the interests that arise from conducting business activities[44] that sustain the corporation's status as a dominant force with integrative functions. The corporate organs have the duty not simply to enhance the financial interests of the shareholders but also to further the broad purpose and economic success of the corporation;[45] this must take into account the legitimate interests of other stakeholder constituencies[46] (eg, the company's employees, suppliers, customers, community and environment).[47]

The piercing doctrine examines the self-reliance of the corporation based on the conduct of the dominant shareholder. The insufficient financing of the company by its owner or shareholder provokes a lack of transparency concerning the substance of the corporate interest. Not only the undercapitalisation but also the destroying influence of the shareholder can damage the self-sufficiency of the company.[48] The devastation of the corporation occurs as a result of the actions of a person (legal or natural) who – through his entrepreneurial activity – creates a quasi-corporate or entrepreneurial interest. This is clearly seen in the piercing theories of US case law, particularly in the alter ego theory, but also in the enterprise theory, where the whole group of companies represents an autonomous entrepreneurial interest. In those cases, the judge recognises first the entrepreneurial interest and then attributes personal liability to its holder.

ii. *The Interest of a Group of Companies*

The US jurisdiction has developed the doctrine of piercing the corporate veil in the relationship between parent companies and their subsidiaries. The case law has developed guidelines as to whether a subsidiary should be treated as an intermediary or as an independent legal personality. These guidelines should be carefully applied only after considering all the particularities of each case. The list of indicative fact-based factors which must be considered by the judge encompasses, among other things, the undercapitalisation of the subsidiary or the economic and entrepreneurial domination of the subsidiary by the parent company. Generally, a combination of financial and operational dependence of the subsidiary by the parent company might lead the subsidiary to a lack of corporate autonomy. According to the alter ego theory, both legal entities lose their

[44] M Jürgenmeyer, *Das Unternehmensinteresse* (Frankfurt, Fachmedien Recht und Wirtschaft, 1984) 236.

[45] W Junge, 'Das Unternehmensinteresse' in HC Taschner, D König, KF Kreuzer and HG Leser (eds), *Festschrift für Ernst von Caemmerer zum 70. Geburtstag* (Tübingen, Mohr Siebeck, 1978) 554: 'Das Unternehmen ist als Interesse an der Rentabilität des Unternehmens und damit seiner dauerhaften Erhaltung zu definieren.'

[46] G Spindler, 'Unternehmensinteresse als Leitlinie des Vorstandshandelns – Berücksichtigung von Arbeitnehmerninteressen und Shareholder Value' (October 2008), boeckler.de/pdf/mbf_gutachten_spindler_2008.pdf.

[47] K Pampoukis, 'The General Corporate Interest as Central Idea in the Institution of Corporate Governance' (2003) *ΕπισκΕΔ* 955 ff.

[48] Areios Pagos 1315/2017, *ΕΕμπΔ* 2018, 321: conduct contrary to the corporate interest.

autonomous existence, and the subsidiary is degraded to the alter ego of the parent.[49] The most important and commonly used theory is the so-called instrumentality[50] doctrine,[51] according to which: 'to establish that a corporation is an alter ego, a party must show that the shareholders disregarded the corporate entity and made it a mere instrumentality for the transaction of their own affairs'.[52]

iii. A Community of Interests

The 'enterprise theory' is also noteworthy, which has gained particular importance because of the important role it played in the *Amoco Cadiz* case.[53] The enterprise theory examines the extent of the parent's financial interference in the subsidiary and concludes that a multinational enterprise group should be regarded as an economic and business entity.

The enterprise theory of US case law approaches the concept of 'community of interests' formulated from the French jurisprudence: ships belonging to the same companies group form a uniform economic reality that is hidden under a judicial montage (*montage juridique*) of separate corporations.[54] These ships are essentially part of the assets of those companies, which, through their common shareholders[55] (the members of the same family), are unified as a 'community of interests'.[56] 'Community of interests'

[49] *Automotriz del Golfo de California, SA de CV v Resnick* (1957) 47 California Reports, Second Series 792 = 306 Pacific Reporter, Second Series 1, 4. This case described the twofold alter ego test to hold individuals or parent companies personally liable: '1. There must be such a unity of interest and ownership that the separate personalities of the corporation and the individual no longer exist and 2. that, if the acts are treated as those of the corporation alone, an inequitable result will follow.' See also *Mesler v Bragg Management Co.* (1985) 39 Cal 3d 290, 301; *United States of America v Ira S Bushey & Sons Inc* (1973) AMC 2639 (21 August; US District Court, District of Vermont).

[50] *GE Lowendahl v The Baltimore and Ohio Railroad Co et al*, 287 NYS 62, 76. Frederick Powell formulated the so-called three-factors-rule containing three conditions which must be fulfilled in order to pierce the corporate veil: '1. Control, not mere majority or complete stock control, but complete domination, not only of finances but of policy and business practice in respect of the transaction attacked so that the corporate entity as to his transaction had at the time no separate mind, will or existence of its own; and 2. Such control must have been used by the defendant to commit fraud or wrong, to perpetrate the violation of a statutory or other positive legal duty, or a dishonest and unjust act in contravention of plaintiff's legal rights; and 3. The aforesaid control and breach of duty must proximately cause the injury or unjust laws complained of.'

[51] *Bergen v St Patrick*, AMC 2024 (9th Cir 1987); *Georg W Benett Bryson & Company Ltd v Norton Lilly & Co, Inc*, AMC 2189 (5th Cir 1974); *Ross Industries Inc v M/V Gretke Oldendorff* (1980) AMC 1397 (21 January; US District Court, Eastern District of Texas).

[52] *United States v Fidelity Capital Corporation*, 920 F 2d 827, 837 (11th Cir 1991).

[53] *In Re Oil Spill by the Amoco Cadiz off the Coast of France on 16 March 1978* (1984) AMC 2123.

[54] M Rémond-Gouilloud, 'L'émanation maritime ou comment faire céder l'écran de la personnalité morale d'un armement?' (1986) *DMF* 333.

[55] I Corbier, *La notion d'armateur* (Paris, PUF, 1999) 118.

[56] In the case of the ships *Brave Mother* and *Brave Themis*, the Court of Appeal of Rennes accepted the affinity of the two vessels based on the indications arising both from the name of the ships themselves and from the directors of the companies, who were the members of the family of the company's chairman. In addition, the companies had common manager, offices and phones and corresponding corporate names: Cour d'Appel de Rennes (France) of 21 June 1989, *navire Brave Mother* (1989) *DMF* 649, Commentaire Bonassies (1990) *DMF* 60, no 27. This judgement was upheld by the Supreme Court of France: Cour de Cassation of 12 February 1991, *navire Brave Mother* (1991) *DMF* 315, Commentaire Bonassies (1992) *DMF* 83. See also Cour d'Appel d'Aix-en-Provence of 11 March 1988, *navires Hakki Morgul et Morgul* (1989) *DMF* 367; Cour d'Appel de Rouen of 26 January 1995, *navire Merzario-Britania* (1996) *DMF* 49.

is the economic and managerial unity (*unité économique et de gestion*) that appears under the veil of different legal persons.[57] The doctrinal foundation of the piercing theory in French case law is essentially based on the theory of 'community of interests', which implies the unity of the interests represented by the group of companies through the pursuit of common entrepreneurial interest. At the same time, this theory is assisted and complemented by the theory of the creation of false appearances (*théorie de l'apparence*) and the theory of fictitious companies. The concealment of reality by the creation of a fictitious non-existent legal construction is the starting point of the reasoning in most of the decisions in French case law. The ship manager who carries on the operation of the ship and at the same time uses the material substrate of this activity to pursue maximum profit possible undertakes the enduring business risk and is the real entrepreneur in the maritime industry. In French law, there are no dividing lines between the theories that lead to the piercing of corporate veil. The core of the 'community of interests' is without doubt the entrepreneurial interest of the whole group of companies. The common economic, social and financial interest of a group of companies, which must be appreciated in the light of a policy developed for the group, is recognised in the French jurisprudence from the French Supreme Court in the *Rozenblum* case.[58]

B. The Emergence of an Entrepreneurial Interest

Piercing theories highlight an individual as the holder of an entrepreneurial interest that appears through the weakening of the real entrepreneurial holder: the corporation. Sometimes, the legal entity is weakened to such an extent that it ceases to be the real operator of the business and its position is taken by the holder of another interest. This interest is distinct and autonomous and is not integrated into the interest of the company or of the group of companies in question.

i. Consisting Elements of the Entrepreneurial Interest

According to the Greek jurisprudence, piercing the corporate veil is permitted by abuse or misuse of the legal personality:[59] 'Criteria indicative of misuse are: a) the

[57] Cour d'Appel de Rouen of 27 June 1991, *navire Ariana* (1992) *Bulletin des Transport* 102: 'les deux navires … sont la propriété des sociétés dont les patrimoines se trouvent unis par une communauté d'intérêts et qu'apparait aussi, derrière la voile des personnes morales, une unité financière et de gestion entre les deux navires'.

[58] Case *Rozenblum*: Cass Crim 4 February 1985, D 1985, jurisp, 478 = Crim. Février 1985, JCP éd G II, 1986, p 20585, note J Didier: 'le concours financier apporté par le dirigeants de fait ou de droit d' une société à une autre entreprise d' un même groupe dans laquelle ils sont intéressées directement ou indirectement doit être dicté par un intérêt économique, social ou financier commun, apprécié au regard d' une politique élaborée pour l'ensemble de ce groupe, et ne doit ni être démuni de contrepartie ou rompre l'équilibre entre les engagements respectifs des divers sociétés concernées, ni excéder les possibilités financières de celle qui en supporte la charge: que tel n' étant pas le cas en l'espèce, les moyens réunis doivent être écartés'. According to the *Rozenblum* doctrine, the existence of the group should be based on the common interest within which the internal relations have a reciprocal consideration with balanced responsibilities of the concerned companies and without exceeding the financial capacity of the group entity. On the attempts to establish the crucial concept of the interest of the groups of companies, see A Rocas 'The Interest of Groups of Companies' (2016) *ΕεμπΔ* 789, 795.

[59] Areios Pagos 2/2013 NOMOS=*ΠειρΝ* 2013, 48; Areios Pagos 149/2013 *ΔΕΕ* 2013, 964; Areios Pagos 330/2010 *ΕπισκΕΔ* 2010, 763; Areios Pagos 309/2009, *ΔΕΕ* 2009, 804.

inadequate finance or undercapitalization of the company, b) the commingling between the company's property and the controller's personal property, c) the fact that the company does not have its own business organization, and at the same time the controller/shareholder acts in his own name and under the covering of the corporate personality.' These indicators of the misuse of the corporate personality are reflective of the aggregate and independent shareholder's activity, which creates a whole unit with its own interest. Also, the above-described facts, as well as the behaviour of the shareholder, comprise the consisting elements of an entrepreneurial interest (ie, the result of an independent, complex mercantile and financial interest colliding with the corporate interest): (a) the profit aimed activity; and (b) the field of activity with the assets belonging to it.

Furthermore, a crucial element of the entrepreneurial interest is the liability of its holder. Every action provokes a reaction and a liability. An individual who enters into a contract and deals for his own benefit, while ignoring the company's organisation and property, generates commercial activity that affects both components of corporate interest: the property of the corporation and its entrepreneurial activity. The substance of the corporate entity is then undermined from its internal organs. The balance of corporate interest is lost when a shareholder develops and prioritises his own interests, particularly when he has external economic interests of such importance that they damage the dependent company. Thus, the shareholder realises profits to the detriment of the corporation. The corporate entity is first disregarded by its shareholders, followed by a judge.

In this sense, the piercing of the corporate veil should not be the sanction for the above conduct of the controller.[60] The judge acknowledges the liability of the holder of the emergent entrepreneurial interest. As established above, corporate interest is self-determining and independent of the individual interests of the company's shareholders. It must be pointed out that the real and sole holder of the corporate interest is the legal person and not the underlying organisation of natural persons who are only the organs that express its will and perform its actions. The activity of the shareholder on his own account cannot be associated with the activity of the company because the shareholder and the company are acting based on independent interests informed by their own, separate activities. Therefore, the dictum of Greek decisions that 'the legal person is an absorbing mechanism of the unfavourable effects of the entrepreneurial activity of natural persons' enables a lack of dogmatic coherence.[61]

ii. The Evasion of the Responsibilities as the Rationale of Piercing Theories

The unfolding entrepreneurial interest creates personal liabilities for its holder, who tries to avoid and evade them through the legal person, which appears in the economic process. It should be stressed that what precisely leads to unfairness is the fact that the holder of the interest refuses to undertake, personally and unlimitedly, the business

[60] According to the German jurisprudence, the abuse of the legal entity leads to a tortious conduct of the abuser (§ 826 BGB): Bundesgerichtshof of 16 July 2007, *BGHZ* 173, 246 (Trihotel-Urteil).

[61] Areios Pagos 2/2013 *ΠειρΝ* 2013, 48 = NOMOS.

risk by fragmenting his activity into different corporate unities while receiving the total business profit.[62] Unfortunately, the Greek jurisprudence accepted as legitimate the practice of fragmentation of business responsibility, as well as the fact that the natural person carries on business activities indirectly concealed by the legal cover of one or more companies. In particular, in relation to the maritime companies, the court decisions contain a logical and legal contradiction by arguing that the entrepreneurial activity does not confer the status of beneficial owner (*efoplistis*) to the natural or legal person who operates a ship, while according to the Greek maritime law, the main characteristic of the beneficial owner (εφοπλιστής, the *efoplistis* legal concept) is the entrepreneurial activity.

Recently the English jurisprudence[63] has contributed to the conceptual difference between the concealment and the evasion of responsibilities. As explained by Lord Sumption in his judgment in *Prest v Petrodel Resources Ltd and Others*:

> There is a limited principle in English law which applies when a person is under an existing legal obligation or liability or subject to an existing legal restriction which he deliberately evades or whose enforcement he deliberately frustrates by interposing a company under his control. The Court may then pierce the corporate veil for the purpose, and only for the purpose, of depriving the company or its controller of the advantage that they would otherwise have obtained by the company's separate legal personality.[64]

This case introduced the distinction between the principles of concealment and evasion:

> The concealment principle is legally banal and does not involve piercing the corporate veil at all. It is that the interposition of a company or perhaps several companies to conceal the identity of the real actors will not deter the courts from identifying them, assuming that their identity is legally relevant. In these cases, the Court is not disregarding the façade but only looking behind it to discover the facts, which the corporate structure is concealing. The evasion principle is different. It is that the court may disregard the corporate veil if there is a legal right against the person in control of it which exists independently of the company's involvement, and a company is interposed so that the separate legal personality of the company will defeat the right or frustrate its enforcement. Many cases will fall into both categories, but in some circumstances, the difference between them may be critical.

Evasion is the only basis for piercing the corporate veil.

[62] Areios Pagos 2/2013, *ΠειρΝ* 2013, 48. The Greek jurisprudence describes the structure of maritime entrepreneurship in Greece as follows: 'It is usual that an entrepreneur who does not want to risk unlimited capital constitutes one or more companies which purchase one or more ships and operate them for their own account either directly or by delegating their management to another company that exists or is established for that purpose and acts on their behalf. In this way, the control of the shipowner/ship management companies is maintained by the same natural or legal person, who participates in their management and as he is the main shareholder indirectly profits from the economic growth of the shipowner company.'

[63] Under English law, there is a limited piercing jurisdiction. See *Salomon v Salomon & Co Ltd* [1897] AC 22; *Woolfson v Strathclyde RC* [1978] SC (HL) 90 (HL); *Adams v Cape Industries plc* [1990] Ch 433; *Ord v Belhaven Pubs* [1998] 2 BCLC 447; *VTB Capital plc v Nutritek International Corp* [2013] UKSC 5, [2013] 2 AC 337. See also B Hannigan, 'Wedded to Salomon: Evasion, Concealment and Confusion on Piercing the Veil of the One-Man Company' (2013) 50 *Irish Jurist* 11.

[64] *Prest v Petrodel Resources Ltd and Others* [2013] UKSC 34, [2013] 3 WLR 1.

iii. Corporate Transparency through the Recognition of the Entrepreneurial Interest

The problem lies in the detachment and business alienation of the shareholder from the company to such an extent that he or another person (natural or legal) becomes the holder of another entrepreneurial unit, which is standing in the international social and economic environment without being integrated into a jurisdiction that regulates its responsibilities and obligations. The natural person develops an independent business activity that goes beyond the business cycle of each company. However, while the risks of business activity are fragmented into different legal entities, the profits from it are channelled to the natural person. Against third parties, this business activity as a whole is not transparent. Its overall responsibility is fragmented into multiple corporate formations and its obligations towards the society are not fulfilled. The independent and autonomous entrepreneurial unit shapes a socio-economic ontology, which cannot be ignored by the judge. Courts are obliged to look for its holder. A comparative study is necessary to demonstrate the core of piercing theories. The red thread unifying piercing theories is the entrepreneurial activity (ie, the profit-aimed activity), which leads to the coherent dogmatic basis of entrepreneurial interest and its holder.[65]

In this sense, the court is not piercing the corporate veil, but is instead recognising the new emergent interest and granting remedies against its holder. In this way, the judge defends justice and protects market transparency and the public interest.

The differential approaches within different jurisdictions share common features. It is not a coincidence that judges from different countries and legal traditions converged on their arguments and conclusions. French courts used the concept of 'society of interests', which is the core of the company, the creative web of company law. Corporate interest becomes particularly clear when considering German legislation and case law. Both qualified de facto companies group liability[66] and company's destruction liability[67] in German law target the substance of corporate/entrepreneurial interest.[68]

IV. Conclusions

By comparing the authorities at the international level, we conclude that the doctrine of piercing the corporate veil applies in cases where there is a lack of transparency concerning the identity or integrity of the corporation. The piercing jurisdiction is a

[65] K Schmidt, 'From Commercial Law to Business Law' (in Greek translation: G Sotiropoulos; *ΕΕμπΔ* 2003) 1, 10; Baur, 'The Importance of the Concept of Enterprise (Unternehmen) in German Law' (in Greek translation P Papanikolaou; *ΕλλΔνη*, 1985) 369, 375.

[66] BGH of 16 September 1985, *BGHZ* 95, 330 (Autokran-Urteil); BGH of 20 February 1989, *BGHZ* 107, 7 (Tiefbau-Urteil); BGH of 23 September 1991, *BGHZ* 115, 187 (Video-Urteil); BGH of 29 March 1993, *BGHZ* 122, 123 (TBB-Urteil).

[67] BGH of 17 September 2001, *BGHZ* 149, 10 (Bremer Vulkan); BGH of 25 February 2002, *BGHZ* 150, 61 ('L-Kosmetik'); BGH of 24 June 2002, *BGHZ* 151, 181 ('KBV'); BGH of 20 September 2004, *DStR* 2004, 2065 ('Klinik').

[68] K Schmidt, 'Die wundersame Karriere des Unternehmensbegriffs im Reich der Konzernhaftung, Überlegungen über Rechtsfortbildung und Begriffsjurisprudenz' (1994) *AG* 189.

glaring example that lacks both clarity and a coherent principle towards unifying the authorities. However, this chapter proposes a new approach to the doctrine of piercing the corporate veil through the concept of corporate/entrepreneurial interest. Tracing the features common to different theories developed under different jurisdictions, it unfolds the structural elements of the concept of corporate/entrepreneurial interest: the property and the profit-aimed activity. In all piercing cases, the judge recognises an entrepreneurial interest which is active and parallel with the corporate interest and causes a lack of transparency. The person who bears the emergent entrepreneurial interest is made responsible for the transactions undertaken by the corporation.

Furthermore, common features of different piercing theories have been illuminated in this chapter into the piercing jurisprudence. To summarise, piercing the corporate veil is allowed: (a) in situations where no other remedy is available; (b) when an individual entrepreneurial interest emerges within the corporation; (c) this entrepreneurial interest undermines the corporation to the extent that it is no longer able to fulfil its own obligations; and (d) the holder of the individual entrepreneurial interest uses the corporation to deliberately evade his own liability. Under these conditions, the judge does not pierce the corporate veil of the company, but he recognises the emergent new interest, restores corporate transparency and grants justice.

According to Heck,[69] 'it is pre-eminently through the judicial decisions that law affects human affairs. Not until the law has been embodied in judicial decisions does it become a living reality'.

[69] Schoch and Fuller (n 37) 37.

PART VI

Conclusion

18

Corporate Transparency in the Technological Frontier

NICHOLAS L GEORGAKOPOULOS

I. Introduction

The fundamental economics of information produce the result that transparency enables optimal activity and optimal matching in contracting. In tension with this benefit to society stands the desire of individual persons and businesses to hide both any drawbacks that would hurt them as well as any advantages the knowledge of which might help their competitors. Securities law imposes broad disclosure obligations, with many beneficial consequences.

After laying this foundation, this chapter continues to study how financial areas of law wrestle with the issues that new technologies pose. Whereas the gain they promise is immense, the risks they pose are not trivial. The path forward is bright, but treading cautiously will avoid dangers.

The closer look to the threats posed by co-location, artificial intelligence, cryptocurrencies, blockchain technologies, automated contracts and distributed automated organisations indicates that the new technologies do not present a radically different paradigm for regulation. Rather, vigilance and porting existing safeguards into the new medium may well be sufficient.

II. Privacy versus Transparency: Fundamentals

Disclosure and transparency have vastly different values when seen from the perspective of the individual versus that of society. Individual people and businesses benefit from secrecy in multiple ways. Individuals benefit primarily by avoiding negative consequences of undesirable traits or information. A job applicant who can hide the existence of a disadvantage may obtain employment for which a candidate without that disadvantage would be better suited. A business that can hide its precarious financial situation will attract counterparties who may have preferred to take less counterparty risk than that to which this contract exposes them.

Successful businesses also benefit from secrecy by reducing the probability that competitors may deduce the recipe for their success. Both as a matter of a process of managing the business and as a matter of a manufacturing process, the individual business will prefer not to disseminate its methods. Secrecy also benefits the individual business with respect to its strategic position regarding future plans; the less its competitors know, the better the competitive position of the business.

Investors in the business are similarly interested from an individual perspective in secrecy. Knowledge of an individual's deep pockets makes the individual a likelier target of various annoyances, such as litigation, solicitations for donations and crime.

However, society's interests about transparency are essentially the opposite. The society's productivity (commercial and not) loses from imperfect matches, whether those are in employment, contracting or personal relations.[1] Contracts should include appropriate adjustments established by the market for all features of the contract, including counterparty risk. To the extent that society decides to reward the investment and skill of innovation with intellectual property, that tends to occur in a balancing of the monopoly power those bestow against the dissemination of knowledge that they produce by the publicity of filing.[2] Trade secret law, the only part of intellectual property law that enables secrecy without extracting dissemination, may be an accidental exception, perhaps due to the historical accident of allowing private ordering with little balancing of its social consequences.[3]

III. Corporate Disclosure

Reaching the treatment of information in the corporate environment, the evolution of argumentation might be seen as counter-intuitive.

Until the late nineteenth century, the initial corporate charters were exceptional acts of state legislatures. Therefore, each charter constituted a unique legislative balancing of commercial gain against the powers that the charter bestowed on that corporation. The transition to routine incorporation at the end of the nineteenth century and the continuously more permissive corporate law (much more pronounced in the US than in Europe) changed that balancing in favour of businesses. The disclosures necessary in the corporate charter are rudimentary and the result was to enable an environment of private ordering, which translated into a lack of transparency. The change arrived with the social pressure to protect investors, initially with state laws culminating with the

[1] See generally RA Posner, 'The Economics of Privacy' (1981) 71 *American Economic Review* 405 (explaining society's interest in the least privacy and most information). The next generations of models assume significant additional complexity to justify privacy, while more recent analysis suggests complete voluntary disclosure. See A Acquisti, C Taylor and L Wagman, 'The Economics of Privacy' (2016) 54 *Journal of Economic Literature* 442.

[2] See, eg, Posner (n 1); P Moser, 'Patents and Innovation: Evidence from Economic History' (2013) 27 *Journal of Economic Perspectives* 23; B Hall, C Helmers, M Rogers and V Sena, 'The Choice between Formal and Informal Intellectual Property: A Review' (2014) 52 *Journal of Economic Literature* 375.

[3] See, eg, Hall et al (n 2); K Linton, 'The Importance of Trade Secrets: New Directions in International Trade Policy Making and Empirical Research' (2016) *Journal of International Commerce and Economics* (September), https://www.usitc.gov/publications/332/journals/katherine_linton_importance_of_trade_secrets_0.pdf.

New Deal's production of federal securities laws starting in 1933, one of the very few dramatic expansions of federal jurisdiction during the New Deal that have survived.[4]

The laissez-faire economists' reaction to the disclosure obligations that securities laws impose was puzzlement over the need for regulation. The market failure that justifies regulation was not obvious. Rather, in a voluntary regime, investors would create a pooling valuation of all stocks. The best corporations would find it worthwhile to disclose and would receive a higher valuation, producing a new pooling of lower valuation for the rest. The result would be a cascade of disclosures that would leave only the worst corporations silent.

However, this argument, which could be called the cascade-to-escape-from-pooling, rests on an assumption of a significant degree of transparency. Investors must be able to observe the profits of corporations with credibility and confidence. They must also be able to easily compare the financial performance of different corporations. However, the standardisation of accounting practices and the obligation to disclose accounting data is a result of securities laws.

Rather, persuasively justified are elements of disclosure provisions that deter and reveal fraud. Related later banking provisions similarly deter money-laundering and tax evasion. Today, given the long-term concern about terrorism, these take additional importance.

A different group of disclosure obligations is justified by facilitating corporate governance. Shareholders vote on directors, some corporate policies and corporate combinations. Yet, the complexity of the decisions makes the cost of becoming informed prohibitive for small shareholders. Disclosure provisions reduce this cost by placing the burden of informing shareholders fully on the corporation. Shareholders receive the information through the corporate disclosure with no effort on their own part and may become informed. Thus, disclosure in these settings overcomes not only a collective action problem but also a free-rider problem.[5]

However, these explanations cover only a fraction of the disclosure rules. The rules that require disclosure for mere accuracy of the stock price remain unexplained, with no regard to possible fraud or any corporate decision. Their explanation consists of two steps: first, the existence of false prices and erring traders; and, second, the deficiency from a social perspective of the corporation's motivation to maintain accurate prices.

[4] State securities laws are known as Blue Sky laws, preventing promoters from selling the blue sky to investors. Federal securities laws constitute of a string of lawmaking beginning with the Securities Act of 1933 and the Securities Exchange Act of 1934. They are a dramatic expansion of federal jurisdiction because according to the US Constitution, federal jurisdiction is enumerated, with the states retaining plenary authority, and the regulation of securities is not included in the enumerated federal powers. The New Deal era brought numerous expansions of federal authority with statutes utilising the jurisdiction over interstate commerce and the mails. Most of those expansions have failed the test of time, being overturned or repealed as federal power shrank in the late twentieth century. Examples of surviving agencies are the Federal Deposit Insurance Corporation and the Securities and Exchange Commission. Examples of agencies no longer in existence are the Federal Works Agency and the Maritime Labor Board.

[5] The collective action problem exists when a single owner would engage in different actions than the several part-owners. In this setting, a single shareholder would expend the resources to become informed about the corporate decision because its impact would justify the expenditure. Small shareholders who only enjoy a fraction of the gain or loss from the decision find the cost of becoming informed to be prohibitive. The free-rider problem aggravates the setting because even if becoming informed is cost-justified, each individual shareholder would rather have others bear that cost and then merely follow their lead.

To lawyers, the existence of false prices and erring traders seems obvious. Some economists do not hesitate to acknowledge the errors of markets. However, some finance scholars start from the evidence about the 'efficiency' of stock market prices, which means their accuracy. Therefore, from the perspective of finance, the question is not trivial, but requires proof. The proof exists in at least three forms. First is the evidence of market crashes. The dramatic change of prices in a single day cannot correspond to a true change in the underlying economic circumstances.[6] Second is the evidence of persistently false prices in various settings. The most famous is that of closed-end funds, which routinely trade at a significant discount to the value of their assets.[7] Less stark deviations from accuracy are numerous and well documented.[8] Third are models of survival of erring traders and their disproportionate influence.[9] Therefore, false prices and erring traders exist.

The existence of false prices and erring traders may justify disclosure rules in many minds. Disclosure provides information about the appropriate price of stocks and aims to counteract errors. Nevertheless, laissez-faire scholars counter that the choice of how intensely to counteract errors need not be made by the regulator, but can and should be made by private firms.

The response to the argument that businesses should establish disclosure policies voluntarily begins by recognising that the value of accurate prices is different for each trader. A key driver of this value is how often each investor trades. Accurate prices have little importance for perpetual holders of securities, as close to perpetual may be the holdings the largest index funds and large endowments, such as those of the wealthiest universities. Perpetual holders of stocks care relatively little for the accuracy of prices because they do not trade. At the opposite extreme are investors who intend to liquidate their positions in the near future. For them, the accuracy of prices is very important because it counteracts the risk of selling at falsely low prices. Investors are averse to risk. Therefore, the possibility of trading at high prices does not cancel out the risk of selling at low prices.

[6] CP Kindleberger and RZ Aliber, *Manias, Panics and Crashes: A History of Financial Crises*, 6th edn (London, Palgrave Macmillan, 2011).

[7] See, eg, JB de Long and A Shleifer, 'The Bubble of 1929: Evidence from Closed-End Funds' (1990) National Bureau of Economic Research Working Paper No 3523; G Gemmill and DC Thomas, 'Noise Trading, Costly Arbitrage, and Asset Prices: Evidence from Closed End Funds' (2002) 57 *Journal of Finance* 2571; F Black, 'An Equilibrium Model of the Crash' in S Fischer (ed), 3 *NBER Macroeconomics Annual 269* (Cambridge, MA, MIT Press, 1988) (considering the 1987 crash as an instance of increased perceived risk).

[8] See, eg, MS Rozeff and WR Kinney, 'Capital Market Seasonality: The Case of Stock Returns' (1976) 3 *Journal of Financial Economics* 379 (identifying the January effect); MR Reinganum, 'The Anomalous Stock Market Behavior of Small Firms in January' (1983) 12 *Journal of Financial Economics* 89; R Roll, 'Vas ist das? The Turn of the Year Effect and the Return Premia of Small Firms' (1983) 9 *Journal of Portfolio Management* 18; R Thaler, 'Anomalies: The January Effect' (1987) 1 *Journal of Economic Perspectives* 197.

[9] See, eg, A Shleifer and RW Vishny, 'Equilibrium Short Horizons of Investors and Firms' (1990) 80 *American Economic Review* 148; A Shleifer and RW Vishny, 'The Limits of Arbitrage' (1997) 52 *Journal of Finance* 35; JB de Long, A Shleifer, L Summers and R Waldman, 'Positive Feedback Investment Strategies and Destabilizing Rational Speculation' (1990) 45 *Journal of Finance* 379 (the existence of noise traders that 'follow the crowd' as for example, does portfolio insurance, may induce rational traders to anticipate such trends, enter in their beginning and initiate them). See also DM Cutler, JM Poterba and LH Summers, 'Speculative Dynamics and the Role of Feedback Traders' (1990) 80 *American Economic Review* 63; JB de Long, A Shleifer, LH Summers and RJ Waldmann, 'Noise Trader Risk in Financial Markets' (1990) 98 *Journal of Political Economy* 703 (the existence of noise traders increases risk; rational traders take that risk into account and therefore take smaller positions, which may be insufficient to correct the effect on prices of noise traders).

Therefore, the corporate disclosure decision should adapt to account for the median holding period of its shareholders. However, this is not a stable setting. First, the executives likely consider themselves long-term shareholders, creating a bias towards less disclosure. More sharply, however, the shorter-term shareholders will find that level of disclosure insufficient and will likely depart for different investments that are better suited to shorter horizons. The result is a policy drift towards less disclosure.

From this perspective, the regulatory imposition of a disclosure regime seeks to reverse the bias of this setting in favour of short-term ownership, and therefore more frequent trading in the stock market. More frequent disclosure makes the market more appealing to shorter-term holders than a securities market left to its own devices.

Thus, disclosure regulation from the perspective of the stock market fits into a theme of reinforcing the vitality of the stock market and fits into a self-reinforcing virtuous cycle.

The virtuous cycle runs from market liquidity to accurate prices, which led to frequent trading, which begets liquidity. The financial forces forming the cycle are that liquidity reduces the reaction of prices to trades in general, but informed trades in particular. The result is that a liquid market is more appealing to informed traders. The resulting increased competition of informed traders produces more accurate prices with less than a proportional increase of the profits of informed traders.[10] An increased accuracy of prices translates into making trading more hospitable for all trades because traders are averse to risk. Trading also becomes more appealing because the increased competition of informed traders reduces the adverse selection transaction cost that informed traders extract from other traders. Finally, the cycle completes with the increased trading activity, leading naturally to greater liquidity. More trading means more trading opportunities for every trader, so traders who seek to trade do not have to make as many concessions (in terms not only of price but also of delay) as they would in a less active market.

IV. Recent Complications

Whereas the conventional explanation of the overarching policy of securities laws towards disclosure is fundamental, the changing technological circumstances have presented new problems for disclosure policy. Some are from the recent past and are discussed here. The next section discusses those that are still evolving.

A. The Decentralisation of Exchanges: Co-location and Alternative Trading Systems

The phenomenon appeared about 25 years ago that computer-driven traders were willing to pay a fee to the exchanges in order to co-locate. To co-locate means placing the

[10] This relation is the result of the analysis by A Admati and P Pfleiderer, which was subsequently empirically confirmed. See A Admati and P Pfleiderer, 'A Theory of Intraday Patterns: Volume and Price Variability' (1984) 1 *Review of Financial Studies* 3; MJ Barclay, RH Litzenberger and JB Warner, 'Private Information, Trading Volume and Stock Return Variances' (1990) 3 *Review of Financial Studies* 233.

traders' computers in the same location as the exchange's trading engines, the exchange's computers. We now understand that the type of trading that these strategies applied was to front-run large institutional orders by a few milliseconds.

The following example provides an illustration of this. Suppose that the limit order book, ie, the standing limit orders that would be next to execute that add up to 1,000 shares supply of some stock are one to sell 200 at $10, a second to sell 200 at $10.05 and so on at increments of five cents until an order to sell 200 shares at $10.20. An order to buy 1,000 shares approaches the exchange and is detected by the co-located computer. The co-located computer buys the 1,000 shares from the existing limit orders and sells them to the new buy order at, say, $10.15. Without the co-located computer, the buy order would have average price of $10.10. The co-located system extracted a small profit. Proponents of co-location argue that the co-located trading also provided a small service and faster and more certain execution compared to gradually exhausting the ladder of limit orders to sell.

Perhaps largely in reaction to co-location trading strategies, institutional investors have moved their trading to *alternative trading systems*, sometimes known as *dark pools*. Alternative trading systems are, in essence, competing exchanges that shield their participants from co-locating traders. The most publicised one is the basis for Michael Lewis's book *Flash Boys: A Wall Street Revolt* (2014). Alternative trading systems are subject to supervision by the Securities and Exchange Commission (SEC), but they do not have an obligation to be transparent. However, in reaction to some abuses by some dark pools, they must disclose various features of their structure.[11]

From the perspective of disclosure and transparency, the strategies of co-location and the market reaction of dark pools is a step backwards. The limit order book is a transparent mechanism for trading, whereas dark pools are not.

B. Artificial Intelligence in Finance

True self-guided artificial intelligence is probably still budding in finance. True self-learning seems rare. Artificial intelligence in finance tends to mean several programming innovations: algorithmic trading, robo-advisors, automated underwriting of loans and insurance products, automated fraud detection, and computing improvements in identity and security.

Algorithmic trading refers to programmed trading by computers. For example, a trading house may have determined that some securities, stocks or bonds respond in certain ways to specific changes in the values of some indices. In other words, the trading house has identified information that gives rise to profitable trades. Algorithmic trading means the programming of a computer to collect information and to trade pursuant to

[11] See, eg, FINRA, 'FINRA Makes Dark Pool Data Available Free to the Investing Public' (2 June 2014), finra.org/newsroom/2014/finra-makes-dark-pool-data-available-free-investing-public. It is important to realise that the shape of the regulation of these evolving issues is itself evolving. See, eg, Equity Market Structure Advisory Committee Customer Issues Subcommittee, *Customer Issues Subcommittee Status Report* (3 April 2017), sec.gov/spotlight/emsac/emsac-customer-issues-subcommittee-status-report-040317.pdf (discussing improvements needed in alternative trading systems (ATS) disclosures).

a strategy. Algorithmic trading is the culprit for the 'flash crash' of 6 May 2010, in reaction to which the SEC implemented a new circuit breaker program, pausing trading when stocks change by 10 per cent.[12] A 2016 rule requires that persons associated with the design, development, modification and supervision of algorithmic trading register as securities traders.[13] The primary motivation for the rule is to ensure the safe operation of algorithmic trading and does not have a significant impact on the transparency of corporations or markets. Analysis also rues the speed of algorithmic trading for its potential to marginalise traditional traders and destabilise markets.[14] Critics also claim that algorithmic trading undermines the efficiency of capital markets due to its focus on narrow information.[15] Some predict convergence in the regulation of algorithmic trading, claiming that the US is likely to follow the path of the European Union (EU), including the requirement of traders to submit source codes, the limitation of a trader's activity in certain financial instruments, and the stricter organisational requirements on trading firms and venues.[16]

Robo-advisors are platforms that offer to retail investors the service of automated financial advice, often paired with algorithmic trading strategies.[17] While many proponents argue that robo-advisors provide financial advice and strategies at minimal cost compared to traditional investment advisors, concerns exist about the rapidly growing technology.[18] Among these is the belief that robo-advisors lack human-to-human interaction, which is argued to be a crucial and comforting part of an investor adviser/client relationship.[19] Personal financial data becoming digitised is a related risk, and robo-advisors present a challenge for financial service authorities to invest in new areas of expertise needed to adequately provide advice concerning financial strategies.[20]

Artificial intelligence also offers new opportunities in the automated underwriting of loans and insurance products. Robo-advisors are already matching consumers to insurance and mortgage services and products, opening up a Pandora's box of problems relating to data security and sharing among providers of services.[21]

Information technology has produced significant improvements in security after initially producing new vulnerabilities. One side of the new security is automated mechanisms for detecting fraud. The SEC reports several programs that use text-search techniques to identify corporate issuers likely to be involved in wrongdoing and big

[12] TCW Lin, 'The New Investor' (2013) 60 *UCLA Law Review* 678, 703–04.

[13] SEC Release 34-77551 (7 April 2016).

[14] M Woodward, 'The Need for Speed: Regulatory Approaches to High Frequency Trading in the United States and the European Union' (2017) 50 *Vanderbilt Journal of Transnational Law* 1359, 1361.

[15] Y Yadav, 'How Algorithmic Trading Undermines Efficiency in Capital Markets' (2015) 68 *Vanderbilt Law Review* 1607, 1615.

[16] Woodward (n 14) 1392–93.

[17] See SEC, Division of Investment Management, 'Guidance Update: Robo-Advisers' (February 2017), sec.gov/files/2017-03/im-guidance-2017-02.pdf.

[18] NG Iannarone, 'Computer as Confidant: Digital Investment Advice and the Fiduciary Standard' (2018) 93 *Chicago-Kent Law Review* 141, 141 (explaining that 'by 2020, robo-advisers will digitally manage $2 trillion in assets, growing over 3,000% from 2015').

[19] ibid 152.

[20] T Baker and B Dellaert, 'Regulating Robo Advice across the Financial Services Industry' (2018) 103 *Iowa Law Review* 713, 715–16.

[21] ibid 729.

data methods for fraud detection.[22] The other side is enhanced security mechanisms in various facets of the operation of financial firms, ranging from clients' log-on to internal monitoring and compliance. But by making an attempt to increase safety through new technologies, companies could possibly open themselves up to liabilities due to a lack of knowledge of quickly evolving statutes and regulations governing cybersecurity.[23] New safety technologies can also be costly for companies.[24] The advancement of enhanced security measures also puts individuals at risk of manipulation due to the amount of personal data that becomes tracked and analysed.[25]

V. New Problems

The advances of telecommunication technology and the computerisation of exchanges led to the co-location problems and the programming issues discussed in the previous section. However, continuing technological advances raise new issues.

A. Blockchain and the One-Second-Takeover

Underlying the excitement about Bitcoin and similar cryptocurrencies is their technology. Cryptocurrencies have as a foundation the practice that all transactions are recorded and reconciled in a decentralised manner. Recent transactions are recorded into electronic *blocks* or ledgers. However, any computer may enrol to maintain the ledger. With some frequency, these ledgers are reconciled.[26] The chain of the ledgers of transactions, the *blockchain*, is thus a complete record of who holds which units of the cryptocurrency and all the transactions that have resulted in the current holdings of the cryptocurrency. A more descriptive name for this process is *distributed ledger technology*, in contrast to conventional ledgers, which a central entity maintains.

NASDAQ and state corporate laws have adopted blockchain technology.[27] At least one corporation has conducted an initial public offering using blockchain technology.[28]

[22] See generally SW Bauguess, 'The Role of Big Data, Machine Learning, and AI in Assessing Risks: A Regulatory Perspective' (21 June 2017 speech), sec.gov/news/speech/bauguess-big-data-ai (discussing such efforts at the SEC).

[23] EG Orlinsky et al, 'Cybersecurity: A Legal Perspective' (2014) *Maryland Bar Journal* 32, 36 (stating that the 'legislature and other regulatory bodies across the country have recently made considerable revisions to cybersecurity related laws and regulations').

[24] ibid (explaining that some jurisdictions mandate an investigation and notification when fraud is detected, and '[t]o comply with the level and method of notification required, the cost incurred by a business can be substantial').

[25] SJ Shackelford et al, 'When Toasters Attack: A Polycentric Approach to Enhancing the "Security of Things"' (2017) *University of Illinois Law Review* 415, 427–28.

[26] At the time of these reconciliations of the many ledgers, a lottery awards one of the computers doing the reconciliation successfully (while also solving a cryptographic problem) a diminishing amount of the cryptocurrency. This is the incentive for participating in maintaining the blockchain.

[27] See, eg, A Friedman, 'The Future of Blockchain' *Financial News* (26 September 2016), sec.gov/spotlight/investor-advisory-committee-2012/friedman-future-of-blockchain.pdf (the CEO of NASDAQ discusses blockchain applications).

[28] D DeConinck, 'Overstock Completes First Public Stock Issuance Using Blockchain' (2017) 36 *Review of Banking & Financial Law* 416 (discussing the offering of bonds in 2015 and stock in Overstock on 2017).

For corporate law, the transition to a decentralised trading of shares on a blockchain framework raises some important issues: the compliance with consequences arising from crossing ownership thresholds (including control) and maintaining the ability of courts to stay, enjoin and void transaction. The corresponding soundbites are the one-second takeover and the powerless courts.

Whereas trading shares on blockchain frameworks still comprise only a small minority of the trading activity, the goal is to create an environment where most shares are traded using blockchain technology. The current trading environment occurs through brokers and clearing houses, imposing some safeguards and delays. When nearly all shares trade on blockchain technologies, enormous changes in positions would become possible instantaneously. Merely understanding which are the important safeguards that brokers currently impose is difficult, because we cannot know the violations that the blockchain would allow. Perhaps the compliance with rules about margin borrowing and against money-laundering appear to be the most important safeguards that the current environment presents, but trading on the blockchain may reveal that conventional trading produces a stronger anti-manipulation environment compared to blockchain trading.

However, taking blockchain trading in its current early form misses the important opportunity to make compliance part of the fabric of trading technology. Crossing some ownership thresholds triggers filing requirements under the securities laws. The identity of some traders, notably statutory insiders, triggers filing obligations. Corporate rights plans (poison pills) produce devastating consequences for buyers who cross specified thresholds. The securities laws impose various obligations to buyers who make tender offers (such as waiting, proration and withdrawal). The examples continue. The next generation of trading technology must produce automatic compliance with all those rules, from updating the SEC filings for buyers to blocking acquirers from accidentally triggering poison pills.

Compliance with court orders is also an important component of the trading environment. The next generation of trading technology should include structures allowing courts to enjoin or stay transactions.

B. Cryptocurrencies and the Return to the Gold Standard

Bitcoin and other cryptocurrencies have not only captured investors' imagination but have also started changing the shape of retail international finance. International payment systems have already adopted cryptocurrency technology to a large extent.[29] However, the capacity of cryptocurrency systems to meet the demands of mainstream finance is argued to be far from adequate, being far from having the capacity to handle

[29] See, eg, A Sayarina, 'Is the International Remittance Industry Headed the Cryptocurrency Way?' *Coinspeaker* (27 April 2018), coinspeaker.com/2018/04/27/international-remittance-industry-headed-cryptocurrency-way = perma.cc/VYD5-3YGY] (discussing the growth of cryptocurrency-based businesses that offer international remittances); SD Klein and FD de Martino, 'Delaware Governor Signs Groundbreaking Blockchain Legislation into Law' (27 July 2017), mofo.com/resources/publications/170727-delaware-blockchain-legislation.html.

transactions with the speed that a modern exchange would require, for example.[30] Nevertheless, the native digital nature of cryptocurrencies means that they are the future.

A major drawback of the present shape of cryptocurrencies is that they do not have the capacity to counter deflation. During a financial crisis, currency tends to become unusually strongly desired. Usually, the reason is an erosion of trust in financial institutions or markets, which produces a run to withdraw and hold currency rather than leave the funds invested. In normal economic times, by contrast, the fact that currency is not a productive investment makes it not so strongly desired. The financial crisis of 2008 illustrates this effect. Financial markets withheld financing to an unprecedented degree and central banks responded by injecting liquidity, essentially creating money, also to an unprecedented degree. Despite the strong response of the central banks, some deflation did occur.[31]

The decentralised nature of cryptocurrencies in their current form means that no entity has the authority of a central bank to increase the supply of the currency in reaction to a financial crisis. Therefore, the current shape of cryptocurrencies is that they cannot provide any relief from deflationary pressures. If central banks began issuing cryptocurrencies, it would be possible to design those cryptocurrencies in a way that the central bank would have the power to counter deflationary pressures, primarily by increasing the money supply.

The architecture of cryptocurrencies enables much more aggressive measures against panics. Pursuant to some indication of a run or at the central bank's choice, an anti-run effect could be triggered, preventing the withdrawal of the greater of some amount or some percentage from every deposit. Granted, such measures may seem overly aggressive, but the prevention of another Great Depression has justified extraordinary measures in the past and the new technologies should allow central banks to increase the number of the tools at their disposal in order to avert depressions rather than reduce them.

In closing, whatever issues cryptocurrencies raise for financial stability law, they are not central to corporate law. Granted, the issue arises whether they are securities versus being commodities. Under US law, the definition of a security is 'the investment of money with the expectation of profit [predominantly] from the effort of others'.[32]

[30] See, eg, Goldman Sachs, 'Is Bitcoin a (Bursting) Bubble?' (Podcast: Exchanges at Goldman Sachs, 10 April 2018), goldmansachs.com/our-thinking/podcasts/episodes/04-19-2018-stongin-himmelberg-currie.html (arguing that the cryptocurrency technologies must improve a lot before they can serve mainstream finance).

[31] See generally BS Bernanke, *The Federal Reserve and the Financial Crisis* (Princeton, Princeton University Press, 2013); see also I Kottasova, '$9 Trillion and Counting: How Central Banks are Still Flooding the World with Money' *CNN Money* (9 September 2016), money.cnn.com/2016/09/08/news/economy/central-banks-printed-nine-trillion/index.html (stating that the Federal Reserve injected $3.9 trillion over the course of three rounds of asset buying between November 2008 and October 2014). Despite the influx of money, deflation appeared; see Federal Reserve Bank of St Louis, Consumer Price Index for All Urban Consumers: All Items, fred.stlouisfed.org/series/CPIAUCSL (showing the Consumer Price Index dropping from 218 in July 2008 to 211 in December 2008, being flat in 2010 and experiencing occasional small drops in 2012 to 2017).

[32] *SEC v WJ Howey Co*, 328 US 293, 301 (1946) ('the test is whether the scheme involves an investment of money in a common enterprise with profits to come solely from the efforts of others'). Appellate courts have subsequently relaxed the definition by replacing 'solely' with 'predominantly' in order to encompass sellers' attempts to defeat the definition by having the buyers join as nominal partners. See, eg, *SEC v Life*

In pure cryptocurrencies, pure in the sense that their value does not depend on entrepreneurial efforts of those who issue the currency, no effort of others exists. This is in sharp distinction to different arrangements, such as the Distributed Automated Organisation (DAO), discussed below. Accordingly, pure cryptocurrencies cannot be securities, but the corresponding contracts, especially derivatives, will tend to fall under the jurisdiction of the Commodities Futures Trading Commission. In the EU, which does not follow this division between securities and other financial contracts, the answer is correspondingly more simple, turning on the definition of financial instruments.

C. Automated Contracts and the One-Second Financial Crisis

Resting on the technologies of the distributed ledger and cryptocurrencies, automated contracts execute when their conditions are met. For example, payment is made upon performance. A contract for the delivery of an item can be linked to the database of the parcel delivery service and when the database indicates that the item is delivered, the payment due upon delivery occurs automatically in the parties' chosen cryptocurrency.

A concern in automated contracts is that the legal system makes some contracts illegal. Whereas automatic payment upon the issuance of a death certificate is welcome in the case of life insurance, the same is not true in the case of a contract for murder. Because parties write the code, automated contracts allow the parties to ensure the performance of contracts that courts would not enforce.[33]

From the perspective of financial regulation, a thorough adoption of automated contracts produces a nightmare scenario of an instantaneous Great Depression. Fortunately, the premises for it are quite different from the present environment.

Imagine a world where much lending has moved to the peer-to-peer model.[34] Individuals lend to individuals. Presumably, in that environment, callable and secured loans would offer lower interest rates and also exist as they do in the current lending market that is centred on financial institutions. Imagine, then, that massive callable secured lending occurs with the collateral being some asset subject to an irrational exuberance. The corresponding automated loans are programmed to automatically call the loan

Partners, Inc, 87 F 3d 536, 550 (DC Cir 1996) ('Howey's third prong should be interpreted broadly to allow an investment contract to exist where the profits come 'predominantly', but not solely, from the efforts of others. See, eg, *SEC v International Loan Network, Inc*, 968 F 2d 1304, 1308 (DC Cir 1992)').

[33] One of the major early uses of Bitcoin was for illegal transactions, and, because identities on the blockchain generally take the form of digital signatures rather than real names, it can be difficult to identify counterparties who create illegal 'smart' contracts. See K Werbach and N Cornell, 'Contracts Ex Machina' (2017) 67 *Duke Law Journal* 313, 347–48, fn 164, 167; see also J Bearman, 'The Rise and Fall of Silk Road: Part II' *WIRED* (May 2015), wired.com/2015/05/silk-road-2 (explaining the story of Silk Road, a Bitcoin exchange commonly used for drug sales and other illegal activity).

[34] See K Judge, 'The Future of Direct Finance: The Diverging Paths of Peer-to-Peer Lending and Kickstarter' (2015) 50 *Wake Forest Law Review* 603, 604 (stating that the strong interest in peer-to-peer lending after the 2008 financial crisis was fuelled by the 'growing trend away from reliance on corporations, banks[,] and large institutions'). But see EC Chaffee and GC Rapp, 'Regulating Online Peer-to-Peer Lending in the Aftermath of Dodd-Frank: In Search of an Evolving Regulatory Regime for an Evolving Industry' (2012) 69 *Washington & Lee Law Review* 485, 505–06 (explaining the 'substantial concerns' of peer-to-peer lending, including difficulties determining borrowers' creditworthiness, problems with unsecured loans based entirely upon repayment by individual borrowers, and the low liquidity of peer-to-peer loans compared to other forms of investment).

when this asset drops below some value and perhaps foreclose. If the debtor does not have the cryptocurrency necessary for the repayment, the automated contract triggers an automated sale of the collateral. At some point in time, the collateral drops in value dramatically on a particular market in the middle of the night. Loans are called automatically, forced sales further aggravate the problem, and the majority of the population wakes up insolvent. Add to this scenario a layer of automated employment contracts that automatically terminate when the employer's financial condition worsens below some point and a swath of the population wakes up unemployed. A financial crisis is in full swing: a very large fraction of borrowers and lenders are insolvent and a large fraction of the population is unemployed. Spending plummets and production halts. The cycle of economic activity slows down severely. The economy enters a severe recession or depression.

Dangers that can be foreseen should be addressed. The web of automated contracting should include safeguards against letting this kind of a scenario unfold. Granted, automated contracts may facilitate illegal contracts and may produce systemic risk. Nevertheless, neither concern relates to corporate disclosure directly.

D. Distributed Automated Organisations

A DAO is a network of computers which perform automated tasks in coordination as an organisation. DAOs represent the next step after the technological steps of the blockchain and the automated contract. They are a web of automated contracts that act in coordination, resting on blockchain technology. A simple example of a DAO would be to simulate a mutual insurance company. The insured enter into insurance contracts that also entitle the insured to some voice and profits. The DAO invests the premiums it receives according to some algorithmic strategies, perhaps influenced by choices of the insured, pays any claims and distributes any gains to the insured.

The advantages of DAOs are analogous to those enjoyed by large corporations, the ability to engage in projects requiring large capital and wide cooperation. However, the principal experience with DAOs is one of being maliciously hacked and robbed. The first DAO, after raising about $150 million in a cryptocurrency, fell prey to a vulnerability that allowed an unknown attacker to transfer about a third of that amount away.[35]

The reaction to this fraud reveals a lot about the capacity of the well-meaning but anarchical society of cryptocurrency programmers. The visibility of all transfers and accounts allowed the community to isolate the transferred amount and preclude future transfers from the account in which it resided. The community calls this a soft fork, presumably in the sense that the software of the currency changed, but that change does not have consequences for others than this account.

[35] SEC, *Report of Investigation Pursuant to Section 21(a) of the Securities Exchange Act of 1934: The DAO* 9 (25 July 2017), sec.gov/litigation/investreport/34-81207.pdf.

The founder also managed to have more than half (actually more than 80 per cent) of the keepers of the blockchain to undo the transaction. The ledger of the cryptocurrency contains a correction, the undoing of the fraudulent transaction. However, a small minority of about 15 per cent of the keepers of the ledger considered that undoing the fraudulent transaction was improper and continued the old ledger without the correction. The result is called a hard fork. The cryptocurrency split into two cryptocurrencies, the original one pursuant to the corrected ledger and a second one pursuant to the uncorrected ledger.

The SEC produced a report after these events.[36] The report shows that the SEC considers the sales that raised the cryptocurrency investments into the DAO to be sales of securities. The report also recounts the events of the fraud and the elements of the way that this DAO was organised (no specific project was intended; rather, the members would submit project ideas, some members would filter those ideas and then the entire membership would vote on the ideas to pursue; the hack occurred before any of this intended activity occurred).[37] However, the vulnerability that allowed the hack is not discussed and the 'hard fork' is treated as a remedy that eliminates the need for SEC intervention.

Looking forward to the inevitably coming of age of government-sponsored cryptocurrencies, the incident of the DAO has optimistic lessons to offer. The danger of fraud may be reduced vastly when all transactions are visible and when accounts can be frozen after they have received improper transfers. A crypto-euro or crypto-dollar would also eliminate hard forks. Of course, from the perspective of transparency, DAOs must be programmed to comply with the transparency obligations of businesses.

VI. Conclusion

The experience with the new technologies has been one of flash crashes, hacks and similar destructive accidents. Nevertheless, technological innovation is neither reversible nor avoidable, and nor is it undesirable. Accidents are bound to occur on the way to the gains that technological innovation promises. Indeed, the internet businesses that have been successful are those that managed to overcome the weaknesses of the medium. Apple's success rests in part in the privacy that it provides to its users, not using their information for marketing. Facebook's success rests in part in the lack of anonymity and in the positive identification of its users. Both Apple and Google track accurately their users' movements from device to device and through space, and offer effective protection from hacking.

To return to the theme of corporate disclosure and transparency, the question is whether the new automated environments that are developing will trigger the transition to a new regime of transparency and disclosure. Corporations are already subject to at least two very different legal regimes. Facing the buyers of their products or services,

[36] See generally ibid.
[37] ibid 3–5, 9.

corporations use the regular contract law regime of *caveat emptor* (buyer beware). Facing the buyers of their securities, corporations are subject to the enhanced disclosure obligations of securities laws, an environment where the seller must disclose, making it the opposite of the buyer beware environment of contract law.

The transition to a digital world has already produced significant regulation regarding the use of information and its safeguarding. The open question that this volume explores in detail from several perspectives is how the transition to a digital environment will influence corporate disclosure and transparency. From the law and economics perspective, the pressure for a new regime is subdued. Rather, the challenge will be the incorporation of the current rules into the new technologies.

19

Towards the End of Anonymity in *Sociétés Anonymes*?

EVANGHELOS PERAKIS

I. Introduction

Talking about the end of anonymity, as a prospect, carries with it a question mark. To the question of whether we are moving towards the end of anonymity, a definitive yes or no answer is not possible, because we do not know if today's trend, which is clearly against anonymity, will continue tomorrow. Everything is moving today faster than in the past, despite the end of history for corporate law proposed by Henry Hansman and Reinier Kraakmann.[1] These professors argued in 2000 that the shareholder-oriented model of the corporation had reached a high degree of uniformity, characterised by five features, namely: (1) full legal personality; (2) limited liability; (3) shared ownership by investors of capital; (4) delegated management; and (5) transferable shares. In *The Anatomy of Corporate Law*, the same authors, accompanied this time by John Armour and Mariana Pargendler, repeated this list, but added that: 'Fully transferable shares do not necessarily mean *freely tradable* shares.'[2] Perhaps they might also have said: 'Fully transferable shares do not necessarily mean *bearer* shares.' But things are evolving and the components of the corporation model have a relative value. One thing we may accept with some certainty is that anonymity, ie, mainly bearer shares, is not a necessary feature of the modern corporation, not a shareholders' right, not an expectation and surely not a characteristic with a moral dimension.

Beginning with anonymity itself: after all the discussion about disclosure, which has a connotation of open air and blue sky, anonymity is an ominous-sounding term with many faces. It is member of a club comprising a host of hidden goodies, like cryptocurrencies, virtual currencies, shadow banking, dark pooling and dark trading. Like these,

[1] H Hansmann and R Kraakman, 'The End of History for Corporate Law' (2000–01) 89 *Georgetown Law Journal* 439.

[2] R Kraakman, J Armour, P Davies, L Enriques, H Hansmann, G Hertig, K Hopt, H Kanda, M Pargendler, WG Ringe and E Rock, *The Anatomy of Corporate Law*, 3rd edn (Oxford, Oxford University Press, 2017) 10.

anonymity does serve a purpose: to do business unnoticed. Whether this is a legitimate purpose remains to be seen. This is the first point.

The second point is that anonymity is not exactly the opposite of disclosure. You can abolish anonymity and still need disclosure, the main example being disclosure not just of an owner, but of the *beneficial* owner. So disclosure does not presuppose anonymity; beyond that, it has to do with apparent entitlements, like nominees, trustees, depositories, intermediaries and proxies. Therefore, disclosure like transparency is a much bigger issue, and the analysis about disclosure has abundantly shown that the areas where disclosure is meaningful transcend the cases of anonymity.

II. *Société Anonyme* and Anonymity

The question now is what is the relation between anonymity, as denoted by the term *société anonyme*, and anonymity, as a feature of that kind of company? The similarity of the terms should not mislead us. The 'anonymous' company (*société anonyme, ανώνυμη εταιρία, naamloze vennootschap, sociedad anónima, sociedade anónima* etc) is a term that has prevailed in some countries of French tradition, including Greece, where the impact of the Napoleonic Code de Commerce has been massive.[3] Sometimes funny translations of the term have been proposed, like the term 'unbennante Gesellschaft' used in 1810 by Johann Nikolaus Brauer in his Commentary of the French Napoleonic Code and the Civil Code of Baden.[4] But one should wonder if any reader of Brauer managed to understand what this literal translation might mean. In most other countries, this type of company has been named after the instrument incorporating the participation, ie, the shares, like *Aktiengesellschaft*, *società per azioni*, company limited by shares etc.

Does the term *société anonyme* or *ανώνυμη εταιρία* imply something different from the anonymity of the shares? The simplest and most plausible answer is, in my view, the one given by Georges Ripert[5] – an old acquaintance but always an authority: it has to do with the partners' liability for the debts of the company. Where the partners are fully liable for the debts of the company, the latter is a *société en nom collectif* or simply *en nom* – meaning that the company is named after the *names of the partners*, who bear the debts and the risk. On the contrary, where the members of the company have no liability, the company is 'anonymous'. This does not mean that the company has no name or that the partners are hiding; it is only a warning that the creditors cannot pursue the partners to pay what the company owes to them. Therefore, anonymity of

[3] In fact. the Napoleonic Code de Commerce was introduced in Greece after (and even during) the Independence War in 1821.

[4] See JNF Brauer, *Erläuterungen über den Code Napoleon und die Großherzogliche Badische bürgerliche Gesetzgebung* (Karlsruhe, Müller, 1810) 389; cited by A Deutsch, in W Bayer and M Habersack (eds), *Aktienrecht im Wandel, Bd 1* (Tübingen, Mohr Siebeck, 2007) 339.

[5] See G Ripert, *Aspects juridiques du capitalisme moderne*, 2nd edn (Paris, Pichon, 1951) 59: 'Cette expression société anonyme est empruntée à l'ancienne langue juridique, mais elle change de sens. Elle désignait dans l'Ancien droit la participation occulte. Elle va maintenant désigner la société dans laquelle il n'y a pas d'associé responsable, donc pas de raison sociale.'

the 'anonymous company' denotes a fact: lack of liability, ie, the second feature proposed by Hansman and Kraakman, and not the fifth feature, ie, free transferability of shares.

III. Strategies of Anonymity

It follows that when anonymity (and the end of it) is examined, it is pertinent to ignore the term *société anonyme* and instead focus on the features of that type of company which allow the investors to go unnoticed, and see if these features are well established or if they are fading out. Therefore, let us see how anonymity is manifested. The most spectacular feature producing anonymity – independently of the term 'anonymous' – is of course bearer shares. We will see that later on in this chapter, but let us first meet some other aspects of anonymity:

(a) First, *secret ballots*: this is rather a question of 'internal' anonymity. A secret ballot takes place when shareholders do not wish to disclose to their fellow shareholders and the company's management how they have cast their votes, especially in cases of elections or nominations. National laws differ as to whether voting has to take place openly or secretly. In many jurisdictions, secret voting used to be the rule, and it is significant that Greek law provides for a minority right to request an open voting.[6]

However, opinions shift in favour of open voting. In Greece, for example, a court decision of 2003 held that secret ballot is the rule.[7] A few years later, an author admitted that secret ballot may still be the rule, but open ballot is gaining ground,[8] whereas in a more recent article, Professor Marinos has concluded that open voting must be the rule,[9] and this evolution corresponds to the need to know how shareholders have voted in order to see, for example, if a resolution of the general meeting is abusive. This rule also seems to be in force in other countries, for example, France, where voting is generally carried out *à mains levées*,[10] or Switzerland, where open voting is considered to be the 'preferred' way of voting,[11] whereas in Germany, the matter is usually decided by the chairman of the general meeting.[12] There are even cases where a shareholder may be obliged to disclose how he voted. An example is given by Article 3g of Directive 2007/36, as amended in 2017 by Directive 2017/828 (SRD II), where it is provided that institutional investors and asset managers are obliged to disclose how they have cast their votes in the general meetings of companies.

[6] Article 39 of codified Law 2190/1920 (art 141 of the new Law 4548/2018).

[7] Single Member Court of First Instance 2327/2003 (2004) *Episkopisi Emporikou Dikaiou* 215.

[8] E Tziva, 'Commentary on Art 31–35 of Greek Company Law' in V Antonopoulos and S Mouzoulas (eds) *Sociétés Anonymes* (Athens, Nomiki Vivliothiki, 2013) art 31 no 10–11. See also A Spyridonos, *Minority Rights in the SA*, 2nd edn (Athens, Nomiki Vivlothiki, 2016) 197.

[9] M Marinos, 'Legality of GM Resolutions in Case of a Secret Ballot and Attendance of Non-shareholders' (2013) *Chronika Idiotikou Dikaiou* 627.

[10] P Merle and A Fauchon, *Droit Commercial: Sociétés commerciales*, 20th edn (Paris, Dalloz, 2017) 607 no 543.

[11] V Roberto and HR Trüb, *Handkommentar zum Schweizer Privatrecht, Personengesellschaften und AG*, 2nd edn (Zürich, Schulthess, 2012) OR 703, 8.

[12] R Ek, *Praxisleifaden für die Hauptvesammlung*, 3th edn (Munich, CH Beck, 2018) 106.

(b) Anonymity can be also achieved by means of contractual arrangements, mainly *shareholder agreements* (or voting agreements or extrastatutory agreements). By such agreements, often bearing confidentiality clauses, the corporate power can be shifted from an apparent majority to a minority shareholder or a third party. National laws treat such agreements as valid within certain limits, such as the violation of provisions of public order. However, many shareholder agreements are not disclosed to third parties and provide for their enforcement by means of sophisticated clauses avoiding the court system.

Shareholders' agreements are sometimes taken into account by the law. For example, the Transparency Directive (Directive 2004/109/EC, as amended) treats as a controlled undertaking any undertaking where a person or entity is a shareholder controlling a majority of the shareholders' voting rights, 'pursuant to an agreement entered into with other shareholders or members of the undertaking in question' (Article 2(1)(f)(iii)). This is the kind of agreement which, if not disclosed, produces anonymity in the broader sense of the term, ie, uncertainty as to the person exercising in fact the corporate power. The same applies to the notification requirement of a shareholder who has concluded an agreement with another shareholder, 'which obliges them [these shareholders] to adopt, by concerted exercise of the voting rights they hold, a lasting common policy towards the management of the issuer in question' (Article 10(a)). This provision is interesting because the issue is not one of disclosure of who owns the shares, but of concerted voting. So, these examples can help us to understand that although a general duty of shareholders to disclose their private agreements has never been enacted,[13] in situations like those involving the Transparency Directive, disclosure is mandatory in order to avoid anonymity.

(c) A third manifestation of anonymity in a broad sense is nominee shareholders. Nominees are frowned upon, for example, by the Anti-Money Laundering (AML) Directive (EU) 2015/849 (recently amended by Directive (EU) 2018/843), which in Annex III contains a list of factors signalling a potentially higher risk of money laundering and terrorist financing, and one of them is 'companies that have nominee shareholders or shares in bearer form'. So here we have two things that are equally risky – nominees and bearer shares.

(d) Other strategies for escaping disclosure regimes can be derivatives, pyramid structures, multiple voting shares, chains of corporate vehicles etc.[14]

These are some examples of anonymity or strategies for concealing the identity of a shareholder; however, bearer shares are the most common strategy.

IV. Bearer Shares

Bearer shares (or unregistered shares or 'anonymous' shares) are so named because the identity of their owner, the shareholder, is neither mentioned on the share

[13] See M Marinos, *Extra-statutory Agreements between Shareholders* (Athens, Sakkoulas 2011) 75.

[14] See M Fenwick and E Vermeulen, 'Disclosure of Beneficial Ownership after the Panama Papers' (2016) *Lex Research Topics in Corporate Law & Economics Working Paper No 2016-3*, papers.ssrn.com/sol3/Papers.cfm?abstract_id=2777152.

certificate, nor is it registered in a shareholders' registry. Normally, they can be transferred by simple delivery of the instrument that incorporates them, although in the case of bearer shares for which no instrument has been issued, their transfer is normally made by ordinary assignment or, if dematerialised, from account to account.

Bearer shares are an old feature of limited companies. It seems that they were already in use in the seventeenth century,[15] whereas in England they were introduced in 1867.[16] Many countries allow this type of shares, for example, France (see Article L 228-1 of the Code de commerce), Germany (§ 23 III 5 of the Aktiengesetz), Italy (Codice Civile 2354) or Spain (art 23-d of Real Decreto Legislativo 1/2010)), but the list is shrinking, as we shall see.

V. Bearer Shares: Pros and Cons in Terms of Company Law

In terms of company law, anonymity has some advantages, the most important being the easy proof of ownership (the possessor is deemed to own) and the easy transfer of the shares. It is also safer and re-assuring to stay unknown. But this is of course a controversial advantage and has a relative value. The need to avoid identification and obscure one's assets may seem under the circumstances to be ethically dubious and cannot provide a complete justification of bearer shares, although one has to be sensitive to fears of blackmailing, kidnapping etc.[17]

Bearer shares have additional problems. First of all, the term 'bearer shares' itself is today difficult to grasp, at least when shares are dematerialised, because – as Philippe Merle asks – who can 'bear' a share that does not physically exist?[18] Going beyond terminology, we can see functional problems associated with bearer shares; for example, bearer shares are blamed for fostering short-termism because they facilitate change of ownership instead of the 'long-term engagement' of shareholders[19] promoted by the recent SRD II.[20] Bearer shares imply provisional participation and lack of interest to serve a company's sustainability, and prevent what the French call *la fidélisation de l'actionnariat* (the loyalty of shareholders),[21] which is promoted by the Directive. Other disadvantages might also be identified, like the vulnerability of the issuing company to hostile takeovers, the need to go through some procedure if the shares are lost etc.

[15] A Cordes and K Jahntz in Bayer and Habersack (n 4) 19.

[16] J Lieder in Bayer and Habersack (n 4) 339.

[17] See U Noack, 'Identifikation der Aktionäre, neue Rolle der Intermediäre – zur Umsetzung der Aktionärsrechte-Richtlinie II' (2017) 20 *Neue Zeitschrift für Gesellschaftsrecht* 561, 567: 'Diese sollte die Übertragbarkeit erleichtern, hatten aber nicht den Zweck, anonymen Aktienbesitz zu ermöglichen.'

[18] Merle and Fauchon (n 10) 323: '[L]es valeurs mobilières n'ayant plus de support matériel, la notion de titre au porteur aurait dû disparaitre: qui peut en effet porter un titre qui n'existe plus?'

[19] On the shareholders' engagement, see B Hannigan, *Company Law* (Oxford, Oxford University Press, 2012) 128.

[20] See B Lecourt, 'L'actionnaire de long terme, nouvelle notion européenne' (2017) *Revue des sociétés* 675.

[21] P Barban, 'L'identification des actionnaires' (2017) *Revue de sociétés* 678.

VI. Dangers of Anonymity: Non-company Law

The main criticism against bearer shares does not originate in company law. There are many considerations *outside* company law which come into play, mainly tax considerations, money laundering, terrorism, criminality financing etc. It is significant that at the European level, the problem of bearer shares is mostly addressed not by any company law directive, but by Article 10 of the AML Directive. In Annex III, this directive considers as factors of potentially higher risk 'companies that have nominee shareholders or shares in bearer forms'. It also requires that: 'Member states shall take measures to prevent misuse of bearer shares and bearer share warrants.'

The emblematic reasons for this distrust are the so-called 'Panama Papers', 'Paradise Papers' and other papers, which have revealed the mobility of capital, the extent of potential misuse of the offshore finance industry, the interconnection of tax with crime and, finally, the vulnerability of the unnamed shares. These 'papers' have contributed to the mood of public scepticism that currently surrounds the financial services industry. Taxation is also a crucial factor, not only as a matter of tax evasion, but also – less importantly – because bearer shares do not make it possible to draw up a complete inventory of the taxpayers' assets.[22] All this can explain that, as time passes, the reaction against bearer shares, as a means of facilitating illicit activity, is turning almost into a crusade.

A. The OECD (Taxation)

One of the champions of this crusade is the Organisation for Economic Co-operation and Development (OECD) and the Global Forum on Transparency and Exchange of Information for Tax Purposes, which works as a branch of the OECD and 'supports governments around the world in enhancing the efficiency of tax enforcement and increasing the level of tax compliance'. The Forum has repeatedly warned governments against bearer shares:

> The size and scale of offshore tax evasion are exposed by the various data leaks that have occurred over the last few years. Many of the schemes involved the issue of bearer shares. The Global Forum has repeatedly warned of the dangers bearer shares pose to good tax administration and has convinced many countries to do away with such regimes, leaving only a handful in place.[23]

In its last report (2017),[24] the Forum was happy to announce considerable progress. Many countries have taken measures against bearer shares, mainly in three ways: they

[22] See Merle and Fauchon (n 10) 322 no 315 ('pour la mise en œuvre de l'impôt sur les grandes fortunes').
[23] See oecd.org/tax/transparency/global-forum-annual-report-2017.pdf.
[24] See ibid.

introduced custodial arrangements, they introduced non-custodial reporting arrangements or they abolished bearer shares altogether.

B. The FATF (Criminality)

Another soldier in the war against bearer shares is the Financial Action Task Force (FATF). The FATF is an intergovernmental body established in 1989 by countries representing most major financial centres. Its objectives are to set standards and promote the effective implementation of legal, regulatory and operational measures for combating money laundering, terrorist financing and other related threats to the integrity of the international financial system. As is noted in its website, the FATF is a 'policy-making body', which works to generate the necessary political will to bring about national legislative and regulatory reforms in these areas.[25] It has elaborated 'International Standards on Combating Money Laundering and the Financing of Terrorism & Proliferation', the so-called 'FATF Recommendations',[26] which the AML Directive closely follows.

The FATF's Recommendation 24, as updated in February 2018, is about 'Transparency and beneficial ownership of legal persons'. It recommends that:

> Countries should ensure that there is adequate, accurate and timely information on the beneficial ownership and control of legal persons that can be obtained or accessed in a timely fashion by competent authorities. In particular, countries that have legal persons that are able to issue bearer shares or bearer share warrants, or which allow nominee shareholders or nominee directors, should take effective measures to ensure that they are not misused for money laundering or terrorist financing.[27]

In the interpretive note to Recommendation 24, the FATF proposes concrete measures for the prevention of misuse:

> 14. Countries should take measures to prevent the misuse of bearer shares and bearer share warrants, for example by applying one or more of the following mechanisms: (a) *prohibiting* them; (b) converting them into registered shares or share warrants (for example through *dematerialisation*); (c) *immobilising* them by requiring them to be held with a regulated financial institution or professional intermediary; or (d) requiring shareholders with a controlling interest *to notify* the company, and the company to record their identity.

This list of measures (prohibition, dematerialisation, immobilisation and notification) is in fact similar to the three measures of the Global Forum, ie, custodial arrangements, non-custodial reporting and outright abolition of bearer shares. Using the list of the FATF, we can see some examples of the measures taken by certain countries.

[25] See www.fatf-gafi.org/about/.

[26] See www.fatf-gafi.org/publications/fatfrecommendations/documents/fatf-recommendations.html.

[27] See www.fatf-gafi.org/media/fatf/documents/recommendations/pdfs/FATF%20Recommendations%202012.pdf.

VII. Examples of National Measures to Prevent Misuse

A. Prohibition to Issue New Bearer Shares and Conversion of Existing Bearer Shares into Registered Shares

A characteristic example is the UK, where bearer shares were abolished as of 26 May 2015 by the Small Business, Enterprise and Employment Act 2015 in order to make company ownership more transparent. In summary, this Act prohibited companies from issuing new bearer shares and directed existing ones to be surrendered and registered. Since May 2015, the company must apply to the court for an order for the shares to be cancelled, paying into court the issue price of the shares plus any accrued dividends up to cancellation.[28]

A similar conversion into registered shares has been provided in Austria (GesRÄG 2011), but only for non-listed companies. As from 1 January 2014, bearer shares are considered to be registered.[29] The Isle of Man also converted in 2011,[30] Hong Kong in 2012[31] and – most importantly – the US in 2007.[32]

Another example is Greece. The recent Law 4548/2018 abolished bearer shares, which will take effect in January 2020. In the meantime, no new bearer shares can be issued.

B. Dematerialisation

An example of dematerialisation is Belgium. On 14 December 2005, the Belgian legislator introduced a gradual abolition of bearer shares. During the first phase, which started on 1 January 2008 and ended on 31 December 2013, new bearer shares of listed companies could no longer be issued and had to be dematerialised. Since 1 January 2014, all bearer shares have been automatically converted into registered or dematerialised shares, depending on the company's articles of association.[33]

C. Immobilisation

Examples of immobilisation can be seen in Luxembourg and Panama. In Luxembourg, according to the Law of 28 July 2014 on the immobilisation of bearer shares, these must be deposited with a professional depositary located in Luxembourg, which can

[28] https://www.lexology.com/library/detail.aspx?g=a8e97ede-6a00-4191-b844-2bcf5ae90e9d.

[29] https://www.luxcsd.com/luxcsd-en/products-and-services/assetservices/austria--austrian-registered-shares/67868.

[30] www.mondaq.com/IsleofMan/x/221004/offshore+financial+centres/The+Companies+Prohibition+Of+Bearer+Shares+Act+2011.

[31] https://www.cr.gov.hk/en/companies_ordinance/docs/part4-e.pdf.

[32] https://www.angloinfo.com/blogs/global/us-tax/the-transparency-noose-tightens-bearer-shares-keep-biting-the-dust/.

[33] See www.ing.be/static/legacy/SiteCollectionDocuments/dematerialisation-of-securities-en.pdf.

be a bank or financial institution, a notary, a lawyer or a Luxembourg Certified Public Accountant (CPA). The custodian must have a bearer shares register indicating the name of each shareholder and the number of shares held by each one. The transfer of bearer shares is made by registering the transfer in the bearer shares register. Bearer shares cannot confer rights (namely, the right to participate or vote in the Shareholders General Meeting and to receive dividends), unless these bearer shares are deposited through a depositary. Until they are, they do not confer any rights.[34]

Even Panama, after the Panama Papers, immobilised bearer shares in August 2013. Anyone in possession of bearer shares issued by Panamanian companies was required either: (1) to deposit his certificates with an authorised custodian, which could be a lawyer, a law firm, a bank or a trust company, which in return issued a custody certificate; or (2) to allow the company to cancel the bearer shares and issue nominative shares.[35] Panama was followed by some other 'similar' countries, such the British Virgin Islands[36] and Singapore.[37]

D. Notification

The case of Switzerland is interesting. In order to achieve transparency that Switzerland needed as a financial centre, the new Article 697i of the Code of Obligations, as amended on 1 July 2015, established a general duty for all owners of non-listed bearer shares to report themselves (*Meldepflicht*) as a condition for exercising their shareholders' rights. This is not a one-time identification, but a permanent duty to identify itself as a shareholder. Every shareholder must submit to the company some personal data, ie, name, address, photo, photocopy of identity card, passport or driving licence. Persons conducting a business have to submit certificates of the relevant commercial registry. On the basis of this reporting, a registry of bearer shares (a '*Verzeichnis*' – Article 697l)[38] has to be kept by each company. This registry includes shareholders who alone or in concert with others hold more than 25 per cent of the capital or the votes. A 'registry of bearer shares' may seem an oddity and a contradiction in terms,[39] but the system is only a first step towards the end of the anonymity of shares in Switzerland. A second step is now expected to take place involving the outright abolition of bearer shares. This is expected to happen in 2019.[40]

These examples do not allow us to say which system is the most effective and also the least troublesome during the transition. The hostility to bearer shares is a fairly recent attitude and experience is lacking in this respect. Therefore, it is understandable that some countries hesitate to proceed with a full abolition and prefer hybrid schemes.

[34] See https://www.fiduciaire-lpg.lu/en/publications/corporate-law/bearer-shares.

[35] See www.step.org/panama's-government-approves-bearer-shares-immobilization-law.

[36] See http://bviincorporation.com/BVI.Business.Companies.Act/Immobilisation.of.Bearer.Shares.

[37] See https://www.startupdecisions.com.sg/singapore/company-law/singapore-companies-amendment-act-2017.

[38] 'Die Gesellschaft führt ein Verzeichnis über die Inhaberaktionäre sowie über die der Gesellschaft gemeldeten wirtschaftlich berechtigten Personen.'

[39] On the problems of a registry of bearer shares, see A Tucci in P Abbadessa and GB Portale (eds), *Il nuovo diritto delle società – Liber Amicorum Gian Franco Campobasso 1* (Milan, Wolters Kluwer, 2007) 619 fn 5.

[40] https://www.lexology.com/library/detail.aspx?g=e7df0e4e-78b1-497c-9715-769ac29cd7e8.

E. Other Measures: '*Titres au Porteur Identifiables*' (France) – The EMCA

This is where France comes in, with its *titres au porteur identifiables* – instruments between registered and bearer shares (Code de commerce L 228-2); such *titres* were introduced in 2001. The company may ask the Central Securities Depository (CSD) to supply identifying information regarding persons holding Titres au Porteur Identifiables (TPI). If the company feels that any person on the list holds shares for somebody else as an intermediary, it can ask such a person to disclose the real shareholder.[41]

It would also be interesting to mention the European Model Corporate Act (EMCA),[42] which was drafted by a group of law professors. This is worth mentioning because it shows some reluctance in suggesting the outright ban of bearer shares.

The group considered advocating a ban on bearer shares along the lines of the Belgian model, but in the end refrained from doing so because in several countries, a deep attachment to bearer shares exists, at least for certain types of company. It remains to be seen whether this will survive the international regulatory tide. For the time being, the EMCA thinks that a balance can be struck between the desire for more transparency while still allowing bearer shares by a system of mandatory disclosure of large (more than three or five per cent) shareholdings, as has been organised for listed companies by the EU Transparency Directive. Such a system could be expanded to non-listed (including private) companies.[43]

VIII. How the Bearer System Fades Out

All in all, registered shares are gaining ground. Ulrich Noack[44] notes that around the shift of the millennium, registered shares experienced a comeback due to what he calls 'hard' (ie, legal) and 'soft' (ie, practical) reasons. For example, the law forbids the issuance of bearer shares, which are not fully paid up or which are issued by certain types of companies, like credit institutions. It should be added that the law can expand the use of registered shares in other situations too, like in France, where shares owned by the board members must be registered (Article L 225-109 of the Code of Commerce).

The soft reasons are abundant. The nature of some companies, like family companies or companies susceptible to being taken over, makes the choice of registered shares almost unavoidable. Conversely, the dream of anonymity and privacy is short-lived and anybody who wishes to find anybody's assets and is willing to spend some money in order to do so will manage at the end of the day to have the information he needs. It is also argued that strategies such as having nominees or bearer shares or even invoking the attorney-client privilege can offer some layers of privacy, but at the end of the day,

[41] Merle and Fauchon (n 10) 323.

[42] papers.ssrn.com/sol3/papers.cfm?abstract_id=2929348.

[43] See EMCA, Chapter 5, Shares, 99 at the end of 'General Comments', papers.ssrn.com/sol3/papers.cfm?abstract_id=2929348.

[44] U Noack in Bayer and Habersack (n 4) 526.

the real entitlement will be found out.[45] Besides, comparing successive lists of shareholders who attended general meetings can provide valuable information about their identity; moreover, the issuance of shares is less and less frequent in the classic form of paper; the owners of shares (especially of listed shares) appear in electronic records and their names can often be retrieved by interested parties in central depositories and other intermediaries. The system of transferring listed shares is not always compatible with anonymity. Tax reasons can also make the bearer system totally ineffective, as occurred in Greece in the past, where the bearer shares could not be transferred unless the tax office was notified.[46] All of these, as well as the fact that a more protectionist climate takes hold internationally, are reasons why the bearer system is fading out. As Ulrich Noack (again) asked, 'Inhaberaktie eine sterbende Aktienart?'[47] (are bearer shares a dying form of shares?). And some authors have asked why bearer shares are still around in the first place.[48]

IX. Indirect Holding

At the end of this chapter, another aspect of anonymity must be mentioned, which is *indirect holding.*[49] Holding shares for somebody else, ie, the actual provider of capital, is a longstanding problem, but is always a hot topic. Intermediaries, and especially the chain of intermediaries, with their sophisticated organisation, as well as omnibus accounts, are creating problems equivalent to those of anonymity. Especially in cross-border situations, through complex chains of intermediaries and through the use of electronic means, the identity of shareholders is often lost. The problem here is not finding who is hiding behind a bearer share, but rather finding who is hiding behind the person appearing to own shares, whether these be bearer or registered. The need to address this problem is the same as for the abolition of bearer shares: indirect holding contributes to tax avoidance, criminality and money laundering.

The problem of indirect holdings is addressed by various systems of identification of the 'ultimate beneficial owner'. For example, under the AML Directive of 2015, such identification is a duty of the company. According to Article 30, any issuer has the duty to hold (and therefore to collect) 'adequate, accurate and current' information not only on the legal owners but also on the beneficial owners of the relevant entity, which is the 'customer'. This applies in principle to shares or voting rights or other means of control, whether they are in registered or in bearer form. Such information must be available at all times in interconnected registries and must be constantly updated. It must be accessible by the competent authorities, the obliged entities (banks etc) and any third party having a legitimate interest. The accessible information must include

[45] See P Nicolosi, 'Can Business Owners Stay Anonymous?', https://www.internetlegalattorney.com/can-business-owners-stay-anonymous.

[46] See how anonymity is frustrated in practice in ibid.

[47] Noack (n 44) 561, 567.

[48] An old question; see MA Frison-Roche and M Jockey, 'Pourquoi existe-t-il encore des titres au porteur?' (1994) *Juris-Classeur Périodique* 344.

[49] On the indirect investors, see Hannigan (n 19) 136.

at least the name, the date of birth, the nationality and the country of residence of the beneficial owners.

Listed companies are in principle exempted (see the definition of 'beneficial owner' in Article 3(6) of the AML Directive), but listed companies are subject to their own identification requirements, especially that of the SRD II.

The AML Directive does not give any hint (as the SRD II does) on how a company will identify its shareholders, let alone the beneficiary shareholders. It is fair to say that the company must make all efforts to collect the necessary information, this obligation being, as argued in France,[50] an obligation of *moyens* (means) rather than of *résultats* (results).

X. Conclusion: The Comeback of Anonymity?

One is tempted to say that the end of anonymity is definitely here. Bearer shares have either been replaced by registered shares or neutralised through an identification procedure. Is that irreversible?

Maybe not. An advantage of bearer shares is that, against all odds, they can give a competitive advantage to the countries where they are available. So theoretically what might happen is something like the following.

In the 'What if' section of *The Economist* of 15 July 2017 – less than two years ago – the newspaper discussed what could happen if Britain exits the UK and becomes what the (anti-Brexit) paper called 'Singapore-on-Thames'. What might the UK do to create a comparative advantage and compete against the EU? Well, said *The Economist*, among other things, bearer shares might be re-introduced, having been abolished in 2015. That is political fiction, of course. But it is a good example to show that irreversibility bears another big question mark, like the question mark in the title of this chapter.

[50] J Lasserre Capdeville, 'L'identification du bénéficiaire effectif en droit des sociétés' (2018) *Revue des sociétés* 7, 12; J Lasserre Capdeville, 'Nouveau décret du 18 avril 2018 à propos de l'identification du bénéficiaire effectif en droit des sociétés' (2018) *Revue des sociétés* 423.

20

Delineating Transparency for Stock Corporations and its Prospects

VASSILIOS TOUNTOPOULOS

I. Introduction: Transparency as a Multi-dimensional Phenomenon

Transparency has long been a central feature of company and capital market regulation on both sides of the Atlantic.[1] In the US, disclosure is considered to be the foundation of federal securities law,[2] while the pivotal role of transparency in the architecture of financial regulation[3] and company law[4] has also been widely recognised in the EU.[5] The importance of transparency is also well recognised in the case law of the European Court of Justice (ECJ). In *Geltl*, the ECJ held that the prompt and fair disclosure of information to the public enhances market integrity,[6] while in *Inspire Art*, it ruled that English disclosure requirements were sufficient to protect people dealing with an

[1] On the importance of transparency, see generally the Organisation for Economic Co-operation and Development (OECD) principles of corporate governance from 2015, according to which 'a strong disclosure regime that promotes real transparency is a pivotal feature of market-based monitoring of companies and is central to shareholders' ability to exercise their shareholders rights on an informed basis'.

[2] See the message of President Franklin D Roosevelt to Congress encouraging the enactment of the Securities Act, noting that a mandatory disclosure regime 'adds to the ancient rule of caveat emptor, the further doctrine, "let the seller also beware". It puts the burden of telling the whole truth on the seller. It should give impetus to honest dealing in securities and thereby bring back public confidence'. S Rep No 73-47 (1933) 6–7 and HR Rep No 73-85 (1933) 1–2.

[3] See H Brinckmann, 'Disclosure System – Foundations' in R Veil (ed), *European Capital Markets Law* (Oxford, Hart Publishing, 2017) 263.

[4] Some authors consider mandatory disclosure rules to be the price for limited liability. See generally on this discussion H Merkt, *Unternehmenspublizität* (Tübingen, Mohr Siebeck, 2000) 317.

[5] See Report of the High Level Group of Companies Experts (2002, available at: papers.ssrn.com/sol3/abstract_id=315322) 34. The Group recognised that recognised that 'requiring disclosure can be a powerful regulatory tool in company law. It enhances the accountability for and the transparency of the company's governance and its affairs'. See also S Kalss and C Klampfl, *Europäisches Gesellschaftsrecht* (Munich, CH Beck, 2015) 89 ff; P Davies and S Worthington, *Gower's Principles of Modern Company Law* (London, Sweet & Maxwell, 2016) 689, 690: 'On the basis that "forewarned is forearmed" the fundamental principle underlying the Companies Act has always been that of disclosure … disclosure is the bed-rock of company law.'

[6] Case C-19/11, *Markus Geltl v Daimler AG*, ECLI:EU:C:2012:397, para 34.

English limited company.[7] Bearing this case law in mind, a discussion was triggered at the beginning of the millennium on whether transparency (disclosure) rules could replace mandatory substantive provisions in company law (*Informationsmodell*).[8]

The situation has now changed dramatically. We are living in the information age, where the information explosion has greatly affected all aspects of social organisation and financial activities. Moreover, the uncovering of financial scandals (eg, the Panama Papers and WikiLeaks), the fight against terrorism as well as the recent frenetic pace of innovation spearheaded by cryptotechnologies have created a totally new landscape at the global level.[9] As a result, the discourse over the transparency of stock corporations goes far beyond classic company and capital market law issues such as the Efficient Capital Market Hypothesis (ECMH)[10] and behavioural finance,[11] which until recently dominated company and capital market law debates. Arguments outside company and capital market law, such as the fight against money laundering and terrorist financing,[12] the response to tax evasion,[13] environmental protection[14] and the protection of human rights,[15] among other things, are shaping public policy discussion on the transparency of stock corporations,[16] especially multinational corporations.[17]

The different aspects and origins of the above-mentioned arguments make it clear that the transparency of stock corporations has become a multi-dimensional phenomenon. The multi-dimensionality of transparency could be considered a by-product of the modern information society. Therefore, in order to better understand the transparency phenomenon, we have to take into consideration the new

[7] Case C-167/01, *Kamer van Koophandel en Fabrieken voor Amsterdam v Inspire Art*, ECLI:EU:C:2003:512, para 135.

[8] Reports of the High-Level Group of Companies Experts (n 5) 34: 'The EU, in considering new – and amending existing – regulation of company law, should carefully consider whether disclosure requirements are better suited to achieve the desired effects than substantive rules.' See on the information model H Merkt, 'European Company Law Reform: Struggling for a More Liberal Approach' (2004) *European Company and Financial Law Review* 3; S Grundmann, 'Ausbau des Informationsmodells im Europäischen Gesellschaftsrecht' (2004) *Deutsches Steuerrecht* 232; U Grohmann, *Das Informationsmodell im Europäischen Gesellschaftsrecht* (Berlin, De Gruyter, 2006) 56; N Vervessos, 'Das Informationsmodell im Gesellschaftsrecht – Überlegungen zur Information als Gläubigerschutzinstrument' in K Riesenhuber, F Klinck and I Karakostas (eds), *Information als Schutzinstrument* (Baden-Baden, Nomos, 2013) 131.

[9] See ch 18.

[10] See generally E Fama, 'Efficient Capital Markets: A Review of Theory and Empirical Work' (1970) 25 *Journal of Finance* 383.

[11] See generally R Schiller, 'From Efficient Markets Theory to Behavioral Finance' (2003) 17 *Journal of Economic Perspectives* 83; L Klöhn, *Kapitalmarkt, Spekulation und Behavioral Finance* (Berlin, Duncker & Humblot, 2006) 140 ff.

[12] See ch 11.

[13] See generally J Wheater, 'New Global Information Exchange Regimes and the Impact on the Financial Industry Worldwide' (2017) 18 *Business Law International* 3.

[14] See ch 7.

[15] See, for example, R Lindsay, A Kirkpatrick and J Low, 'Hardly Soft Law: The Modern Slavery Act 2015 and the Trend towards Mandatory Reporting on Human Rights' (2017) 18 *Business Law International* 29.

[16] See, eg, J Parkinson, 'Disclosure and Corporate Social and Environmental Performance' (2003) 3 *Journal of Corporate Law Studies* 3.

[17] See OECD Guidelines for multinational enterprises 2011. See also D Szabó and K Sørensen, 'Non-financial Reporting, CSR Frameworks and Groups of Undertakings: Application and Consequences' (2017) 17 *Journal of Corporate Law Studies* 137.

macro-economic environment. Although this can help us explain the special features of transparency issues, it cannot always give us practical answers to specific questions. Delineating transparency when it comes to stock corporations, its rationales, limitations and perspectives as an integrated phenomenon remains a complex and multi-parametric equation.

That being said, as a general remark, we have to highlight that the goal of this book is to provide some insights that will allow policy makers and legal scholars to better understand the transparency of stock corporations as an integrated phenomenon. Again, this book has not attempted to answer all questions relating to transparency; besides, the question of transparency is not a binary one.[18] Its aim was to pose the main issues of transparency from different (but not exhaustive) perspectives and angles. Having done this, the question now is whether we can find a common denominator to approach the transparency phenomenon in stock corporations. In order to answer this question, the first step is to abstractly define transparency.

II. Definition, Forms and Features

In the EU legal environment, there is no single and generally accepted definition of transparency.[19] Besides, due to the broadness of the term and its extended scope of application, such a definition would not be possible. Accordingly, at the EU level, there are no systemised or codified provisions on transparency as an integrated phenomenon.[20] Nonetheless, the principle of transparency (openness) applies both vertically[21] and horizontally in public[22] and private[23] law. The degree, intensity and extent of transparency required by various provisions vary considerably. The specific characteristics of transparency are linked both to the letter and the aim of the provision in question. Hence, it is obvious that the Anti-Money Laundering (AML) Directive has a completely different perception of transparency from trade secret law.

[18] On the ad hoc analysis required for the disclosure of information in competition law, see, eg, Case C-536/11, *Bundeswettbewerbsbehörde v Donau Chemie*, ECLI:EU:C:2013:366, para 34.

[19] See generally on the multiple notions of transparency H Merkt, *Unternehmenspublizität* (Tübingen, Mohr Siebeck, 2000) 6.

[20] There are, of course, some special and sectoral laws. See, for example, Regulation (EC) No 1049/2001 of the European Parliament and of the Council of 30 May 2001 regarding public access to European Parliament, Council and Commission documents [2001] OJ L145/43 (Public Access Regulation).

[21] See also Recital 2 of the Public Access Regulation: 'Openness enables citizens to participate more closely in the decision-making process and guarantees that the administration enjoys greater legitimacy and is more effective and more accountable to the citizen in a democratic system. Openness contributes to strengthening the principles of democracy and respect for fundamental rights as laid down in Article 6 of the EU Treaty and in the Charter of Fundamental Rights of the European Union.'

[22] According to the settled case law of the ECJ, the principle of transparency, as generally applied in public law, requires every measure with legal effects to be clear and precise and be brought to the notion concerned. See Joined Cases 205–215/82, *Deutsche Milchkontor and Others v Germany*, EU:C:1983:233, para 30; Case C-212-217/80, *Administatione delle Finanze delle Stato v Srl Meridionale Industria Salumi*, EU:C:1981:270, para 10.

[23] See generally on the application of the principle of transparency in private law K Riesenhuber, F Klinck and I Karakostas (eds), *Information als Schutzinstrument* (Baden-Baden, Nomos, 2013).

With regard to its extent and intensity, transparency may be full or limited. Full transparency means that all issues/events have to be disclosed to the public.[24] On the other hand, transparency may be limited when it refers to some events only (eg, material events) or is addressed to some persons only (eg, shareholders or authorities). Moreover, disclosure can be divided into periodic and event-driven (ad hoc) types. Periodic disclosure must be made at a specific time, while event-driven (ad hoc) disclosure refers to material changes occurring between periodic disclosure obligations. Where disclosure has to be made to shareholders or investors, the information usually has to be disclosed to the recipients simultaneously in order to ensure equal treatment.[25] Again, the degree, extent and intensity of the transparency pursued differ according to the scope and aim of each provision. Specific legislative provisions also determine the time and the duration of the transparency as well as other aspects.

Another issue refers to the possibility of the national legislator to go beyond the obligations laid down in European legislation. This question has to be decided on an ad hoc basis and is tidily connected to the nature of each European legislative act (directive or regulation) and its minimum or maximum harmonising character.[26] Accordingly, the ECJ in its ruling in *Inspire Art* held that 'without affecting the information obligations imposed on branches under social or tax law, or in the field of statistics, harmonisation of the disclosure to be made by branches, as brought about by the Eleventh Directive, is exhaustive, for only in that case can it attain the objective it pursues'.[27]

From a technical point of view, transparency is the result of a process, one which is usually ongoing and complex. This process is usually (but not necessarily) based on mandatory disclosure.[28] Nonetheless, companies in responding to market demands often apply voluntary disclosure that goes beyond minimum disclosure requirements.[29] In both cases, disclosure has to meet specific requirements. It is generally accepted that not every form of disclosure has positive effects on the smooth functioning of the market. The information to be disclosed has to meet some minimum qualitative and quantitative criteria. As a general principle, the information disclosed has to be timely, accurate and complete,[30] while the means of transparency also play a decisive role. Without appropriate means, information cannot be widespread and information asymmetries arise.

[24] See, for example, Case C-97/96, *Verband deutscher Daihatsu-Händler v Daihatsu Deutschland GmbH*, EU:C:1997:581, paras 19, 20 and 22; and Joined Cases C-435/02 and C-103/03, *Axel Springer AG v Zeitungsverlag Niederrhein GmbH & Co Essen KG and Hans-Jürgen Weske*, EU:C:2004:552, paras 29, 33.

[25] OECD, *G20/OECD Principles of Corporate Governance* (Paris, OECD Publishing, 2015) 41.

[26] See generally on this issue J Schürnbrand, 'Vollharmonisierung im Gesellschaftsrecht' in B Gsell and C Herrestahl (eds) *Vollharmonisierung im Privatrecht* (Tübingen, Mohr Siebeck, 2009) 273. See also A Brüggemeier, *Harmonisierungskonzepte im europäischen Kapitalmarktrecht* (Tübingen, Mohr Siebeck, 2018) 131 ff.

[27] See for example Case C-167/01, *Inspire Art Ltd*, ECLI:EU:C:2003:512 para 69.

[28] See H Merkt, *Unternehmenspublizität* (Tübingen, Mohr Siebeck, 2000) 12, 13: 'Publizität ist mithin eines der Mittel mit denen Transparenz erreicht werden kann'; T Jutzi, *Unternehmenspublizität* (Bern, Stämpfli, 2017) 26: 'Die Herstellung und Steigerung von Transparenz können gar als eigentliches Ziel der Publizität bezeichnet warden.'

[29] See ch 3.

[30] See generally T Bonneau and F Drummond, *Droit des marchés financiers*, 3rd edn (Paris, Economica, 2010) 522.

III. Means

Transparency may be achieved by a variety of means. In European company law, transparency was traditionally achieved via official company registries and the publication of financial statements. At the EU level, company registries and financial statements are closely interrelated, since the information contained in financial statements cannot be widely disseminated without public registries. Nonetheless, the use of registries for the dissemination of corporate information is not a common practice outside Europe. As was mentioned in Chapter 1, only 52 per cent of jurisdictions worldwide require that annual accounts be submitted to registries.

The rationale for this seems to be that in these jurisdictions, the mandatory disclosure of annual accounts as well as an integrated system of dissemination of information is not considered necessary, especially for companies that are not large enough. In small enterprises, the information burden has to be shifted to participating and contracting parties. Potential shareholders, creditors and business partners should require the information needed directly from the company as a condition for investing or providing a loan. By doing so, small enterprises are freed of expensive legislatively mandated disclosure requirements.

At the EU level now, the European legislator seems to endorse a more information-driven approach. Mandatory disclosure of annual financial statements, narrative reporting, a corporate governance statement included in the management report,[31] capital market disclosure obligations[32] and AML provisions all reflect the importance of transparency for stock corporations at the EU level. Along the same lines, the Shareholders Directive[33] shifts the burden of the dissemination of information to issuers. At the same time, the European legislature aims to create a European-wide integrated system for the flow of information based on technological developments, which can enable remote access to information and make the interconnection of registries possible.

IV. Rationales

Transparency of stock corporations is a regulatory tool linked to many positive effects. First of all, transparency as 'soft law' is non-costly for the supervisors and well accepted by stock corporations, since it does not prescribe change in their underlying behaviour. Moreover, transparency can enable (i) people participating in or (ii) doing business with the company to take decisions based on correct and accurate information. At the same

[31] See art 20 of Directive 2013/34/EU of the European Parliament and of the Council of 26 June 2013 on the annual financial statements, consolidated financial statements and related reports of certain types of undertakings [2013] OJ L182/19–76.

[32] See chs 5 and 6.

[33] Directive (EU) 2017/828 of the European Parliament and of the Council of 17 May 2017 amending Directive 2007/36/EC as regards the encouragement of long-term shareholder engagement [2017] OJ L132/1-25 (Shareholders Directive).

time, transparency can address: (a) information asymmetries, as well as the principle agent problem;[34] (b) resolve conflicts of interests;[35] (c) enhance minority control; and at the same time (d) influence the behaviour of companies.[36] The latter is especially the case when companies are obliged to disclose their policies (if any) and performance with respect to environmental and ethical standards.[37] Focusing on public policy reasons, transparency can also serve to promote enforcement and the supervision of corporations.[38]

Based on the functions of transparency, it becomes clear that the goals of corporate transparency are manifold. If we want to abstractly systematise the goals of transparency based on the protected persons, we could generally say that transparency aims at protecting: (a) shareholders and investors;[39] (b) creditors (especially those supplying finance to the corporation via the markets); and (c) the public interest,[40] especially the market and the price formation mechanism, by ensuring the dominance of the rational pricing of securities. Nonetheless, the provisions imposing disclosure obligations do not always pursue the same goals. Hence, shareholders' rights to be informed aim at protecting shareholders and not creditors. However, the goals of provisions imposing disclosure are not tightly separated. A disclosure obligation can (directly or indirectly) pursue many goals.[41] As a result, disclosure obligations can be used in several different, but complementary, ways.[42]

Although all these goals are abstractly legitimate and recognised in the case law of the ECJ, it seems that there is not always a causal connection between the legitimate aim pursued and the (extent of) transparency required by the legislation. So, for example, it is not clear why according to the AML Directive the major shareholders of corporations should be publicly disclosed even in the case of not listed corporations.[43] Moreover, the disclosure obligations imposed on small and medium-sized enterprises (SMEs) are in many cases disproportionate. Disclosure requirements place unreasonable administrative and financial burdens on enterprises.

[34] See P Mahoney, 'Mandatory Disclosure as a Solution to Agency Problems' (1995) 62 *University of Chicago Law Review* 1047; J Armour, H Hansmann and R Kraakman, 'Agency Problems and Legal Strategies' in R Kraakman et al (eds), *The Anatomy of Corporate Law: A Comparative and Functional Approach*, 3rd edn (Oxford, Oxford University Press, 2017) 38.

[35] See ch 8.

[36] See G Cromme as cited by Av Werder in *Deutscher Corporate Governance Kodex* (Munich, CH Beck, 2018) 382: 'Was man nicht mit guten Gründen und guten Gewissens der Öffentlichkeit mitteilen kann, das soll man auch erst gar nicht tun.'

[37] See ch 7.

[38] In cross-border situations, the exchange of information between supervisory authorities is also necessary for effective supervision. See in this regard Case C-15/16, *Baumeister*, ECLI:EU:C:2018:464, para 27; Case C-140/13, *Altmann and Others*, EU:C:2014:2362, para 27.

[39] See ch 2.

[40] See also L Enriques and S Gilotta, 'Disclosure and Financial Market Regulation' in N Moloney et al (eds), *The Oxford Handbook of Financial Regulation* (Oxford, Oxford University Press, 2015) 534, considering transparency as a synonym for the prevention of opportunism and fraud.

[41] *Axel Springer AG* (n 24) para 50: 'the provisions as to disclosure which it imposes on certain types of capital companies pursue the double objective of public interest laid down by Article 54(3)(g) of the Treaty, that is to say the protection of third parties against the financial risks … and the establishing in the Community of minimum equivalent legal requirements as regards the extent of the financial information that should be made available to the public by companies.'

[42] J Armour (n 34) 38.

[43] On the disclosure of major shareholdings in listed companies, see ch 6.

V. Limitations

Transparency is a regulatory tool with endogenous limits. The failure of transparency over the course of the financial crisis is clear evidence of this. Furthermore, transparency can be very costly for issuers.[44] The cost for issuers is not limited to production and verification of the information. Transparency can lead to revealing trade secrets and competitors can use the information to the firm's disadvantage.[45] Moreover, transparency can lead to an increase in both compliance costs and liability risk. Failure to disclose (even unintentionally) can form the basis for legal actions (usually in the form of class actions) against the issuer. The experiences from the other side of the Atlantic reveal the liability risk for issuers.[46]

At the same time, the consequences of transparency for investors and the market are not always positive. Behavioural dynamics can weaken disclosure benefits for investors. In the same vein, disclosure in the banking sector can harm the smooth functioning of the market and impact on financial stability. This is so because the confidence of depositors is of utmost importance for the banking sector. Hence, a fully transparent bank (especially when it comes to the disclosure of requests for emergency liquidity assistance) could shatter this confidence, putting financial stability at risk and causing a bank run.[47]

Consequently, transparency has to be weighed against other parameters in order to ensure a positive outcome. An overdose of transparency (not only in relation to banks) will result in information overload,[48] with negative effects for both investors and the market. Along the same lines, it has been pointed out that the volume of disclosures is rising much faster than the amount of meaningful information.

Moreover, in competition law, there is much scepticism about transparency.[49] The reason is that transparency and information exchange can be destructive to competition by leading to coordination and collusive behaviour. This is especially the case when information exchanges create transparency about future prices, quantities, capacity, cost and demand.

That being said, it becomes clear that we need some preventative tools against to ward off the negative consequences of transparency.[50] Antitrust law aside, as mentioned

[44] See also W Schön, 'Corporate Disclosure in a Competitive Environment: The Quest for a European Framework on Mandatory Disclosure' (2006) 6 *Journal of Corporate Law Studies* 259, 276; F Easterbrook and D Fischel, 'Mandatory Disclosure and the Protection of Investors' (1984) 70 *Virginia Law Review* 671: 'they give larger issuers an edge, because many of the costs of disclosure are the same regardless of the size of the firm or the offering'.

[45] See also Schön (n 44) 293 ff.

[46] F Easterbrook and D Fischel, 'Mandatory Disclosure and the Protection of Investors' (1984) 70 *Virginia Law Review* 669, 707. See also ch 5.

[47] See art 17(5) of Regulation (EU) No 596/2014 of the European Parliament and of the Council of 16 April 2014 on market abuse (Market Abuse Regulation) [2014] OJ L173/1–61.

[48] Justice Thurgood Marshall, writing for the court in *TSC Industries v Northway*, explained, 'management's fear of exposing itself to substantial liability may cause it simply to bury the shareholders in an avalanche of trivial information – a result that is hardly conducive to informed decision-making'. *TSC Industries, Inc v Northway*, 426 US 438, 448–49 (1976).

[49] See ch 14. See also Schön (n 44) 288 ff.

[50] See generally V Pfisterer, *Unternehmensprivatsphäre* (Tübingen, Mohr Siebeck, 2014) 303 ff.

previously, these tools seem to be legislation on personal data and trade secret protection.[51] The protection of both data and trade secrets is well established at the EU level. Regulation (EU) No 2016/679 recognises data protection as a fundamental right, while Directive (EU) 2016/942 recognises the importance of trade secrets for business competitiveness as well as for research and development, and innovation-related performance. Nonetheless, the protection of these rights is not absolute. There are numerous specific provisions both at the EU and national level giving priority to the public interest and requiring disclosure with regard to corporations. As stated by Justice Jackson, 'corporations can claim no equality with individuals in the enjoyment of a right to privacy'.[52] Again, fighting corruption and tax evasion[53] are the decisive arguments for promoting transparency at all levels.

VI. Enforcement

Disclosure obligations are valuable only if corporations fulfil their disclosure obligations by making timely and accurate disclosures. Therefore, enforcement is essential in order for disclosure to achieve its goal. Nonetheless, the enforcement regime for disclosure varies extensively within different legal orders.[54] Moreover, the enforcement strategies are highly diversified. Some legal orders focus on public enforcement, while others focus on private enforcement.

At the EU level, the enforcement of disclosure is mainly based on public enforcement. The recent financial crisis revealed the need for a stricter supervision regime. Hence, the sanctions provided in the new European legal framework (specifically in the field of capital market law) are draconian.[55] The severe pecuniary sanctions, the disgorgement of profits and public disclosure of the sanctions imposed are some of the new weapons in the arsenal of the competent authorities in order to ensure that sanctions remain dissuasive for those infringing the relevant transparency provisions. It remains to be proven whether these severe sanctions can and will always achieve their goal.

At the same time, both legal scholars and national case law seem to consider private enforcement as a necessary complement to public enforcement. The main arguments

[51] See chs 12 and 13.

[52] *US v Morton Salt*, 338 US 632, 652. See also Joined Cases C-92/09 and C-93/09, *Schecke GbR v Land Hessen*, ECLI:EU:C:2010:662, para 87.

[53] See, for example, Case T-47/02, *Danzer v Council of the European Union*, ECLI:EU:T:2006:167, para 44: 'It follows that, even if it were to be accepted that the disputed provisions are such as to undermine, to a certain extent, the protection of business secrets, the principles of free competition and property rights, the obligations they impose on the companies in question do not constitute excessive and unacceptable intervention which undermines the very substance of those rights and accordingly cannot be regarded as disproportionate in the light of the general interest objective referred to in Article 44(2)(g) EC. The same is true for the alleged breach of the right to protection of personal data, which encompasses fiscal secrecy, without it even being necessary to consider whether a fundamental right to protection of personal data exists for legal person.'

[54] See chs 15 and 16. See also R Veil and A Brüggemeier, 'Kapitalmarktrecht zwischen öffentlich-rechtlicher und privatrechtlicher Normdurchsetzung' in H Fleischer et al, *Enforcement im Gesellschafts- und Kapitalmarktrecht* (Tübingen, Mohr Siebeck, 2015) 277.

[55] See ch 15.

are twofold. First, the competent authorities do not always have the means to reveal violations of disclosure requirements and proceed against the violators. Second, private investors always have incentives and motives to detect violations of rules of transparency and ask for indemnification for harm suffered. Nonetheless, at the European level, there is not yet a unanimous approach on the importance of private enforcement for the proper functioning of the market. In relation to private enforcement, it is also striking that in the majority of legal orders, opacity and lack of transparency, if used to mislead the counterparties of the legal entity, are sanctioned through the lifting of the veil.[56]

VII. Prospects

This book has demonstrated that at the European level, the disclosure rules have become more stringent over time. In recent years, transparency obligations for stock corporations have been extended. Nonetheless, the new disclosure rules are not stand-alone developments; quite the opposite in fact. The recent developments fit within an evolutionary chain towards increased transparency requirements with regard to stock corporations.[57] Accordingly, the transparency rules are quite likely to become even more stringent in the near future. Besides, everything is moving in the direction of a transparent society (*gläserne Gesellschaft*).[58] The transparent corporation has already become the central figure of the new European legal framework on company law and beyond.

Focusing on this trend, it is necessary to make the following remarks:

(a) It seems that the pressure for more transparency in the functioning of stock corporations has its main roots outside company and capital market law. Of course, transparency is advocated to protect investors and ensure the smooth functioning of the markets; however, they are not the overarching arguments found in the policy discussion. As this book has made clear, AML and tax law are the main pressure tools to promote transparency in stock corporations.[59] The disclosure of the beneficial owners of shares under the AML Directive as well as the recent abolition of bearer shares in many European jurisdictions is clear evidence of this fact.[60]

(b) Transparency is also strongly affected by the evolution of technology and the globalisation of the economy. On the one hand, cryptotechnologies promote privacy, while on the other hand, technological developments make the processing, access to and storage of data easier at a global level. Due to the huge magnitude and volume of information, the role of information intermediaries has become crucial.[61]

[56] See ch 17.

[57] See on the ownership disclosure A Schouten and M Siems, 'The Evolution of Ownership Disclosure Rules across Countries' (2010) 10 *Journal of Corporate Law Studies* 451, 452.

[58] See on the original term '*gläserner Bürger*' G von Westphalen, 'Auf dem Weg zum gläsernen Bürger? Das Volkszählungsgesetz 1982' (1983) *Die Neue Ordnung* 136.

[59] See chs 11 and 19.

[60] See ch 19.

[61] See generally J Armour et al (eds), *Principles of Financial Regulation* (Oxford, Oxford University Press, 2016) 118 ff.

(c) The globalisation of the economy makes it clear that the transparency of corporations is not only a European issue. It does not make any sense to promote transparency for European corporations, while leaving offshore and multi-national companies operating under opaque rules. Besides, the opacity of offshore companies was the main reason for enhancing transparency in the European AML legislation. In any event, offshore companies should not be given competitive advantages in relation to European companies.

(d) The reasons favouring the use of transparency as a tool inside and outside company law are well documented. There is general consensus that the fight against tax evasion, terrorist financing, corruption as well as the protection of investors/creditors and the smooth functioning of the market are linked to transparency.

(e) At the same time, the Panama Papers and WikiLeaks meant that action was required and the legislator both at the European level and at the national level was obliged to respond. The immediate and cheap regulatory answer was the imposition of disclosure obligations.

(f) Nonetheless, the means and the extent of transparency required are in some cases highly questionable. The transparency required by legislation often goes far beyond what is necessary to achieve the legislative goal. It is not an overstatement to say that transparency is often used as a response to populism. Characteristic examples are the disclosure of any short position higher than 0.5 per cent of a company's shares as well as the provisions of the new AML Directive on the disclosure of major shareholdings and beneficial owners of non-listed corporations to the general public. We do not consider that there are persuasive arguments for the disclosure required in the above-mentioned cases being viewed as proportional in relation to the goal pursued.[62]

(g) It is also clear that the necessary safeguards must be established to protect the fundamental rights and freedoms of individuals from transparency. The data protection legislation and the trade secret protection legislation are the main tools to protect individuals from the negative aspects of transparency. Unfortunately, it seems that these legislative acts are not always apt to fulfil this goal.

(h) One way to strike a balance between the contradictory interests of transparency and confidentiality is the principle of proportionality[63] as enshrined in EU legislation and the case law. As a general principle, the principle of proportionality applies in all steps of the legislative and regulatory process. It dictates that the lawfulness of a measure is subject to the condition that the measure in question is appropriate and necessary in order to achieve the objectives legitimately pursued by the legislation in question. As explicitly stated in the case law of the ECJ, 'when there is a choice between several appropriate measures, recourse must be had to the least onerous, and the disadvantages caused must not be disproportionate to the aims pursued'.[64]

[62] See chs 5 and 11.

[63] See generally on this principle A Barak, *Proportionality* (Cambridge, Cambridge University Press, 2012) 131 ff; G Huscroft, B Miller and G Webber (eds), *Proportionality and the Rule of Law* (Cambridge, Cambridge University Press, 2014).

[64] Case C-331/88, *R v Minister of Agriculture, Fisheries and Food ex parte Fedesa*, EU:C:1990:391, para 13.

(i) Insofar as the application of the principle of proportionality to transparency issues is concerned, special emphasis should be placed on: (aa) the content and the extent of the information required in relation to the goal pursued; and (bb) the nature of the corporation concerned. It is beyond any doubt that SMEs should not be overburdened with disclosure obligations. The new legal framework on financial statements, market abuse and prospectuses recognises the particularities of SMEs,[65] but there is still much to do in order to ensure a balanced system that on the one hand informs and protects investors and on the other hand facilitates capital formation. This seems to be the Holy Grail for researchers in the policy discussions concerning transparency.

VIII. Conclusion

All in all, the transparent corporation is not a literary metaphor. If not a reality at present, the transparent corporation is a real prospect in the not too distant future. Transparency, if correctly applied, can improve the functioning and the governance of corporations and protect the public interest. A necessary precondition for this is to apply transparency according to the principle of proportionality. If not, transparency will have negative consequences for both European corporations and the internal market. We should not underestimate the famous Brandeis quote that exposure to sunlight can disinfect.[66] Nonetheless, we should always bear in mind that overexposure to sunlight can also cause burning. This is also the moral of this book.

[65] See chs 5 and 9. See also G Ferrarini and A Ottolia, 'Corporate Disclosure as a Transaction Cost: The Case of SMEs' (2013) 9 *European Review of Contract Law* 363; R Veil, *Kapitalmarktzugang für Wachstumsunternehmen* (Tübingen, Mohr Siebeck, 2016) 3 ff; L Enriques and S Gilotta, 'Disclosure and Financial Market Regulation' in Moloney et al (n 40) 529.

[66] See L Brandeis, *Other People's Money and How the Bankers Use it* (Seven Treasures Publications, 2009) 65: 'Sunlight is said to be the best of disinfectants; electric light the most efficient policeman.'

INDEX